D1609181

THE ILLUSTRATED ENCYCLOPEDIA OF BILLIARDS

THE ILLUSTRATED ENCYCLOPEDIA OF BILLIARDS

MIKE SHAMOS

LYONS & BURFORD, PUBLISHERS

Design by Catherine Lau Hunt

Printed in the United States of America

10 9 8 7 6 5 4 3 2 1

Library of Congress Cataloging-in-Publication Data

Shamos, Michael Ian.
    The illustrated encyclopedia of billiards / Michael Ian Shamos.
       p.   cm.
    Includes bibliographical references.
    ISBN 1-55821-219-1
    1. Billiards—Encyclopedias. I. Title.
GV891.S53 1993
794.7'2—dc20   93-13787
                                  CIP

To my parents, Marion and Morris,
on their 50th anniversary

C·O·N·T·E·N·T·S

A·C·K·N·O·W·L·E·D·G·M·E·N·T·S

A project of this magnitude requires the assistance of numerous people and organizations. I will do my best to name those who have made the most significant contributions, and I regret the omission of many others.

Robert Byrne, author of the best and most enjoyable billiard volumes of the last 75 years, has been my muse and creative idol, as well as a friend. He has shared many insights and engaged in numerous debates with me over the fine points of billiard terminology and technique. My file of correspondence with Bob is almost as thick as this book and is filled with his wisdom and suggestions. Five years ago, when this book was in draft, I offered him the chance to become a coauthor. He shrewdly turned me down with the observation that "collaborations mean twice the work for half the money." In this case, I fear, it would have been much more than twice the work—I thought the book was nearly finished in 1987, but I was off by five years. Bob also made the crucial suggestion that the entries should contain interesting anecdotes as well as the more standard form of definition. Because of his suggestion, the book was much more fun to write and, I hope, to read.

Mike Panozzo, the editor of *Billiards Digest*, allowed me to examine archival copies of *Billiards Magazine* and the *National Bowler's Journal*, both of which are critical parts of the written record of American billiard history. Mike has also provided photographs and many other favors. I am most grateful for the opportunity he has given me to write a regular column for the *Digest*, which allows me needed freedom to ramble on about such historical topics as strike my fancy.

Dick Meyers and his late wife Mildred assembled a large collection of books and memorabilia that they referred to as the "Billiard Archives." If they had lacked the patience to put such a trove together, this book could not have been written.

The Billiard Archive, a nonprofit organization I established in Pittsburgh, labors on to preserve the game's history. As Curator, I have access to a large collection of source material on cue games. The Archive now holds over 800 books on billiards. No other facility in the U. S. is known to possess more than 250. Without these materials, there would have been no book.

The Firestone Library of Princeton University provided my first introduction to billiard history. Its open-stack sporting book room and extensive magazine collection allowed me to discover at my own pace the long heritage of the game. The remainder of the Princeton campus provided the emerald tables so necessary for my practical research.

The Hillman Library of the University of Pittsburgh maintains an open microform collection that includes the principal indexed American newspapers, which were invaluable in tracing the development of U.S. billiard terminology. I was fortunate to have been allowed unlimited access to this resource, which permitted me to investigate billiard news reporting in depth. The large number of references to newspaper articles in the text is a tribute to the strength of the university's holdings.

Clement F. Trainer, one of our premier billiard historians and author of a thorough treatment of the 18.2 Balkline championships, has challenged me with questions and permitted me to peruse his files of correspondence with the players of the 1930s. He once asked if I could figure out why carom billiards was called Straight-Rail. It wasn't a trick question, since he didn't know the answer himself, despite considerable searching. Clem found the answer in these pages. Before he died in 1991 at the age of 89, he graciously completed a review of the manuscript and offered critical suggestions.

The Billiard Congress of America (BCA), the game's governing body, has recognized the work of the Archive and has encouraged its participation in BCA projects. It has honored me by allowing me to serve on its Statistics and Records and Hall of Fame Committees.

Charlie Ursitti, promoter and referee, has regularly sent me copies of players' scrapbooks, photographs and thousands of articles over the years. His dedication to research into the history of the game exceeds my own. Pocket billiards has no greater friend than Charlie.

All but six of the diagrams in this book have been reproduced directly from original sources, primarily 1898 Thatcher, 1913 Daly, 1978 Byrne, 1957 Holt, 1979 Robin and 1989 Koehler. My thanks go to Bob Byrne, Eddie Robin, and Jack Koehler for their kind permission to reprint these illustrations, which are products of their painstaking work.

Cygnet Publishing Technologies, Inc., a Pittsburgh software company specializing in desktop publishing and typesetting systems, and Carnegie-Mellon University provided invaluable help in maintaining the manuscript in computerized form.

Ted Ronca, a companion from my playing days at Princeton, has been tireless in assisting me in acquiring material for this book. He has pointed me to fascinating connections between billiard terminology and other fields. See "Toad-in-the-Hole" for an example.

Tony Annigoni, manager of the Q Club in San Francisco, has provided detailed information on gambling terminology and methods of handicapping, as well as some hugely entertaining road experiences.

Specialized information has been supplied by Tom ("Dr. Cue") Rossman, Mike Panozzo (photographs), Ken Macher (on Ralph Greenleaf), Adrienne Gefsky (on colloquial terms used in Pennsylvania), Marilyn Fish (on the ivory industry and the career of Michael Phelan), Warren Masui (on pocket games played in Hawaii), and Frank Masland IV (on "no count" and handicapping techniques).

Elizabeth Holmes, a billiard writer in Healdsburg, California, has been a regular contributor of source material on women's billiards and an engaging conversationalist on numerous topics, both historical and contemporary. I greatly value her insights.

Willie and Flora Mosconi invited me to their home and allowed me to examine their large collection of billiard articles and memorabilia, including extensive records of pocket competition in the 1940s and 1950s. To his great credit, Willie has never claimed the distinction of being the greatest pocket billiard player who ever lived. But he is.

As always, my family—Julie, Josselyn and Alex—exhibit a tolerance for my playing and writing activities that exceeds anything I could have hoped for. I love you for it.

F·O·R·E·W·O·R·D

This book took so long to complete—nine years—that I feel compelled to explain why I ever wrote it. The reason is simple—I had no choice in the matter. Billiards has been a passion of mine since 1964.

I was fascinated by the game as a child, although I only rarely had the chance to hold a cue. My best friend, Clifford Hauptman, had a pool table with carom plugs that could be inserted to block the pockets for a game of Three-Cushions. We watched as our fathers sent the cue ball around the table, hitting five or more rails to complete a score. We had no idea how they could even visualize such shots, much less execute them. Playing that game seemed to require some cosmic combination of physics, intuition and technique.

I entered Princeton University in 1964, a time when there were plenty of pocket and carom tables on campus, at least 20 of each. I took more readily to billiards than to pool and made the game a part of my daily routine. I approached billiards the same way that I did other academic subjects—I went to the library to read up on it. Fortunately, Firestone Library at Princeton had an extensive collection of sporting books, including a small shelf of old billiard volumes. It was there that I first saw *Daly's Billiard Book* from 1913, which has since been reprinted in paperback. What a collection of shots it had! Hundreds of them, with detailed explanations of how to control the movement of all three balls. I was struck by the fact that a huge amount of knowledge lay submerged in these books that I was not likely to pick up in a pool hall.

But that was not for lack of trying. I spent a fair amount of time around the rooms of New York, particularly McGirr's, which was a real crossroads of humanity. It stayed open 23 hours a day, being forced by law to close from 5:00 to 6:00 A.M. Near Times Square and the Theatre District, it seemed to pulse to the beat of the city. You could play Pool, Billiards or Snooker, and each game attracted its own spectrum of followers. Actors and musicians would show up to mix with businessmen, hustlers, college students and criminals. By playing there I was exposed to the craft and custom of all three games, which only increased my thirst for information. I saw Jimmy the cue man maintain the bins of house cues, all segregated by weight. I watched gamblers, loiterers, and kibitzers, all of whom had a profound, if unschooled, knowledge of the game. But most of all I studied the shots, and to this day I still marvel at what people can do with a billiard ball.

Misspent though some of my youth may have been, it was not a total loss. I majored in physics at Princeton and wrote a thesis on gravitation theory under Professor John Wheeler. But my mind never strayed very far from billiards. I won the university Three-Cushion championship in 1967 and 1968 and took the Association of College Unions Northeast Regional Three-Cushion title in an all-day shootout at Steele's in Newark in 1968. That room was so dangerous that some of the spectators had to pay a ransom just to be allowed to leave.

Fate took me to Vassar College for graduate study. The school was not yet coeducational and billiards was not popular, but I met my future wife, Julie, there. In 1970, I became the first male to be awarded a graduate degree from Vassar and left for a government stint in Washington. I entered Yale for a Ph.D. in computer science in 1972 and began teaching at Carnegie-Mellon University in 1975. The educational imperative inspired me to collect a law degree from Duquesne University in 1981 and I ultimately left full-time teaching to start a pair of computer software companies and practice law. I then learned that many attorneys harbor a fondness for billiards. Many players maintain a respectable outside career, but some use it simply as a cover for their real devotion.

My interest in the historical side of the game led me to start collecting antiquarian items, like books, photographs and ephemera. By 1983, I had collected about 75 books and 30 prints, enough to provide fascinating reading but not a major holding by any means. That year, Dick Meyers of San Pedro, California, was offering for sale the largest collection of billiard memorabilia in the United States. Putting sanity aside, I felt that I had to have it, and made what turned out to be the winning bid. My excitement was only slightly dampened when I learned later that it had been the *only* bid. In 1983, billiards was not very popular, and it was uncertain whether the game would survive to the end of the decade. In New York it almost didn't. The number of public rooms in Manhattan had dwindled to two by 1986, down from thousands during the 1930s.

The collection, in 43 shipping cartons, duly arrived in Pittsburgh. As I unpacked the hundreds of books and began to catalog them by computer, it struck me that no record of the game as extensive as this existed anywhere in the country. What was missing from the books was filled in by the artwork, which included an extensive trove of prints and photographs. The collection at this point had achieved a "critical mass," valuable enough as a historical resource to warrant substantial further investment.

To justify my essentially sole stewardship over these materials, I vowed to use them for research and to publish the results of my studies. A few months later, I established the Billiard Archive, a nonprofit organization dedicated to preserving the game's history, and have served as its curator ever since. I tried to make good my promise. The problem was that when I started reading the older books (those written before 1900), I couldn't understand them. I would encounter sentences like, "double the ball with left twist and force for the winning hazard" which was thoroughly unintelligible. It took me quite a while to figure out that it just meant "play the bank shot with left draw." Working out such puzzles clarified many confusing points. During the nineteenth century, "break" referred either to the position left after a shot (in the U.S.) or to a run of consecutive points (in Britain), not the opening shot of the game, which is its present meaning. When playing at McGirr's, I often heard old-timers call a shot a "scratch" on a carom table. I had no idea it was possible to scratch on a table without pockets until I learned that "scratch" also meant a lucky shot.

I began keeping a glossary of the terms I didn't understand and the ones that seemed to have unusual or ambiguous meanings. The list grew steadily, and I began to rely on it heavily after I started writing for *Billiards Digest* in 1988. During the last four years, the manuscript has been a virtual obsession, but I began to despair of ever seeing it in print, since it is not easy to curl up with a book whose material is presented in alphabetical order. The recent rise in popularity of billiards, however, created an appetite among publishers for titles on the subject. I became aware that Lyons & Burford was under contract to publish the Official Rule Book of the Billiard Congress of America and offered to add this one to its catalog. Matters proceeded very swiftly from that point; the only chore that remained was updating the manuscript to be current through the end of 1992. I give you this book that you may share my fascination with the game.

I would greatly appreciate receiving corrections or supplementary material from readers, particularly information about games and terminology not listed in the book. I have enjoyed writing it so much that a second edition seems inevitable. Please write to me at the Billiard Archive, 605 Devonshire Street, Pittsburgh, PA 15213.

U·S·I·N·G T·H·I·S B·O·O·K

This book attempts to define the whole of billiard terminology in the English language in a historical context. The practical reasons for the introduction of each term are traced as thoroughly as possible. The definitions were compiled from original sources by reviewing several thousand books, manuscripts and articles. They record the actual usage of words in a billiard context. A work of this nature is doomed to chronic incompleteness. I have accepted from the outset that I would strive to be thorough but was certain to fail.

No attempt is made to trace etymology, that is, how a word developed in English from other linguistic sources. However, extensive attention is devoted to changes in the meanings of terms over time, and an effort is made to explain their evolution. Using this book, the reader should be able to read and understand any material on billiards ever written in English.

The format of the book is alphabetical, to facilitate rapid reference. It is really an annotated index of the subject. Although many of the entries resemble dictionary definitions, most are actually brief encyclopedia articles containing anecdotes, quotations, and analysis along with citations from actual sources.

Through the use of extensive cross-references, the reader should be able to look up any word or concept related to billiard games and be led to others, eventually obtaining a thorough explanation of not only the original but several related notions. I have adopted the admittedly annoying habit of dividing explanatory material among the several synonyms of a term (for example, see "14.1 Continuous" and "Straight Pool"). This requires the reader to look up all its listed equivalents (which are listed for convenience) to obtain a complete picture. It is hoped that the inconvenience will be adequately repaid with added insight.

It has been impractical to collect or record terminology of a local or narrowly regional nature. I have attempted to fashion authoritative definitions, but errors have necessarily occurred, particularly because slang terms rarely appear in print and knowledge of them has to be based on personal experience, which is sure to be faulty. This book is intended to be neither a history of billiards nor a complete exposition of the subject, which would run to numerous volumes, but a glossary. Textual material accompanying the definitions is anecdotal and should not be considered complete. Original artwork has been used for illustrative purposes wherever it was available.

It has been necessary to omit much that would have been of interest. Although many billiard players and personalities are mentioned in the text, no biographies have been included. Likewise, match and tournament results and a variety of records are referred to where appropriate, but a thorough listing of them would take another decade to compile and would take us far afield. Instructional material, of which there is certainly no shortage in the published corpus of billiard works, is neither appropriate in a book of this type nor within my capability to provide.

The word "billiards" refers to a wide variety of games played with balls on a table having cushions. Although there is a technical distinction between games in which pockets are used (commonly but inaccurately known as "pool" games) and those in which no pockets are used (commonly but also inaccurately known as "billiard" or "carom" games), this book uses "billiards" to refer to both styles unless the context requires precision. The term "pool" is *never* used alone in this book to refer to a type of game (except in this section) because, as the reader will see, it is highly ambiguous. The use of "pocket billiards" in its place should not be interpreted as reflecting a moral stance, but simply an effort to distinguish between the pocket and pocketless forms. I might have used the term "cue sports," which includes cue games that are neither pocket nor carom games (e.g. Casin) in the title of the book, but the phrase is relatively new and might not have been understood properly.

Game rules are constantly changing. A statement of a rule in a definition means only that the rule was in effect at the cited time in some version of the specified game according to some referenced source. This book should never be quoted as authority for any current rule. The reader is referred instead to official sources, such as the *Official Rule Book* of the Billiard Congress of America.

FORMAT OF ENTRIES

An entry may begin with a parenthetical opening indicating the game or games to which the term pertains and whether the term is obsolete, colloquial, or slang. If a term has several definitions, they are numbered and given in order of frequency of use. That is, the first definition is the most common usage. Parts of speech are not indicated explicitly unless there is possible ambiguity.

When a term is the name of a billiard game, a bare outline of the mode of play is given, along with any unusual rules. However, the reader should not expect to be able to play a game simply from the description given here. The references should be consulted.

Any technical terms used in a definition that are themselves defined elsewhere in this book are highlighted in small capital letters, except the following extremely common terms: ball, billiard, cue, cue ball, cue stick, pocket, and table. Names of games are always capitalized or highlighted. Other terms, when not highlighted, are used in their ordinary English senses. A highlighted term may differ in grammatical form from that used in the corresponding entry. For example, BANKING may be used, but the main entry is BANK.

"See," when used in a definition, means that the cited term is essential to an understanding of the definition. "See also" means that the cited term is related to the term being defined. "Also" means that the cited term is a synonym of the term being defined. "Cf." indicates that the reader should compare the cited term to the main term because their meanings are different, perhaps only subtly.

Not every entry is a definition. Some are brief articles on miscellaneous billiard topics. See, for example, CHURCH; COUNTRIES, NAMES OF; DEATH; LEFT-HANDED PLAY; NICKNAME; SHIP, BILLIARDS ABOARD; and WOMEN IN BILLIARDS.

INDEXING ORDER

Indexing is strictly alphabetical. Hyphens, commas, and other punctuation marks are ignored unless two consecutive entries differ in no other way. For example, "B.B.C. Co." appears as if it were written as "BBC Co." Spaces are significant. Numerals, such as "14.1," are indexed as if spelled out fully in words ("fourteen point one"). An entry is capitalized if capitalization is appropriate for its principal (first) meaning.

SPELLING

American orthography is employed throughout except that British spelling (e.g., "baulk") is used when discussing British games or topics. There is necessarily some overlap, and the spelling that seems most appropriate in context is used. The common American/British pairs are balk/baulk, center/centre, and color/colour.

CITATIONS

References to original works are provided where they are known. Usually at least three citations are given for each term: (1) the earliest known to the author; (2) an intermediate citation, usually from around 1900; and (3) a recent reference. All billiard works cited can be found in the bibliography at the end of this volume. It is incorrect to quote this book as authority for the earliest date of use of a particular term, except in the unusual circumstance that the birth of the term can be fixed with precision (e.g., SPACE GAME). If no citation is supplied for a definition or factual claim, the material is based on my opinion or recollection.

Two different citation formats are used. Books are cited by giving the year, author and page, in that order. For example, "1807 White 29" means White's 1807 treatise, page 29. A single lower-case letter is added after the year if ambiguity would otherwise result. Anonymous works are cited in the same way, with an abbreviated title in place of the author's name.

If a year is known only approximately, it is followed by the letter "c" (meaning "circa") or may be indicated as 186x, meaning sometime in the 1860s. If the date is not known to within five years, it is omitted. For citations to the Oxford English Dictionary (OED), the year given refers to year cited in the OED itself, not the date of publication of the OED edition. For example, "1710 OED" means that the OED contains a citation to the term in a billiard context dated 1710. The principal source used by the OED for billiard references was Bennett's 1873 *Billiards*. This work is too late to be of substantial use in fixing earliest dates of usage. Therefore, no OED citation is given unless it predates all other known sources.

Magazines and newspapers are cited by giving the year, title, date of issue (in parentheses), and page. Example: 1935 *Newsweek* (Nov 30) 22 refers to the November 30, 1935 issue of *Newsweek* magazine, page 22. For newspapers, section, page, and column references are also given. Thus, 1931 NYT (Aug 16) X 3:6 refers to the August 16, 1931 issue of the *New York Times*, section X, page 3, column 6. If a work is not listed in the Bibliography or the list of abbreviations, then its title is italicized.

APPENDICES

At the rear of the book are lists of important billiard numbers and the games, organizations, and persons mentioned in the text. A bibliography of works cited is also included.

OTHER GLOSSARIES

The idea of publishing a list of billiard terms with definitions is not new. Such glossaries appear in many works. One of the earliest is in 1807 White. Others may be found in 1857 Phelan, 1866 Crawley, 1873 Bennett, 1885c Cook, 1978 Byrne, 1989 Koehler, and 1992 OR. The most extensive of them contains fewer than 250 terms; this book, by contrast, has more than 2200 entries. 1971 Ardévol is an extensive Spanish language compilation of terms, but its emphasis is on technique rather than linguistic usage.

A·B·B·R·E·V·I·A·T·I·O·N·S

=	Indicates synonymous terms.
abbrev.	abbreviated
AH	*American Hoyle*
Amer.	American
Annals	*Annals of Gaming*
b.	born
BA	Billiard Association
BBM	*Bowling and Billiard Magazine*
BD	*Billiards Digest* (magazine)
Bill.	Billiards, billiard
BM	*Billiards Magazine*
BR	*Official Billiard Reporter* (magazine)
Brit.	British
BSCC	*Billiards and Snooker Control Council*
BSTE	*Billiards and Snooker Teasers Explained*
Burwat	*The Burwat Billiards View* (magazine)
BYB	*Billiard Year-Book for 1910*
Canad.	Canadian
cf.	compare. Means that the reader should compare and contrast this entry with the cited one.
colloq.	colloquial
d.	died
def.	definition
diag.	diagram
e.g.	for example
Ency. Brit.	Encyclopedia Britannica
Eng.	English
esp.	especially
fig.	figure
fr.	from
Fr.	French
HDB	*History and Description of Billiards*
HRB	*Handbook of Rules of Billiards*
ITP	*International Tournament Pool*
KTG	*Know the Game Billiards and Snooker*
KTGP	*Know the Game Pool*
MB	*Modern Billiards*
NBJ	*National Bowler's Journal* (magazine)
NBN	*National Billiard News* (magazine)
n.c.	not cited
n.d.	no date
NYDT	*New York Daily Tribune* (newspaper)
NYT	*New York Times* (newspaper)

OBG	*Official Billiard Games Rule Book*
obs.	obsolete. A term is marked as obsolete if a reader is likely to encounter it only in a historical context and not with reference to current play.
OED	*Oxford English Dictionary*
OR	*Official Rule Book for All Pocket & Carom Games*
org.	organization
PBA	Professional Billiards Association *Tournament Promoter's Handbook*
PBM	*Pool and Billiards Magazine*
PC	private communication
Phil.	*A Philosophical Essay on the Game of Billiards*
pl.	plate
pr.	pronounced
RGRG	*Rules Governing the Royal Game of Billiards*
sl.	slang
Souv.	*American Billiard Championship of America, Souvenir*
Span.	Spanish
vol.	volume
WB	*World of Billiards*
WPBA	Women's Professional Billiard Association *Player Manual*
WPBSA	World Professional Billiards and Snooker Association *Official Diary Yearbook 1988/89*
WSD	*Webster's Sports Dictionary*

T·E·R·M·S

à cheval

(Balkline, Fr.) International referee's CALL when the object balls lie astride a BALKLINE, and there is thus no limit on the number of consecutive points that may be scored. Literal French meaning: "on horseback," or "astride." 1981 Rottie 136. See also DEDANS, ENTRÉ, RENTRÉ, RESTÉ DEDANS.

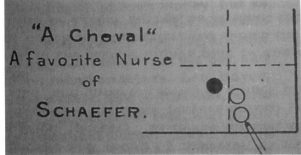

à cheval

A la Guerre

(game, obs.) Billiard game popular in the mid-1600s, also known as the WAR GAME. See JEU DE GUERRE.

A la Royale

(game, obs.) ENGLISH BILLIARDS slightly modified to permit three players to participate. The players alternate cue balls, and the first to make the allotted number of points receives a stake from the other two. All FORFEITS score to both of the other players. Usually played to 50 points. Also known as the GAME OF THREE, referring to the number of players. 1839 Kentfield 36, 1850c White & Bohn 48, 1856 Crawley 108.

AABA

(org.) = AMERICAN AMATEUR BILLIARD ASSOCIATION.

AAU

(org.) = AMATEUR ATHLETIC UNION.

ABA

(org.) = AMERICAN BILLIARD ASSOCIATION.

above

(Brit. games) Nearer to the TOP of the table. 1957 Holt 6. The British and American systems for identifying directions on the table are the reverse of one another. The "top" in Britain is the foot in the U.S. Cf. BELOW.

absence

(Brit. games) A player who is temporarily absent from the playing room may appoint a representative, usually called a SECOND, to look out for his interests and call FOULS. 1987 BSCC S23.

ACA

(org.) = AMERICAN CUEMAKERS ASSOCIATION.

Accu-Stats

A method of measuring players' performances in Nine-Ball competition, developed by Pat Fleming of Accu-Stats Video Productions, 119 Clark Street, Bloomingdale, New Jersey 07403. Also, a computer program for this purpose. See TOTAL PERFORMANCE AVERAGE. Some recorded statistics include average misses per 100 balls pocketed, RUN-OUT opportunities, position errors per 100 balls pocketed, KICK performance average, and breaking efficiency. Accu-Stats also produces narrated videotapes of pocket and carom billiard matches.

ace

1. (Pocket Bill., colloq.) The ONE-BALL. 1878 NYT (Apr 21) 1:7. See also DEUCE. 2. One of four specially marked balls in POKER POCKET BILLIARDS. 1946 OR 72. 3. A very skillful player. "He's an ace at billiards."

act of God

A disturbance of playing conditions by a force beyond human control, such as an earthquake. It is generally reckoned that a player must accept the consequences of an act of God and has no right to have the balls replaced as he would in a case of INTERFERENCE. See REPLACEMENT. Cf. NONPLAYER INTERFERENCE.

action

1. Spin on the ball; ball motion of any type. 1913 Daly 31. "He got tremendous action on that shot." In Carom Billiards, sometimes meaning excessive force, resulting in spreading the balls apart and ruining a potential GATHER. 1925 Hoppe 6. 2. A wager on a billiard game. 1970 Fensch 158. A situation involving GAMBLING. 1967 Polsky 101. "He's giving hundred-dollar action."

Action Eight-Ball

(game) = HOT EIGHT, especially as played at Chalker's Billiard Club in Emeryville, California. 1993 Holmes PC. Also HURRICANE EIGHT-BALL.

action room

A POOL ROOM in which GAMBLING is commonplace and money players are readily available. 1967 Polsky 35, 1979 Grissim 249.

ACU-I

(org.) = ASSOCIATION OF COLLEGE UNIONS INTERNATIONAL, the sponsor of INTERCOLLEGIATE BILLIARDS in the United States.

address

To position oneself at the table in preparation for a STROKE. According to the regulations, a player is said to have "addressed" the ball when any part of his body, cue or clothing has touched the table prior to a shot. 1986 Quinn 88. The concept is useful in resolving certain thorny rules situations, such as what happens if a ball drops into a pocket as the INCOMING PLAYER is preparing to stroke. If he has addressed the cue ball, the fallen object ball is replaced; if he has not addressed the cue ball, the object ball is credited to the previous player, whose inning continues. The idea behind this rule is that once the incoming player touches the table, any ball that falls cannot be credited to the OUTGOING PLAYER. See also IN CONTROL, INNING, MOTION, TURN, VISIT.

The use of "address" in the sense of preparing to hit a ball dates from the mid-nineteenth century. OED.

adjust

To move a ball, especially the cue ball, with one's hand or the side of the cue stick when it is legal to do so, as when the ball is IN HAND. 1986 OR. In most games, moving the cue ball with the POINT of the cue is either a shot or a NUDGE, depending on the circumstances. This is not necessarily true in English Billiards, where it is permissible to position the cue ball with the tip of the cue if the player's intention is clear to the REFEREE. 1988 WPBSA.

advice

See ASSISTANCE.

AEBF

(org.) = AUSTRALIAN EIGHT-BALL FEDERATION.

African-American players

Billiard games have been popular among African-American players since at least the 1860s. Many of these players have exhibited considerable skill. However, primarily because of discrimination by the billiard establishment, no African-American participated in any world-caliber professional competition until Cisero Murphy won a World Straight Pool tournament (unsanctioned) in Burbank in 1965. Writing of a different black player, 1966 Fats states, "James Evans is the greatest Negro pool player who ever lived, and the only reason why he never won a lot of those world tournaments was because they wouldn't let him play on account of his color." Evans ran a room in Harlem, but was known all over New York. He once ran 15 balls without allowing the cue ball to touch a cushion. George "Rotation Slim" Hairston got his nickname in 1926 by beating a local Rotation player in Chicago. He was famous for his Bank Pool and One Pocket play but was never asked to enter a sanctioned event.

Black players were often mocked in artwork, particularly the prints of Currier & Ives, whose "Darktown" series portrayed them as bumbling and primitive. 1991 BD (Dec) 64. The failure of tournaments to invite minority players led to the formation in 1916 of the COLORED AMATEUR BILLIARD PLAYERS' ASSOCIATION. Unfortunately, almost no information has survived concerning this organization.

after-position

(Brit. games, obs.) = POSITION. 1908 Mannock II 30, 1925 Peall. The arrangement of the balls after a shot. The LEAVE.

afterwrap

That portion of the BUTT of a cue stick lying between the WRAP and the BUTT PLATE or BUTT CAP. 1983 NBN (Mar) 18. Cf. FOREWRAP.

ahead session

A MATCH in which the first player to lead by a predetermined number of games is the winner. 1979 Grissim 250. See FIVE AHEAD for an example. See also FREEZE-OUT, SESSION. Cf. RACE, in which the first player to win a prescribed number of games is the victor.

aiming

The act of lining up the cue stick in preparation for shooting. Aiming comprises the distinct steps of (1) determining where the cue ball should go and (2) making it go there. Very little has been written on precisely *how* to aim—most sources deal with determining where the cue ball should contact the object ball and do not discuss what the player must do with his eyes in order to achieve the desired result. Because of the distance between the eyes, the effect of parallax must be taken into account. To demonstrate the phenomenon, try aiming with one eye only, then open and close your right and left eyes alternately, noting how much the cue ball seems to shift in the process. Aiming should be done with the dominant eye. Cues have been manufactured with a line drawn on the shaft to assist the player in sighting, although this aid is of questionable value. Another approach that has been tried is to manufacture special balls with markings that assist in aiming. See ZIGZAG BALL.

There is little tutorial material about methods for lining up the eye, stick, and POINT OF AIM. Experienced players use a variety of practical techniques for this purpose. For example, a common rule of thumb is that to achieve a QUARTER-BALL hit, you aim the edge of the cue stick at the edge of the object ball. (Aiming the *center* of the cue stick at the edge of the object ball results in a HALF-BALL hit.) See also CLOCK SYSTEM, WHIZ WHEEL SYSTEM.

Further complicating the process is the fact that the cue ball does not necessarily move in the direction in which the cue stick is aimed. The effects of ROLL, SQUIRT, SWERVE, and THROW must be taken into account.

Although aiming has been known to be of paramount importance for centuries, there is still no agreement on exactly where the player should be looking at the actual moment of striking. Authorities differ vehemently as to where the player's eyes should last fall before the shot is made. Among those who feel that the cue ball should be

glanced at last are: 1858 Mardon 362, 1922 Fry, and 1925 Hoppe 198. All these references are to carom rather than pocket games, and a distinction has been drawn between the two games in terms of cue ball aiming. Hoppe notes that a disturbing tendency on carom FOLLOW SHOTS is to glance last at the SECOND OBJECT BALL, and says that this temptation is to be avoided. A large number of authors prefer to sight the first object ball last: 1807 White 13, 1839 Kentfield 5, 1866 Crawley 18, 1904 Dawson, 1924b Newman 30, 1935 Levi ix, 1935 Smith 68, 1948 Mosconi, 1980 Davis 38, 1984 Williams 12. This split in opinion makes aiming, along with the HALF-BALL ANGLE and TRANSMITTED SIDE questions, one of the three great controversies in billiards.

For a method of aiming BANK SHOTS, see PROJECTING THE POCKET. For a different kind of aid, see GLASSES. In all billiard games, the use of physical devices to assist in aiming is prohibited, as is making marks on the table or cushions or the placement of objects on the rails to serve as targets. 1992 OR 49.

air ball

(colloq.) A shot during which the cue ball contacts no object ball, which constitutes a TABLE SCRATCH in Pocket Billiards. See also FIELD GOAL.

air gun

(colloq.) A HUSTLER who is out of money (one who has no BARRELS) is said to be shooting an "air gun," a weapon that fires harmlessly.

airplane billiards

Billiards played in an airplane that is in flight. On December 16, 1929, the first recorded attempt to play pocket billiards aloft was made by Ralph Greenleaf on a 2½ × 5 foot table in a Ford trimotor flying at 100 mph over Detroit. He had trouble sinking balls at the start, but the experiment was ultimately a success—he had a high run of 9. 1929 NYT (Dec 17) 37:3. That night, after landing, Greenleaf shattered the (terrestrial) championship HIGH RUN record of 111 at 14.1 Continuous by running 126 UNFINISHED against Frank Taberski. The event set off a mini-explosion in airborne billiards. The following year, Charlie Peterson made 100 points at Straight-Rail in 28.5 seconds while aloft; he later expressed a desire to play in a submarine! 1931 NYT (Aug 16) x 3:6. Willie Hoppe and Jake Schaefer Jr. once agreed to play a match of 18.2 Balkline in an airplane, but the contest appears not to have taken place. Publicity associated with the aerial game suggested at the time that billiards might be tried as a recreation on long cross-country flights. It is safe to predict that this idea will not be resurrected. See also SHIP, BILLIARDS ABOARD.

Alabama Eight-Ball

(game) EIGHT-BALL in which the 1- and 15-balls must be pocketed in designated SIDE POCKETS. 1977 Fels 133. The rule enhances the game's defensive possibilities, since a player may avoid a loss by placing SAFETY on the 8-ball. The original game of Eight-Ball was played this way. Cf. LAST POCKET OPTION, MISERY, MISSOURI, ONE AND FIFTEEN IN THE SIDE. For a list of other states named in billiard games, see STATES, NAMES OF.

albino

(sl.) The cue ball, so named because it is pure white. 1988 Rossman 34. Also WHITEY.

alignment system

(Artistic Bill.) A method of recording the position of the balls so that a shot can be set up repetitively and precisely. 1987 Jewett 1. See COORDINATES, NOTATION.

All-In Game

(game, obs.) = ENGLISH BILLIARDS. So-called probably because *all* methods of scoring (WINNING HAZARDS, LOSING HAZARDS, and CAROMS) counted for points. 1889 Drayson 100.

all on the black

(Snooker) Situation in which the players' scores differ by fewer than seven points so whoever pots BLACK will win unless there is a FOUL or SNOOKER. 1910a Ritchie 106, 1954 KTG 34. If the difference in scores is exactly seven and one player pots black to TIE, the black is spotted and lots are drawn to determine who will be IN HAND for a SUDDEN DEATH finish. 1986 KTG 31. Also BLACK BALL GAME.

all-round cannon

(Eng. Bill.) A shot AROUND THE TABLE, resulting in a CANNON. 1889 Drayson 42, 1901 Roberts 47.

alternating break

A convention whereby the BREAK rotates among the players in a series of games. In particular, if there are only two players, the break alternates between them. 1992 OR 43. This tends to equalize the advantage in games in which the break is desirable, such as Nine-Ball. It is commonly adopted for Eight-Ball competition. Cf. LOSER BREAKS, WINNER BREAKS.

amateur

One who does not make a living at the game, whether as a player or otherwise. The distinction between an amateur and a PROFESSIONAL was formerly of importance, particularly in Balkline during the period 1910–1925, when separate tournaments were held for these two groups and different sanctioning bodies governed the respective competitions.

The first organized amateur Straight-Rail competition was sponsored in 1887 by the Racquet and Tennis Club of New York and won by Orville Oddie Jr., later a leading Balkline player. 1899 Souv 10. Amateur 8.2 Balkline began in 1891; 14.2 Balkline in 1893.

In the first few decades of the twentieth century, amateur Balkline competition was so sophisticated that four classes of championships were held: Classes A, B, C, and D. Class A was the highest level; the Class A winner was recognized as the amateur champion of the United States. Class D was reserved for novice players. A player's AVERAGE was a good indicator of what class he was likely to compete in; Class A players would average approximately 15 at 18.2 Balkline, Class B about 10, and Class C about 6. Only a handful of players occupied Class A at any particular time. In 1899, only five so qualified.

In Three-Cushions, amateur competition was held in the United States in every decade from 1910 through the 1970s. Amateur LEAGUE play was held before 1920. The first world amateur Three-Cushion tournament was held at Reims, France, in 1928 and won by Edmond Soussa. The most celebrated amateur in the history of billiards was the incomparable Raymond Ceulemans, who won the world title at least 19 times.

Amateur Athletic Union (AAU)

(org.) The governing body of amateur billiards in the United States up to 1899, when the NAABP was formed after a dispute with roomkeepers George Slosson and Maurice Daly. The AAU's first sanctioned tournament, at 14.2 Balkline, was won by Florian Tobias in 1897. 1899 Souv 16.

ambidextrous

Able to wield a cue stick with either the right hand or the left. A valuable skill enabling the player to avoid awkward BEHIND-THE-BACK SHOTS or having to use the MECHANICAL BRIDGE. Its benefit is mentioned in 1924a Newman 118.

Many famous players were ambidextrous. Maurice Vignaux could NURSE with either hand. 1880 NYT (May 3) 8:1. Jacob Schaefer Sr. could even play a FREE-HAND MASSÉ with the opposite hand. 1890 NY Herald (Mar 1) 8:1. Willie Hoppe, however, was not ambidextrous. 1972 Byrne. Among pocket players, Jimmy Caras and Erwin Rudolph were ambidextrous; Ralph Greenleaf was not. 1931 BM (Jun) 12, 1938 NBJ (Nov). See also LEFT-HANDED PLAY.

On April 30, 1873, in Norwich, Connecticut, the first left-handed match for right-handed players was held at Straight-Rail. The winner averaged 10, which was front-page news at the time. 1873 NYT (May 1) 1:3.

In 1906, Mark Twain, a perennial billiard fan and player, attended a match in New York pitting George B. Sutton against Willie Hoppe. At the conclusion of play, Twain told the following story: "Once in Nevada, I dropped into a billiard room and began to knock the balls around. The proprietor, who was a red-haired man, with such hair as I have never seen anywhere except on a torch, asked me if I would like to play. I said 'Yes.' He said, 'Knock the balls around a little and let me see how you can shoot.' So I knocked them around and thought I was doing pretty well when he said, 'That's all right, I'll play you left-handed.' It hurt my pride but I played him. We banked for the shot and he won it. Then he commenced to play, and I commenced to chalk my cue to get ready to play and he went on playing, and I went on chalking my cue; and he played and I chalked all through the game. When he had run his string out I said: 'That's wonderful! Perfectly wonderful! If you can play that way left-handed, what could you do right-handed?' 'Couldn't do anything,' he said, 'I'm a left-handed man'." 1925 Hoppe 110. See also 1925 *Literary Digest* (Jul 25) 55.

American Amateur Billiard Association (AABA)

(org.) This rival of the NATIONAL ASSOCIATION OF AMATEUR BILLIARD PLAYERS was formed in the 1918 in the United States with William Gershel as its first president. 1918 NYDT (Mar 27) 14:2. A second, unrelated organization with the same name was established in February, 1927.

American Billiard Association (ABA)

(org.) Former sanctioning body for U.S. carom tournaments, particularly Three-Cushions. It merged in 1988 with the BFUSA to form the UNITED STATES BILLIARD ASSOCIATION.

American Cuemakers Association (ACA)

(org.) Formed in 1992 by Leonard Bludworth to unite cuemakers into a guild to promote and preserve the art of cue manufacture. Address: 7614 Edna Street, Houston, Texas 77087.

American Four-Ball Billiards, American Four-Ball Game

(game, obs.) An American version of English Billiards but played with four balls instead of three: a PLAIN white ball, a SPOT WHITE, a DARK RED and a LIGHT RED. The game was played on carom tables and both four- and six-pocket tables in several variations. On carom tables and sometimes on pocket tables, only caroms counted: a carom on two reds was worth three points; on a white and a red, two; and on the white and both reds (called a DOUBLE CAROM), five. In another version, both caroms and WINNING HAZARDS counted; the number of points scored depended on the ball or balls pocketed and the ball first contacted. Thirteen points could be won on a single stroke, called a THIRTEEN-STROKE, by caroming onto and pocketing all the object balls. 1850 Phelan 23. Also known as the AMERICAN GAME.

Because multiple points could be earned for a single stroke, winners of Four-Ball events frequently scored more points than the GAME TOTAL because all points earned were credited. For example, the final score in a 1500-point match might be 1503 to 1342.

The opening position had the light red on the HEAD SPOT (which became known as the LIGHT-RED SPOT), the dark red on the FOOT SPOT, and the opponent's white on the POOL SPOT, five inches from the FOOT RAIL in the center of the table. 1864 AH 420, 1891 MB 276. Also known as the AMERICAN GAME, FOUR-BALL GAME, REVOLUTION GAME, or occasionally just as Billiards. These names were also applied to the carom versions. Cf. FOUR-BALL CAROMS, KOREAN GAMES, YOTSU-DAMA. See also AROUND THE TABLE.

The American Game was the principal billiard amusement in the United States in the mid-nineteenth century. An early version employed two white balls, a red, and a blue, with different scoring. 1839 Kentfield 46. The first public matches for money prizes at any form of billiards began at the American Four-Ball Game in 1854. 1891 MB 368. Competition took place on tables of the following sizes:

DATES	TABLE SIZE	NUMBER OF POCKETS
1854–1863	6 × 12	6
1863–1869	6 × 12	4
1869–1873	5½ × 11	4
1873–1876	5 × 10	0

The first champion of America was Dudley Kavanagh in 1863; the title was sponsored by Phelan and Collender. It then passed to Louis Fox, John Deery, Joseph Dion, and John McDevitt in succession over the next five years. No player ever regained the title after having lost it. A second championship series, known as the Diamond Cue, was initiated in 1869 and won by Deery, A. P. Rudolphe, Frank Parker, Cyrille Dion, Maurice Daly, Albert Garnier, and Cyrille Dion again, who held it for two and a half years until 1876. 1904 MB 225.

With the rise of the Three-Ball Game in the 1870s, interest in the four-ball variety declined precipitously. Reporting on a four-ball match in 1876, during which C. Dion and Rudolphe made extremely long RUNS, the *New York Times* declared, "The contest last night fairly kills the four-ball game." 1876 NYT (Apr 8) 7:3. In fact, no first-class competition was ever held again.

American Pocket Billiard League

(org.) An organization promoting the game of HOT EIGHT. Address: 8441 Monroe Avenue, Stanton, California 90680.

American Poolplayers Association (APA)

(org.) The organization of 115,000 members (in 1992) that coordinates the Bud Light Pool League, the American Pool League and the Canadian Pool League, all of which are devoted to BAR POOL. 1993 PBM (Jan) 60.

American Four-Ball Billiards (Currier & Ives)

American Game

1. (game, obs.) The AMERICAN FOUR-BALL GAME. 1839 Kentfield 46, 1857 Phelan 170. The American Game was introduced in England by a Mr. Stark, a New York player, and was played with a blue ball instead of a light red. 1856 Crawley 74. 2. (game, obs.) The three-ball carom game, also known as FRENCH CAROMS, as opposed to English Billiards, in which HAZARDS also counted. 1919 Hoyle 624 .

American Handicap

(Brit., obs.) A ROUND-ROBIN tournament. 1889 Drayson 93.

American Pyramid Pool

(game, obs.) A pocket game played with fifteen object balls RACKED in the shape of a triangle, or PYRAMID. The first player to pocket eight balls (more than half of 15) is the winner. Balls need not be CALLED on the opening stroke. Failure to DRIVE two balls to cushions on the opening stroke costs one point. The game is derived from the English game of PYRAMIDS. Tournaments were held in the U.S. in the early 1880s, but the game was largely supplanted by CONTINUOUS POOL beginning in 1888. 1884 MB 299, 1890 HRB 80, 1916 RGRG 57. Also known as American Pyramid Fifteen-Ball Pocket

Billiards or EIGHT-BALL PYRAMID. In modern usage, the game is called BASIC POCKET BILLIARDS.

The first tournament at American Pyramid Pool was held in 1882, BEST OF 41 games. Albert Frey was the winner.

American series

(Straight-Rail) The RAIL NURSE, known to the French as SÉRIE AMÉRICAINE because it was perfected by American players. 1889 Vignaux, 1980 BD (Nov/Dec) 20. The term is still in use outside the United States but is confusing because "series" is not used in English to mean either "run" or "nurse."

American Snooker

(game) Snooker whose rules have been modified to be consistent with other American pocket games. In American Snooker, the BAULK COLOURS are spotted on the HEAD STRING, whose location differs from that of the BAULK-LINE. In Snooker, no cushion need be struck by any ball so long as the BALL ON is contacted; in American Snooker the cue ball must hit the ball on, after which a ball must either be pocketed or contact a cushion. In American Snooker, the PINK is initially spotted so that it is touching a RED. In the British game, the pink is not in contact with any other ball. JUMP SHOTS are legal in American Snooker, but forbidden in Snooker. 1946 OR 75, 1965 Fats 60.

For variations, see also GOLF, LIABILITY, PAY BALL, PINK BALL.

American spot

(Amer. Four-Ball Bill., obs.) The SPOT on which the LIGHT RED is placed, just ABOVE the BAULK-LINE. 1869 Roberts 165. On American tables, the balk region occupies one-fourth of the table area, on English tables only one-fifth. Thus, when American Four-Ball is played on an English table, the light red must be placed somewhat above the BAULK-LINE SPOT, that is, closer to the TOP, to maintain proper proportions. Also known as the HEAD SPOT, STRING SPOT, UPPER SPOT, WHITE SPOT, and, in Three-Ball Billiards, the WHITE-BALL SPOT.

American Three-Cushion Billiard League

(org.) A professional LEAGUE formed on October 30, 1927, with Jack Doyle, a New York room owner, as president.

ammunition

(colloq.) Money, bankroll for gambling, one's ARMY. 1983 Linhard. See also BARREL.

Amusette

(game, obs.) A makeshift billiard game played on a dining or other table covered with a cloth. Clamps are used to set up borders around the table that consist not of cushions but of strings or bands in a manner resembling a boxing ring. Advertisements for this apparatus date back at least to 1883. Also IMPROMPTU BILLIARDS, PARLOR BILLIARDS.

7

Amusette

anchor

1. (Balkline) An ANCHOR SPACE or the ANCHOR NURSE. The term dates from 1890. 2. (Eng. Bill.) The ANCHOR CANNON.

anchor block

(Balkline) A variety of BALKLINE MARKER used to trace the outline of an ANCHOR SPACE on the cloth of a billiard table. See BALKLINE for a discussion of the anchor.

anchor cannon

(Eng. Bill.) A NURSERY position in which the object balls are JAWED in such a way that they are in contact with the ELBOWS of a pocket but are not FROZEN to one another. Invented by American Frank Ives, it was used by him to defeat John Roberts, Jr. in their 6000-point challenge match in 1893, during which Ives ran 2540 at the nurse. 1925 Hoppe 32. Tom Reece, in a match against Joe Chapman of 500,000 UP in 1907, ran it for 85 hours and 49 minutes over a period of five weeks, scoring an unofficial BREAK of 499,135. 1974 Lindrum 124. It is also called the CRADLE CANNON. 1908 Mannock II 418, 1912 Levi III 584, 1979 Everton 23. The term ANCHOR derives from the fact that the object balls do not move during the shot and thus appear to be "anchored" to the pocket. Cf. JAM CANNON. The term sometimes refers to the related stroke known in the U.S. as the ANCHOR NURSE.

anchor nurse

(Balkline) A STATIONARY NURSE in which the two object balls are resting astride a BALKLINE—one FROZEN to the rail, the other at a short distance from the rail. The two-shot repetitive sequence consists of (1) KISSING from the first ball and grazing the second ball with the cue ball without moving it, then (2) playing back to the original position by grazing the free ball and caroming off the second ball, which remains frozen to the rail. 1890 NY Herald (Feb 25) 9:1. After a few shots, the free ball becomes "anchored" to its location, hence the

name. The history of the stroke is obscure; some sources credit it to A. P. Rudolphe, but at least one other traces it back to Samuel Jakes in 1875, prior to the drawing of balklines. 1929 BM (Aug). There is no doubt, however, that Frank Ives was the greatest practitioner of the anchor nurse and his run of 487 at it in 1894 led to the introduction of PARKER'S BOX, a development that preceded the ANCHOR SPACE. 1908 Mannock II 20, 1913 Daly 164. Cf. CHUCK NURSE.

anchor space

(Balkline) A RESTRICTED SPACE consisting of a seven-inch square marked in CHALK on the table and whose side is centered at the intersection of a cushion and a BALKLINE. There are thus eight anchor spaces in most Balkline games, six at 71.2 and four at 28.2. 1916 RGRG 16, 1976 WSD 6, 1977 OR 10. When both object balls lie in the same anchor space, they are treated as if they were IN BALK, and the referee announces, "in anchor." The original anchor space, known as PARKER'S BOX, was introduced to prevent the ANCHOR NURSE, whose boring nature threatened billiards as a spectator sport. The anchor space is twice as large as the 3½ × 7-inch Parker's Box. The expansion to this size occurred in 1914 for the first 14.1 Balkline Tournament to prevent the CHUCK NURSE. 1924 NYT (Jan 10) 10:7. In METRIC BALKLINE, the anchor space has a side of length 178 millimeters. For more history, see 18.2 BALKLINE. About restricted spaces generally, see INTERDICTED AREA.

anchored

1. (Balkline) = IN ANCHOR, lying in the same ANCHOR SPACE. 1916 RGRG 16. 2. = JAWED.

and out

See OUT, UNFINISHED.

angle

1. (Pocket Bill.) The relationship of the lines of travel of the cue ball and the object ball. 1977 Martin 205. A deviation from a straight line, useful in obtaining POSITION. "I need an angle to get on the seven." See also the compounds below. When the cue ball, the object ball, and the pocket all lie in a line, an angle can be created by CHEATING THE POCKET. 2. A corner of the PLAYING SURFACE of a billiard table, where the CUSHIONS meet. 1807 White 3. See CROTCH. 3. = POCKET ANGLE. 4. = The angle formed by the CUSHION FACING. 5. = CUT ANGLE. 6. (obs.) The JAW of a pocket, one of the surfaces of the pocket opening. The "long angle" is the jaw that is farther from the shooter; the "short angle" is the nearer. 1970 Knuchell 236.

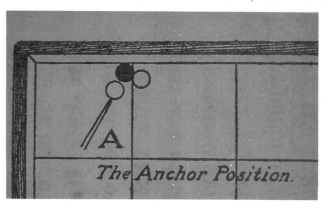

The Anchor Position.

anchor nurse

Angle Game

(game) Another name for THREE-CUSHION BILLIARDS, apparently derived from the fact that knowing the angles at which balls travel around the table is essential to success at this game. 1924 BM (Jul).

angle of incidence

The angle subtended by a cushion and the line of travel of a ball as the ball strikes the cushion. Used in a billiard context at least as early as 1653 in the French treatise *Récréations Mathématiques*. Cf. ANGLE OF REFLECTION, to which it is not necessarily equal.

angle of reflection

The angle between a cushion and the path of a ball as the ball rebounds from the cushion. See ANGLE OF INCIDENCE. In optics, the angle of reflection of light equals its angle of incidence. The same is not necessarily true in billiards, even when no English is used, as was recognized in 1806 Phil 22 and 1807 White 15: "This, however, is by no means the case with bodies equally moveable and elastic." The angle of reflection may be affected by speed, spin and the properties of the ball and cushion. The reason that the angles are not equal is explained in 1989 Koehler. The cushion deforms as it is struck by the ball and produces a reaction force that is greater in the direction from which the ball arrived. This causes the ball to rebound at an angle that is more nearly perpendicular to the cushion.

angle shot

(Pocket Bill.) A CUT SHOT, one in which the object ball is struck off-center to cause it to move in the desired direction. 1992 OR 5.

angled ball

(Pocket Bill., Snooker) A ball, either the cue ball or an object ball, that is positioned in the JAW of a pocket so that some other ball (usually the BALL ON) cannot be struck by it directly. 1900 WB (Nov 14) 11, 1974 Lindrum 138, 1978 BSCC 47, 1982 OR. A ball is said to be "angled" with respect to that part of the table from which a straight shot will not hit it. 1885 Cook 7, 1896 Broadfoot 105, 1946 OR 82. Under modern Snooker rules, a player is angled only if his line to each ball on is obstructed by a pocket. 1988 WPBSA. If the cue ball is angled, the REFEREE calls, "angled ball." 1992 OR 95. See also CALL, CORNER HOOKED, OBSTRUCTION. In modern British colloquial usage, KNUCKLED.

angled pot

(Brit. games) = CUT SHOT, one in which the object ball is not struck at its centre. 1991 Everton 64.

angles, know the

To understand the way in which balls travel around the table, and thus be able to make billiard shots. 1850 Phelan 17. "Nothing is so essentially requisite to constitute a good player, as a perfect knowledge of the angles of the table." 1807 White 29. The phrase has entered the English language to mean "having a particular skill."

announcement

1. = CALL. 2. (Forty-One) The claim by a player that he has won the game, whereupon he exhibits his PRIVATE NUMBER BALL so that the claim may be verified. 1992 OR 82.

APA

(org.) = AMERICAN POOL PLAYERS ASSOCIATION.

APBU

(org.) = ASIAN POCKET BILLIARDS UNION.

apex

(pocket games) The part of the PYRAMID that rests on the FOOT SPOT. 1992 OR 5. Hence the APEX BALL, or HEAD BALL, the ball that is spotted on the FOOT SPOT at the start of the game. 1896 Broadfoot 391. See also APEX BREAK, an anachronism whose use is confined to MISTER AND MRS. POCKET BILLIARDS.

apex ball

(pocket games) The ball at the APEX of the TRIANGLE and that is spotted on the FOOT SPOT at the start of a game. Also HEAD BALL.

apex break

(pocket games) A BREAK SHOT in which the only requirement is that the cue ball must contact the APEX BALL. It is not necessary to drive either the cue ball or any object ball to a cushion. This break is used in MISTER AND MRS. POCKET BILLIARDS.

appearance money

Compensation offered to a player to appear in a tournament, regardless of the player's performance or position in the final standings. The practice is condemned because it is thought to decrease competitiveness—a player need not play hard to win if money is guaranteed. In 1913, the NAABP proposed to bar any player who accepted appearance money. 1913 NYT (Jan. 20) 9:7. Cf. DUMP, SAVER.

applause

The showing of appreciation by the SPECTATORS or the opponent for a well-executed shot or successful game through the making of noise. Common methods in-

9

clude the clapping of hands or snapping of fingers. A player may bang the butt of his cue on the floor or tap a piece of chalk against his cue. Snapping and tapping are employed when other games are in progress to minimize the disturbance to players at neighboring tables. The BUMPER was introduced during the 1880s to reduce the noise made by butt-banging.

Apple

(game) A ROTATION game, popular in Hawaii, in which the 5, 10, and 15 are MONEY BALLS. A player who fails to CONTACT the lowest-numbered ball first may be forced to shoot again, but the incoming player is not given BALL IN HAND. 1991 Masui PC.

apron

1. A decorative panel hanging beneath the RAILS of a table, designed to conceal the FRAME. Also SKIRT. 2. A garment, often made of billiard cloth, that is worn around the waist of a billiard player to protect his clothing from wear and any chalk dust that might be lying on the rails. 3. A piece of cloth attached to a SKIRTED RACK to protect the playing surface as balls are being RACKED.

arch

1. (obs.) The IRON, PASS, PASS IRON or PORT. A target similar to a croquet wicket used on early billiard tables. The term was already falling into disuse in 1773 and was obsolete by 1807. 1974 Hendricks 25. 2. (obs.) A comb-like fitting for a Bagatelle table, used in the game of Mississippi.

army

(sl.) Hustler's term for his playing money or bankroll. 1970 Fensch 158. Also AMMUNITION, CHEESE, or WAD.

Around the Clock

(game) A CAROM game in which a player must make a DIRECT CAROM, a CUSHION CAROM, a two-cushion shot, a three-cushion shot, a two-cushion shot, a cushion carom, and a direct carom, in that order, though not necessarily in the same inning, in order to win. 1992 Segal PC.

Around the Horn

(game, obs.) A game played with three CUE STICKS placed as obstacles on the table, the object being to make one's designated ball come to rest in a marked circle at the upper end of the table without contacting any cue stick or the ball of any other player. 1888 NYT (Jun 6) 3:5.

around the table

1. Said of a shot in which a ball follows a diamond-shaped path, circling the table and CONTACTING three or more adjacent cushions in succession. 1977 Martin 205. The phrase was "round the table" in 1873 NYT (Jun 24) 5:3. 2. (game) A rule variation in the AMERICAN FOUR-BALL GAME, first tried in 1865, under which scoring could be accomplished by both CAROMS and POCKETINGS. 1904 MB 214.

artificial bridge

= MECHANICAL BRIDGE. 1850 Phelan 19, 1864 AH 400, 1982 OR. The instrument consists of a shaft approximately the same length as a cue stick with a BRIDGE HEAD affixed to the tip. The bridge head has several smooth notches on which to rest the cue during stroking.

Artistic Billiards

(game) A spectacular style of carom billiard competition comprising a set collection of 68 FANCY SHOTS, each of which is accorded an integer score ranging between 4 and 11, indicating its degree of difficulty. Every shot is performed by all contestants, who are ranked by the total number of points scored. Three attempts are permitted for each shot; the full score is awarded if the shot is made on any of the three attempts. All the shots require extreme English or a forceful stroke. The balls are placed accurately (sometimes to within a tolerance of two millimeters) in prescribed positions by the referee at specified COORDINATES located by means of a TEMPLATE. It is also known as FANTASY BILLIARDS or FANTAISIE CLASSIQUE, a discipline whose origins are more than a century old.

The shots are classified into MASSÉ SHOTS, JUMP SHOTS, etc. and are so difficult that the easiest of them is a challenge for most ordinary players. The maximum possible number of points that can be scored is 500. World title competition began in 1986. The record in world title play is 355, by Raymond Steylaerts in 1984. The highest score ever achieved in competition is 404, by Jean Reverchon of France in 1991. The governing body of the sport is the CIBA, which until 1990 required that ivory balls be used in competition. Players compete in two categories, based on their level of skill. The current threshold is an average of 220 points.

On some shots a small PIN is used as an obstacle and the player is required to make the cue ball pass on a designated side of the pin.

The vocabulary of Artistic Billiards is principally French, and many of its terms have no direct equivalent in English. See COUP FOUETTÉ, MASSÉ COULÉ, PIQUÉ.

10

See 1987 Jewett for diagrams of the shots of this remarkable game.

Asian Pocket Billiards Union (APBU)

(org.) The Asian governing body for pocket games. These games have not been popular in the Far East, where carom games predominate, but the situation is changing rapidly.

assistance

Players may not receive assistance or advice during a game. See also COACHING, SECOND. An infraction is treated as UNSPORTSMANLIKE CONDUCT. 1982 OR 51. This rule is very old—1674 Cotton 32 provides that "A stander by though he betts, shall not instruct, direct or speak in the Game without consent, or being first asked." 1807 White 76 describes attempts by players to subvert the rule by the use of surreptitious gestures and signals. In team play, team members may confer, but not "whilst the striker is at the table." 1987 Hales 68, 1987 BSCC S22. This rule is modified in SCOTCH DOUBLES. Assistance may take the form of recommending a shot or even warning a player that he is about to shoot with the WRONG BALL. Requests for refreshments, equipment and the like must be made through the REFEREE or a tournament official. The player may not accept such items from anyone else without permission.

For assistance in lining up a shot, see AIMING.

Association of Billiards and Snooker Referees

(org., Brit.) Professional body founded in Great Britain in 1977 to administer referee training and qualification programs. See REFEREE.

Association of College Unions International (ACU-I)

(org.) The governing body of certain intercollegiate sports and games in the United States, including billiards. Originally just the Association of College Unions, it has sponsored pocket and carom competition since 1932. National titles were formerly awarded in Straight-Rail, Three-Cushions, and Straight Pool. Now the only competitive form is Eight-Ball.

Association of Snooker Writers (ASW)

(org., Brit.) An organization of over 100 journalists covering Snooker. It confers annual Player of the Year and Service to Snooker awards.

ASW

(org., Brit.) = ASSOCIATION OF SNOOKER WRITERS.

11

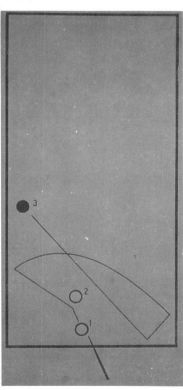

Artistic Billiards (1)

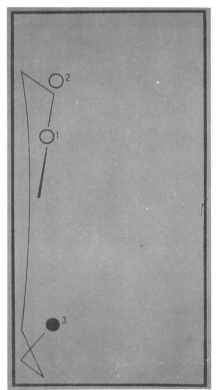

Artistic Billiards (2)

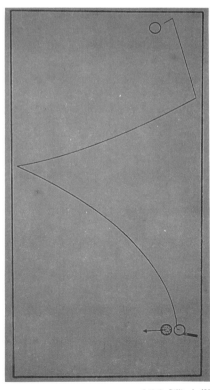

Artistic Billiards (3)

Australian Eight-Ball Federation (AEBF)

(org.) The governing body of Eight-Ball in Australia.

automatic return

= BALL RETURN. A system of GUTTERS for returning pocketed balls to a central GULLY. 1988 Rossman 99.

average

A numerical measure of a player's skill; the average number of points per INNING achieved by a player over a defined period such as a game, match, or tournament. Averages began to be kept around 1857. 1891 MB 368. The term "average" appears in 1865 NYT (Jan 21) 8:3. The average is called a "decimal" in 1889 Drayson. See GRAND AVERAGE, HIGH AVERAGE, HIGH GRAND AVERAGE, HIGH INDIVIDUAL AVERAGE, HIGH SINGLE AVERAGE, INDIVIDUAL AVERAGE, SINGLE AVERAGE, TOTAL PERFORMANCE AVERAGE.

If a player's probability of making a shot is p, his expected run length r (that is, his average, assuming no limitation on the number of points he may score) is given by $r = p / (1 - p)$. To prove this, let $q = 1 - p$, his probability of missing a shot. The probability of a run of length n is $p^n q$, since the player must first make n successful shots and then miss. His expected run length is therefore $\sum_{n=0}^{\infty} n\, p^n q = \dfrac{p}{1 - p}$. Similarly, the shot probability can be computed from the average r via the relationship $p = \dfrac{r}{1 + r}$. For numerous results on computing various probabilities based on averages under handicaps, consult 1947 Bottema 15.

According to the above relationships, a Three-Cushions player who averages 1.00 is making half of the shots he attempts. A player with an average of 0.5 is making one-third of his shots. The record competitive average in a 50-point game was 3.125 for over half a century, achieved by Otto Reiselt in 1926 and tied by Sang Lee in May 1992. It was then shattered by Sang Lee, who scored 19-11-9-11 for 50 in 4 innings in a handicap game in September 1992 at SL Billiards in Queens, New York. 1993 *World Report 3-Cushion* (Jan) 10.

The loser of a match may have a higher average than the winner if the winner breaks and thus plays one more inning than the loser. For example, if A wins, 100 to 99 in 10 innings, his average is 10 but the loser's average is 99/9 = 11. A situation such as this actually occurred in the Hoppe-Horemans match at 18.2 Balkline in 1921. The anomaly is no longer possible in international competition because the non-breaker is allowed an inning from the BREAK SHOT if he is not the first player to score the required number of points. See EQUAL IN-NINGS. A game can now result in a DRAW if the second player ties the score in his last inning.

It is possible for the winner and loser of a match to have the same average. This has happened occasionally. However, only once have the winner and loser tied for both average and high run in a title match. This occurred in 1863, when Dudley Kavanagh beat Philip Tieman at American Four-Ball on a four-pocket table. They both ran 203 and averaged 33⅓. 1941 NBJ (Jan).

away

(Snooker) Forfeited, as applied to points scored; that is, "given away." For example, "5 away" means that a penalty of five points has been assessed for an infraction of the rules. 1954 KTG 33. Points away are given to the opponent, not subtracted from the offender's score, so negative totals cannot result.

BAA

(org.) The BILLIARD ASSOCIATION OF AMERICA. A former governing body of American billiards.

BACC

(org.) = BILLIARDS ASSOCIATION AND CONTROL COUNCIL.

back double

(Snooker) = CUTBACK DOUBLE. 1988 Meadowcroft 54. Also CROSS DOUBLE.

backer

A banker for a money player. 1900 WB (Nov 14) 6, 1970 Fensch 158. Also called a STAKEHORSE. The backer generally pays all losses and keeps a percentage of any winnings. The relationship between a HUSTLER and his backer can be stormy. The hustler is reluctant to accept merely a small share of his winnings but may be perfectly willing to let the backer bear the losses. The backer, for his part, may find himself the victim of a DUMP by his player. The term was in use in a general betting sense in the sixteenth century. See GAMBLING.

backspin

= DRAW, LOW. 1913 Daly 34. Spin imparted to a ball by striking it below center so as to cause it to spin "backwards," *e.g.*, on a horizontal axis and in such a way that the ball tends to return after striking another ball.

backswing

The portion of a player's STROKE in which the cue stick is pulled backwards in preparation for hitting a ball. Edouard Horemans, a top balkline player during the 1920s and 30s, was unique in not employing a backswing at all; he placed the tip of the cue very near the ball and simply shoved the stick forward.

back-up

1. = BACKSPIN, DRAW, LOW. So named because the cue ball "backs up" after striking an object ball. 2. (Bill.) A ball is said to "back up" when it enters a corner with REVERSE ENGLISH, thereby narrowing the angle at which the ball will exit. 1898 Thatcher 80, 1978 Byrne 196.

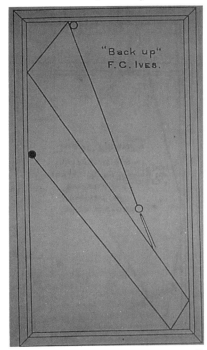

"Back up" F.C. Ives.

back-up (def 2)

Backwards Pool

(game) A pocket billiard game in which the object is to shoot an object ball at the cue ball to carom the cue ball into a pocket. Also BILLIARD POOL, CAROM POOL, CHINESE POOL, CONTRA POOL, INDIAN POOL, IRISH POOL, KISS POOL, LOOP, REVERSE BILLIARDS. Cf. CUE BALL POOL.

bad hit

A HIT that does not conform to the rules. 1989 Koehler 250. An invalid CONTACT, or no contact, between the cue ball and the required object ball, especially in Nine-Ball. Cf. GOOD HIT.

baffle

= BALL BAFFLE.

bag

= CUE BAG.

Bagatelle

(game, obs.) 1819 OED. A game similar to Billiards but played on a special table known as a Bagatelle Board having a semicircular area at one end in which there are nine numbered holes or CUPS, each number signifying the points to be scored by pocketing a ball in the corresponding cup. Table sizes of 6 × 1½ and 10 × 3 are known, as well as intermediate lengths. The table width is usually approximately one-third of its length. The cups are about 2½ inches in diameter, the balls 1⅞ inches. The baulk-line, sometimes called the DEAD-BALL LINE, lies approximately one-fifth of the distance from the end of the table. The table BED is commonly of slate. Occasionally, a BRIDGE with multiple ARCHES is used in addition to the cups.

The game is played with nine balls: one red, four black and four white. Players commence the game by STRINGING FOR LEAD, but rather than attempt to BANK the cue ball, they try to drop it in a hole. The player sinking his ball in the highest numbered hole leads. A black ball is placed on a spot nine inches in front of hole number one. Each player plays all eight balls up the table, scoring only when a ball has touched the black and then entered a cup. Holing the black doubles the score otherwise achieved on that stroke. Balls that miss the black, roll back across the balkline or are forced off table are DEAD for the player's round. 1837 Walker 89, 1881 MB 296, 1893 HRB 109, 1960 Ency. Brit. Known infrequently as SEMI-BILLIARDS.

During the late nineteenth century, Bagatelle evolved to resemble modern pinball. The table had a glass top and the balls bounced off fixed obstacles to land in holes. Also PIGEON-HOLE GAME.

Bagatelle was a diversion and never highly regarded by billiard players: "Bagatelle is to Billiards what Draughts [checkers] is to Chess, and he who plays at the superior game seldom practices much at the other." 1862 Crawley. There is currently an effort to revive Bagatelle, since it can be played in much less space than billiards. This is true because balls are struck from one end of the table only, so the table may be placed against a wall without obstructing the game.

For Bagatelle and related games, see BILIARDINO, CANNON GAME, CAROMBOLETTE, COCKAMAROO, ENGLISH BAGATELLE, FRENCH GAME, HIGH NUMBER POOL, IRISH CANNON GAME, LA BARRAQUE, MISSISSIPPI,

13

Bagatelle

MONTE CARLO, PARISIAN POOL, PIGEON HOLE AND JENNY LIND, POOL FOR 31 POINTS, RUSSIAN BAGATELLE, SANS EGAL, SEMI-BILLIARDS, TROLL MADAME, TROU MADAME.

baize

A coarse woolen CLOTH having a long NAP and used to cover billiard tables. Employed figuratively in the phrase "the green baize" to refer to the billiard table itself. 1881 NYT (Apr 12) 5:4.

Balabushka

The legendary cuemaker George Balabushka (d. 1975). He began his career by converting one-piece Brunswick stock models into superb jointed cues, known for simple elegance and unequaled BALANCE. A cue of his is known as a "Balabushka" in the same sense that a violin made by Antonio Stradivari is called a "Stradivarius." The Balabushka supposedly sported by Tom Cruise in the film *The Color of Money* was not actually a Balabushka but was a Joss cue.

balance

1. According to cuemaker Ray Schuler, "balance" is that property of a cue stick that makes it feel lighter in use than simply an equivalent dead weight. 1983 NBN (Mar) 18. This concept is rather ethereal. In physical terms, balance relates to the moment of inertia of the stick, or its tendency to resist rotating about the BALANCE POINT. 2. = BALANCE POINT.

balance point

The center of gravity of the cue stick, usually about 18 inches from the BUTT end. 1992 OR 5. Sometimes known as just the BALANCE. 1866 Crawley 9. The cue should be held somewhat behind the balance point or, in ONE-HANDED PLAY, just at that point.

balk

A specific marked area on a billiard table in which play is variously restricted or in which the cue ball must be placed in certain circumstances. An INTERDICTED AREA, RESTRICTED SPACE. See also entries under BALKLINE, BAULK, CROTCH, IN BALK, IN BAULK and OUT OF BALK.

1. (Pocket Bill.) The area between the HEAD STRING and the HEAD RAIL, also known as the KITCHEN. The area from which the ball can be played when it is IN HAND. When the last remaining object ball is IN BALK and the cue ball is in hand, either an object ball must be spotted (in certain games) or the cue ball must be made to leave the balk before it may lawfully strike the object ball. 1976 WSD 22, 1977 Martin 205. When the cue ball is required to leave the balk area, it need not contact a cushion or another ball first; the striker may massé the cue ball so that it returns to hit a ball in balk. 2. (Balkline) An area defined by lines drawn parallel to the cushions at a specified distance. A BALK SPACE or PANEL.

balk space

(Balkline) An area defined by lines (known as BALKLINES) drawn on the surface of the table and within which the number of caroms that can be made without driving at least one object ball out of the space is limited. A PANEL. See, generally, BALKLINE. See also CADRE, INTERDICTED AREA, RESTRICTED SPACE.

Balkline

1. (game) Any of a large variety of carom games in which the table is divided into regions (BALK SPACES) by lines (BALKLINES) drawn on the cloth. The number of points a player may score while both object balls lie in the same region is restricted. 1879 NYT (Nov 12) 5:5, 1881 MB. It can be viewed as a variation of STRAIGHT-RAIL designed to make play more difficult and thus reduce the length of RUNS to enhance spectator interest in the game. 1976 WSD 40. 2. A line marked on the cloth to define a balk area or BALK SPACE. 1946 OR 87, 1976 WSD 23, 1977 Martin 205. See ANCHOR SPACE, BALK, CENTER SPACE, CROTCH, INTERDICTED AREA, PANEL, RESTRICTED SPACE. The table markings for Balkline are made with tailor's CHALK or lead pencil. 1881 NYT (Apr 12) 5:4, 1883 NYT (Mar 11) 14:1. A reliable method of drawing the lines is to hold the chalk against the edge of a frame called a BALKLINE MARKER, which is then made to slide along the cushion.

The story of the Balkline game could easily fill a thick volume. The version below is a streamlined historical account. A summary of Balkline developments can be found in 1888 NYT (Oct 28) 20:1; an extensive history appears in 1898 Thatcher.

Balkline was introduced to combat the growing skill of Straight-Rail practitioners at NURSING, or compiling extremely long runs (in the hundreds) by means of delicate shots to keep the balls under close control. Such displays were boring to the spectators and diminished the competitive nature of the game, since a player who achieved a nurse position might finish the game out and prevent his opponent from taking another shot.

Crotching, the practice of freezing the object balls in a corner and caroming repeatedly, was first prohibited in 1862. 1891 MB 374. The CROTCH, a defined (but usually unmarked) space near the corners, was the first BALK SPACE. Three shots were allowed in the crotch before at least one of the object balls had to be driven out. It has always been the case that a ball that must be driven out of balk is allowed to return.

Barring the crotch inspired the development of the RAIL NURSE, in which the balls are moved around the table slowly by means of strokes that preserve the orientation of the balls while replicating the position a short distance down the rail. This nurse led to experimentation with a host of restrictive arrangements and variations on the basic Balkline layout pictured here. Note that the central rectangle in Balkline is not a balk space and there is no limit on the number of caroms that may be made with the balls inside it.

To many modern carom players, Straight-Rail seems so challenging that taking steps to increase its difficulty seems wholly unnecessary. However, the skill of dedicated players was so great that they could score essentially at will.

A Balkline game can be given a numerical designation consisting of two numbers separated by a period, such as 18.2. The first number specifies the distance, either in inches or centimeters, at which the balklines are drawn from the cushion. The second number tells how many shots are allowed while both object balls lie in the same balk space. This notation appears in the 1904 edition of *Modern Billiards*, but not in any prior edition. In this book, a third number is occasionally added to indicate how many shots are allowed IN ANCHOR; thus 14.2.5 means 14-inch balklines, two shots in balk, and five shots in anchor. See ANCHOR SPACE. If no third number is given, it is assumed to be equal to the second number, so 18.1 is an abbreviation for 18.1.1. The first popular Balkline game was 14.2; 14 inches is the distance between adjacent diamonds on a 5 × 10 table.

For specific game rules and anecdotes, see 8.2, 12½.2, 14.1, 14.2, 18.1, 18.2, 28.2, 38.2, 39.2, 42.2, 45.1, 45.2, 47.1, 47.2, 57.2 and 71.2 BALKLINE. Other games that have been played at various times include 10.2 and 12.2. An interesting version designed to limit long runs is FIVE AND TEN. For a frivolous variation, see LIBERTY BILLIARDS.

Balkline was the dominant carom game from 1883 until the late 1930s, when it was supplanted by Pocket Billiards and Three-Cushions. It was a favorite for AMATEUR play; competition in the U.S. was divided into four separate classes. Balkline is still popular in Europe and the Far East. For referee's calls in international Balkline, see À CHEVAL, DEDANS, ENTRÉ.

Following is a brief chronology of the game.

15

CHRONOLOGICAL HISTORY OF BALKLINE BILLIARDS	
YEAR	BALKLINE EVENT
1874	Diagonal lines at each corner are drawn to prevent the RAIL NURSE in tournament play. 1913 Daly 13.
1875	Balkline played by Rudolphe and the Dions with a six-inch continuous line, suggested by Benjamin Garno, later the editor of *Modern Billiards*. 1912 MB 264. See CONTINUOUS BALKLINE.

CHRONOLOGICAL HISTORY OF BALKLINE BILLIARDS	
YEAR	BALKLINE EVENT
1879	Advent of the CHAMPION'S GAME. A 14″ × 28″ diagonal drawn in each corner is used to frustrate the RAIL NURSE.
1879	Handicapping by drawing balklines at different distances proposed but not tried until 1888. 1888 NYT (Oct 7) 17:6.
1883	Four balklines at a distance of eight inches from the cushions to divide the table into nine rectangles suggested by Randolph Heiser. Vignaux beats Daly at 8.2 in the first public Balkline match at Chicago, March 26.
1884	The Space Game, a bizarre honeycomb of balk spaces, is tried in public. This variation is never played competitively again.
1885	Twelve-inch lines tried, then 14-inch. 1899 Souv 42. However, 14.2 is not played by major players again until 1888.
1886	Ten-inch lines used. 1912 MB.
1888	Fourteen-inch lines played against eight-inch lines as a HANDICAP. The odds between equal players are reported to be 8:5.
1891	12½.2 played on a 4½ × 9 table. (This gives the same geometric proportions as 14.2 on a 5 × 10.)
1894	Ives runs 487 at the ANCHOR NURSE, which leads to PARKER'S BOX, named after Charles Parker of Chicago, and the game of 14.2.10. The game of 28.2 is invented.
1896	Eighteen-inch balkline, 18.2.5, introduced by Daly. 1983 Malsert 99. First tournament at 18.1.1. The game of 71.2 is invented by F. Ferrandin.
1906	Willie Hoppe (age 18) beats Maurice Vignaux (age 59) for the 18.1 World Championship.
1907	Professional tournaments at 14.1 Balkline suggested, but not played until 1914.
1910	Hoppe plays 18.1 to Cutler's 18.2 in a handicap match in New York. 1910 NYT (Oct 29) 12:5.

CHRONOLOGICAL HISTORY OF BALKLINE BILLIARDS	
YEAR	BALKLINE EVENT
1914	Anchor space enlarged to 7″ × 7″. Willie Hoppe wins first professional 14.1 Balkline tournament. Tom Foley suggests dividing the table into four quadrants to stop Hoppe. 1914 NYT (Mar 21) 11:6.
1937	First and last U.S. professional tournaments held at 28.2 and 71.2 Balkline.
1958	The 47 centimeter game is introduced to make the widths of the balk spaces along the short rail equal. 1983 Malsert 99.

balkline marker
1. (Balkline) Device to aid in marking the table with chalk or pencil for BALKLINE play, consisting of a frame with slats at various distances that is slid along the cushion so that its edge traces a straight line. 1908 Brunswick 94. The chalk or pencil is held against the marker as it is moved. See also ANCHOR BLOCK, MARKER.
2. (Balkline) A scoring official (the MARKER) at a game of BALKLINE.

balkline marker

balkline nurse
(Balkline) A RUNNING NURSE designed to avoid the effect of the BALKLINES, permitting a repetitive position in spite of the BALK restrictions. 1894 NY Herald (Jan 10) 13:3, 1913 Daly 184. The most celebrated of these is the LINE NURSE, sometimes known just as the LINE.

balkline table
(Balkline) An ordinary CAROM TABLE whose cloth has been ruled with BALKLINES. Otherwise, no special table is used for Balkline.

ball
A solid sphere used in billiard games. 1674 Cotton. A BILLIARD BALL. Over the centuries, a wide variety of

materials has been used for billiard balls, including wood, clay, steel, ivory, celluloid, crystalate, and plastic materials. Ivory was the material of choice from 1627 until well into the twentieth century. An extensive history of balls and their development can be found in 1974 Hendricks.

Substantial technology is involved in ball manufacture, which involves applying such markings as numbers and stripes, turning the balls into ROUND, polishing them, and choosing sets matched by weight. It is critical that balls be round and of uniform density so they will run TRUE. "If your Balls are not completely round you can neither expect good proof in your play." 1674 Cotton. Currently, balls are turned to a tolerance of five thousandths of an inch. 1975 Billiard Facts 29.

For several centuries, no better substance was known for billiard balls than ivory, and to this day billiard balls of many different materials are referred to as "ivories." The problems associated with obtaining and using ivory led to an extensive search for a substitute, motivated in part by a prize of $10,000 reportedly offered by a New York billiard table manufacturer. John Wesley Hyatt developed the celluloid ball in 1868, but it is not clear whether the prize was ever awarded. Hyatt formed the Albany Billiard Ball Company and conducted numerous experiments to perfect his materials. Celluloid itself was not really suitable because of its tendency to explode.

At the turn of the century, there was outcry over the use of ivory. Curiously, however, the concern was not the large-scale slaughter of elephants but the fear that humans would be injured on dangerous hunting expeditions. In recent years, regard for the elephant population has led to international restrictions on ivory traffic, which in turn has resulted in the demise of the ivory ball. Recently, the CIBA relaxed its rule requiring the use of ivories in Artistic Billiards competition.

The size of balls has increased over the years. Early English games were played with 1⅞" balls. By 1830, this had grown to 2", then to 2¹⁄₁₆" by the end of the century. In the U.S. in 1890, the size of carom balls was 2⅜". The Korean four-ball game is played with 65.5 mm balls (about 2⁷⁄₁₆"). These are extremely heavy—the weight of a ball increases with the cube of its diameter. BAGATELLE boards were supplied with 1⅝" balls. Before a competitive match, billiard balls would be weighed and their size checked using a MEASURING RING. In issuing a CHALLENGE, the size of the balls to be used had to be specified. Below is a table of ball sizes and weights for various games.

SIZES AND WEIGHTS OF BALLS USED IN VARIOUS BILLIARD GAMES		
GAME	**SIZE, WEIGHT**	**REFERENCE**
Carom Billiards	2⅜" 2²⁵⁄₆₄" 2²⁷⁄₆₄" 2⁷⁄₁₆" 61–61.5 mm 7–7½ oz. 205–225 grams	1982 OR 1946 OR 3, 1978 Stone 8 1976 WSD 24 1982 OR WBA 2 1981 Rottie 27
English Billiards	1⅞–2" 2¹⁄₁₆–2³⁄₃₂" 57.5 mm 5 oz. ± 0.5 g. per set	1839 Kentfield 3 1978 BSCC 23 1978 BSCC 23
Pocket (U.S.)	2¼" 2⁵⁄₁₆" 5½–6 oz.	1913 Stoddard 10, 1946 OR 3 1916 RGRG 5 1976 WSD 24, 1982 OR

Snooker	2¹⁄₁₆"
	2⅛" (Amer.)
	52.5 mm
	  + 0.05 − 0.08
	5–5½ oz
	Tolerance
	  ± 3 grams/set
		1982 OR
		1946 OR 3
		1987 BSCC 38

In international carom tournaments, the difference in weight between the lightest and heaviest ball of a set cannot exceed one gram.

Balls began to be colored in 1771 by staining. Numbered balls were used for the game of Hazards in 1773. Balls of several different colors were employed in the English game of Pool in the early 1800s and are shown in plates from Mingaud's 1827 handbook of TRICK SHOTS. 1807 White 4 indicates that one of the two white cue balls in Billiards was marked with a black spot.

In Pocket Billiards, balls whose numbers differ by eight are of the same color; the ball with the higher number has a stripe. The current color sequence is yellow, blue, light red, purple, orange, green and dark red. These are just the colors of the spectrum with dark red substituted for indigo. The eight-ball is black, then the colors are repeated for the striped balls. In 1899, the three-ball was pink and the five-ball brown. In 1935, Brunswick experimented with purple cloth and created a set called "spectro balls" whose colors were tan, deep blue, maroon, lavender, brown, yellow, green, and pink. 1935

NBJ (Sep). See SEVEN-BALL for a color change necessitated by television.

In international carom tournaments, the SPOT BALL has been replaced by an unspotted yellow ball. To learn what happens if a ball splits into more than one piece during a shot, see BROKEN BALL.

The REFEREE may clean the balls at his own volition or at the request of a player. See also POLISH.

For differences in balls used for various games, see BILLIARD BALL, POOL BALL, SNOOKER BALL.

For expressions and concepts based on "ball," see also AIR BALL, ANGLED BALL, APEX BALL, BANDED BALL, BIG BALL, BILLIARD BALL, BLACK BALL, BREAK BALL, BROKEN BALL, BUNKER BALL, CALLED BALL, CAROM BALL, CHANGED BALL, CLEAR BALL, COMPANION BALL, COMPOSITION BALL, CORNER BALL, CUE BALL, DEAD BALL, FINE BALL, FIRST OBJECT BALL, FOLLOWING BALL, FREE BALL, FULL BALL, GAME BALL, GROUP BALL, GUTTER BALL, HALF-BALL, HEAD BALL, JUMP BALL, KEY BALL, KILLED BALL, KING BALL, LARGE BALL, LIFTED BALL, LINE BALL, LIVE BALL, LOOSE BALL, MONEY BALL, NEAREST BALL PLAYABLE, NOMINATED BALL, NUMBERED BALL, OBJECT BALL, OFF THE BALLS, ON BALL, OVERSIZE BALL, PARK THE BALL, PAY BALL, PENALTY BALL, PLAIN BALL, PLAY BALL, POCKETED BALL, POOL BALL, PRIVATE BALL, PYRAMID BALL, QUARTER-BALL, RECOVERY BALL, RED BALL, SCORE BALL, SECOND OBJECT BALL, SHAKE BALL, SNOOKER BALL, SPINNING BALL, SPOT BALL, STILL CUE BALL, STOP BALL, STROKE BALL, SUSPENDED BALL, TALLY BALL, TOUCHING BALL, UNBANDED BALL, WHITE BALL, WRONG BALL, ZIGZAG BALL and the compounds below.

ball and pocket

A shorthand term for the rule in CALL-SHOT GAMES requiring the player to name the ball he intends to pocket and the pocket in which it will fall. No other details of the stroke need be specified.

ball baffle

(Bar Bill.) A device to prevent HOLED balls from being returned to the player once time has expired.

ball bridge

A FINGER BRIDGE for supporting the cue stick so a stroke can be made over an intervening ball. 1946 Brunswick.

ball cleaner

1. A mechanical polishing device used to clean billiard balls by buffing. 2. Any solvent used to remove CHALK and other stains from billiard balls.

ball holder

A BALL RACK for storing billiard balls either when they are not in use or during a game for scoring purposes. 1876 Collender 14. The balls pocketed by each player are stored on different shelves so that the scores can easily be determined at a glance. The fourth billiard ball (the LIGHT-RED) used in the Four-Ball Game was commonly stored in the gas fixture above the table during Three-Ball play.

ball in hand

(Pocket Bill., Brit. games) Following the commission of certain FOULS or the occurrence of irregularities, the INCOMING PLAYER is said to have "ball in hand," meaning that he is permitted to place the cue ball by hand anywhere inside a specified area of the table. In general, anywhere within BALK. 1807 White 107. In Pocket Billiards, a ball in hand may be placed anywhere behind the HEAD STRING, in an area known as the KITCHEN. The cue ball is in hand at the commencement of the game and following any SCRATCH in which the cue ball enters a pocket. In certain games, such as NINE-BALL and SEVEN-BALL, which require a particular ball to be struck first, a ball in hand may be placed anywhere on the table. In English games, a ball in hand may be placed anywhere within the D. See also IN HAND entries.

ball in motion

See MOTION.

ball off

A JUMP BALL or JUMPED BALL, one that has been knocked off the table and remained off, or has left the table and hit a person or an object not considered part of the table EQUIPMENT. 1977 Martin 206. See also OFF THE TABLE.

ball on

1. (Pocket Bill., Snooker) Generally, the object ball with which the cue ball may or must make first CONTACT. 1916 RGRG 41, 1974 Lindrum 138. See also ON. The original term was "ball played on" (see, *e.g.*, 1900 May 97), which was contracted to "ball on" in common usage by 1925. The phrase does not appear in the official 1909 rules of the BILLIARDS ASSOCIATION.

The definition varies somewhat depending on the game being played, as in EIGHT-BALL, NINE-BALL and ROTATION. In Snooker, a ball is ON if it may be legally struck first by the cue ball. While REDS remain on the table, the striker is alternately on reds and COLOURS. 1992 OR 5 defines the ball on to be any color a player *intends* to pocket, but this is too restrictive because a player can be on a ball but have no intention of pocketing it, preferring instead to LAY A SNOOKER.

18

2. (Pocket Bill.) Said of a straight-in shot, one in which the cue ball, object ball and pocket all lie in a straight line. 1964 Crane & Sullivan 88. Cf. ANGLE.

Ball Pool

(game, obs.) The original name for pocket billiard games in the U.S. during the late nineteenth century, referring particularly to FIFTEEN-BALL POOL.

ball rack

1. A rack for holding billiard balls, usually mounted on a wall. Some have a mechanical device for releasing the balls, which then roll conveniently down into the player's hand. 1908 Brunswick 116. See also BALL HOLDER. 2. A RACK or TRIANGLE.

ball rack

ball return

(Pocket Bill.) A bin or holder, usually suspended below the FOOT of the table, into which pocketed balls roll for ease of retrieval or RACKING. The ball enters the return by means of GUTTERS or TROUGHS that run under each pocket. Ball returns were known in the 1700s, when they ran along the outside periphery of the table. On early French tables, pockets were not cut into the cushions but consisted simply of holes in the slate. Balls entering these holes would drop through a leg of the table and appear at the mouth of an ornamental lion head carved into the leg. See also GULLY, TROUGH. A table without a ball return is said to have DROP POCKETS, *i.e.*, pockets into which balls drop and remain in place. (*See illustration bottom of this page.*)

ball-to-ball cannon

(Eng. Bill.) A CANNON in which the cue ball contacts both object balls before contacting any cushion. A DIRECT CANNON. The number of legal consecutive ball-to-ball cannons is limited to prevent lengthy BREAKS achieved through NURSERIES. 1919 Cut-Cavendish 102. See CONSECUTIVE CANNONS.

ball to nothing

(Snooker) = SHOT TO NOTHING. 1938 Clifford.

balls struck simultaneously

1. (Snooker) Two balls, other than two REDS or a FREE BALL and the BALL ON, may not be struck simultaneously. The reason for this is that the ball on must be struck *first*. It is therefore a foul if the ball on is not

ball return

clearly contacted *before* any other ball. See DOUBT. There is no such prohibition in other games, unless there is a requirement that a specific ball be hit first, as in NINE-BALL or ROTATION. Cf. SPLIT HIT. 2. (Eng. Bill.) For purposes of scoring, if both object balls are struck simultaneously, the white is considered to have been hit first. This creates a presumption against the player, since he would earn one more point if the red were contacted first. 1941 Levi 245. See DOUBT.

banana shot

(Snooker, colloq.) A shot for POSITION in which the cue ball is struck with extreme TOP at a ball lying near a cushion. The cue ball follows forward to the cushion, rebounds, and then stops. 1983 Davis 73.

band

1. (pocket games) A broad stripe, usually white in color, around the equator of a ball that serves as background for the ball's number. See also BANDED BALL. 2. (Brit.) = CUSHION. 1926 BM (Mar) 49.

banded ball

(Pocket Bill.) A STRIPE, one of the pocket billiard balls numbered 9 through 15 and having a broad colored band around its circumference. 1977 Martin 206. See also BALL. Cf. SOLID, UNBANDED BALL.

bank

1. A BANK SHOT, one in which a ball strikes a cushion before hitting another ball or entering a pocket. 1674 Cotton 41, 1850 Phelan 21, 1881 MB 22. Also used as a verb, as in "bank it in the side." 2. A CONTACT between a ball and a cushion, as in "two-bank shot," "off three banks." 3. A CUSHION, so called by analogy with the bank of a river. On early tables, the cushions were straight vertical walls reminiscent of riverbanks as opposed to the beveled cushions of today. 4. The opening LAG or STRING for BREAK, in which the players send their cue balls against the FOOT RAIL, the one coming to rest nearest the HEAD RAIL being the winner. 1871 NYT (Apr 27) 1:5, 1941 Hoppe 75. "He won the bank."

Bank Billiards

(game) CAROM BILLIARDS in which the cue ball must contact at least one cushion before hitting any ball. 1911 HRB 49, 1946 OR 17, WBA 13. This differs from CUSHION CAROMS in that the latter requires only that the cue ball make a cushion contact sometime prior to completing the shot. Originally known as the BANK-SHOT GAME. See also EIGHT AND EIGHT, THREE-CUSHION BANKS.

Bank Pool

(game) A SINGLE-RACK pocket game in which all shots must be BANK SHOTS of the object ball off at least one cushion. The first player to score eight balls wins. 1965 Fats 30, 1992 OR 63. Banking the cue ball does not count unless an object ball is also banked. All shots must be CLEAN BANKS. INCIDENTAL CONTACT between a ball and a cushion does not count as a bank. Also called BOUNCE POOL or just BANKS or BUMPS.

Bank Pool tournaments are held occasionally. Because of the difficulty of making the shots and the excellent opportunities for DEFENSE, a Bank Pool game can progress rather slowly. For a tournament in Decatur, Illinois, in 1980, the length of games was reduced to five balls to shorten play. The skill of Eddie Taylor, the "Knoxville Bear," at Bank Pool is of legendary proportions.

The number of different possible initial racks in Bank Pool is 15!, or 1,307,674,368,000 (just over a trillion).

bank shot

1. Generally, a shot in which a ball contacts a cushion before a score is effected. Also just a BANK. 1865 NYT (Jun 4) 5:4. The term "bank" originally referred to the border of the table. The particular meaning of "bank shot" varies depending on which game is being discussed. In Carom Billiards, it is a shot in which the striker's cue ball hits a cushion before contacting any ball. This is universally referred to as a bank shot but is properly called a BRICOLE. In Three-Cushions, a bank shot may cause the cue ball to hit many cushions before contacting a ball and may be aimed using a DIAMOND SYSTEM. Tom Rossman's 1988 book contains over 50 pages on banking systems. See also UMBRELLA. Banking is discussed as early as 1674 Cotton 41.

In Pocket Billiards, the standard definition of a bank, originally known as a DOUBLET, is a shot in which the object ball contacts a cushion before entering a pocket. 1986 OR. Such a narrow specification is appropriate for the game of BANK POOL, in which a banked object ball may not contact any other ball on its way to the pocket. In general, a bank shot is one in which a contact between a ball and a cushion is essential to making the shot. It is certainly not merely a shot in which some ball contacts a cushion, as this happens on virtually every shot. A special type of bank, known as a KICK SHOT, is one in which the cue ball contacts a cushion before hitting an object ball (that is, a bricole).

Bank shots are rarely played in tournament Straight Pool events because of the greater possibility of a miss. 1930 BM (Jan) 4, 1948 Mosconi 65.

See also BRICOLE, CLEAN BANK, CROSS, CROSS-CORNER,

CROSS DOUBLE, CROSS-SIDE, DOUBLE, DOUBLE BANK, DOUBLE DOUBLE, DOUBLET, DUB, INCIDENTAL CONTACT, KICK SHOT, LONG BANK, NATURAL BANK, PROJECTING THE POCKET, RAIL-FIRST, REFLECTED HAZARD, SHORT BANK, STRAIGHT BACK, TREBLE, TRIPLE.

2. The LAG or STRING for BREAK. 1942 Cochran 106. See BANK.

Bank-Shot Game

(game) = BANK BILLIARDS. Carom Billiards in which the cue ball must CONTACT a cushion before touching any ball. 1890 HRB 62, 1891 MB 308, 1916 RGRG 20. Cf. the closely related BRICOLE GAME, which is English Billiards with a bank requirement.

Bank the Nine

(game) A HANDICAP form of Nine-Ball requiring the stronger player to BANK the nine in order to win the game.

Banks

(game) = BANK POOL, BOUNCE POOL. A Pocket Billiard game in which all shots must be BANK SHOTS. 1984 Tevis. Occasionally used to refer to BANK BILLIARDS or THREE-CUSHION BANKS, depending on the context. See also NINE-BALL BANKS, ROTATION BANKS.

Banks, Kisses, and Combinations

(game) = HONOLULU, INDIRECT.

BAPTO

(org.) = BRITISH ASSOCIATION OF POOL TABLE OPERATORS.

Bar Billiards

(game) A style of game played on special equipment, similar to a BAGATELLE table, having nine holes, four SKITTLES and a red ball. White balls are shot from baulk. The ball must first hit another ball, then some ball must enter a hole. A player continues shooting until he fails to score, fouls or upsets a skittle. The number of points scored for holing a ball depends on which hole is involved. Likewise, each skittle carries its own penalty. Cf. BAR POOL.

The table is narrow and can be located in a relatively small space, even with two sides adjacent to walls because it is necessary to shoot from only one end. The game is a bar amusement, often played with an automatic timer that prevents play from continuing after time runs out. See BALL BAFFLE, NINE-HOLE SNOOKER. Older versions of this game were known as RUSSIAN BAGATELLE, SKITTLE BILLIARDS and SNOOKERETTE.

Bar-Hole Game

(game, obs.) CRAMP GAME of English Billiards in which one HOLE (pocket) is BARRED to a player, meaning that he may make no HAZARDS into the designated pocket. 1775 Annals 111. 1807 White 50 gives the advantage as 6 points in 21 between otherwise equal players, but this depends on which hole is barred. The game was obsolete by the 1860s. Crawley found the game "uninteresting," but he was not fond of cramp games in general. 1866 Crawley 235. The Bar-Hole Game is, of course, a precursor of ONE-POCKET.

Bar Pool

(game) Pocket billiards, almost always Eight-Ball, as played in bars, usually on COIN-OPERATED TABLES. The rules tend to be informal and subject to substantial local variation (see HOUSE RULE). Also known as the BAR-TABLE GAME. See also LEAGUE.

bar table

A table, generally 3½ feet × 7 feet in size and usually coin-operated, intended for use in bars, where space is at a premium and the dominant game is Eight-Ball. Hence, BAR POOL or the BAR-TABLE GAME. See also LEAGUE.

Bar-Table Game

(game) = BAR POOL. 1978 Fels 133.

barber

(usually Bill., colloq.) A narrow miss, often made deliberately (and illegally) for safety purposes. A "close shave." Also WINDY. Cf. DELIBERATE SAFETY, INTENTIONAL MISS.

barge pole

(Brit. games, colloq.) = LONG-BUTT. 1897 Payne 34.

Barraque, La

(game, obs.) = PARISIAN POOL. A game played on the PARISIAN POOL BOARD, normally to 200 points. The ball must strike a cushion outside the STRING, run up the incline, pass over a brass plate onto the board, and drop into one of 12–15 CUPS to score the number of points marked on that cup. Players alternate single shots. 1890 HRB 106, 1891 MB 352.

barred

1. Forbidden. At various times, certain billiard strokes have been barred, such as the MASSÉ (1862), PUSH (1862), CROTCH (1862), and JAW SHOT (1864). Barred implements have included the MACE (1865) and the MECHANICAL BRIDGE (1865). It is also possible for a pocket to be barred in such HANDICAP contests as the BAR-HOLE GAME. 2. (Brit. games) Limited. For exam-

ple, shooting when the balls are CROTCHED. The stroke itself is not actually illegal, but multiple consecutive repetitions are disallowed beyond a specified limit. See SPOT-BARRED GAME. See also SHARP.

barrel
(colloq.) A quantity of cash equal to the current stake being played for. At $100 per game, a player with $500 in his pocket is "shooting with five barrels," meaning he can lose five games before being wiped out. See also AIR GUN.

base
1. That portion of a table supporting the BED. The BASE FRAME. 2. The flat bottom surface of a cue TIP, which is in contact with the FERRULE. 1965 Fats 77. Cf. CROWN.

base frame
The structural members that support the heavy slate BED of a table. 1979 Sullivan 182. See BASE.

Baseball
(game) A carom game in which each player has CHOICE OF CUE BALL each inning and shoots until he misses three times (corresponding to "outs"). Each point is equivalent to a "single" in baseball. A game consists of nine INNINGS. 1943 NBJ (Jan).

Baseball Pocket Billiards
(game) Pocket billiard game designed to emulate certain aspects of baseball. It is played with 21 object balls, numbered 1–21, which are RACKED in six rows in an enlarged triangle. The one-ball is spotted on the FOOT SPOT, which is called HOME PLATE. The nine-ball is known as the PITCHER. Each player is given nine INNINGS (in both the billiard and baseball senses) in which to score RUNS. His total of points scored in an inning is the sum of the values of all balls pocketed. If a player sinks all balls remaining on the table, the balls are racked and his inning continues. 1925 RGRG 48, 1946 OR 69, 1965 Fats 57. A flyer published by Brunswick in 1912 listing the rules described Baseball Pocket Billiards as "the most fascinating game of the twentieth century." See also BASEBALL SET.

Baseball set
A set of six pocket billiard balls numbered 16–21 and intended to be used with an ordinary 15-ball rack to play BASEBALL POCKET BILLIARDS.

Basic Pocket Billiards
(game) A SINGLE-RACK game played with a cue ball and 15 object balls. The first player to pocket a total of eight balls wins. Balls, but not pockets, must be CALLED. 1946 OR 27. A ONE-BALL BREAK is utilized. Substantially the

same game as AMERICAN PYRAMID POOL, or EIGHT-BALL PYRAMID.

basket
1. A POCKET NET; the container that captures pocketed balls. There is no specification for the capacity of a pocket, but a typical basket holds nine balls. 2. (obs.) = POOL BASKET.

baulk
1. (Brit. games) A marked area on a billiard table from which the cue ball must be played when it is IN HAND. 1800 OED, 1807 White 3, 1839 Kentfield 3. That portion of the table between the BAULK-LINE and the BOTTOM RAIL, constituting one-fifth of the table area. See also BALK, IN BAULK. 2. (Eng. Bill.) A desirable situation in which the opponent's cue ball is OFF THE TABLE and both other balls are within the BAULK-LINE. 1807 White 66. The STRIKER must play from the D and is not allowed to hit either ball directly. See MAKE A BAULK.

baulk circle
(Brit. games) = D. 1873 Bennett 18. On a REGULATION TABLE, this is a semicircle of approximate radius 11 inches, centered at the middle of the BAULK-LINE and lying entirely in the BAULK. 1866 Crawley 15. Also known as the BAULK SEMICIRCLE, HALF-CIRCLE, SEMI-CIRCLE or STRIKING RING.

baulk colour
(Snooker) A ball (a COLOUR) that is spotted on the BAULK-LINE at the beginning of a FRAME: the YELLOW, the BROWN, or the GREEN. 1975a Lowe 13, 1979 Everton 100. Also SMALL COLOUR.

baulk cushion
(Brit. games) The SHORT RAIL at the BAULK END of the table, nearest the D. The BOTTOM CUSHION. 1973 Spencer 66.

baulk end
(Brit. games) The BOTTOM, or lower, end of the table, containing the BAULK area. In American games, the HEAD of the table. 1974 Lindrum 138. See also BAULK CUSHION.

baulk-line
(Brit. games) A line drawn across the lower end of the table to define the BAULK, about 2½ feet from and parallel to the BOTTOM cushion. 1839 Kentfield 3, 1866 Crawley 15. The distance is 29 inches on a standard Snooker table. 1975a Lowe 13. The regulation distance is one-fifth the length of the playing area or, on metric tables, 700 millimetres. 1978 BSCC 23.

In order to counter the monotonous effect of NURSERY CANNONS in English Billiards, a rule was introduced in 1932 requiring the player to cross the baulk-line with his cue ball after every 150 points or lose his turn. In 1935, the rule was modified to require such a crossing during the last 20 of each 200 points. See LINE RULE.

baulk marker

(Brit. games) A template for drawing the D. 1957 BSTE 3. Cf. BALKLINE MARKER.

baulk pockets

(Brit. games) The two CORNER POCKETS within the BAULK, that is, BELOW the BAULK-LINE. 1869 Roberts 165.

baulk semicircle

(Brit. games) = D, BAULK CIRCLE, HALF-CIRCLE, SEMI-CIRCLE, or STRIKING RING.

baulk spot, baulk-line spot

(Brit. games) Spot located in the center of the BAULK-LINE. 1866 Crawley 7, 1873 Bennett 18, 1976 WSD 23. The BROWN is placed on the baulk spot at the commencement of a Snooker frame. Also known as the MIDDLE SPOT IN BAULK. In American games, the HEAD SPOT.

BBC

1. The Brunswick-Balke-Collender Company. See BRUNSWICK. 2. The British Broadcasting Company, credited with contributing to the huge increase in popularity of Snooker in Great Britain though its television series POT BLACK.

B.B.C. Co. Pool

(game, obs.) A forerunner of Eight-Ball, the game is played with seven yellow, seven red, one black and one cue ball. The object is to pocket the black after having pocketed all seven balls of one color. 1908 HRB 120, 1916 RGRG 67. The black is racked behind the APEX ball. Balls pocketed on the BREAK count. "B.B.C." refers to the Brunswick-Balke-Collender Company, a major manufacturer of billiard tables and equipment in the late nineteenth century and the predecessor of the modern Brunswick Corporation. The game was introduced by Brunswick and was still referred to by its original name as late as 1925. The sets are no longer sold, the public having realized that a regular set of pocket balls, including seven SOLIDS, seven STRIPES, and an eight-ball, serves just as well.

BBIA

(org.) = BILLIARD AND BOWLING INSTITUTE OF AMERICA.

BCA

(org.) = BILLIARD CONGRESS OF AMERICA.

bead

= BUTTON.

Beat the Breaker

(game) A version of Three-Cushions with scoring resembling bowling, invented by Harry Sims, former U.S. national Three-Cushion champion. The game consists of ten "frames," each of which begins with a BREAK SHOT. The player may shoot until he misses, then may shoot again until he misses. A player who scores on the first attempt may score a maximum of 10 points for the frame. A run of 10 on the first attempt earns a bonus of 10. A player who misses on the first attempt may score any number of points on his second attempt. The player who is in the lead after 10 frames is the winner.

bed

The flat, level surface of a billiard table, which is covered with cloth. 1839 Kentfield 3, 1863 Phelan & Berger 90, 1976 WSD 36, 1979 Sullivan 182. The playing area of a table, exclusive of the cushions. 1977 Martin 4, 1982 OR. The height of a billiard table is measured from the floor, or bottom of a LEG, to the bed. See TABLE. Originally, table beds were made of wood, usually oak, which gave rise to the term BILLIARD BOARD as a synonym for billiard table. Beds were later made of marble and metal. Finally, around 1827, use of SLATE began.

If the bed is composed of more than one slate, the maximum permissible difference in height between adjacent pieces is 0.005". 1992 OR 2.

Inexpensive table beds may be made of imitation slate or an aluminum honeycomb structure designed to provide sturdiness with very little weight. There is no substitute for weight in a bed, however; it is crucial that the table not move when it is leaned upon, which cannot be achieved in a light table unless it is rigid and bolted to the floor.

bed cloth

The cloth used to cover the BED of a table. Cf. RAIL CLOTH.

behind the back

A method of shooting ordinarily unreachable shots by stroking with the cue stick held behind the back as the player sits on the rail. 1915 Reece & Clifford 128. This stance is mentioned in 1878 NYT (Dec 28) 8:1, but is of much earlier origin, as demonstrated by prints from the eighteenth century. A usually clumsy and showy ma-

23

behind the back

neuver better avoided by shooting with one's other hand. 1898 Thatcher 196 advises players to refrain from shooting behind the back entirely. See AMBIDEXTROUS.

behind the eight-ball

= SNOOKERED, HOOKED. Thought by many to refer to an Eight-Ball player whose cue ball is blocked by the eight-ball and so is unable to play any legal shot directly, since the eight-ball cannot be used to play a COMBINA-TION. 1979 Grissim 250. According to Charles C. Peterson, however, the expression came into use in 1919, long before Eight-Ball was known by that name. It derived from a version of Kelly Pool, known as Kelly Rotation, in which players chose small balls called PILLS to determine order of play and PRIVATE NUMBER BALL. A player drawing any position after eighth ("behind the eight-ball") had little chance to win because he could not shoot until at least some opponent had an opportunity to win by sinking his own ball. (This is true since eight is more than half the number of balls on the table.) "Behind the eight-ball" has entered American colloquial speech to mean "in a difficult position."

bell

(obs.) A device in RUSSIAN BAGATELLE that signals when a ball has entered a certain CUP. In FORTIFICATION BILLIARDS, a bell is used to indicate that a ball has entered a fort. According to 1674 Cotton, a STRING and a bell were used as a substitute for the KING.

below

(Brit. games) Nearer to the BOTTOM cushion. 1957 Holt 6. Note that in American usage this is the HEAD of the table. Cf. ABOVE.

best game

That game of a TOURNAMENT in which a player required the least number of INNINGS to score the requisite number of points. 1941 Hoppe 74. Sometimes a separate prize is offered to the player whose best game of a competition was shortest (measured in innings). A player who wins no games has no "best game," which explains why this statistic is occasionally missing from tournament results for some players.

best of

A method for deciding the winner of a match. "Best of 31 games" means that the first player to win more than half of 31 games (that is, 16) is the winner of the match. Best of $2n-1$ games is the same as RACE to n games.

betting

See GAMBLING.

bevel

(Brit. games) See CHAMFER.

BFUSA

(org.) = BILLIARD FEDERATION OF THE USA, which merged in 1988 into the USBA.

Biathlon

A form of competition in which a player must participate in both Three-Cushions and the Five-Pin Game. A world championship is held at this event. Cf. PENTATHLON, TRIATHLON.

big

1. (Eight-Ball) Any of the balls numbered 9–15. Also HIGH, STRIPE. Cf. LITTLE. 2. See BIG BALL.

big ball

(Bill.) An object ball that lies near a cushion or in a corner so that it can be hit either directly or off one or more nearby cushions. A ball so placed is effectively a larger target than it would be if lying in the center of the table. 1913 Daly 78, 1941 Hoppe 74, 1964 Cottingham 144. In Three-Cushions, a ball is considered big only if a rail it lies near need not be contacted for a valid COUNT. In older British usage, LARGE BALL.

Big Ball. Ball 1 is big because it presents a large effective target to cue ball C.

big ball

Big Four Pool

(game) = HIGH-LOW-JACK GAME, SEVEN-UP POOL. 1902 Burrowes 7. The "big four" refers to the four different ways of scoring in this game.

big pocket

(pocket games, colloq.) = SIDEBOARD. 1992 Billing 92.

Bigs and Littles

(game, colloq.) = STRIPES AND SOLIDS, *i.e.*, EIGHT-BALL. 1990 Rushin 8. See also BIG, LITTLE.

Biliardino

(Bagatelle game) Billiards played on a small table similar to a BAGATELLE table. 1975 *Dizionario Enciclopedico Italiano*.

billard

The French and German word meaning BILLIARDS. In French, also the word for "billiard table." The game itself is referred to as "jeu de billard" or "billardspiel," respectively.

Billard Nicolas

(game) A billiard-like game played on a small circular table with miniature balls. No cue sticks are used; the balls are blown into pockets using jets of air expelled from nozzles through the use of rubber bulbs. Each player sits behind a pocket and may use his nozzle to prevent the ball from entering, much in the manner of a goalie. Also known as PUFF BILLIARDS, the game was popular in Paris in the late nineteenth century. 1976 Duteil 43. Cf. BLOW POOL, a wet and somewhat disgusting game in which the cue ball is ejected from a player's mouth.

Billiard Nicolas

billiard

1. A CAROM. 1976 WSD 39, 1977 Martin 206, 1982 OR. "He made a billiard." 2. (*adj.*) Of billiards. Used in such combinations as BILLIARD BALL, BILLIARD TABLE, etc. Debate has arisen as to whether the correct adjectival form is "billiard" or "billiards." 1924 BM (Oct) 29. The former is vastly more common and, in the author's opinion, correct. See BILLIARDS.

Billiard and Bowling Institute of America (BBIA)

(org.) An industry trade association for both bowling and billiards in the U.S. and Canada, formed during the

25

1930s. Address: 200 Castlewood Drive, West Palm Beach, FL 33408–9960.

There has long been a connection between billiards and bowling. Many bowling alleys contain billiard tables, several manufacturers supply both billiard and bowling equipment, and for decades a publication known as the *Bowlers' Journal and Billiard Revue* was devoted to news of both games.

Billiard Archive

(org.) A non-profit organization set up by Mike Shamos to preserve the history of Billiards, Pool, and Snooker. The Archive maintains a large collection of books, prints, photographs, artifacts, and memorabilia, some dating back to the early 1600s, that reflect the technical and sociological development of billiards. Access may be granted to qualified researchers upon application and payment of a research fee. Contact: The Billiard Archive, 605 Devonshire Street, Pittsburgh, PA 15213.

Billiard Association of America (BAA)

(org.) A former governing body of American billiards and predecessor of the BCA. It was established in 1941 as the successor to the NATIONAL BILLIARD ASSOCIATION OF AMERICA. Its first president was Charles C. Peterson.

billiard ball

A ball used in playing billiards. 1637 OED. Sometimes used particularly to describe a ball used in carom games, as opposed to a POOL BALL, which is for pocket play. A billiard ball is larger and heavier, usually 62.5 millimeters in diameter and weighing 7–7½ ounces. See BALL.

billiard block

= CAROM PLUG, POCKET BLOCK, POCKET STOP.

billiard board

1. A billiard table. Named for the wooden playing surface common before the introduction of SLATE. 1674 Cotton. The term was used as early as 1588 in reference to the Duke of Norfolk, who kept at Howard House, "a billyard bord covered with greene cloth." 1967 Polsky 9, 1979 Everton 10. About 1605, King James I ordered a "billiarde bourde." 1954 KTG 3. See also BAGATELLE, PARISIAN POOL BOARD. 2. A flat piece of wood containing holes that is placed on a billiard table to provide targets for playing certain game variations. See BILLIARD BOARD GAME.

billiard board game

A game played on a billiard table on which a thin board with holes has been positioned against an END RAIL to serve as a target. The player must BANK or carom a ball into a hole on the board, thereby scoring an indicated number of points. These games were popular by 1916 and such boards are still sold. They include Amos & Andy, Barnyard Golf, Black Jack, Hatta-Boy, Keno, MAC'S SOLITAIRE, PIGEON-POOL, Roulo, Rummy, SCOTCH POOL, Star, and Turf.

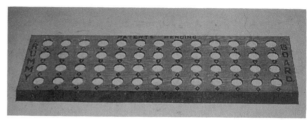

billiard board game

Billiard Bowls

(game) An unusual game that attempts to simulate lawn bowls on a billiard table. It is played with wooden balls specially made for the purpose. The balls are rolled on the table by hand; no cue sticks are used. A large circle is drawn with pipe-clay at the TOP end of the table. The object is to roll a ball from BAULK so that it hits the side and TOP RAILS and lands inside the circle. The player or team having the most balls inside the circle at the finish wins. This gives rise to the defensive play of attempting to knock the opponent's balls out of the circle. 1924 Smith 120, 1927 Clifford 51.

billiard cloth

CLOTH used to cover the BED and cushions of a billiard table.

Billiard Congress of America (BCA)

(org.) The governing body of billiards in the United States. A trade association and tournament sanctioning body formed in 1948 as the successor to the Billiard Association of America. Its voting members are principally manufacturers. The BCA promotes billiards, sponsors an annual trade show, publishes the official rule book of billiards, and organizes tournaments. It maintains the HALL OF FAME to honor great players and contributors to the industry. Address: 1700 S. 1st Avenue, Suite 25A, Eastdale Plaza, Iowa City, IA 52240.

billiard cue

1. = CUE STICK. A distinction is sometimes drawn between a billiard cue and a POOL CUE, the former being specially designed to be more suitable for Three-Cushion Billiards, in which the balls are heavier and must be struck harder and with substantial spin. A cue for billiards is shorter and has a thicker shaft, but usually a smaller diameter TIP and a FAST TAPER. 2. (obs.) A monthly billiard magazine published by Michael Phe-

26

lan from 1856 to 1874. 1938 Mott 203, 1967 Polsky 24. Surviving copies are exceptionally rare; the author is only aware of four of them.

Billiard Federation of the USA (BFUSA)
(org.) A former U.S. sanctioning organization for THREE-CUSHIONS and a member of the UMB. It was formed in 1966 and merged with the ABA to form the USBA in 1988.

billiard hall
= BILLIARD PARLOR.

billiard marker
1. = MARKER. One who marks the points made by each player. 1775 OED. "The billiard marker, whose skill was immense/ Might perhaps have won more than his share" 1876 Lewis Carroll *The Hunting of the Snark*. The job of marker in a billiard room was not particularly strenuous and provided plenty of idle time during which markers would practice their play. They were usually excellent players, and customers were warned not to wager with them. A number of champions began as markers, including Maurice Daly, who started in Dudley Kavanagh's room in New York. Markers were regarded as professionals and thus ineligible to enter amateur tournaments. 2. = MARKER. A device for keeping the score of a billiard game.

billiard-mast
(obs.) A billiard MACE. 1731 OED. Also MAST.

billiard notebook
A blank book with the outline of a billiard table on each page, used for recording SHOT DIAGRAMS. One such book was published by A. Webster in England in the nineteenth century. 1904 Mannock I 35.

billiard parlor
A ROOM, public or private, in which billiards is played. 1869 Kavanagh 67. In public rooms, tables have been rented by the hour, the cue, or the game at various times. In Great Britain, some parlors have installed coin-operated meters that shut off the lights over the table when time runs out. Often just a PARLOR. See BILLIARD ROOM, TABLE TIME.

billiard player
One who plays billiards. A BILLIARDIST; A CUEIST. Sometimes used in contrast to a POOL PLAYER, one who plays pocket billiards.

Billiard Player, The
A periodical published by the Billiards Association and Control Council in Britain beginning in the 1920s.

Billiard Players Association (BPA)
(org.) A defunct players' organization formerly operated by George Jansco, the promoter responsible for the famed JOHNSTON CITY hustlers' tournaments of the 1960s and 1970s. Among its members was Fred Astaire. Abbreviated BPA. 1967 Polsky 15.

Billiard Pool
(game) Pocket billiard game in which the object is to strike a numbered ball with the cue stick causing it to carom off the cue ball and into a pocket. Also called BACKWARDS POOL, CAROM POOL, CHINESE POOL, CONTRA POOL, INDIAN POOL, IRISH POOL, KISS POOL, LOOP, or REVERSE BILLIARDS. (The spelling of "loop" is the reverse of "pool.") 1981 BD (Jan/Feb) 46. Cf. CUE BALL POOL.

billiard room
1. A BILLIARD PARLOR. 1848 OED. Such places have existed since the beginnings of the game. 1674 Cotton says of England that there were "few Towns of note therein which hath not a publick Billiard-Table." Often just a ROOM. The employees of a billiard room include the COUNTER MAN, CUE MAN, DAY MANAGER, HOUSE MAN, NIGHT MANAGER and TAKER. 2. A room devoted to billiard play, particularly in a private home or club.

Billiard Room Proprietor's Association of America (BRPAA)
(org.) A tournament-sponsoring organization composed of New York area ROOM owners, which staged the World 14.1 Continuous Pocket Billiard competition during the years 1963–1968, when there was no world title sanctioned by the BCA. 1982 OR 159.

billiard shot
A CAROM, that is, a shot in the game of Billiards. Often, just a BILLIARD. In Pocket Billiards, a carom that is used to pocket a ball or to obtain a suitable POSITION. 1985 Marguglio 215.

billiard spot
(Brit. games) In English Billiards, the location at which the red ball is spotted at the beginning of the game and after being pocketed. 1954 KTG 10, 1976 WSD 41. Also called the ENGLISH SPOT, it is marked on the longitudinal center of the table at a position $\frac{1}{11}$ of the length of the playing surface from the TOP cushion. On a metric table, this is 320 mm from the top cushion. 1978 BSCC 23. On a 6′ × 12′ table, the distance is 12¾ inches. 1924 Aiken 31, 1976 WSD 41. On a 5′ × 10′ table, 10½ inches. 1946 OR 78. In Snooker, it is where the BLACK is spotted. 1954 KTG 6, 1976 Charlton 101. Hence, the BLACK SPOT. Also the LOSING SPOT, TOP SPOT, WINNING

AND LOSING SPOT, and (except in the U.S.) the RED SPOT. Generally, see SPOT.

billiard stick

= CUE STICK. 1817 OED.

billiard table

A table used for playing billiard games, having boundaries called RAILS surrounding a level playing surface that is covered with CLOTH. 1674 Cotton. See TABLE. The term was already in use by 1576, when Mary, Queen of Scots, imprisoned at Fotheringay Castle, complained of being deprived of her billiard table. 1954 KTG 3. Sometimes used to mean a CAROM TABLE as opposed to a POCKET TABLE.

billiardist

(obs.) A BILLIARD PLAYER, a CUEIST. 1865 NYT (Feb 12) 8:3.

billiards

The origin of the word "billiards" is obscure, but it was apparently derived from the French *bille*, meaning "ball" or *bilart*, a type of stick. Variants of the term appear in English printed works by the year 1591, the modern spelling by 1598. See 1873 Bennett and 1974 Hendricks for etymological treatments. The evolution of the game itself is equally mysterious. Sources in Europe generally ascribe the invention of the game to other European countries. The *Académie des Jeux*, a French work, stated that the game appeared to have been invented in England. The Great Soviet Encyclopedia credits the game to India or China. It was played in Russia during the time of Peter the Great, around 1700. There is no evidence that billiards was played in ancient Egypt, in spite of the fact that Shakespeare has Cleopatra speak the line, "Let us to billiards." See also BILLIARD.

1. (game) A generic term for any game played on a billiard table, specifically one employing small solid balls, generally on a rectangular table having a smooth cloth-covered horizontal surface, the balls being driven about, according to the rules of the game, by means of long tapering sticks called cues. Billiards (including pocket billiards) is the third most popular participant sport in the United States, after bowling and basketball. During 1991, at least 39,232,000 played the game at least once (source: BCA). 2. = CAROM BILLIARDS. A form of game involving CAROMS only, as distinguished from POCKET BILLIARDS, therefore referring to STRAIGHT-RAIL, BALKLINE, THREE-CUSHIONS, and related games. 3. In Britain, the game of ENGLISH BILLIARDS. 1807 White.

Billiards and Snooker Control Council (BSCC)

(org.) The world governing body of amateur English Billiards and Snooker, those games that are played on an English Billiards table. Formerly the BILLIARDS ASSOCIATION AND CONTROL COUNCIL, its name was changed in 1971. Unfortunately, the Council went into receivership in 1991. The corresponding professional organization is the WORLD PROFESSIONAL BILLIARDS AND SNOOKER ASSOCIATION.

Billiards and Snooker Foundation

(org.) British organization formed in 1969 to teach young people the games of English Billiards and Snooker.

Billiards and Snooker Trades Association

(org.) British trade organization, roughly comparable to the BILLIARD CONGRESS OF AMERICA.

Billiards Association

(org.) British organization formed on February 14, 1885, chiefly to promulgate rules. John Roberts Jr. and Sr. were its leading members.

Billiards Association and Control Council (BACC)

(org.) British organization formed in 1919 by merger of the BILLIARDS ASSOCIATION and the BILLIARDS CONTROL CLUB. It later became the BILLIARDS AND SNOOKER CONTROL COUNCIL.

Billiards Control Club

(org.) Organization formed in 1908 by British amateur players, later merged with the BILLIARDS ASSOCIATION to form the BILLIARDS ASSOCIATION AND CONTROL COUNCIL.

Billiards Digest

A bimonthly American billiard publication, produced in Chicago by Luby Publishing, Inc. It began in 1978 as successor to the NATIONAL BOWLERS JOURNAL AND BILLIARD REVUE and covers the spectrum of U.S. cue sports with glossy pages and a good deal of interior color. The current publisher, Mort Luby Jr., is from a prominent bowling and billiard publishing family—both his father and grandfather owned magazines in the field. Michael E. Panozzo is the only editor the magazine has ever had. Columnist George Fels is Consulting Editor. Robert Byrne and your author are Contributing Editors. Address: 200 S. Michigan Avenue, Suite 1430, Chicago, IL 60604.

Billiards Golf

1. (game) A variation on ENGLISH BILLIARDS. The red ball is placed on the CENTRE SPOT. The player shoots from the D and must POT the red into each pocket in

clockwise order, beginning with the top left, in the fewest possible number of strokes, the red being respotted each time it is sunk. Also known as SNOOKER GOLF. Cf. GOLF, GOLF BILLIARDS. 2. (game) A French game similar to BUMPER POOL. 1976 Duteil 42.

Billiards Professionals Association

(org.) Organization of British billiard markers and professionals associated with private clubs, not including players of the top rank, who belonged to the BILLIARDS ASSOCIATION AND CONTROL COUNCIL. It was the Billiards Professionals Association that sponsored the first professional Snooker tournament in 1923. 1986 Everton 50.

Billiards Worldcup Association (BWA)

(org.) Administrative body overseeing the Worldcup championship and rankings. Based in Geneva, Switzerland, it conducts an international professional tour of top carom players.

bills

(colloq.) American college term for Billiards.

bitoquet

(obs.) A rake-like instrument used to avoid making a PUSH STROKE. 1807 White 10, 1906 Hotine 116. Also spelled "bistoquest" or "bistoquet." 1974 Troffaes. Probably related to the Old French *hoquet*, meaning a curved stick, from which the word "hockey" is derived.

black

1. (Snooker) Color of the ball, valued at 7 points, that is spotted at the beginning of the game on the BILLIARD SPOT (hence, BLACK SPOT); also, the name given to that ball. Used in expressions such as ALL ON THE BLACK and BLACK-BALL GAME. 2. (Pocket Bill.) Color of the eight-ball. 3. One of the three balls used in GOLF BILLIARDS, where it functions as the BUNKER BALL. 4. (Bill.) The SPOT BALL. See BLACK BALL. 1894 NY Herald (Jan 10) 13:3. Cf. WHITE.

Black and Pink Pool

(game) BLACK POOL augmented with a pink ball, which is spotted on the PYRAMID SPOT. A player potting the BLACK or PINK receives a LIFE from each other player. 1896 Broadfoot 423.

Black Ball

1. (game) = EIGHT-BALL. 1965 Fats 26, 1974 ITP 26. Also used to refer to the eight-ball itself. 2. (Snooker) The BLACK. 3. (Bill.) Any cue ball that is not completely white, regardless of its color. This term usually denotes the SPOT WHITE, a white ball having a small black dot for identification. 1883 NYT (Mar 10) 5:1. Because the mark

on the ball is difficult to see, the spot white has been superseded in international tournament play by a solid YELLOW ball. We thus have the anomaly that the yellow ball is called the "black ball" even though it has no black mark on it at all. 4. (Bumper Pool) A game played by installing a special game board over the surface of a BUMPER POOL table and using balls 1–9 and a black ball. 1960 Schmidt 33.

black ball game

(Snooker) Situation in which whoever pots the BLACK will win the game. See ALL ON THE BLACK. 1983 Bills 10.

black players

See AFRICAN-AMERICAN PLAYERS.

Black Pool

(game, obs.) A precursor of Snooker, similar to LIFE POOL, but in which there is no pool and each player has an unlimited number of LIVES. The BLACK is placed on the CENTRE SPOT, the white on the LOSING SPOT. If a ball is pocketed, its owner must pay a life to the striker. After each player has played once, any ball may be played at, and, if a ball other than black is pocketed, the striker may then elect to play at black. If he is successful, each player pays him a life. 1862 Crawley 120, 1889 Drayson 105, 1896 Broadfoot 419, 1919 Hoyle 642, 1979 Everton 60. The black was known as the ROVER, since any player was allowed to strike at it. Since the object was to sink black after every other ball, the connection with the eventual game of Snooker is clear. 1986 Trelford 22. The game is also known as SHELL-OUT. Cf. BLACK AND PINK POOL, BLUE POOL, EVERLASTING POOL, PERPETUAL POOL, SELLING POOL.

black spot

(Snooker) Where the BLACK is spotted; a point in the longitudinal centre of the table and 12¾" from the TOP CUSHION. 1975a Lowe 13. The BILLIARD SPOT, ENGLISH SPOT, LOSING SPOT, TOP SPOT, WINNING AND LOSING SPOT, and (except in the U.S.) RED SPOT.

blackleg

(obs.) A swindler or SHARPER. 1771 OED, 1775 Annals.

blank

1. (obs.) An unsuccessful inning; one in which no point is scored by a player. 1873 *Bill. Cue*, 1873 NYT (Jun 26) 1:4. He is said to have scored a "cipher," "duck egg," "goose egg," or "naught." See also OPEN, def. 6. 2. An unfinished portion of the BUTT of a cue stick, after being SPLICED but before being TURNED. Some suppliers specialize in supplying blanks to cuemakers.

Blazz

(game, pr. BLAZE) A pocket game played with 16 object balls, eight red and eight STRIPES numbered 11–18, invented by Thomas J. Wozniak of Akron, Ohio, to provide greater spectator interest than Nine-Ball, in which the next object ball to be struck is always predetermined. The 16, 17, and 18 are black, yellow, and blue, respectively. The objective is to pocket a red (worth one point), followed by a numbered ball (worth its number). Unlike in Snooker, reds and stripes are alternated across players, so the incoming player may have to hit a stripe on his first shot. Balls legally pocketed are not respotted. The game may be played continuously for points or may be scored by frames, in which case the first player scoring 63 wins the frame. Blazz incorporates a number of innovations. For example, the player who sinks the last ball of a frame may "steal" the next break shot from his opponent by leaving the cue ball within the diamond-shaped rack area. "Blazz" is a trademark of Grand Prix Billiards, Inc.

Blind

(game) A pill ROTATION game, popular in Hawaii, using pills numbered 10–20. The game is "blind" since a player does not draw a pill until after completing his run. The object is to have one's run plus the value of the pill drawn equal 31. A player whose total exceeds 31 is eliminated from the game. A player may "stand" with any total without risk of scoring more points and possibly going over 31. 1991 Masui PC. Cf. STRAIGHT.

blind draw

A method of pairing players in a tournament that ensures a random placement. 1982 OR. An unfortunate side-effect of a blind DRAW may be that the top two players in the tournament face each other early instead of in the final match, decreasing spectator interest. Cf. SEEDING.

blindfolded shot

A TRICK SHOT in which the object balls are covered with a handkerchief and are thus not visible to the shooter. 1908 Hood 11. The shot is set up so that it can be made by aiming the cue ball directly at a DIAMOND. Note that the performer is not blindfolded.

block

1. A unit of play in MATCHES that extends over interrupted periods of play, such as afternoon and evening sessions or over successive days. Each block is played until some player's cumulative score reaches a multiple of the block length. If 125-point blocks are being used, the first session ends when one player reaches 125. The

second block ends when some player (not necessarily the winner of the first block) reaches 250, and so forth.

In Pocket Billiards, the striker who first reaches the block total continues play until all balls on the table except one have been pocketed. The STRIKER receives credit for all balls legally pocketed. The purpose is to reduce the number of balls whose positions must be marked to two: the cue ball and the BREAK BALL. Because of this rule, a block may end with one player having scored more than the requisite number of points. When play resumes at the commencement of the next block, the striker's INNING continues. 1965 Fats 40, 1974 ITP 41, 1976 WSD 45. In Carom Billiards, the positions of all three balls are marked in pencil on the cloth at the completion of each block.

The use of blocks to divide long matches began in 1876 in the Three-Ball Game, although the term "block" was not used at that time. 1876 NYT (Jun 7) 7:4. Before then, competitions were 1500-point marathon events lasting 10 hours or more. The term "section" was used in 1881 NYDT (Apr 16) 8:2, but is now obsolete. The word "block" appears in 1891 MB 657. A RUN may extend over multiple blocks.

2. A plug for obstructing pockets to permit carom games to be played on a pool table. Also known as a BILLIARD BLOCK, CAROM PLUG, or POCKET STOP.

3. A technique used in carom games to control the motion of the first object ball as it rebounds from a cushion. The cue ball and/or the second object ball is positioned so as to block the returning object ball to prevent it from going astray on a GATHER SHOT. 1913 Daly, 1925 Hoppe.

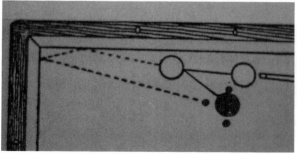

block (def. 3)

4. An ANCHOR BLOCK.

Blow Pool

(game) = MOUTH BILLIARDS. Cf. BILLARD NICOLAS, PUFF BILLIARDS.

blue

1. (Snooker) Color of the ball, valued at 5 points, that is spotted at the beginning of the game on the CENTRE SPOT (hence, BLUE SPOT); also, the name given to that ball, as in "pot the blue" or "pot blue." Also used in Canadian Snooker. 2. (Pocket Bill.) The color of the two-ball and ten-ball. See BALL, BLAZZ. 3. The most common color of cue CHALK. Blue chalk was introduced in 1828. 4. Occasionally, a color of cloth, particularly in European and Asian carom tournaments. 5. (obs.) One of the balls used in BLUE PETER; BLUE POOL; CARLINE; CUE ROQUE; DEVIL-AMONG-THE-TAILORS; ITALIAN SKITTLE POOL; RED, WHITE, AND BLUE; and the RUSSIAN GAME. See also AMERICAN FOUR-BALL BILLIARDS.

Blue Peter

(game, obs.) A variation of LIFE POOL for three players, but played with a fourth ball, the BLUE, which is placed on the CENTRE SPOT. After a hazard, the striker may attempt a "Blue Peter," that is, to pot the blue. If successful, he receives a stake from each player and may try again if the blue is the nearest ball to the cue ball. 1869 Roberts 242, 1916 HDB 73.

Blue Pool

(game) A predecessor to Snooker, played with 15 REDS and a blue ball, which is spotted at the CENTRE SPOT. The striker TAKES a red and the BLUE alternately. Potting the blue is worth two points, and the ball is respotted after being sunk. 1927 Clifford 53.

blue spot

(Snooker) = CENTRE SPOT. Where the blue ball is spotted at the beginning of play. 1975a Lowe 13. Also known as the MIDDLE SPOT.

body English

Gesticulations made by the STRIKER, after the cue ball has broken contact with the cue stick, in a futile attempt to influence the path of the balls, which take no notice of such goings-on. The 1881 edition of *Modern Billiards* warned players against "indulging in ridiculous and unnecessary contortions in following the progress of their ball." See also LIGHTING.

Boston, Boston Pool

(game) = CHICAGO, ROTATION, SIXTY-ONE. 1900 May 61, 1959 Tevis. Billiard games were occasionally named after the place in which they were known to be played or thought to have originated. See also CITIES, NAMES OF.

bottle

A container, formerly of leather but now commonly of plastic, that is used to hold PILLS for distribution in games requiring each player to have a PRIVATE BALL or in which the order of play is determined by LOT. Cf. POOL BASKET. It may also be used as a target in such games as BOTTLE POCKET BILLIARDS.

Bottle Pocket Billiards, Bottle Pool

(game) Played with a cue ball, two object balls numbered "1" and "2," and a SHAKE BOTTLE. The bottle is not used to hold PILLS as usual in PIN POOL, but is itself a target in this game. The one- and two-balls are spotted at the left and right diamonds nearest the FOOT POCKETS and FROZEN to the FOOT RAIL. The bottle is placed inverted on the CENTER SPOT. The object is to score exactly 31 points by caroms (worth one point) and to pocket an object ball (for one or two points, determined by the value of the ball sunk). A carom of the cue ball that subsequently knocks over the bottle scores 5 points. If an object ball knocks the bottle over, no score results. A pocketed ball is replaced on the RED-BALL SPOT or, if that spot is occupied, then at the 1-ball diamond or 2-ball diamond, in that order. A player whose score exceeds 31 is said to BURST, and his score is reset to zero. A carom that flips the bottle upright wins the game. 1892 HRB 122, 1916 RGRG 73, 1919 Hoyle 649, 1946 OR 53, 1982 OR 79. The rules given above are based on those formulated at the Manhattan Athletic Club in the 1890s.

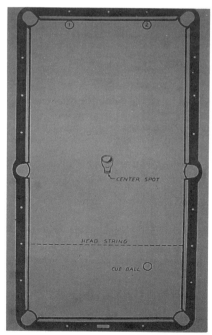

Bottle Pocket Billiards

31

bottom

1. (Brit. games) = DRAW. 1957 Holt 36. Cf. TOP. 2. (Brit. games) The BAULK END of the table; that part of the surface that is behind the BAULK LINE. 1895 Buchanan 2, 1913 Stoddard 8. Cf. TOP. 3. In American games, the FOOT of the table. 1850 Phelan 23.

bottom pocket

(Brit. games) A pocket at the BOTTOM end of the table. Unfortunately, an American would call one of these a HEAD POCKET. To him, a "bottom" pocket would be a FOOT POCKET. But don't the Yanks and the Brits drive on different sides of the road? Cf. TOP POCKET.

Bouchon Pool

(game) ("Bouchon" is the French word for "cork.") Played with three carom balls and three CORKS, each at least 1½″ long and placed upright on the table at the CENTER SPOT, HEAD SPOT and FOOT SPOT. Each player antes a coin; the pool money is stacked on top of the center cork. The red ball is spotted at the POOL SPOT, five inches from the TOP RAIL. The object is to hit the red, drive it against one or more cushions and cause it to knock down the center cork so that the cork falls clear of its spot without knocking down any other cork. If he succeeds, the pool is his. The second player uses the other WHITE and may BANK either object ball. Player three may shoot with any ball. If a player misses, he must add a coin to the pool that is stacked on the center cork, which becomes progressively less stable with each shot. 1890 HRB 103, 1891 MB 349, 1916 HDB 127. This game was a Parisian favorite. Also known as CORK POOL. See also BUMBLE-PUPPY.

bounce

1. (Bill.) A CONTACT in which a ball leaves the bed of the table and rebounds vertically from a cushion one or more times. In games requiring cushion contacts, such as THREE-CUSHIONS, consecutive bounces on the same cushion count as only a single contact. 2. A rebound from a cushion. But see INCIDENTAL CONTACT. See also BOUNCE POOL, BUMPS.

Bounce Pool

(game) Another name for the game of BANK POOL, BANKS, or BUMPS. 1972 Byrne 27. The name refers to the fact that in a BANK SHOT the ball BOUNCES (def. 2) off a cushion.

Bowery shot

(colloq., obs.) A PUSH, GERMAN-TOWNER or TIMBER-LICK. 1865 Phelan 67. The origin of the term is unknown, but the Bowery is a neighborhood of New York City that was home to POOL ROOMS and billiard manufacturers in Phelan's time.

bowling

A game whose history in the twentieth century is intertwined with billiards. See BILLIARD AND BOWLING INSTITUTE OF AMERICA.

Bowlliards

(game) A SHORT RACK pocket billiard game played with a cue ball and 10 object balls, which are racked in the first four rows of the TRIANGLE. Scoring is similar to bowling. At the beginning of each INNING the striker has a FREE BREAK. Any balls pocketed on the break are spotted, but the shooter may continue until he has pocketed a maximum of 10 balls, with two chances being given each inning. Pocketing all 10 in one run scores a STRIKE, in two runs a SPARE. The object is to score the highest point total in 10 innings. 1992 OR 70. Also called Bowlards. See also COCKED HAT, TEN PINS.

The number of different possible initial racks in Bowlliards is 10!, or 3,628,800.

box

1. (Balkline) A marked rectangular area on a billiard table. An ANCHOR SPACE or PARKER'S BOX. Used rarely to refer to a BALK SPACE. 2. The package in which billiard balls are sold. An everyday term such as this would not normally merit mention, but the box is sometimes used an obstacle in carom trick shots (see diagram). See also BOX BILLIARDS. 3. Container mounted below the playing surface of early billiard tables to capture any balls falling through a HAZARD. 1674 Cotton 25. The predecessor of the POCKET. 4. (obs.) Term for the scorekeeper or MARKER.

Box Billiards

(game) A variant of THREE-CUSHIONS in which the rectangular ball BOX is placed on the CENTER SPOT as an obstacle. The stake is anted into the box after each point. In order to score and collect the pool, the striker must make his carom in such a way that no ball hits the box. 1984 BD (Apr) 20. *See illustration on next page.*

Boy Meets Girl

(game) = MISTER AND MRS. POCKET BILLIARDS, a HANDICAP game intended to equalize the supposed difference in skill between men and women. 1979 Sullivan 183. Also called Boy vs. Girl. 1964 Crane & Sullivan 84.

BPA

(org., obs.) = BILLIARD PLAYERS ASSOCIATION.

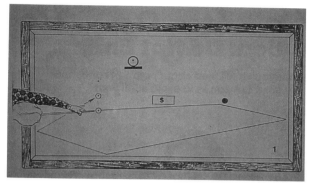

Box Billiards

bracket

A set of players in a tournament DRAW; a branch of the tree of matches. Players in different brackets meet in later ROUNDS. For example, the LOSERS' BRACKET in a DOUBLE ELIMINATION tournament is the one for players that have already lost one game and will be eliminated if they suffer another loss.

break

1. The first, or opening, shot in a billiard game following the LAG. 1992 OR 6. The first stroke from the defined position in which the balls are placed for the beginning of a game. In pocket billiard games, the first shot of a new RACK or FRAME. In English Billiards and Snooker, the BREAK-OFF. Originally a British term, it had to be explained to American readers by Dudley Kavanagh in *The Billiard Cue* in 1869. "Breaking the balls" formerly meant replacing them in the starting position. 1807 White 146, 1866 Crawley 133. See also BREAK SHOT, CRUSH, SNAP. 2. (Pocket Bill., Snooker) To separate the racked balls or a CLUSTER of balls by scattering them with another ball. 1881 MB 22, 1976 WSD 55. In Snooker, a SPLIT. See BREAK SHOT. 3. (Brit. games) A RUN; a consecutive series of successful strokes; the number of points thus scored. 1866 Crawley 72, 1885 Cook 7, 1896 Broadfoot 105. "He led after a break of 43." Also called a CLUSTER or STRING. 4. An interruption in a RUN. A faulty position during play of the RAIL NURSE. 1878 NYT (Mar 17) 5:4, 1919 Hoyle 625. See also BREAK DOWN. 5. (colloq.) A lucky event; a FLUKE. 6. (obs.) The position of the balls after a stroke has been played. 1844 Mardon pl. xxxii, 1850 Phelan 21, 1881 MB 22. This is the origin of the expressions "bad break" and "tough break." Also LEAVE, LIE, SHAPE. 7. See BROKEN BALL.

break ball

(14.1 Continuous) The last object ball remaining on the table after the other 14 have been pocketed, which is to be sunk on the ensuing BREAK SHOT so that the game can be continued after the remaining balls have been RACKED. 1948 Mosconi 78, 1976 WSD 56. The idea of a break ball was devised by Jerome Keogh in 1910. Before that time, the striker who pocketed the last ball of a FRAME would shoot at a full TRIANGLE of balls to open the next frame. See also FREE BALL. The ball used to get POSITION on the break ball is the KEY BALL.

break certificate

(Brit. games) The Billiards Association and Control Council issues a certificate upon request for any witnessed BREAK of at least 50 points in English Billiards or 33 in Snooker. 1988 Morrison 21.

break cue

(Pocket Bill.) A cue stick for making powerful BREAK SHOTS, used to preserve the tip and JOINT of the player's regular cue. 1985 Marguglio 215. The principal attribute of a break cue is durability, not quality. The correct WEIGHT for a break cue is a matter of some dispute, but experiments indicate that a very heavy cue (say, 24 oz.) is not advisable because the player's stroke will be slowed significantly. See 1989 BD (Aug) 12. After breaking, the player will resume using his RUN STICK.

break down

1. To UNSCREW a jointed cue. See also CONCESSION. 2. (Eng. Bill.) To fail to score, causing the striker's BREAK to end. 1954 KTG 10.

Break Game

(game, Brit.) A CRAMP GAME equivalent to NO COUNT. 1909 BYB 87, 1911 Roberts 254. That is, a player does not score unless he makes a BREAK exceeding a prescribed minimum.

break-off

(Brit. games) The British term for the opening shot, used to avoid confusion with BREAK, which in Britain means a RUN of points, but in American parlance refers to the first shot of a game. 1957 Holt 8, 1965 Pulman 56. Also known as the LAY-OFF. *See illustration on next page.*

break shot

1. The BREAK; the first shot of a game. A stroke from a formal opening position to put the balls in play. 1894 NY Herald (Mar 25) 7:4, 1992 OR 47. Generally, the winner of the LAG or other method for deciding who plays first may elect whether to play the break shot

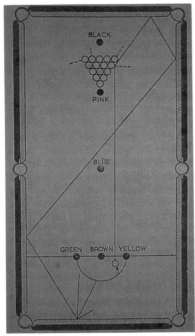

break-off (Snooker)

himself or assign the duty to his opponent. In some games, such as NINE-BALL and all varieties of Billiards, it is considered an advantage to break because of the likelihood of scoring. In others, such as Pocket Billiards, the break shot is usually assigned to the opponent because of the difficulty of pocketing a ball on the opening shot and the skill required to execute a SAFETY BREAK accurately from this position. Still other games allow the break shot to be used to either offensive or defensive advantage. See also ALTERNATING BREAK, LOSER BREAKS, WINNER BREAKS.

In Pocket Billiards, the cue ball must hit an object ball and then either an object ball must be pocketed or at least two object balls must contact cushions. Failure results in a BREAKING VIOLATION and a forfeiture of two points. In 1883, the break shot at FIFTEEN-BALL POOL, a predecessor of 14.1 CONTINUOUS, required the driving of three balls to cushions. The number was reduced to two in 1887. 1891 MB 649. There are now six different types of breaks in pocket games. See APEX BREAK, CLOSED BREAK, FREE BREAK, ONE-BALL BREAK, OPEN BREAK, and TWO-BALL BREAK (of which there are two subtypes), OPEN BREAK. In English Billiards and Snooker, the opening shot is known as the BREAK-OFF or LAY-OFF.

In games such as Eight-Ball and Nine-Ball, it is essential to pocket a ball on the break shot and obtain a wide spread of the object balls while controlling the cue ball. A break of this sort is usually stroked very hard, which has given rise to a number of colloquialisms suggesting force. See CRUSH, SNAP.

2. A shot that pockets a ball but whose intended side effect is to separate a RACK or CLUSTER. See also BREAK, SCATTER SHOT. The shot that begins each rack in 14.1 Continuous. Sometimes the term "secondary break shot" is used when a cluster other than the full rack is involved. 1977 Fels 41. In Snooker, a SPLIT.

break stick
= BREAK CUE. Cf. RUN STICK.

breaker
The player who BREAKS and thus OPENS the game or LEADS. 1977 Martin 207.

breaking violation
(Pocket Bill.) Failure to comply with the special rules that apply to the OPENING BREAK. 1983 Rule Book 253, 1992 OR 6. The penalty varies depending on the game being played. In Eight-Ball, the INCOMING PLAYER may accept TABLE IN POSITION or break himself from a RERACK. 1992 OR 43. In Straight Pool, the penalty is two points and the incoming player may accept table in position or compel the offender to play another break shot from a rerack. 1992 OR 55. In Nine-Ball, failure to contact the one-ball on the break is not a foul; the striker breaks again from a rerack. 1992 OR 48.

breeches, pair of
See PAIR OF BREECHES.

breeches stroke
(Eng. Bill.) The shot resulting in making a PAIR OF BREECHES. 1957 Holt 28.

breeze
(colloq.) = FEATHER. 1973 Mizerak 79, 1977 Martin 207.

bricole
(obs., Fr., pr. bree-COAL) A RAIL-FIRST shot, particularly one in which the cue ball contacts a rail before hitting any other ball. 1807 White 28, 1919 Hoyle 20. A type of BANK SHOT, the other being a DOUBLET. The term appears in French rules posters before 1700: "On emploie ce mot pour signifier le chemin que la bille fait, après avoir frappé une des bandes du billard. [This word is used to mean the path taken by the ball after having struck one of the cushions of the table.]" Its meaning in French is "rebound." The word was being used in English by 1591. The BRICOLE GAME, distantly related to Bank Pool, is described in 1775 Annals. See also "The History of Billiards" in 1889 *Eng. Ill. Mag.*

1807 White makes it clear that accurate banking depends on being able to hit the cue ball without imparting unwanted spin. In modern pocket games, a bricole is known as a KICK.

Bricole Game

(game, obs.) A CRAMP GAME, played with two balls, in which the player is obliged to BANK his own cue ball and then pocket the adversary's ball. If the cue ball touches the other ball before hitting a cushion, one point is forfeited. If the cue ball SCRATCHES or jumps off the table after hitting the adversary's ball, two points are lost. If it touches the other ball before hitting a cushion and then scratches or leaves the table, the penalty is three points. 1775 Annals 95, 1807 White 49, 1839 Kentfield 74, 1856 Crawley 98. The HANDICAP is said by White to be worth about 8 or 9 points in 16. According to 1866 Crawley 235, playing Bricole against the Winning and Losing Game is equivalent to giving 17 in 25. Cf. BANK BILLIARDS, or the BANK-SHOT GAME, which is Carom Billiards played by banking the cue ball, and the DOUBLET GAME, in which the object ball, not the cue ball, must hit a cushion.

bridge

1. The position of the hand in guiding the TIP end of the cue stick. 1674 Cotton advises the player to "Hold your stick neatly between your two fore fingers and your thumb," but he does not use the term "bridge," which apparently dates from 1806 Phil 30. This work states that wrapping the forefinger over the shaft of the cue is not recommended because of the moisture on a player's hands. The opposite hand, used to hold the BUTT end of the cue, is formed into a position known as the GRIP.

Bridging predates the invention of the cue and was used in MACE play when it was necessary to reverse and elevate the instrument and strike with the tail of the mace.

The original cue bridge was formed simply by resting the cue on the first joint of the thumb. Later, the cue was placed in the "V," or crease, between the thumb and forefinger. Still later, the forefinger was wrapped around the shaft to guide the cue. 1974 Hendricks 25. This last bridge was used extensively by William Cook. 1908 Roberts 62.

The "length" of a bridge refers to the distance between the hand and the ball being struck, although it is never stated exactly from which part of the hand the measurement is to be made. Various authorities propose bridges of differing lengths, depending on the game and shot being played. 1867 Dufton 23 recommended six inches. According to 1948 ABC 13, a bridge for STRAIGHT-RAIL should be five inches long; for THREE-CUSHIONS six and a half inches; and

for Pocket Billiards and Snooker, seven inches. Extremely long bridges (*e.g.*, 14 inches) can be used in ARTISTIC BILLIARDS and the FREE-HAND MASSÉ. No bridge at all is used in JACK-UP POOL.

Although much has been written about the position of the fingers in making a bridge, there has been scant discussion of what position the arm of the bridge hand should occupy while striking. To achieve a completely solid bridge, San Francisco room owner and tournament player Tony Annigoni rests his entire forearm on the table. Virtually all other players place only the wrist on the cloth.

The length of the bridge is important because it affects the accuracy of AIM, damping of SHAFT vibration during the stroke, length of FOLLOW-THROUGH, and other physical parameters that alter the motion of the cue ball.

See also BRIDGE BOUCLÉE, BUCKLED BRIDGE, CLOSED BRIDGE, FINGER BRIDGE, FINGERTIP BRIDGE, LONG BRIDGE, LOOP BRIDGE, MASSÉ BRIDGE, NATURAL BRIDGE, OPEN BRIDGE, RAIL BRIDGE, SHORT BRIDGE, TRIPOD BRIDGE, V-bridge, and the compounds below.

2. A rod with a special HEAD on which the player's cue stick may be rested as he shoots; a MECHANICAL BRIDGE. 1879 NYT (Feb 8) 8:3. In British usage, a REST.

See also ARTIFICIAL BRIDGE, BALL BRIDGE, INTERLOCKING BRIDGE, LONG TACKLE, MECHANICAL BRIDGE, STICK BRIDGE, SUBSTITUTE BRIDGE, and the compounds below.

3. To support the tip of the cue with the hand or a MECHANICAL BRIDGE. 1976 WSD 58. "I can't bridge over the ball."

4. (Bagatelle, obs.) A comb-like structure used on a BAGATELLE table. See MISSISSIPPI. Cf. ARCH.

bridge bouclée

(pr. boo-KLAY) Modern BRIDGE in which the forefinger is wrapped around the SHAFT of the cue to steady it in delivering the stroke. 1896 Broadfoot 109, 1957 Holt 53. The cue rests on the third joint of the middle finger. Also known as a BUCKLED BRIDGE, CLOSED BRIDGE or LOOP BRIDGE. Cf. OPEN BRIDGE, V-BRIDGE.

bridge hand

The hand that is used by the player to grip and steady the SHAFT of the cue stick at its tip end. For a right-handed player, the left hand is normally the bridge hand. Cf. GRIP HAND.

bridge head

That part of the MECHANICAL BRIDGE that rests on the table and supports the shaft of the cue. Also, just the

HEAD or REST HEAD. Rules vary as to whether the striker is to be penalized if the bridge head should fall off accidentally and contact a ball during a stroke. See PLAYER RESPONSIBILITY FOUL.

bridge-hook

A device for hanging the MECHANICAL BRIDGE under the table, where it is easily accessible to the players. 1876 Collender 7. The device is visible in prints as early as 1868. See also BUTT HOOK.

bridge stick

The MECHANICAL BRIDGE or, sometimes, just its SHAFT. 1965 Fats 9.

British Association of Pool Table Operators (BAPTO)

(org.) The governing body of ENGLISH EIGHT-BALL POOL.

broken ball

A ball that breaks into more than one piece during a shot. Since the advent of cast phenolic balls, this is a rare accident. However, it was seen occasionally in the days of ivory balls. There is legend to the effect that a carom is complete if any fragment of the cue ball touches the second object ball, but there has never been any official rule covering the situation.

brown

(Snooker) Color of the ball that is valued at four points and spotted at the beginning of the game at the BAULK SPOT (hence, BROWN SPOT), in the middle of the BAULK-LINE; also, the name given to that ball. See also BAULK COLOUR. For an aid in remembering where to spot the brown, see GOD BLESS YOU.

brown spot

Unofficially, the SPOT on which the BROWN is placed. The BAULK SPOT, MIDDLE SPOT IN BAULK.

BRPAA

(org.) = BILLIARD ROOM PROPRIETOR'S ASSOCIATION OF AMERICA.

Brunswick

A prominent American manufacturer of billiard tables and supplies established by John Brunswick, a cabinet-maker. He began making PIGEON-HOLE TABLES around 1840, then in 1845 turned to billiard tables. The company's history can be found in the book, *One Hundred Years of Recreation*. In 1858 the company was renamed J. M. Brunswick & Bro., then in 1874 J. M. Brunswick & Balke Company. This entity merged with H. W. Collender in 1879 and was renamed in 1884 the Brunswick-Balke-Collender Company, or B.B.C. Co.

Its modern descendant is the 1960 Brunswick Corporation, a billion-dollar conglomerate with a small but famous billiard division. H. W. Collender was itself an 1871 descendant of Phelan & Collender, formed in 1856 from the merger of the first two important American manufacturers. 1992 PBM (Aug) 64. Brunswick tables began to be used in tournaments in 1867. 1912 MB 222.

Brunswick led the campaign against the use of the word "pool" in the early decades of the twentieth century, managing to have "Pocket Billiards" substituted, at least in official usage. A major industry force, it controlled billiard tournaments, exhibitions, and equipment specifications through the 1950s and is still very influential.

To "shoot from Brunswick" meant that the striker's cue ball was frozen to the center of the head cushion, next to the MANUFACTURER'S NAMEPLATE, which, more often than not, read "Brunswick." 1930 BM (Jan) 14.

Brunswick Ten-Pin Billiard Game

(game) Played with a cue ball and ten SKITTLES in the shape of bowling pins, which are set up in the form of a triangle. The object is to knock over as many pins as possible with the cue ball in two strokes, which constitute a FRAME. A game consists of 10 frames, with scoring as in bowling. 1915 *Bill. News* (Aug) 3. Cf. BOWLLIARDS, COCKED HAT, TEN PINS.

brush

Implement used for cleaning the table CLOTH, to remove accumulated lint and CHALK at the end of the day or between games. 1896 Broadfoot 83. Brushing should be "with the nap," *i.e.*, from BOTTOM to TOP. See also FLY, VACUUM CLEANER.

BSCC

(org.) = BILLIARDS AND SNOOKER CONTROL COUNCIL.

bubble

(Brit.) A maneuver in which the cue ball is aimed at the POINT or ELBOW, in the hope of making it take the looped path as shown. The shot is risky, but sometimes useful to ESCAPE from a SNOOKER. 1981 Quinn 66. *See illustration on next page.*

bucket

(colloq., U.S. and Brit.) A POCKET that is abnormally wide and thus accepts balls easily. 1988 Rossman 97. Also SEWER or WASTEBASKET.

buckled bridge

= BRIDGE BOUCLÉE, CLOSED BRIDGE. 1924c Inman 20. Cf. OPEN BRIDGE, V-BRIDGE.

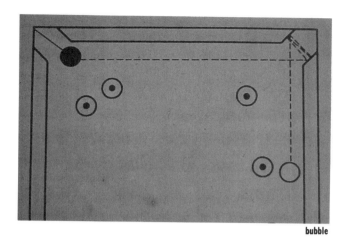

bubble

Bull Dog Game

(game, obs.) A hybrid game consisting of both caroms and winning and losing HAZARDS. Similar to COWBOY POOL, but played with the two-, three- and five-balls. The two is placed on the HEAD SPOT, the three on the FOOT SPOT, and the five on the CENTER SPOT. Forty points are to be scored by HAZARDS and caroms, then 10 points by caroms only. The score for a hazard is the numerical value of the ball pocketed. The last shot must be CALLED and must be a SCRATCH of the cue ball off an

object ball. 1911 HRB 104, 1916 RGRG 71. Cf. FORTY-FIVE, SCRATCH POOL, THIRTY-EIGHT, THIRTY-ONE POOL.

Bumble-Puppy

(game, obs.) A variation on CORK POOL in which a three-inch circle is drawn in chalk around the CORK. Each player who fails to knock over the cork must place a COIN upon it. When the cork is hit, the successful striker keeps only those coins falling outside the circle. A coin is considered outside if more than half of it lies beyond the circle. 1896 Broadfoot 430.

bump

The curved side of a pocket opening on an ENGLISH BILLIARDS table. 1924 Aiken 48, 1924c Inman 20, 1936 Newman 28. Also ELBOW or SHOULDER. Cf. POINT.

bumper

1. A soft covering, frequently rubber, applied to the BUTT end of a cue stick, attached to the BUTT CAP. 1965 Fats 19. Patented in 1880, its function was to prevent damage to the wood of the butt and eliminate the noise made when the butt contacts the floor during APPLAUSE. 2. (Bumper Pool) A rubber-trimmed obstacle or peg. 3. (Brit.) A cushion. 1937 NBJ (Oct).

Bumper Pool

(game) Pocket billiard game played on a small, rectangular table with a hole at each short end and whose playing surface contains cushioned pegs that serve as obstacles. 1965 Fats 67, 1976 WSD 61. The game is

37

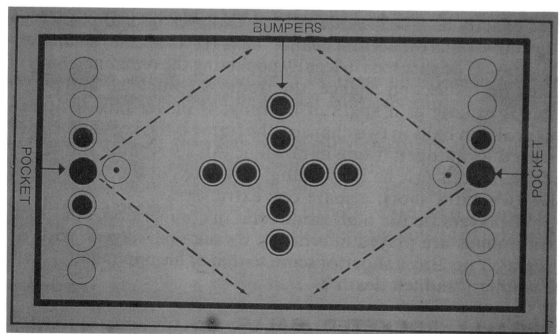

Bumper Pool

played with five red and five white balls, one of each being specially marked. No cue ball is used, the object being to BANK all the balls of one color into a player's designated pocket. 1992 OR 72. "Bumper Pool" is a registered trademark of the Valley Company, Bay City, Michigan. It is familiarly known as BUMPERS. See also BLACK BALL.

Bumpers

(game, sl.) = BUMPER POOL.

Bumps

(game, sl.) A Chicago-area expression for BANK POOL.

bunch

(pocket games, colloq.) The several object balls used in a game. The HEAP, PACK, PYRAMID, RACK, or STACK. Sometimes, a CLUSTER, def. 1.

bunker ball

(Golf Bill.) The name given to the black ball, whose function is somewhat analogous to that of a bunker in golf. The player whose cue ball contacts the bunker ball during a shot has one point added to his score as a penalty. See also HAZARD.

burn mark

A small elliptical discoloration on the CLOTH of a billiard table caused by friction with the cloth when a ball is struck sharply. These marks are often confused with PITS, which result from balls bouncing on, or being driven down into, the cloth.

burst

1. In certain games, to score more than the number of points required for game and hence have one's score reset to zero as a penalty. 1850 Phelan 45, 1881 MB 22, 1992 OR 82. One who has burst is said to be DEAD. Examples of games utilizing burst are: BOTTLE POOL; FIVE-PIN GAME; FORTY-ONE POCKET BILLIARDS; ITALIAN BILLIARDS; KELLY POOL; NIGGER POOL; PIN POOL; PLANT GAME; POOL FOR 31 POINTS; RED, WHITE, AND BLUE; RUSSIAN BILLIARDS; SENTINEL POOL; SKITTLE POOL; THIRTY-ONE POOL. 2. The BREAK, the opening of the PACK or PYRAMID. 1880 NYT (Dec 31) 5:3, 1884 MB 22.

business

1. (sl.) Players are "doing business" when they are engaged in a DUMP. 1989 Annigoni PC. 2. (colloq., obs.) Dilatory tactics designed to unnerve one's opponent. 1930 BM (Jan) 16. A form of SHARKING.

bust

1. (pocket games, colloq.) A BREAK SHOT. 1916 BM (Jan) 55, 1973 Mizerak 79, 1977 Martin 207. The usage dates at least from the 1880s, when a Currier & Ives lithograph titled "Bustin' the Pool" appeared showing a black player whose break shot went awry. In modern usage it refers particularly to a shot that separates a CLUSTER. 2. (colloq.) = BURST.

bust-in

(Brit., colloq.) = BUST. 1937 NBJ (Oct).

bustaway

(Brit., colloq.) A BREAK that ends the game. A RUNOUT. 1937 NBJ (Oct).

butt

1. The handle of a cue stick; the end that is thicker than the TIP and is gripped by the player to provide motive force for the stroke. The butt is usually made from harder woods, such as ebony, cherry, and tulip. 1881 MB 17. This handle is often covered with a WRAP to absorb moisture and render the player's GRIP more certain. The butt end of the cue was formerly used for striking the ball, in order to avoid putting on unwanted SIDE. 1836 Tillotson 6, 1866 Crawley 7, 1873 Bennett 456, 1920 Levi II 20. It was specially beveled to enable the player to slide it along the cloth accurately. 1925 Macmillan 26. Using the butt in this way ceased around 1899 and is now prohibited. It has been common up to the present day to express admiration for a shot or run by banging the butt end of the cue against the floor several times as a substitute for applause. This practice is described in 1883 NYT (Apr 2) 1:5, but is undoubtedly much older. See also BEVEL, CHAMFER, CUE-BUTT, GRIP, PRONG, WRAP. 2. A type of mechanical bridge or rest. 1954 KTG 16. See also HALF-BUTT, HALF-REST, QUARTER-BUTT. 3. A species of long cue stick, used in conjunction with the LONG REST to reach shots that would otherwise be impossible. 1897 Payne 34, 1924 Ogden 269. Also LONG-BUTT. 4. (Brit., obs.) A tipless cue made broad at its base, which is beveled and leathered so that it may lie flat on the table and propel the ball in a straight line without imparting spin. 1866 Crawley 12. A mace-like cue.

butt cap

A protective cover applied to the BUTT end of a cue stick. Cf. BUMPER

butt hook

(Eng. Bill.) A contrivance for hanging the BUTT below the table, where it will be easily accessible to the players. 1975a Lowe 14. See also BRIDGE HOOK.

butt plate

1. A ring of protective material fastened to the BUTT of the cue to prevent splintering or damage at the end. 2. An attachment to the butt for increasing the weight of the cue. 1908 Brunswick 53. See also WEIGHT.

button

(obs.) A BEAD, resembling a button, used on the SCORE STRING to record a player's point total. Figuratively, a point scored. 1888 NYT (Jun 24) 11:6. "He tallied 48 buttons."

BWA

(org.) = BILLIARDS WORLDCUP ASSOCIATION.

bye

The privilege given to a player of bypassing one or more rounds of a tournament. 1683 OED. A bye is given to a SEEDED player to lessen his chances of losing early and being eliminated. A bye must be awarded if the number of players entered in an elimination tournament is not even.

cadre

(Balkline, Fr.) In French, a BALK SPACE. Literally, "square."

Calculagraph

A clocking device used in public billiard rooms for measuring the amount of time that a table has been in use. It contains two clock mechanisms, one of which prints an empty clock face; the other prints arrows indicating elapsed time and amount owed. It eliminated the need for subtracting hours and minutes to calculate TABLE TIME, thus speeding up room operations. This mechanical aid has given way to microcomputers in many establishments. The practice of charging for table use by the hour instead of by the game originated in 1867. See 1867 NYT (Aug 23) 5:5. *See illustration in next column.*

Calcutta

(colloq.) A pari-mutuel gambling arrangement in which odds are established by having bettors bid for the chance to win a pool should their selected player win

Calculagraph

the tournament. After deduction of a percentage for the promoter, the pool is awarded to the bettors choosing the eventual top finishers. During the selection phase prior to the tournament, as each player's name comes up it is assigned to the highest bidder. A favored player will attract a high bid, a long-shot a low one. See 1988 BD (Feb) 52 for an explanation of the technical operation of a Calcutta.

In most states, a Calcutta is illegal as a form of lottery or game of chance. This does little to diminish its popularity, however, since the authorities appear to take no interest in the practice. The Calcutta is the modern descendant of "pool selling," a notorious form of public betting at billiard matches during the last half of the nineteenth century. Bettors and pool operators alike were sometimes the victims of DUMPING, a scam that still thrives today.

California Pool

(game, obs.) A game played on a CAROM TABLE with four balls—two white and two red. The red balls are placed in the two corners at the FOOT end, a white object ball at the center of the FOOT RAIL, and the cue ball on the HEAD SPOT. The object is to use the cue ball to drive all four balls into a square region whose side is one diamond in length and located in the head corner at the striker's left in the fewest number of strokes. 1884 MB 307. Cf. WESTERN POOL. For a list of states named in billiard games, see STATES, NAMES OF.

call

1. A required oral nomination by a player of the stroke he intends to play next. 1881 MB 320, 1965 Fats 22. "He called the five-ball in the side." See BALL AND POCKET, CALL-SHOT GAME, GENTLEMAN'S CALL, VASO AMEND-

MENT. The general rule is that all balls called on a shot must be pocketed, or the player's inning ends. If a single ball is called but it and others are pocketed, in most games credit is given for all balls pocketed. There is therefore no reason to call more than one ball. Cf. SLOP. 2. An oral announcement by the referee or MARKER, *e.g.*, "safety allowed." Sometimes a decision by a referee in a contested situation. "What was his call?" See ANGLED BALL, CROSS-CORNER, CROSS-SIDE, FOUL, FREE BALL, FROZEN, GAME, IN, IN ANCHOR, IN BALK, NOT FROZEN, OPEN TABLE, OUT, POOL, SAFETY, SAFETY ALLOWED, SAFETY NOT ALLOWED, THREE-POOL, TOUCHING BALL. For referee's calls in international Balkline, see À CHEVAL, DEDANS, ENTRÉ, RENTRÉ, RESTÉ DEDANS. 3. To claim, as in "He called a foul."

call-shot game

Game in which the STRIKER is obliged to announce, or CALL, in advance the shot he intends to play. Some games require both ball and pocket to be named; others require naming the ball only. See BALL AND POCKET. If the ball to be pocketed is obvious, it need not be called in modern games. See GENTLEMAN'S CALL. If a referee is present, he will make the call, which, if incorrect, must be corrected by the player before striking. Formerly, a shot on which a ball was pocketed but not called was treated as a SAFETY. 1916 RGRG 51. If more than one ball is called on a shot, all the balls called must be pocketed for any to count. If all the called balls are pocketed on a shot, any other balls pocketed on the same stroke count even if not called, regardless of the order in which the balls enter pockets. See also VASO AMENDMENT. Cf. SLOP.

In modern play, there are four different calling requirements, depending on the type of game being played. In BASIC POCKET BILLIARDS, the ball only (not pocket) need be called. In BANK POOL, the ball, pocket, and other details of the stroke, including all cushions to be contacted, must be named. Just ball and pocket must be called in EIGHT-BALL, 14.1 CONTINUOUS, BOWLLIARDS, EQUAL OFFENSE, HONOLULU, and LINE-UP. As a general principle, no calling is required in SET-ORDER GAMES and in the following: ONE-POCKET, SIX-BALL, SEVEN-BALL, NINE-BALL, TEN-BALL, FIFTEEN-BALL, ROTATION, BOTTLE POOL, BUMPER POOL, COWBOY POOL (except that the pocket must be called on the 101st point), CRIBBAGE, ELIMINATION, FORTY-ONE, MISTER AND MRS. POCKET BILLIARDS, PEA POOL, and SNOOKER. Except in BANK POOL, no details of a stroke other than ball and pocket need ever be designated in pocket games (but see NAMING-STROKE GAME). This principle is often altered by HOUSE RULE.

The need for calling arose in the game of HAZARDS, in

which a player who failed to make a shot had to pay a forfeit to the owner of the ball he missed; it was thus necessary to identify the player to be paid. The first tournament in which calling both ball and pocket was required occurred at SIXTY-ONE POOL in 1884. Pockets used to be numbered for calling purposes, beginning with pocket "1" at the leader's left and proceeding clockwise around the table. Shooting the seven-ball in the right-hand side pocket would be called "seven in five." 1886 NYT (May 12) 2:5.

Curiously, pocket games are not the only ones in which calling is required. See CALL-SHOT THREE-CUSHIONS.

Call-Shot Rotation

(game) ROTATION in which pockets must be CALLED. 1987c OBG 18. Generally, Rotation is a game of SLOP, in which shots need not be called and luck is an important factor. Requiring shots to be called remedies this deficiency.

Call-Shot Three-Cushions

(game) THREE-CUSHIONS in which all rail CONTACTS must be named in advance of the stroke. 1979 Stone 92. There is thus no BIG BALL in this game. The high run is 16 by Gus Copulos at Detroit in 1930.

called ball

(pocket games) An OBJECT BALL a player has designated as one he intends to pocket. 1878 NYT (Apr 21) 1:7, 1976 WSD 65. In most CALL-SHOT GAMES, a shot is successful only if the called ball enters the CALLED POCKET. See CALL, DESIGNATED, FREE BALL, NOMINATED, VOLUNTEER.

called pocket

(pocket games) The pocket into which a player has announced his intention to SINK a CALLED BALL. 1976 WSD 65. The first tournament in which pockets had to be called was held in 1884. Before then, only balls had to be called. See BALL AND POCKET, CALL, CALL-SHOT GAME, DESIGNATED, NOMINATED.

Canadian Snooker

(game) A variation of Snooker played with 15 reds and five POOL BALLS: the yellow, green, brown, blue, and black (but not pink). All balls other than black have the same value as in Snooker; the black is valued at six. A player may play at any ball at any time without forfeit if he POTS it. However, if he fail to do so, the penalty is the value of the ball played at if the ball would not have been ON at Snooker. 1900 May 96, 1916 HDB 71.

cannon

British term for a CAROM, which scores two points at English Billiards. Also spelled "canon." 1806 OED,

1839 Kentfield 26, 1976 WSD 66. See also ALL-ROUND CANNON, ANCHOR CANNON, BALL-TO-BALL CANNON, CLOSE CANNON, CONSECUTIVE CANNONS, CRADLE CANNON, CUSHION CANNON, DIRECT CANNON, DOUBLE CROSS CANNON, DROP CANNON, GATHERING CANNON, INDIRECT CANNON, JAM CANNON, KISS CANNON, LACE CANNON, NURSERY CANNON, PENDULUM CANNON, RICOCHET CANNON, ROCKING CANNON, SCREW CANNON, SQUEEZE CANNON, STAB CANNON, STEEPLECHASE CANNON, SWITCHBACK CANNON, UP-AND-DOWN.

Cannon Game
(Bagatelle game, obs.) Three balls are used: the white, spot-white and black. The black is spotted, and the nonstriker's ball is placed midway between holes 1 and 9. The object is to make CANNONS and to cause balls to fall into the holes, but if a ball falls in and no cannon is made, points score to the opponent. A cannon scores two points. Holing the OBJECT WHITE scores, two; the black scores three. Missing the object white scores one point to the opponent; missing the black scores five. 1878 Crawley 154, 1900 May 68. Cf. IRISH CANNON GAME.

canon
(obs.) = CANNON. 1862 Crawley 18.

Canons Against Hazards and Canons
(game, obs.) CRAMP GAME in which the player giving the HANDICAP must score by CANONS only, while his opponent may make both canons and HAZARDS. 1856 Crawley 98.

carambole
1. A CAROM. 1775 OED, 1807 White 9, 1974 Lindrum 10. Also used adjectivally, as in CARAMBOLE GAME, meaning a game consisting of caroms. 2. The red ball in carom games. Said to derive from the Spanish carambola, a type of small fruit. 1775 OED.

Carambole Game
1. (game) = The FRENCH GAME, consisting of CAROMS only, usually played on a table without pockets. 1775 Annals 95, 1856 Crawley 100. 2. Any game in which caroms count, such as the WINNING AND LOSING CARAMBOLE GAME. 3. (game, obs.) An English game, played by 1773, in which caroms and WINNING HAZARDS counted for points. 1974 Hendricks 25.

Carline, Caroline
(game, obs.) The RUSSIAN GAME, played with two white and three colored balls: the black, blue and red. It is similar to the AMERICAN GAME, with scoring by WIN-NING HAZARDS and CANNONS. The black ball, known as the "Carline," is placed at the beginning of the game on the CENTRE SPOT. The red ball is placed on the WINNING AND LOSING SPOT, the blue on the BAULK-LINE SPOT. The player must stroke the red ball first. Three points are scored for hazarding the red or blue in a CORNER POCKET; six for holing black in a MIDDLE POCKET. Three points are forfeited for holing the RED. A cannon between WHITE and a colored ball scores two points; between two colors, three. Successive cannons count serially on the same shot, so many points can be credited on a single stroke. 1775 Hoyle, 1820 OED, 1839 Kentfield (different rules), 1866 Crawley 212, 1881 MB 294.

The name of the game is derived from Karolin, the German word for the yellow ball. This origin is now blurred because a black ball has been substituted for the yellow. 1807 White 56, 1856 Crawley 108. The Spanish version, Carolina, is played with one PIN placed on the CENTER SPOT and a green, a yellow, and two white balls.

carom
The word is derived from the French caramboler, whose definition is, "toucher avec sa bille les deux autres billes [to touch the two other balls with one's own]". See CARAMBOLE.

1. A contact between the cue ball and two other balls. 1779 OED, 1807 White 9, 1857 Phelan 63, 1881 MB 23. A CANNON. Occasionally spelled "carrom." Cf. CASIN. A DOUBLE CAROM is a carom in which the cue ball hits three object balls. See AMERICAN FOUR-BALL BILLIARDS. 2. (Pocket Bill.) A shot in which the object ball strikes another before entering a pocket or in which the cue ball hits one object ball before pocketing another. 1948 Mosconi 65, 1977 Fels 59, 1980 Balukas 194. Also called a BILLIARD SHOT.

carom ball
(Bill.) The second ball hit by the cue ball during a shot; this contact completes the CAROM. 1913 Daly 46, 1919 Hoyle 621. Also known as the SECOND OBJECT BALL or SCORE BALL. Cf. FIRST OBJECT BALL.

Carom Billiards
(game) Any of a number of games in which the object is to cause the player's cue ball to contact two or more object balls, thus effecting a CAROM. 1941 Hoppe 74. Commonly used as a synonym for STRAIGHT-RAIL, FRENCH CAROMS, or the THREE-BALL GAME. Advanced versions impose various restrictions on the player, such as the requirement in THREE-CUSHIONS

that the cue ball make three distinct CONTACTS with rails before completing the carom. Cf. BALKLINE, ENGLISH BILLIARDS.

carom plug

A device for blocking the pockets of a pocket billiard table so as to convert it into a CAROM TABLE. 1908 Brunswick 95. Also known as a BILLIARD BLOCK, POCKET BLOCK or POCKET STOP. This method of transforming a table for billiard play is quick but generally unsatisfactory, since the optimum height of a cushion depends on the diameter of the balls being used. (See CUSHION.) Since billiard balls are larger than pocket billiard balls, the rails will necessarily be at the wrong height. There is also no effective method of joining the cushion portions of the carom plug to the table cushions, which results in the creation of two "dead" regions on the rails adjacent to each pocket. A slower but more effective means of utilizing a pocket table for carom games is to replace the rails entirely. Carom plugs were already well known in the 1850s. See also COMBINATION TABLE, CONVERTIBLE TABLE. Cf. POOL STOP.

Carom Pool

(game) A pocket billiard game in which the object is to shoot an object ball at the cue ball to carom the cue ball into a pocket. Also BACKWARDS POOL, BILLIARD POOL, CHINESE POOL, CONTRA POOL, INDIAN POOL, IRISH POOL, KISS POOL, LOOP, REVERSE BILLIARDS. Cf. CUE BALL POOL.

carom table

(Bill.) A billiard table without pockets, for playing CAROM games. 1860 Leslie's (Apr 7) 247:2. Cf. POCKET TABLE.

carombole

An alternative spelling of CARAMBOLE.

Carombolette

(game, obs.) A game combining the luck of BAGATELLE with the skill required for pocket games. 1898 HRB 101. The Bagatelle table was modified for this purpose through the use of a device called a POOL STOP. *See illustration in next column.*

carrom

(obs.) A variant spelling of CAROM. 1779 OED, 1845 Hoyle 227, 1893 HRB 12.

carry-through

(Brit.) = FOLLOW, TOP. 1926 BM (Mar) 29.

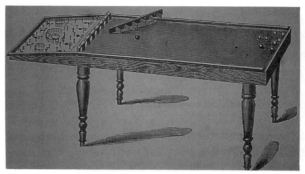
Carombolette

case

= CUE CASE. A protective container for storing a cue stick, frequently lined with velvet or other material to prevent nicks and scratches and hermetically secure to keep out moisture.

case game

(colloq.) A game situation in which each player needs only a single point to win. 1985 BD (Feb) 40. Also CASEY JONES, DOUBLE CHEESE, HILL GAME, TV game.

Casey Jones

(colloq.) = CASE GAME. Also DOUBLE CHEESE, HILL GAME, TV game.

casin

1. A French term for a three-ball billiard shot in which a score is earned by causing one object ball to hit the other, as opposed to a CAROM, in which the cue ball contacts both object balls. This word has no English translation but the concept is really that of a COMBINATION on a table without pockets. Some European games are centered on this type of shot. Also, a particular French game played with PINS. Casin games are immensely popular in Europe and the Latin countries. An annual world championship is conducted. See 1971 Ardévol for details of many pin games having untranslated names. 2. (game) A mixed carom billiard game requiring nine different types of shots: direct carom, cushion carom, two-cushion shot, three-cushion shot, red ball shot, a "free" (unrestricted) carom, left-handed shot (or right-handed for left-handed players), rail-first and a casin. The striker must announce in advance the stroke he intends to play and may not call the same type twice in succession. The number of points credited for each stroke may depend on its type. 1983 Malsert 163. See also RAZZLE-DAZZLE. 3. (game) A Spanish game played on a six-pocket table with five pins, two white balls and a smaller white ball known as a "casin." Two extra SPOTS are used in this game, each located one ball diameter from the center of each SHORT RAIL. 1971 Ardévol 367.

casin game

A game in which points may be scored by driving one object ball into another, that is, by effecting a CASIN.

CEB

(org.) = CONFÉDÉRATION EUROPÉENNE DE BILLARD.

center ball

Stroke in which the cue ball is hit at its center so as to avoid imparting ENGLISH. 1807 White, 1965 Lassiter 36. The use of center ball improves accuracy and the present instructional trend is to discourage the use of English unless it is necessary for some specific reason, such as to POSITION the cue ball or THROW the object ball. Also PLAIN BALL.

center of percussion

A point on an object that, when struck, will cause the object to rotate only and not shift its position by translation. 1727 OED. The idealized center of percussion of a sphere (billiard ball), not accounting for frictional effects, at a point on its surface at a height $7/10$ of a diameter from its base. A billiard ball struck at its center of percussion theoretically moves off by rotation only, without sliding along the cloth. This height is optimal for placement of the cushion NOSE, since it prevents the balls from either bouncing or flying off the table. In practice, the cushions are placed lower because of the elasticity of the rubber, which would cause balls to become trapped underneath the nose at that height.

center pocket

= SIDE POCKET, MIDDLE POCKET. 1856 Crawley 106. Curiously, the pocket is not at the center of the table, but lies in the center of a SIDE RAIL.

center space

(Balkline) The central rectangle on a BALKLINE TABLE, formed by the intersection of two sets of parallel balklines. The center space is not a BALK SPACE, however. The number of consecutive caroms that may be made while either ball lies inside the space is unlimited. 1884 MB 309, 1946 OR 18. See BALKLINE.

center spot, centre spot

A SPOT located midway between the two SIDE, or MIDDLE, pockets. 1866 Crawley 7, 1873 Bennett 18. The spot in the exact center of the playing surface of a billiard table, where the blue ball is spotted in SNOOKER. 1992 OR 6. Hence, the BLUE SPOT or MIDDLE SPOT. The center spot began to be used about 1850 to place balls when other spots were occupied. 1850 Phelan 32. Prior to that time, any ball whose spot was occupied would be held off the table until its spot became free. 1845 Hoyle.

In ENGLISH BILLIARDS, the RED is spotted at the centre spot if both the BILLIARD SPOT and PYRAMID SPOT are occupied. 1954 KTG 12. When the striker's ball is FROZEN to either object ball, the red is placed on the BILLIARD SPOT and the opponent's ball on the centre spot. 1889 Drayson 99.

In Pocket Billiards, if the cue ball lies in the RACK at the end of a FRAME and the BREAK BALL occupies the HEAD SPOT, the cue ball is spotted at the center spot. 1946 OR 51.

In THREE-CUSHIONS, if the cue ball is FROZEN to the opponent's cue ball, the player has the option of shooting away from the frozen ball or having both balls spotted, in which case the opponent's cue will go on the center spot. This also occurs if the opponent's ball becomes a JUMP BALL.

center string

(Pocket Bill.) An imaginary line connecting the centers of the SIDE RAILS on a billiard table and passing through the CENTER SPOT. 1946 OR 5. The author can find no present use for this line at all, though it is frequently defined and is used in many glossaries and rule books. 1992 OR 4. Its earliest appearance seems to be at 1925 RGRG 31, in a rule providing that, after a foul, the INCOMING PLAYER "may request the referee to place the object ball nearest the center string line on the center spot on the table." This rule tends to prevent a player from achieving a positional advantage by means of a foul. In the Caras-Rudolphe challenge match for the World Pocket Billiard title in 1936, the rule was expanded to give the incoming player BALL IN HAND behind the HEAD STRING at the beginning of each inning, regardless of whether his opponent had fouled; he could also ask the referee to move the object ball lying closest to the center string onto the center spot. As recently as 1982, the center string still played a role in the rules. See IN HAND BEHIND THE HEAD STRING. Generally, see STRING.

center table

(Bill.) The square portion of the playing surface of a table bounded by the LONG RAILS, the HEAD STRING, and the FOOT STRING. In Straight-Rail, it is undesirable to position the balls in this area because of the difficulty of manipulating them there. One should use, by contrast, the SHORT TABLE. 1913 Daly 81.

centered ball

= LINE BALL. 1976 Regulation 62.

central stroke

= CENTER BALL. 1839 Kentfield 13, 1884 Bohn 525.

43

centre

(Brit.) See terms beginning with "center."

century, century break

(Brit. games) A sequence of 100 uninterrupted points. 1876 NYT (May 20) 2:4, 1884 OED, 1973 Spencer 121. The first century break recognized at Snooker was one of 113 by Con Stanbury in 1922. The first player to record a thousand centuries was Horace Lindrum in 1970. The first century by a woman in a title event was 103 by Allison Fisher on May 23, 1987.

chalk

1. An abrasive substance used on the cue tip to increase friction between the tip and the cue ball to prevent a MISCUE. Chalk is formed into cubes by molding or cutting and is surrounded on five sides by paper for grasping. A depression is made in the exposed face that can be used effectively to grind particles onto the tip.

If a ball carries unwanted chalk on its surface, the effect of THROW when it contacts another ball can increase dramatically. 1987 BD (Jan). Balls must therefore be CLEANED regularly to prevent an accumulation of chalk.

chalk (Indifference, 1823. Earliest etching showing chalk being applied to a cue tip)

Sometimes this is done while a game is in progress. See also LIFTED BALL.

Cue chalk is not actually made of chalk (calcium carbonate), but is composed of a gritty powder, usually silica, combined with a colorant and suspended in a fixative, all of which is baked in an oven to give the cube a conveniently hard form. All these materials alter the characteristics of the final product. Chalks of different colors from the same manufacturer may behave very differently. The fact that chalk is abrasive means that continued use will eventually wear away the tip of the cue. Continued contact between the chalk and the FERRULE will wear it away as well.

A piece of chalk that is not on the BED of the table is considered part of the table EQUIPMENT for purposes of determining when a ball is a JUMP BALL. If a ball jumps the table, hits a piece of chalk (that is not on the bed), and returns to the table, it is not treated as a jump ball. 1992 OR 38. Contact between a ball and a piece of chalk that is on the bed constitutes INTERFERENCE.

Under international rules, chalk may not be placed on the rail of the table while a player is shooting. This keeps the table clean and prevents any possible use of the chalk cube as a target or aiming aid.

There are many stories concerning the discovery of the usefulness of chalk. According to one version, one Jack Carr is reported to have made a fortune in the 1820s selling a TWISTING POWDER that would permit the user to perform magical feats with the cue ball. 1981c Clare 5. However, the story appears to be apocryphal, since it does not appear in any work contemporaneous with Carr, and chalk was being applied to the ends of cues even before the invention of the leather tip. 1806 Phil 22, 1807 White 6. Sometimes this was done by twisting the cue into a plaster ceiling. White chalk was used originally, with blue chalk appearing in 1828 and green chalk in 1843. In the 1860s, eating billiard chalk was a common remedy for indigestion. 1861 *Leslie's* (Apr 20) 347:3. Chalk was made of calcium carbonate until 1893. For a somewhat less bizarre use of chalk, see APPLAUSE.

Although chalk is universally supplied free to patrons of billiard rooms, at various times vending machines have been produced to dispense chalk cubes on deposit of coins. In England in the 1930s, the price was one penny per piece (at that time, 1/240 of a pound Sterling). 1933 Burwat (Mar) 28.

Substantial effort has been made over the years to develop a cue tip that would not require chalking, but without real success. Numerous patents have been granted for such inventions, some of which consist of mixtures of rubber and sand.

Modern brands of chalk differ considerably in composition, color, and grittiness. Some of the better known are Master, National Tournament, Standard, Sterling, Superior, and Triangle.

2. A powdery substance, normally not containing any chalk but made of TALCUM POWDER, used on the BRIDGE HAND to absorb moisture and decrease friction between the fingers and the shaft of the cue. Also called HAND CHALK.

3. A material used for ruling lines on the cloth for games such as Balkline that require the drawing of lines. A line can be drawn parallel to a cushion with a device known as a BALKLINE MARKER. The ANCHOR SPACES were drawn using an ANCHOR BLOCK as a template. Tailor's chalk was often used for this purpose. 1881 NYT (Apr 12) 5:4. For the first use of chalk lines on a billiard table, see CROTCH.

chalk cup

A holder for CUE CHALK, frequently attached to the table in some manner. A variety of CHALK HOLDER. 1863 Phelan & Berger 105, 1876 Collender 25.

chalk grip

= CHALK HOLDER. 1925c Grote & Hubbell 31.

chalk hanger

A counterweighted device with pulleys, designed to keep cue chalk off the table rails but conveniently available to the players. The chalk is placed in a CHALK HOLDER that is suspended above the table and retracts out of the way when not in use. In British usage, a CHALK SUSPENDER. *See illustration on next page.*

chalk holder

A cup for holding a piece of CUE CHALK, usually tied to the table and hanging over the edge so as to be readily available to players.

chalk shot

Any of a type of illegal TRICK SHOT in which chalk is applied to the contact point between two balls, producing an unexpected result. A variety of GAFF SHOT. An example is at 1981 Varner 95. Chalk increases the friction at the contact point between the balls, lengthening the time they remain in contact and increasing the amount of SPIN that is transferred from one ball to the other.

chalk suspender

(Brit.) = CHALK HANGER.

chalk hanger

chalk up

1. To prepare for play, from the act of chalking the tip of the cue before stroking. 2. To mark up points, derived from the use of chalk on a small slate by BILLIARD MARKERS to tally players' scores. 3. Title of a billiard publication of the A. E. Schmidt Company, a manufacturer of tables.

challenge

1. A demand against a CHAMPIONSHIP titleholder that he defend his CROWN within a certain time period or lose it by FORFEIT. A challenge in a prize match formerly had to be accompanied by a remittance of the proposed stake, also called a forfeit, which would be held by a third party until the outcome of the match was decided. Many titles changed hands in the nineteenth century because of the failure of champions to defend them. The majority of pocket and billiard titles were transferred in the United States by challenge rather than by being won in TOURNAMENT play, although there has not been a title challenge since 1966, when Luther Lassiter successfully defended his World Pocket Billiard title against Cisero Murphy.

Challenges were subject to elaborate rules regarding time limits for acceptance, location of the contest and posting of stakes. 1911 HRB 38. The size of the proposed balls, for example, had to be stated in the challenge. Once the money was posted, the match became "pay or play, death alone relieving the principals from the contract." 1916 RGRG 31. The champion could not be compelled to play in June, July, or August and had the

right to name the hall in which the challenge would take place. Match arrangements were handled by the players' representatives, known as SECONDS.

2. (Eng. Bill) A statement by the NONSTRIKER that he believes a ball lying near the LIP of a pocket is about to FALL. If it falls after such a challenge, but before the striker shoots, it must be replaced in its original position. This concept and the term "challenge" appear at 1807 White 148. See MOTION. Challenging is both impossible and unnecessary in the United States, where a player is credited with pocketing a ball if it falls within a specified time after its apparent motion has ceased.

chamfer

(Brit.) The bevel at the BUTT end of a cue stick, which permits the player to strike a ball by sliding the cue along the cloth in the manner of a MACE. The chamfer on modern British cues is used for decoration and to identify the manufacturer. 1688 OED (non-billiard).

Champion Billiard Players' League

(org.) A body formed in 1914 by Willie Hoppe and other top professionals to conduct matches in 150 U.S. cities. 1914 NYT (Jun 21) IV 2:1.

Champion's Game

(game, obs.) A variation on STRAIGHT-RAIL billiards in which a diagonal BALK SPACE is drawn at each corner to curb the RAIL NURSE. If the centers of both object balls lie in the same space, the player must drive at least one of them out of the space by his second shot, *i.e.*, he has TWO SHOTS IN. A precursor of Balkline, the Champion's Game was based on an expansion of the CROTCH drawn at the corners of the table for a Three-Ball tournament in 1874. The crotch was originally a triangular area with 5½-inch sides. In the Champion's Game, first played in 1879, the line was drawn twice as far from the corner on the long rail as on the side rail. The sizes used were 14 × 28 in 1879, 18 × 36 18 × 36 in 1884, and 20 × 40 in 1885. 1879 NYT (Nov 18) 5:5, 1891 MB 561, 1925 BM (Sep) 22. The first match at this game (February, 1879) was won by George Slosson; the last match (January, 1885) was lost by Slosson, who was still playing in 1946! There was some discussion in 1883 of playing this game without actually drawing lines on the table, to avoid marking up the cloth. 1883 NYT (Mar 11) 14:1. The invention of the Champion's Game is credited to Benjamin Garno, a professional player who edited the handbook *Modern Billiards* for many years. The HIGH RUN record is 398 by Slosson against Maurice Vignaux in Paris, 1882.

Although the purpose of the Champion's Game was to defeat the rail nurse, it was unsuccessful. Jacob Schaefer

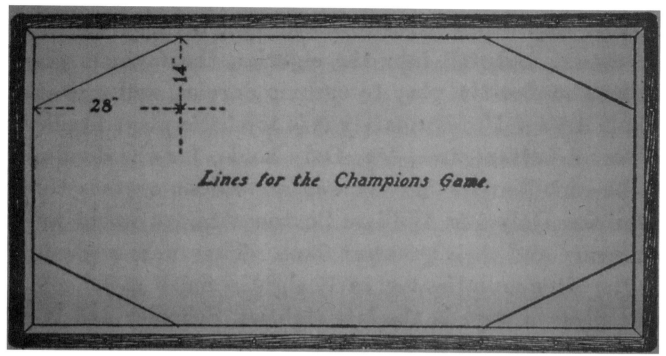

Champion's Game

Sr. mastered the technique of reversing the direction in which the balls are moved during the rail nurse. He was then able to shuttle them back and forth between the diagonals at will. Rectangular balklines were needed to eliminate RAIL PLAY. See BALKLINE.

championship

A prize or award donated by a sponsor, to be won according to specified rules under competitive conditions or by FORFEIT. To be recognized as a title, the championship must be sanctioned by an accepted sanctioning organization or governing body. In various cue sports, zero, one, or multiple rival sanctioning organizations have existed simultaneously, which has resulted in more than one person holding the "championship," which is antithetical to good sense.

A championship is continued according to the terms of its donation, which may provide for a fixed term of years or may allow a player who defends the corresponding title a certain number of times in succession or over a fixed period to retire with permanent possession of it. In the U.S., there has never been a self-perpetuating title. After a championship expires, the title becomes vacant. It is not retained by the last person to hold it at expiration. For example, there is currently no U.S. champion at 18.1 Balkline.

A championship is usually first decided by TOURNAMENT. Once a titleholder has been established, the title may be subject to CHALLENGE or the titleholder may be compelled to enter a new tournament in order to win the title again.

During the 1920s and 1930s, winning a world title brought not only a cash prize but also a salaried position performing billiard exhibitions for one year. In some cases, the title was not subject to challenge, so the incumbent would hold it until the next tournament.

The first world billiard championship was at the THREE-BALL GAME in New York in 1873, won by Albert Garnier. The currently acknowledged U.S. Straight Pool championship is the U.S. OPEN, held irregularly but carrying high prestige.

Championship Game

(game) = 14.1 CONTINUOUS POCKET BILLIARDS. 1946 OR 39. At different times, various game styles have been known as the "Championship Game," usually the one thought to provide the highest test of billiard skill. Cf. CHAMPION'S GAME.

changed ball

(Eng. Bill.) Situation in which the striker has played the wrong cue ball, which is a FOUL, and this fact is subsequently discovered. 1807 White 149, 1845 Hoyle 222, 1856 Crawley 39. The penalty varies depending on the game being played. In some games, if the discovery is made during the INNING of the OFFENDING PLAYER, he forfeits all points scored during that inning. If his opponent plays before the error is detected, the points

47

count, but the new striker will not be charged with a foul for changing balls himself as a result of the opponent's mistake. In other games, all scores count prior to the shot on which the foul is discovered, the player's inning ends, and points are deducted for a single foul. See also WRONG BALL.

changing balls

1. (Bill.) Substituting one or more balls for those in use in a game. The balls *must* be replaced by the REFEREE at the request of a player and with the consent of his opponent. The balls *may* be replaced by the referee on his own initiative at any time, despite any objection by the players, if he believes that they are not acceptable for play. This rule is more important if IVORIES are being used, because it is rare for COMPOSITION BALLS to require replacement during a game. A ball that has become soiled or marked with chalk is usually not changed but is cleaned and replaced. See also BALL MARKER. 2. Playing with the wrong cue ball. 1836 Tillotson 8. See CHANGED BALL, WRONG BALL.

cheat the pocket

(Pocket Bill.) To MANUFACTURE an angle out of an otherwise straight shot by aiming the object ball at one side of the pocket rather than at its center, thus enabling the cue ball to be positioned. 1977 Martin 65, 1992 Billing 90.

48

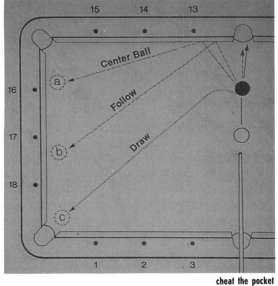

cheat the pocket

cheating

See also DIRTY POOL. Cheating at billiards has been endemic since the early days of the game. (See TRAIL, for example.) Although it is difficult (but not impossible) to alter the course of the balls while the opponent is watching, the EQUIPMENT can be tampered with in advance to give one player an advantage. The following methods have been used, but the reader is warned that employing them may be both morally and physically harmful:

- Equipment. Substitution of a faulty ball; shaving the SLATE to guide balls more readily into the SIDE pockets. 1866 Crawley 47. Making PITS in the cloth near the rails to help maintain the balls in a NURSE position. (Albert Garnier did this in the 1870s. See RAIL NURSE.)
- Misracking. Intentional tampering with the RACK by either player. See RACK. An extensive list of such methods can be found in 1987 NBN (Jul).
- Scoring. Failure to keep score correctly, particularly when a SCORE STRING is in use. See RUB THE WIRE.
- Moving balls. A crude form of cheating that consists of rearranging the still balls while the opponent's attention is focused on the shot in progress. See STILL CUE BALL.
- Moistening the CUE CHALK. A bit of saliva on the tip of the index finger is rubbed into the concave surface of the cue chalk. This will prevent the chalk from adhering to the tip and increase the chances of a MISCUE by the opponent. A countermeasure is for the player to retain a piece of chalk in his possession at all times.
- Screening. Obscuring the view of the REFEREE with one's hands or body to conceal an infraction. See COAT.
- Selective miscueing. A deliberate MISCUE to hide what is actually an INTENTIONAL SAFETY.

Check-Check

(game) A PILL game, played in Hawaii since at least the 1960s. The balls in the rack are not all FROZEN, but are placed in such a way that the APEX BALL and the left and right balls in each row form a "V." The remaining six balls are racked in a triangle close to, but not touching, the other nine. Each player selects two pills from a BOTTLE and wins by sinking the balls corresponding to his pills. The 1, 8, and 15 are free balls. If a player sinks the 1, he must play in rotation in increasing numerical order. If he sinks the 15, he must thereafter play in decreasing order. If he sinks the 8, he may play either upward or downward from 8. 1991 Masui PC.

check side

(Brit. games) = REVERSE ENGLISH, COUNTER, HOLD-UP, OPPOSING SIDE, WRONG-WAY ENGLISH. 1908c Cook Jr. 78. SPIN that acts to narrow the angle of rebound of the ball after CONTACT with a cushion, as measured between the line of travel of the ball and a perpendicular to the cushion. 1924 Aiken 31, 1954 KTG 22. The effect is to "check," or hinder, the action of the ball.

cheese

1. (sl.) One's money or bankroll. Also AMMUNITION, ARMY, or WAD. 1985 BD (Feb) 52. A locution popularized by Minnesota Fats, as in, "I never lost when we played for the cheese." 2. (sl.) The state of being in the ONE-HOLE, in which a player needs only one point for victory. DOUBLE CHEESE means that both players need only one point to win. See also ON THE HILL.

cheval

(Balkline, Fr.) See À CHEVAL.

cherry

= CRIPPLE, DUCK, HANGER, MINNIE, PUPPY, SET-UP, or SITTER.

Chicago

1. (game) A form of ROTATION in which the balls are not racked but are placed FROZEN to the rails at various predetermined DIAMONDS in numerical order counterclockwise about the table. The striker must hit the lowest-numbered ball on the table first and receives credit for the numerical value of any balls pocketed on the stroke. The custom in the city of Chicago was for the lowest-scoring player to pay for general refreshments and the next lowest to pay for the TABLE TIME. 1890 HRB 88, 1916 RGRG 63. Also called BOSTON POOL, CHICAGO POOL, or MEXICAN ROTATION. 1900 May 61. The term "Rotation" derives from the arrangement of the balls in the game of Chicago and not from the fact that the balls are struck in numerical sequence. Other U.S. cities appearing in names of billiard games are BOSTON and

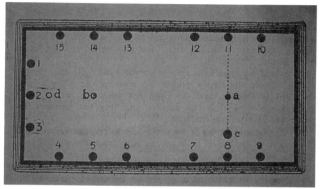

Chicago

HONOLULU. 2. (game) A synonym for ROTATION. 1979 Sullivan 99. General references: 1890 HRB 88, 1891 MB 334, 1919 Hoyle 633.

Chicago Pool

(game, obs.) The version of CHICAGO in which the object balls are placed in contact with the cushions instead of being racked. 1890 HRB 88.

Chinese Billiards

(game, obs.) A game similar to BAGATELLE, played on an inclined table. 1896 Cady 6.

Chinese Pool

1. (game) A casual pocket or carom game in which the cue ball is not stroked but is instead rolled down the

49

Chinese Pool (Taberski)

groove formed by two cue sticks held parallel to one another. 1893 NYDT (Nov 19) 18:4, 1908 Hood 16, 1916 BM (Jan) 61. The origin of the name is unknown, but may relate to the chopstick-like appearance of two cues held together. It was common at the turn of the century to apply the adjective "Chinese" to anything that was done in a different or unusual fashion. Jimmy Caras and Frank Taberski were particularly skilled at the game and were able to run whole racks without difficulty. Also known as CHOPSTICKS POOL. See also RAILROAD SHOT. 2. = BACKWARDS POOL, BILLIARD POOL, CAROM POOL, CONTRA POOL, INDIAN POOL, IRISH POOL, KISS POOL, LOOP, REVERSE BILLIARDS. Cf. CUE BALL POOL.

Chinese table

(obs.) A circular novelty table popularized during the early nineteenth century. See generally TABLE.

Chinese table

Choice of Balls

1. (game) A form of THREE-CUSHIONS in which the INCOMING PLAYER is permitted to select either cue ball as the one he will use for his entire INNING. See CHOICE OF CUE BALL. 2. (game, obs.) A CRAMP GAME using only two balls, usually the WHITE WINNING GAME, in which the weaker player may choose either ball as his cue ball on each shot, but the stronger player must use the same cue ball throughout. 1807 White 49, 1856 Crawley 98, 1867 Dufton 234. Said to present an "incalculable advantage" to the player receiving the HANDICAP. 1862 Crawley 98. In 1866 Crawley 234, this is not a cramp game, and either player may strike at or with either of the white balls.

choice of cue ball

1. (Bill.) The right given to the winner of the LAG to select which cue ball, SPOT or PLAIN, he will use for the duration of the game. This custom is very old, probably

dating back to the seventeenth century. 1807 White 60, 1871 NYT (Apr 27) 1:5. Under international rules, cue ball assignment is either determined by LOT or by the convention that the OPENING BREAKER must use the BLACK BALL. 2. (Three-Cushions) A three-cushion game in which the INCOMING PLAYER may choose either cue ball on the opening shot of his INNING as the one he will use for the entire inning. A French idea, this variation was tried in 1929 and has made occasional appearances thereafter. 1929 NYT (Dec 16) 37:3. Its purpose is to speed up play and reduce the use of SAFETIES. Points are easier to score because of the choice of balls. Safeties are less desirable for two reasons: It is more difficult to leave the opponent without a shot, and the player shooting a safety gives up a substantial chance to make a point himself. In its extreme form, the game of Choice of Balls is played with three white balls, the player being allowed to select any of the three as his cue ball. 1929 NYT (Feb 18) 32:3. Cf. CROSS CUE TOURNAMENT, OPTIONAL CUE BALL, STREAMLINED BILLIARDS.

choke

(colloq.) To lose concentration at a critical juncture; to collapse under psychological pressure. 1979 Grissim 250. See CLUTCH, PSYCH.

Chopsticks Pool

(game) = CHINESE POOL, a game in which the cue ball is rolled off two cue sticks in a fashion somewhat reminiscent of a pair of chopsticks.

chuck nurse

(Bill.) A STATIONARY NURSE in STRAIGHT-RAIL, in which the cue ball is repeatedly caromed off a ball that

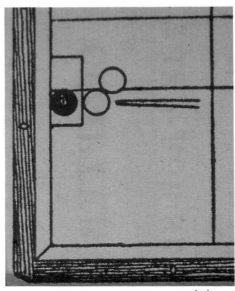

chuck nurse

remains FROZEN to a cushion, while the SECOND OBJECT BALL is rocked but not moved from its position. 1913 Daly 160, 1946 OR 89, 1979 Sullivan 183, 1992 OR 6. In 1912, W. A. Spinks ran 1010 UNFINISHED at this nurse in 18.2 BALKLINE. Derived from an obsolete use of the word "chuck," meaning "direct impact," referring to the manner in which the cue ball is kissed off the first object ball. In English Billiards, a ROCKING CANNON.

church

The relationship between billiards and organized religious bodies has fluctuated cyclically since the 1860s. Clergymen were quick and correct to denounce dissolute and criminal behavior that occurred in POOL HALLS, but were wrong in ascribing such conduct to immoral factors in the game of billiards itself. After a time, it was realized that the inherent appeal of billiards to young men could be used as a recruiting tool for religious purposes, and tables were installed in church basements. At the height of billiards' popularity, however, an amazing tract was published by the Reverend John A. Phelan (no relation to Michael Phelan) entitled, "Pool, Billiards and Bowling Alleys as a Phase of Commercialized Amusements in Toledo, Ohio." It appeared in 1919 and contains vituperative diatribe against pool halls, which are characterized as "meeting places of underworld mashers, cadets, procurers, gangsters, gunmen, thieves and criminals of all sorts." Phelan concedes that there is a place for the game in a regulated Christian life, but deplores public establishments, which he asserts in 196 pages are a blot on decent society.

Phelan's comments were echoed by clergy and politicians around the country, which began to turn the regulatory tide against billiards until the 1990s. Numerous ordinances were enacted imposing stringent licensing, zoning, and other restrictions on pool halls. Many of them survive today and still impose obstacles to new billiard development. One of the reasons that the Chelsea area of New York is densely populated with rooms, while they are still relatively sparse in the rest of Manhattan, relates to zoning, a holdover from the days of tight political control.

There seems to have been no particular comment from the church concerning billiards before the advent of organized pool halls, which were a nineteenth-century phenomenon. In fact, billiards was popular among churchmen long before that time, including Martin Luther and the French Bishop of Langres, who was apparently something of a hustler in the early 1600s. 1974 Hendricks 1. In the 1850s, it was the measure of morality of a town how many houses of worship it contained compared with the number of billiard par-

lors. In *Moby Dick* (1851), Herman Melville noted that Lima, Peru, was a corrupt place, despite having "churches more plentiful than billiard-tables." 1992 Holmes PC.

CIBA

(org.) The COMMISSION INTERNATIONALE DE BILLARD ARTISTIQUE, the world governing body of ARTISTIC BILLIARDS. 1982 BD (Sep/Oct).

circus shot

(obs.) A spectacular but unlikely shot, very pleasing to the SPECTATORS. 1925 Hoppe 109. One that is exorbitantly fancy. Cf. FANCY SHOT, GAFF SHOT, TRICK SHOT.

cities, names of

The following billiard games incorporate names of cities: BOSTON, CHICAGO, HONOLULU. See also COUNTRIES, NAMES OF and STATES, NAMES OF.

clamp

= CUE CLAMP.

clean

1. (pocket games) A shot is clean if the object ball touches no cushion or other object ball before being pocketed. See also CLEAN BANK. A POCKET DROP is clean if the ball encounters no interference in falling into the pocket; in particular, it does not tend to rebound from the pocket back onto the PLAYING SURFACE. See also POCKETED BALL. 2. See CLEANING.

clean bank

(Bank Pool) A BANK SHOT in which the object ball enters a pocket without touching any other object ball. 1992 OR 7. In the game of BANK POOL, all shots must be clean banks. See also INCIDENTAL CONTACT.

clean the table

(pocket games) = CLEAR THE TABLE. To sink all the remaining balls on the table in a single turn or, in 14.1 CONTINUOUS, all but the BREAK BALL. 1989 Koehler 252. Cf. RUN OUT.

clean up

(Brit. games, colloq.) To RUN OUT. 1981 Quinn 85. See also BUSTAWAY, GET OUT, OFF THE BALLS, OUT.

cleaning

The act of removing debris from an item of EQUIPMENT, such as a ball or the cloth. A ball that is IN PLAY may be cleaned only by the REFEREE, since the act of touching such a ball would constitute a FOUL. The STRIKER, however, may clean a ball that is IN HAND. 1957 Holt 207. When a ball must be cleaned, its location is marked with a POSITION MARKER. In the U.K., cleaning may be requested by a player. 1978 BSCC S24. In the U.S., the referee must clean any "visibly soiled ball." 1992 OR 52.

Balls and cloth should normally be cleaned after each use, since foreign matter alters their characteristics. In some rooms, new balls may be requested after each game of Three-Cushions. Balls are cleaned by the application of ball polish and manual rubbing or by the use of a BALL CLEANER. Cloth is best cleaned by brushing and use of a VACUUM CLEANER.

clear

1. To remove balls manually from a DROP POCKET so it does not become too full to receive additional balls. 1988 PBA 22. It is the player's responsibility to ensure that the referee performs this function. 1992 OR 52. (The player himself may not touch pocketed balls. See OUT OF PLAY.) 2. To execute a shot that has the effect of moving an object ball that was OBSTRUCTING a pocket opening. 3. Unobstructed, OPEN. "You're clear," meaning that no ball or portion of the table is interfering with your shot. Also FREE. 4. (Bill.) = CLEAR BALL.

clear ball

1. (Bill.) The unmarked white ball; the PLAIN, as distinguished from the SPOT BALL, SPOT WHITE, or BLACK BALL. 1992 OR 7. Although the clear ball is not actually transparent, lucite balls that are literally clear have been manufactured for novelty purposes. Aiming at them is extremely difficult, so they are not useful for practical play. 2. (Snooker) A ball that can be struck directly by the cue ball at both of its extreme left and right edges. A ball on which a player is not SNOOKERED. 1956 BSTE 20. See also OBSTRUCTION.

clear the table

(Pocket Bill., Snooker) To sink all the remaining balls on the table in a single BREAK or RUN. 1862 Crawley 105, 1881 NYT (Jan 8) 5:5, 1957 Holt 141. To CLEAN THE TABLE. In 14.1 CONTINUOUS, to pocket all the balls up to the BREAK BALL. Cf. RUN OUT, which means to score all points needed for game, which may involve more or fewer balls than remain on the table.

clearance

(Snooker) The act of POTTING all the remaining balls on the table (other than the cue ball) in a single BREAK. A TOTAL CLEARANCE is one in which all 21 object balls are potted.

clip

(Snooker) To hit the BALL ON very THIN, especially in order to bring the cue ball back into BAULK for a SAFETY. 1988 Davis 143. See also FAN, FEATHER, FINE BALL.

clock system

1. A method for specifying the type of ENGLISH to be applied to the cue ball by using the face of a clock as a reference. For example, low LEFT is "7 o'clock English," while pure FOLLOW is "12 o'clock English." 2. A DIAMOND SYSTEM in which the type of ENGLISH to be used is computed from the diamond positions of the object balls. The positioning of the cue tip is given in terms of def. 1, above.

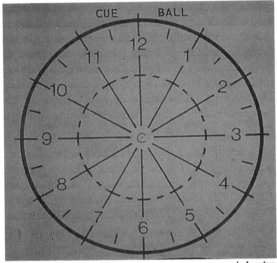

clock system

close cannon

(Eng. Bill.) = NURSERY CANNON; a CANNON calling for close manipulation because the balls are very near one another and the position must not be disturbed in order to preserve the BREAK. 1904 Mannock I 250, 1925 Reece 84, 1954 KTG 16.

close draw

DRAW SHOT in which the cue ball is very near the FIRST OBJECT BALL, thus preventing a legal FOLLOW-THROUGH. 1884 MB 251. Commonly played as a NIP to avoid a PUSH.

closed break

(Pocket Bill.) A BREAK SHOT in which a player receives credit for a pocketed ball only if it has been CALLED. 1913 Burrowes 5. "Closed" refers to the fact that it is desirable not to spread the PACK widely on such a shot, since the player cannot score himself and would only offer opportunities to his opponent. Cf. FREE BREAK, OPEN BREAK.

closed bridge

A positioning of the fingers of the BRIDGE HAND in which the shaft of the cue is encircled by a curled finger. See also BRIDGE BOUCLÉE, LOOP BRIDGE. A closed bridge provides better guidance for the cue stick during the stroke, but this style of bridge is not favored by Snooker players. Cf. OPEN-HAND BRIDGE, V-BRIDGE.

closed-hand bridge

= CLOSED BRIDGE.

cloth

The fabric covering the BED of a billiard table, on which the balls roll. Tables have been covered with cloth since the fifteenth century. In one of the more gruesome incidents in billiard history, the body of Mary, Queen of Scots was wrapped in the cloth from her billiard table when she was decapitated in 1576. 1974 Hendricks 1. In 1588, the Duke of Norfolk owned at Howard House "a billyard bord covered with greene cloth." 1967 Polsky 9. It is not known authoritatively when the rails of the table were covered with cloth, but it has probably been so ever since the game was brought indoors.

Originally chosen to simulate the appearance of grass, green has been the most popular color for billiard cloth since at least the sixteenth century. It happens that the human eye has lower sensitivity to green light, and this color enables us to play for long periods without visual fatigue. Contrast between the balls and the cloth is thought to be important for aiming, but this hardly seems plausible in view of the choice of green for the six-ball and fourteen-ball and one of the Snooker CO-LOURS. In 1935, Brunswick introduced a purple cloth with the name I-Rest, claiming that it eliminated after-image and caused less eye fatigue. The color was tried at the World Three-Cushion Championship that year, but it never caught on. 1935 NYT (Dec 8) v 7:2.

The properties of the cloth strongly affect play. A SLOW cloth is one that offers resistance to the motion of the balls. It requires the player to drive the balls harder, which reduces aiming accuracy. A FAST cloth, by contrast, allows the balls to be struck softly, but presents so little resistance that it is difficult to make the cue ball stop. In general, fast cloth is essential for three-cushion play, but a medium speed is appropriate for pocket billiards.

Billiard cloth is often erroneously called "felt," but felt is never used because it would tear too readily. The finest cloths are made of 100% worsted wool, similar to the type used in men's suits. The firm of Iwan Simonis of Verviers, Belgium, is probably the most famous manufacturer of billiard cloth. The company is approximately as old as billiards itself, a predecessor having been formed in 1453. Its preferred source of wool is the Australian Merino sheep. Spinning and weaving wool is a complex process requiring many steps and chemical treatments.

Before the Industrial Revolution, cloth was a precious commodity and the rules of the game exacted penalties for damaging it. 1674 Cotton contains a rule forbidding a player to drop ash from his pipe on the cloth.

The effect of the cloth on the impact and rolling of balls is poorly understood and the subject of much speculation. How tightly should the bed cloth be stretched? Should the same cloth that covers the bed also be used to cover the cushions? See also BED CLOTH, BURN MARK, FEATHER STRIP, NAP, PIT, RAIL CLOTH, SLIDE.

Cloth, particularly a slow cloth, may be profoundly affected by high humidity, which slows the rolling of the balls even further. Moisture may be driven from the cloth by HEATING the bed of the table.

Tables are typically outfitted with new cloth before a tournament. Because of the effect of SLIDE, new cloths behave differently from those that have been broken in and extraordinary spin effects can be achieved on new cloths.

Whether the cloth can be changed during a MATCH, when, and by whose direction have been debated. In one infamous case, a player took matters into his own hands. After the eighth BLOCK of a match with Willie Hoppe in 1925, Robert Cannefax complained that the cloth was too slow and demanded that it be changed. Hoppe, who was leading, refused to agree. Cannefax himself produced a pocketknife and tore the cloth, which he felt sure would compel the organizers to install a new one. Instead, a FORFEIT was declared and Cannefax was suspended by the National Three-Cushion Billiard League for a year. 1925 BM (Jul) 35. During the SUSPENSION, he performed a traveling comedy billiard act in theatres. Cannefax became ill during the tour and died in 1928 without returning to tournament billiards.

cluster

1. (Pocket Bill., Snooker) A collection of balls that are either FROZEN or so close together that no clear shot is possible on any of them. A cluster represents a potential obstacle to a RUN and thus must be OPENED with a BREAK SHOT or SPLIT if the INNING is to continue. 1977 Fels 62. 2. (Bill.) To GATHER, that is, to make the balls come together closely in a small region of the table. 1878 NYT (Jan 24) 2:1. 3. A run of points. "He put together a cluster of 134." 1907 NYT (Mar 7) 10:3. Also a BREAK or STRING.

clutch

(colloq.) To fail to perform at a critical time, to CHOKE; to suffer a sudden loss of control or concentration and thereby miss a shot. See also PSYCH.

coaching

The act of giving advice to the STRIKER. In certain games, such as ENGLISH EIGHT-BALL POOL, coaching is completely forbidden. In various team games, the striker's partner alone may coach him on a shot, but only before the ball has been ADDRESSED. 1981 Quinn 117. See ASSISTANCE.

coat

(colloq.) A player is said to "coat" the REFEREE when he positions himself or his clothing so as to obscure the official's view of a shot or an infraction by the player. 1972 Byrne 171. In all billiard games, the player is not presumed to have made a point. If the referee does not see the shot, he may declare the player's INNING at an end. See DOUBT. However, the referee may seek the advice of the SPECTATORS as to the outcome of the shot.

cochonnet

(*Fr.*, pr. ko-shun-NAY) A smaller billiard ball used as a target in such games as PÉTANQUE.

Cockamaroo

(Bagatelle game, obs.) = RUSSIAN BAGATELLE. 1878 Crawley 154.

Cocked Hat

(game, obs.) A bowling-like game similar to TEN PINS, except that only three pins are used, formed in the shape of a 9-inch triangle. 1902 Burrowes 20.

cocked-hat double

(Snooker) A BANK SHOT or DOUBLE in which the object ball hits the side, end, and side rails and falls in a MIDDLE pocket, tracing what appears to be the outline of a cocked hat in the process. 1936 Davis 24, 1957 Holt 171, 1986 Davis 69. *See illustration in next column.*

coin

A small metal disk having value, with multiple uses in billiard games. See also LINE BALL.

1. The most common use of coins is in connection with COIN-OPERATED TABLES. 2. A coin is used when decisions are required by LOT, as in determining order of play or who is to BREAK. The coin should not, however, be tossed so that it falls on the cloth, since the rilled edge may tear cloth fibers. 3. A coin is used to claim WINNERS, that is, to indicate a desire to play against the winner of the current game. The coin is placed prominently on the rail of the table for this purpose. 4. Coins are used casually for scoring purposes in unrefereed matches where it is necessary to keep track of games won. Each player places a coin underneath the cushion NOSE opposite a DIAMOND, in a position where it cannot

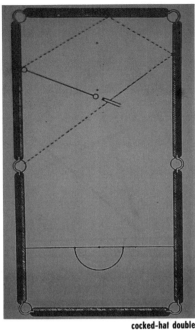

cocked-hat double

interfere with any balls. On winning a game, the coin is moved to the next diamond. One player moves the coins clockwise, the other counterclockwise. The current score can easily be read visually. 5. Coins are used as targets in certain games, such as BOUCHON POOL, BUMBLE-PUPPY, and CORK POOL. 6. (obs.) Coins were used as an ante in LIFE POOL and were stored during play in the MARKING BOARD, from which they were dispensed at the conclusion of the game.

coin-operated table

A table, usually smaller than regulation size, that dispenses a single RACK of balls on deposit of one or more COINS. The object balls that enter pockets during play are not returned to the GULLY, while the cue ball, which is of slightly larger diameter, is returned if it should be pocketed. The difference in size of the cue ball can be exploited; see Robert Byrne's article at 1988 BD (Aug) 15. Knowledgeable players can derive the maximum use from such a table if they engage in a primarily defensive game such as ONE-POCKET. Also known as a "coin-op" table or BAR TABLE. See also BAR POOL, BAR-TABLE GAME, OVERSIZE BALL, QUARTER TABLE.

Because pocketed object balls cannot be SPOTTED, but are trapped by the table, the rules of most games (except Eight-Ball, which is ideal for coin-operated play), must be modified as a result.

collar

A FERRULE at the JOINT of a TWO-PIECE CUE. 1983 NBN (Mar) 18. Though it is a true ferrule in the sense of a fitting that protects the wood, the collar is never known by that name, to avoid confusion with the ferrule at the tip end of the cue.

collision-induced English

Spin imparted to a ball during a glancing collision with another ball. 1989 Koehler 252. Cf. CUSHION-IMPARTED SIDE.

color

1. (Snooker) A colored, or non-red, ball. Also COLOUR. 2. The hue of a ball. Balls are colored so they may be distinguished from one another. In Pocket Billiards, STRIPED and SOLID balls of the same color differ by eight in numerical designation. For example, both the two- and ten-balls are blue. For a discussion of the color of the cloth, see CLOTH. For ball colors, see BALL.

Color-Ball Pool

(game) = LIFE POOL. 1919 Hoyle 639. Also called ENGLISH POOL, FOLLOWING POOL, LAST PLAYER, LIVE POOL or just POOL.

Color of Money, The

1. The title of a 1984 novel by Walter Tevis, a sequel to his earlier book, THE HUSTLER. The 1986 film version starred Tom Cruise and Paul Newman, who reprised his role as Eddie Felson and won an Academy Award. The movie is credited with causing a resurgence of "upscale" pocket billiards during the late 1980s. See also WEIGHT. 2. Green, the same color as billiard cloth.

Colored Amateur Billiard Players' Association

(org.) Organization formed in New York in 1916 to meet the needs of black billiardists. 1916 BM (Jan) 63.

colour

1. (Snooker) A coloured ball other than a RED. 1929b Davis 34. A POOL BALL. 2. (obs.) A flag used in FORTIFICATION BILLIARDS to identify FORTS belonging to different SIDES.

colour-blind

(Snooker) The rules compel the REFEREE to identify for a colour-blind player the colour of any ball on the table. 1978 BSCC 57.

combination

1. (Pocket Bill.) A shot in which the cue ball drives one object ball into another to cause the CALLED BALL to be pocketed. 1878 NYT (Apr 21) 1:7, 1976 WSD 87. A shot in which the cue ball first strikes a ball other than the one to be pocketed. 1992 OR 7. It is as difficult to define a combination precisely as it is to define a BANK SHOT. The gist is that there must be some contact between two balls other than the cue and the called ball that is

essential to making the shot. Cf. CASIN, PLANT, SET. 2. (Eng. Bill.) A shot in which the player scores in two or more ways, *e.g.*, by making a CANNON and a HAZARD on the same stroke. 1954 KTG 10, 1976 WSD 87. An example is a DOUBLE HAZARD. 3. (Three-Cushions, very rare) A TIME SHOT. 1898 Thatcher 38. 4. (Bill., very rare) A TRICK SHOT in which two or more players participate, each one shooting a ball. 1878 NYT (Feb 8) 8:4. Several outstanding examples of this type of shot were featured in the 1948 film short, "Super Cue Men," performed by Jimmy Caras and Willie Mosconi.

combination set

A set of carom balls consisting of two white IVORY cue balls and one synthetic red object ball, the purpose of the substitution being to save cost. 1919 BM (Apr) 7.

combination table

A table that can be used for both pocket and carom games, or as both a dining table and a billiard table. Tables with these dual functions have been depicted in engravings back as far as 1640. Play of both Pocket and Carom Billiards can be achieved on an ordinary table through the use of CAROM PLUGS or replaceable rails. See also CONVERTIBLE TABLE. 1893 HRB 12. *See illustration on next page.*

Commanding Game

1. (game, obs.) CRAMP GAME of English Billiards in which the method of making certain shots must be called (*i.e.*, commanded) in advance by the STRIKER. 1876 Crawley 96. See also NOMINATION GAME. 2. (game, obs.) CRAMP GAME in which the adversary may choose the ball to be used by the STRIKER. 1807 White 52, 1839 Kentfield 38, 1862 Crawley 96. Said in 1856 White & Bohn 39 to be equivalent to giving 12 points in 16.

commercial table

A table designed for the rigors of use in a public room or in other high-activity locations. Cf. HOME TABLE.

Commission Internationale de Billard Artistique (CIBA)

(org.) The world governing body of ARTISTIC BILLIARDS.

Common Game

(game, obs.) = The WINNING GAME or WHITE WINNING GAME. 1773 *Covent Garden*, 1974 Hendricks 25. In the early nineteenth century, the WINNING AND LOSING CARAMBOLE GAME, that is, ENGLISH BILLIARDS. 1807 White 60.

communicated side

(Brit. games) SIDE transferred to the object ball through friction with the spinning cue ball. 1911 Roberts 52.

55

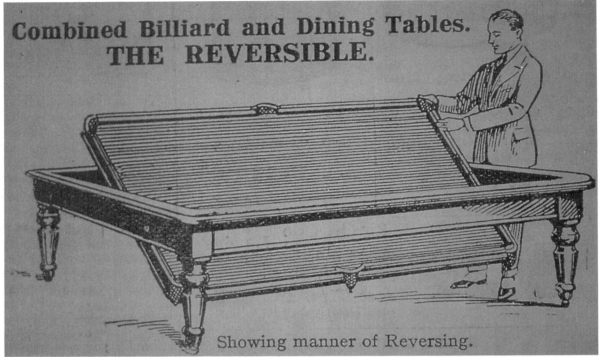

Combined Billiard and Dining Tables.
THE REVERSIBLE.

Showing manner of Reversing.

combination table

See TRANSMITTED SIDE for an account of the lengthy controversy surrounding this concept.

companion ball

(Cribbage) Two object balls constitute a CRIBBAGE if their numerical total is 15. One ball is then said to be the companion ball of the other. 1992 OR 76. For example, the 6 and 9 are companion balls.

company

The SPECTATORS or GALLERY. A collection of RAIL BIRDS.

composition ball

A billiard ball made of a synthetic (*i.e.,* non-IVORY) material. 1941 Levi 202. See BALL. Composition balls were allowed in British competitions beginning in the late 1920s. 1985 Morrison 11. See also MUD. One composition ball, known as "compo-ivory," actually contained ground ivory fragments.

compulsory stroke

(Eng. Bill.) A stroke that a player is compelled to make under the rules because of his having deliberately interfered with the balls in the hope of obtaining a tactical advantage. For example, the player may jam a ball against the cushion with his arm and try to claim that it was his shot, acknowledging the foul but leaving his opponent in a poor position. The player is then compelled to make a fair stroke with the tip of the cue, but is not allowed to score and his inning ends. That is, no COUNT can be made on a compulsory stroke. Failure

to make the required stroke when so directed by the referee results in a forfeiture of points for each offense. 1916 RGRG 8. Cf. PLAY AGAIN RULE, ROLLOUT.

concession

An acknowledgment by a player that he or his team has lost the game or match. This may be done as a gentlemanly gesture when one's deficit is too great to overcome even though victory may still be technically or mathematically possible. It is common in Nine-Ball to concede when the opponent faces a HANGER on the nine-ball, much as one concedes a short putt in golf. But the usual rule in TOURNAMENT play is that balls cannot be conceded and all games must be played out or the conceding player FORFEITS.

In professional games, to UNSCREW the joint of one's cue (except to change shafts) is taken as a signal of concession, since the only other reason for so doing would be to annoy the striker. Returning one's cue stick to the rack is likewise an admission of defeat, and one with a long history. According to 1836 Tillotson 9: "Putting down the cue when the striker is within a few points of Game argues it lost, and the striker may claim the Game." See also RACK UP.

Not all concessions are involuntary or the result of an infraction of the rules. For a stunning example, see SPORTSMANSHIP.

condom

(sl.) The jocular name for the removable rubber sleeve used as a GRIP. A RUBBER. The allusion is enhanced by the manner of applying the sleeve to the cue, which involves rolling it up and unrolling it in position.

condone

(Brit. games) To fail to CALL a FOUL on one's opponent, causing the game to proceed as if no infraction had occurred. A foul that is not called prior to the next stroke is condoned. 1987 BSCC s19.

Confédération Européenne de Billard (CEB)

(org.) The European Billiard Confederation, the sanctioning body of European carom tournaments.

consecutive cannons

(Eng. Bill.) The number of consecutive CANNONS a player may make not in conjunction with a HAZARD is 75. 1978 BSCC 36. The REFEREE must warn the STRIKER when 70 cannons are reached. If he fails to do so, the player may make five additional cannons after being warned. 1987 BSCC B16. In certain kinds of competition, the limit on consecutive cannons is 35. 1960 Ency. Brit. The limit was originally 25 (1919 Cut-Cavendish 105), but was raised over the years, finally reaching 75 in 1971. This rule was introduced to eliminate long NURSERY breaks, which were boring to spectators. See also CONSECUTIVE HAZARDS, LINE RULE.

consecutive fouls

More than one foul made in successive turns at the table by the same player. Rules vary in different games as to the penalty or remedy for consecutive fouls. In 14.1 CONTINUOUS, a FIFTEEN-POINT PENALTY was formerly assessed for three consecutive fouls. This sanction was replaced in 1977 by a loss of either 20% of the total number of points needed for game or by subtracting one point and giving the INCOMING PLAYER cue ball IN HAND anywhere on the table, at his option. See also ON A FOUL, SUCCESSIVE FOULS. 1982 OR.

consecutive hazards

(Eng. Bill.) The number of consecutive HAZARDS a player may make without an intervening CANNON is 15 in professional and amateur championships. 1978 BSCC 36. If more than one ball is pocketed on a single stroke, only a single hazard is counted for purposes of this rule. The REFEREE must warn the STRIKER after 10 hazards. 1987 BSCC B15. In ordinary games, the limit on consecutive hazards is 25. 1960 Ency. Brit. This rule, which has frequently been altered, prevents lengthy breaks consisting of successive SPOT HAZARDS. See also CONSECUTIVE CANNONS. Cf. SPOT-BARRED GAME, TWO-POT RED RULE.

contact

1. A collision of a ball with the FACE of a cushion to which it is not already FROZEN. In games requiring one or more cushion contacts such as BANK POOL, CUSHION CAROMS, and THREE-CUSHIONS, it is important to be able to define when a valid contact has occurred. In carom games, any contact with the face of a cushion counts, but multiple consecutive BOUNCES on the top of a single cushion count collectively as one contact only. In Bank Pool and related games, a contact is not valid if it is an INCIDENTAL CONTACT. See also DOUBT. 2. A collision between two balls, also known as a HIT. Carom games require a definitive contact between the cue ball and two or more object balls, so it is essential to be able to determine when such a contact has occurred. A ball that is moving rapidly past another may move that ball with a rush of air without actually contacting it, and it is unlikely that such motion would fail to be taken as a hit (although it isn't one). REFEREES tend to rely on the clicking sound made by the glancing of two balls, although no rule specifies how contact is to be detected. See DOUBT. 3. The touching of the cue tip to the cue ball, also known as a HIT. In pocket billiards, the contact must be no more than momentary to be legal. 1990 OR 37. See MOMENTARY CONTACT, PUSH. See also CONTINUOUS STROKE.

contact point

See POINT OF CONTACT.

Continuous

(game) = 14.1 CONTINUOUS POCKET BILLIARDS, in which scoring is tallied over more than one RACK, as opposed to SINGLE-RACK games such as BASIC POCKET BILLIARDS. Cf. CONTINUOUS POOL.

continuous balkline

1. (Balkline) A single BALKLINE having the shape of a rectangle and located at a constant number of inches from the rails, say, eight. The BALK SPACE so formed extends from the rails to the line; within this space only two caroms are allowed without forcing an object ball out of the space. 1881 MB 23.

This style of line was first proposed in 1873, but its manner of use was very unusual. When both object balls lay between the cushion and the line, the player was required to either (1) contact a cushion before hitting the second object ball or (2) hit a cushion and another ball after making a carom. In 1875, the proposal was made to allow a player three shots while both balls were within the line. 1883 NYT (Mar 25) 5:1. See BALKLINE.

2. (game) The name of a game played on a table having a continuous balkline. It served as a transitional phase between the CHAMPION'S GAME and BALKLINE.

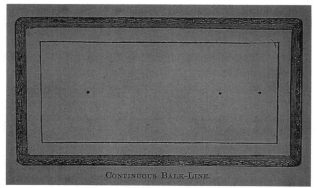

CONTINUOUS BALK-LINE.

Continuous Balkline

Continuous Pocketings

(game, obs.) = FIFTEEN-BALL CONTINUOUS POCKET BILLIARDS. 1916 RGRG 49, 1927 Katch 52. This was one of the names given to the game before 14.1 CONTINUOUS was adopted as the tournament game in 1911.

Continuous Pool

(game, obs.) A pocket billiard game in which scoring is "continued" from one FRAME to the next until the requisite number of points for game is attained, as distinguished from BASIC POCKET BILLIARDS, which lasts for only a single frame. Each ball counts, and a player's score at any point is the total number of balls he has pocketed, less any penalties assessed for FOULS. The player who pockets the last ball of a frame must begin the next frame by shooting at a full PACK. There is no BREAK BALL. 1890 HRB 70, 1891 MB 316, 1919 Hoyle 632. Cf. 14.1 CONTINUOUS POCKET BILLIARDS, in which a break ball is used and a single player's RUN may extend over more than one RACK.

"Continuous" does not refer to the fact that a run can continue over more than one rack, but reflects instead that SCORING is continued over racks, as opposed to previous pocket styles, which were all SINGLE-RACK games.

Continuous Pool was introduced by an Englishman who felt that the method of scoring at FIFTEEN-BALL POOL was unfair in that the player sinking the most balls is not necessarily the winner. He observed this during a match between Albert Frey and James L. Malone and offered a stake of $200 if the players would replay the match, counting only the total number of balls pocketed

by each player. The first tournament was held in 1888, Albert Frey winning. 1913 NYT (Feb 23) V 4:6. The exhibition high runs are 97 on a 10-foot table and 118 on a 9-foot, both by William Clearwater. The tournament high run at this game is 81 by Alfredo De Oro in 1910. 1910 NYT (Dec 1) 12:3. The record still stands because Continuous Pool was supplanted by 14.1 Continuous the next year and no further title competition has been held since.

continuous stroke

(pocket games) A stroke in which the cue stick is moved smoothly, with no hesitation or jerking action. A shot was formerly legal in most pocket billiard games if it was made with "one continuous stroke of the cue." This rule has been replaced by one disallowing anything beyond MOMENTARY CONTACT with the cue ball. The continuous stroke concept has never been applicable in carom games. See PUSH.

Contra Pool

(game) A pocket game in which the object balls are used as cue balls and must be caromed off the white ball into a pocket. The white is spotted at the HEAD SPOT and the first ball stroked is the APEX BALL. 1902 Burrowes 19. It is called "Contra" Pool because it is in a sense the reverse of Pool. The game has been reinvented several times. See BACKWARDS POOL, BILLIARD POOL, CAROM POOL, CHINESE POOL, INDIAN POOL, IRISH POOL, KISS POOL, LOOP, REVERSE BILLIARDS. Cf. CUE BALL POOL, ROTATION CONTRA POOL.

convertible table

= COMBINATION TABLE. 1908 Brunswick 96.

coo

= COUP, def. 2. 1836 Tillotson 2.

coordinates

A method of recording the positions of the balls so that others may attempt the same shots without the need for diagrams. See also KEY SHOT, NOTATION, TELEGRAPHIC BILLIARDS.

An early formal system used by de Rivière in his 1891 book divides the table into 128 squares by an 8 × 16 rectangular grid. The boxes are designated A1 through A16, B1 through B16, etc., through H16. 1910 Russell also uses an 8 × 16 structure, but of slightly different form. Boxes are numbered 1 to 32 in a 4 × 8 array; each box is then subdivided into four squares labeled A, B, C, and D counterclockwise from the lower left. 1983 Malsert 43 uses pure geometric coordinates measured in centimeters with the lower left corner as origin and the x-coordinate corresponding to distance along the SHORT RAIL.

In ARTISTIC BILLIARDS, it is essential for the referee to be able to set up the balls precisely for several attempts at the same shot by multiple players. 1987 Jewett 1. The table is divided into 16 sectors, labeled A through P and measuring one diamond by two in size. Each sector is partitioned into 72 squares, each of side ⅔ inch, arranged in a 6 × 12 configuration. There are thus 1152 regions in all—a 24 × 48 array of squares. In each sector, the squares are marked from 1 to 156. The last digit is always in the range 1 to 6 and indicates distance along the long rail. The leftmost digit or digits are 0 . . . 5, 10 . . . 15, but the zero occurring alone is not written. Thus A05 is written simply as A5. A further refinement adds the suffix 7, 8, or 9 in parentheses, indicating the center of the top side of the square, the upper right corner, and the center of the right side, respectively. Top and right are viewed with respect to the long rail adjacent to the square's sector. The total number of distinct specifiable locations is therefore 3360. (Figuring out why this is less than 3 × 1152 = 3456 is left as an exercise for the reader.) This system is somewhat complicated; in practice its use is simplified considerably by employing a TEMPLATE.

cork

A soft, absorbent material exhibiting several uses in billiards.

1. Cork is sometimes used as a WRAP on the GRIP of a cue. 2. A cork is used as a target in such games as BOUCHON POOL and CORK POOL.

Cork Pool

(game) Played with three balls and a CORK, which is placed on the CENTER SPOT and used as a target. The red ball is placed on the BILLIARD SPOT. Each player then places a penny on top of the cork as a stake. Each shot must be a CANNON off the red to the cork. When the cork is knocked over, the STRIKER wins the ante. If a player misses or commits a FOUL, he must add a penny to the cork. 1896 Broadfoot 429, 1924 Smith 116, 1927 Clifford 59. Use of a coin in this manner on a billiard table is not recommended. See COIN, def. 2. In Dutch, "kurkspel." See also BOUCHON POOL, BUMBLE-PUPPY, CORONATION CORK POOL BILLIARDS.

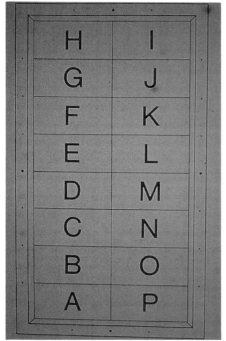

coordinates (1)

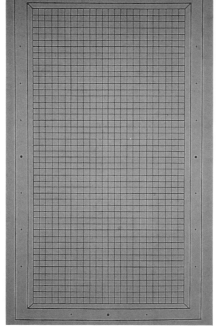

coordinates (2)

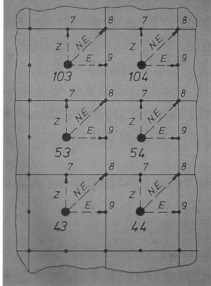

coordinates (3)

corner

1. (pocket games) A CORNER POCKET, as in the player's call, "ace in the corner." 2. (Bill.) One of the four places on a CAROM TABLE at which two perpendicular cushions meet. See CROTCH. A ball shot directly into the corner is likely to behave unpredictably.

corner ball

(pocket games) Any ball, excluding the APEX BALL, that is racked at one of the corners of the RACK.

corner five

(Three-Cushions) The standard DIAMOND SYSTEM, FIVE-AND-A-HALF SYSTEM or FIVE SYSTEM, called the "corner five" because it assigns a CUE-BALL NUMBER of five to the corner of the table, which is not marked by any diamond.

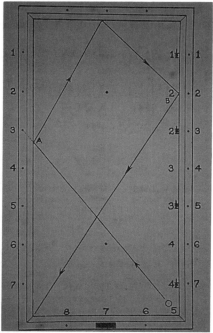

corner five

Corner Game

(game) A two-ball carom game that originated in France in which players must BANK the cue ball against the left side and foot cushions before hitting the single object ball. The goal is to drive the object ball into a marked area in the left corner at the head of the table in the fewest number of shots. Players of this game utilized an aiming system that was the precursor of the DIAMOND SYSTEM. 1893 NYDT (Jan 8) 19:4, 1898 Thatcher 231, 1946 OR 89, 1977 OR. It was introduced into the U.S. by Maurice Daly in 1893. The principal American exponent was W. H. Catton, who won the Three-Cushion title in 1899.

corner hooked

See ANGLED BALL. 1992 OR 7.

corner pocket

(pocket games) A pocket located at one of the four corners of the playing surface of a pocket billiard table. 1807 White 119, 1857 Phelan 110, 1992 OR 4. Often just "the corner." Cf. SIDE POCKET.

Coronation Cork Pool Billiards

(game) A British game played with three billiard balls, PRIVATE NUMBERS, and a CORK colored red and white. The cork is placed on the MIDDLE SPOT. Scoring is as in English Billiards; knocking the cork down after the cue ball strikes another is worth 10 points. Knocking the cork down before the cue ball has hit another costs 11 points. To win, a player's score plus the value of his private ball must equal GAME TOTAL (either 63 or 126) exactly; the game is lost if the total is exceeded. There are complex rules dealing with respotting the cork after it has been knocked down. 1986 Rhys 95.

count

1. (Bill.) A CAROM. 1866 NYT (May 26) 5:2. "The ball traveled around the table to complete the count." A successful shot, primarily in carom games. 1967 Polsky 81. To make a successful shot, to score. 1850 Phelan 29. In Pin Pool, knocking over the PIN. 1881 MB 23. 2. The current score, as in, "What's the count?" 1941 Hoppe 74. 3. The number of points scored for a particular shot; in Pocket Billiards, one point; in Snooker and English Billiards, the count varies depending on the nature of the shot. 1861 *Leslie's* (Sep 26) 318:3, 1976 WSD 90, 1980 Balukas 194.

counter

1. A device for keeping the score of a billiard game. Also, one of the beads strung on a wire known as the SCORE STRING and used as a MARKER for keeping score. 1850 Phelan 19, 1857 Phelan 34. 2. The desk at a BILLIARD ROOM at which players obtain balls and chalk and pay for TABLE TIME, staffed by the COUNTER MAN. 3. A PILL marked with the number of a ball for use in PILL POOL games. 4. (obs.) = REVERSE ENGLISH, OPPOSING SIDE. 1866 Crawley 83, 1868 *London Soc.* (Apr) 375. So called because the spin makes the ball run "counter" to its natural direction. See also CHECK SIDE, HOLD-UP, WRONG-WAY ENGLISH.

counter man

An employee of a BILLIARD ROOM who supervises activity and is responsible for clocking TABLE TIME and collecting money. Also HOUSE MAN. In Britain, a TAKER.

counting string

A WIRE or STRING mounted above the table and fitted with sliding markers for keeping track of points scored by the players. 1970 Knuchell 237, 1977 Martin 208. A variety of COUNTER. Also known as a SCORE STRING.

countries, names of

The following billiard games incorporate names of countries: AMERICAN SNOOKER, CANADIAN SNOOKER, CHINESE POOL, DANISH BILLIARDS, DUTCH POOL, ENGLISH BILLIARDS, FRENCH CAROMS (see also FRENCH BILLIARDS and succeeding entries), GERMAN PYRAMID GAME, INDIAN POOL, IRISH POOL, ITALIAN POOL, MEXICAN ROTATION, RUSSIAN POOL, SCOTCH POOL, SPANISH GAME. Cf. STATES, NAMES OF.

coup

1. A French term meaning "stroke" or "shot." 2. (Bill., obs.) A stroke in which the cue ball runs into a pocket, or goes off the table, without touching either of the other balls. 1770 OED, 1836 Tillotson 2, 1866 Crawley 17. The penalty in English Billiards was a forfeiture of three points. The term is used in the expression, RUN A COUP, meaning to cause or make a coup. 1896 Broadfoot 105, 1897 Payne 90.

coup fouetté

(pr. coo fwet-TAY) A French term meaning "whip shot," used to refer to a FORCE FOLLOW in ARTISTIC BILLIARDS. For these shots, the cue ball is placed at a distance no greater than five millimeters from the FIRST OBJECT BALL. It is easy to foul by making a PUSH SHOT

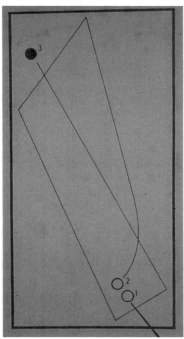

coup fouetté

from this distance, and the REFEREE is obliged to rule first on the validity of the HIT before determining whether the carom was completed successfully. A push is avoided by allowing the cue stick to glance away from the ball before it can strike the second object ball.

coup sec

(pr. coo SEHK) A stroke executed without a FOLLOW-THROUGH, used to avoid a PUSH when the cue ball lies very close to the object ball. 1891 Garnier 73, 1913 Daly 28. The term is French, meaning "sharp stroke," often mistranslated as "dry stroke," which is meaningless. See also NIP.

court-plaster

The material of which the SPOTS on the cloth formerly were made. 1896 Broadfoot 83, 1913 Stoddard 9. Court-plaster is a piece of silk coated with isinglass used as a skin patch and so called because it was worn by ladies at court. An important property of a spot is that it be thin enough not to interfere with the motion of the balls. Physical spots are no longer permitted in international play because of the possibility of such interference, so pencil marks are now used instead.

cover

1. (Bill.) Situation in which all three balls lie in a straight line, with one of the object balls between the cue ball and the other object ball. An undesirable result in STRAIGHT-RAIL or BALKLINE since a DIRECT CAROM is not possible, which increases the difficulty of the shot. Also called a "covering" (1924a Newman 248), LINE-UP or TIE-UP. 1896 Broadfoot 105, 1908 Mannock II 17, 1915 Reece & Clifford 180, 1935 Smith 39. 2. To affix a billiard cloth to the BED of the table or to the rails. "You need to have the table covered." 3. = TABLE COVER. A protective material that is spread over the BED of the table to prevent dust from collecting on the playing surface. 1911 Roberts 2. Dust on the table will otherwise accumulate on the balls and cause unwanted and unpredictable THROW and ROLL. 4. (pocket games) To obstruct. "If each pool ball is covered by a pyramid ball, the player is said to be snookered." 1889 Drayson 111. A pocket is "covered" if it is blocked by a ball. 1981 Quinn. A SPOT is covered if it is OCCUPIED. 1861 *Leslie's* (May 11) 411:3. *See illustration on next page.*

Cowboy Pocket Billiards, Cowboy Pool

(game) A hybrid of English Billiards and Pocket Billiards, played to 101 points with four balls: a cue ball and the one-, three- and five-balls. The one is placed on the HEAD SPOT, the three on the FOOT SPOT, and the five on

cover

the CENTER SPOT. Pocketing a ball scores its numerical value; a carom on two balls is worth one point, a carom on three balls two. Hence the maximum possible score on any stroke is 11, made by caroming on all three balls and sinking all of them. For a scratch or foul, the striker loses all points scored during his run, not just those made on the foul stroke. The player may score his first 90 points in any manner, points 91–100 by caroms only, and must score the last point by scratching off the one-ball into a CALLED pocket (a LOSING HAZARD). 1908

Cowboy Pocket Billiards

HRB 105, 1916 RGRG 65, 1977 OR 72. In one variation, the player must scratch off the one-, three-, and five-balls in succession to win. 1913 Stoddard 154.

Cowboy appears to have originated around 1900, but is derived from THIRTY-EIGHT, which was introduced as a diversion in 1885. The first printed rules appeared in 1908, about the same time as the Eight-Ball rules. 1913 Stoddard describes a version that is played to 103 points. A minor Cowboy tournament was held in 1914. Where its name came from is still a mystery. Cf. BULL DOG GAME, FORTY-FIVE, SCRATCH POOL, THIRTY-EIGHT, THIRTY-ONE POOL.

cradle cannon

(Eng. Bill.) = ANCHOR CANNON. A NURSERY CANNON in which two object balls are JAMMED at the MOUTH of a pocket, which permits repetitive scoring. 1912 Levi 582, 1924 Ogden 269, 1974 Lindrum 17. The stroke was introduced by Walter Lovejoy on January 18, 1907. 1931 Burwat (Jan). Differs from the JAM in that the balls are not touching one another and the cue ball is not passed *across* both balls. 1908 Mannock II 424. But see JAM CANNON for a different view. In 1907, Tom Reece made an unfinished BREAK of 499,135 at the anchor cannon, which is unofficial because press and public were not present throughout. This accomplishment required a full month, and its aftermath was the outlawing of the stroke by the BILLIARDS ASSOCIATION. W. Cook holds the official record of 42,746, made in 1907. Such long breaks were possible because the balls settled

62

in hollows in the cloth from which they could be dislodged only by deliberate action.

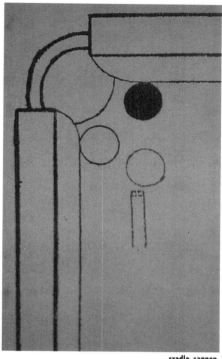

cradle cannon

cramp

1. (obs.) A HANDICAP, as in CRAMP GAME, one in which the player giving the handicap is thereby "cramped." 1839 Kentfield 36. 2. (obs.) A CUE CLAMP, as in "cue cramp." 1886 Kentfield 92.

cramp game

(obs.) = A game with a HANDICAP, in which one player is thus "cramped" by being restricted or disadvantaged in some way. 1839 Kentfield 36, 1850c White & Bohn 35, 1856 Crawley 19. Any game described in this book as a cramp game is likely to be obsolete.

cramp stroke

1. (obs.) A shot in which the BUTT of the cue must be elevated because of a cramped position, as when the cue ball is FROZEN to a cushion. Called a "cramped stroke" in 1896 Broadfoot 188. 2. (obs.) = A FANCY SHOT, a MASSÉ. 1856 Crawley 88. A TOUR DE CUE, violent SCREW, PUNCH, or very strong side stroke. 1866 Crawley 117.

crash

(Brit.) To hit the balls very hard.

crawl

= DRAG. 1954 Davis 88.

crawl stroke

(Snooker) Shot in which the cue ball is rolled up behind a nominated FREE BALL to leave the opponent snookered. A ROLL-UP. This maneuver was deemed unfair because the opponent is made to pay twice for one infraction: He gives a free ball and then also finds himself snookered. It was made illegal by a rule change in 1934. 1985 Everton 47.

Crazy Eight

(game) EIGHT-BALL with relaxed rules, such as allowing the eight-ball to be used in making COMBINATIONS.

Crazy Pool

(game) A variation on ROTATION in which a player who misses a shot forfeits the value of the ball aimed at. 1946 *Atlantic Monthly* (Aug) 134.

Cribbage, Cribbage Pocket Billiards, Cribbage Pool

(game) A single-rack pocket billiard game that incorporates some ideas from the card game of Cribbage. For this purpose, a "cribbage" is a pair of balls whose numerical total is 15. The break is an OPEN BREAK. The object is to score five cribbages (out of a possible eight), each being made in two consecutive shots (or on the same shot). The 15-ball may be pocketed only when no two-ball cribbages remain and it alone counts as a cribbage. 1946 OR 58, 1973 Mizerak 63, 1982 OR 87. This game may sound contrived, but it presents interesting positional challenges and is excellent as a practice exercise. Also known as FIFTEEN POINTS or PAIR POOL. See also COMPANION BALL, ON A CRIBBAGE, SUCCESSIVE FOULS.

In racking, the 15-ball must be placed in the center of the third row. No two of the three corner balls may total 15, which gives $14 \times 12 \times 10 \times 2 \times 11! = 134,120,448,000$ different racking arrangements.

cripple

A ball that is resting near a pocket opening; hence, an easy shot. 1964 Crane & Sullivan 89, 1977 Martin 208. Also called a CHERRY, DUCK, HANGER, MINNIE, PUPPY, SET-UP, or SITTER.

crisp

A table is "crisp" if it exhibits no LONG ROLL. See also SHORT TABLE.

croak

(Canad., sl.) To MISCUE. 1988 NBN (Nov) 8.

cross

(obs.) A BANK SHOT or DOUBLET in which a ball is made to cross the table in the short direction. 1850 Phelan 21,

1881 MB 23. The term survives in some of the compounds below.

cross-corner

(Pocket Bill.) A type of BANK SHOT in which the object ball travels across the table (that is, in the short direction) into a corner pocket. Also, a CALL in those pocket billiard games requiring the pocket to be NOMINATED, meaning that the object ball will first contact a LONG RAIL opposite the striker and then enter a corner pocket on the side of the table at which the striker is standing. 1989 Koehler 252. Cf. CROSS-SIDE.

cross cue tournament

(Bill., obs.) Carom tournament in which the incoming player has choice of cue ball on the first shot of each inning. Said to have been originated by C. C. Peterson in his hall in St. Louis. 1928 Brunswick. Cf. CHOICE OF CUE BALL, OPTIONAL CUE BALL.

cross cues

To oppose one another in a billiard game. 1878 NYT (Jul 27) 2:4. "Garnier and Daly will cross cues tonight." Crossed cue sticks were often used as a logo to symbolize billiards.

cross double

1. (usually Snooker) A BANK SHOT, or DOUBLE, in which the object ball "crosses" the table in the short direction to enter a pocket. 1976 Reardon 122. Used particularly when the target is a MIDDLE POCKET. 1975a Lowe 93. 2. (Brit. games) A bank shot in which the cue ball "crosses over" the face of the object ball before the object ball moves off toward the intended pocket. 1986 Davis 67. A CUTBACK DOUBLE.

cross loser

(Eng. Bill.) A LOSING HAZARD made by sending the cue ball across the table after it contacts a cushion. 1957 Holt 20. Cf. LONG LOSER.

cross rest

(Brit. games) A REST whose HEAD is in the shape of an "X," or cross. *See illustration in next column.*

cross-side

(Pocket Bill.) Player's or referee's CALL designating a particular type of BANK SHOT in which the object ball crosses the table in the short direction to enter a SIDE POCKET. 1989 Koehler 252. The instruction "cross it into the side pocket" occurs at 1850 Phelan 78. Cf. CROSS-CORNER.

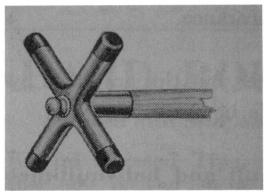

cross rest

cross-table shot

(Three-Cushions) A shot accomplished by driving the cue ball across the table (*i.e.*, between the long rails) twice in an attempt to score. 1910 NYT (Oct 21) 7:3, 1958 OR, 1992 OR 7. Called an "accordion" by the French, referring to the shape of the path taken by the cue ball during the shot. 1983 Malsert 128. In British parlance, a DOUBLE CROSS CANNON.

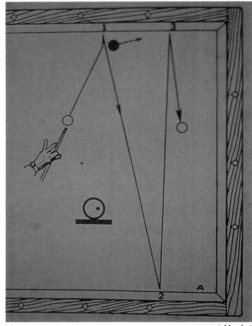

cross-table shot

crossover player

A player who is adept at more than one distinct style of billiard game, particularly both pocket and carom versions. 1990 BD (Jun) 52. There have been only five crossover champions, that is, players who won national or world championships at both pocket and carom games. They are:

AMERICAN CROSSOVER CHAMPIONS	
PLAYER	CHAMPIONSHIPS WON
Joseph Dion	Straight-Rail, Fifteen-Ball Pool (1878)
Thomas Hueston	Continuous Pool (1905, 1906–1909), Three-Cushions (1908, 1910)
Alfredo De Oro	Fifteen-Ball Pool (1887, 1888), Continuous Pool (1889–93, 1896, 1899–1900, 1904–05, 1908, 1910–11), 14.1 Continuous (1912, 1913), Three-Cushions (1908–11, 1913–19)
John Horgan	Continuous Pool (1906), Three-Cushions (1911–12)
Johnny Layton	14.1 Continuous (1916), Three-Cushions (1921–23, 1928, 1930, 1934)

Many players have excelled at both pocket and three-cushion billiards. Ralph Greenleaf, Irving Crane, Andrew Ponzi, Joe Procita and Willie Mosconi qualified as competitors in the World Three-Cushion Tournament. Greenleaf tied for third in 1942 behind Willie Hoppe and Welker Cochran; Mosconi was fourth in 1947.

crossover shot

(Snooker) A SAFETY PLAY consisting of sending a CO-LOUR twice across the table diagonally to land at the center of the TOP RAIL while the cue ball travels DOWN the table into BAULK. 1973 Spencer 94. The result is that the opponent has a long shot to make and the BALL ON cannot readily be pocketed. *See illustration in next column.*

crotch

1. (Bill.) The CORNER of a CAROM TABLE. 1866 NYT (May 26) 5:2, 1881 MB 25. Specifically, a triangular area defined by points lying along the cushions and 4½ inches from each corner. The number of caroms that can be made while both object balls lie in the marked area is restricted, usually to three. 1916 RGRG 13, 1976 WSD 102, 1992 OR 7. See, generally, BALK SPACE, INTERDICTED AREA, JAW SHOT, RESTRICTED SPACE.

Two object balls that both lie in the same crotch are said to be "crotched." 1866 NYT (May 26) 5:2, 1869 Roberts 27.

The crotch was introduced in 1862 but no line defining it appeared on the table. The crotch was first drawn with

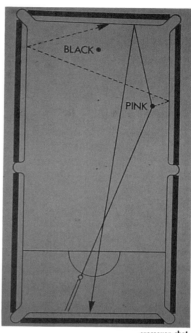
crossover shot

chalk on the table in a match in Montreal between Joseph Dion and M. Foster on January 28, 1869. These were the first lines actually drawn with chalk on a billiard table. 1941 NBJ (May/Jun). The crotch was introduced because players had mastered the art of assembling the balls in the corner for prodigious runs. "Carme got all the balls together in a corner of the table, and was proceeding to count indefinitely." 1866 NYT (May 26) 5:2. In 1870, the practice of "crotching" was barred permanently, but actual lines were rarely drawn, and sometimes the crotch was taken to be a square rather than a triangle. In his first public appearance in the United States, Maurice Vignaux won a Three-Ball tournament in New York in November 1874 in which a 5½-inch triangular crotch was drawn with chalk, three shots permitted. See CROTCH LINE. 2. The opening of a pocket, more frequently called the JAW. 1891 MB.

crotch line

(Bill.) A line defining the CROTCH, usually (when drawn) running diagonally between a SIDE RAIL and an adjacent END RAIL to create a triangular area on a CAROM TABLE within which consecutive caroms are restricted in Straight-Rail. 1958 OR. Under present rules, it is 4½ inches from the corner.

crow

(obs.) = FLUKE or SCRATCH. Said to derive from the expression, "the man who shot at the pigeon but killed the crow," thus connoting a lucky and unintended result. 1885c Cook 9. Also GARBAGE SHOT or SLOP SHOT.

crown

1. The rounded portion of the cue TIP that contacts the ball. 1965 Fats 77, 1974 ITP 77. See TIP for an explanatory diagram. 2. The shape formed by the PRONGS at the BUTT of a cue stick, which resembles a crown. 1977 Martin 208, 1983 NBN (Mar) 18. 3. The figurative mantle of a CHAMPIONSHIP, said to be "held" by the winner. "She won the last three games to take the crown." Sometimes "title crown." 4. The convex shape of a table RAIL, which may be bowed slighty upward. Such a rail is also said to be "crowned." 1993 PBM (Jan) 56.

crush

(Nine-Ball, colloq.) The BREAK SHOT, so called because of the tendency of players to use as much force as possible on this shot. See also ORANGE CRUSH.

crutch

(colloq.) = MECHANICAL BRIDGE. 1978 Byrne 13, 1992 OR 7. One of a number of terms for the bridge implying (incorrectly) that the user is somehow handicapped or lame if he uses it. Also LADIES' AID, OLD MAN'S AID, SISSY STICK.

cue

1. = CUE STICK, the instrument used to propel billiard balls. 1749 OED. The word "cue" is derived from the French *queue*, meaning "tail" and referring to the end, or shaft handle, of the MACE. When the ball lay near a cushion, the player would frequently turn his mace around and strike the ball with the thin handle. This usage ultimately led to the development of the cue stick itself. 1974 Hendricks, 1979 Grissim 35. 2. The CUE BALL, one of the balls used in Billiards. The ball the player is striking with his cue stick. 1924 Aiken 31. 3. To stroke, or prepare to stroke, a ball.

cue bag

A protective container for a cue stick; a CUE CASE. 1928 Brunswick.

cue ball

The ball a player strikes with his cue stick. 1807 White 12, 1941 Hoppe 74. Generally, the ball that may legally be used to set other balls in motion. It was once called the "active ball." 1806 Phil 11. Another obsolete synonym is "stroke ball." Cf. OBJECT BALL, OBJECT WHITE. The cue ball is usually white. In games requiring multiple cue balls, such as carom billiards, the balls are either colored differently or distinguished by the presence of small markings, particularly DOTS. See also SPOT WHITE, WHITE. In less refined speech, the cue ball is sometimes the ALBINO, the ROCK, or WHITEY.

In general, cue balls are made to be more durable than object balls. The cue ball on a COIN-OPERATED TABLE is slightly larger and heavier than the object balls.

cue-ball number

(Three-Cushions) A concept used in applying the DIAMOND SYSTEM. The location at which the player's cue ball is lying is assigned a number, based on the diamonds, that depends on its position and the direction in which it is to be struck. Subtracting the number of the target diamond on the first cushion from the cue ball number gives the number of the diamond that the cue ball will contact on the third cushion.

Cue Ball Pool

(game, obs.) A SINGLE-RACK pocket billiard game in which the cue ball is pocketed by caroming it off an object ball. The object ball is then removed from the table and the striker plays again from the STRING. His score is the sum of the numbers on the object balls so removed. 1913 Burrowes 17. The British equivalent is the LOSING GAME OF PYRAMID. Cf. BACKWARDS POOL, BILLIARD POOL, CAROM POOL, CHINESE POOL, CONTRA POOL, INDIAN POOL, IRISH POOL, KISS POOL, LOOP, REVERSE BILLIARDS.

cue-ball spot

(Bill.) Either of the two SPOTS located 6 inches to the right and left of the HEAD SPOT on the HEAD STRING. For the OPENING BREAK, the player's cue ball must lie on the head string somewhere between the cue-ball spots.

cue band

A wrapper that can be fitted onto the BUTT of a cue stick to identify the owner. 1935 Brunswick.

cue-butt

(Eng. Bill., obs.) = QUARTER-BUTT. A stick that is larger in diameter than the cue, about five feet long, and leathered at the bottom. 1873 Bennett 27. Used for striking the ball so as not to impart ENGLISH. See BUTT for the origin and demise of this function.

cue cabinet

An item of furniture with drawers for storing CUE STICKS horizontally. 1908 Brunswick 122.

cue case

A protective container to hold a cue stick, usually for traveling. Also known as a CUE BAG.

cue chalk

CHALK used on the tip of a cue. Cf. HAND CHALK.

cue clamp

Apparatus used during the process of tipping a cue stick to hold the TIP on the shaft until any necessary cement hardens. 1863 Phelan & Berger 92, 1876 Collender 22. A tremendous amount of ingenuity has been applied to the development of these devices. The difficulty in producing an effective clamp is that it must grasp the end of the cue tightly but without gouging or marring the soft wood of the shaft. In obsolete usage, a CRAMP. Modern fast-setting adhesives make the use of a clamp unnecessary.

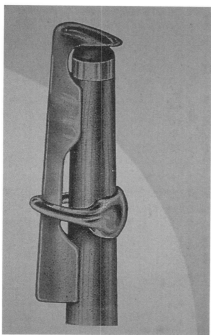

cue clamp

cue cutter

Device for removing the CUE TIP and glue from the SHAFT of the cue stick and for shaping the TENON. 1863 Phelan & Berger 105, 1876 Collender 20. This implement is useful in removing a worn or damaged tip without harming the FERRULE.

cue drawer

Part of a CUE CABINET. A drawer with recesses installed to hold butts and shafts of cue sticks.

cue extension

= EXTENSION. 1988 Morrison & Smith 4.

cue joint

The JOINT of a sectional cue stick. In a two-piece cue, the place at which the SHAFT is screwed into the BUTT. 1908 Brunswick 51.

cue leather

A CUE TIP made of leather. 1863 Phelan & Berger 105, 1881 MB 33, 1893 HRB 18. Captain Mingaud is credited with being the first to apply leather to the tip of a cue, supposedly a piece cut from an old bridle. This occurred sometime during the period 1807–1818. Self-adhesive cue leathers were developed in the mid-nineteenth century.

cue man

An employee of a billiard room whose function is to care for the HOUSE CUES and cues belonging to customers. He keeps the tips shaped and replaces them when necessary.

cue point

A fitting, often of IVORY, attached to the shaft of the cue stick and on which the TIP is fastened. The FERRULE. 1897 Brunswick 27, 1908 Brunswick 52. See also POINT.

cue rack

An apparatus for storing cue sticks vertically, usually mounted on a wall. Vertical storage prevents warping of the cue SHAFT from uneven pressure. 1908 Brunswick 120. Wall-mounted racks for holding maces were used in the early 1700s. Circular cue racks, in which cues are stored in a conical arrangement, were known by 1830.

67

cue rack (circular)

cue rest

= MECHANICAL BRIDGE. 1983 Rule Book 250. See also REST.

Cue Roque, Cue-Roquet

(game, obs.) A billiard game played on a table with 22 small brass posts as obstacles and four balls (white, red, yellow and blue). The game exhibited some of the features of croquet (hence its name) in that the posts acted as wickets. 1915 Brunswick. The term "roquet" as used in croquet refers to a contact between the player's ball and another ball.

using the thin shaft of the MACE to strike at balls lying near the cushion. It evolved as a separate instrument during the period 1680–1780. In 1775 Annals 93 it is described as a "thick stick, diminishing gradually to a point of about half an inch diameter. It is the only instrument in vogue abroad, and is played with amazing address by the Italians, and some of the Dutch." The tip was unknown in the eighteenth century and, for this reason, only good players were allowed to use the cue out of fear that lesser players would tear the cloth. 1869 Roberts 21. See also JEFFERY.

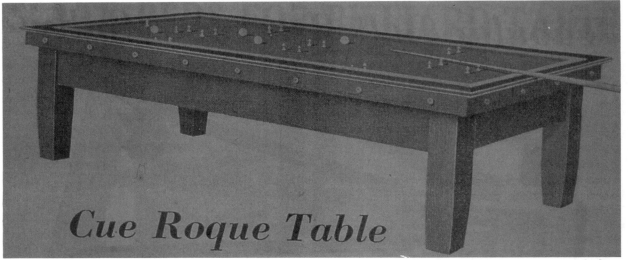

Cue Roque Table

Cue Roque

cue sports

The internationally accepted and politically correct designation for all games played with cue sticks on billiard tables, particularly POCKET BILLIARDS, CAROM BILLIARDS, CASIN, AND SNOOKER.

cue stick

A tapered instrument for stroking the CUE BALL, usually made of wood and approximately 57 inches long. Also known as a BILLIARD STICK, A STICK, or just a CUE. Colloquially, is it sometimes referred to as one's TOOL, WAND, or WEAPON. See diagram and also entries for individual parts: AFTERWRAP, BALANCE, BALANCE POINT, BUMPER, BUTT, BUTT CAP, BUTT PLATE, COLLAR, CROWN, CUE BAND, DRESS, EXTENSION, FERRULE, FORE-WRAP, FRONT, HANDLE, HUSTLER, INLAY, JOINT, JOINT CAP, MERRY WIDOW, ONE-PIECE CUE, POINT, PRONG, RING, SCREW-ON TIP, SHAFT, SPLICE, SPLICED CUE, TAPER, TENON, TIP, UNDERWRAP, VENEER, WEIGHT, WINDOW, WRAP. The definitions of many of these terms are based on the writings of Ray Schuler, a Chicago cuemaker whose articles appeared in the *National Billiard News*.

The cue stick developed from the common habit of

The JOINTED CUE or TWO-PIECE CUE appeared in 1829 and became popular in the late nineteenth century for convenience in carrying and storage. Since then, cues of up to five pieces have been made. The practice of loading a cue with lead to alter its weight is traced by Mitchell to 1833. It is common in Europe to alter a cue's weight by inserting a ring-shaped weight over the tip and sliding it down toward the butt. Herman Rambow, a member of the BCA Hall of Fame, is credited with several advances in cue construction. He was granted a patent in 1925 for a cue whose weight could be altered without shifting the BALANCE POINT.

Cue sticks have been made of a wide variety of woods, including ash, maple and ramin, and of other materials such as aluminum and graphite. Butts are often of walnut, ebony, or rosewood. An immense amount of creativity goes into decorating cues with complex inlays of wood, ivory or mother-of-pearl. There is no necessary relationship between the degree of ORNAMENTATION of a cue and its playing quality. 1867 Dufton 18 cautioned players that "Ornamental inlaid cues are generally not so well balanced, and are seldom used by good players."

The butt of a cue is often spliced because it is not

desirable to make a cue out of a single type of wood. A cue made entirely of maple (a good shaft material) would be too light; one made entirely of rosewood or ebony would be too heavy. The splice is made by fitting together two positions composed of long, thin triangles known as POINTS or PRONGS. These provide additional strength by increasing the surface area to which glue may be applied when joining the pieces. See also BLANK.

There is much lore associated with cue manufacture; sticks from certain makers such as Herman Rambow and George Balabushka are of legendary quality and price. See AMERICAN CUEMAKERS ASSOCIATION. The debate still rages over whether a cue with a flexible or a stiff shaft is preferable, whether the construction of the joint matters (*i.e.*, wood-to-wood, wood-to-metal, metal-to-metal), whether or not the prongs at the butt play a role in shock absorption, and so forth. The question in general is how different physical properties of a cue affect its playing qualities. See BALANCE, DEFLECTION, SPINE, SQUIRT, STIFFNESS.

A stick that is available in a public room is known as a HOUSE CUE. One that is made to order for a player is a CUSTOM CUE.

Unscrewing the joint of one's cue during a match is treated as a gesture of CONCESSION.

The common practice of rolling a cue on the table to determine whether it is straight is misleading; a visual inspection should be performed instead by sighting down the cue and rotating it slowly.

The lengths of American cues average 57 inches but may fall in the range of 48 to 60 inches. The 57-inch length has been a de facto standard for over a century, even in Britain. 1867 Dufton 18. There are no length limitations. In British games, there is no upper limit on length but it is a foul to strike with a cue shorter than 910 millimeters (about 3 feet). 1987 BSCC S8. The reason for this is that a player named Alec Brown once produced a "fountain pen cue" just a few inches long in a Snooker competition before World War II. The cue was useful in shooting over a cluster of balls that would have been impossible with an ordinary REST. The instrument was banned by the referee and the rules were changed shortly thereafter to prevent its reappearance. 1974 Lindrum 125, 1983 Davis 109. A cue was formerly known in Britain as a SHOOTER-STICK. For differences in

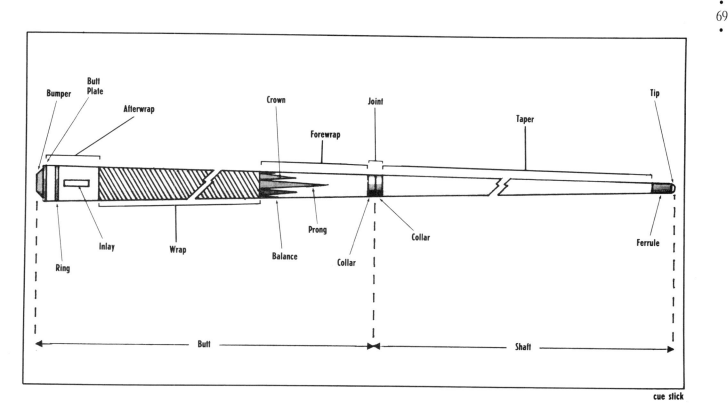

cue sticks intended for different games, see BILLIARD CUE, POOL CUE, SNOOKER CUE.

American billiard cues generally weigh between 15 and 22 ounces; Snooker cues usually fall in the 12- to 18-ounce range. No rules specify allowable weights. By 1833, weighted cues were being sold by Thurston's. 1850 Phelan 19 recommends that a player's cue should weigh 2½ times as much as the ball being struck. The diameter of the cue tip is also not specified in the rules, but is normally between 11 and 15 millimeters.

It is not unusual to find a cue that is more expensive than the table on which it is being used. Custom cues now begin at around $500; collectors have forced the price of cues made by the finest cuemakers to over $3000. A surprising number of cues sell for just under $10,000 in the United States, and there are stories of cues with jewels and precious metals that have sold in the Orient for five times that amount. There is always interest in cues made by such famed craftsmen as Rambow, BALABUSHKA, Martin, and SZAMBOTI. These instruments are felt to have properties that are not readily duplicated.

Special cues have been made for a variety of purposes. A cue was designed whose tip was propelled by compressed air and could thus strike a ball without being moved. 1925 BM (May) 18. A cue with a square cross-section has been fashioned for shooting from the rail. Special heavy cues are used for BREAKING (see BREAK CUE), and light cues are produced for making JUMP SHOTS (see JUMP CUE) and for use in ARTISTIC BILLIARDS. Short, thick, heavy cues are used for MASSÉ shots. A cue for normal stroking is known as a RUN STICK. See also TELESCOPING CUE.

It is, of course, possible to propel the ball with instruments other than the cue stick and even with parts of the body. Although these alternatives fall outside the rules, see FINGER BILLIARDS, FOOT BILLIARDS, MOUTH BILLIARDS, NOSE and UMBRELLA. The use of a walking-stick as a cue is mentioned in 1807 White 156.

cue straightener
A brake used to bend the SHAFT of a cue stick until it regains a straight shape.

cue tip
The material covering the end of the SHAFT of a cue stick, used to make contact with the ball. See TIP.

cue trimmer
Device for shaping CUE TIPS. 1876 Collender 21. It may consist simply of a piece of sandpaper carried in a holder or may resemble a miniature lathe that attaches to the shaft of the cue.

cue up
To prepare to play or to place a ball in a position for a SHOT. To STROKE.

cue wafer
An adhesive disk for fastening a CUE TIP to the SHAFT. 1863 Phelan & Berger 105, 1876 Collender 22. A perennial problem in affixing tips to cue sticks, reduced through the use of wafers, was the even application of glue.

cue wax
Adhesive for attaching a CUE TIP to the SHAFT of the cue, used before cements were generally available. 1863 Phelan & Berger 105, 1891 MB 26, 1893 HRB 18.

cueist
One who wields a cue stick. A BILLIARD PLAYER. 1870 OED. Also BILLIARDIST, CUEMAN.

cueman
1. A billiard player, a CUEIST. 2. = CUE MAN, an attendant in a BILLIARD ROOM who is responsible for caring for the cue sticks, sanding, filing, and retipping them when necessary.

cup
1. (Bumper Pool) A POCKET. 1992 OR 72. 2. A pocket on a BAGATELLE table, BUMPER POOL table or the PARISIAN POOL BOARD. The cup is often just a circular depression in the table with no hole through which a ball may drop. In some games, the cups are numbered and a player holing a ball receives a number of points equal to the numerical value of the target cup.

curfew
1. The time at which a billiard room is compelled to close under law, or after which minors may no longer be present. Although a number of cities permit 24-hour operation, closing times vary from 1:00 a.m (Chicago) to 5:00 a.m. (Atlantic City). 2. An hour at which play must cease in a competition, usually imposed by local ordinance or as a condition of the promoter's license. Curfews have occasionally caused serious disruption in championship events. When Edward Ralph won the first national Straight Pool crown in April 1912, he was immediately challenged for the title by Alfredo De Oro, the third-place finisher. A 600-point match over three nights was set to begin on May 29 in Trenton, New Jersey, near Ralph's hometown of Hightstown. The third BLOCK was in progress on Saturday night with Ralph ahead 587 to 583 and still at the table when the

clock struck midnight. Because of the city's Sunday blue laws, the game had to be terminated and the match was cancelled. A REPLAY was held in the same hall two weeks later with De Oro the victor, 600 to 408. 1912 MB 374. Despite many attempts over the next decade, Ralph never again won the title.

curve shot

A shot in which the path of the cue ball is made to curve slightly by elevating the BUTT of the cue and applying ENGLISH, usually to avoid an intervening ball. 1989 Koehler 253. A partial MASSÉ. In British usage, a SWERVE.

cushion

1. The border surrounding the playing surface of a billiard table, from which the balls rebound. 1674 Cotton, 1807 White 3. Also BAND, BANK, BUMPER or GUM. Popularly, but erroneously, known as a RAIL. (The rail is made of wood and is the top boundary of the table, to which the cushions are attached.) For cushion parts, see FACE, NOSE.

The technology of cushions has always played an important role in the quality of billiard play. The earliest tables had flat wooden boundaries called "banks," because of their resemblance to river banks. Later, they were lined with leather. By the time of Cotton in 1674, the walls were covered with cloth and were "swel'd or stuft with fine flox or cotton." Hair and LIST were also tried. The introduction of India RUBBER in 1835 was revolutionary, because the rebound could be made uniform all around the table. The subsequent discovery of vulcanization by Goodyear in 1839 made rubber cushions durable and reliable ones were available during the 1840s.

Abraham Bassford patented an air-pump cushion, which consisted of a rubber tube that had to be blown up

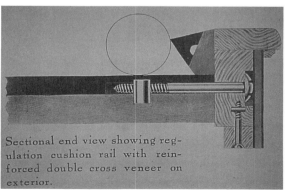

Sectional end view showing regulation cushion rail with reinforced double cross veneer on exterior.

cushion

every day with a pump. The "combination cushion" of rubber, leather, and cork, first manufactured by Phelan in 1855, was used in the famous Phelan-Seereiter match of 1859. 1892 HRB 20. A great deal of ingenuity was devoted to methods of attaching the rubber firmly to the rail, until a suitable glue was found.

Experimentation with cushions continues to this day. Cushions faced with steel, canvas, and whalebone have been tried. For more on the composition of cushions, see 1869 Kavanagh 62, 1981c Clare 9.

To obtain a clean rebound of the ball from the cushion, without causing the ball to jump, the NOSE of the cushion should strike the ball at its CENTER OF PERCUSSION, which is at a point ⅖ of a ball radius above the center. UMB standards require the height of the cushions for carom games to be between 36 and 37 millimeters. Since carom balls and pocket balls are of different sizes, it is not possible to play both games properly on the same table (even with CAROM PLUGS) unless the cushions are changed. Tables with interchangeable rails have been made that solve this problem.

The physics of cushions is important but imperfectly understood. When a ball strikes a cushion, two principal phenomena operate. First, the cushion is deformed by the impact, causing the ball to remain in contact with it for some time, depending on the resilience of the cushion. This contact time also depends on the speed at which the ball is traveling. Simultaneously, friction operates between the ball and the cloth covering of the cushion. It is thus possible for a ball shot obliquely into a cushion without English to acquire English by virtue of the contact.

The width of a regulation cushion is two inches. 1975a Lowe 13.

2. To place or leave a ball close to, or resting against, the cushion.

3. (U.S., colloq.) To make the ball hit the cushion before making a carom or after contact with one of the balls. "He cushioned it."

cushion cannon

(Eng. Bill.) A CANNON in which the cue ball contacts a cushion before its first contact with the SECOND OBJECT BALL. 1866 Crawley 90. A CUSHION CAROM or INDIRECT CANNON.

cushion carom

A CAROM in which the cue ball strikes at least one cushion before completing the COUNT. A CUSHION CANNON or INDIRECT CANNON. 1872 NYT (Sep 4) 5:5, 1881 MB 23, 1893 HRB 57.

71

Cushion Caroms

(game) A billiard game in which each COUNT must be effected by means of a CUSHION CAROM, *i.e.*, the cue ball must contact at least one cushion before hitting the second object ball for the first time. 1879 NYT (May 19) 5:1, 1916 RGRG 19, 1941 Hoppe 74, 1992 OR 107. A miss of both balls results in a deduction of one point. DOUBT as to whether a cushion has been contacted is resolved against the striker. 1916 RGRG 19. Sometimes erroneously referred to as "One-Cushion" (although it is known this way in various foreign languages: *una banda* (Spanish) or *einband* (German)).

The original version of Cushion Caroms was called the INDIRECT GAME and was played in the 1820s. 1888 NYT (Oct 28) 20:1. A descendant of the DOUBLET GAME, it was revived later in the century as part of an effort to curb the monotonous effect of the RAIL NURSE in STRAIGHT-RAIL. At this it was only partially successful, since it gave rise instead to the RUB NURSE, a delicate position in which the cue ball is repeatedly banked into the rail to contact two balls lying nearby. In the first public exhibition of the game in Boston in October, 1867, Joseph Dion defeated John McDevitt. Jacob Schaefer Sr. won the first public MATCH, also in Boston. The first tournament was held in 1878 in St. Louis. The only world tournament ever held (New York, 1881) was won by J. Dion, who averaged 3.40 and had a high run of 45.

During the period 1883–1897, an unusual rule was in effect. A cushion carom was valid even if the cue ball hit the second object ball before contacting a cushion, provided that the cue ball later hit a cushion and then touched either object ball for a second time.

Frank Ives's tournament high run record of 85 survived for many decades. 1931 BM (Nov) 26. Charles C. Peterson made 104 in an EXHIBITION in 1915. The modern high run is 199 by Francis Connesson.

Willie Hoppe professed a fondness for Cushion Caroms as a practice game. He was also the last U.S. champion, reigning during the period 1933–1944. The only U.S. titleholders apart from Hoppe were J. Dion, William Sexton, Maurice Daly and George Slosson. The game is not played in the U.S. today but is part of international competition. See PENTATHLON.

cushion facing

A piece of rubber or leather that is used to cover the beveled edges at the ends of a CUSHION. 1991 Conway 25. PBTA specifications require the angle formed by the cushion facing to be 75 degrees, plus or minus one degree. The cushion facing angle should not be confused with the CUT ANGLE.

cushion-first

= RAIL-FIRST. See also BANK SHOT, BRICOLE, KICK SHOT.

Cushion Game

1. (game, obs.) CRAMP GAME of English Billiards in which the stronger player must make every score off a cushion in some fashion. 1909 BYB 87. Cf. CUSHION CAROMS, in which the underlying game is ordinary Carom Billiards. Contrast also the NON-CUSHION GAME, in which the player must *prevent* his cue ball from contacting any cushion. 2. (game, obs.) CRAMP GAME of English Billiards in which the STRIKER must play his ball from atop the RAIL at the BAULK end of the table. 1807 White 57. The disadvantage is estimated by 1850c White & Bohn to be 6 points in 16.

cushion-imparted side

(Brit.) Spin applied to a ball by virtue of a glancing contact with a cushion. 1912 Levi iii, 1913 Stoddard 77. In American usage, "cushion-induced English." 1989 Koehler 253.

cushion nose

= NOSE.

cushion pot

1. (Brit. games) A POT accomplished by hitting the ball RAIL-FIRST. 1920 Levi 246. 2. (Brit. games) A POT of a ball that is FROZEN to a cushion.

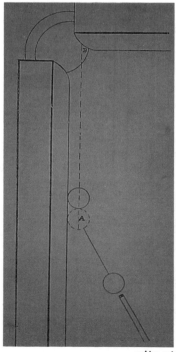

cushion pot

cushion profile

The cross-sectional shape of the cushion rubber, particularly of its NOSE.

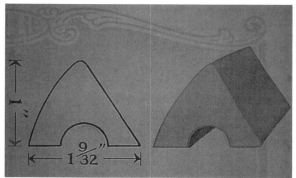

cushion profile

cushion rail

A RAIL to which a CUSHION is attached, as opposed to a SIDE RAIL, which hangs from the cushion rail and acts as an APRON. 1957 Holt 5.

cushion rest

A REST, or MECHANICAL BRIDGE, constructed so that it can be used to strike at a ball lying near a cushion. Part of the rest laps over the cushion for support. 1873 Bennett 28, 1897 Payne 33.

cushion side

(Brit.) Spin applied to the cue ball on the same side as the cushion lies in relation to the FIRST OBJECT BALL. If the cushion lies to the left side of the object ball, then cushion side is LEFT ENGLISH. 1889 Drayson 46.

cushion spot

A mark made on a RAIL to delineate the BAULK-LINE. 1873 Bennett 18. A DIAMOND, DOT, NAIL, RAIL MARKER, SIGHT, or SPOT. Normally, the word "spot" alone refers to a mark made on the CLOTH.

cushioned

(obs.) FROZEN to a cushion. Said either of a ball or a player whose ball is so placed. 1770 OED. "He's cushioned."

custom cue

A cue stick that is made to the customer's order, usually specifying WEIGHT, length, TIP diameter, TAPER, type of WRAP, and decoration. Cf. HOUSECUE.

cut

1. (pocket games) To cause an object ball to move off at an angle to the line of cue ball aim by hitting it off-center, particularly if the hit is THIN, *i.e.*, thinner than HALF-BALL. An ANGLE SHOT. 1807 White 31, 1874 NYT (Sep 23) 5:4. A CUT SHOT. Also used in the compounds OVERCUT and UNDERCUT. See also LINE OF CENTERS, THROW. 2. = FINE BALL. 1850 Phelan 21. A stroke in which the object ball is barely touched by the circumference of the cue ball. As a verb, to drive an object ball at a sharp angle by a very THIN hit. 1976 WSD 104, 1977 Fels 28, 1979 Grissim 250.

cut angle

The angle formed by adjacent sides of a pocket, around the point as a radius. PBTA specifications require a corner pocket cut angle of 140 degrees and a side pocket cut angle of 105 degrees, each to within a tolerance of one degree. See also CUSHION FACING.

cut pot

(Brit. games) A POT that is accomplished by a very THIN hit on the object ball. 1957 Holt 33.

cut shot

A shot involving a CUT. 1881 NYT (Jan 23) 27, 1989 Koehler 253, 1992 OR 8. An ANGLE SHOT. In Britain, an ANGLED POT.

Cut-Throat Pocket Billiards

(game) = ELIMINATION. 1974 OR 74, 1979 Sullivan 184. Also called SCREW YOUR BUDDY.

cutback double

(Snooker) A DOUBLE into a MIDDLE pocket made by CUTTING a ball sharply into the cushion nearly across from the pocket. 1973 Spencer 106. The cue ball lies closer to the CENTRE STRING than does the object ball, which therefore must be "cut back" toward the pocket. 1954 Davis 64, 1986 Davis 67. Also just BACK DOUBLE or CROSS DOUBLE. *See illustration on next page.*

D

(Brit. games) A semicircular area within the BAULK, from which the cue ball is put into play at the com-

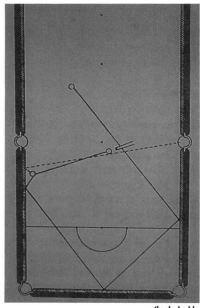

cutback double

mencement of the game or after a LOSING HAZARD, so called because of its shape. Also known as the BAULK CIRCLE, BAULK SEMICIRCLE, DEE, HALF-CIRCLE, SEMI-CIRCLE, STRIKING POINT or STRIKING RING. On a regulation SNOOKER TABLE, the radius of the D is 11½ inches. 1975a Lowe 13. It is 9⅜ inches on a 10-foot table. 1946 OR 78. The radius is 292 millimeters on a METRIC TABLE, or ⅙ the width of the playing surface. 1978 BSCC.

The D is illustrated in 1807 White, but is not named there, and no explanation of its origin has yet been given. This author can add little but to note a resemblance between the D and the shadow cast by the ARCH on early tables.

Danish Billiards

(game, obs.) A variation on PIN POOL that was popular in Hollywood during the 1930s. Five pins are placed as in Pin Pool. The cue ball may not touch any pins, which can be struck only by object balls and other pins. Each pin knocked down counts two points; the center pin alone scores five, and downing all pins in a single stroke scores 15 points. A carom is worth four. The penalty for a FOUL or SCRATCH is two. The game is played to 50 points. 1934 NBJ (Dec).

dark red

1. The name given to a CAROM billiard ball that is colored solid dark red. Also known as the DEEP RED. One of three balls used in carom games; one of four used in the FOUR-BALL GAME. Cf. LIGHT RED. 2. (pocket games) Color of the 7 and 15 balls. Cf. RED.

dark-red spot

= FOOT SPOT, where the DARK RED is spotted in the AMERICAN FOUR-BALL GAME. 1850 Phelan 47, 1864 AH 419. Also called the FOOT SPOT, PINK SPOT, PYRAMID SPOT, RED SPOT (Bill.), or WINNING SPOT.

day manager

A BILLIARD ROOM employee who oversees the day shift. Cf. NIGHT MANAGER.

daylight

(colloq.) Space or clearance enabling a ball to be hit or pocketed. 1990 White G-2. "There's enough daylight to sink it."

DBU

(org.) = DEUTSCHE BILLARD UNION.

dead

1. Said of a shot that is straight on and thus cannot be missed, especially a COMBINATION SHOT. 1807 White 87, 1894 NY Herald (Mar 25) 7:4, 1982 OR. A DUCK or SET-UP. 2. Not lively, as a "dead rail." 1893 HRB 27. A "dead draw" in Billiards is a DRAW SHOT in which the cue ball rolls slowly up to the SECOND OBJECT BALL. 1913 Daly 35. See DEAD BALL. 3. Said of a ball that is not IN PLAY or is inactive. 1807 White 28. A ball becomes dead when it LEAVES THE TABLE, is pocketed or has been interfered with. A KILLED BALL. 4. Said of a ball that has stopped rolling or is moving very slowly. 1807 White 23. 5. (Life Pool, obs.) A player is dead when he has lost all three LIVES and thus must STAR to continue play. 1850 Phelan 41, 1924 Smith 109. Also KILLED. 6. (Pin Pool) One's status when he has BURST. 1850 Phelan 45. 7. (Kelly Pool) A player is "dead" when another player has pocketed his ball. A dead player is not out of the game; he cannot win, but must shoot in turn and can kill others. 1916 RGRG 61.

dead ball

1. A stroke causing the cue ball to stop or to roll very slowly after it contacts the object ball, used to achieve POSITION. 1913 Daly 26, 1941 Hoppe 74, 1992 OR 8. In Billiards, a dead ball will move the second object ball only very little. In Pocket Billiards, a dead ball is used to keep the cue ball near the location formerly occupied by the object ball. See also IN PLAY, KILLED BALL. Cf. STOP BALL.

Invention of the dead ball stroke is credited to Dudley Kavanagh during the period 1859–1860. 1890 NY Herald (Feb 20) 9:5. 1925 Hoppe 208 advises making this shot with the forearm rather than the wrist.

2. A ball that is stroked without any ENGLISH. Also, the name of a DIAMOND SYSTEM for calculating the path taken by such a ball—the DEAD BALL SYSTEM.

3. A ball that is not IN PLAY. 1807 White 28. A ball that is IN HAND or is OFF THE TABLE. 1881 MB 23.

4. (Eng. Bill.) A ball that comes to rest FROZEN to a rail or another ball. 1924 Ogden 269, 1941 Levi 29.

5. A ball that has lost its resiliency and thus does not rebound readily when struck at another. 1913 Stoddard 10.

dead-ball line
(Bagatelle, obs.) The BAULK-LINE. If a ball returns behind the dead-ball line, it becomes a DEAD BALL, hence the name. See also BAR BILLIARDS.

dead-ball massé
A MASSÉ in which the cue ball travels very slowly upon being struck. It is performed by essentially allowing the vertical cue stick to fall through the ball by its own weight. 1908 Mannock II 51. The stroke can be used to impart extreme ENGLISH with very little forward speed.

dead ball system
(Three-Cushions) A DIAMOND SYSTEM for determining the path taken by a ball that is shot without ENGLISH. 1977 Gilbert 10.

dead full
Describing the contact or concussion of two balls along their LINE OF CENTERS. 1850 Phelan 21, 1900 WB (Dec 5) 56. A stroke in which the center of the cue ball is aimed directly at the center of the object ball. Also FULL, FULL BALL.

dead spread
(Bill.) A DEAD BALL shot in which the cue ball caroms off the first object ball at an angle of approximately 90 degrees and crawls slowly over to the second object ball for the COUNT and a GATHER. 1913 Daly 47. See SPREAD.

dead straight
Said of a shot in which the object ball, cue ball, and pocket are all in a straight line. 1869 Roberts 107. See also COVER.

dead stroke
1. A stroke causing the cue ball to stop or move very slowly after contact with the object ball. 1873 Bennett 193. See DEAD BALL. 2. (colloq.) A player is "in dead stroke" when he is shooting very well and apparently cannot miss. 1977 Martin 209. At the top of one's game. 1979 Grissim 250. See also FREE STROKE.

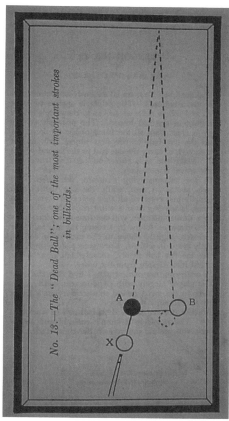

No. 18.—The "Dead Ball"; one of the most important strokes in billiards.

dead spread

dead trail
(obs.) A variety of TRAILING stroke made with the MACE. 1807 White.

death
A number of players have been so devoted to the game that they literally died while in the act of playing. In some cases the end has come of natural causes, which was the case with Onofrio Lauri (1971) and Luther Lassiter (1988). Sadly, some players have taken their own lives shortly after performances they believed were substandard, including Louis Fox (1865; see also FLY) and Louis Roberts (1991). Harold Worst played in the world pocket billiard tournament in 1966 while terminally ill with cancer and died less than three months later.

dedans
(Balkline, Fr.) International referee's call when the object balls lie in the same BALK SPACE and one of them must be driven out on the player's next shot. 1981 Rottie 136. Literal French meaning: "in." See also À CHEVAL, ENTRÉ, RENTRÉ, RESTÉ DEDANS.

dee
(Brit. games) = D.

deep red
= DARK RED. 1850 Phelan 47, 1916 RGRG 14.

default
= FORFEIT.

defense
That aspect of the game concerned with preventing the opponent from scoring, usually by positioning one or more balls to create a difficult shot. See SAFETY PLAY. Cf. OFFENSE.

deflection
The bending of the SHAFT of a cue stick as the TIP contacts a ball. See also SPINE, SQUIRT, STIFFNESS. 1983 NBN (Mar) 18.

delay
An undue suspension of play by the STRIKER. The referee may place a reasonable time limit on strokes and thus penalize delay. 1916 RGRG 55. The penalty for an infraction varies with the game. In Pocket Billiards, one minute is thought to be sufficient time in which to complete a shot. 1946 OR. In Britain, TIME WASTING. See also FORFEIT, FIVE-POINT PENALTY, UNSPORTSMAN-LIKE CONDUCT.

In 1890, Frank Ives was to play J. F. B. McCleery in a 3000-point match of Straight-Rail in a single night. Ives was off his game and found himself unable to make long runs without resting his arm. In order to give himself the necessary time, he hit on the tactic of laboriously walking around the table the long way before each carom to chalk his cue and walking the long way back to deliver his shot. This resulted in an intolerable slow-down in the match. When his opponent complained, Ives was admonished by the referee, whereupon Ives challenged the official to produce a copy of the rule forbidding slow play. When no printed copy of the rules could be found, a messenger was sent to obtain one. By the time he returned, Ives had rested sufficiently to complete and win the match. 1925 BM (Jul). This would have been a FORFEIT under modern rules.

The term for repeated and intentional delay is SLOW PLAY, which is annoying to spectators as well as to the referee and the opponent. Efforts have been made at various times to control such behavior by imposing a TIME LIMIT on each shot.

delayed taper
= PROFESSIONAL TAPER, SLOW TAPER. Cf. FAST TAPER.

deliberate foul
= INTENTIONAL FOUL.

deliberate safety
(Three-Cushions) A stroke on which no legitimate attempt is made to score and an effort is made to leave the opponent without a shot. Also INTENTIONAL SAFETY. Under earlier rules, only one consecutive deliberate safety was allowed. The second such stroke was a FOUL resulting in the loss of a point. The penalty for each additional deliberate safety was two points. 1925 RGRG 20. The purpose of this rule was to encourage offense. Because the loss of a point is a substantial penalty in Three-Cushions, players sometimes resorted to subterfuge to disguise what was actually an intentional safety. See CHEATING. Referees had to be alert to this behavior and use their own familiarity with the game to determine the player's real intent.

In the 1944 World Three-Cushion championship, the first deliberate safety was penalized by loss of a point, the second by loss of five more points.

designated
= CALLED, NOMINATED. The ball or pocket named by a player as the intended target of his shot.

deuce
(Pocket Bill., colloq.) The TWO-BALL. 1878 NYT (Apr 21) 1:7. Cf. ACE.

Deutsche Billard Union (DBU)
(org.) = The governing body of billiards in Germany.

devil
The black PIN in SKITTLE games, so called because a player who upsets it loses his LIFE.

Devil-Among-the-Tailors
(game, obs.) A SNOOKER variant similar to SHELL-OUT. 1924 Smith 107. The 15 REDS are racked and the blue or black ball is placed on the CENTRE SPOT. The player takes a red and the COLOUR alternately, earning five points for potting the colour.

diamond
A marker embedded in the rail of a table to assist the player in aiming. 1941 Hoppe 74. Also known as a CUSHION SPOT, diamond sight, DOT, NAIL, RAIL MARKER, SIGHT, or SPOT. There are 20 diamonds on a carom table, six on each LONG RAIL and three on each SHORT RAIL. A pocket table has 18 diamonds; the ones normally located where the side pockets fall are absent.

The practice of using nails or other markers attached to the rails of the table is quite old, but their use was originally limited to defining the two ends of the BAULK-LINE. 1775 Annals. Nails evolved into DOTS by 1839.

Diamonds were never common on English tables. When they were used, only six were present: two pair to mark the baulk-lines and another to define the longitudinal center line. 1873 Bennett still shows only two spots in use. Modern Snooker tables have no rail spots at all.

The utility of diamonds for aiming does not seem to have been noticed prior to 1850, when they began to appear on American tables, probably introduced by Phelan. (See the frontispiece in 1850 Phelan.) There is a hint of the concept in 1807 White, but that was before the invention of the cue tip and widespread use of English. The idea of setting the diamonds flush with the rails is discussed in 1855 *Scientific American* (Dec 23). Before that, they were laid atop the rails. Originally rectangular in shape, the markers soon became elongated diamonds. 1863 Phelan 260. Today they are often simply circular in shape. As late as 1898, Thatcher noted that in diamonds "probably most persons . . . see only an ornamentation to relieve the idea of bareness."

Despite their age, diamonds have no official role in American rules. The BCA Official Rule Book requires diamonds only to mark the ends of the CENTER STRING, the FOOT STRING, and the HEAD STRING, although one can infer that more diamonds were contemplated. Little attention has been given to how large the diamonds should be or exactly where they should be placed. The international (UMB) rules call only for the rails to "contain inlays situated at regular intervals representing one-eighth of game area length." PBTA specifications state that the center of a diamond should be $3^{11}/_{16}$ inches from the tip of the cushion NOSE. There is no analogous BCA regulation.

Diamonds are often used as a visual guide in making BANK SHOTS in both Billiards and Pocket Billiards. They have also given birth to a profusion of DIAMOND SYSTEMS for use in Three-Cushions. See also DIAMONDS COVERED.

diamond rack

A RACK or FRAME in the shape of a diamond to conform to the 1-2-3-2-1 racking format of NINE-BALL.

diamond system

Any SYSTEM of aim computation involving the DIAMONDS. 1979 Robin 335. The term "diamond system" was in use by 1924.

There is no subject in the history of Billiards that is more murky than the origin of the diamond system. Diagrams showing the path taken by a ball banked around the table appear in 1807 White to teach the "angles of the table," but nothing more advanced appeared in print for over a hundred years. Every player alive during the 1920s seems to have heard a different story. Alfredo De Oro claimed to have invented a diamond system in Cuba before coming to the U.S., which would put its creation around 1883. 1926 BM (Apr). Pierre Maupome, world amateur Three-Cushions champion in 1910, said *he* brought it from Mexico. W. H. Catton exhibited a "system" for the CORNER GAME in 1895 that had his opponents scrambling to develop systems of their own. 1898 Thatcher 232. (Catton won the Three-Cushions title in 1899.) Charles W. Henry, a fancy-shot exhibition player, gave diamond system demonstrations in 1916. 1916 BM (Mar) 16. Clarence Jackson, called the "King of the Bank Shots," popularized the FIVE-AND-A HALF SYSTEM and published a booklet on it. Versions of the diamond system first began to appear in print during the 1920s. Some diagrams are given in 1924 BM (Oct). The Cannefax Charts, a pamphlet of 10 diagrams illustrating 35 SYSTEM SHOTS, appeared around 1926. The first book devoted to the system was 1928 Barry. The experts agree on at least one fact concerning the diamond system— the system expounded in Hoppe's 1941 book, *Billiards as It Should Be Played*, was neither known to nor played by Hoppe. 1972 Byrne 163.

The objective of a diamond system is to permit a player to determine where his cue ball should contact the first cushion of a three-cushion shot in order to complete the carom successfully. The system reduces the computation of the aim point to a matter of arithmetic based on numbers assigned to the diamonds. This technique depends on the fact that a ball hit into a cushion at a certain angle and speed and with particular English will travel reliably around to and rebound from the third cushion at a specific point.

The most popular system, known as the 5½ system because of its scheme of numbering the diamonds, is based on the observation that a ball located in a corner, when banked into a long rail at a point three diamonds from the far corner with normal speed and RUNNING ENGLISH, will exit from the third rail two diamonds down from the end rail and will continue into the corner adjacent to the one from which the cue ball was originally struck. Applying the system involves a knowledge of the possible paths the cue ball may take and how to make corrections for various conditions, including the properties of the specific table being used.

The player first determines a quantity known as the CUE-BALL NUMBER, which is the point at which the desired cue-ball path intersects the cushion from which the cue ball is being shot. The player then decides from which diamond on the third cushion the cue ball must emerge. The diamond to which the cue ball is aimed is then calculated by subtracting this number from the cue-ball number.

Many other diamond systems have been devised to cover special cases, such as THREE-ON-TWO SHOTS. See, generally, 1977 Gilbert and CLOCK SYSTEM, CORNER FIVE, DEAD BALL SYSTEM, DOUBLE-THE-RAIL, END RAIL SYSTEM, FIVE-AND-A-HALF SYSTEM, FIVE SYSTEM, MAXIMUM ENGLISH, NO ENGLISH SYSTEM, PLUS SYSTEM, RC MARKS SYSTEM, REVERSE SYSTEM, SHORT-ANGLE SYSTEM, THREE-FOUR SYSTEM, TWICE AROUND SYSTEM, UMBRELLA SYSTEM. Carl S. Conlon, a habitué of the world Three-Cushions circuit, has collected details of scores of different systems. For a collection of systems for banking in Pocket Billiards, see 1988 Rossman.

In 1935, the suggestion was made to draw lines on the table connecting opposing diamonds, which would result in dividing the playing surface into 32 squares. 1935 NBJ (Dec). It was probably unknown at the time that the idea was anticipated by a diagram in 1807 White.

The diamond system has been subjected to tedious analysis. A 1958 book by Antonio Cilione devoted entirely to the diamond system contains 187 pages of elaborate mathematical calculations. However, the success of the system depends on both a reproducible stroke and appropriate compensation for individual table differences.

Diamonds Covered
(game) A variant of THREE-CUSHIONS in which the diamonds are masked so as to be invisible. Although this would seem to make the game slower and more difficult, it was actually introduced in the 1920s to speed up competition by preventing players from taking the time to make elaborate DIAMOND SYSTEM calculations. 1929 NYT (Dec 16) 37:3.

After the diamond system was developed, a dispute arose as to whether it was of any real use. Jake Schaefer Jr. held the opinion that it was superfluous. (Despite this attitude, Schaefer left notes describing his own variations of the diamond system.) Welker Cochran and Otto Reiselt played two 600-point matches: one with the diamonds covered, which was won by Cochran; Reiselt won the other. Johnny Layton beat Cochran both ways under similar circumstances. 1930 BM (Jan) 32.

ding
(colloq.) A nick or dent in the SHAFT of a cue, usually caused by banging the stick accidentally against a hard object. Small dings can be removed either by applying water to the ding to expand the wood fibers or by rubbing

the ding hard with a glass rod to generate heat, which also expands the fibers. "Ding" is an old word for a knock or blow.

Dion's nurse
(Bill.) A STATIONARY NURSE practiced by Joseph Dion having two alternating positions in which one object ball is close to the cushion and the other is out about one ball diameter from the cushion. 1913 Daly 10. A forerunner of the RAIL NURSE.

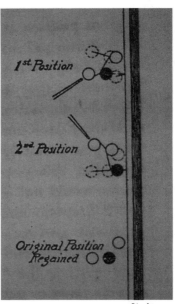

Dion's nurse

dip
(obs.) = JUMP SHOT. 1836 Tillotson 56, 1856 Crawley 92, 1866 Crawley 36. It is named from the act of dipping the TIP of the cue by raising the BUTT and striking the cue ball above its equator. See also HIGH OBLIQUE STROKE.

direct cannon, direct carom
(Eng. Bill.) CANNON in which the cue ball contacts both object balls without hitting a cushion. A BALL-TO-BALL CANNON. 1866 Crawley 89, 1899 Souv 40, 1957 Holt 38, 1976 WSD 66. Cf. INDIRECT CANNON.

direct English
= FOLLOW. 1976 WSD 161.

dirty pool
(colloq.) Foul play at billiards consisting of actions that are contrary to or that stretch the rules. 1979 Grissim 251. Used popularly by extension to mean illicit activity in any sport or game. See also CHEATING.

discount

(obs.) An American method of HANDICAP scoring in which all points made by a player are both added to his own score *and* simultaneously deducted from his opponent's score. 1857 Phelan 66, 1869 Kavanagh 14, 1884 MB 23, 1916 RGRG. The word "discount" is also used as a verb meaning to grant such a handicap. See also NO COUNT, a related SPOT, and ODDS.

In DOUBLE DISCOUNT, twice the number of points scored is deducted from the odds-giver. 1857 Phelan 66, 1869 Kavanagh 15, 1891 MB. In TREBLE DISCOUNT, three times the number of points scored is deducted from the odds-giver. 1857 Phelan 66, 1869 Kavanagh 15, 1891 MB. In GRAND DISCOUNT, the odds-giver has his score reset to zero whenever when his adversary scores. 1869 Kavanagh 15, 1891 MB. In ROYAL DISCOUNT, the odds-giver has his score reset to zero whenever he misses. He must therefore make all the points needed for game in a single RUN. 1891 MB. This is equivalent to playing for the entire GAME TOTAL at no count.

DiscPool

(game) A game played on a rotating 5-foot by 5-foot table using round discs instead of balls. 1992 PBM (Oct) 51. Regular cue sticks are used; the table has a pocket at each of the four corners. The game is the subject of U.S. Patent No. 5,131,664.

disqualification

A player may be disqualified from a game, match or tournament for repeated willful violations of the rules or conduct inimical to the game of billiards. The disqualified player receives no points, even though he may have scored, and is ineligible for any record or prize, including those for AVERAGE and HIGH RUN, that he may have earned prior to disqualification. When his opponent is disqualified, the player is credited with the number of points he scored prior to the disqualification. 1946 OR 14. In cases of extreme behavior, a player may even be barred from future competition. For an example, see CLOTH. In Snooker, the non-offender has added to his score the value of all balls remaining on the table, each RED being valued at eight points (since the player might have potted black after each red), plus 147 points for each unplayed frame. 1987 Hales 50, 1987 BSCC S23. See also FORFEIT, LOSS OF GAME, PENALTY, UNSPORTSMANLIKE CONDUCT.

Divided Pockets

(game, obs.) CRAMP GAME in which the stronger player is assigned one or two pockets, the weaker player receiving the others. 1909 BYB 87. Each player must make all of his HAZARDS into only his assigned pockets or face loss of

turn and forfeiture of the hazard to his opponent. Cf. ONE POCKET TO FIVE, TWO POCKETS TO FOUR.

division

(Life Pool, obs.) A situation in which only two players remain in the game and both have equal numbers of LIVES remaining. The pool is then divided between them and the game ends. 1836 Tillotson 6, 1856 Crawley 123.

dodge

(colloq.) To play a SAFETY, to avoid making a shot. 1858 NYT (Jan 5) 2:3. Also DUCK, def. 3.

dog

1. A difficult shot or LEAVE; a STIFF. 2. To CHOKE. 1936 NBJ (Jan), 1979 Grissim 251. "He dogged the shot." 3. To play beneath one's ability in order to HUSTLE the opponent. See also DUCK, LEMON, LET UP, LIE DOWN, STALL.

dot

= DIAMOND, CUSHION SPOT, NAIL, RAIL MARKER, SIGHT, or SPOT. 1977 Martin 209.

double

(Brit. games) = BANK SHOT, DOUBLET, REFLECTED HAZARD. 1839 Kentfield 39, 1885 Cook 7, 1976 Charlton 78. A shot in which an object ball contacts a cushion before entering a pocket. The term is also used as a verb. See also BACK DOUBLE, COCKED-HAT DOUBLE, CROSS, CROSS DOUBLE, CUTBACK DOUBLE, DOUBLE DOUBLE. A double involves only a single contact with a cushion and should not be confused with a DOUBLE BANK, which involves two cushion contacts. Colloquially known as a DUB. See INCIDENTAL CONTACT. Cf. TREBLE.

double bank

A BANK SHOT in which a ball hits two cushions before falling into a pocket or counting. 1876 NYT (May 23) 5:5, 1977 Martin 72, 1992 Billing 91. Also a DOUBLE DOUBLE or TREBLE. Cf. DOUBLE. *See illustration on next page.*

double baulk

(Eng. Bill.) The situation in which both object balls are IN BAULK and the INCOMING PLAYER has BALL IN HAND. The incoming player now has his cue ball in the D and will not be able to shoot at any ball directly. 1874 NYT (Sep 23) 5:4, 1896 Broadfoot 105, 1957 Holt 68. He may try PLAYING ACROSS to escape this dilemma. See also MISS IN BAULK. Cf. SINGLE BAULK. *See illustration on next page.*

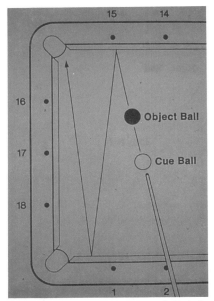

double bank

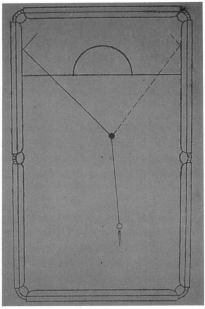

double baulk

double carom

(Amer. Four-Ball Bill., obs.) A CAROM in which the cue ball contacts all three object balls. 1896 Cady 18. The term was in use much earlier.

double-chance shot

(colloq.) = TWO-WAY SHOT. 1879 NYT (Jun 23) 5:3, 1898 Thatcher 13.

double cheese

(sl.) The situation in which both players are ON THE HILL, that is, each needs only a single point or score for

victory. The phrase is derived from the fact that whoever scores first will win the CHEESE. See also CASE GAME, CASEY JONES, HILL GAME, TV GAME.

double, cocked-hat

See COCKED-HAT DOUBLE.

double cross cannon

(Eng. Bill.) CANNON in which the cue ball travels across the table twice to complete the COUNT. 1904 Mannock I 312. Cf. CROSS-TABLE SHOT.

double discount

(obs.) A method of giving a HANDICAP in which the superior player deducts two points from his score for every point scored by the opponent. 1857 Phelan 66, 1865 NYT (Feb 10) 2:1. See DISCOUNT.

double double

(Brit. games) A two-cushion BANK SHOT in which the object ball travels twice across the table. 1856 Crawley 19, 1884 Bohn 542, 1941 Levi 210. Also called a TREBLE. The term was in use by 1827. Cf. DOUBLE, DOUBLE BANK.

double draw

A shot played with so much DRAW that the cue ball reverses direction after contacting a cushion and rolls back toward the cushion again. 1992 OR 8. When a ball is drawn into a cushion, the draw subsequently acts as FOLLOW with respect to that cushion. Cf. SNAKE SHOT, in which follow is used. *See illustration on next page.*

double elimination

A style of TOURNAMENT in which a player is eliminated upon losing two games. Cf. KNOCK-OUT, ROUND-ROBIN, SINGLE ELIMINATION, SPLIT DOUBLE ELIMINATION.

The first time a world 14.1 pocket title was decided by double elimination occurred in August 1976 at the PPPA World Open, Larry Lisciotti winning.

double hazard

(Eng. Bill.) A stroke on which both a WINNING HAZARD and a LOSING HAZARD are made. 1807 White 42, 1839 Kentfield 31. Sometimes, a HAZARD in which any two balls are potted. 1881 MB 24. See also FOLLOWING BALL, PAIR OF BREECHES, WHITE LOSING GAME. Not related to a DOUBLET HAZARD, which is a BANK SHOT.

double hit

An illegal shot in which the cue ball is struck twice by the tip of the cue stick. 1992 OR 9. This may result from a PUSH if the cue ball rebounds into the advancing cue stick after hitting the object ball. The stroke has been

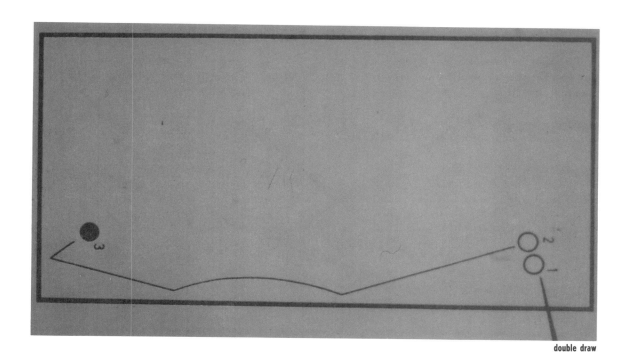

double draw

prohibited since the earliest days of billiards. 1674 Cotton states: "He that . . . strikes his Ball twice together . . . loseth one."

double kiss

A shot in which a ball contacts the same ball twice in succession, particularly when one lies near a cushion. 1991 Raftis 40. Usually known simply as a KISS.

double round-robin

A style of ROUND-ROBIN tournament in which each entrant plays every other player twice. 1992 OR 9. This arrangement is frequently used in high-level invitational tournaments involving a small number of players because it eliminates the luck of the DRAW and reduces the effect of chance on the outcome of the competition, as no player can be eliminated in the early matches.

An international 18.2 Balkline tournament in New York in 1931 utilized a double round-robin format, Welker Cochran winning. This method was first used for a world pocket billiard championship event in Detroit in 1942, at which Willie Mosconi won his first championship tournament title.

A quadruple round-robin was used to decide the 1923 U.S. National Three-Cushion title. Each of four players, Tiff Denton, Johnny Layton, Otto Reiselt and Robert Cannefax, played against each other player in four different cities. Denton was the winner with an 8–4 record. It was the only time he won the title.

double strength

(Eng. Bill.) A stroke in which the cue ball is forced UP and DOWN, or the force required to make such a shot. 1885c Cook 9.

double-the-corner

(Three-Cushions) A shot in which the cue ball makes four cushion contacts using only two rails in the corner, that is, it hits both of the cushions in the corner twice.

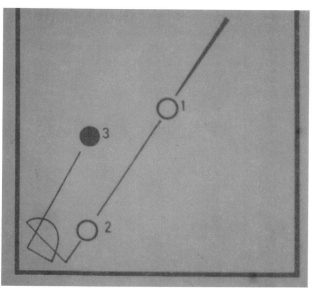

double-the-corner

81

One of the required strokes in the ARTISTIC BILLIARDS repertoire. Raymond Ceulemans is able to make the cue ball hit six or eight cushions on two. Also FOUR-ON-TWO. Cf. THREE-ON-TWO.

double-the-rail

(Three-Cushions) A shot in which the cue ball makes three cushion contacts using only two different rails, which means that one of the cushions is hit twice (doubled). It is accomplished by using REVERSE ENGLISH so that the ball returns to the first cushion after contacting a second. 1916 BM (Feb) 26. Also known as a THREE-ON-TWO shot. Cf. SNAKE SHOT, in which the cue ball first hits the same rail twice, then contacts a third. The double-the-rail system is a type of DIAMOND SYSTEM used to compute the path taken by the cue ball during a three-on-two or double-the-rail shot.

doublet

(Brit. games, obs.) = BANK SHOT, DOUBLET HAZARD, REFLECTED HAZARD. 1807 White 40, 1862 Crawley 21, 1884 Bohn 542. See also CROSS. Cf. BRICOLE.

Doublet Game

(game, obs.) A CRAMP GAME, played with two balls, in which each hazard involves a "reverberation from a cushion." 1807 White 51. The object ball, not the cushion, is struck first by the cue ball. 1856 Crawley 98. Said in 1850c White & Bohn 38 to be equivalent to giving 5 points in 16 against the WHITE WINNING GAME, or 10 in 16 against the WINNING AND LOSING GAME. 1839 Kentfield 39, 1862 Crawley 97. A version is also played with three balls in which scoring is by LOSING HAZARDS and CANNONS. Every shot must be made by a DOUBLET from the cushion after an *object* ball is struck. A losing hazard without a doublet scores against the striker; a WINNING HAZARD results only in loss of turn. 1866 Crawley 214. Cf. BRICOLE GAME.

doublet hazard

(Eng. Bill., obs.) = DOUBLET, a WINNING HAZARD made by BANKING the object ball. 1807 White 5, 1915 Reece & Clifford 27. In modern parlance, a BANK SHOT. The French used a special table for a game consisting of doublet hazards only, having a single hole cut in the bed at the center of the table. Cf. DOUBLE HAZARD, a completely unrelated concept.

doubt

Uncertainty as to whether a rule has been complied with. In deciding whether there has been a valid COUNT, doubt is resolved against the STRIKER. 1892 HRB 63. The general concept is that when a positive act is required for a score, the player is not given the benefit of any doubt.

The rationale for the rule of doubt is that the striker has a definitive obligation to obey the rule, and he will not be credited with points if compliance is uncertain. There may be doubt as to whether a cushion or ball has been contacted, whether a ball lies on a line or which of two balls has been struck first. Matters of fact that are in doubt are decided by the REFEREE or MARKER.

For example, in Three-Cushions, the cue ball must make three distinct cushion contacts before hitting the SECOND OBJECT BALL. If it appears to hit the third cushion and the second ball simultaneously, the rule of doubt applies and the shot does not count. In Eight-Ball, the striker must first contact a ball of his own GROUP. If there is any question whether he has been successful in doing so, the shot is not legal.

On the other hand, doubt as to whether a FOUL has occurred is resolved in favor of the striker. If the referee does not clearly observe the foul, it did not take place. There is thus a PRESUMPTION OF INNOCENCE in billiards. But see INSTANT REPLAY.

A recent change to the professional Nine-Ball rules contravenes the rule of doubt. See SPLIT HIT. The British do not follow the rule, but give the benefit of doubt to the striker. 1956 BSTE 32.

dowel

A peg inserted between two pieces of SLATE to ensure accurate alignment. Slates that are not doweled may slide past one another at the SEAM, creating a small cliff if the portions are unequal in thickness. Use of dowels guarantees that the slates as installed in the table are in the same orientation as when they were machined at the factory.

down

1. Behind in the score. "You're five games down." Cf. UP, def. 2. 2. (Brit. games) Toward the BOTTOM cushion. In American games, toward the FOOT of the table, hence, DOWN THE TABLE. Cf. UP, def. 5. 3. Pocketed. "The five is down, so you're on the six." 4. (Pin Pool) A PIN is said to be down if it is lying on the TABLE, is entirely off its spot, or is leaning against a ball, cushion, or another pin.

down the table

In American games, toward the FOOT of the table. 1878 NYT (Jan 24) 2:1, 1970 Knuchell 238. Also DOWNTOWN. In English games, toward the BOTTOM (the opposite direction). Cf. UP THE TABLE.

downtown

= DOWN THE TABLE. Cf. UPTOWN.

drag

(primarily Brit., rare in U.S.) BACKSPIN used to slow the progress of the cue ball. 1873 Bennett 194, 1885 Cook 9, 1924 Aiken 65, 1989 Koehler 254. Also CRAWL, JAB, SKID SHOT, STAB. LOW applied to the ball to cause it to run TRUE. 1895 Buchanan 74, 1896 Broadfoot 202, 1954 KTG 23. STOP BALL, English that causes the cue ball to stop after striking an object ball. 1913 Daly 34, 1976 WSD 122. The distinction between DRAG and DRAW is that with drag the backspin is lost by the time the first object ball is contacted; the cue ball then has rolling motion only. 1920 Levi II 173. Cf. DRAW.

draw

1. Spin imparted to the cue ball to cause it to come back after striking an object ball. 1866 NYT (Mar 27) 8:4, 1881 MB 23, 1976 WSD 123. Hence a "draw shot" is one in which draw is used; a shot in which the cue ball appears to be "drawn" back from the object ball by means of BACKSPIN. Draw is applied by striking the cue ball below its center, sometimes by elevating the BUTT of the cue. A shot is said to have been played with DRAW if any backspin at all is applied; the cue ball need not actually recoil. Also called BACK-UP or, in English games, BOTTOM, LOW, PULL, RETURN, SCREW, SCREW-BACK, or TWIST. See also CLOSE DRAW, DOUBLE DRAW, FORCE DRAW, NIP, PINCH, POWER DRAW, SPREAD DRAW, SUCK. Very rarely, REVERSE ENGLISH. Cf. DRAG, JAB, STAB, STUN.

Draw was apparently the first kind of spin whose effect was understood and used by billiard players, imparted by means of the JEFFERY in the 1790s even before the cues had tips. It was called "twisting" in 1806 Phil, FORCE in 1850 Phelan. During the 1860s, Michael Phelan taught his students how to apply draw by placing two balls six inches apart and making a chalk mark on the cloth halfway between them. The student was told to stroke so as to make the tip of the cue stick touch the mark. 1925 Hoppe 190.

2. A TIE, NULL, or STALEMATED game. Such an occurrence is possible playing by international carom rules, under which each player is given the same number of innings in which to score. If the second player ties the score from his BREAK SHOT in the last inning, the game is a draw. See EQUAL INNINGS. This rule arose out of a controversy beginning in 1925, when Jake Schaefer Jr. beat Erich Hagenlocher by running 400 points in 18.2 Balkline from the OPENING BREAK. Hagenlocher never got a chance to shoot. 1925 BM (Mar). Drawn games have not been possible in Snooker since 1919, when a rule was added providing for the BLACK to be spotted at the end of the FRAME if the players' scores are equal. 1985 Everton 47. See also SUDDEN DEATH.

A draw used to be possible in English Billiards even if the players' scores were not tied! This occurred when neither player reached GAME within a specified time limit. 1917 NYT (Dec 23) I 14:6.

3. A set of player pairings for matches in a TOURNAMENT. See also BYE, SEEDING. A BLIND DRAW is one in which the pairings are chosen at random.

draw shot

A shot in which DRAW is applied to the cue ball. 1873 NYT (May 17) 1:3. In British usage, a carom made by the use of draw is called a SCREW CANNON.

dress

To prepare the TIP of a cue stick so it is in the proper condition for playing. In particular, to trim the tip so it is flush with the FERRULE. 1983 NBN (Mar) 18.

dress code

Regulations regarding the style of clothing that is allowed to be worn in tournament play. The promoter specifies a dress code, which varies depending on the venue of the event, time of day, and whether the competition is being televised.

In women's professional play, Dress Code A (formal) requires tuxedo or full-length evening gown or other formal clothes and dress shoes. Dress Code B permits dress slacks and sweaters, collared blouses, and dress shoes, but no jeans, cords or sneakers. Dress Code C (casual) allows colored jeans, but not blue jeans, and permits sneakers. 1987 WPBA 14.

drift

= TABLE ROLL. 1980 BD (Sep/Oct) 56. Also FLOAT.

drill

To make a shot definitively, in such a way that it was never close to missing. "He really drilled it." See also NAIL.

drive

1. To cause a ball to contact a rail. "The opening player at Pocket Billiards must drive two balls." 2. (Bill.) A shot in which an object ball is sent away from the cue ball for a calculated distance for positional purposes, often to rebound from a cushion and return to effect a GATHER. 1881 MB 24, 1941 Hoppe 74.

drop

1. (colloq.) To POCKET. "Drop the six and lay for the seven." 2. = FALL. 3. To maneuver a ball, usually through a narrow space. "Drop it in behind the eight." 4. A handicap in Eight-Ball in which a player or his

opponent is permitted to remove a certain number of balls from the table.

drop cannon

(Eng. Bill.) A particular type of shot for POSITION consisting of a BALL-TO-BALL CANNON in which the first object ball is driven off a long rail and meets the cue and second object ball farther up the table, the purpose being to GATHER the balls between the TOP pockets. 1903 WB (Apr 15) 278, 1904 Mannock I 336, 1957 Holt 84, 1974 Lindrum 50. The balls seem to "drop" together. "Dropping" a ball to the other end of the table for safety reasons is mentioned several times in 1807 White.

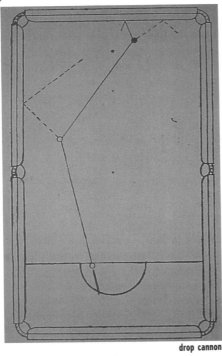

drop cannon

drop pocket

A pocket that collects balls in a NET instead of returning them to a GULLY. 1979 Grissim 251. The pocket hangs, or drops, beneath the BED. Cf. POCKET DROP.

dub

(Snooker, colloq.) A DOUBLE or BANK SHOT.

duck

1. An easy shot, one that cannot be missed. 1988 Rossman 98. Also a CHERRY, CRIPPLE, HANGER, MINNIE, PUPPY, SET-UP or SITTER. 2. To lose or miss deliberately. A maneuver by a HUSTLER to conceal his true ability from the opponent. See also DOG, LEMON, LET UP, LIE DOWN, STALL. 3. A SAFETY. 1941 Hoppe 74. (From the idea of "ducking," or avoiding, the shot.) Also used as a verb. The construction "three and duck" means a style

of HANDICAP in which a player is not permitted to run more than three points, his INNING ending on a miss or his third stroke, whichever comes first. Also DODGE. See also STOP.

dump

To lose deliberately to collect a wager or to achieve an advantage for another player in the standings. Also said of a game lost in this manner: "It was a dump." 1967 Polsky 49. Kavanagh reported in 1869 *Billiard Cue* 67 that Pierre Carme and A. P. Rudolphe arranged a dump in a match they played on November 18, 1868. See also BUSINESS. Cf. LEMON, SAVER.

A dump becomes financially advantageous when two players collude to maximize the sum of the prize money to be won and their share of any side bets. They then divide the total without regard to bettors or backers. For example, suppose that A and B are competing for a $5000 first prize in which A is heavily favored to win. If there is $10,000 in side action on B at 3:1 odds and $10,000 on A at 1:1, then if the players collude and A dumps to B, allowing him to win, the players will share $35,000. If A wins, the players share only $15,000. Such are the risks in billiard betting. See also CAL-CUTTA.

Another type of dump occurs when a player deliberately loses to enhance the record of another. Suppose that two players from the same country are participating in a round-robin tournament. When they must play against each another, the player with the poorer record at that point may dump to the player with the better record to improve that record further and increase the chance of a victory for their common country. A countermeasure against such tactics is to pair such players early in the final round before a dump can be profitable.

duplex pocket

(Brit.) A DROP POCKET fashioned with overlapping NETS so that balls can be removed without the need to reach one's hand down into the pocket from the table bed. 1905 Orme.

Duplicate Billiards

(game, obs.) A version of 18.2 BALKLINE in which the players are given an equal number of innings, which they commence by playing predetermined shots. Much like duplicate bridge, this form of competition permits the comparison of players who never face one another at the table. An amateur Duplicate tournament was held in New York in 1911. 1931 BM (Oct). Cf. EQUAL OF-FENSE, KEY SHOT BILLIARDS, TELEGRAPHIC BILLIARDS.

Dutch Pool

(game, obs.) A pocket billiard game played with a cue ball and four object balls: two one-balls and two two-balls. These are spotted as the PINS would be in SENTINEL POOL. Sinking a ball scores its numerical value. A carom on two balls is worth one point, on two balls two points. After an object ball is pocketed, it is returned to its spot. 1902 Burrowes 7. See also NIGGER POOL.

E

edge nurse

1. (Bill.) The PASS NURSE. 1913 Daly 61, 208. In British usage, the SQUEEZE CANNON. 2. (Bill.) RUDOLPHE'S NURSE. A STATIONARY NURSE in which the object balls are FROZEN to the rail and the cue ball is "edged" by them without disturbing their position. 1980 BD (Nov/Dec) 20.

effect

(obs.) = ENGLISH, SPIN. 1881 NYT (Feb 27) 2:3. In French, *effet*. 1827 Mingaud, 1835 Coriolis. The French term is still in use; the English word was only rarely employed.

egg

(colloq.) A BILLIARD BALL. 1988 Rossman 98. The metaphor was particularly apt in the days of ivory balls, which had an off-white color resembling eggs and were often ovoid instead of spherical. In most pool rooms, pocket balls are still stored in trays that are sometimes called "egg trays."

Eight and Eight

(game, obs.) A carom game, invented in Minneapolis by Frank Johnson, in which a player must make eight bank shots and eight three-cushion shots, in any order. Before attempting a three-cushion bank, the player must specify which category he is trying for. 1945 NBJ (Feb).

eight and out

(One-Pocket) Describing the act of winning the game by sinking all eight balls in a single RUN. See OUT.

Eight-Ball

1. (game) One of the most popular SINGLE-RACK pocket billiard games, played with 15 object balls and a cue ball. The object balls are divided into two GROUPS called the SOLIDS, which are numbered 1–7, and the STRIPES, numbered 8–15. At the start, the eight-ball is racked at the center of the TRIANGLE and one ball from each group is racked at each of the rear corners. An OPEN BREAK is used, and the first successful striker must choose one of the two groups. The object is to sink the eight-ball after having pocketed all the balls in one's group. The eight-ball itself may not be used for a COMBINATION shot after groups have been determined. 1986 OR 53. The game is also known as BIGS AND LITTLES or STRIPES AND SOLIDS.

Sometimes the game is scored by assigning three points for a win plus one point for each ball of the opponent's group remaining on the table at the finish. 1976 WSD 40. This is known as the POINT SYSTEM.

Eight-Ball is descended from B.B.C. CO. POOL, which was played under the same rules, but with yellow balls and red balls in place of the stripes and solids, and was still known by this name as late as 1925. 1991 Shamos 43. Despite widespread play, the game was not added to the official rule book until after 1940. Eight-Ball is now so universally played that many beginners know no other pocket game and believe it to be synonymous with "pool."

Eight-Ball is extensively played in LEAGUES, particularly on BAR TABLES. The game can be played without spotting any balls, which makes it ideal for COIN-OPERATED TABLES. Although Eight-Ball receives little respect from professionals as a competitive test, championship tournaments are nonetheless conducted regularly.

The popularity of Eight-Ball has led to an unusually large number of rule variations. See ALABAMA EIGHT-BALL, CRAZY EIGHT, ENGLISH EIGHT-BALL POOL, HARD EIGHT, LAST POCKET OPTION, MISERY, MISSOURI, OFF, ONE AND FIFTEEN IN THE SIDE, OPEN TABLE, PLAYER'S EIGHT-BALL, POINT SYSTEM, ROTATION EIGHT-BALL, SOFT EIGHT, STALEMATED GAME. See also BEHIND THE EIGHT-BALL, an expression that surprisingly is not related to the game of Eight-Ball.

A game similar to Eight-Ball can be played with nine balls instead of 15 using an ordinary Nine-Ball rack, the eight-ball, four stripes, and four solids. 1989 Raftis 150. See HOT EIGHT.

The number of different possible initial racks in Eight-Ball is $2 \times 7 \times 7 \times 12! = 46,492,156,800$.

2. The solid black ball at POCKET BILLIARDS.

3. = AMERICAN PYRAMID POOL, BASIC POCKET BILLIARDS. Also known as EIGHT-BALL PYRAMID, which refers to the fact that eight balls must be pocketed for a victory. 1916 RGRG 49. The first tournament was held in 1882, Albert Frey winning. The game is not related to modern Eight-Ball.

Eight-Ball Pyramid
(game, obs.) = AMERICAN PYRAMID POOL. See EIGHT-BALL.

eight-ball spot
(Eng. Eight-Ball Pool) The spot on which the eight-ball is positioned when the object balls are racked. It is located at the intersection of the diagonals connecting the top and middle pockets, that is, at the PYRAMID SPOT. Note that the APEX BALL is not racked on this spot in English Eight-Ball Pool. 1985 KTGP 4. Other names: DARK-RED SPOT, FOOT SPOT, PINK SPOT, WINNING SPOT.

8.2 Balkline
(game, obs.) BALKLINE played with four LINES, drawn at a distance of eight inches from the cushions. The game was suggested by Randolph Heiser as an improvement over Continuous Balkline. In the first public Balkline contest of any kind, Maurice Vignaux beat Maurice Daly at 8.2 in Chicago on March 26, 1883. The eight-inch game gave way quickly to 14.2 Balkline after a brief flirtation with 10-inch and 12-inch lines. For a brief period, a HANDICAP at Balkline was given by using both 8-inch and 14-inch lines on the same table. The weaker player used the former, the stronger player the latter. The record high run is 329 by Vignaux against Jacob Schaefer Sr. in Paris in 1884.

eight safe
(Nine-Ball) A HANDICAP at Nine-Ball, in which the weaker player is guaranteed a DRAW if he sinks the eight-ball legally. That is, he is "safe" if he pockets the eight. Also SAFE EIGHT.

eight-shot, eight-stroke
(Eng. Bill., Amer. Four-Ball Bill.) A shot on which eight points are scored. In English Billiards, this can be done by hitting the red ball first, holing it, making a cannon, and pocketing the striker's ball, or by hitting the red and holing all the balls without making a cannon. 1890 HRB 110. In American Four-Ball, it is done by caroming on all the balls and pocketing a RED and the WHITE. 1850 Phelan 22.

eight to hop
(Nine-Ball) A HANDICAP at Nine-Ball. See HOP THE EIGHT for an explanation.

18.1 Balkline
(game) A version of BALKLINE in which the lines are drawn 18 inches from the cushions and when both balls lie IN BALK or IN ANCHOR the player must drive one of them out on his next shot. See NO SHOT IN, ONE SHOT IN. The metric version of 18.1 is 45.1 BALKLINE, whose lines fall approximately 17¾ inches from the cushions. Cf. 18.2 BALKLINE.

The first tournament at 18.1 was held in Chicago in May 1896, only six weeks after the introduction of 18.2 in New York. Albert Garnier was the victor over Jacob Schaefer Sr. and Frank Ives. The first world championship was played in New York in November 1897, George Slosson winning, but there were no foreign entrants. In challenge matches that followed, the title passed to Schaefer, then to Ives.

In 1900, the leading professionals declared themselves against the game, claiming that it was too difficult to play. 1900 NYT (Sep 2) 17:6. Nevertheless, a second world championship tournament took place in New York in December 1901, with Schaefer winning. Slosson took the title by DEFAULT in 1903 when Schaefer failed to post the $250 stake required by the rules. Maurice Vignaux wrested the championship from Slosson in March 1904 in Paris. This set the stage for the spectacular match of January 15, 1906, in which 18-year-old Willie Hoppe defeated Vignaux, the "Lion of France," for the 18.1 title.

The championship changed hands 10 times during the next 20 years, finally reposing with Hoppe again for the period 1927–1944, after which no further competition was held. The other players who held the title were George B. Sutton and Ora Morningstar. The tournament high run remains 212, achieved by Jake Schaefer Jr. in 1926. Although Welker Cochran holds the EXHIBITION records for HIGH RUN (353), SINGLE AVERAGE (150), and GRAND AVERAGE (61), he never won the 18.1 title.

18.2 Balkline
(game) A style of BALKLINE in which the lines are drawn 18 inches from the rails and if both balls are IN BALK or IN ANCHOR the player must drive one of them out on or before his second shot. See also DUPLICATE BILLIARDS, TWO SHOTS IN. Cf. 18.1 BALKLINE, 45.2 BALKLINE, ONE SHOT IN.

The 14-inch line was widened to 18 inches because of a popular feeling that 14.2 BALKLINE was too easy a game

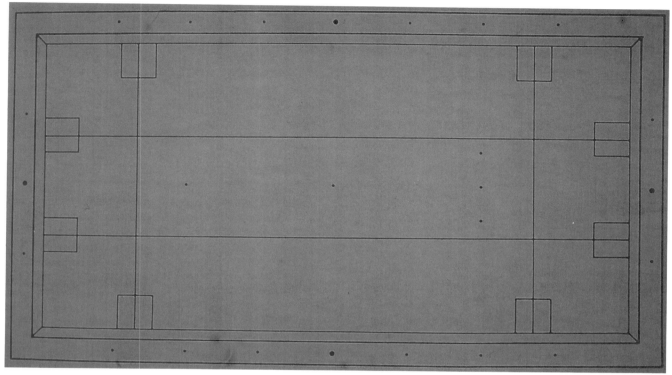

18.2 Balkline

for professional competition. The first 18.2 tournament (18.2.5, with PARKER'S BOX) was played in New York in March 1896. Jacob Schaefer Sr. and Frank Ives tied for first place, and no playoff was ever held. The next significant contest was for the Championship of France in Paris in March 1902. Louis Cure, who had run 100 at Straight-Rail when he was 12 years old, was the victor.

The first world championship was played at Paris in February 1903. Three players tied for the lead at the end of regulation play. Maurice Vignaux, who had the highest GRAND AVERAGE, refused to play off for the title, claiming that the tie-breaking rules made him the winner by virtue of his average. Litigation ensued, and nine months later Vignaux was awarded the title by a French court. All future world championship tournaments were held in the United States. Willie Hoppe first won the title in 1908 in a challenge match against George Sutton, but he held it for only a week, not winning again until 1910. The only players to hold the title subsequently were George Slosson, Ora Morningstar, Calvin Demarest, Jake Schaefer Jr., Edouard Horemans, Erich Hagenlocher and Welker Cochran. For a complete treatment of every professional world championship game of 18.2 Balkline ever played, extending over 14 tournaments, see 1971 Trainer.

After the 1903 tournament, only two shots were allowed IN ANCHOR. In 1919, the ANCHOR SPACE was increased in size to a seven-inch square.

The tournament high run at 18.2 is 400 by Jake Schaefer Jr., when he ran out the game from the break against Hagenlocher in 1925. Cochran had an EXHIBITION high run of 684 in 1926. In an exhibition in 1930, Schaefer ran 400 from the break in four consecutive games, for a sequence of 1600 unbroken points. Roger Conti ran 837 in 1929, but this record has not been recognized in the U.S. 1929 NYT (Oct. 19) 15:7.

elbow

(Eng. Bill.) The curved corner or MOUTH of a pocket on an ENGLISH BILLIARDS table. 1869 Roberts 167. Also BUMP or SHOULDER. See BUBBLE for a shot aimed at the elbow.

elevation

The angle at which the cue stick is held, relative to the plane of the table. During a MASSÉ shot, increasing the elevation reduces the distance traveled by the cue ball before any applied spin takes effect and increases the amount of DRAW or FOLLOW imparted.

eleven-shot, eleven-stroke

(Amer. Four-Ball Bill., obs.) A shot scoring 11 points, which may be accomplished by caroming on all the balls and pocketing both REDS. 1850 Phelan 22. No such shot is possible in English Billiards since the maximum number of points that can be scored on a single stroke is 10.

Elimination

1. (game) A pocket billiard game for three or five players. The 1-ball is placed at the foot spot, the 6 and 11 at the corners of the rack. For three players, the ball GROUPS consist of the 1–5, 6–10 and 11–15. For four players they are 1–3, 4–6, 7–9, 10–12, and 13–15. A player is eliminated when all balls of his GROUP have been pocketed. The last surviving player is the winner. Also called CUT-THROAT POCKET BILLIARDS or SCREW YOUR BUDDY. 1974 OR 74, 1992 OR 77. An excellent game for an odd number of players. As with any THREE-HANDED GAME, however, collusion is possible between any pair of players to the detriment of the third.

The number of different possible initial racks in Elimination is $2 \times 12! = 958,003,200$.

2. A method of determining the winner of a TOURNAMENT by successively dropping (eliminating) players who have lost a specified number of games. See DOUBLE ELIMINATION, SINGLE ELIMINATION.

end

1. The area of a billiard table lying near a SHORT RAIL. 2. A CORNER POCKET, also known as an END POCKET. 3. (obs.) A unit of play in early billiard games, roughly corresponding to a modern INNING. The length of games was five ends if played by daylight, three ends by candlelight. 1674 Cotton. This was probably because of the high cost of candles. See also LIGHTING.

end pocket

= A CORNER POCKET; a pocket at one END of the table. 1881 NYT (Jan 23) 2:7. Cf. SIDE POCKET.

end rail

A SHORT RAIL; a rail at one END of the table. Sometimes used to refer specifically to the FOOT RAIL. 1864 AH 419, 1989 Koehler 254. Cf. SIDE RAIL.

end rail system

(Three-Cushions) A DIAMOND SYSTEM used to compute the path taken by the cue ball after it first contacts an END RAIL. Cf. PLUS SYSTEM.

end table

The SHORT TABLE, that area between a STRING and the nearest END RAIL, constituting one-fourth the area of the full table. Frank Ives developed the idea of keeping the balls in carom games within the end table to maintain control over them, since it is much easier to GATHER the balls in a smaller space. 1925 Hoppe 236.

English

= SPIN or TWIST applied to the cue ball by striking it off center. 1873 NYT (Jun 26) 5:3, 1881 MB 24, 1896 Broadfoot 191, 1941 Hoppe 74. The origin of this term is unknown, but it may have developed when English visitors introduced spin to the U.S. in the nineteenth century. The British refer to English as SIDE. English could be applied to the ball sparingly with a tipless cue or the JEFFERY, and it is described in the literature prior to the invention of the leather tip. 1806 Phil 21: "A *lateral* twist or rotation also, may be given, by striking the ball *sideways*, with the point of the cue chalked as before." 1807 White cautions against hitting the cue ball on the side but describes the application of HIGH and LOW and an elementary form of JUMP SHOT. In American usage, "English" encompasses DRAW and FOLLOW as well as SIDE. Cf. BODY ENGLISH.

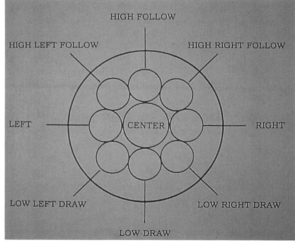

English

The quantity of English applied to a ball can be measured in units of tip width or just "tips." "Two tips" of English means that the outer edge of the cue tip is aimed at the cue ball at a distance of two tip widths from center. (The center of the tip is actually at a distance of one and a half cue tips from the center.) See also CLOCK SYSTEM.

English may be transferred between balls (TRANSMITTED SIDE) or induced by a glancing contact with a cushion

(CUSHION-IMPARTED SIDE) or with another ball (COLLISION-INDUCED ENGLISH).

See also DIRECT ENGLISH, INSIDE ENGLISH, LEFT ENGLISH, MAXIMUM ENGLISH, NATURAL ENGLISH, OUTSIDE ENGLISH, REVERSE ENGLISH, RIGHT ENGLISH, RUNNING ENGLISH, WRONG-WAY ENGLISH.

English Bagatelle

(Bagatelle game) BAGATELLE played with a special KING BALL, which must be struck by some other ball at the beginning of each round before any score is possible. 1898 HRB 101.

English Billiards

(game) A game played with three balls on a table having pockets, in which points are scored by making CANNONS, WINNING HAZARDS and LOSING HAZARDS. 1976 WSD 39. CANNONS count two points, WHITE HAZARDS two and RED HAZARDS three. 1869 Kavanagh 10, 1890 HRB 109. The player is credited with all points earned on a particular stroke, which yields a maximum of 10 (see TEN-SHOT). In Britain, the game is known simply as Billiards; in other countries it is the ENGLISH GAME. Also ALL-IN GAME, COMMON GAME.

English Billiards is an amalgam of three games: the WINNING GAME, the LOSING GAME and the CARAMBOLE GAME. Consequently, it was formerly called the WINNING AND LOSING CARAMBOLE GAME. The Winning Game was played with two white balls; a player scored points by potting his opponent's ball. Holing one's own ball resulted in a loss of points, which gave rise to the Losing Game, or one in which the object was to make those hazards that were "losing" in the Winning Game—that is, to pot one's own ball after having hit the opponent's. The Carambole Game was played with three balls, including a red; the object was to carom on the two object balls only. These games became popular in England after 1770 and had fused into the present game of English Billiards by about 1800.

Before organized professional play began in 1870, champions were designated by acclamation. Jonathan Kentfield reigned from around 1820 to 1849, when he refused a challenge from John Roberts Sr. Roberts was champion from 1849 to 1870, when he lost to William Cook in the first professional match. The first U.S. stake match was also held in 1870. 1891 MB 664. For a further historical account, see 1979 Everton. The other champions through 1983 have been John Roberts Jr. (1870, 1871, 1875–77, 1885), Joseph Bennett (1870, 1880–81), Charles Dawson (1899–1900, 1901, 1903), H.W. Stevenson 1901, 1909–11), Melbourne Inman (1908–09, 1912–19), Willie Smith (1920, 1923), Tom New-

man (1921–22, 1924–27), Joe Davis (1928–32), Walter Lindrum (1933–34), Clark McConachy (1951), Rex Williams (1968–76, 1982–83), and Fred Davis (1980). Every champion through 1980 was the author of a book on billiards. In the U.K., English Billiards has largely given way to Snooker but is still played by loyal devotees.

A women's professional title was offered starting in 1931, won by Joyce Gardner (1931–33, 1935–39), Ruth Harrison (1934, 1939), and Thelma Carpenter (1940, 1949–50).

The vocabulary of English Billiards is rich, as might be expected of a game with such a long history. See, for example, BAULK, BREAK-OFF, CANNON, CONSECUTIVE CANNONS, CONSECUTIVE HAZARDS, CUSHION GAME, D, DOUBLE BAULK, FLOATING WHITE TECHNIQUE, FOLLOWING CANON, FORCED OFF, IN-OFF, LINE RULE, NURSERY CANNON, PUSH CANON, PUT HIM IN, ROCKING CANNON, SPOT-BARRED GAME, SPOT-STROKE, TWO-POT RED RULE, WHITECHAPEL. For game variations see À LA ROYALE, AMERICAN FOUR-BALL BILLIARDS, BAR-HOLE GAME, BILLIARDS GOLF, BRICOLE GAME, COMMANDING GAME, LOSING GAME, MAN-OF-WAR GAME, NAMING STROKE GAME, NOMINATION GAME, ONE POCKET TO FIVE, RED WINNING CARAMBOLE GAME, SIDE AGAINST SIDE, TWO POCKETS TO FOUR, WHITE BALL AGAINST THE RED, WINNING HAZARDS AGAINST ALL HAZARDS AND CANONS.

English Eight-Ball Pool

(game) EIGHT-BALL modified for play on an ENGLISH BILLIARDS table. 1986 Quinn 87. The differences between the English and American styles are minor and largely cultural. For example, in the English version, a player who is SNOOKERED as the result of his opponent's foul stroke may play from the D. The game defines a "snooker" in an unusual fashion—see OBSTRUCTION. When the balls are racked, the eight-ball, in the center of the PACK, not the APEX BALL, is racked on the PYRAMID SPOT. See EIGHT-BALL SPOT. Do not confuse this game with English Pool, an obsolete pocket game of historical significance in the development of Snooker.

The governing body of English Eight-Ball Pool is the BRITISH ASSOCIATION OF POOL TABLE OPERATORS.

English Game

= ENGLISH BILLIARDS, as referred to outside of England.

English Pool

(game, obs.) = LIFE POOL, COLOR-BALL POOL, FOLLOWING POOL, LAST PLAYER, LIVE POOL or just POOL. 1857 Phelan 217, 1891 MB 362. The game originated around 1819. 1974 Hendricks. Cf. ENGLISH EIGHT-BALL POOL, a modern style.

English Pyramids

(game, obs.) = PYRAMID GAME, an English game strongly resembling AMERICAN PYRAMID POOL.

English spot

(Eng. Bill.) A SPOT in the lateral center of the table and approximately 13 inches from the TOP RAIL (12¾ inches on a REGULATION TABLE; 320 millimeters or ¹⁄₁₁ of the table length on a METRIC TABLE). 1857 Phelan 165, 1978 BSCC 22. The name of this spot arises out of its use in English Billiards as the spot on which the RED is placed after being pocketed. Also known as the BILLIARD SPOT, BLACK SPOT, LOSING SPOT, RED SPOT (Eng. Bill.), TOP SPOT, WINNING AND LOSING SPOT, or just the SPOT.

English table

A table used for playing ENGLISH BILLIARDS, normally 12 feet in length and having curved ELBOWS at its six pockets. A SNOOKER TABLE.

entré

(Balkline, Fr., pr. ahn-TRAY) International referee's CALL when the object balls first enter the same BALK SPACE. Literal French meaning: "entered." 1981 Rottie 136. See also À CHEVAL, DEDANS, RENTRÉ, RESTÉ DEDANS.

EPBF

(org.) = EUROPEAN POCKET BILLIARD FEDERATION.

equal innings

(Bill., usually Three Cushions) A rule ensuring that both players will have an equal number of innings in which to shoot, regardless of who plays the OPENING BREAK. If the player who opened the game is the first to reach the requisite number of points, his opponent is given an additional inning in which to reach the same total. If he succeeds, the game is a DRAW. WBA 5. This rule applies in all UMB events. There were calls for such a provision for decades, dating back at least to a suggestion by Frank Cohn of Chicago in 1920. 1920 BM (Mar) 45. The opening break is a great advantage; one's opponent may never get to shoot. The game is thought to be much fairer if the players have equal chances.

It is often asked why the second player can only draw and not win. The reason for this is that the RUN of the first player is halted when he reaches GAME, so it would be unjust to allow the second player to exceed the GAME TOTAL. A variation would be to permit each player to continue shooting to the end of the run after reaching the number of points needed for game.

USBA rules do not provide for equal innings, so the rule is not common in the United States.

Equal Offense

(game) A pocket billiard game in which conditions are equalized so that the performances of different players can be compared even though they have not met head-to-head. Each player shoots for 10 innings exactly, opening with a FREE BREAK each time. Any balls pocketed on the break are spotted but the player then continues shooting with cue ball IN HAND BEHIND THE HEAD STRING, proceeding until he misses, fouls, or pockets the maximum number of balls allowed for an inning. The winner is the player with the highest score at the end of 10 innings. The game is copyrighted by Jerry Briesath, a proprietor member of the Billiard Congress of America. 1977 OR 86, 1978 Byrne 170, 1984 BD(Apr) 20. Since there is no defense in this game, it can be played solitaire and competitions can be held involving players thousands of miles apart. Cf. DUPLICATE BILLIARDS, SOLITAIRE POOL, TELEGRAPHIC BILLIARDS.

equipment

The items used in playing a billiard game, including the balls, table, cues, CHALK, etc. The equipment must conform to regulations and must be used for its intended purpose. For example, the MECHANICAL BRIDGE can be used only to support the shaft of the cue stick and not to strike any ball. These materials may not be used to annoy the opponents, to disrupt the game, or to affect the other equipment adversely.

Whether an object is an item of equipment can be of importance in determining what happens if a ball should come in contact with the object during a shot. For example, if a ball leaves the table bed, hits a piece of equipment and returns to the table, it is still IN PLAY and is not considered a JUMP BALL. For this purpose, any lighting fixture suspended over the table is considered to be equipment. If the ball contacts anything other than a piece of equipment before returning to the table, it is no longer in play. The UMB rules differ. If a ball leaves the bed of the table and contacts anything other than a CUSHION (even the wood of the RAIL), the striker's INNING ends.

escape

(Snooker) A legal shot made by a player who is SNOOKERED. 1973 Spencer 101. That is, a shot in which the player "escapes" from the effects of the snooker. See also GET OUT.

European Billiard News

The official publication of the EUROPEAN POCKET BILLIARD FEDERATION. Address: A-5600 St. Johann, Hauptstrasse 53, Postfach 32, Austria. Chief editor: Ralf Teppan.

European Pocket Billiard Federation (EPBF)

(org.) The governing body of pocket billiards in Europe. It promulgates equipment specifications and sanctions tournaments. Its official publication is EUROPEAN BILLIARD NEWS.

European taper

= STRAIGHT TAPER. So called because it is used by European Three-Cushion players. Cf. DELAYED TAPER, PROFESSIONAL TAPER.

even up

1. As applied to a game, meaning that no HANDICAP has been given. 1979 Grissim 251. "They're playing even up." See also HEADS UP, LEVEL, UP. 2. Said of scores or players that become tied during a competition.

Everlasting Pool

(game, obs.) LIFE POOL in which there is no collective stake, or POOL, and players are free to enter or leave the game at any time. Each player has an unlimited number of LIVES and there is thus no STAR. When a player's ball is pocketed, he pays a forfeit to the striker and plays from BAULK at his next opportunity. The black ball is placed on the CENTRE SPOT. When the striker pockets any ball other than black, he may then play at black to receive the value of a life from each player. 1867 Dufton 222, 1916 HDB 74. Also called PERPETUAL POOL or SELLING POOL. Cf. BLACK POOL.

exhibition

A performance staged to demonstrate a player's skill, as opposed to a game held for competitive reasons. An exhibition may be a solo show or may be a game or MATCH involving opponents. Rules may be lax, but the essential feature of an exhibition that distinguishes it from private play or a PRACTICE GAME is that an exhibition is scheduled and announced in advance, so that the press and SPECTATORS may be present to verify any events that take place. Some outstanding billiards has been played at exhibition, whose format is particularly conducive to the breaking of high run records because a player need not halt play when GAME TOTAL is reached. See also UNFINISHED. Willie Hoppe's Three-Cushion run of 25 and Willie Mosconi's Pocket Billiard high run of 526 were both made in exhibition play.

Experts' Game

(game, obs.) A variation of carom billiards designed to suppress NURSING. See RED, WHITE, AND BLUE.

extended spider

(Brit. games) A type of REST. A SPIDER that has been modified so that the cue stick is supported several inches beyond the arch of the rest. See also SPAN REST, SWAN NECK.

extendible cue

A cue stick whose length can be altered during play to avoid the need for the mechanical bridge. One version is the TELESCOPING CUE. Another model has a piston-like apparatus inserted in the butt for adjusting the length continuously like a trombone.

extension

A handle that can be fitted easily over the BUTT of a cue stick to increase its effective length. 1988 Davis 11. This device is preferred by many players to the MECHANICAL BRIDGE because it allows the cue to be held and bridged in the normal fashion. Cf. EXTENDIBLE CUE, TELESCOPING CUE.

An extension may also be used with a REST, which is useful in Snooker because of the size of the table; such a need does not arise on 9-foot pocket tables. 1990 Taylor 113.

91

face

The area of the CUSHION against which the balls strike. 1873 Bennett 17. Originally, the face was flat and vertical like a wall; only later were beveled cushions introduced. See BANK, NOSE.

facing

= CUSHION FACING.

fair stroke

A STROKE made in accordance with the rules. 1974 Lindrum 139. It used to be the case in English Billiards that "All strokes made with the point of the cue are fair." 1836 Tillotson 5. This rule was expunged from the AMERICAN FOUR-BALL GAME in 1867 when the PUSH was BARRED. 1893 HRB 32. It is thus no longer true that all such strokes are fair. See, for example, JUMP SHOT, MOMENTARY CONTACT. Cf. FOUL, FOUL STROKE.

fall

1. The inner line of the pocket, where the slate terminates. 1873 Bennett 17. The curved edge of the bed of the table that forms the MOUTH of the pocket. 1978 BSCC 25, 1974 Lindrum 139. This boundary is called the "fall" because any ball whose center passes over it will fall into the pocket. See also NAIL, POCKET ANGLE, POCKET DROP. 2. To enter a pocket. 1913 Burrowes 5. "After what seemed like an eternity, the ball eventually fell." Also DROP.

fan

1. = FEATHER, to hit a ball very THIN. 1978 Byrne 202. Also CLIP, FINE BALL. 2. A devotee of the game, given to incessant viewing or playing.

fancy shot

A shot requiring props or unusual skill, played for audience satisfaction rather than the assurance of a score; a crowd-pleaser, a TRICK SHOT. 1857 Phelan 147, 1881 NYT (Jan 21) 2:5. See also ARTISTIC BILLIARDS, CIRCUS SHOT, GAFF SHOT, STROKE SHOT. Some sources distinguish fancy shots from trick shots, defining the latter to be shots in which illegal props or strokes are used.

In the 1920s and 30s, organized fancy shot competitions were held; Charles C. Peterson and Isidro Ribas (Spain) both claimed the (unofficial) world title. The format of fancy shot tournaments required each player to submit 50 shots, for a total of 100. Each player had to attempt all 100 shots. Making a shot on the first attempt was worth one point, on the second attempt, two, on the third, three, and on the fourth attempt, five. The player with the lower point total was the victor. 1932 BM (Feb) 8. Because the opponent would not see a player's submitted shots for the first time until the tournament, contestants would practice in secret for weeks before a match.

Fancy shot competition is popular in Korea, where top players maintain a grueling exhibition schedule and perform shots of even greater difficulty than those in the Artistic Billiards program.

Fantaisie Classique

(game) = ARTISTIC BILLIARDS (literally, "classical fancy"). This competitive form was developed by Charles Faroux and Louis Roig, who developed a set program of fancy carom shots to be performed by competitors. See also FANTASY BILLIARDS.

Fantasy Billiards

1. From the French *fantaisie*, meaning fancy or whimsical, mistranslated as "fantasy." TRICK SHOTS or FANCY SHOTS (coups de fantaisie), often involving extreme application of MASSÉ. 1880 Mangin 242. 2. (game) = ARTISTIC BILLIARDS. 1982 BD (Sep/Oct), 1987 Jewett.

fast

1. Lively or active, said of a table. 1839 Kentfield 24 (who uses "fast-running"), 1858 Mardon 402. Also applied to the cushions, balls or cloth. 1867 Dufton 16, 1913 Stoddard 8. 2. Said of a rapid shooter, one who spends little time in aiming or practice stroking. See also MACHINE GUN. 3. Impatient for ACTION; willing to play for high stakes. A quality of a HUSTLER, *e.g.*, the character "Fast Eddie" in 1959 Tevis. 4. Said of a TAPER that increases in diameter rapidly in progressing along the SHAFT from the TIP to the JOINT. 1983 NBN (Mar) 18. Cf. SLOW. 5. (obs.) = FROZEN. 1869 Roberts 273, 1884 MB 306, 1890 HRB 51, 1916 HDB 88. See also TOUCHING BALL.

fast taper

A TAPER in which the diameter of the shaft increases quickly in moving from the tip to the joint. Cf. SLOW TAPER.

feather

1. To hit a ball very THIN. 1924 Ogden 270, 1992 OR 9. Also CLIP, FAN, FEATHER STROKE. A few players are specialists at thin stroking; others try to avoid such shots as much as possible. Among Three-Cushion players, Abel Calderón has developed feather shots into an art form. 2. A tiny practice or warm-up stroke preparatory to shooting. 1973 Spencer 19, 1984 Williams 9. Touching the ball accidentally during preliminary stroking was not originally a FOUL. 1807 White 68. The rule is otherwise in 1836 Tillotson 6. See also FIDDLE, NUDGE, TOUCH, WAGGLE, WARM-UP.

feather strip

A strip of wood, square in cross-section, that is placed in a groove routed in the RAIL of a table just above the point at which the RUBBER is affixed and used to hold the RAIL CLOTH in place. The feather strip is covered by the cloth and is thus normally not visible.

feather stroke

1. A shot in which one ball just grazes another. See FEATHER. 2. (obs.) = QUILL STROKE. 1896 Broadfoot 370.

Fédération Française de Billard (FFB)

(org.) The French governing body of billiards.

Fédération Luxembourgeoise des Amateurs de Billard (FLAB)

(org.) The Luxembourg governing body of billiards, founded March 25, 1928.

Federation of Billard Players

(org.) Group headed by Willie Hoppe and formed to stimulate interest in BALKLINE. 1931 BM (Mar) 45.

felt

Cloth material erroneously believed to be used to cover billiard tables, hence, figuratively, the CLOTH itself. Occasionally expanded to mean the table or game of billiards. "He is a master of the felt." The usage is curious because billiard cloth contains no felt.

ferrule

The segment of a cue stick below the TIP, fastened to the SHAFT on a projection known as the TENON. The ferrule forms a flat base for attaching the tip and prevents the shaft from splintering. 1977 Martin 210. See diagram under CUE. In the U.S., cues intended for pocket games normally have long ferrules made of white material, formerly ivory. A fibrous material is sometimes used today. In the U.K., short brass ferrules are universal. See also CUE POINT. A ferrule at the JOINT of a cue is known as a COLLAR.

FFB

(org.) = FÉDÉRATION FRANCAISE DE BILLARD.

fiddle

= FEATHER, NUDGE, WAGGLE, WARM-UP. To move the cue stick back and forth in preparation for shooting. Edouard Horemans, a Belgian who became 18.2 Balkline champion of the world, abhorred the habit of fiddling and would not take practice strokes prior to shooting because he believed them to be detrimental. See also TOUCH.

field goal

(colloq.) A shot, particularly a carom BANK SHOT, in which the cue ball misses both object balls by passing between them. Unlike in football, no points are awarded for a field goal in billiards. Cf. AIR BALL.

Fifteen-Ball

(game) A SINGLE-RACK pocket billiard game derived from PYRAMID POOL and played with 15 object balls but in which the player pocketing a ball scores as many points as the numerical designation of the ball pocketed. In racking, the 15-ball is placed on the FOOT SPOT, with other high-numbered balls near the 15. The first player to score 61 points wins. 1850 Phelan 47. There is no requirement resembling that of ROTATION under which the first ball contacted must be the lowest-numbered ball on the table. 1859 Phelan, 1976 WSD 39. A TWO-BALL BREAK without CALL is utilized. Also called BALL POOL, FIFTEEN-BALL POOL, or SIXTY-ONE POOL, referring to the number of points needed for victory.

At present, the racking requirements in Fifteen-Ball are rather vague. Although the 15-ball must go on the foot spot, the rules state only that "the higher numbered balls are placed at the front of the rack near the 15-ball." Assuming that this means that the 10–14 are to go in rows two and three and that the remaining nine balls are placed in the last two rows, then the total number of possible arrangements is $5! \times 9! = 43,545,600$. If it means that no row can have any ball with a higher number than any in a preceding row, the number drops to $2! \times 3! \times 4! \times 5! = 34,560$.

The game was introduced at Bassford's room in New York, probably in the 1830s. 1925 BM (Jul). The first championship tournament was held in New York on April 20, 1878; Cyrille Dion beat Gotthard Wahlstrom in the BEST OF 21 games. In 1880, in order to discourage SAFETY PLAY, a rule was added requiring that the cue ball touch some object ball on each shot, and then an object ball must be pocketed or one of the balls must hit a cushion. In 1888, Fifteen-Ball gave way to CONTINUOUS POOL, in which the total number of balls pocketed, not the number of games won, determined the winner. In 1910, the BREAK BALL was suggested by Jerome Keogh, and modern Pocket Billiards was born. Fifteen-Ball is thus a direct ancestor of 14.1 CONTINUOUS.

Fifteen-Ball Continuous Pocket Billiards

(game, obs.) The forerunner of 14.1 CONTINUOUS POCKET BILLIARDS and the first game to utilize a BREAK BALL to allow a RUN to continue through a RACK. Also known as CONTINUOUS POCKETINGS. 1916 RGRG 30. Cf. CONTINUOUS POOL, FIFTEEN-BALL.

Fifteen-Ball Pool

(game) = FIFTEEN-BALL.

fifteen-point penalty

1. (Pocket Bill.) An extra PENALTY formerly assessed against a player for committing three consecutive SCRATCHES. The balls are re-racked and the player is compelled to play an opening BREAK SHOT. 1946 OR 45. The total number of points deducted is 18, three for the three scratches plus 15 for the added penalty. The present penalty is more severe. See CONSECUTIVE FOULS. The 15-point penalty still applies in Line-Up.

Why was the penalty 15 points? The penalty for three consecutive scratches in AMERICAN PYRAMID POOL was forfeiture to the opponent of all object balls remaining on the table. This was, of course, a maximum of 15. The penalty remained in Continuous Pool but was changed to the set value of 15 points in 1919. For a time during the 1920s, the penalty was imposed for just two consecutive fouls. In 1929 this was restored to three fouls. It was not unknown for a player to accumulate over 70 points in penalties in a game of 125 points.

2. Penalty for committing an INTENTIONAL FOUL in pocket billiard games. 1946 OR 49. The points are subtracted from the player's score and the incoming player may accept TABLE IN POSITION or, at his option, have the balls replaced at the locations they occupied prior to the foul. 1977 OR 64. The offender is not required to play a BREAK SHOT.

Fifteen Points

(game) = CRIBBAGE POCKET BILLIARDS, PAIR POOL. 1964 Cottingham 47. So called because a "cribbage" consists of a pair of object balls whose numbers total 15.

57.2 Balkline

(game) The scaled equivalent of 71.2 BALKLINE as played on a 2.5-meter table instead of a regulation 3.1-meter (10-foot) table. 1981 Rottie 135.

file

A tool used to shape and roughen the cue TIP so it will hold chalk more readily. The file was used to shape the wooden end of the cue and chalk was applied even before the tip was invented. 1807 White 28.

fine ball

A THIN hit, a grazing contact between two balls. 1839 Kentfield 8, 1884 Bohn 524. A CUT. 1850 Phelan 21. The expression "playing fine" is used in 1807 White 36, "fine cut" in 1907 Levi 269. See also CLIP, FAN, FEATHER.

finesse

(Eng. Bill.) SAFETY PLAY. 1904 Mannock 434. More generally, delicate play. Originally a term for a defensive play in the game of croquet. 1875 OED.

Finger Billiards

Billiards in which the cue ball is propelled by use of the hand instead of a cue stick. Also known as HAND BILLIARDS or hand-stroke billiards.

Although this form of play is something of a curiosity, the accomplishments of hand players have been prodigious. Extraordinary effects can be produced because much more English can be imparted to the ball with the fingers than with a cue. The reason for this is that the duration of contact between the hand and the ball is

much longer than the momentary impact produced by a cue stick. The only way to impart spin to a ball with a level cue is to push it forward at the same time.

Finger Billiards was practiced before the cue tip was invented, so it is likely that players were aware of the effects of extreme spin long before it was possible to duplicate them with the cue. 1807 White 156 warned readers of SHARPERS who offered to play with their fingers only. Pardon recalled "seeing a one-armed man in France who could *throw* the ball from his hand with such certainty as to be able to play the canon game against ordinary players who scored all the canons and hazards with the cue." 1856 Crawley 102.

It later became usual to permit the finger player to place his cue ball anywhere on the table before each shot. Under such a rule, the finger players rivaled the very best cue players at Straight-Rail and were able to achieve runs in the thousands. Napoleon, who had a billiard table even in exile on St. Helena, was said to be fond of playing by hand. President Grant once witnessed a hand exhibition by the British player John Roberts. 1908 Roberts. The phrase "finger billiards" appears in 1873 NYT (Oct 29) 12:5.

Finger play was popularized in England by the French player Adrien Izar. 1869 Roberts 222. He put on a program in New York with Cyrille Dion that even included a show of NOSE billiards. 1875 NYT (Sep 4). Jacob Schaefer Sr. was also a practitioner of the finger game, along with Yank Adams, A. P. Rudolphe and Hugo Kerkau, who was also known for his run of 7000 (with a cue) at the RAIL NURSE. 1878 NYT (Feb 8) 8:4, 1898 Thatcher 236. Adams could give any cue player 500 points in a thousand and win.

The apex of finger billiards was reached around 1900. R. De Kuyper specialized in fancy shots, and Three-Cushion champion Eugene Carter performed hand exhibitions with a special set of small balls he called "Carter's Little Liver Pills." 1992 BD (Oct) 90. His obituary in 1902 WB declared that "Carter could hold a company better than any billiard entertainer past or present."

In an amazing display of skill and determination, George H. ("Handless") Sutton was able to play "finger" shots even though he had lost both hands in an accident. He grasped the ball between the stumps of his arms and spun it wildly, often applying too much English in this manner.

Modern finger exponents have been Arthur Thurnblad, once world Three-Cushion champion; Isidro Ribas, a noted trick shot artist; Juan Navarra; Cue Ball Kelly; and Mike Massey. Using his fingers, Ribas could make a ball

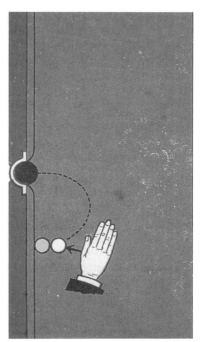

Finger Billiards

spin on a plate for over five minutes. 1935 NBJ (Mar) 24. See also FOOT BILLIARDS, NOSE. Cf. RONDO.

finger bridge
A BRIDGE made with the fingers of the hand, as opposed to the MECHANICAL BRIDGE. May be either a LOOP BRIDGE or a V-BRIDGE.

fingertip bridge
A BRIDGE used for shooting over balls in which the fingertips are placed nearly perpendicular to the table and the cue is supported with an outstretched thumb. 1979 Sullivan 47.

first object ball
(Bill.) The first ball CONTACTED by the cue ball. 1880 Garnier ix, 1913 Daly 43, 1941 Hoppe 74. See OBJECT BALL. Cf. CAROM BALL, SCORE BALL, SECOND OBJECT BALL.

fish
(sl.) A HUSTLER'S term for a MARK, PIGEON, or SUCKER; one who can be "caught" or "hooked." A victim who can be persuaded to bet money on billiard games and can be counted on to lose. An inferior player who is not alert to the fact that he is outclassed and who returns frequently for more beatings. 1967 Polsky 43, 105.

fishing rod
(Brit. games, colloq.) = LONG REST. 1915 Reece & Clifford 126.

Five Ahead
(game) A method of conducting a match at NINE-BALL, in which the first player to lead by five games wins. 1984 Mizerak. See AHEAD SESSION, FREEZE-OUT. Cf. RACE.

five-and-a-half system
(Three-Cushions) The most popular DIAMOND SYSTEM, used to calculate the path taken by a ball that is aimed at a long rail with medium force and RUNNING ENGLISH. The name comes from the method of numbering the diamonds used to measure cue ball position. The scheme assigns the number 1½ to the first diamond and adds ½ for each diamond down the rail, reaching the number 5 in the corner. The spot on which the white object ball is placed is at position 5½. Also known as the FIVE SYSTEM or CORNER FIVE.

Five and Ten
(game) BALKLINE game in which a player earns one point for a run of five, and two points for a run of ten, but no run greater than ten is allowed. 1944 NBJ (Mar). Not to be confused with NICKEL AND DIME.

five-inch line
(Bill.) An imaginary line located five inches from each rail and used as an aid for maintaining the balls in position for the RAIL NURSE. 1913 Daly.

Five-Pin Game, Five-Pin Pool
(game) = PIN POOL. So called because the game is played with five pins or SKITTLES—one white and four black. The white pin is placed on the CENTER SPOT, and each of the other four is placed one skittle length away. Three balls are used, with BURST at 31 and ROYAL. Also known as ITALIAN BILLIARDS.

five-point penalty
(14.1 Continuous, obs.) A PENALTY of up to five points assessed by the referee for ungentlemanly conduct or dilatory behavior. 1945 OR 46. See UNSPORTSMANLIKE CONDUCT. Cf. FIFTEEN-POINT PENALTY.

five-shot, five-stroke
(Eng. Bill., Amer. Four-Ball Game) A shot during which five points are scored by the striker. In English Billiards, this may be accomplished by a cannon that pots the red or by hitting the RED, making a CANNON and potting the striker's ball. In American Four-Ball, it can be made by pocketing a red and caroming on white or caroming on all three balls. 1850 Phelan 21.

five system
(Three-Cushions) The FIVE-AND-A-HALF SYSTEM, the most popular DIAMOND SYSTEM. Also CORNER FIVE.

95

FLAB

(org.) = FÉDÉRATION LUXEMBOURGEOISE DES AMATEURS DE BILLARD.

flat draw

Low English that widens the angle of rebound of the cue ball after contact with an OBJECT BALL. 1992 Billing 91.

flat joint

A cue JOINT that is formed by mounting a screw in the butt end, leaving exposed wood surrounding the screw so that wood meets wood when the cue is screwed together. 1992 Billing 6. Cf. PILOTED JOINT.

flight

A grouping for competitive purposes of players in a round of a TOURNAMENT, similar to a "heat" in a track event. The outcome of the flight results in the elimination of a group of players from the field. The remaining players progress to further rounds. Flights can be used for SEEDING purposes. If two highly ranked players are entered in the same tournament, a BLIND DRAW might cause them to meet each other in the first game. To prevent this, the players could be assigned to different flights, ensuring that they will not face off until later in the competition.

flite

= FLIGHT.

float

= DRIFT. 1991 Raftis 41.

floating white technique

(Eng. Bill.) A method for controlling the balls in TOP-OF-THE-TABLE play to achieve a position in which the RED can be POTTED and a CANNON on the white scored simultaneously for five points. The idea is to maneuver the OBJECT WHITE (whose position "floats" rather than remaining fixed) so that it remains near the billiard spot instead of being driven to the top cushion. Floating white is difficult to play but yields excellent results, because the red and white remain close together. 1991 Everton 41.

fluke

(Brit. games) A stroke made by a lucky accident, a SCRATCH. The term is said to have originated among whalers who, having missed the body of a whale with a harpoon, might catch it by a tail fluke. 1857 OED, 1873 NYT (Jun 26) 1:4, 1885 Cook 9. Also used as a verb, as in "He miscued and fluked the white." See CROW, GARBAGE SHOT, LUCK SLOP SHOT.

fly

A pernicious insect, seemingly given to disturbing billiard players who are in the act of shooting. In a match at the FOUR-BALL GAME between Louis Fox and John Deery played in Rochester, New York, on September 7, 1865, a fly kept landing on Fox's cue ball. Fox repeatedly shooed it away, but when he finally undertook to hit the ball, he miscued. Deery thereupon ran out the game to win 1500 to 1465. Fox, despondent, ran from the hall and apparently jumped into the nearby Genesee River and was drowned. His body was found frozen in the ice the following spring. 1883 NYT (Nov 25) 5:1, 1949 Coronet (Sep) 158-159. Billiard players have been bothered by flies ever since.

A source of much fly trouble was that many of them would be killed by soaring too close to the gas lamps illuminating the table and their carcasses would litter the cloth. H. W. Stevenson, the English Billiards player, played a match in Ceylon around 1900 in which the table had to be BRUSHED twice for this reason. 1928 Bill. Player (May).

Willie Hoppe related that in his match for the 18.2 Balkline championship against Ora Morningstar in 1906, he raised his cue no fewer than 18 times to shoot and a fly lighted on the ball each time. However, Hoppe, possibly mindful of the Fox disaster, eventually won the game, 500-207. 1925 Hoppe 106.

In the 1935 World Three-Cushion Tournament, Johnny Layton lost his last three games after becoming disconcerted when a fly landed on his cue ball. 1935 Newsweek (Nov 30) 22. He never again won the title.

follow

1. Spin, or ENGLISH, that causes the cue ball to roll forward after contact with an object ball. 1850 Phelan 21, 1881 MB 23, 1941 Hoppe 74. It is applied by striking the cue ball above its center. The term is used as a verb but not as a noun in 1807 White 84. Also called DIRECT ENGLISH, FOLLOWING STROKE, HIGH, or HIGH STROKE. 1976 WSD 161. Called "walking" in 1806 Phil, later CARRY-THROUGH in British usage. 2. (obs.) To have another chance to play after a successful shot. See FOLLOWING GAME.

follow on

(Eng. Bill.) = FOLLOW-THROUGH; the stroking of the cue stick through the position occupied by the cue ball. 1895 Buchanan 29.

follow shot

Shot in which HIGH, or FOLLOW, is used, causing the cue ball to "follow" the first object ball after contacting it. 1875 NYT (Nov 17) 5:3, 1992 OR 9. Cf. DRAW SHOT.

follow-through

1. A continuous stroke of the cue stick through the position occupied by the cue ball to impart speed or ENGLISH, as opposed to checking or jerking the cue back after striking the cue ball. 1913 Daly 28, 1992 OR 9. Follow-through is important because stopping the cue tip soon after contacting the cue ball requires the player to begin decelerating the cue earlier, creating a punchy hit in which it is difficult to aim the shot accurately. A follow-through is also indispensable in imparting EN-GLISH. Cf. NIP. 2. (Eng. Bill.) = FOLLOW ON.

following ball

(Eng. Bill.) A cue ball that follows the object ball into the same pocket for a LOSING HAZARD after a WINNING HAZARD. 1866 Crawley 83. See DOUBLE HAZARD.

following canon

(Eng. Bill.) A carom made by a FOLLOW SHOT. 1889 Drayson 29.

following game

Any billiard game in which the striker is permitted to shoot again after making a successful shot. That is, the player may "follow" himself after scoring. In the original FRENCH CANNON GAME, players alternated strokes regardless of whether points were scored on a given shot and thus were allowed exactly one shot per INNING. 1807 White 124, 1845 Hoyle 228. See also ONE AND STOP.

Following Pool

(game, obs.) = LIFE POOL. 1919 Hoyle 639. Also called COLOR-BALL POOL, ENGLISH POOL, LAST PLAYER, LIVE POOL or just POOL. The name does not relate in any way to a FOLLOWING GAME, but reflects the fact that the players in the pool follow one another in a prescribed order based on the color of each player's ball. The game has been known to accommodate 13 participants at one time.

following stroke

(Eng. Bill.) = HIGH STROKE with FOLLOW-THROUGH, that is, FOLLOW. 1836 Tillotson, 1862 Crawley 19, 1885c Cook 9. Also called DIRECT ENGLISH or HIGH.

foot

1. = FOOT OF TABLE. Confusingly, this is the same as the TOP of an English Billiards table. The use of the term dates to about 1875. See compounds based on "foot," such as FOOT RAIL and FOOT SPOT. 2. A support component on which the table (particularly the PEDES-TAL) rests. On modern tables, a foot is held by a machine bolt, which can be rotated for leveling.

foot billiards

Billiards in which the cue stick is held and manipulated with the feet. This style was practiced with considerable skill by disabled soldiers who would lie on hospital gurneys for this purpose. The toes of one foot are used as a BRIDGE and the cue is grasped with the other foot. The usual FOOT ON FLOOR rule is waived in this game. Cf. HAND BILLIARDS.

foot of table

That end of the table opposite the HEAD; the end not marked by the MANUFACTURER'S NAMEPLATE. In POCKET BILLIARDS, object balls are RACKED at this end. 1875 NYT (Nov 19) 5:4, 1881 MB 24, 1977 Martin 210. Sometimes just FOOT. It is important to distinguish between the head and the foot on tables whose cloths have a NAP, which induces a preferred direction on which the player must be able to rely. On napless cloth, the distinction is arbitrary.

foot on floor

Rule specifying that at least one of the striker's feet must be touching the floor at the moment he strikes the cue ball. 1978 BSCC 26. This requirement is universal in billiard games except in very informal settings and has been so since at least 1674 Cotton: "He that sets not one foot upon the ground when he strikes his Ball shall lose an END." Failure to do so is a foul. The rule is so old that its origin is unknown. However, during the seventeenth century tables were of very flimsy construction, and it is likely that a player who climbed upon one would destroy it. The rule may therefore have been an attempt to preserve the equipment. For another rule of this type, see CLOTH.

In an early version of the rules for the THREE-BALL GAME, a player who had ball IN HAND was required to keep his entire body, including his feet, between the two end corners of the table. 1859 Phelan 195. Normal foot attire is required. It is a violation of the rules to play while wearing shoes that would permit one to circumvent the requirement. 1992 OR 37.

foot pocket

A pocket at the FOOT of the table. In British usage, a TOP POCKET. Cf. HEAD POCKET. In One-Pocket, no ball is credited to either player unless it enters a foot pocket. In professional Straight Pool, more than 90% of the object balls are pocketed in the foot pockets. Occasionally, runs of over 100 are seen in which only the foot pockets are used.

foot rail

The SHORT RAIL at the FOOT of a billiard table that is not marked with the MANUFACTURER'S NAMEPLATE. 1875

NYT (Nov 19) 8:3, 1946 OR 95. See also FOOT OF TABLE. Cf. HEAD RAIL.

foot spot

The SPOT midway between the foot cushion and the CENTER SPOT, where the APEX BALL of the TRIANGLE is racked in pocket billiard games and where illegally pocketed balls are spotted. 1976 WSD 164. Use of this term began about 1875. In carom games, the red ball is spotted on the foot spot. See diagram under SPOT. Also called the DARK-RED SPOT, PINK SPOT, PYRAMID SPOT, RED SPOT (Bill.), or WINNING SPOT. Cf. HEAD SPOT.

foot string

An imaginary line perpendicular to and connecting the SIDE RAILS, passing through the FOOT SPOT. 1946 OR 5, 1992 OR 42. Although the foot string is carefully drawn in table diagrams illustrating the rules of billiards, the author has not found a single use for the foot string in any game.

Football Pool

(game) A pocket game played on a special table with six pockets, three along each SHORT RAIL. Each player uses a team of eleven objects (six object balls and five fixed obstacles) in a confrontation that resembles a game of football, with similar scoring based on touchdowns, field goals, and safeties. Invented by Lawrence A. McKenzie of Jacksonville, Florida.

football shot

(pocket games) A type of TRICK SHOT in which balls are lined up so as to obstruct a pocket but so that hitting one

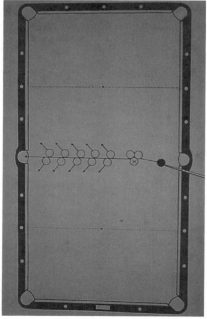

football shot

of them will knock the others out of the way to allow a ball to be pocketed. So called because the effect resembles offensive line blocking in football.

for the time

A method used by two or more players to determine who will pay for TABLE TIME in a public billiard room, indicating that the loser will pay the check. 1967 Polsky 37. "Let's play for the time." In this manner, good players can play for free without being required to HUSTLE. In 1917, J. Clinton Ransom reported that "the time-honored custom of the loser paying for the use of the table is gradually going out of fashion." 1992 BD (Feb) 4. Cf. SPLIT THE TIME.

force

1. The amount of strength with which a STROKE is played. 2. An adjective meaning "hard" in the sense of "forceful" in all following definitions beginning with "force." It is used particularly when the cue ball lies close to the object ball and a hard stroke is required to achieve the required ACTION. In British usage, a FORCER. 3. (obs.) A shot in which the cue ball retrogrades after contact with the object ball; a DRAW SHOT. 1850 Phelan 20, 1881 MB 23, 1976 WSD 164.

force draw

Powerful DRAW, usually used when the cue ball is close to the object ball, appearing (incorrectly) to drive the cue ball through the position formerly occupied by the object ball before the cue ball begins to move backwards. 1946 OR 91. "Forced draw" is found in 1977 Martin 211, but this usage is only rarely encountered.

force follow

Powerful FOLLOW, usually when the cue ball is close to the object ball, and by which the player drives the cue ball through the position formerly occupied by the object ball. 1881 NYT (Nov 25) 5:1, 1992 OR 9. "Forced follow," for example in 1977 Martin 211, is an uncommon variation. See also COUP FOUETTÉ, MASSÉ COULÉ. *See illustration on next page.*

force massé

Powerful MASSÉ.

forced off

(Brit.) Said of a ball that has become a JUMP BALL, the latter being an American expression. 1987 BSCC S12, 1988 WPBSA. Also LOST.

forcer

(Eng. Bill., colloq.) A stroke in which the cue ball is hit very hard. 1908c Cook Jr. 39. A FORCE shot or FORCING SHOT. Also TRAVELER.

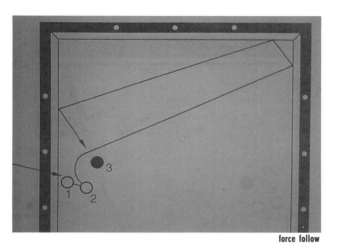

force follow

forcing hazard
(Eng. Bill.) A LOSING HAZARD made by a FORCING SHOT. 1885c Cook 9.

forcing shot
(Eng. Bill.) Shot in which the natural rebound angle of the cue ball from the first object ball is altered by striking the cue ball very hard. 1910a Ritchie 116. A FORCE shot or FORCER.

forewrap
That portion of the BUTT of a cue stick lying between the WRAP and the JOINT. 1983 NBN (Mar) 18.

forfeit
1. To have points subtracted from one's score or added to the opponent's score as a penalty for a FOUL. 1976 WSD 165. 2. To lose the game by failure to continue or comply with the rules. A player who refuses to play loses the game. 1807 White 72. A player who makes one stroke in a game must finish that game, or consent to lose it. 1866 Crawley 133. A player may have his game forfeited by the referee if he leaves the playing area without the referee's permission, for persistent UNFAIR CONDUCT, or for refusal to play. After five minutes of such refusal, the REFEREE must call a forfeit. See DELAY. No forfeit can be called for SPECTATOR behavior. 1916 RGRG 12. A forfeit is a DISQUALIFICATION. The disqualified player receives no score and none of his statistics are be recorded or credited. A player whose opponent forfeits is eligible for any prize for HIGH RUN or other accomplishment, and he is treated as the victor for all purposes. See also LOSS OF GAME. Depending on the circumstances, a player on whom a forfeit is imposed for rule violations may be subject to SUSPENSION. Sometimes a forfeit is also called a DEFAULT.

Forfeits have played a significant role in determining championships. George Sutton won the World 18.1 Balkline title on three separate occasions without playing a single game. On one of them, Willie Hoppe forfeited to him and lost a $250 stake. At the World Pocket Billiard Tournament in 1933, the referee called a forfeit on Ralph Greenleaf in his game against Jimmy Caras when he continued to insist that Caras had touched the cue ball with his hand during a shot. Prior to this tournament, Greenleaf had not lost a championship game in three years.

3. (obs.) A money STAKE posted in advance of a match, which a player will lose if he fails to compete. See CHALLENGE.

fornicator
(obs.) A term used in seventeenth-century billiard games. One whose ball has passed through the back of the PORT and is thus obliged by the rules to pass twice through the fore part. 1674 Cotton 31. This word implies no obscenity; it is derived from the Latin *fornix*, meaning "arch." Thus a fornicator is one whose ball has gone through the ARCH.

fort
(obs.) A structure used in FORTIFICATION BILLIARDS resembling a military fort and through which a ball must pass in order to effect a score. 1807 White 160, 1974 Hendricks 26. See BELL.

Fortification Billiards
(game, obs.) An early billiard game having a military flavor and played on a table furnished with FORTS, batteries, and a PASS through which balls attacking a fort must travel. There are two sides, known as the English quarter and the French quarter. The object is to take forts by causing one's ball to enter the fort and ring a small BELL. The game was listed in 1779 Hoyle and remained popular until the 1820s. It was totally obsolete by 1850. 1807 White 57, 1974 Hendricks 26.

Forty-Five
(game, obs.) A game similar to COWBOY POOL, but only half as long. It is played to 51 points, as opposed to 101 in Cowboy. The first 45 may be made in arbitrary fashion, the next five must be by caroms alone, and the final point is earned by a LOSING HAZARD off the one-ball. 1913 Burrowes 12.

45.1 Balkline
(game, obs.) The metric (centimeter) equivalent of 18.1 BALKLINE. Supplanted in Europe in 1958 by 47.1 BALKLINE. 1983 Malsert 99. Cf. 45.2 BALKLINE.

45.2 Balkline

(game, obs.) The metric (centimeter) equivalent of 18.2 BALKLINE. Supplanted in Europe in 1958 by 47.2 BALKLINE. The record high run was 1214 by Roger Conti. 1983 Malsert 99. Cf. 45.1 BALKLINE.

Forty-One Pocket Billiards

(game) Pocket billiard game played with a SHAKE BOTTLE and PILLS numbered 1 through 15 or, in some variations, 6 through 18. Each inning consists of a single shot. A player wins when his score, when added to the number on the pill he has chosen by lot, equals 41 exactly. If his score plus the pill number ever exceeds 41, he has BURST, his score is reset to zero, all the balls he has pocketed are spotted, and he chooses a new pill. Missing all the balls or pocketing the white is a SCRATCH and the striker owes a ball to the table, meaning that his next successful shot will not count and the ball pocketed will be spotted. If all the balls become pocketed, the player whose score is closest to 41 is the winner. 1890 HRB 87, 1916 RGRG 68, 1973 Mizerak 64.

47.1 Balkline

(game) Metric Balkline, ONE SHOT IN, in which the three BALK SPACES at the END RAILS are equal in width at 47.416 centimeters. WBA 10. Cf. 45.1 BALKLINE, in which the middle balk space at each end rail is slightly wider than the corner spaces. 45.1 was supplanted by 47.1 in 1958. Roger Conti's high run at 47.1 was 416. 1983 Malsert 100. Cf. 47.2 BALKLINE.

47.2 Balkline

(game) Metric Balkline, TWO SHOTS IN, in which the three BALK SPACES at the END RAILS are equal in width at 47.416 centimeters. WBA 10. Cf. 45.2 BALKLINE, in which the middle balk space at each end rail is slightly wider than the corner spaces. The change from 45.2 dates from 1958. Cf. 47.1 BALKLINE, 42.2 BALKLINE. *See illustration in next column.*

42.2 Balkline

(game) The scaled equivalent of 47.2 BALKLINE as played on a 2.8-meter (9-foot) table instead of a regulation 3.1-meter (10-foot) table. 1983 Malsert 105.

foul

An infraction of the rules. 1807 White 67, 1850 Phelan 21, 1941 Hoppe 75. A stroke made in violation of the rules. 1881 MB 24, 1896 Broadfoot 105, 1976 WSD 168. This last definition is not strictly correct, however, since it is not necessary to make a stroke in order to foul.

The penalty for a foul may include termination of the striker's INNING, a forfeiture of points, addition of points to the opponent's score, or more severe sanctions. See

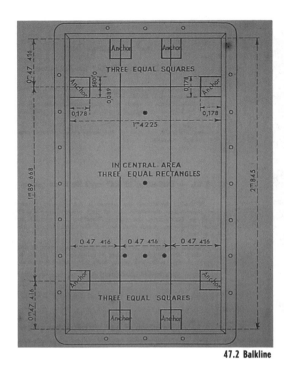

47.2 Balkline

DISQUALIFICATION, FORFEIT, and PENALTY. In general, only a single foul is assessed against a player for multiple infractions at one time, usually the one for which the penalty is most severe. 1986 OR 44.

Several acts have constituted fouls since printed rules appeared in 1674. Among these are shooting with both feet off the ground, sinking one's own ball, striking a ball while any ball is moving or hitting the cue ball twice. Originally, touching a ball unintentionally was not a foul. 1807 White 68. Some very specific transgressions have appeared in lists of rules at various times, including allowing pipe ash to drop on the cloth, blowing on the balls, practicing the lag, or placing marks on the cloth or cushions to assist in aiming.

Occasionally a player will call a foul on himself, sometimes when he is the only one aware of the infraction. A notable incident occurred during the International 18.2 Championship in New York in April 1906 when the French player Louis Cure, playing against Jacob Schaefer Sr., sat down on his own after a brief run of 11, mystifying the gallery. When it was explained to the audience that he had called his own foul, the audience gave him a deafening cheer for his SPORTSMANSHIP. Cure went on to win the game, 500 to 380. 1906 NYT (Apr 17) 10:3.

See also BALL IN HAND, CONSECUTIVE FOULS, CUE STICK (relating to length), DELIBERATE FOUL, FIFTEEN-POINT PENALTY, FORFEIT, FREE BALL, INTENTIONAL FOUL, INTERFERENCE, LAG, LOSS OF GAME, MOTION, NUDGE, ON A FOUL, PENALTY, PENALTY POINTS, PLAYER RESPON-

SIBILITY FOUL, REFEREE, SAFETY ALLOWED, SCRATCH, SERIOUS FOUL, SETTLING, SHOOT OUT, STANDARD FOUL.

foul stroke

A stroke during which a FOUL is committed. 1807 White 67. Normally no points can be scored on a foul stroke—the player's inning terminates and a penalty is incurred. Cf. FAIR STROKE.

Four-Ball Caroms

(game) A carom game played with four balls: the DEEP RED on the FOOT SPOT, the LIGHT RED on the STRING SPOT, and two white balls IN HAND. A carom on two balls counts one point; a carom on all three balls counts two. 1898 HRB 42, 1916 RGRG 14. The game was popular during the period 1825–80. Sometimes known as the AMERICAN GAME. 1862 Crawley 126. It is basically the AMERICAN FOUR-BALL GAME played on a carom table. Modern four-ball styles exist. 1992 OR 107. See also YOTSUDAMA, the Japanese word for "four balls."

Four-Ball Game

(game, obs.) = AMERICAN FOUR-BALL GAME, REVOLUTION GAME. 1845 Hoyle 221, 1974 Hendricks 26. In 1839 Kentfield 46, the game is played 31 UP with one red, one blue and two white balls. In other sources, the game is played with two red balls.

Four Game

(game, Brit.) A style of play at various English games involving two teams of two players each, whose members alternate strokes after each WINNING HAZARD. 1775 Annals 96, 1807 White 56. Also called a FOUR MATCH. The idea of allowing four players to participate is mentioned in 1674 Cotton 32, which cites a penalty for striking out of turn. Also FOUR-HANDED GAME.

four-handed game

A game with special rules permitting four players to participate. 1869 Kavanagh 9. The first four-handed match on record in the U.K. pitted John Roberts Sr. and William Dufton against Hughes and Joseph Bennett in 1866. 1934 Burwat (Jan) 133. A public four-handed stake match was held in Chicago in 1872. 1872 NYT (Mar 27) 1:1. Cf. FOUR GAME.

Four-Handed Snooker

(Snooker) Snooker with four participants, divided into two sides of two players each. The players strike alternately, subject to special rules in case of ties. 1987 BSCC S21.

Four Match

= FOUR GAME.

four-on-two

(Three-Cushions) A shot in which the cue ball makes four rail contacts on only two different cushions. A compulsory shot in ARTISTIC BILLIARDS. See also DOUBLE-THE-CORNER. Cf. THREE-ON-TWO.

Four Pockets

(pocket games) A practice game in which object balls may not be pocketed in the two HEAD POCKETS, but must be sunk in either the foot or side pockets. Played with five to fifteen object balls, depending on the skill of the player. Each ball pocketed counts for one point, but the player receives a bonus of five points for running all balls. Five more points are earned for making the cue ball pass through the rack area on the last shot of the rack.

four-shot, four-stroke

(Eng. Bill., Amer. Four-Ball Bill.) A shot during which the striker scores four points. In English Billiards, this may be done by pocketing both white balls without a CANNON or by hitting the WHITE, making a cannon, and potting a white. 1890 HRB 110. In American Four-Ball, it is made by pocketing the white and caroming onto a red. 1850 Phelan 22.

14.1 Balkline

(game) A variety of BALKLINE in which the lines are drawn 14 inches from each rail and when both balls are in the same BALK SPACE the player must drive at least one of them out on his first shot, *i.e.*, he has ONE SHOT IN. Cf. 14.2 BALKLINE.

In 1907, long after 14.2, 18.1, and 18.2 BALKLINE had been introduced for professional competition, 14.1 Balkline was suggested as a compromise between the difficult game of 18.1 and the comparatively easy game of 18.2. Championships at this style began in 1914. The world title was held by continuously by Willie Hoppe until 1944, after which no further tournaments were held. The high run is 303 by Willie Hoppe in 1914.

There is absolutely no connection between 14.1 Balkline and 14.1 CONTINUOUS. Even the numerical designations "14.1" have different meanings in these two games.

14.1 Continuous, 14.1 Continuous Pocket Billiards

(game) = STRAIGHT POOL. A CALL-SHOT GAME of Pocket Billiards that facilitates continuous scoring. When only one object ball is left on the table, the remaining 14 are RACKED and the player may continue by sinking the last ball (known as the BREAK BALL) and BREAKING the racked balls. The 14.1 TRIANGLE is arranged with the one-ball at the right rear, the five-ball at the left rear and the others at random. 1925 RGRG 28, 1982 OR 66. (See RACK.) It is also known as 14.1 RACK, STRAIGHTS, POCKETS, RACK POOL, or, ambiguously, just POOL. The game is almost always begun with a SAFETY BREAK. Cf. BASIC POCKET BILLIARDS, which is a SINGLE-RACK game.

The number of different initial racking arrangements is 13! = 6,227,020,800. Two of the balls are in fixed positions; the remaining 13 may be placed arbitrarily.

14.1 Continuous is an offspring of CONTINUOUS POOL, a style introduced in 1888 but without a break ball. The player sinking the last ball of each FRAME was entitled to strike at a full triangle to commence the next one. Because of the risk of failing to pocket a ball on such a shot, safety play became commonplace, which reduced the length of RUNS and slowed the game down. In 1910, Jerome Keogh, the Continuous Pool champion, suggested the expedient of leaving the last ball free to be used to break the others. He referred to this idea as the OPEN BREAK. 1910 NYT (Oct. 26) 6:5. The first competition at "Continuous Pool with One Ball Free" was held on November 6, 1911, Alfredo De Oro winning. 1911 NYT (Nov 11) 11:6. Of the free ball format, the *New York Times* reported, "This warrants any amount of manoeuvring for position on the last ball, which provided a decidedly interesting factor in the game." In 1912, the name of the game was changed to Pocket Billiards and it was adopted as the official tournament game, replacing Continuous Pool. The designation "14.1," meaning "14 racked, one ball free," began to be used in the mid-1920s. 1988 BM (Jun) 26. The use of the word "continuous" in this context does *not* refer to the ability of the player to continue a run through more than one rack—it means only that the player's score is cumulative throughout the game and is not reset to zero after each rack, as it was in FIFTEEN-BALL POOL.

The HIGH RUN at 14.1 Continuous is usually accepted as 526 by Willie Mosconi in EXHIBITION at the East High Billiard Club in Springfield, Ohio, in 1954, breaking his previous record of 365. He also holds the two prior records of 355 and 322. There are inconsistent accounts crediting Mike Eufemia with a run of 625 balls at the Logan Billiard Academy in Brooklyn, New York, on February 2, 1960. On several occasions in tournament competition, a player has run out 150 points in the first inning; the most recent such run occurred at the 1992 U.S. Open in New York in August 1992, when Mike Sigel accomplished the feat against Mike Zuglan and eventually won the tournament. The tournament high run is 182 by Joe Procita in 1954 versus Mosconi on a 10-foot table. (The record for 125-point games is 127.) See also MARGIN. The only player ever to hold the

World Junior, World Amateur and World Professional titles is Arthur Cranfield. Former world champions include Joe Balsis, Jimmy Caras, Irving Crane, Alfredo De Oro, Ralph Greenleaf, Luther Lassiter, Andrew Ponzi, Erwin Rudolph, and Ralph Taberski. From 1917 to 1956, only eight different people held the world title, even though it was contested on 69 occasions.

14.1 is regarded by many players as the purest form of pocket billiards. It requires intense concentration, superb position play, defensive maneuvering, and all-around shot-making ability. Luck is virtually no factor in the game. Despite the wide popularity of Nine-Ball, Straight Pool tournaments continue to be held regularly. American players dominate world 14.1 play; the only foreigner ever to win the U.S. Open tournament was Oliver Ortmann in 1989. Top U.S. players include Allen Hopkins, Ray Martin, Steve Mizerak, Jim Rempe, Mike Sigel, Nick Varner and Dallas West. The American women's field is headed by Jean Balukas, Loree Jon Jones, and Ewa Mataya.

The number of different possible initial racks in 14.1 Continuous is 13! = 6,227,020,800.

14.1 Rack

(game) = CONTINUOUS, 14.1 CONTINUOUS, RACK POOL, STRAIGHT POOL, STRAIGHTS. 1934 Storer 78.

14.2 Balkline

(game) Variety of BALKLINE in which the lines are drawn 14 inches from each rail and when both balls are in the same BALK SPACE the player must drive at least one of them out by his second shot, *i.e.*, he has TWO SHOTS IN. After a brief experiment with 12-inch lines in 1884, a tournament at 14.2 was held in April 1885. George Slosson won with a high run of 148 and an AVERAGE exceeding 18. Cf. 14.1 BALKLINE. Why was 14 inches chosen? It's the distance between adjacent diamonds on a 5 × 10-foot table.

It is curious that 14.1 BALKLINE was not played until 1914, almost 20 years after 18.1 BALKLINE was introduced. The first TELEGRAPHIC BILLIARDS match was at 14.2 Balkline.

frame

1. (Snooker) A unit of play, during which all the balls are pocketed or one player has secured a win. 1954 KTG 24, 1957 Holt 140, 1976 WSD 171. A frame ends when (1) a player or team has conceded; (2) the last black has been potted or fouled, except when this results in a tie; or (3) when a player or team has been disqualified. 1987 Hales 64. See also WANTING A SNOOKER. The term "frame" is thought to derive from the triangular frame used to rack the balls. 1990 Taylor 113. (See def. 3,

below.) See also CONCESSION. 2. One RACK of balls in POCKET BILLIARDS. 1888 NYT (Dec 13) 2:7. 3. (Pocket Bill.) The TRIANGLE that is used to RACK the balls. 1850 Phelan 47, 1990 Taylor 113. 4. That part of the table that supports the slate bed. (See diagram under TABLE.) 5. (rare) An INNING; a player's turn at the table.

free

= OPEN. A ball is free if it can be contacted directly by the cue ball. See also FREE BALL, OBSTRUCTION.

free ball

1. (Snooker) An arbitrary ball NOMINATED in place of the BALL ON by an INCOMING PLAYER who has been SNOOKERED as a result of his opponent's FOUL stroke. 1927 Clifford, 1954 KTG 31, 1975a Lowe 109. Also NOMINATED BALL, OBSTRUCTION. The purpose of the rule, adopted in 1919, is to prevent a player from profiting by his own FOUL. However, the incoming player may not himself lay a snooker with the nominated ball (unless only pink and black remain on the table); to do so would be to make the opponent pay twice for his foul. 1936 Davis 87, 1990 Taylor 114. If a RED is nominated as a COLOUR and potted, it is replaced, which is an exception to the general rule that reds are never spotted. Cf. LIFT, PLAY AGAIN RULE, TAKE UP. Also, the referee's call when the incoming player is SNOOKERED as the result of a foul stroke. 1992 OR 95.

Through the use of a free ball, it is theoretically possible to score 16 points on a single stroke at Snooker. The striker, ON reds, NOMINATES a color as a red and pots it along with all 15 reds!

2. (game) = OPTIONAL CUE BALL. 1923 BM (Jul).

3. (Bill., obs.) The object ball that remains a short distance from the rail in playing the ANCHOR NURSE. The other ball is FROZEN and hence not "free."

4. (Volunteer Snooker, obs.) A BALL ON, which the striker may attempt to pot, without forfeit if he misses. Distinguished from a ball VOLUNTEERED out of turn, or PENALTY BALL, which if not pocketed results in a foul. 1978 BSCC 62.

5. (14.1 Continuous, obs.) The original name given to the BREAK BALL by its inventor, Jerome Keogh, in 1910. 1911 NYT (Nov 7) 11:6.

free break

(Pocket Bill.) An OPENING BREAK in which it is prudent and desirable to achieve a wide spreading of the balls (instead of playing a SAFETY) in the hope of sinking one or more balls or leaving a difficult position for the INCOMING PLAYER. Any balls pocketed either count or are respotted and the player continues shooting, de-

pending on the game being played. There is no requirement that any minimum number of balls must contact cushions. Examples of games using a free break are BOWLLIARDS and EQUAL OFFENSE. 1982 OR 16. Cf. BREAK, CLOSED BREAK, OPEN BREAK, SAFETY BREAK.

Free Game

(game) = STRAIGHT-RAIL. This style is said to be "free" because there are no balk spaces, required cushion contacts, or other restrictions. This term is more commonly seen in translation, such as the French *partie libre* and German *freie Partie*.

free-hand massé

A MASSÉ stroke in which the bridge hand does not rest on the table bed but is held free or braced against the player's body. Also known as a GRAND MASSÉ. 1914 Taylor 17, 1925 Hoppe 244. See also MASSÉ BRIDGE. Cf. PETIT MASSÉ. *See illustration on next page.*

free play

The use of a table without charge. See TABLE TIME. A common problem for billiard room management is to prevent employees from allowing friends to play for free. Sometimes good players, instructors or other desired visitors (such as the chief of police or clergymen) are encouraged to patronize a room by being granted free play.

free stroke

A player is in "free stroke" when he is shooting smoothly and accurately. 1977 Martin 211. See also DEAD STROKE.

free table

(Eng. Eight-Ball Pool) = OPEN TABLE, in the sense of American EIGHT-BALL. 1988 Morrison & Smith 31.

freeze

(Bill.) A situation in which two or more balls come to rest in contact with one another. 1875 NYT (Nov 16) 8:3, 1916 RGRG 7, 1922 BM (May) 21. Used rarely when a ball and a cushion are in contact. See FAST, FROZEN, KISSING, TOUCHING BALL.

freeze-out

(colloq.) An AHEAD SESSION; a match in which a player wins the entire stake when he achieves a lead over his opponent of a predetermined number of games. 1938 NBJ (Mar), 1959 Tevis 111. For example, a player wins a "10-game freeze-out" the first time he has won 10 more games than his adversary, which may occur at a score of 10–0, 15–5, 23–13, etc.

free-hand massé 1 (engraving)

free-hand massé 2 (Hoppe)

French Billiards

A generic term applied to a collection of games originating or currently popular in France.

1. = CAROM BILLIARDS, FRENCH CAROMS, STRAIGHT-RAIL. 1976 WSD 40, WBA. Sometimes played on a table having pockets, but in which case only caroms count. 2. (game, obs.) Caroms and WINNING HAZARDS played on an English Billiards table. Played prior to 1734 only with MACES and balls, with no PORT or KING. In a version fashionable in France, hazards counted against the player and scoring was by DOUBLET CANNONS. 1856 Crawley 100, 1862 Crawley 122, 1974 Hendricks 26.

French Cannon Game, French Carom Game

(game, obs.) Played with two white balls and a red on an ENGLISH TABLE. HAZARDS cause forfeitures in complicated ways. 1857 Phelan 191. In France, it was played without pockets. 1866 Crawley 215. Cf. FRENCH CAROMS, played on a table with no pockets.

French Caroms

(game, obs.) = CAROM BILLIARDS, STRAIGHT-RAIL. Billiards on a pocketless table. Cf. FRENCH CANNON

GAME, in which a pocket table is often used. So called because the game became popular in France around 1850.

French Corner Game

(game) = CORNER GAME.

French Following Game

(game) A slight variation on ENGLISH BILLIARDS. The name is intended to distinguish the game from French styles in which a player was allowed only one stroke at each turn of play, regardless of whether he scored or not. 1845 Hoyle 228. See FOLLOWING GAME.

French Game

1. (game) = FRENCH BILLIARDS, FRENCH CAROMS, STRAIGHT-RAIL. Billiards played on a CAROM TABLE. 1856 Crawley 100. 2. (game, obs.) The three-ball WINNING GAME in which a player having BALL IN HAND is not confined to the BAULK SEMICIRCLE, but may play from anywhere within baulk. 1839 Kentfield 45, 1862 Crawley 122, 1865 Phelan 191. The FRENCH WINNING GAME. 3. (game, obs.) The DOUBLET GAME. 1857 Phelan 188. 4. (Bagatelle game, obs.) Played 100 or 101

UP. The red ball is placed on the spot. The player strikes with the other colored ball and plays until he fails to hole a ball or game score is reached. 1878 Crawley 153.

French Pocket Billiards
(game, rare) = ROTATION. 1927 Katch 55.

French stroke
(obs.) = MASSÉ. 1867 Dufton 28. Known by this name undoubtedly because the French originated and popularized this technique.

French terms
The French language has spawned many billiard terms either now used in English or for which there is no English synonym. See À CHEVAL, À LA GUERRE, BAGATELLE, BILLARD, BOUCHON POOL, BRICOLE, BRIDGE BOUCLÉE, CADRE, CASIN, COCHONNET, COUP, COUP FOUETTÉ, COUP SEC, DEDANS, ENTRÉ, LA PÉTANQUE, LE PRÉSIDENT, MASSÉ, MASSÉ COULÉ, MASSÉ DÉTACHÉ, PASSE, PIQUÉ, PLON-PON, QUEUE, RENCONTRÉ, RENTRÉ, RESTÉ DEDANS, ROUGE, SANS ÉGAL, SÉRIE AMÉRICAINE.

French tip
Cue TIPS from France have long been reputed to be of the best quality. The tip itself was invented in France prior to 1818. French tips were first sold in England by Thurston's in 1838. 1974 Hendricks 36. They were recommended in 1866 Crawley 8 and are still manufactured and sought today. The French firm of Chandivert carries on the tradition.

French Winning Game
(game, obs.) A game of WINNING HAZARDS in which a ball IN HAND may be placed anywhere behind the BAULK-LINE and is not confined to the SEMICIRCLE. When playing from hand, neither foot can be placed beyond the limits of the table. (See FOOT ON FLOOR.) The NONSTRIKER'S ball at start is on the WINNING SPOT, not the UPPER SPOT. Two points are scored for a WINNING HAZARD, two are forfeited for a LOSING HAZARD or COUP and one point is lost for a MISS. 1866 Crawley 214. Sometimes known as just the FRENCH GAME.

fringe
Decorative material used as an exterior border adornment for billiard table POCKETS. 1908 Brunswick 79. Sometimes known as "pocket fringe." Fringe is also used to decorate billiard table lamps.

front
The SHAFT of a cue stick. 1983 NBN (Mar) 18.

Front to Back
(Game) A difficult form of One-Pocket in which each player is assigned one of the HEAD POCKETS into which he must sink balls instead of one of the FOOT POCKETS.

frozen
1. In CONTACT, permanently touching. The term "frozen" can apply to two balls or to a ball and a cushion. 1866 NYT (Sep 10) 8:3, 1941 Hoppe 75. See FAST, FREEZE, KISSING, TOUCHING BALL. The reason that frozen balls are a problem is the certainty of a PUSH if the cue ball is shot at the frozen object ball.

In Snooker, if the cue ball is frozen to a ball and the striker is ON that ball, he is considered to have hit it even if he shoots away from the ball (the TOUCHING BALL rule). 1941 Levi 225. In English Billiards, when the cue ball is frozen to another ball, the red is placed on the LOSING SPOT and the adversary's ball on the CENTRE SPOT, while the striker plays from baulk. 1889 Drayson 99. In Straight-Rail and Balkline, if the player's cue ball is frozen to an object ball, he may play a BREAK SHOT. If he does not, the cue ball is not considered to have touched the object ball to which it is frozen unless it hits

105

frozen

that ball after contact has first been broken. In THREE-CUSHIONS under international and modern American rules, only the two frozen balls are SPOTTED. (Formerly, all three balls were spotted for a break shot when any two were frozen.) In Three-Cushions, if the cue ball is driven into a cushion to which it is frozen, the contact does not count. In Cushion Caroms the rule is otherwise. 1893 HRB 62.

2. (Bill.) CALL by the REFEREE indicating that the striker's cue ball is frozen to an object ball. 1916 RGRG 13. Cf. NOT FROZEN. Officials have experienced enormous difficulty in determining whether two balls are frozen, sometimes having to light MATCHES to illuminate the balls. 1879 NYT (Feb 11) 8:4. In an Ives-Schaefer match in Chicago in November 1893, a magnifying glass was used to detect frozen balls. 1893 NYT (Nov 30) 3:4. Maurice Daly, an excellent player and frequent referee, conducted a tournament in 1913 in which frozen balls were separated by a card to permit the player to shoot instead of having the balls spotted. 1913 Daly 4.

full

Said of a HIT that is nearly head on, with the center of one ball aimed at the center of another. "Hit it full." See also FULL BALL.

full ball

A stroke in which the HIT is full, that is, the center of the cue ball is aimed at or very close to the center of the object ball. 1807 White 17, 1866 Crawley 49, 1973 Mizerak 81. Cf. HALF-BALL, QUARTER-BALL. In English Eight-Ball Pool, a full ball shot is one in which a direct hit can be made at the center of the object ball. 1985 KTGP 31. See OBSTRUCTION.

full massé

A MASSÉ stroke performed with the cue stick held nearly perpendicular to the plane of the table. 1881 MB 47, 1946 OR 93. Cf. HALF-MASSÉ.

full rack

A RACK consisting of a full complement of balls, usually 15 in number. Cf. SHORT RACK.

furl

A decorative ring around the shaft of the cue stick and to which the TIP is applied; a misspelling of FERRULE. 1973 Mizerak 81, 1980 Balukas 195.

gaff shot

A FANCY SHOT requiring the use of props or an illegal substance, such as saliva or CHALK. 1985 BD (Aug) 51. See also CHALK SHOT, SPIT SHOT.

gallery

The COMPANY or the SPECTATORS observing a billiard game, who may be consulted regarding disputes that arise during play.

gambling

The nearly irresistible habit of wagering money or items of value on the outcome of billiard games. The practice is described in the earliest billiard literature and is largely responsible for the game's negative image. Some sources, dating back at least to 1807 White, even provide tables of odds for BETTING on players of varying skills. The vocabulary of billiard gambling is treated extensively at 1983 BD (Nov) 20.

The world of bettors is inhabited by many different types of characters who feed in various ways on gambling activity, each described by a colorful name. The TOUT advises bettors on whom to bet and collects a percentage of any winnings for this service. The tout often gives contradictory information to different bettors to guarantee himself a payoff regardless of the outcome of the match.

The STEER MAN or WHEEL MAN attempts to bring bettors together to create ACTION on a game. He may be compensated by taking a percentage of the winnings or by placing a bet himself on the outcome.

A KNOCKER tries to prevent certain wagers from taking place to protect the interests of certain players or BACKERS.

A SWEATOR is one who has bet on a game and is concerned about his prospects and thus perspires from nervousness while it is being played.

Because of its antiquity and pervasiveness, gambling has given rise to an extensive argot. See, for example, AIR GUN, BARREL, CALCUTTA, CHEATING, DOG, DUMP, FISH, HUSTLER, LEMON, MARK, ODDS, OPEN GAME, OVER/UNDER, RING GAME, SAVER, SHARK, SHARP, STALL, THROUGH-TICKET. *See illustration on next page.*

gambling

game

1. A unit of competitive play at billiards. One complete contest between two or more players. One or more games may constitute a MATCH, and one or more matches a TOURNAMENT. A game itself may comprise several FRAMES. A game of Nine-Ball formally begins when the referee has RACKED the balls and ends when the outcome has been decided, whether by FORFEIT, by DISQUALIFICATION, or at the end of the shot on which the nine is legally pocketed. 1992 OR 53. 2. A billiard contest defined by a specific set of rules, as in "the game of Nine-Ball." 1674 Cotton 23. For a list of over 400 different billiard games, see Appendix B at the back of this book. Games are broadly divided into POCKET GAMES, CAROM GAMES, and CASIN GAMES. POCKET GAMES are further subdivided into CALL SHOT and SET-ORDER GAMES. For countries and states whose names appear in the titles of billiard games, see COUNTRIES, NAMES OF and STATES, NAMES OF. 3. Marker's call to signify the end of the game when a player has won. 1866 NYT (Sep 10) 8:3, 1890 HRB 110, 1897 Payne 35. "That's game." 4. (Eng. Bill., obs.) A player is said to "play the game" when he plays the proper stroke. 1885c Cook 9, 1897 Payne 35. "It's the game to play an in-off from baulk." 5. (High-Low-Jack Game, obs.) The

act of pocketing the most balls in one frame, for which a bonus of one point is awarded. See also BIG FOUR POOL, SEVEN-UP POOL.

game ball

A ball that, if pocketed, will cause the shooter to win the game. 1992 OR. For example, in NINE-BALL, the nine is the game ball. In 14.1 CONTINUOUS, the ball that will give the striker the requisite number of points for game is the game ball. Sometimes known as the MONEY BALL or PAY BALL in SINGLE-RACK games.

game board

See BILLIARD BOARD GAME.

game clock

A clock used in such events as WORLD TEAM BILLIARDS, in which the contest ends after a certain amount of time has elapsed; the team that is ahead at the finish is the winner. See also TIME LIMIT.

Game of Three

(game, obs.) = À LA ROYALE. 1839 Kentfield 36, 1850c White & Bohn 48, 1866 Crawley 150.

game off the balls

(Eng. Bill.) A single BREAK resulting in completion of the game from the current position. 1869 Roberts 168, 1885c Cook 10. See also OFF THE BALLS. "He made game off the balls." In American usage, to RUN OUT.

game on the wire

See ON THE WIRE.

game total

The total number of points that a single player or team must earn in order to win a billiard game. In tournament Straight Pool, this is currently 150 points. From 1924 to 1954 it was 125 points.

garbage shot

(Pocket Bill.) = SLOP SHOT. 1979 Grissim 251. A shot that is made by luck rather than skill, especially when one hits the PACK hard in a game not requiring CALLED shots, in the hope that at least one ball will enter a pocket. Also CROW, FLUKE, SCRATCH.

gas

(sl.) = LEGS, SPEED. A ball fails to have enough "gas" if it is shot too slowly. Cf. OIL, which refers to spin rather than speed.

gather

(Bill.) A shot that causes the billiard balls to come to rest near one another so that the next shot can easily be made. A form of POSITION PLAY. Through the use of gather, the player can execute long sequences of shots, especially in Straight-Rail. "He made an attractive

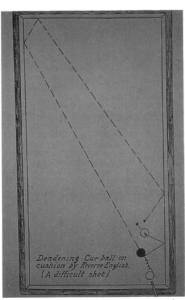

Deadening Cue-ball on cushion by Reverse English. (A difficult shot)

gather

gather." 1873 *Billiard Cue*. Also used as a verb: "He gathered them at the end rail." See GATHER SHOT.

An 1855 treatise by the Frenchman Claudius Berger discusses gather shots. In EXHIBITION, he would draw a circle in chalk on the table and announce prophetically that he would make a carom and cause all three balls to stop within the circle. 1890 NY Herald (Feb 20) 9:5. Berger referred to a gather as a "reunion," which is quite descriptive. 1860 *Leslie's* (Nov 10) 393. Gather shots form the subject of virtually the whole of 1913 Daly.

gather shot

(Bill.) A shot whose result is to bring the cue ball and object balls close to one another; a GATHER, GATHERING CANNON, or GATHERING SHOT. 1992 OR 10.

gathering cannon

(Eng. Bill.) A CANNON that GATHERS the balls for the player; a GATHER SHOT.

gathering shot

(Bill.) = GATHER SHOT. 1876 NYT (May 25) 7:4, 1881 MB 24, 1919 Hoyle 625.

gear

(Penetration Nine-Ball) See IN GEAR.

general average

= GRAND AVERAGE. 1873 NYT (Jun 29) 5:4.

Gentleman's Call

(pocket games) A rule in informal games, especially Eight-Ball, that a shot need not be CALLED orally if the striker's intention is obvious. BANK SHOTS and COMBINATIONS are never considered obvious. 1992 OR 42.

German Pyramid Game

(game, obs.) A pocket game played with 21 balls RACKED in a triangle. After the first stroke, the player may play with any ball at any other ball. Pocketing all the balls in one BREAK scores double. 1856 Crawley 106. Scoring is by WINNING HAZARDS only, except for the final stroke. Three balls must be holed in each pocket, leaving two others to be disposed of at pleasure. The last stroke must consist of both a winning and a losing hazard. Scoring is complex, essentially solitaire for each player. 1866 Crawley 222. Also known as PYRAMIDEN-PARTIE.

German-towner

(colloq., obs.) = BOWERY SHOT or TIMBER-LICK. A PUSH SHOT. 1865 Phelan 67. Although Germantown was a section of Philadelphia, how this place name gave rise to the term is obscure.

get

To obtain a position, as in "getting the rail," meaning to maneuver the balls appropriately for the RAIL NURSE.

get on

1. To obtain position for, *e.g.*, "Try to get on the five-ball." To "get on the spot" means to obtain a suitable position for the SPOT-STROKE. 2. To back a player financially or to place side bets that he will win. 1898 Thatcher 226. "Get on me, Bert. I can't lose." 1959 Tevis.

get out

1. To RUN OUT the game from the current position. "He can easily get out from here." See also CLEAN UP, GAME OFF THE BALLS, OFF THE BALLS. 2. To ESCAPE from a SNOOKER, that is, to contact the BALL ON in spite of having been snookered. 1965 Pulman 73.

give a miss

(Eng. Bill.) To perform a particular type of SAFETY in which the striker fails to hit any ball, thus incurring a penalty and giving up an opportunity to score in order to leave his opponent in a difficult position. 1807 White 112, 1858 Mardon 385. The opponent is said to SCORE A MISS when this occurs. See also INTENTIONAL MISS, MISS, MISS IN BAULK.

glasses

1. A special type of spectacles were made for billiard playing, as a player tends to peer over the rim of ordinary glasses as he bends over to shoot. 1915 Reece & Clifford 1–7. Few professionals in the U.S. have worn glasses while playing. Notable exceptions were Jerome Keogh, the inventor of 14.1 Continuous, and Frank Taberski. A number of top Three-Cushion players wore glasses while playing, including Jay Bozeman, Tiff Denton, and Clarence Jackson ("King of the Bank Shots"). Champions Willie Hoppe and Johnny Layton wore glasses while away from the table, but not while competing. A few Snooker players use spectacles, particularly Dennis Taylor (whose large lenses have become his trademark), Joe Johnson, and Fred Davis. 1990 Taylor 2. Drinking glasses are sometimes used as obstacles for TRICK SHOTS, particularly in carom games. The performer must have confidence in what he is doing, for a miss can lead to shattered glass all over the table.

Go-Back Game

(game, obs.) CRAMP GAME in which the player giving the HANDICAP must win during a single inning only. So named because the stronger player's score "goes back" (*i.e.*, is reset) to zero after a miss. See ROYAL DISCOUNT. Sometimes it refers to a game in which a player must win the game during one interval in his opponent's scoring. That is, whenever his opponent scores, the player's score is reset to zero. Also called the PULL-DOWN GAME. 1839 Kentfield 37, 1862 Crawley 96, 1909 BYB 87. This latter version is the equivalent of GRAND DISCOUNT.

God Bless You

(Snooker) A mnemonic phrase used by Snooker players to recall the correct placement of the BAULK COLOURS—the **G**reen, **B**rown, and **Y**ellow—which are spotted in that order from left to right on the D.

Golf

A generic term for billiard games that attempt in some fashion to emulate the game of golf, generally by requiring the player to pocket a ball or balls in each pocket of the table. The player who uses the least number of strokes is the winner. Many versions of this game exist, played with varying numbers of balls.

1. (game) A pocket billiard game, usually played on a SNOOKER TABLE. Each player is assigned a numbered object ball, which he must pocket in each of the six pockets in numerical order using the least number of strokes, beginning with hole one at the right head pocket. A shot costs one stroke, a foul three. The cue ball is placed on the HEAD SPOT at the start, the object ball on the CENTER SPOT. When the object ball is pocketed it is respotted, but the cue ball remains where it came to rest. 1978 Fels, 1982 OR 95. Cf. BILLIARDS GOLF, GOLF BILLIARDS, SNOOKER GOLF. 2. (game) A British game played with the six Snooker COLOURS, a white ball and a RED. The eight balls are divided into four pairs, consisting of black and pink, blue and brown, green and yellow, and red and white. The first ball of each pair serves as a cue ball. The object ball is placed on the CENTRE SPOT and the player has ball IN HAND. The goal is to pot the object ball into each of the pockets in clockwise order, beginning at the top left, using the fewest number of strokes. 1986 KTG 36. Cf. SNOOKER GOLF.

Golf Billiards

(game) A pocket billiard game played with a white cue ball, a red ball and a black object ball called the BUNKER BALL. The pockets are numbered one through six counterclockwise from the right middle pocket. The cue ball is placed on the HEAD SPOT, the red on the CENTER SPOT, and the black on the FOOT SPOT. The player must hole the red ball in pockets one through six in succession. The object is to obtain the lowest score for 18 holes, playing three times around the table. Penalties are exacted if the cue ball comes to rest in various HAZARDS, which are marked spaces on the table representing such obstacles as water, sand traps, and railroad tracks. Scratching the cue ball into a pocket costs three strokes. Contact between the cue ball and the black ball (the BUNKER BALL) costs one stroke. 1916 RGRG 77.

golf course

A set of obstacles intended to be used on a POCKET TABLE to create a facsimile of the game of golf, with HAZARDS and other obstructions. 1930 Des Moines.

Golf Pocket Billiards, Golf Pool

(game) Essentially the same game as GOLF. The red ball is placed on the CENTER SPOT, the white on the HEAD SPOT. The object is to sink the red ball in all six pockets in the least number of strokes. 1908 HRB 116, 1916 RGRG 76, 1965 Fats 52. Cf. BILLIARDS GOLF, GOLF BILLIARDS, SNOOKER GOLF.

good

Successful, said of a shot. "It was good" means that the shot scored. 1883 NYT (Jun 13) 5:5. This usage is still current. See also GOOD HIT.

good hit

1. A valid CONTACT between the cue ball and an object ball, especially in Nine-Ball. 1989 Koehler 255. Cf. BAD HIT. 2. (Three-Cushions, colloq.) An exclamation by the opponent or SPECTATORS to congratulate a player on making a difficult contact with the object ball.

grain

1. The NAP of the cloth. 2. The natural growth pattern visible in an IVORY ball.

grand average

The average number of points per inning made by a player during all games of a match or TOURNAMENT. 1865 NYT (Jun 4) 5:5, 1888 NYT (Dec 3) 5:6. See also AVERAGE, HIGH GRAND AVERAGE. Originally known as "general average."

grand discount

(obs.) A method of giving a HANDICAP in which the superior player loses all his points each time his adversary scores. See DISCOUNT, GO-BACK GAME, PULL-DOWN GAME.

grand massé

MASSÉ shot in which the BRIDGE HAND is not rested on the table but is held at the player's thigh or waist, or out over the table. Likewise (rarely) "grand piqué." 1908 Mannock II 43. Also FREE-HAND MASSÉ. Cf. PETIT MASSÉ.

Granito

Brand name of a high-quality CLOTH made in Spain, comparable to SIMONIS.

grease

(sl.) Extreme ENGLISH, also called JUICE, OIL, SPIN, or STUFF.

green

1. The usual color of billiard cloth, at least as far back as 1588, and probably since the beginning of the game. See CLOTH. Green was originally used to simulate the appearance of grass, the surface on which the precursors of billiards were played. (See GROUND BILLIARDS.) The fact that green is restful to the eyes may account for the continued popularity of this color. Abstractly, the term refers to the amount of cloth visible between the cue ball and the object ball, hence the distance between them. 1985 Marguglio 219. "You're looking at a lot of green." 2. (Snooker) Color of the ball that is valued at three points and spotted at the beginning of the game to the left (as viewed from the BOTTOM of the table) of the BROWN at the intersection of the D and the BAULK-LINE; also, the name given to that ball. See also BAULK COLOUR. For an aid in remembering where to spot the green, see GOD BLESS YOU. 3. (Pocket Bill.) The color of the six- and fourteen-balls. 4. The color of money; hence, figuratively, cash, money for betting. 1984 Tevis. "Let's see some green."

green spot

(Snooker) The SPOT on which the GREEN is placed, at the left intersection of the D and the BAULK-LINE. Cf. YELLOW SPOT.

grip

1. The manner in which the BUTT end of the cue stick is held in the hand. The position of the hand that grasps the cue stick. 1941 Hoppe 75, 1992 OR 10. For carom and pocket play, C. C. Peterson advised holding the cue at the BALANCE POINT, though most players hold it slightly farther back. In Snooker, the recommended grasping point is three to four inches from the butt. 1991 Everton 26. 2. That portion of the BUTT of the cue that is held with the hand, possibly having a WRAP of silk, IRISH LINEN, twine, CORK, or LEATHER. In some cases there is no wrap; the butt is plain or may be carved in a way that enhances its ability to be held securely. *See illustration on next page.*

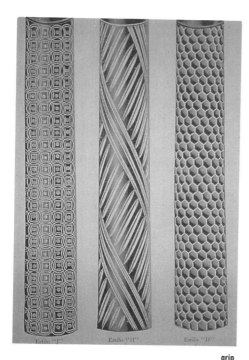

grip

grip hand

That hand used by the player to grasp the butt of the cue stick. Cf. BRIDGE HAND.

Ground Billiards

1. (game, obs.) The original game of billiards, played on the ground with MACES, the PASS, and the KING during the fifteenth century. 1985 Clare 6. 2. (game) A modern style of billiards played on a 30-foot × 60-foot clay court. See "Ground Billiards" in 1951 *Recreation* (Sep) 206.

group

1. (Eight-Ball) A series of balls that is either PLAIN (the seven SOLIDS, numbered 1–7), or BANDED (the seven STRIPES, 9–15). The collection of balls that a player must pocket to earn the right to shoot at the eight-ball to win the game. 1992 OR 48. 2. (Snooker) A row of balls in the TRIANGLE, *e.g.*, the "five-group" is the row consisting of five balls. 1954 KTG 26. 3. One of the collections of numbered balls assigned to players in ELIMINATION. 1992 OR 77.

group ball

(Eight-Ball) One of the balls in the GROUP consisting of either STRIPES or SOLIDS. Every ball other than the eight-ball and the cue ball is in one of these two groups.

guest

(Brit.) A SPECTATOR. 1937 NBJ (Oct).

gully

(Pocket Bill.) A bin at the FOOT end of the table to which pocketed balls run through GUTTERS and collect for ease of RACKING. See also BALL RETURN, TROUGH.

gully boot

A right-angled fitting leading from the bottom of a pocket into a channel running to the GULLY.

gully table

A table in which pocketed balls follow a return system and gather in a single place known as a GULLY. Distinguished from a table having DROP POCKETS and POCKET NETS, which the players must walk around to each pocket to retrieve pocketed balls. 1992 OR 10. A gully table is of greatest convenience for games in which balls are spotted at the FOOT SPOT, such as 14.1 CONTINUOUS and NINE-BALL. See also BALL RETURN, GUTTER.

gum

(colloq.) A CUSHION. The cushion was originally fashioned from rubber made of tree gum. "Stuck on the gum" means "frozen to a rail." Also RUBBER, def. 1.

gutter

(Pocket Bill.) A system of canals beneath the table for returning balls that have been pocketed to the GULLY on a table having a BALL RETURN. 1978 Byrne 182. Also TROUGH.

gutter ball

(Pocket Bill.) A SCRATCH in which the cue ball enters a pocket. A disparaging term used by analogy to bowling. See GUTTER.

half-ball

A stroke in which the center of the cue ball is aimed exactly at the edge of the object ball. 1807 White 16, 1839 Kentfield 12, 1866 Crawley 49, 1891 MB 31. "No stroke is more important to master, or indeed easier, than the half-ball, because the point of aim is sharply defined." 1896 Broadfoot 133. Said incorrectly to produce in each ball an equal motion with regard to direction and speed. 1884 Bohn 524. The actual behavior of the balls following a half-ball contact is of great

111

controversy in the billiard literature. See HALF-BALL ANGLE. The half-ball hit was a mainstay of the Three-Cushion play of Willie Hoppe and Welker Cochran.

half-ball angle

The angle at which the cue ball rebounds from its original direction after a HALF-BALL contact with an object ball. 1954 KTG 34. Though it is easy to define, the determination of the value of this angle has generated a great deal of argument during the last 150 years. For the theoretical case of perfectly elastic balls on a frictionless table, it is straightforward to show that the half-ball angle ought to be 30 degrees. It is the angle whose sine equals 0.5. 1807 White 19 (quoting from an unidentified French source) and 1839 Kentfield 13 state erroneously that the half-ball angle is 45 degrees. This confusion probably resulted from the incorrect belief that the motion of the balls after such a contact must be symmetrical. The error has been repeated by many sources.

a NATURAL-ANGLE STROKE. 1807 White 17. See also HALF-BALL.

half-butt

(Brit., obs.) An instrument for striking the cue ball that is approximately eight feet in length, longer than the QUARTER-BUTT but shorter than the LONG-BUTT. 1873 Bennett 27, 1896 Broadfoot 97, 1924c Inman 98. A long cue, properly tipped and leathered at its base, that is used either as a BUTT or a cue, in which case a longer REST (called a HALF-REST) is employed in conjunction with it. 1866 Crawley 12. A half-butt is visible in the engraving "Billiards," by E. F. Lambert, dated 1827. See also LONG TACKLE.

half-circle

(Eng. Bill., Snooker) = D, BAULK CIRCLE, BAULK SEMICIRCLE, STRIKING RING, or just the SEMICIRCLE. So called because of its shape.

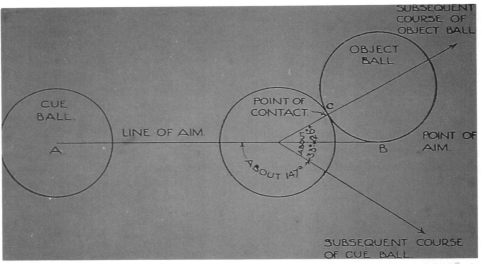

half-ball angle

Around 1900, a number of brief computations from readers appeared in the British periodical *World of Billiards*, all yielding differing results as authors attempted to account for a multiplicity of effects such as the inelasticity of balls, friction between balls, spin, friction with the cloth, and the like. There are inconsistent analyses in 1924 Ogden 270 and 1925 Macmillan 50, the former obtaining an angle of 40 degrees, the latter 26 degrees. An accurate but partial analysis appears in 1835 Coriolis 27, but no convincing treatment of the full problem has ever been published.

half-ball stroke

A shot in which the center of the cue ball is aimed at the edge of the OBJECT BALL. 1895 Buchanan 36. Also called

half-follow

A stroke played with overspin that is midway between a full FOLLOW and a simple DIRECT CAROM played without ENGLISH. 1880 Garnier x. The shot can be aimed approximately by directing the center of the cue ball at the point where the LINE OF CENTERS drawn between the two object balls intersects the surface of the FIRST OBJECT BALL. 1898 Thatcher 192, 1925 Hoppe 200.

half-inning

A single player's TURN at the table in a game having more than one player. The term INNING may refer either to a single player's turn or to one round of turns by all players. The first inning means the first opportunity for all players to shoot. The first half-inning means the first opportunity for the first player. "He ran out during the first inning" may apply to the second player. The distinction between an inning and a half-inning is rarely made in practice.

half-massé

A MASSÉ shot in which the cue is elevated only partially, usually to an angle between 45 and 67.5 degrees. 1882 NYT (Apr 28) 2:6, 1946 OR 93. Cf. FULL MASSÉ.

half-push

(Eng. Bill., obs.) A stroke in which the cue stick remains in contact with the cue ball as the cue ball contacts an object ball. By contrast, in a PUSH stroke the cue ball moves the first object ball aside so that the shot can be made. The half-push is used when the balls are within an inch or two of one another and is aimed as a HALF-FOLLOW. 1873 Bennett 309, 1895 Buchanan 104. It was formerly a legal stroke. 1896 Broadfoot 228.

half-rest

A REST employed in conjunction with the HALF-BUTT. 1866 Crawley 12. It is curious that a half-rest is longer than a rest, but shorter than a LONG REST. Properly called the "half-butt rest," but contracted to "half-rest."

Hall of Fame

The BILLIARD CONGRESS OF AMERICA maintains a Hall of Fame honoring individuals who have made significant contributions to billiards through either meritorious service to the billiard industry or championship playing performance. Through 1992, only 29 individuals have been inducted. The youngest man inducted was Mike Sigel at age 35; the youngest woman was Jean Balukas at 26. The other player members, with dates of induction, are Joe Balsis (1982), Lou Butera (1986), Jimmy Caras (1977), Welker Cochran (1967), Irving Crane (1978), Alfredo De Oro (1967), Ralph Greenleaf (1966), Willie Hoppe (1966), Luther Lassiter (1983), Johnny Layton (1976), Steve Mizerak (1980), Willie Mosconi (1968), Charles C. Peterson (1966), Andrew Ponzi (1988), Erwin Rudolph (1987), Jacob Schaefer Sr. (1968), Jake Schaefer Jr. (1968), Frank Taberski (1975), Nick Varner (1992), Dorothy Wise (1981), and Harold Worst (1970).

The meritorious service entrants (and the accomplishments for which they were recognized) are John Brunswick (1990, founding of J. M. Brunswick & Bro., predecessor of Brunswick Corporation), Minnesota Fats (1984, popularization of billiards in the 1960s), John Wesley Hyatt (1971, invention of celluloid for billiard balls), Benjamin Nartzik (1967, promotion of billiards during the 1960s), Herman J. Rambow (1979, cue-

maker to champions), and Walter Tevis (1991, for writing *The Hustler* and *The Color of Money*).

Separate halls of fame are maintained by the BOWLING AND BILLIARD INSTITUTE OF AMERICA and the WOMEN'S PROFESSIONAL BILLIARD ASSOCIATION.

Hand Billiards

(game) Billiards played by hand, without any cue sticks. See FINGER BILLIARDS. Also called "hand stroke billiards" in 1908 Roberts. The balls are rolled and spun with the bare hand.

hand chalk

White chalk or TALCUM POWDER used to dry the hands and reduce friction between the fingers and the shaft of the cue. See also CHALK, but there is no actual chalk in hand chalk.

hand, in

See IN HAND.

hand out

An expression meaning that a player's INNING or turn at the table has ended. 1845 Hoyle 225. "His hand is out." See LOSE ONE'S HAND, OUT.

handicap

1. A modification in the scoring or rules of a game to compensate for differences in skill among players. 1982 OR. Although the idea is very old, the first public tournament in which the players were handicapped did not occur until 1871. 1912 MB 231.

Handicapping is essential in hustling, where the victim is usually aware that the hustler is better, so a means must be employed to make the victim think he has a chance.

A prodigious number of handicapping methods have been devised. See BALKLINE, CRAMP GAME, DISCOUNT, DUCK, NO COUNT, ODDS, RECEIVING, SCRAMBLE, SPOT, SPOT THE BREAK, WEIGHT. Games with built-in handicaps: BAR-HOLE GAME, DIVIDED POCKETS, GO-BACK GAME, HANDICAP SWEEPSTAKES, JACK-UP POOL, MISTER AND MRS. POCKET BILLIARDS, PLAYER'S EIGHT-BALL, PULL-DOWN GAME. Cf. EVEN UP, LEVEL, STRAIGHT-UP, UP.

One of the strangest handicaps was used in a professional tournament in 1890 in which the table was marked with two sets of balklines, at 8 and 14 inches from the cushions. The stronger player had to use the 14-inch lines. 1890 NY Herald (Jan 19) 25, 1990 BD (Feb) 20.

2. An infirmity that interferes with one's normal ability to play billiards, such as a missing limb or other deficiency. The history of billiards is replete with examples of the handicapped achieving an unbelievable degree of skill at the game. Perhaps the outstanding example is George H. "Handless" Sutton, who lost both arms below the elbow in a sawmill accident while a teenager. He eventually became a traveling exhibition player, able to play all but top champions 100 or NO COUNT at Straight-Rail. He also performed finger shots with a high degree of dexterity even though he had no hands, let alone fingers. He accomplished these shots by spinning the balls with the stumps of his arms.

handicap (George H. Sutton)

Handicap Sweepstakes

(game, obs.) An English game for players of varying strengths. Each player is given a HANDICAP by being assigned a certain number of points to earn. The first player to achieve his total is the winner of the stake and must pay for the table. 1850c White & Bohn 47, 1856 Crawley 106. Essentially a nineteenth-century version of SCRAMBLE.

handle

The BUTT of a cue stick, particularly the GRIP. 1879 NYT (Feb 9) 12:2.

hanger

A ball that is perched at the edge of a pocket and poised to fall in. 1937 NYT (Dec 21) 30:2, 1978 Stone 94. Hence, an unmissable shot, one that is "hanging" on the edge. Also called a CHERRY, CRIPPLE, DUCK, MINNIE,

PUPPY, SET-UP or SITTER. Sometimes also used by extension to refer to an easy shot on a carom table, even though no pockets are present.

hanging

(pocket games) Said of a ball that is about ready to drop into a pocket or is situated very near a pocket opening. See CHALLENGE, def. 2.

Hard Eight

(Eight-Ball) Rule variation in which a player, upon sinking his last GROUP BALL, must make a GOOD HIT on the eight-ball or lose the game. 1990 White G-3. Cf. SOFT EIGHT.

harpoon stroke

(obs.) A MASSÉ in which the cue stick is held nearly perpendicular and the cue ball hit with considerable force. 1867 Dufton 75. So called because the posture suggests use of a harpoon.

hazard

1. Originally, a pocket or hole in a billiard table through which a ball may fall. 1598 OED. The sinking of a ball in a pocket. 1674 Cotton, 1807 White 9, 1850 Phelan 20, 1976 WSD 206. A WINNING HAZARD is one in which an object ball is pocketed, a LOSING HAZARD one in which the cue ball is pocketed. A DOUBLE HAZARD consists of pocketing two balls in the same stroke. 2. (obs.) Any stroke made with the point of a cue; an attempt at a shot. 1862 Crawley 18. 3. (obs.) A POOL, POT, or collective STAKE. That which is risked or "hazarded." A bet. 4. (Golf Bill.) A marked area of the table, carrying a penalty to any player whose cue ball comes to rest within it. Used in the sense of a hazard at golf.

hazard-table

(obs.) A BILLIARD TABLE with pockets, *i.e.*, a table on which HAZARDS can be made. 1820 Egan. A POCKET TABLE. The term is also used to refer to a dice table, creating the same sort of confusion as POOL ROOM.

Hazards

1. (game, obs.) Pocket billiard game in which each player is assigned a distinct (*e.g.*, numbered or colored) ball. A player whose ball is HOLED must pay a forfeit to the STRIKER. One who misses a shot forfeits half the HAZARD (that is, the STAKE) to the person whose ball he was attempting to pocket. 1773 *Covent Garden*, 1974 Hendricks 25. The first CALL-SHOT GAME, a precursor of modern pocket games. Nominating a ball was required to determine who should receive the forfeit in case of a miss. 2. (game, obs.) CRAMP GAME in which only WINNING HAZARDS count. 1775 Annals 96. After a

successful shot, the striker must play at the ball nearest the cue ball. 1807 White 51. According to 1856 Crawley 99, "A good game for ladies and gentlemen in a country house." Cf. NEAR BALL, NEAREST BALL POOL.

head

1. The part of the MECHANICAL BRIDGE that rests on the table and supports the shaft of the cue, also known as the BRIDGE HEAD or REST HEAD. 2. The HEAD OF TABLE. Cf. FOOT.

head ball

(Pocket Bill.) The ball located at the APEX of the RACK and that rests on the FOOT SPOT. 1891 MB 360, 1977 Fels 79. Also known as the APEX BALL.

head of table

In American usage, the END of the table bearing the MANUFACTURER'S NAMEPLATE, and from which the BREAK SHOT is played. 1857 Phelan 185, 1875 NYT (Nov 20) 2:5, 1881 MB 24. Also called the HEAD, but known as the BOTTOM in English games. See also NAP.

head pocket

(Pocket Bill.) One of the two pockets at the HEAD of the table. In British usage, a BOTTOM POCKET. Cf. FOOT POCKET.

head rail

The SHORT RAIL nearest the HEAD SPOT, on which the MANUFACTURER'S NAMEPLATE is placed. 1946 OR 95, 1989 Koehler 255. Called the "head cushion" in 1857 Phelan 165. See diagram under TABLE.

head spot

A SPOT located at the center of the HEAD STRING, one-quarter of a table length from the HEAD RAIL. 1916 RGRG 49, 1992 OR 10. Where the WHITE is spotted in billiard games and where the BREAK BALL is spotted in 14.1 CONTINUOUS if it lies IN THE RACK at the end of a FRAME. Also called the AMERICAN SPOT, LIGHT-RED SPOT, STRING SPOT, UPPER SPOT, WHITE-BALL SPOT or WHITE SPOT. Cf. FOOT SPOT.

head string

(Pocket Bill.) An imaginary line, perpendicular to the LONG RAILS and passing through the HEAD SPOT, that defines the BALK area, or KITCHEN. 1946 OR 28, 1992 OR 10. Also known as the STRING LINE or just the STRING.

heads up

(colloq.) Referring to a game in which no handicap is in effect. "Let's play heads up." See also EVEN UP, LEVEL, UP.

heap

(pocket games, colloq.) A BUNCH, PACK, PYRAMID, RACK, or STACK.

heating

In the days of IVORY balls, tables were heated to prevent warping of the balls or changes in their condition during the game. Queen Victoria's table had zinc tubes that could be filled with hot water. 1839 Kentfield 3. Electric heating was first used in U.S. title play in an 18.2 BALKLINE match between Jake Schaefer Jr. and Welker Cochran in December 1927. Under current international carom rules, tables must be equipped with a heating system to remove moisture from the slates and cloth so that the table will remain FAST, which is particularly important for Three-Cushion play. The playing surface is normally kept at approximately 5°C (9°F) above room temperature. 1981 Rottie 154.

held

(obs.) = POCKETED. In the nineteenth century, "holed," meaning "pocketed," became corrupted to "hold." Hence "held," the past tense of "hold," also had this meaning. 1859 *Leslie's* (Oct 1) 273:2.

help

(Three-Cushions, colloq.) An unintentional KISS that assists a player in scoring. Sometimes requested of the gods of billiards by a player who believes he will otherwise miss the shot, as in "A little help, please."

Hi-Cue

(game) A modern pocket billiard game invented by John Furda, played with four solid-color balls, one striped "wild" ball, the balls numbered one through nine, and an extra five-ball. The game consists of 10 innings, with a player allowed three shots in each inning. The players alternate, taking two innings at the table each turn. Many combinations of point values may be earned on a single shot. For example, sinking any solid or stripe on the first shot of an inning is worth 25 points. 1983 BD (Aug) 16. Cf. HIGH CUE.

hickey

(Golf) A FOUL. 1992 OR 100.

hidden set

(Snooker) A SET in which the first ball to be hit is obstructed by another ball. 1910b Ritchie 28, 1957 Holt 179. The shot is played by caroming the cue ball into the obstructed ball off another ball. If contact is made, success is assured because the shot is a set. *See illustration on next page.*

115

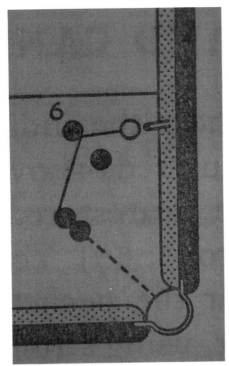

hidden set

high
1. = FOLLOW. Overspin introduced to the cue ball by
striking it "high," that is, above center. This tends to
make the cue ball travel faster and farther and to
continue its forward progress even after striking an
object ball or cushion. Also DIRECT ENGLISH, FOLLOW-
ING STROKE, HIGH STROKE. Cf. HALF-FOLLOW, LOW. 2.
(Pocket Bill.) One of the object balls numbered 9–15.
Also BIG, STRIPE. Cf. LOW. 3. (obs.) The name for the
15-ball in the HIGH-LOW-JACK GAME.

high arch rest
(Brit. games) = SPIDER. A type of MECHANICAL BRIDGE
designed for bridging over balls, originally used in the
game of PYRAMIDS, where clusters of multiple balls can
prevent effective use of the ordinary REST. 1866 Crawley
10.

high average
= HIGH SINGLE AVERAGE. The highest average number
of points per INNING made by a player in any single game
of a tournament. See AVERAGE.

high cue
(colloq.) = FOLLOW. Cf. HI-CUE, LOW CUE.

high grand average
The highest GRAND AVERAGE attained by any player in a
TOURNAMENT. 1941 Hoppe 75.

High-Low-Jack Game
(game, obs.) A FULL-RACK pocket billiard game. The
15-ball is known as HIGH, the 1-ball the LOW, and the
9-ball the JACK. Sinking any of these balls is worth one
point. The player sinking the most balls in a frame
scores GAME, also worth one point. The player first
scoring seven points is the winner. At the break, the 1,
9, and 15 are placed in a triangle at the center of the
PACK, with the 15 nearest the FOOT SPOT. 1890 HRB 86,
1916 RGRG 74, 1919 Hoyle 633. PILLS are used to
determine order of play. An amateur tournament at this
game was held in New York in 1885. 1891 MB 670. It is
also known as BIG FOUR POOL, after the four ways of
scoring—High, Low, Jack, and Game, and as SEV-
EN-UP POOL.

High Number Pool
(Bagatelle game, obs.) Played on the PARISIAN POOL
BOARD. 1891 MB 352. Each member of the pool takes
one stroke. The player whose ball lands in the highest-
numbered CUP wins. In case of a tie, a PLAYOFF is held.
1890 HRB 106.

high oblique stroke
(Eng. Bill., obs.) = OBLIQUE STROKE, JUMP SHOT. 1807
White 25, 1866 Crawley 35. Early in the eighteenth
century, players found that it was necessary to elevate
the BUTT of the cue in order to shoot at a ball lying near
a cushion. If the cue ball is struck above its center from
such a position, it will jump from the cloth. This stroke
was the forerunner of the MASSÉ, which results when the
ball is contacted off-center to the left or right and at a
higher angle of elevation. See also DIP. Cf. PERPENDIC-
ULAR STROKE.

high run
The largest number of consecutive points scored by a
player in any single turn at the table. 1941 Hoppe 75.
The RUN may be measured over a GAME, TOURNAMENT,
or lifetime. Originally "longest run," then "highest
run." 1888 NYT (Dec 3) 5:6. See also ROOM HIGH.

high single average
= HIGH AVERAGE, the highest SINGLE AVERAGE attained
by any player during a TOURNAMENT. 1941 Hoppe 75.
The game in which a player achieves this is known as his
BEST GAME. Sometimes known as "best average." 1891
MB 381.

high stroke
(Brit. games) HIGH, FOLLOW. 1807 White 24, 1856
Crawley 15, 1866 Crawley 34.

Highs and Lows

(game) = EIGHT-BALL, so named because the object balls are divided based on numerical value into the HIGHS, numbered 9–15, and the LOWS, numbered 1–7. Also BIGS AND LITTLES, STRIPES AND SOLIDS.

hill

See HILL GAME, ON THE HILL.

hill game

(colloq.) A situation in which both players each need only a single point for victory. Also CASE GAME, CASEY JONES, DOUBLE CHEESE, TV GAME. See also ON THE HILL.

hit

1. CONTACT between the cue stick and the cue ball, between two balls or between a ball and a cushion. Examples: "nice hit," "thin hit." The term has been in use in this context since before the year 1600. Cf. STRIKE. See MOMENTARY CONTACT. 2. A collision of a ball with the FACE of a cushion to which it is not already FROZEN. See CONTACT, def. 1. 3. A collision between two balls. See CONTACT, def. 2.

hit the ball

(Nine-Ball) A rule, used in professional play, requiring the STRIKER to contact the lowest-numbered ball on the table first. If he does not, the INCOMING PLAYER is awarded cue ball IN HAND anywhere on the table. 1984 Mizerak 52. See also ONE SHOT OUT. Cf. PLAY AGAIN RULE, ROLLOUT, SHOOT OUT.

hold

1. = HOLD-UP, REVERSE ENGLISH. 1977 OR 17. Spin that tends to work against the natural motion of the ball as it rebounds from a cushion. 2. = STOP, STOP BALL. 1992 OR 10. 3. Pocketed. See HELD.

hold-up

= REVERSE ENGLISH. 1978 Byrne 47. Motion imparted to the cue ball to keep it from following a normal course after hitting an object ball. 1976 WSD 214, 1982 OR. English that makes the ball slow down when it hits a rail. 1978 Byrne 183. Also known as CHECK SIDE, COUNTER, OPPOSING SIDE, and WRONG-WAY ENGLISH.

hole

1. A POCKET. Also used as a verb. 1674 Cotton 24, 1775 Annals 91, 1807 White 61, 1884 MB 23. The term is used particularly in reference to BAGATELLE. See also HOLD. 2. (game, sl.) = ONE-HOLE, ONE-POCKET.

home-and-home match

(obs.) A MATCH conducted in two parts, one in each player's home city. The first such match in the U.S. was held in 1862. 1912 MB 210. The format is thought to be fairer, as it equalizes the home advantage.

home plate

(Baseball Pocket Bill.) Designation for the FOOT SPOT, where illegally pocketed balls are spotted. 1925 RGRG 48, 1946 OR 70.

home run

(Baseball Pocket Bill.) The act of pocketing the balls one though nine, in that order, without a miss. The term was in use in 1912.

home table

1. A table intended for home use, generally made of less sturdy materials than a COMMERCIAL TABLE. 2. The table on which a player regularly practices, regardless of whether it is actually in a home. More often the table is in the player's favorite PARLOR.

Honest John

(Nine-Ball) = ROLLOUT, so called because the shooter must always make an "honest" effort to hit the required object ball.

Honolulu

(game) A single-rack pocket game in which each shot must be made by a BANK, a KICK, a KISS, or a COMBINATION. Each ball CALLED and legally pocketed is worth one point; the first player to score eight is the winner. A kick is legal only if the cushion involved is not adjacent to the pocket in which the object ball falls. A TWO-BALL BREAK with call is utilized. 1992 OR 83. Also known as BANKS, KISSES, AND COMBINATIONS or INDIRECT. See also INCIDENTAL CONTACT.

hook a snooker

(Snooker) To LAY A SNOOKER, leave the opponent SNOOKERED. 1977 Fels 83.

hooked

Obstructed. See ANGLED, CORNER HOOKED, JAWED. 1979 Grissim 251, 1989 Koehler 256. Used in this sense when the obstacle is a portion of the table. In Snooker, unable to make direct contact with the BALL ON because of the presence of another ball. See also IN JAIL, OBSTRUCTION, SNOOKERED, TIED UP.

hop the eight

(Nine-Ball, colloq.) A HANDICAP in which the weaker player, having pocketed the seven-ball, is permitted either to play at the eight-ball or to "hop over" the eight and play directly at the nine-ball to win the game. Cf. LAST TWO.

Hot Eight

(game) A game similar to Eight-Ball but played with a SHORT RACK of nine balls arranged in the conventional Nine-Ball diamond. The eight-ball is racked in the center, with the solids 1–4 placed in counterclockwise order and the stripes 9–12 placed in clockwise order around the eight-ball. The table is OPEN until the first ball is legally pocketed to determine the striker's GROUP. Group balls must be contacted in numerical order. A PUSH-OUT is allowed after the break; all fouls are penalized by BALL IN HAND. A player may shoot at the eight-ball once that player's group balls have been pocketed. More information on this game can be obtained from the AMERICAN POCKET BILLIARD LEAGUE. Also known as ACTION EIGHT-BALL.

house

A BILLIARD ROOM, usually public, particularly its management. "The house doesn't allow massé shots."

house cue

A cue stick available for use by the public in a billiard parlor. House cues are generally unjointed and of inferior quality because of indifferent maintenance. 1977 Fels 2. In fairness to room operators, investment in better equipment is often unproductive because customers may be careless in handling it. The current trend, however, is to supply two-piece house cues and even to allow customers to rent custom cues at reasonable rates, such as a dollar an hour. Cf. SNEAKY PETE.

house man

1. = COUNTER MAN. 2. The best player in a room, willing to play any stranger for money. Walter Tevis in 1955 *Bluebook* 11.

house pro

A player of high playing and instructional ability employed by a billiard room to assist customers in improving their level of performance by giving lessons, arranging exhibitions, conducting tournaments, and the like. Players who are making progress frequently spend a great deal of time practicing, particularly at off-hours, so this activity tends to build a solid clientele that increases table utilization. The house pro may also operate a pro shop on the premises selling cues and billiard supplies.

house rule

A LOCAL RULE, one that applies only in a particular billiard room, such as a requirement that all balls in NINE-BALL must be CALLED or a custom that a player who scratches must buy a round of drinks. Many a player has lost money on being informed that he has violated a house rule of which he was unaware. The notion of a "Rule of the House" is mentioned at 1680 Howlett 190. One of the most unusual house rules known to the author is in effect in a small bar on the island of St. John in the U.S. Virgin Islands. A sign on the wall reads, "Ball on floor—play the juke box."

hug the rail

A ball "hugs the rail" when it travels along and in contact with a cushion or runs close to the cushion and repeatedly inclines toward it. 1850 Phelan 21, 1881 MB 24, 1977 OR 16. ACTION in which a ball rolls along the cushion or makes multiple successive contacts with the same cushion. 1946 OR 93. Phelan believed, incorrectly, that hugging could occur only on a defective table: "This is an infallible sign either that the bed of the table is faulty, or that the table itself is not level." 1857 Phelan 65. A ball can easily be made to hug the rail by causing the cue ball to strike the cushion just before the ball and by using NATURAL ENGLISH.

hustler

1. A money player who induces others to play for high stakes by concealing his real ability. 1973 Mizerak 81. A player who seeks to persuade less-skilled individuals to gamble at billiards. 1979 Sullivan 186. A player with predatory instincts, a SHARK or BLACKLEG. One who wins through trickery or deceit that falls short of CHEATING. The term is not used, but the concept is fully described, in 1775 Annals. See SHARPER.

The word "hustler" itself was in use in the U.S. around 1825. It originally referred to a pickpocket, or one who jostles another to rob him. Its use in billiards is thus figurative, but powerfully suggestive.

The essence of hustling is hiding one's true SPEED and playing only as well as necessary to win when desired. It is essential for the hustler to make his good shots look lucky and his misses accidental rather than deliberate. See GAMBLING. He may miscue occasionally to appear careless. A Three-Cushions hustler may shoot purposely into kisses to avoid scoring. For hustling techniques, see DOG, LEMON, LET UP, PROPOSITION BET, STALL. The victim of a hustle is known as a FISH, MARK, PIGEON or SUCKER. A hustler who is shooting to his full ability is said to be playing STAND-UP. See also ROAD PLAYER, SLICK.

2. A JOINTED CUE that is disguised to resemble a HOUSE CUE so it can be used by a hustler without his opponent knowing that he is actually using a quality cue. Also SNEAKY PETE.

Hustler, The

A well-known 1959 novel by Walter Tevis about pool hustling. Made into a 1961 movie starring George C. Scott, Jackie Gleason and Paul Newman as "Fast Eddie" Felson, it is credited with causing a mini-renaissance for pocket billiards in the U.S. A grimy black-and-white film, it featured a collection of memorable characters such as Minnesota Fats and Bert Gordon, Eddie Felson's backer. The sequel, *The Color of Money*, a 1984 novel produced as a film in 1986, won Paul Newman his first Academy Award and is the first instance of a film actor playing the same character in two performances given 25 years apart.

IBSF

(org.) = INTERNATIONAL BILLIARD AND SNOOKER FEDERATION.

illegally pocketed ball

A ball that has entered a pocket as the result of a stroke that is in contravention of the rules. The status of such a ball varies greatly, depending on which game is being played. It may remain OFF THE TABLE (a RED in Snooker), be SPOTTED (14.1 Continuous), be held off the table until its spot becomes VACANT, be held off the table until the completion of the striker's INNING (balls not in a TARGET POCKET in One Pocket), be credited to the opponent (balls in the opponent's pocket in One-Pocket), or result in LOSS OF GAME (pocketing the eight out of turn in Eight-Ball).

Impromptu Billiards

(game, obs.) A makeshift version of billiards intended to be played on any ordinary convenient table. Similar to AMUSETTE or PARLOR BILLIARDS. One of these game sets was supplied to Queen Victoria for the royal yacht. See also SHIP, BILLIARDS ABOARD.

in

1. Generally, a ball is said to lie "in" a designated area of the table if its point of contact with the cloth lies in the area. Thus a ball IN HAND may legally be placed so that a portion of the ball lies beyond the HEAD STRING provided that its center is strictly behind (and not on) the head string. Whether the actual line bounding an area is considered to be within the area differs in different games. See LINE BALL. 2. (Balkline) A CALL made by the MARKER when the object balls are IN BALK. 1897 NY Herald (Nov 28) V 11:1, 1916 RGRG 16. 3. (Eng. Bill.) POCKETED. See PUT HIM IN, meaning to sink the opponent's ball. See also WHITECHAPEL.

in anchor

(Balkline) CALL made by the MARKER when both object balls lie within the same ANCHOR SPACE. 1916 RGRG 16. The term dates from the introduction of PARKER'S BOX in 1894.

in balk

1. (Balkline) Situation in which both object balls lie in the same BALK SPACE and the number of shots a player may make without moving at least one outside the space is restricted. See ONE SHOT IN, TWO SHOTS IN. A ball lying on a BALKLINE is IN BALK. If both lie on the same line, they are considered to be in the same balk space but the player may elect which of the two balk spaces they are in. See BALK. Cf. BAULK, IN BAULK. 2. (Balkline) CALL made by the MARKER when both object balls lie in the same BALK SPACE. If the call is not made when required, any carom made by the striker will count even if no ball is driven from the balk space. 1897 NYT (Dec 4) 4:5.

in baulk

(Eng. Bill.) Located BELOW the BAULK-LINE, *i.e.*, in the space between the baulk-line and the BOTTOM RAIL. Inside the baulk area. 1866 Crawley 15. A ball in baulk cannot be played at by a player whose ball is IN HAND. See BAULK, DOUBLE BAULK. Cf. BAULK, IN BALK, KITCHEN.

in control

A player is said to be "in control" of the table from the time he ADDRESSES the cue ball up to the time the next incoming player addresses the cue ball. 1981 Quinn 116. The player is generally responsible for, and receives credit for, events that occur while he is in control of the table. See also INNING, MOTION, TURN, VIBRATION POT, VISIT.

119

in gear

(Penetration Nine-Ball) Situation in which fewer than four object balls remain on the table and fouls are penalized by giving the incoming player cue ball IN HAND BEHIND THE HEAD STRING.

in hand

1. (Pocket Bill.) Situation in which the STRIKER may place the cue ball anywhere within a defined area before shooting. 1845 Hoyle 224, 1976 WSD 200. Usually, anywhere on the playing surface, but sometimes behind the HEAD STRING, depending on which game is being played. See IN HAND BEHIND THE HEAD STRING, KITCHEN. In some games, the cue ball may not be placed in contact with an object ball. 1987 PBM (Dec) 37. The ball is said to be "in hand" because it may legally be touched and moved by the player prior to his stroke, an act that would otherwise constitute a FOUL. 2. (Brit. games) Situation in which the player may place the cue ball anywhere within the D and must play at a ball out of BAULK or hit a cushion out of baulk. 1807 White 107, 1866 Crawley 15, 1978 BSCC 47. See also OFF THE TABLE. 3. (Nine-Ball) A rule variation in which the INCOMING PLAYER after a foul stroke may place the cue ball anywhere on the table. See also HIT THE BALL, ONE SHOT OUT. Cf. SHOOT OUT.

in hand behind the head string

(Pocket Bill.) Situation in which the player may place the cue ball anywhere between the HEAD STRING and the BOTTOM RAIL, in an area known as the KITCHEN. Thus, "in the kitchen." This condition arises, for example, after an opposing player's SCRATCH. 1992 OR 11. When the cue ball is placed in the kitchen it must be stroked so that it leaves the kitchen before hitting any cushion or ball. An exception occurs when there is a ball outside the kitchen but the cue ball will hit it before leaving the kitchen. Shooting at such a ball was formerly legal only if the object ball traveled at least to the CENTER STRING. 1982 OR 47.

in jail

(colloq.) = HOOKED, TIED UP. See JAIL. See also SNOOKERED.

in-off

(Brit. games) = LOSING HAZARD. 1870 NYT (Feb 13) 4:4, 1924 Aiken 31, 1954 KTG 32. So named because the cue ball goes "in" a pocket "off" (after hitting) the object ball. In Pocket Billiards, a type of SCRATCH. *See illustration in next column.*

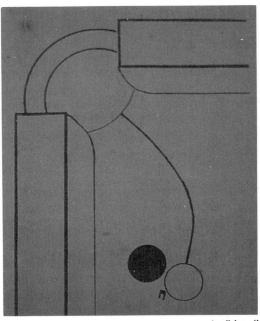

in-off (massé)

in play

Said of a ball that is not DEAD but is instead a potential participant in the shot being attempted. In English Billiards, a ball that is not IN BAULK when the striker is IN HAND. 1911 Roberts 6. In Snooker, a ball does not come into play if, in the opinion of the referee, the striker is attempting to position it with the cue stick. 1987 BSCC S10. In this connection, see also NUDGE. Cf. OUT OF PLAY.

in position

See TABLE IN POSITION.

in stroke

Said of a player who is playing well or stroking smoothly. 1941 Hoppe 75. Said when a player is ON. Cf. OFF, OUT OF STROKE.

in the kitchen

(pocket games) See KITCHEN.

in the money

A player is said to finish a tournament "in the money" if he wins a cash prize due to his final standing. Merely winning a prize for HIGH RUN or BEST GAME does not constitute an in-the-money finish.

in the rack

(14.1 Continuous) Said of a ball that is lying in such a position that it would cause INTERFERENCE with the RACKING of the other 14 balls. 1992 OR 11. The ball need not lie literally within the rack area to be considered "in the rack."

incidental contact

A grazing contact between a cushion adjacent to a pocket and a ball that is proceeding toward that pocket. Incidental contact alone is not sufficient to constitute a BANK SHOT. 1992 OR 64. See also HONOLULU. There is no concept of incidental contact in carom games; all cushion contacts count, no matter how fleeting (except for the rule that multiple BOUNCES on top of the same cushion are treated as a single contact, and the first contact with a cushion to which the cue ball is FROZEN does not count at all).

The need for the notion of incidental contact arose in the obsolete STOP GAME, in which a player was penalized if his cue ball hit a cushion. (He had to "stop" his ball before it touched the rail.) On LOSING HAZARDS, however, if the cue ball brushed the rail on the way to the pocket, the shot was deemed valid and no penalty was imposed. So the general rule in pocket games is that incidental contact does not count as a cushion hit, either in games requiring contact (BANK POOL) or in those penalizing contact (STOP GAME).

incline

1. The angle formed between the cue stick and the BED of the table as a player is striking. MASSÉ shots are those in which the cue is highly inclined, usually at an angle exceeding 45 degrees. 2. (Brit. games, obs.) A small amount of SIDE. 1873 Bennett 126.

incoming player

The PLAYER whose turn it will be to shoot at the end of the STRIKER'S current INNING. 1946 OR 5. In a two-player game, the incoming player is also known as the NONSTRIKER. The distinction between the incoming and outgoing player becomes important when an object ball falls into a pocket after first appearing to have stopped rolling. See also ADDRESS. Cf. OUTGOING PLAYER.

Indian Billiards

1. (game, obs.) Game played on an English Billiards table with a red ball worth three points and spotted on the BLACK SPOT, a brown worth four points and spotted at the right of the D, a green worth six and spotted at the left of the D, and a yellow worth nine and spotted at the CENTRE SPOT. 1924 Ogden diag. 120. 2. (game, obs.) A game introduced by the manufacturer Burroughes & Watts, played 200 UP with five balls, each of which is associated with a pocket. A curved line is drawn at a distance of two inches from each pocket. Any ball stopping within this arc is spotted unless it is the ball belonging to the pocket.

Indian Pool

1. (game, obs.) = RUSSIAN POOL. 1924 Smith 92, 1954 KTG 35, 1976 WSD 365. Also called SLOSH, TOAD-IN-THE-HOLE. 2. (game) = BACKWARDS POOL, BILLIARD POOL, CAROM POOL, CHINESE POOL, CONTRA POOL, IRISH POOL, KISS POOL, LOOP, REVERSE BILLIARDS. Cf. CUE BALL POOL.

Indirect

(game) = BANKS, KISSES, AND COMBINATIONS or HONOLULU. 1992 Billing 78.

indirect cannon

(Eng. Bill.) A CANNON in which the cue ball contacts a cushion before hitting the SECOND OBJECT BALL. 1976 WSD 66. A CUSHION CAROM. "Indirect" was used with this meaning in 1867 NYT (Dec 17) 3:1. Cf. DIRECT CANNON.

Indirect Game

(game) = CUSHION CAROMS. 1888 NYT (Oct 28) 20:1.

indirect pot

(Snooker) A POT in which the object ball enters the pocket after hitting another object ball. 1957 Holt 177. The equivalent of a KISS SHOT in Pocket Billiards. See also PLANT.

inlay

A method of decorating the BUTT of a cue stick by setting material into a groove cut in the wood. Cf. VENEER.

inning

The duration of a player's stay at the table from the time he first contacts the cue ball until his turn is ended by a MISS, FOUL, or completion of the game or BLOCK. 1864 NYT (Apr 10) 8:4, 1941 Hoppe 75, 1946 OR 92. The term was used in the game of cricket as early as 1746. See also HAND OUT, SPACER. See ADDRESS, IN CONTROL, TURN, VISIT. Cf. HALF-INNING.

The definition of "inning" is imprecise; it is unclear whether a player's inning commences (1) when he ADDRESSES the cue ball or (2) when he contacts the cue ball or commits a foul. It is likewise uncertain when an inning ends. See MOTION. Once the game begins, is it always someone's inning?

The professional Nine-Ball rules define an inning as beginning when it is legal for a player to stroke and ending at the end of a shot on which he misses, fouls, or wins the game. 1992 OR 53. The question is what happens during the first five seconds after it is legal to shoot, when any ball that drops spontaneously will be credited to the OUTGOING PLAYER. Whose inning was it?

121

The notion of inning is generalized somewhat in BOWL-LIARDS to conform to that of an inning of bowling. The striker is given two chances to make runs in a single inning. See also TEN PINS. In the old game of CONTINUOUS POOL, an "inning" was synonymous with a FRAME of 15 balls. 1889 NYT (Feb 26) 5:1.

inside

Between a ball and the cushion to which it is closest in a given direction. Used to describe English or the direction taken by the cue ball in a type of UMBRELLA shot at Three-Cushion Billiards. Cf. OUTSIDE.

inside English

ENGLISH on the same side of the cue ball as the direction in which the object ball is being CUT. 1989 Koehler 256. Cf. OUTSIDE ENGLISH.

inside leather

A LEATHER that covers the stitching on the inside of a pocket. Sometimes "pocket leather." Cf. SHIELD.

inside umbrella

See UMBRELLA.

installer

One who sets up a billiard table. Also MECHANIC.

instant replay

A method of reviewing events during a billiard game to determine whether a FOUL was committed. If a match is being videotaped, the tape may be used to verify that a foul occurred only if no infraction was observed by the REFEREE. If the referee saw the foul, the tape may not be used to reverse the decision.

intentional foul

One of a certain group of FOULS that, when committed deliberately, results in the imposition of additional sanctions or PENALTIES. Also known as a DELIBERATE FOUL. In general, an intentional foul is one made purposely and designed to alter the path of the cue ball or ball to be pocketed or to affect the position of a ball that is IN PLAY. The idea is that an intentional act merits greater punishment than an accidental one. The referee warns the player at the first offense; a second in the same match results in a FORFEIT. 1986 OR 44. See FIFTEEN-POINT PENALTY for an obsolete sanction.

Not all fouls committed willfully are classed as intentional fouls. For example, a deliberate SCRATCH carries no extra penalty. See also DELIBERATE SAFETY.

intentional miss

A type of SAFETY in which the player deliberately misses a shot in order to obtain a tactical advantage, such as by leaving a difficult shot for the opponent. Certain games, such as NINE-BALL and SNOOKER, have rules intended to prevent a player from benefiting from an intentional miss. See, for example, FREE BALL, PLAY AGAIN RULE, TAKE UP.

The intentional miss is illegal in Snooker and carries a penalty. 1978 BSCC 49. The CALLING of intentional misses is a difficult aspect of refereeing because the official must determine the subjective intent of the player based on his own knowledge of the game and not simply on objective facts, such as whether or not a ball was contacted. See also INTENTIONAL SAFETY.

intentional safety

(Three-Cushions) = DELIBERATE SAFETY. See also INTENTIONAL MISS.

Interclub Billiard League

(org.) Formed in 1916, an organization of private clubs in various U.S. cities, all having billiard facilities. Membership was limited to 15 clubs, which served as sites for matches and tournaments. 1916 NYT (May 16) 14:8.

Intercollegiate Billiards

1. Competitive billiards at the college level. In the first recorded American college match, Harvard freshmen beat a Yale team in 1860, a few years after the rivalry between Oxford and Cambridge was initiated. See also ASSOCIATION OF COLLEGE UNIONS INTERNATIONAL. 2. (game) A competitive format designed for college team play, adaptable to both carom and pocket billiards. Play commences from a standard BREAK SHOT and the contestants alternate turns for 15 innings, the object being to score as many total points as possible.

interdicted area

(Bill.) A region of the table in which play is restricted in some way, usually by placing a limit on the number of consecutive points that may be scored while both object balls lie in the area. 1881 NYT (Mar 27) 2:2, WBA 7. Examples: ANCHOR, BALK SPACE, CROTCH, PARKER'S BOX. See also BALKLINE, CHAMPION'S GAME, PANEL, RESTRICTED SPACE.

interference

1. A disturbance of playing conditions, either by one of the players or by some outside influence. 1946 OR 10, 1983 Rule Book 252. Examples of interference rules are:

- Touching or influencing the course of a ball in play in any manner except by legal contact between the cue stick and cue ball constitutes interference. 1807 White 68. Jimmy Marino, a top player of the 1970s, once fouled by allowing his long hair to touch a ball. 1982 BD (Sep/Oct) 24.
- Any object or substance on the table for which the player is responsible (such as a piece of chalk) may be removed by him before it touches a ball. See also PLAYER RESPONSIBILITY FOUL.
- Any substance foreign to the game for which the striker is not responsible may be removed by the REFEREE on request. This action was formerly required to be taken without raising any ball off the table and without the assistance of any player. 1916 RGRG 10. In a match between Jacob Schaefer Sr. and A. P. Rudolphe in 1879, the white ball ran over a small piece of chalk during the 126th shot of a RUN by Schaefer. He entreated the referee to remove the debris, which could be done only by moving the ball. This brought furious protest from Rudolphe, but there was no rule covering the point. The referee moved the ball, cleaned off the cloth, and Schaefer eventually ran 170 and won the match. 1879 NYT (Jan 24) 8:1. This action would be permissable today.
- After interference, the incoming player may accept TABLE IN POSITION or have the balls placed in the position "they obviously would have obtained had there been no interference." 1916 RGRG 10. See REPLACEMENT, RESTORE. In the mid-nineteenth century, the incoming player could compel the offender to play a BREAK SHOT.
- The NONSTRIKER must stand at least four feet from both the STRIKER and the table and must not annoy the striker.
- In case of NON-PLAYER INTERFERENCE, the balls are replaced by the referee and the striker incurs no penalty. 1916 RGRG 10. The referee may request the offender to leave the premises; if he fails to do so, the match may be postponed by the referee and the players must comply.
- Intentional interference is UNSPORTSMANLIKE CONDUCT. 1982 OR 49. In 14.1 CONTINUOUS, this results in the penalty for CONSECUTIVE FOULS.
- An ACT OF GOD does not constitute interference.

2. A ball "interferes" with the SPOTTING or RACKING if the required action cannot be performed without moving the ball, which is not permitted. Sometimes elaborate rules are necessary to specify what is to be done in various instances of such interference. In 14.1 CONTINUOUS, for example, the interference rule for racking occupies an entire page. 1986 OR 72. See IN THE RACK, OCCUPIED, SPOTTING.

interlocking bridge

A MECHANICAL BRIDGE so designed that the HEADS of two or more of them can be joined or interlocked to form a higher bridge for shooting over intervening balls to achieve the effect of a SPIDER. 1973 Mizerak 18. The rules of some games limit the number of bridges that can be used on a given shot, usually to two.

intermission

A SUSPENSION of play for the convenience of the players or SPECTATORS. The rules of some tournaments prohibited intermissions entirely. 1911 HRB 43a. During the 1935 World Three-Cushion title tournament, a break of 10 minutes was taken following the HALF-INNING of the first player to reach 25 points. 1937 NBJ (Sep). Also RECESS.

International Billiard and Snooker Federation (IBSF)

(org.) The world amateur governing body of English Billiards and Snooker. Originally the WORLD BILLIARDS AND SNOOKER COUNCIL, its name was changed in 1973. The countries associated with this body are: Australia, Bangladesh, Belgium, Canada, Egypt, England, Fiji, Hong Kong, Iceland, India, Isle of Man, Kenya, Malaysia, Malta, Mauritius, Netherlands, New Zealand, Northern Ireland, Pakistan, Republic of Ireland, Scotland, Singapore, Sri Lanka, Sudan, Sweden, Thailand, United States, Wales and Zimbabwe.

International Pocket Billiards Association (IPBA)

(org.) Formed in 1975 to upgrade tournament activity and establish a professional pocket billiard tour.

Interstate League

(org.) A LEAGUE of professional Three-Cushion players that organized competition beginning in 1914. Its participants in 1916 included such future champions as Robert Cannefax, Augie Kieckhefer, Jess Lean, Charles McCourt, and George Moore. 1916 BM (Jan) 42. During 1923–26, no world title competition was held, and the winner of the Interstate League was recognized as the U.S. national champion.

IPBA

(org.) = INTERNATIONAL POCKET BILLIARDS ASSOCIATION.

Irish Cannon Game, Irish Game

(Bagatelle game, obs.) Played with three balls, CANNONS counting two points and WINNING HAZARDS as marked on the ball holed. If the player's cue ball enters a CUP, points are forfeited to the adversary. 1878 Crawley 154, 1900 May 69. It differs from the CANNON GAME in that scoring is possible even if no cannon is made.

Irish linen

A fabric commonly wrapped around the butt of a cue stick to act as a GRIP. A WRAP must absorb perspiration slightly so the grip does not feel moist; failure to do this is one of the deficiencies of rayon but one of the advantages of Irish linen.

Irish Pool

(game) = BACKWARDS POOL, BILLIARD POOL, CAROM POOL, CHINESE POOL, CONTRA POOL, INDIAN POOL, KISS POOL, LOOP, REVERSE BILLIARDS. Cf. CUE BALL POOL.

iron

1. The metal rim used to attach a pocket to the rail. A POCKET IRON. 2. To apply a hot iron to the CLOTH to remove moisture. 1896 Broadfoot 83, 1911 Roberts 3, 1975a Lowe 13. See HEATING. The practice of ironing was not universally favored. 1883 J. *Liverpool Polytechnic Soc.* 93. 1906 Hotine even describes the need for ironing the balls. 3. (obs.) = PASS, PASS IRON or PORT. The use of this device was obsolescent in 1773 and thoroughly obsolete by 1807. 1974 Hendricks 25.

Italian Billiards

(game) = FIVE-PIN GAME, ITALIAN SKITTLE POOL.

Italian Skittle Pool

(game) A game played with two white balls, a red, a blue and five numbered SKITTLES. It is played to 31 points with BURST. Knocking down the center PIN while leaving the other four pins standing is called a ROYAL (a NATURAL or RANCHE in other games) and wins the game. 1866 Hardy, 1867 Dufton 223, 1869 Roberts 244. Also called ITALIAN BILLIARDS.

ivories

(colloq.) Billiard balls, so named because they were formerly made of IVORY. 1873 NYT (May 17) 1:3, 1888 OED.

ivory

A material, obtained from the tusks of elephants, from which billiard balls are made. Hence, by extension, a billiard ball itself. See IVORIES. A set of balls is sometimes referred to as "the ivory herd."

Ivory billiard balls were known in 1627 and probably much earlier. At the time of 1674 Cotton, ivory was used not only for balls but for the PORT, KING, and portions of the MACE. Marie Antoinette is reported to have owned a cue stick made entirely of carved ivory. Ivory was not in common use, however, until 1820. By 1860, the demand for ivory in billiard ball manufacture was so great that a prize was offered for the discovery of a

suitable substitute. This led to the development of celluloid by John Wesley Hyatt. See BALL, COMBINATION SET.

Ivory is a dense, tooth-like material between horn and bone in character, possessing a natural gelatin that contributes to its polish. Only the highest-quality material is used for billiard balls. It is obtained from female elephants in what was formerly Zanzibar, now Tanzania. 1839 Kentfield advises, "that from the Cape of Good Hope is best." An average tusk can be expected to yield only three to five balls. There is a large amount of waste because of cracks in the tusks that result in unusable sections.

Ivory has a grain structure that renders the balls susceptible to warping, splitting and even shattering. 1881 MB 17. They are sensitive to changes in temperature and may expand and contract unevenly, which can make play impossible. In the winter of 1907–08, George B. Sutton and Ora Morningstar played a match in an unheated hall. As the room became colder, the balls turned unwieldy and the game set a new record for low AVERAGES. 1925 Hoppe 123. Players used to be advised by manufacturers not to buy ivory balls during fall or winter and not to use them for one week after purchase. 1893 HRB 6. See HEATING.

Except in ARTISTIC BILLIARDS competition, ivory balls are rarely used today. A mystique has built up around their supposed ability to retain English even after multiple contacts with the cushions. Ivories differ from plastic balls in their elasticity, which changes the angle at which the balls separate after a collision, and in coefficient of friction, which affects their ACTION off a rail.

jab

(Eng. Bill.) = STAB. 1925 Peall 45.

jack

1. One of a number of specially marked balls in the game of POKER POCKET BILLIARDS. 1946 OR 72. 2. (obs.) The name given to the nine-ball in the HIGH-LOW-JACK GAME.

Jack-Up Pool

(game) Pocket Billiards in which one or both players shoot with one hand held in a trouser pocket and in which the cue stick may not be rested on a RAIL. An extreme HANDICAP. 1959 Tevis *The Hustler*. See ONE-HANDED PLAY.

jail

(colloq.) "In jail" means to have one's ball blocked by other balls. Also HOOKED, SNOOKERED.

jam

1. (Eng. Bill.) = JAM CANNON. 2. (Bill.) A kiss off a ball FROZEN to a cushion. 1910 NYT (Oct 21) 7:3. 3. (very rare) A player is "jam up" when he is shooting well. 1977 Martin 213.

jam cannon

(Eng. Bill.) NURSE performed with the object balls JAMMED, that is, FROZEN, to one another and to the JAW of a pocket. 1908 Mannock II 417, 1909 BYB 58, 1924 Ogden 228. Also spelled "jamb." 1895 Buchanan. In 1891, Tom Taylor made BREAK of 1467 with the aid of this cannon. 1912 Levi 587. The stroke was later outlawed. Cf. ANCHOR CANNON.

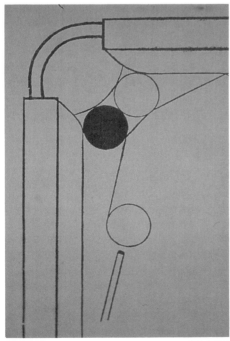

jam cannon

jammed

(Eng. Bill.) Said of two balls that are touching each other and different SHOULDERS of a pocket. 1867 NYT (Jun 11) 1:7, 1909 BA Rules 22, 1916 HDB 53. See JAM CANNON.

jar stroke

(Eng. Bill.) A shot in which the cue ball is struck with FOLLOW at a ball near a rail, after which the cue appears to hug the rail or contact it repeatedly. 1895 Buchanan 106. See also RICOCHET CANNON, SERPENTINE MASSÉ, SMASH-IN, SNAKE SHOT, SQUIB.

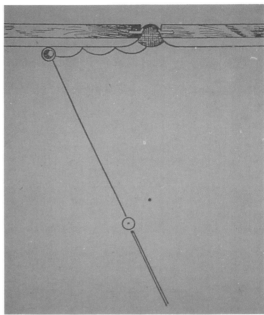

jar stroke

125

jaw

A corner of a CAROM TABLE or the opening of a pocket on a POCKET TABLE. 1850 Phelan 21, 1958 OR. 1881 MB 25 says that "jaw" is used only to refer to the pocket opening. To "jaw a ball" means to have it ricochet back and forth at the pocket opening without falling or to position it for the JAW SHOT. 1857 Phelan 65, 1979 Grissim 252. See JAWED. Cf. CROTCH.

jaw shot

A carom shot at balls held in the JAW. 1946 OR 92, 1976 WSD 235. This shot caused one of the earliest problems in competitive billiards, since a player who achieved the position could score indefinitely, making a mockery of the game. The stroke was BARRED in 1864. See also CROTCH.

jawed

1. LOCKED, FROZEN in the JAW. 1867 NYT (Jun 11) 1:7, 1979 Grissim 252. See also SUSPENDED BALL. 2. Said of a ball that fails to DROP in a pocket after bouncing back and forth against the JAWS. 1992 OR 11.

jeffery

(obs.) A cue stick whose shaft is cut obliquely at the POINT, thus beveled so as to permit the cue ball to be struck below center. This device was invented about 1790, prior to the introduction of the cue tip. 1873 Bennett 9. Later, the end of the cue was rounded on one side to increase the area of contact between the stick and the ball. 1839 Kentfield 2.

jenny

(Eng. Bill.) A LOSING HAZARD off a ball lying near a LONG RAIL into a pocket adjacent to that rail. The ball is usually BELOW the middle pocket and 6 to 12 inches away from the cushion. 1807 White 36, 1862 Crawley 20, 1911 Roberts 17. A LONG JENNY is one played into a

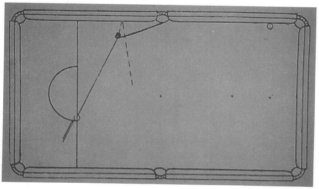

jenny (short)

corner pocket; a SHORT JENNY is played into a middle pocket. When performed delicately, the position can be repetitive and may lead to a long BREAK. See also QUILL STROKE.

Jenny Lind

(game, obs.) A game played with five balls, devised to circumvent a New York ordinance prohibiting the FOUR-BALL GAME. 1879 NYDT (Feb 24) 6:3. The name of a popular Swedish singer of the nineteenth century. Cf. PIGEON HOLE AND JENNY LIND.

Jeu de Guerre

(game) = WAR GAME. Also called À LA GUERRE.

jigger

(obs., sl.) = MECHANICAL BRIDGE. 1847 OED, 1866 Crawley 10, 1885 Cook 10.

Johnston City

A small town in Illinois that was the site of a long series of annual HUSTLERS' tournaments from 1961 to 1972, promoted by the brothers George and Paul Jansco. These events included competition at One-Pocket and Nine-Ball at a time when Straight Pool was the only sanctioned tournament form. Although officially unrecognized, the Johnston City matches were of great significance because they brought together skilled players who rarely entered conventional tournaments. To

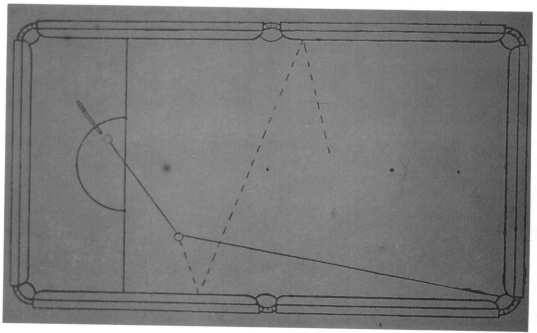

jenny (long)

many players of the period, "Johnston City" is synonymous with competitive pocket billiards at its highest level.

joint

The fitting at which a TWO-PIECE CUE, or JOINTED CUE, can be broken down; the piece that joins the BUTT and the SHAFT. 1965 Fats 75. Joints may be "piloted" or "flat-faced," referring to the manner in which the butt and shaft are placed in contact. The question whether a metal-to-metal or wood-to-wood joint is superior is not yet settled. The issue concerns the efficiency of transmitting force across the boundary between two materials having differing speeds of sound. See FLAT JOINT, PILOTED JOINT.

joint cap

A protective cap screwed on the male or female component of the JOINT of a cue to protect it from damage while in storage. 1990 White 2–9. What incident might occur while the cue is in its CASE that would harm the joint without thoroughly mangling the other portions of the cue has never been satisfactorily explained, so it is safe to conclude that joint caps are really for decorative purposes. Cf. JOINT PROTECTOR.

joint protector

A fitting that screws into or over the end of a shaft or butt to protect the COLLAR as well as the screw. Cf. JOINT CAP, which does not extend over the side of the joint but merely covers its end.

jointed cue

A cue stick that can be taken apart for ease of carrying. Also called a TWO-PIECE CUE, although jointed cues with as many as five sections have been made. Jointed cues were being sold by Thurston's in 1829. 1974 Hendricks 36. Cf. ONE-PIECE CUE.

juice

(sl.) = SPIN, especially extreme spin or ENGLISH. Also GREASE, OIL, STUFF.

jump ball

A ball that has left the table and come to rest elsewhere or has left the table and contacted an object that is not part of the permanent billiard furnishings, regardless of where it comes to rest. 1850 Phelan 21, 1983 Rule Book 252. Also known as a JUMPED BALL or a BALL OFF. A ball that has jumped the table is said to be LOST; it is not IN PLAY. In British usage, FORCED OFF. Cf. LEAVE THE TABLE, SUSPENDED BALL.

Since the earliest days of billiards it has been illegal to jump a ball off the table. 1674 Cotton provides: "He that

. . . strikes either Ball over the Table loseth one." There are now a variety of modern rules covering jump balls. In American games, if a ball hits any non-table equipment, it is a jump ball even if it later returns to the table. 1992 OR 38. Under international THREE-CUSHION rules, when all the balls jump the table, the INCOMING PLAYER'S cue ball is placed on the HEAD SPOT, the red on the FOOT SPOT and the opponent's cue ball on the CENTER SPOT. WBA 15. If a spot is OCCUPIED, the ball that would have been placed there is put instead on the spot reserved for the interfering ball. In ENGLISH BILLIARDS, jumping the cue ball off the table after counting was formerly not a foul (but is now); it was replaced on the STRING SPOT, RED SPOT, or CENTRE SPOT, in that order, if the proper spot was occupied. 1916 RGRG 7.

In Bumper Pool, the penalty for a jump ball is that the incoming player may place the ball anywhere on the table and may also DROP two of his object balls.

jump cue

A cue stick that is light and short (for example, nine ounces and 35 inches) used for making JUMP SHOTS. The cue need not be long because little follow-through is required. It can be unwieldy to use a regular cue for such shots because of the need to elevate the butt yet use a short stroke.

jump shot

A shot in which the cue ball jumps from the bed of the table and returns to complete the shot. 1859 *Leslie's* (Jan 15) 107:1, 1881 MB 25, 1941 Hoppe 75. In the early days of 14.1 CONTINUOUS, jump shots were not permitted. 1916 BM (Mar) 45. Under present rules, a jump shot is legal if the cue ball is struck above its center by raising the butt of the cue. It is illegal if the ball is struck below center because this is believed to imply (alas, incorrectly) that some part of the SHAFT of the cue stick must have contacted the ball to cause it to jump; contact is legal only between the tip of the cue stick and the cue ball. 1956 BSTE 18. The jump shot is illegal in English Billiards and Snooker if the cue ball jumps over another ball. 1978 BSCC. However, since 1958 the jump has been allowed if it occurs after the cue ball has legally hit a BALL ON. 1985 Morrison 25, 1987 BSCC S13. See also DIP, LEAP, SCOOP SHOT, STEEPLECHASE CANNON.

In Bumper Pool, it is illegal to jump a ball over another ball or a BUMPER. 1992 OR 73.

Jump shots were known before the invention of the cue. In connection with the game of TRUCKS, played with large mace-like sticks, 1674 Cotton 44 gives the instruction, "to make your jump over his . . . you must strike a strong stroke, sloping downwards, which will make your

127

Ball mount aloft." Because of the height of the cushions, early cue players were forced to raise the butt of the cue when shooting at a ball lying near a rail. It was observed that this stroke caused the ball to leave the table briefly. Jump shots were performed as tricks during the eighteenth century and were made with a motion of the cue called the HIGH OBLIQUE STROKE. 1807 White 25. 1806 Phil 13 teaches that "low application of the point will detach the ball from the table." (It might well have mentioned that there is also risk of detaching the cloth from the table.) The term "jump" appears in 1829 Plan 11 and 1850 Phelan 53.

The jump shot is one of the few areas of billiard technique in which substantive progress has been made during the last 20 years. Accomplished players can jump a POOL BALL entirely over another even if the distance between the balls is less than half an inch. The jump is an important tool in Nine-Ball, where failure to contact the required ball results in a severe penalty. It is the rise of tournament Nine-Ball that has spurred the development of the jump shot, which has little utility in Straight Pool. A poll of professionals found that Sammy Jones and Pat Fleming are regarded as among the most skilled jump players.

128

jumped ball
= JUMP BALL.

Karolin
The German name for the yellow ball. See CARLINE.

Keeley
(game) = KELLY POOL. 1922 BM (May) 15.

Kegel-Partie
(game) = SKITTLE BILLIARDS. The German word *Kegel* means "skittle." 1876 Bogumil 382. See also KUGEL-PARTIE for the story of a misnomer.

Keilley Game
(game) KELLY POOL to 31 points with the SHAKE BOTTLE, BURST, and PRIVILEGE. 1916 RGRG 61.

Kelly Pool
(game) = PEA POOL, PILL POOL. 1911 HRB 84, 1974 ITP 31. Also known as KEELEY, the KEILLEY GAME or Killy. 1916 HDB 113. Many variations exist—one is played with only 10 balls; another requires the lowest-numbered ball to be contacted first. An early version known as Kelly Rotation gave rise to the expression BEHIND THE EIGHT-BALL. In 1930, the cartoonist Clare Briggs published a book of drawings showing players at Kelly Pool. *See illustration on next page.*

key ball
1. (14.1 Continuous) The ball pocketed immediately before the BREAK BALL, on the KEY SHOT. So named because of the crucial role it plays in permitting the striker to achieve a good position for the upcoming BREAK SHOT. 1948 Mosconi 78. 2. (Pocket Bill.) The third ball from the pocket in COMBINATION shots involving three or more balls. 1948 Mosconi 60. This ball is "key" because the LINE OF CENTERS, defined by it and the ball closest to the pocket, determines the approximate line along which the object ball will travel. *See illustration on next page.*

key shot
1. (14.1 Continuous) The shot on the KEY BALL; an attempt to set up a good BREAK SHOT. 1979 Sullivan 186. 2. (game) = KEY SHOT BILLIARDS.

Key Shot Billiards
(game) A method of conducting intercollegiate billiards competition remotely, so the players do not have to be in the same room, or even the same country, during the match. A prearranged set of shots is attempted, each being set up using a chart as a guide. Beginning from each position, the player continues shooting until he either misses or scores 10 points. His score is the total number of points made over all shots. The results are communicated between the competitors by telegraph. 1938 *Popular Science* (Jun) 56, 1946 Brunswick 15.

The first tournament was held at the University of Wisconsin in 1932 with 10 universities participating. 1932 BM (Feb) 16. Pocket Billiards can also be played in this fashion. See also DUPLICATE BILLIARDS, TELEGRAPHIC BILLIARDS. For a related game allowing comparison of players who have never faced one another over the table, see EQUAL OFFENSE.

kick
1. A KICK SHOT. 2. (Nine-Ball, colloq.) The act of fouling by knocking the cue ball to a position in which the opponent has a difficult shot. See ROLLOUT. 3. (Brit. games) A phenomenon in which the cue and object balls do not separate at the expected angle after making

Kelly Pool (Cartoon by Clare Briggs)

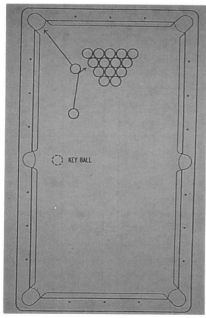

key ball

contact. This is thought to be caused by a foreign substance, such as chalk, lying at the point at which the balls touch. 1985 Morrison 64, 1990 Taylor 114.

kick shot

(Pocket Bill.) A type of BANK SHOT in which the cue ball contacts a cushion before hitting a ball. 1992 OR 11. See also BRICOLE. Kick shots have become important in pool since the introduction of tournament Nine-Ball. They were of little significance in Straight Pool except in SAFETY PLAY, in which no real attempt is generally made to pocket the object ball.

kill

1. To hit a ball very hard and thus, by sacrificing accuracy, risk missing the shot. 2. To hit a ball softly or with ENGLISH in such a way that it becomes DEAD after contact with another ball or a rail. 3. (obs.) To cause a player to become DEAD, as by losing his third LIFE in LIFE POOL. 1850 Phelan 41.

kill shot

A DEAD BALL shot; one in which the motion of the cue ball is greatly reduced by contact with the object ball.

killed ball

(obs.) A DEAD BALL, one that is not IN PLAY. 1884 MB 23.

Killer

(game) A modern European FULL RACK pocket game for 2–15 players based on ideas from the obsolete game of Life Pool. Each player begins with three LIVES. The BREAKER may shoot again if no ball is pocketed on the break. A miss or a foul results in the loss of a life. When all balls have been pocketed, they are racked and the striker breaks. The last player with one or more lives wins the game. 1992 Holmes PC.

king

1. (obs.) A pointed ivory stick used as a target in billiards in the seventeenth and early eighteenth centuries. 1674 Cotton 27. Cf. PORT. Its function has been taken over by PINS and SKITTLES. 1979 Everton 10. 2. (Poker Pocket Bill.) One of a set of specially marked balls, meant to correspond to the king in a deck of cards. 1946 OR 72. 3. (Eng. Bagatelle, obs.) A special ball that must be struck before any score can be made. The KING BALL. 1898 HRB 101.

king (1694) The subject in the engraving happens to be King Louis XIV

king ball

(Eng. Bagatelle, obs.) A special ball that must be contacted by another ball before any score is possible. 1898 HRB 101. Sometimes just KING.

kiss

Generally, a contact between two billiard balls. 1. A second contact between the cue ball and an object ball or between two object balls. 1836 OED, 1850 Phelan 20, 1881 MB 24, 1941 Hoppe 75. A contact between balls that alters their path or position, whether planned or accidental. 1807 White 96, 1875 NYT (Nov 16) 8:3, 1992 OR 11. See also DOUBLE KISS, HELP, KISS-IN, KISS-OFF, KISS-OUT. An unanticipated kiss usually results in a failed shot. However, USBA rule 16 makes it clear that in Three-Cushions a COUNT is valid even it results from an unintentional kiss: "All kiss shots are fair, whether they deprive a player of an imminent score, or whether they assist in a score." 1992 OR 112. Three-Cushion players who lose a shot to a kiss have the annoying habit of saying, "It would have made." Cue-maker Ray Schuler has the perfect response — "So what?" 2. A rebound off a ball that is close to or FROZEN to a rail or another ball. 1806 Phil 41, 1839 Kentfield 23, 1863 Phelan & Berger 37. A KISS-BACK SHOT. In British usage, a RUN OFF. 3. (Pocket Bill.) A CAROM. 1973 Mizerak 81, 1976 WSD 245, 1980 Balukas 196. 4. A light contact between two balls. "The shot can be made if you just kiss it." 5. A FREEZE. "They are kissing," meaning that the balls are FROZEN.

kiss-back shot

A shot in which the cue ball caroms back off a ball that is close to or FROZEN to a cushion. 1978 BD (Nov/Dec) 18. A KISS, KISS CANNON, or KISS STROKE.

kiss cannon

(Eng. Bill.) A CANNON made by reflecting the cue ball off a ball that is FROZEN to a rail. 1911 Roberts 208, 1935 Smith 51. In American usage, a KISS-BACK SHOT. A cannon in which the first object ball forces the second into the cue ball to complete the COUNT. 1954 KTG 23, 1957 Holt 92. The term "kiss carom" appears at 1879 NYT (Jan 29) 8:5. Cf. CHUCK NURSE.

Kiss-Cannons

(game) A game played with two balls on a CAROM TABLE in which the object is to make the cue ball hit the other ball twice. The game was popularized somewhat during the 1890s by May Kaarlus, a famous exhibition player whose specialty was fancy carom shots. Also known as PLON-PON or the TWO-BALL GAME.

kiss-in

A KISS that results in a successful count instead of the player being deprived of a score as in a KISS-OUT. See also HELP. When intentional, this is known as a TIME SHOT. When unintentional, the striker may act as if it were planned all along. Such posturing is unnecessary, since the shot counts without regard to the player's intent. See KISS, def. 1.

kiss-off

Accidental contact between two balls that spoils a shot. 1879 NYT (Jan 28) 8:3, 1942 Cochran 88. A KISS-OUT.

kiss-out

Accidental contact, or KISS, between two balls that causes a shot to fail, in which case the player is said to have been "kissed out." 1867 NYT (Jun 11) 1:7, 1992 OR 11. The kiss-out is an important cause of missed shots in THREE-CUSHIONS. A KISS-OFF. Cf. KISS-IN.

Kiss Pool

(game) = BACKWARDS POOL, BILLIARD POOL, CAROM POOL, CHINESE POOL, CONTRA POOL, INDIAN POOL, IRISH POOL, KISS POOL, LOOP, REVERSE BILLIARDS. 1984 BD (Apr) 20. Cf. CUE BALL POOL.

kiss-pot

(Brit. games) A legal shot in which the cue ball contacts the object ball twice to send it into a pocket. 1957 Holt 36. A variety of TIME SHOT in which the interval between ball contacts is very short.

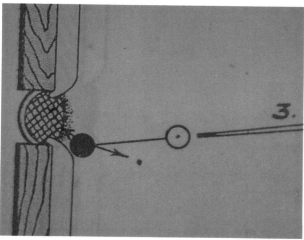

kiss-pot

kiss shot

Generally, a shot in which a KISS is utilized deliberately to effect a score.

1. A shot in which the cue ball is CAROMED off a ball that is FROZEN to a rail. 1873 NYT (May 17) 1:3. A KISS-BACK SHOT or KISS CANNON. 2. (Pocket Bill.) A shot in which an object ball is made to CAROM off another ball on its way to the pocket. In Snooker, an INDIRECT POT. When the object ball is frozen to another, this is known as a PLANT. 3. (Bill.) A shot in which the second object ball

is moved from its original position before being contacted by the cue ball, or in which the cue ball contacts the first object ball twice before completing the count. A species of TIME SHOT.

kiss stroke

(obs.) A KISS-BACK SHOT; one in which the cue ball is made to KISS off a ball that is FROZEN to or near a rail. 1863 Phelan & Berger 37. Sometimes simply a KISS.

kissing

Said of two balls that are in contact, or FROZEN. See FAST, FREEZE, TOUCHING BALL.

kitchen

(pocket games) The BALK area; that portion of the table lying between the HEAD STRING and the HEAD RAIL, in which the player may place a ball that is IN HAND BEHIND THE HEAD STRING. The kitchen does not include the head string itself. 1980 OR 43. Once slang, this term is now gaining respectability because of its appearance in the Official Rules of the BCA.

When one is forced to play from the kitchen, what must the cue ball be made to do before the shot will be considered legal. In Nine-Ball, the cue ball must leave the kitchen (possibly by a BANK or MASSÉ) before it may legally contact any ball within the kitchen. In Eight-Ball, after a scratch following a legal break, the rule specifies that the cue ball must contact a cushion before returning to contact a ball in the kitchen. 1992 OR 43. A massé in this situation is therefore ruled out.

The origin of the term has been an object of speculation for a long time. Jim Vitalo, of Willow Springs, Illinois, explains that many American homes during the late 1800s did not have room for a separate billiard table. It was common to employ a COMBINATION TABLE that could be used for both dining and billiards. This table would have to be placed in the dining room, which was often barely large enough to contain it. To increase the clearance available for BREAK SHOTS, the table would be positioned so that the HEAD RAIL was facing the doorway to the kitchen. This would allow the player to take a more comfortable backswing. He was thus literally "in the kitchen" when shooting from the HEAD STRING.

Klondike

(game, obs.) A game similar to Bagatelle, played on a table of approximate dimensions 7'5" by 3'2" with special troughs known as "alleys." A ball is shot to the semicircular end; points may be scored as it returns toward the player. 1908 HRB 117.

131

knock-out

1. A shot in which a ball dislodges another ball from the rail or other obstructed position. Used to MANUFACTURE a subsequent shot when none would be available otherwise. 1981 Quinn 71. 2. The BREAK SHOT in games in which it is an advantage to spread the balls from the PACK rather than to play a SAFETY on the break. See also FREE BREAK, OPEN BREAK. 3. A form of TOURNAMENT in which a player is eliminated upon losing one game. Also SINGLE ELIMINATION. Cf. ROUND-ROBIN.

knocker

(sl.) One who attempts to dissuade bettors from backing certain players, as by alerting them to a player's true SPEED or warning of a potential DUMP. See GAMBLING.

knuckled

(colloq.) In Britain, an ANGLED BALL is also said to be "knuckled." 1990 Taylor 113.

Komori taper

A TAPER, preferred by Three-Cushion players, in which the diameter of the shaft increases linearly from tip to joint. In other words, when laid on the table, the shaft will lie flat because its profile is a straight line. Named for Japanese Three-Cushion champion Junichi Komori. Cf. DELAYED TAPER, PROFESSIONAL TAPER.

Korean games

The Koreans are enthusiastic carom players. They have created variations of the game that are unknown elsewhere. One is a four-ball game with two red and two white balls. The object is to make a carom on the two reds without touching the other white with the cue ball. Korean carom balls are larger, at 65.5 millimeters, than any Western billiard ball.

A six-ball version is played with two white cue balls and four colored object balls: black, red, yellow, and blue. A foul results in the player's score being reset to zero.

There is also a nine-ball game similar to the six-ball style but that uses seven colored balls: black, two blues, two yellows, and two reds. The black is placed on a small stand; a foul results if it is knocked off. From two to ten points can be scored by caroms; the number of points depends on the colors of the object balls involved. 1992 Segal PC.

Kugel-Partie

(game) = KEGEL-PARTIE, SKITTLE BILLIARDS. 1856 Crawley 103, 1866 Crawley 220. This is undoubtedly a misnomer; the word *Kugel* in German means "ball," while *Kegel* means "skittle."

132

La Barraque

See BARRAQUE, LA.

La Pétanque

See PÉTANQUE, LA.

lace cannon

(Eng. Bill.) A CANNON in which the cue ball travels across the table two or more times, as if it were lacing a boot. 1889 Drayson 54, 1910a Ritchie 106, 1976 Reardon 114.

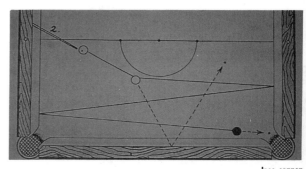

lace cannon

ladder

A means of determining a RANKING of players based on their competitive performance. The players are listed in sequence. Any player may challenge the one immediately above himself on the list; should he win, their positions are reversed. Advancement is thus analogous to climbing a ladder.

ladies' aid

(colloq.) A disparaging term for the MECHANICAL BRIDGE. 1973 Mizerak 82, 1977 Fels 9. Also called the CRUTCH, OLD MAN'S AID or SISSY STICK.

lag

1. A procedure to determine which player will begin the game, that is, who will LEAD. From behind the HEAD

STRING, the players simultaneously drive balls to the FOOT RAIL and back. The winner is the one whose ball comes to rest closest to the HEAD RAIL. 1930 BM (Jun), 1941 Hoppe 75. Also called the BANK or STRING. In British games, the players lag from the BAULK-LINE.

The shooting of balls to select the opening striker is a very old custom described in 1674 Cotton 26. The term "lag" itself is much younger. (The author has found no reference to it prior to 1930.) The object formerly was to run one's ball as close as possible to the KING without touching the far cushion. Later, the winner was the player who left his ball closest to, but not touching, the far cushion.

It is illegal to interfere with the opponent's ball on the lag and a player loses the lag if his ball enters a pocket. 1836 Tillotson 1. The rule in the FOUR-BALL GAME was that the second player to lag had to hit his ball before his opponent's ball touched the first cushion. 1891 MB 277. This was to prevent the later player from obtaining an advantage by seeing how well his opponent had lagged. In some games, it was a foul to practice the lag under the guise of testing the balls. 1893 HRB 60. In BILLIARDS, the red ball may not be contacted on the lag. 1916 RGRG 7. A player loses the lag if his cue ball fails to contact the FOOT RAIL, enters a pocket, or jumps the table. 1982 OR. If the two cue balls touch, the player whose ball is clearly out of line is the loser. 1916 RGRG 7. Under some sets of rules, a player loses if his cue ball crosses the LONG STRING, regardless of whether it hits the opponent's ball.

The winner of the lag normally has choice of cue balls and the LEAD, if he wishes to accept it. 1893 HRB 31. 1941 Hoppe relates a curious 1926 incident in which two players competing for the 18.2 Balkline title, Jake Schaefer Jr. and Erich Hagenlocher, both apparently forgot that the winner of the lag has the option of assigning the break to his opponent. The players were nervous and neither wanted to break. Each therefore deliberately tried to lose the lag! Schaefer won and, *thinking himself unlucky*, broke and ran out the game, 400–0.

Under modern Three-Cushion rules, the opening striker (not necessarily the winner of the lag) must use the BLACK BALL. In some countries, the balls are not spotted after the lag, but the winner must play from the position in which the balls come to rest. See also LEAD.

Many players have difficulty determining who has won the lag. Trying to measure the distances involves much blinking and squinting. A simple method was explained to the author by Allen Gilbert, many-time U.S. Three-Cushion champion. The player should position himself behind the head rail at a point midway between the two cue balls. He should then bend at the knees and lower himself slowly, glancing back and forth from ball to ball. The ball whose point of contact with the cloth is first obscured by the rail is closest to it.

2. (Bill.) A three-cushion BANK SHOT. 1982 OR.

3. (Pocket Bill.) A maneuver in which a ball is deliberately made to roll slowly toward a pocket so that it will either drop or remain near the pocket to be sunk at a later opportunity. 1985 Marguglio 220.

large ball
(Brit.) = BIG BALL. 1889 Drayson 43.

Last Player
(game, obs.) = A popular version of LIFE POOL in which the striker must shoot at the ball used by the "last" (that is, the preceding) player. 1839 Kentfield 40, 1889 Drayson 101. Also known as COLOR-BALL POOL, ENGLISH POOL, FOLLOWING POOL, LIVE POOL, or just POOL. Cf. TWO-BALL POOL.

Last-Pocket Eight-Ball
(game) EIGHT-BALL in which the eight-ball must be holed in the pocket in which the player's last GROUP BALL fell. 1977 Fels 115, 1982 OR 56. This rule, called the LAST POCKET OPTION, adds an extra component of strategy to the game.

last pocket option
(Eight-Ball) Optional rule requiring the player to pocket the eight-ball in the same pocket as his last GROUP BALL. 1982 OR, 1983 Rule Book 255. EIGHT-BALL played with this rule in effect is called LAST-POCKET EIGHT-BALL. See also MISERY, MISSOURI, ONE AND FIFTEEN IN THE SIDE.

last two
(Nine-Ball) A HANDICAP in which the weaker player wins the game if he pockets either of the last two balls remaining on the table. Note that one of these must be the nine-ball, but the other is not necessarily the eight, which may have been pocketed earlier. This SPOT is therefore not the same as HOP THE EIGHT.

lay
To obtain POSITION. "Sink the five and lay for the six."

lay a snooker
(Snooker) To create a SNOOKER; to leave a position in which one's opponent is SNOOKERED, that is, to leave the opponent unable to hit any BALL ON with a straight shot of the cue ball. 1954 KTG 27, 1965 Pulman 67.

133

This tactic is somewhat analogous to laying a trap, which (incorrectly in this context) suggests stealth rather than skill.

lay-off

1. The act of reducing one's risk on a wager by spreading the ACTION to other bettors. 2. (obs. in U.S.) = BREAK-OFF, LEAD, OPENING BREAK. 1875 NYT (Nov 16) 8:3, 1916 RGRG 20.

layout

(pocket games) The arrangement of the balls on the table at a given time. 1977 Fels 68. Also called the POSITION or PATTERN. Cf. LEAVE, which tends to refer to the position for the next shot rather than the situation as a whole.

lead

1. The first proper shot of the game following the LAG or STRING. The BREAK, BREAK SHOT, or OPENING BREAK. 1674 Cotton 26, 1775 Annals 28, 1863 Phelan & Berger 45. In AMERICAN FOUR-BALL BILLIARDS, the lead was very specialized. 1893 HRB 31. The LEADER was not permitted to score, and the second player had to accept the position left to him. See also PLAY OFF. 2. The number of points or games by which one player's score exceeds his opponent's.

leader

The player who makes the first stroke of a game. See LAG, LEAD, STRING.

leading stroke

(obs.) = OPENING BREAK. 1884 MB 23.

league

An association comprising teams or individual players who compete regularly against one another, usually for a league championship. More than one million people currently belong to Eight-Ball leagues in the U.S.

Professional leagues were common during the first half of the twentieth century. The city of Chicago supported its own Three-Cushion league during the 1920s. Two world champions emerged from its ranks: Augie Kieckhefer and Arthur Thurnblad. Occasionally, league play was even used to award championship titles. During the lull between annual world Three-Cushion tournaments, the INTERSTATE LEAGUE brought top competitors to a regular circuit of major cities. From 1923 to 1926 there was no world tournament, and the national title was decided by a grueling Interstate League schedule that lasted 180 games in 1926. It was in one of these matches that Otto Reiselt set the American record for BEST GAME in 50 points when he finished in 16 innings

for an AVERAGE of 3.125. This record was not equaled until May 1992, when Sang Lee tied it in an exhibition tournament in New York.

League play was also occasionally used as a competitive form in Straight Pool. In 1924, 15 players each played 120 games over a period of six months to reduce the field to four finalists who then PLAYED OFF for the national championship, which was won by Ralph Greenleaf. Frank Taberski took the title in 108 games the following year after Greenleaf suffered a nervous breakdown. Nothing has yet topped the marathon competition of 1941 in which Willie Mosconi won his first championship with a record of 176–48 after 224 games. Andrew Ponzi, who came in second, was more than 30 games behind Mosconi with a record of 144–80. Mosconi ran 125 and OUT seven times during that season. No U.S. professional title has been determined by league play since 1941.

leap

(Eng. Bill., obs.) = JUMP SHOT, HIGH OBLIQUE STROKE, STEEPLECHASE CANNON. 1896 Broadfoot 250.

leather

1. = TIP, as in CUE LEATHER. 1884 MB 19. See TIP for the history of tipping cues. Leather was used for tips by 1818. 2. A material used for the WRAP of a cue stick. 3. A decorative trim used on billiard tables. A "black leather" is used for covering POCKET IRONS, a "red leather" for the insides of pockets. 1908 Brunswick 78. See also INSIDE LEATHER, SHIELD.

leave

The POSITION left by the previous shot. 1873 *Billiard Cue*, 1896 Broadfoot 319, 1941 Hoppe 75, 1992 OR 12. "'Jever take 'n try to give an ironclad leave to yourself from a three-rail billiard shot?" 1957 Willson *The Music Man*. Also AFTER-POSITION, BREAK, LIE, PO, SHAPE. Cf. LAYOUT, PATTERN.

leave the table

1. Said of a ball that loses contact with the BED of the table. A ball that leaves the table temporarily is not necessarily a JUMP BALL, since it may return without striking a foreign object and still be considered IN PLAY. 2. To retire from the playing area during one's INNING. In tournament play, permission to do this must be requested from the referee.

ledge

(obs.) = RAIL. 1674 Cotton.

left

= LEFT ENGLISH. "Play it with high left." Cf. RIGHT.

left English

SPIN applied to the ball by striking it to the left of center, which causes the ball to rebound to the left after striking a cushion. See ENGLISH. Also known as LEFT. Cf. RIGHT ENGLISH.

left-handed play

Playing left-handed can be a useful skill for a right-handed player, since it eliminates the need for the MECHANICAL BRIDGE in many situations. See also AMBI-DEXTROUS. Considerable practice is required to develop a feel for using the opposite arm.

Most billiard champions have been right-handed. Left-handed Three-Cushion champions have included Al-fredo De Oro, Charles Ellis, Augie Kieckhefer, and Leon Magnus. Left-handed pocket champions have included Arthur Cranfield, Cyrille Dion and Ruth McGinnis. Edouard Horemans was the only left-handed 18.2 Balkline player to win the world title.

left rail

The LONG RAIL to the player's left as seen from the HEAD of the table. 1946 OR 95. Cf. RIGHT RAIL.

leg

That part of a table that touches the floor and supports the BASE FRAME. Tables have been constructed having from four to 15 legs. The leg may be of many different shapes and is frequently carved or decorated. In French tables of the mid-nineteenth century, a channel ran through the upper portion of the leg for use as a BALL RETURN. Table legs can be very distinctive and are useful as a means of identifying antique tables.

legal object ball

A ball that may be struck first by the cue ball without penalty. A BALL ON. 1985c Game Rules. In Straight Pool, all object balls are legal at all times, except when the striker has CUE BALL IN HAND BEHIND THE HEAD STRING. In Nine-Ball, by contrast, there is never more then one legal object ball, that being the lowest-num-bered ball on the table. In Eight-Ball, when the table is OPEN, any object ball is legal. When the table is no longer open, only balls of the striker's GROUP are legal.

legs

(colloq.) Running speed, energy, ability to keep rolling, as in "not enough legs," meaning that the ball has insufficient speed or, occasionally, ENGLISH to com-plete the shot. 1885 NYDT (Apr 24) 5:3, 1907 NYT (Mar 6) 7:1. The term is still in common use but rarely appears in print.

lemon

(sl.) The act of a HUSTLER in concealing his true playing ability. 1967 Polsky 47. Winning in a lazy or amateur-ish manner or losing deliberately. 1976 WSD 256. See also DOG, DUCK, LET UP, LIE DOWN, STALL. Cf. STAND-UP.

Le Président

See PRÉSIDENT, LE.

let up

(colloq.) To fail to play as well as one is able. 1927 Katch 50.

1. To CLUTCH, meaning to lose one's form suddenly and unintentionally. 2. To play beneath one's ability in the hope of attracting a favorable betting situation. To LEMON. See also DOG, DUCK, HUSTLER, LIE DOWN, STALL.

level

1. Said of a table that is flat and balanced so that the balls will roll properly. The importance of a level table is stressed in 1674 Cotton: "there are very few Billiard-Tables which are found true; and therefore such which are exactly level'd are highly valuable by a good player. . . . Bunglers many times by knowing the windings and tricks of the table have shamelessly beaten a very good Gamester."

A table that is not level will cause the balls to DRIFT as they roll, making aiming difficult. See ROLL, TABLE ROLL. A rise of five-thousandths of an inch per foot is acceptable, which is about one-twentieth of an inch over the length of the table. Anything greater than this will produce a detectable roll. An 18-inch machinist's level is a suitable tool for leveling a table. A typical carpenter's level is too crude to be of use. (This was not the case a century ago; 1867 Dufton 16 recommended using a "spirit level.") On American tables, the most common method of leveling was to insert thin slats of wood, called SHIMS, under the legs. This technique does not allow for very fine adjustment and cannot easily be performed by one person. Modern tables provide adjust-able feet under the legs that can be raised and lowered by rotation. However, this still allows for adjustment at only four points.

European tables have more sophisticated leveling mechanisms. Søren Søgård sets its slates on steel I-beams and provides 18 bolts that are easily adjusted by a single person using a wrench. It has become common to use a surveyor's transit for leveling such tables, but this seems unnecessary.

2. (Brit. games) Equal, EVEN UP. Said when the players have the same score. 1985 Arnold 208. A "level game" is one with no HANDICAP, in which both players need the same number of points to win. 1901 WB (Apr 3) 326. In the U.S., HEADS UP.

Liability

(game) A multi-player game, usually a variant of American Snooker, in which a striker who fails to hit the BALL ON pays a forfeit to the next player in rotation rather than to all players or the one who caused the snooker.

Liberty Billiards

(game, obs.) An amusing variation of Balkline developed by Charles C. Peterson during World War I. The table layout consisted of a map of the battlefield areas of France and Germany, including Paris and Berlin, with ordinary 18-inch balklines superimposed. Actual lines of battle were also drawn, dividing the table into a number of different areas for handicapping purposes. 1918 BM (Nov). This was not the first time that billiards took on a military flavor; see FORTIFICATION BILLIARDS and JEU DE GUERRE.

lie

= LEAVE, the position of the balls following a shot. 1977 Martin 214. Also AFTER-POSITION, BREAK, PO, SHAPE.

lie down

(colloq.) To play more poorly than one is able in order to entice the opponent into further play for higher stakes. In 1674 Cotton, to "lie abscond." See also DOG, DUCK, HUSTLER, LEMON, LET UP, STALL.

life

(obs.) In LIFE POOL and its variants, a chance or opportunity to play. 1836 Tillotson, 1839 Kentfield 40, 1924 Smith 109. Each player began the game having three lives. A life was lost when a player's ball was pocketed by another or when he committed a foul. 1881 MB 26. Additional lives could be purchased through the mechanism of the STAR.

life board

(obs.) A MARKING BOARD for keeping track of lives (see LIFE) in games such as LIFE POOL. 1908 Brunswick 124. A POOL BOARD.

Life Pool

(game, obs.) An extremely popular English game having a collective stake and as many as 13 participants. Each player shoots with a ball of a distinctive color and begins the game having three lives (see LIFE). He loses a life by committing a FOUL or by having his ball legally pocketed by another player. The first player to lose all

three of his lives may obtain a temporary reprieve by STARRING, which is the purchase of additional lives. When these are lost, he is eliminated. The last player remaining in the game wins the stake, which is known as the POOL. 1839 Kentfield 40, 1924 Smith 107, 1979 Everton 60.

Life Pool is a distant ancestor of Snooker. It first appears in British rule books about 1819, when it was simply called Pool. 1974 Hendricks. It is played on an English Billiards table. 1890 HRB 116. The first player places his ball on the WINNING AND LOSING SPOT. The second player plays with his own ball at the first player's ball, the third at the second player's, and so forth, unless the striker is IN HAND, in which case he plays at the nearest ball out of baulk. When the striker loses a life, the next player plays at the ball nearest his own. A life is lost if the player pockets his own ball, misses the ball played on, plays at or with the wrong ball, or has his ball pocketed by the next striker. If a player's shot is blocked so that he cannot hit the required ball, any intervening balls are taken up. This is the origin of the LIFT rule.

The game is variously known as COLOR-BALL POOL, ENGLISH POOL, FOLLOWING POOL, LAST PLAYER, or LIVE POOL. For the specialized terminology of Life Pool, see DEAD, DIVISION, KILL, LIFE, MAIDEN POOL, POOL, PRIVILEGE, PURCHASE, STAR.

For some game variations, see BLACK AND PINK POOL, BLACK POOL, BLUE PETER, EVERLASTING POOL, INDIAN POOL, NEAREST BALL POOL, PENNY POT, PERPETUAL POOL, PINK POOL, RUSSIAN POOL, SELLING POOL, SHELL-OUT, SINGLE POOL, SKILL POOL, SLOSH, TOAD-IN-THE-HOLE.

lift

(Amer. Snooker) A player's right, following a FOUL by his opponent that leaves him SNOOKERED, to remove any ball or balls that interfere with his aim. Any LIFTED BALL remains off the table for the duration of the shot (not the INNING). 1946 OR 82. The purpose behind allowing a lift is to prevent a player from achieving an advantage from his own foul. See TAKE UP. Cf. FREE BALL, NEAREST BALL PLAYABLE and PLAY AGAIN RULE for different solutions to the same problem.

lifted ball

(Amer. Snooker) A ball that has been temporarily removed from the table as a result of a LIFT. It is usual but unwise to rest the lifted ball in the depression in a piece of CHALK while it is off the table. This allows particles of chalk to accumulate on the balls, which interferes with their impact, greatly increasing the effect of THROW.

light hit

= THIN HIT. 1979 Grissim 251, 1989 Koehler 256. The term does not refer to the strength of the shot, but to the obliqueness of contact between the cue ball and the object ball.

light red

(Amer. Four-Ball Bill., obs.) One of the four balls used in American billiard games of the early nineteenth century. The light red is spotted at the beginning of the game on the HEAD SPOT, which is also sometimes known as the LIGHT-RED SPOT. See also BALL HOLDER. Cf. DARK RED, DEEP RED.

light-red spot

(Amer. Four-Ball Bill., obs.) = HEAD SPOT, where the LIGHT RED is spotted in the AMERICAN FOUR-BALL GAME. 1850 Phelan 47, 1864 AH 419. The AMERICAN SPOT, STRING SPOT, UPPER SPOT, WHITE-BALL SPOT or WHITE SPOT.

lighting

The means of illuminating the PLAYING SURFACE of the table. Improvements in table lighting have kept apace of other technical billiard developments. It is important for the level of light to be sufficient for aiming, that shadows be totally absent, and that the light not be so harsh as to tire the eyes during extended sessions of play. 1890 HRB 15.

Billiards was originally played outdoors. When it moved inside, candle illumination was used. Presumably because of the cost of tallow, games were shorter when played by candlelight than by daylight. 1674 Cotton 25. See END. This was reportedly the origin of the expression, "the game's not worth the candle." 1924 BM (Jan) 31. Candles had an annoying tendency to drip on the cloth, balls and players, so candle-holders were provided with circular shields to catch the wax. These shields reduced the amount of light provided, and candles gave way to oil lamps in the 1830s. Gas fixtures were used several decades later. These were bright, noisy, hot, and dangerous. Thomas Wallace burned himself severely on a gas fixture in 1883 while attempting a MASSÉ SHOT, and the rules were altered to permit the REFEREE to hold the fixture aside at the player's request. 1883 NYT (Feb 15) 2:4, 1916 RGRG 10.

Electric light displaced gas in the early twentieth century, but this did not eliminate the massé risk. In 1912, Edouard Roudil, a French amateur balkline champion, was in New York for an international tournament. While trying a massé shot during his first game, "[h]is

cue was held in a perpendicular position over the table and as he was about to smash the ball the head of his cue stick struck a chandelier and a shower of broken glass fell over his head and face." 1912 NYT (Feb. 13) 12:7.

The choice between incandescent and fluorescent lamps presents a problem. Although fluorescent bulbs have a convenient shape for billiard lighting, their "cooler" temperature is not satisfactory. 1985 Clare 28. Present international rules require a minimum illumination of 520 lux and a maximum of 600 lux on the cloth (approximately 48 to 56 foot-candles). WBA 2. The ideal height for a lighting fixture is said to be between 5'8" and 6' from the floor, but this certainly depends on its characteristics. 1881 MB 14, 1916 HDB 52. This height was not sufficient to keep Melbourne Inman from breaking lamps with his BODY ENGLISH. 1935 *Newsweek* (Jan 19) 21.

Limited Game

(game, obs.) CRAMP GAME in which the table is marked with a line along its longitudinal center across which the STRIKER'S ball may not pass without his incurring a penalty. 1807 White 52 calls it "uninteresting, and rarely played." From 1856 Crawley 99: "With scientific players an interesting game; with inferior players merely a funny one." Any CANNON or HAZARD made on the prohibited side is forfeited to the opponent. A decade later Crawley had become more critical: "It is a slow, stupid and unscientific game!" 1866 Crawley 230.

limited rail

(Bill., obs.) Referring to any carom billiard game in which the RAIL NURSE has been curtailed or eliminated by the drawing of a BALKLINE, particularly the TRIANGULAR BALKLINE of the CHAMPION'S GAME. 1881 NYT (Mar 23) 5:6. The game in which there was no restriction on the rail nurse became known as STRAIGHT-RAIL or UNLIMITED RAIL game. See also ANCHOR BLOCK, BALKLINE MARKER.

line

1. A straight mark drawn on the cloth, such as a BALKLINE or STRING LINE. The line is usually made with CHALK or pencil. See RULES. 2. (Balkline) The LINE NURSE. To "get the line" means to obtain a position favorable for this nurse.

line ball

A ball whose center lies exactly on a BALKLINE, STRING LINE, or other marked boundary on the table. 1836 Tillotson 7, 1866 Crawley 15, 1896 Broadfoot 105. Uncertainty about on which side of the line the ball will be considered to fall is generally resolved against the striker. See DOUBT. In ENGLISH BILLIARDS, a line ball on the BAULK-LINE is not playable from BAULK. In Pocket Billiards, however, the HEAD STRING is not considered to be in the balk area, or KITCHEN. In Snooker, a line ball is not IN BAULK. In BALKLINE, if a ball lies in one of the spaces adjacent to the line ball, then both are considered to be in the same BALK SPACE. 1881 MB 25. See also IN BALK. If two line balls lie on the same line, they are in balk but the player may elect which of the two balk spaces they are in. In some games, a ball is in balk if any part of the ball, not just its center, overhangs the balk space.

In 1911 Roberts 18, the following method is given for determining which side of a line a ball lies on: Place two COINS, one on either side of the ball. When the ball is removed, it can easily be seen which coin is closer to the line.

line nurse

(Balkline) A multiple-shot RUNNING NURSE position in which the object balls are on opposite sides of a balkline, with one ball in the center space so that there is no restriction on the number of consecutive CAROMS that are allowed. 1890 NYDT (Feb 21) 7:5, 1906 NYT (Oct 19) 10:3, 1913 Daly 184. This nurse, perfected by George Butler Sutton, consists of making several soft shots before driving the first object ball to a rail. As the cue ball returns, it gently pushes the second object ball over to achieve a repetitive position. Also known as the BALKLINE NURSE or just the LINE. See also LINE RUSHING.

line of centers

An imaginary line connecting the center of the object ball with the center of the cue ball when it is in contact with the object ball. If no side English is used, the object ball will travel away approximately along the line of centers (except for the effect of THROW). Called the POTTING LINE in ENGLISH BILLIARDS. 1924 Smith 30.

line rule

(Eng. Bill.) A rule requiring the player to make his cue ball cross the BAULK-LINE at least once in every 200 points of a break. It was introduced to reduce monotonous CANNON scoring. 1935 Smith 44. See also CONSECUTIVE CANNONS.

line rushing

(Balkline) Generally, the making of points while the object balls are astride a BALK-LINE. A maneuver similar to the LINE NURSE in which one of the object balls is driven to a cushion and back to contact the cue ball so the position is repeated. 1890 NYDT (Feb 21) 7:5.

line score

A numerical record of the number of points scored by the players in each INNING, usually presented as two horizontal rows of numbers. The line score can be augmented with notations indicating SAFETIES, FOULS, and other penalties. The line score of George B. Sutton's match against Willie Hoppe in the 1906 world 18.2 balkline championship reads:

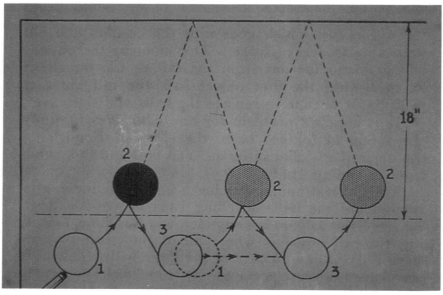

line nurse

Sutton	128	14	0	124	234	Total: 500.	Average: 100.0
Hoppe	11	50	53	0	4	Total: 118.	Average: 23.6

The match is notable for many reasons: Sutton's average of 100 was a world record, this was Hoppe's first attempt at the 18.2 title, and Mark Twain entered the arena during Hoppe's second inning to take his seat as a spectator. 1925 Hoppe 105.

Line-Up

1. (game) A pocket billiard game utilizing a TWO-BALL BREAK with CALL in which all balls made during a RUN are "lined up" on the LONG STRING at the completion of a player's turn. Also, the method of spotting balls in this game. 1965 Fats 48. Said somewhat loosely to be the forerunner of 14.1 CONTINUOUS. 1992 OR 85. This is true only in the sense that Line-Up was an earlier game in which long runs were possible. By 1916, the high run was 154 by Emmett Blankenship. 1916 BM (Feb). By 1930, a claim of 284 was made by Abner Finn. 1930 BM (Feb).

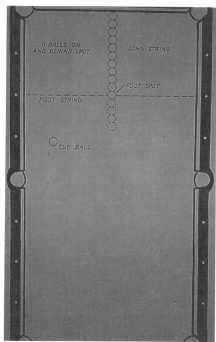

Line-Up

The number of different possible initial racks in Line-Up is $13! = 6,227,020,800$.

2. (Straight-Rail) An adverse position in which the three balls all lie in a straight line with an object ball in the middle of the three, leaving neither a DIRECT CAROM nor a FOLLOW SHOT. 1906 NYT (Oct 19) 10:3. Also COVER, TIE-UP.

3. The "lineup" is the roster of entrants in a tournament, once match pairings have been decided upon. See SEEDING.

lip

The edge or MOUTH of a pocket. 1989 Koehler 258. The FALL; the edge of the pocket at which balls may drop in.

list

(obs.) A band or strip of cloth used as a stuffing in early billiard cushions, before the advent of rubber. 1866 Crawley 7. The strips were glued together to form a multilayer material. 1979 Grissim 38.

little

(Eight-Ball) Any of the balls numbered one through seven. Also LOW, SOLID. Cf. BIG.

Little Corporal, Little Midget

(game, obs.) Carom Billiards with a PIN (the Little Corporal) set up in the center of the table. Knocking down the pin scores five points; caroms count for one. A ball must be hit by the cue ball before it knocks over the pin. The pin must be set up wherever it falls. 1890 HRB 99, 1902 Burrowes 11, 1916 RGRG 29. The player shoots until he fails either to carom or knock down the pin.

live ball

1. A ball that is IN PLAY, not DEAD, still spinning or in MOTION. 1946 OR 92, 1965 Fats 72, 1977 Martin 214. Cf. DEAD BALL. 2. A ball that is moving or spinning rapidly. Cf. DEAD BALL.

Live Pool

(game, obs.) = LIFE POOL. 1927 Clifford 56.

local rule

= HOUSE RULE.

lock

(colloq.) A cinch or sure thing. 1979 Grissim 251. A player has a "lock" on a game or proposition when he is certain to win it. Sometimes a "lock cinch." Also LOCKUP. A "lock table" is one with wide pockets. 1959 Tevis 109.

locked

= JAWED. 1983 Rule Book 252.

locksmith

(colloq.) A player who will bet only if he is offered LOCKUP ACTION that is, in other words, a sure thing.

139

lockup

1. (colloq.) A LOCK, a cinch. 1967 Polsky 51. A game or wager that cannot be lost, as in the expression, "lockup action." See also LOCKSMITH. 2. A position in which a player has no practical shot or is too far behind to have a chance of winning. 1989 Raftis 13. The state of being TIED UP.

long

1. Referring to a shot in which the cue or object ball travels too far or comes off a cushion at too wide an angle to complete the shot. Said of a missed shot that could have been made if less RUNNING ENGLISH had been applied to the cue ball. Cf. SHORT. Also, a shot in which the ball lands farther down the rail than it would have if struck with NATURAL ENGLISH. 1982 OR. 2. A shot in which a ball must travel a great distance, *e.g.*, a "long massé."

long bank

(usually Pocket Bill.) A BANK SHOT that travels the length of the table into a corner pocket; one in which the object ball crosses the CENTER STRING, as opposed to a CROSS-SIDE or CROSS-CORNER bank, in which the object ball travels across the table. 1882 NYT (Mar 9) 2:4, 1977 Fels 49. Cf. SHORT BANK.

long bridge

1. A BRIDGE in which the hand is set on the table at some distance, usually more than seven inches, from the cue ball. The bridge itself is not what is long; the term refers to the length of the span from the bridge to the ball. 1806 Phil 30. Cf. SHORT BRIDGE. 2. A MECHANICAL BRIDGE whose shaft is approximately eight feet in length. The LONG REST. It is used to reach shots on a large table, such as a SNOOKER TABLE. 1881 MB 25. Cf. SHORT BRIDGE.

long-butt

(Brit., obs.) A cue that is longer than a HALF-BUTT. 1873 Bennett 27, 1896 Broadfoot 97. A cue made long enough to reach from one end of an ENGLISH TABLE to the other. The device is depicted in an 1827 engraving. Sometimes this cue and its rest are referred to together as the "long-butt-and-rest." See also BARGE POLE, LONG TACKLE.

long jenny

(Eng. Bill.) A LOSING HAZARD into one of the TOP POCKETS when the object ball lies near a side cushion. 1924 Aiken 31. See also JENNY, SHORT JENNY.

long loser

(Eng. Bill.) A LOSING HAZARD into a corner pocket, in the course of which the cue ball must travel the length of the table. 1895 Buchanan 44, 1910a Ritchie 40. A LOSER into the TOP pocket from BAULK. 1873 Bennett 74, 1957 Holt 27. Cf. CROSS LOSER.

long rail

A SIDE RAIL, twice as long as a SHORT RAIL or END RAIL. 1879 NYT (Nov 23) 2:4.

long rest

(Eng. Bill., Snooker) A type of MECHANICAL BRIDGE having a long shaft, approximately 3.6 meters (12 feet) in length, for use on large tables. 1954 KTG 16. Also FISHING ROD, LONG BRIDGE. Cf. LONG-BUTT, LONG TACKLE, REST.

long roll

The tendency of a ball to roll so that it misses a shot in the LONG direction. A table exhibits "long roll" if the DIAMOND SYSTEM must be corrected when playing on it by shooting into a lower-numbered diamond than expected. 1978 Byrne 183. Sometimes this behavior is caused by table roll, but it is more commonly an artifact of the cushion RUBBER or RAIL CLOTH. See also NAP. Cf. SHORT ROLL.

long string

(14.1 Continuous, Line-Up) An imaginary line extending from the center of the FOOT RAIL to the FOOT SPOT (and beyond, if necessary) that is used for SPOTTING balls. 1946 OR 93, 1977 Martin 215. In tournament play, the long string is not imaginary but is marked on the cloth with pencil up to the foot spot.

long stroke

1. A stroke played with substantial FOLLOW-THROUGH. 2. (obs.) A type of TRAILING stroke in which the cue ball is shoved along the cloth while the MACE remains in contact with it. 1775 Annals. See also LONG TRAIL.

long tackle

(Brit.) A collective term for the extra-length cues and RESTS used in Snooker when the cue ball is far from the striker, such as the LONG-BUTT and the LONG REST.

long trail

(obs.) A TRAILING shot made with the MACE. 1807 White.

Loop

1. (game) = BACKWARDS POOL, BILLIARD POOL, CAROM POOL, CHINESE POOL, CONTRA POOL, INDIAN POOL, IRISH POOL, KISS POOL, REVERSE BILLIARDS.

The name "loop" is "pool" spelled backwards. Cf. CUE BALL POOL. 2. The area formed by the thumb and forefinger in holding the cue stick with the BRIDGE HAND. 1977 Fels 16. See also BRIDGE BOUCLÉE, CLOSED BRIDGE, LOOP BRIDGE.

loop bridge, looped bridge
= BRIDGE BOUCLÉE, CLOSED BRIDGE. 1949 Davis 83, 1984 Karnehm 48. A bridge for guiding the cue stick in which the shaft is grasped in a LOOP formed by the thumb and forefinger. Cf. OPEN BRIDGE.

loose
1. A pocket is "loose" if it approaches or exceeds the maximum regulation width. 1985 Marguglio 220. That is, the pocket will accept balls more readily. Cf. TIGHT, def. 1. 2. (colloq.) A player is "loose" if he is stroking smoothly and playing well or betting freely. Cf. TIGHT, def. 4. 3. NOT FROZEN. See LOOSE BALL.

loose ball
(Carom games) A ball that is not FROZEN to any other and is therefore not spotted in the event the two are frozen.

lose one's hand
(obs.) To have one's turn at the table terminate, especially by a MISS or FOUL. When this occurs, the player's hand is said to be OUT. 1916 RGRG 52. See also HAND OUT.

lose the white
(Eng. Bill.) To pocket the opponent's cue ball, which by the rules must remain OFF THE TABLE, thus reducing one's opportunities for scoring as only the player's cue ball and the red ball remain IN PLAY. 1904 Mannock I 327, 1954 KTG 12. See also PUT HIM IN, WHITECHAPEL.

loser
(Eng. Bill.) = LOSING HAZARD, synonym for IN-OFF. A loser played off the white ball is called a WHITE LOSER, one off the red a RED LOSER. Cf. WINNER.

loser breaks
A convention that the loser of one game of a series is permitted to BREAK for the next game. 1992 OR 51. This tends to negate the break advantage in games in which the break is helpful, such as Eight-Ball. Cf. ALTERNATING BREAK, WINNER BREAKS.

loser play
(Eng. Bill.) Play consisting primarily of LOSING HAZARDS. 1954 KTG 16.

losers' bracket
A term used in connection with a SPLIT DOUBLE ELIMINATION tournament. It consists of the set of players who have lost exactly one game and will be eliminated upon a second loss. Cf. WINNERS' BRACKET.

Losing Carambole
(game, obs.) Billiards in which only CARAMBOLES and LOSING HAZARDS count. 1807 White 54. Also known as the LOSING GAME.

Losing Game
(game, obs.) ENGLISH BILLIARDS in which only CANONS and LOSING HAZARDS count. WINNING HAZARDS cause a forfeit to the opponent. 1773 *Covent Garden*, 1775 Annals 94, 1807 White 9. Played 18 UP. Also known as LOSING CARAMBOLE. It is called the "Losing" Game because losing hazards originally caused the loss of a point in early billiard games. Cf. WINNING GAME.

losing game hazard
(Eng. Bill., obs.) = LOSING HAZARD, a HAZARD played in the LOSING GAME. 1807 White 9.

Losing Game of Pyramid
(game, obs.) PYRAMIDS in which only LOSING HAZARDS count and the player removes a ball of his election after each such hazard. 1850c White & Bohn 45, 1867 Dufton 209. Also called LOSING PYRAMIDS or LOSING HAZARD PYRAMID. The American version is called CUE-BALL POOL.

losing hazard
(Eng. Bill.) A LOSER, a shot in which the STRIKER'S ball enters a pocket after hitting an object ball. 1807 White 31, 1839 Kentfield 12, 1866 Crawley 70. A HAZARD played in the LOSING GAME. A losing hazard off the white ball (a WHITE LOSER) scores two points, a RED LOSER three. Also known as an IN-OFF or (obs.) a LOSING GAME HAZARD. Cf. WINNING HAZARD.

In Pocket Billiards, a losing hazard is a SCRATCH. In Snooker it is a FOUL.

Losing Hazard Pyramid
(game, obs.) = LOSING GAME OF PYRAMID or LOSING PYRAMIDS. 1867 Dufton 209. Occasionally known as Losing Hazard Pool. 1916 HDB 75.

Losing Pyramids
(game, obs.) Pyramid game in which points are made by LOSING HAZARDS off PYRAMID BALLS. Each time a losing hazard is made, the player may remove one pyramid ball. WINNING HAZARDS, MISSES and COUPS count against the player. 1866 Crawley 200, 1881 MB 288.

Also called LOSING GAME OF PYRAMID or LOSING HAZARD PYRAMID.

losing spot

(Eng. Bill.) = RED SPOT, located between 12½ and 13 inches from the TOP RAIL. 1873 Bennett 19. Also known as the BILLIARD SPOT, BLACK SPOT, ENGLISH SPOT, TOP SPOT, WINNING AND LOSING SPOT, or just "the spot."

loss of game

A severe PENALTY imposed for certain infractions of the rules. The transgression may be innocent, such as prematurely sinking the eight prematurely in EIGHT-BALL, or deliberate, as in an INTENTIONAL FOUL or SERIOUS FOUL. See also DISQUALIFICATION, FORFEIT, UNSPORTSMANLIKE CONDUCT.

lost

1. Said of a JUMP BALL that has left the table or come to rest on a cushion. 1864 AH 433. 2. Pocketed. See LOSE THE WHITE.

lot

A random method of determining the starting player and order of play in billiard games, frequently by COIN toss or selection of a PILL. 1992 OR 12. Cf. LAG.

love game

A SHUTOUT; a game in which one player fails to score. 1850 Phelan 21, 1884 MB. See also WHITEWASH. In ENGLISH BILLIARDS, a game in which no HAZARD is made by one side. 1836 Tillotson 10, 1856 Crawley 155.

low

1. ENGLISH applied by hitting the cue ball below center to impart BACKSPIN. It is frequently referred to as DRAW, but a fine distinction is made between applying DRAW and simply hitting the ball low. Known as LOW STROKE in 1807 White 23. 2. (pocket games) One of the balls numbered one through seven; a SOLID. Cf. HIGH. 3. (obs.) The name for the one-ball in the HIGH-LOW-JACK GAME.

low cue

(colloq.) = DRAW. Cf. HIGH CUE.

low stroke

A stroke played with LOW. 1807 White 23, 1862 Crawley 19, 1884 Bohn 525. A near-synonym is DRAW.

lower cushion

In American games, the FOOT RAIL. 1863 Phelan & Berger 43. In English Billiards, the BOTTOM cushion, which is at the BAULK END.

lower table

(Eng. Bill.) The area of the table at the BAULK END, between the BAULK-LINE and the LOWER CUSHION. Cf. UPPER TABLE.

luck

A beneficial effect of the laws of probability, bestowing on the player the gift of a shot to which he would not have been entitled simply by virtue of skill. See also FLUKE, SLOP SHOT.

Luck Rotation

(game) Version of ROTATION in which the player wins by sinking the 15-ball after first hitting the lowest-numbered ball on the table on the same stroke.

mace

(obs.) An early instrument for striking a billiard ball, consisting of a solid wooden head with a flat face and attached to a thin wooden handle that permits the device to be shoved along the table to propel the ball. The first maces resembled curved mallets evidently borrowed from the lawn games from which Billiards developed.

The word "mace" is a translation of the French *masse* (without an accent), a term that originally meant "hammer." Maces are illustrated in engravings dating back to the mid-1600s. They were also known in English as MASTS or just STICKS. 1727 OED, 1775 Annals 93.

The shaft of the mace was generally angled up so that a player could hit the ball without bending over to grasp the handle. Because the mace presented a flat surface to the ball, it was impossible to use it to impart spin. It was also difficult to hit a ball lying near a cushion. For this reason, players would turn the mace around to hit with the tip of the shaft, which was known as the "tail" or, in French, "queue." Around 1680, the "cue," as it was known in English, became a separate instrument and was further refined. See POINT AND POINT. At first, only good players were allowed to use the cue because of the risk of tearing the cloth with a slender untipped stick. The mace fell slowly into disuse. By the late 1700s, it was used primarily by ladies. It was still recommended

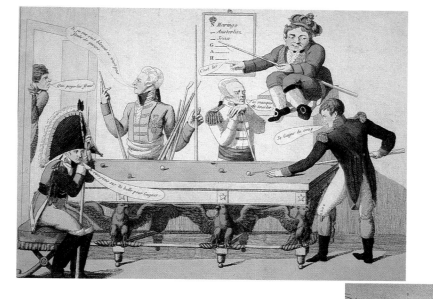

"Une Partie Russe [A Russian Game]."

Colored copperplate engraving, c. 1810. A complex political cartoon using billiards as backdrop. Napoleon sits at lower left. "Partie Russe" means "Russian Billiards," a version played with five balls; it also refers to Napoleon's desire to send his armies to Russia. The players mutter thoughts about the game, each a pun on an aspect of Napoleon's campaign. The general (center) is saying, "I miscued," meaning that he lost a battle. The scorekeeper tallies Napoleon's victories.

"A Game at Pyramids."

Colored lithograph from *St. Stephen's Review*, December 20, 1884. The British game of pyramids—now incorporated into snooker—was a close cousin of American pocket billiards, which it predated. Those depicted include Bismarck, the Mahdi (the Expected One, in desert attire) and Mr. Gladstone (the British Prime Minister.)

" 'I will bet a hundred to ten that you miss,' said Agnew."

Colored wood engraving on the cover of *Tip Top Weekly*, December 16, 1899, illustrating a Frank Merriwell story. The striker is indeed trying a difficult shot—he must massé the cue ball around the red to make the carom. Billiards was often used as the arena for tales having a moral message—for example, fortitude and gentlemanly conduct can win out over a dissolute and loutish opponent.

"My dear boy! There's more in this shot than meets the eye!"

Postcard by Paul Finkenrath, c. 1910. Billiard art is replete with scenes of waiters being hit by cue sticks, with humorous results.

"Yes, I'll be home by ten, Bertha!!"

British postcard, c. 1970. A familiar scene—the husband rarely returns at the promised time when out playing billiards with his friends.

"The Billiard Table."

Aquatint etching by Thomas Rowlandson, 1823; a plate from the book, *The Tours of Dr. Syntax.* By now, the mace was largely obsolete in England, even for ladies. Coeducational billiard play was then socially acceptable, and the game was regarded as good, clean fun. Its status has varied from chic to depraved in regular cycles throughout its 500-year history.

"Les Joueurs du Bon Genre. La Poule [Gentlemanly Players. Pool]."

Colored copperplate engraving, c. 1810. Billiards in France on a six-pocket table with three small balls. The pockets are cut into the table bed, not the rails. The coloring was added later and is not accurate—yellow balls were not used in three-ball billiards until the late 20th century. Two rules posters adorn the walls. The man at right is keeping score on a marking tablet.

"Thomas Hueston. "

Mecca cigarette card, c. 1911. Hueston was one of only five players to ever hold national or world titles in both pocket and carom billiards, and one of only three who held them simultaneously. The other two were Joseph Dion and Alfredo De Oro. See CROSSOVER PLAYER. Cards such as these are rare and highly collectible. The Mecca series are prized for their rich colors.

"Willie Hoppe."

From the series, *Great Moments in Sports*, comes this dramatic poster of the world's great carom champion, who dominated all phases of the three-ball game at various phases in a long career lasting nearly 50 years. Hoppe's life was detailed in a 1925 autobiography, *Thirty Years of Billiards*, at a time when his many three-cushion triumphs still lay ahead of him. He remained a champion for another 25 years.

"Mayst thou thy Christmas happily begin/And ne'er despair shouldst thou not always win."

Trade card for G. A. Schwartz, a Philadelphia toy store, 1886. The children are playing a version of BAGATELLE and keeping score on a tally sheet. The artful message is that it would be a good idea to buy the kids a table for Christmas.

"Au Salon."

Colored lithograph by Jean Droit, c. 1910. An elegant turn-of-the-century club scene. This print is a personal favorite of the author and is the only work displayed in his office at the Billiard Archive. The artist also drew the famous posters for the Paris Olympics of 1924, seen in the film, "Chariots of Fire."

"Wart-Salon im Apartement Seiner Majestät des Kaisers."

Chromolithograph, 1865. An official rendering of the billiard room of Schönbrunn Palace, the summer home of the emperors of Austria-Hungary located near Vienna. The game is Russian Billiards, played with two white balls, a red ball, a yellow ball, and a blue ball. The exquisite eight-legged table contains a drawer for storing cues and supplies, so that a cue rack, which would have detracted from the appearance of the room, was not necessary.

"Interior of the Residency Billiard Room."

Colored lithograph by C. H. Mecham, 1857. The aftermath of the Sepoy Mutiny attacking the British Raj in Lucknow, India. The room shows extensive cannon damage. The table, while missing half of a leg, is still standing and could probably be repaired. The artist was a British army lieutenant who drew the scene from life.

"Billiard Room of the Grand Union Hotel, at Saratoga, N.Y."

Hand-colored wood engraving from Frank Leslie's *Illustrated Weekly*, July 24, 1875. A perfect depiction of billiards played in male surroundings in the resort and racing town of Saratoga. Only carom billiards is being played. The tables are illuminated at night by gas fixtures having four jets. The man at the left who appears to be holding a very long cue is actually the MARKER, who keeps score by moving beads on the overhead score string which runs the length of the room.

"The Billiard Room at Ménil-Hubert."

Oil on canvas by Edgar Degas, 1892. An impression of the billiard room at the home of the artist's friend. Billiards has been the subject of paintings by Van Gogh, Gauguin, Braque, and many lesser-known artists, as well as prints by innumerable others.

"Tribulation."

Colored lithograph by Osborn (fils), c. 1860. The wife has come with her child to the billiard parlor to beg her husband for money. He ignores her, except to complain that her yelling might make him miscue. Episodes like these must have been regular occurrences, judging from the frequency with which they are depicted in artwork.

"Ich Mache Nur Collee; Ich Spiele Nur Zur Lust. [I make only caroms; I play only for pleasure]."

German watercolor, c. 1745. The lady is playing with a mace. Her male opponent (not visible) is using a cue. The table has six holes cut in the bed through which balls may fall. Green cloth has been used since the game was brought indoors from the lawn during the 15th century.

"More Important. You don't mean to say that Jack thinks May a good player!"

Colored lithograph from Puck, c. 1924. Women at carom billiards, a polite game for the social set. The dichotomy between pocket billiards (a game for the masses) and caroms (a respectable game) was reinforced by such images.

"Billiards."

Hand-colored wood engraving from *The School of Recreation*, 1710. Early British billiards using two white balls. The table has no pockets—only two arches similar to croquet wickets, each known as a pass. The table boundaries were flat vertical walls covered with cloth, but unpadded. The sticks being used are primitive MACES, used to shove rather than strike the balls.

"Progress of Gaming."

Colored copperplate engraving, c. 1790. The risks of gambling. Billiards, roulette, and tric-trac (backgammon) in a public salon. A fight has broken out at right, and a sword is about to be drawn. The billiard game is English Billiards, played with three small balls (one is not visible) on a six-pocket table. A MACE or a cue might have been used for a particular shot, depending on the skill of the player and the requirements of the shot. The player at center is holding a long mace, while the striker is using a cue.

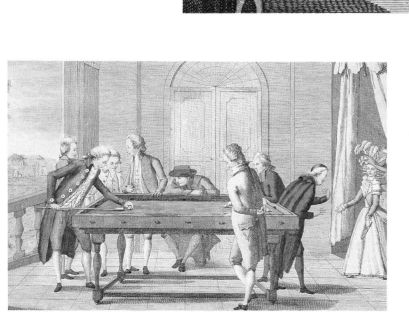

"Il Trucco."

Hand-colored copperplate engraving, c. 1800. The game of Trucks, a close cousin of billiards, at an Italian villa. The table has eight pockets, cut like mouse holes directly into the rails. The sticks are straight MACES. Many balls are used in this game; the man at right center is holding several balls behind his back. Ladies were welcome in such elegant surroundings.

"Billiards," by E. F. Lambert.

Hand-colored copperplate engraving, 1827. English Billiards. This image bears intense study because of what it reveals about equipment of the period—including the table, pockets, scoring devices, and particularly, the lighting. The oil lamps are mounted on a rotating fixture that could be turned during the game in order to cast more light on a specific part of the table. The level of detail is so fine that it permits measurement of the cue lengths and table markings.

"Joyeuses Pâques [Happy Easter]."

French postcard. A different sort of chicken and egg problem—you can't make a carom without breaking some eggs. There is also a subliminal pun operating here; in French, the same word, "poule," means both "pool" and "hen," so many French billiard images somehow manage to depict chickens.

Joyeuses Pâques

"Eene party biljart [A billiard game]."

Colored lithograph, 1869. Scenes of animals playing billiards are undeniably amusing. This image is one of a series of twelve showing the two insects in perfect imitation of human poses.

mace (c. 1730)

as a standard table accessory in 1893 HRB 12 but was essentially obsolete by 1900.

The length of the mace was approximately four feet, but variations up to eight feet were known for use on long shots. Maces were made with an aiming line cut into the center of the head for lining up a shot. An off-center hit would result in the mace twisting in the player's hand and altering the path of the cue ball.

The mace was the precursor of the MECHANICAL BRIDGE. The curved portion of the mace head was used to rest the cue.

Mace technique was very sophisticated, considering the primitive nature of the tool. The mace and the ball were to be slid along the table together—a sharp stroke, such as one might give with a cue, was originally a foul. 1807 White 8. Cheating was possible by unduly prolonging contact with the ball, however, an act that is still a FOUL even with a cue. See DEAD TRAIL, LONG STROKE, LONG TRAIL, RAKING, SHOVE, SWEEP, TRAILING, TURN-UP.

machine gun

1. (Pocket Bill.) The name of a TRICK in which the cue ball is made to carom quickly off all the other balls in succession, thus imitating the sound of a machine gun.

1965 Mosconi. Yank Adams, a FINGER BILLIARDS player of the late nineteenth century, could play this shot by rolling the cue ball with his hand. 1916 BM (Nov). The Korean fancy shot expert Suk Yoon Kim makes this shot with a massé stroke and is able to hit 17 billiard balls, which are larger and heavier than pocket balls. 2. (Pocket Bill.) The name of an exhibition shot in which the object balls are made to enter a pocket rapidly and rhythmically, resulting in a sound similar to that of a

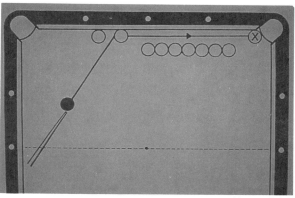

machine gun (def. 1)

machine gun. 3. Nickname of a player who shoots rapidly, especially Lou Butera, who is famous for the speed (and accuracy) of his game. See also FAST.

Mac's Solitaire
(game) = SCOTCH POOL. 1928 BR (Apr) 15.

maiden pool
(obs.) Situation in LIFE POOL in which one player takes the entire pool while his three lives are still intact. 1896 Broadfoot 409.

make
1. To complete successfully or to POCKET, as in "He made the shot," "He made 10 balls before missing," or "The shot didn't make." 2. (colloq.) To promote a money game by introducing the players, serving as a BACKER, and/or proposing a HANDICAP. "He'll make a game for you."

make a baulk
(Eng. Bill.) A defensive maneuver in which both the RED and the STRIKER'S ball are made to land behind the BAULK-LINE. 1839 Kentfield 24, 1869 Roberts 165. In case the INCOMING PLAYER'S ball is off the table, he will be IN BAULK and unable to strike at any ball directly. See also DOUBLE BAULK.

Man-of-War Game
(game, obs.) ENGLISH BILLIARDS played with three white balls, each belonging to a different player. 1919 Hoyle 644.

manager
1. An employee of a billiard room responsible for its overall operation and profitability. Cf. DAY MANAGER, NIGHT MANAGER. 2. An individual who supervises a player's career, deciding which tournaments should be entered and which private games should be played, and is generally responsible for keeping the player in top form. In the U. S., it is unusual for a player to be able to afford a manager. This was not the case in the 1920s, nor is it true in the U.K.

mandatory warning
A WARNING that must be issued by the REFEREE prior to an infraction of the rules in order for that infraction to be punishable as a SERIOUS FOUL.

manufacture
To maneuver a ball into a position suitable for a subsequent shot. 1948 Mosconi 84, 1978 Byrne 152. A BREAK SHOT in 14.1 CONTINUOUS may be manufactured by kissing an object ball into a favorable position for breaking the next rack. An ANGLE may be manufactured

144

by curving the path of the cue ball so that it strikes the cushion at the desired point.

manufacturer's nameplate
A small plaque, usually of brass, containing the manufacturer's ensign and by convention attached to the table on the HEAD RAIL (BOTTOM RAIL). The nameplate may not be placed arbitrarily because it is used as a reference in covering the table to orient the NAP of the cloth and is relied on by players to be affixed properly.

margin
The amount by which the winner's SCORE exceeds the loser's, measured in either games or points. The record margin in a 150-point Straight Pool tournament match is 163; the margin can exceed the GAME TOTAL if a NEGATIVE SCORE is possible. See −13 in Appendix A. The record margin in a 50-point championship Three-Cushion match is 47, achieved by Johnny Layton in beating Jess Jacobs, 50 to 3, in the 1931 world tournament in Chicago.

mark
1. To tally the score of a game, a function performed by the MARKER. 2. To indicate the position of a ball that has been removed from the table so it may be replaced precisely at its original location. A device called a POSITION MARKER is used for this function. 3. To place MARKINGS on the table. See also RULES. 4. The intended victim of a hustle. A FISH, PIGEON, or SUCKER. 1967 Polsky 105.

marker
1. (Brit. games) An individual who administers, and keeps score in, billiard matches. 1770 OED, 1807 White 73, 1836 Tillotson 9. So called because he marks the score on a slate or other device. Also known as a BILLIARD MARKER. In very obsolete usage, a BOX. In tournament play, both a marker and a REFEREE are used, each performing a distinct function. 1983 Rule Book 251.

The marker has many duties, including handing the REST to the players, announcing the state of the game (e.g., "in anchor"), removing potted balls from the pockets and seeing to it that the rules are observed. 1974 Hendricks 28. Before the marker became commonplace, decisions regarding rules and play were made by the COMPANY, the group of SPECTATORS observing the game.

Although normally considered a safe occupation, the role of marker is fraught with unexpected dangers. In 1947, A. James was marking when he was knocked

marker (c. 1730)

unconscious by a JUMP BALL hit by Joe Davis, many times world Billiards and Snooker champion.

2. A device for indicating the score, as by beads (BUTTONS) on a wire (the SCORE STRING) or dials sunk into the rails (a RAIL MARKER). A scoring bead is also known as a "marker."

3. A POSITION MARKER, a device for marking the location of a ball that must be removed from the table and replaced in its original location.

4. Frame for drawing lines on a TABLE; a BALKLINE MARKER or BAULK MARKER.

5. (colloq.) Receipt for a gambling debt; an IOU.

marker frame

A type of MARKING BOARD consisting of a frame with parallel horizontal wires holding beads used for tallying the score. 1908 Brunswick 80. Similar in appearance to an abacus and often mounted on a wall, it can be used to maintain the score for several players simultaneously.

marker, rail

See RAIL MARKER.

marker stand

A freestanding apparatus similar to a MARKER FRAME, used in residences where it is not desirable to string

markers above the table or mount a scoring device on the wall. 1908 Brunswick 89.

marker stretcher

A turnbuckle used to keep the MARKING STRING tight. 1925c Grote & Hubbell 31. Cf. STRETCHER.

marker stretcher

marking board

A device for keeping score for multiple players. 1866 Crawley 12, 1869 Roberts 170. Wooden boards with holes into which pegs were inserted, similar to cribbage boards, were used in the early 1700s. Several types of boards are listed in 1896 Broadfoot 99: (1) a counter with dials embedded in the rails, activated by pressing a button to tally a score; (2) two linear slides for marking the score in twenties and units; (3) an elaborate piece of furniture to record scores and the status of colors for LIFE POOL, sometimes combined with a CUE RACK. A device was once made for marking KELLY POOL that could record scores of 0–31 points for each of 12 players.

marking string

A wire stretched above the table, on which marking beads or BUTTONS are strung for keeping score. They are moved by the player with the tip of the cue stick at the end of his INNING. Traditionally, the beads denoting the player's last run are kept separate from his cumulative score to permit verification prior to his next turn. The string usually consists of 50 beads for each player, every fifth bead being of a different color from the remaining beads for visibility. See also MARKER, SCORE STRING, SCORING, STRING.

In championship Balkline tournaments, it was forbidden to have a marking string over the table. 1911 HRB 43a. The score was called out by the referee and displayed on a scoreboard.

markings

RULES or lines drawn on the CLOTH for use in certain billiard games. Chalk marks are made for the convenience of players, as in BALKLINE. Pencil marks are for the use of the referee, as for the outline of the RACK in 14.1 CONTINUOUS and for various SPOTS. Among the

145

tools used for markings are the ANCHOR BLOCK and BALKLINE MARKER.

masse

(obs., pr. MAHSS, spelled with no accent on the final "e.") The French word for MACE, originally meaning "hammer." 1807 White 11. It is sometimes used in English for MASSÉ when diacritical marks are not available to the printer.

massé

(pr. mah-SAY) A shot involving the extreme application of ENGLISH, achieved by raising the BUTT of the cue at a high angle, usually exceeding 45 degrees, and striking the cue ball from above. 1977 Martin 215. See ELEVATION. The cue ball is effectively squeezed out between the cue stick and the cloth, the friction of which imparts tremendous spin with very little forward speed. A ball hit in this manner can describe a sharply curving path on the table. Cf. PIQUÉ, in which little or no SIDE ENGLISH is used.

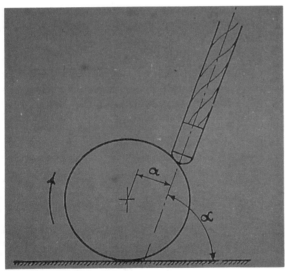

massé

The term is derived from the French verb "masser," meaning "to hammer." Cue players of the early 1700s found that they had to raise the butt of the cue to strike at balls lying near the cushions. It was discovered that the balls could be made to jump in this fashion and the technique became known as the HIGH OBLIQUE STROKE. 1807 White 25.

After the introduction of the leather tip at the beginning of the nineteenth century, it became possible to execute the high oblique stroke with side English and thus cause the ball to curve. This stroke was demonstrated by Mingaud to the astonishment of crowds all over Europe.

The term "masser" was used in Mingaud's 1827 book of TRICK SHOTS. Its first appearance in English is in a rare and obscure anonymous pamphlet of 1829 entitled *Plan of the 44 Strokes of the Game of Billiards to Teach the Use of the Queue Tipped with Leather.* The first study of the physics of the massé was published in 1835 by the Frenchman G. G. Coriolis, who had witnessed one of Mingaud's demonstrations. In Phelan's 1850 treatise it is called the PERPENDICULAR STROKE, referring to the extreme angle at which the cue is held. Improved by the French, the massé was used in the 1850s to effect delicate GATHER SHOTS in French Caroms. It was featured in exhibitions by Claudius Berger in a tour of the United States in 1860. 1925 BM (Sep) 18. Banned temporarily in 1862, the massé was a key factor in Garnier's capture of the world three-ball championship in 1873. 1988 BD (Aug). The word "massé" appeared in 1865 NYT (Apr 4) 2:4, and its definition was added to the 1866 edition of Phelan's *Game of Billiards.*

During the 1870s, the massé was also known as the "crush stroke," because it was played with considerable force, scattering the balls. 1925 Hoppe 242. The delicate massé was developed into a high art by Jacob Schaefer Sr. At his death in 1910, the *New York Times* noted in an obituary that "His massés were at times marvels of conception and skill."

The massé is an inherently spectacular shot because the path of the ball seems to defy intuition. "The very pinnacle of the billiard-ladder is attained with a raising of the cue-butt to its greatest height." 1908 Mannock II 23. The shot is difficult and requires a high degree of touch, which makes it among the most challenging techniques in the repertoire. "It is almost impossible to give a verbal description of these strokes; and players who aspire to make them, should put themselves, for a day at least, under the tuition of a competent instructor." 1857 Phelan 147.

Raising the cue for a massé can involve unexpected risks. See LIGHTING.

Massé is used infrequently in Snooker, Three-Cushions, and Pocket Billiards but is common in Straight-Rail and Balkline, in which it is used for NURSING and POSITION PLAY. The development of the massé in English Billiards was enhanced by the barring of the PUSH STROKE, since players then had to massé to avoid a FOUL. 1908 Mannock II 27.

Some spectacular massé shots are required in ARTISTIC BILLIARDS. See also DEAD-BALL MASSÉ, FREE-HAND MASSÉ, FULL MASSÉ, GRAND MASSÉ, HALF-MASSÉ, HARPOON STROKE, MASSÉ COULÉ, MASSÉ CUE, MASSÉ DÉ-

TACHÉ, PERPENDICULAR STROKE, PETIT MASSÉ, SERPENTINE MASSÉ.

massé bridge

A bridge used to hold the cue during a MASSÉ shot. There are two classes of such bridges depending on which sort of massé is being attempted. For the PETIT MASSÉ, the bridge is difficult to form, since it must be high and OPEN. For the GRAND MASSÉ, the player may sit on the rail and make a bridge on his thigh. Where a long bridge is required, the player may make a loop with the forefinger and use the other fingers to grasp his clothing for stability. For a FREE-HAND MASSÉ, the bridge is either made out in the air (with no support at all) or held against the body.

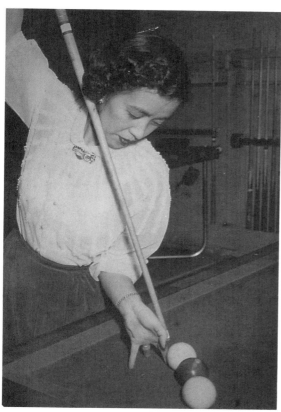

massé bridge (Masako Katsura)

massé coulé

(pr. mah-SAY coo-LAY) A French term meaning "follow massé." The stroke is accomplished by striking the cue ball from above but forward of its North Pole, which imparts extreme FOLLOW.

massé cue

A short, heavy cue (for example, 48 inches, 26 ounces) with a thick shaft and broad tip for playing MASSÉ shots. A short cue is more comfortable for such shots because the FOLLOW-THROUGH is only a few inches and there is

no reason to have to manipulate a cue of the usual length. The weight is required for forceful shots. Delicate massés can be made with a light cue. The idea is that the cue must be able to be handled easily in a vertical position. A massé cue invented by Mannock was two-thirds the length of an ordinary cue and weighed 17 ounces, most of which was offset toward the shaft end. 1908 Mannock II 44. This may not have been the first such cue, but no earlier reference has surfaced.

massé détaché

(Bill., pr. mah-SAY day-tah-SHAY.) A MASSÉ played away from an object ball that is FROZEN to the cue ball. WBA 11. Literally, "detached massé." The objective is to cause the cue ball to reverse direction and hit the ball to which it was frozen, which constitutes a legal shot. Failure to SHOOT AWAY from a frozen ball is a FOUL in carom games.

massé shot

A shot on which MASSÉ is used. Room proprietors have an inordinate fear that massé shots will damage their equipment and display the familiar sign reading, "No massé shots allowed." This is a concern of long standing. 1857 Phelan 147 warns: "[w]e must still caution the novice that the penalty, should he attempt them, will very likely be a rupture of the cloth."

mast

(obs.) A MACE, also known as a BILLIARD-MAST. 1731 OED.

match

1. A competitive series of one or more billiard GAMES between two players or teams. Several matches involving more than two players may constitute a TOURNAMENT or championship event. The first match for a money stake in the U. S. was held in 1854, when Joseph N. White beat George Smith at American Four-Ball Billiards for $200. The first public match to which admission was charged occurred in 1859 in Detroit, at which Dudley Kavanagh defeated Michael Foley for $1000. The idea of extending a single match over more than one day's play originated in France in 1867 and was tried in the U.S. in 1874. See also BLOCK, SESSION. In a HOME-AND-HOME MATCH, games are played in both players' home cities.

A match formally begins when the players are prepared to LAG and ends when the outcome has been decided, whether by FORFEIT, DISQUALIFICATION, or regular play. 1992 OR 53.

147

2. An incendiary instrument used by the referee to determine whether two balls are FROZEN by holding the flame behind them.

Match of Four

(game, obs.) = FOUR MATCH. Billiards by four players divided into two teams. 1839 Kentfield 36, 1850c White & Bohn 49, 1866 Crawley 149. See also HANDICAP SWEEPSTAKES.

maximum

1. (Bill.) = MAXIMUM ENGLISH. 2. (Snooker) = MAXIMUM BREAK.

maximum break

(Snooker) The longest sequence of points that can be made in one turn at the table. This is generally taken to be 147, the score obtained by sinking a red and the black alternately 15 times, followed by TAKING THE COLOURS, for a total of $15(1 + 7) + 2 + 3 + 4 + 5 + 6 + 7 = 147$. 1941 Levi 257.

The first reported maximum was made by Murt O'Donoghue in New Zealand in 1934, but it is not officially recognized. Leo Levitt, an amateur, made the first official maximum in 1948. The first professional maximum was by Joe Davis in a match against Willie Smith on January 22, 1955. Tony Meo, at the age of 17, became the youngest player to achieve one. The highest break by an amateur is 141 by G. Thompson in 1953. 1984a BSCC 113.

A break of 155 can theoretically be made if the OUTGOING PLAYER has left a snooker for the striker as the result of a foul stroke. The INCOMING PLAYER may then take a color as a FREE BALL, which will be treated as if it were a red for scoring purposes, but will be re-spotted. He then takes BLACK and is eight points to the good before commencing a normal maximum break of 147. Note that a player who makes a break of 155 will have a score of at least 159 because of the points he is credited with as a result of his opponent's foul. No player is known to have made such a break; the greatest on record is 152 by Kirk Stevens in 1984. 1987 Thorburn 125.

A maximum break at SNOOKER PLUS is 210 points.

maximum English

(Three-Cushions) The greatest amount of ENGLISH a player can apply to the cue ball without miscueing. The "maximum English system" is a DIAMOND SYSTEM used to calculate the path taken by a ball that is struck with maximum English, as opposed to the usual system that is based on ordinary RUNNING ENGLISH.

measuring ring

A flat metal ring whose inside diameter is machined accurately, used to verify the size of billiard balls and determine whether they are TRUE. 1935 Brunswick. These days a spherical micrometer is preferred.

mechanic

A professional who maintains and installs billiard tables. One who is able to SET UP, SEAM, COVER, and LEVEL tables as well as repair and replace table parts. Certain mechanics are much sought after because of their ability to bring a table quickly into condition for tournament play. These people may be flown thousands of miles for such an assignment. Also INSTALLER.

mechanical bridge

A cue-like stick with a notched plate at the tip end known as the BRIDGE HEAD or REST HEAD, which a player may use to support the shaft of the cue in shooting over a ball or in making a shot he otherwise could not reach. 1973 Mizerak 82. The use of such a device is made necessary by the rule that at least one of the player's feet must be touching the floor at the moment the cue ball is struck. The mechanical bridge is part of the table EQUIPMENT. It is handed to the player by the REFEREE, but the player himself is responsible for any foul he may commit with it through mishandling. See PLAYER RESPONSIBILITY FOUL.

The mechanical bridge and its variants are also known as the ARTIFICIAL BRIDGE, BRIDGE STICK, CROSS REST, CUE REST, CUSHION REST, EXTENDED SPIDER, HIGH ARCH REST, INTERLOCKING BRIDGE, JIGGER, LONG REST, RAKE, REST, SHORT BRIDGE, SPAN REST, SPIDER, STICK BRIDGE, SUBSTITUTE BRIDGE, or SWAN NECK. It is disparagingly known as the CRUTCH, LADIES' AID, OLD MAN'S AID, or SISSY STICK.

The first mechanical bridge was the MACE, whose use as a bridge for the cue was described by John Dew in 1779. The mechanical bridge was prohibited for a time in FRENCH CAROMS. 1860 *Leslie's* (Mar 10) 233:2. It was BARRED in the U.S. in a match in 1865. 1898 Thatcher advises against using it, suggesting instead that the player develop the ability to shoot with either hand. Willie Hoppe rarely resorted to the mechanical bridge. One difficulty in manipulating it is that there is very little friction between the cue stick and the bridge head, making the stroke hard to control. Players may go to extreme lengths to avoid using the device. See BEHIND THE BACK, EXTENDIBLE CUE, EXTENSION, TELESCOPING CUE.

Many players are unaware that one or more mechanical bridges may be stacked one upon another to form a higher bridge, although some games impose a limit on the number of bridges that may be so stacked. Mechanical bridges are now made that are designed to be held entirely in the hand to guide the cue.

Men's Professional Billiards Association (MPBA)

(org.) Organization of U.S. professional pocket billiard players. Formerly the Professional Billiards Association, its name was changed in 1989. It merged with the PROFESSIONAL BILLIARDS TOUR ASSOCIATION in 1991.

merry widow

A cue stick whose BUTT is made or appears to be made from a single piece of wood and thus has no SPLICE. 1983 NBN (Mar) 18. The origin of the term is unknown, but cuemaker Paul Rubino offers two explanations: (1) the solid butt was frequently made from ebony, which was also used in women's corsets intended for use with dark clothing (as worn by widows); and (2) the solid butt is "happy" not to be married (spliced) to a piece of maple.

Metric Balkline

(game) BALKLINE in which the distance at which the lines are drawn from the rails is expressed in centimeters, *e.g.*, 39.2, 42.2, 45.1, 45.2, 47.1, 47.2, 57.2, 71.2. In Europe, balkline distances have always been measured this way, with earlier games having 20-centimeter (8-inch) and 35-centimeter (14-inch) lines.

metric table

A table built to or marked according to metric specifications, *i.e.*, with distances in centimeters or millimeters. 1978 BSCC 22.

Mexican Rotation

(game) = CHICAGO. 1868 NBJ (Nov) 57.

middle hazard

(Eng. Bill) A HAZARD into a MIDDLE POCKET or SIDE POCKET. 1873 Bennett 67.

middle pocket

(Eng. Bill.) = SIDE POCKET. 1807 White 35, 1897 Payne 60, 1957 Holt 6. A pocket in the middle of a LONG RAIL or SIDE RAIL. Rarely, a CENTRE POCKET.

middle spot

(Eng. Bill.) = CENTRE SPOT. The SPOT located at the exact center of the playing surface of the table. 1895 Buchanan 2. Where the BLUE is placed at the beginning of a frame of Snooker. Hence, the BLUE SPOT. It is also used for spotting balls in certain games when the other spots are OCCUPIED. Cf. MIDDLE SPOT IN BAULK.

middle spot in baulk

(Eng. Bill.) The SPOT at the centre of the BAULK-LINE. 1895 Buchanan 2. Also BAULK SPOT, BAULK-LINE SPOT. Called the "centre spot in baulk" in 1836 Tillotson 20. Not to be confused with the MIDDLE SPOT.

mingo

(Span.) A Spanish term for the red ball. Named after Monsieur Mingaud, a French TRICK SHOT artist of the early nineteenth century and reputed inventor of the leather cue TIP.

minnie

(obs.) = CHERRY, CRIPPLE, DUCK, HANGER, PUPPY, SET-UP, SITTER. An unmissable shot. 1941 Hoppe 75, 1977 Martin 208. Also spelled erroneously as "mini."

miscue

A shot or attempted shot in which the TIP of the cue slips off the cue ball as the stroke is being delivered. 1850 Phelan 19, 1873 Bennett, 1881 MB 25, 1941 Hoppe 75. A faulty stroke in which the cue glances off the ball. 1976 WSD 273. It is caused by insufficient friction between the cue tip and the cue ball, usually the result of a defective tip, improper chalking, or the application of excessive ENGLISH. Occasionally spelled as MISS-CUE or "missed cue." In Canadian slang, a CROAK.

A miscue is a stroke, and the player must accept its consequences. If the FERRULE touches the cue ball, it is a FOUL. If the stroke is fair and results in a COUNT, the player receives credit for the shot and continues play.

A miscue can be faked on occasion to achieve a tactical advantage. A HUSTLER may miscue to attain a good defensive position without appearing skilled. In Three-Cushions, a player may miscue to avoid being charged with an INTENTIONAL SAFETY. 1972 Byrne.

Among professional players, a miscue is extremely uncommon, particularly in games characterized by controlled stroking, such as 14.1 CONTINUOUS and BALKLINE. Willie Hoppe miscued in competitive balkline play only about once a decade. Thus an event of unprecedented rarity occurred on the afternoon of December 4, 1937, when, during his match against Jake Schaefer Jr. for the 71.2 BALKLINE championship of the U. S., Hoppe miscued in two consecutive innings! He went on to win the title anyway. 1937 NYT (Dec 5) V 1:3. Miscues are more common in Three-Cushions because extreme English is frequently used, which requires striking near the edge of the cue ball.

Misery

(game) = EIGHT-BALL played with the ONE AND FIFTEEN IN THE SIDE rule. 1988 Lange PC. Cf. ALABAMA EIGHT-

149

BALL, LAST POCKET OPTION. The name probably resulted from confusion with MISSOURI.

misrack

Failure to position the balls properly in the RACK. This may occur if adjacent balls are not FROZEN, or if the balls themselves are in the wrong locations, for example, in Eight-Ball if the eight is not in the center of the third row. There is no rule covering the situation in which it is discovered after a BREAK SHOT that the balls were misracked.

miss

1. Failure to make a successful shot, which ends the player's INNING. The consequences differ in different games. In pocket games, a miss simply results in the loss of turn, provided that other requirements of the stroke are met, and no FOUL is assessed. In carom games, a miss that constitutes a DELIBERATE SAFETY is a foul. 2. (Eng. Bill., carom games) A foul stroke in which the cue ball fails to hit either object ball. 1836 Tillotson 2, 1850 Phelan 21, 1916 RGRG 7. The accidental or intentional missing of the object ball. 1866 Crawley 16. A stroke in which the cue ball fails to touch any other ball or when the cue ball, played from hand, strikes any part of a ball IN BAULK without first hitting a ball or cushion out of baulk. 1978 BSCC 25. The penalty is one point unless the cue ball enters a pocket for a COUP, which costs three points. See also GIVE A MISS, INTENTIONAL MISS, MISS IN BAULK, SCORE A MISS. 3. (Snooker) Deliberate failure to hit the BALL ON. The non-offending player has the choice of playing from the position left or having the cue ball replaced in its prior position and forcing the offending player to shoot again. 1987 BSCC S19. It is not a MISS (but it is a foul) if it is impossible for the striker to contact the ball on.

miss-cue

(obs.) = MISCUE. 1858 NYT (Jan 5) 2:3 (the first *New York Times* article on billiards), 1885 Cook 11, 1896 Broadfoot 106.

miss in baulk

(Eng. Bill) A defensive MISS played so that the STRIKER'S ball comes to rest IN BAULK and hence cannot be played at by the INCOMING PLAYER. 1911 Roberts 7. A common opening stroke. 1844 Mardon 29, 1896 Broadfoot 285.

Mississippi

(Bagatelle game, obs.) Played on a table having a comb-like BRIDGE pierced with nine or more numbered ARCHES. The object is to send balls through the arches after hitting a cushion. If the ball then goes into a CUP, the player scores both the value of the arch and that of the cup. 1863 Phelan & Berger 95. For a list of states named in billiard games, see STATES, NAMES OF.

Missouri

(game) A variant of Eight-Ball played with the ONE AND FIFTEEN IN THE SIDE rule. Also known as MISERY. For a list of states named in billiard games, see STATES, NAMES OF.

Mister and Mrs. Pocket Billiards

(game) A SINGLE-RACK pocket billiard game with a built-in HANDICAP in which women are free to shoot at any ball but men are required to shoot in rotation, that is, in numerical order. Played to 61 points, with each ball scoring its numerical value. It was designed to equalize the supposed difference in playing ability between the sexes. 1945 OR 65, 1965 Fats 55, 1976 WSD 277, 1992 OR 86. An APEX BREAK is used. The game combines the features of ROTATION and BASIC POCKET BILLIARDS. Also called BOY MEETS GIRL.

The number of different possible initial racks is $11! = 39,916,800$ because the rack setup is identical to that used for Rotation.

mixed doubles

A form of team TOURNAMENT competition in which each team consists of a man and a woman. In general, the players on a team shoot in alternate INNINGS. Also SCOTCH DOUBLES.

Mixed Game

(game) A competition combining several different billiard games, the aggregate score of which determines a winner. In 1914, such a tournament was held at Mussey's consisting of 18.2 Balkline, Red Ball, Cushion Caroms and Three-Cushions. 1926 BM (Mar) 23. Cf. BIATHLON, PENTATHLON.

momentary contact

In order for a stroke to be legal in pocket billiards, the cue tip must not remain in CONTACT with the cue ball any longer than the split second necessary to propel the ball, or else the shot constitutes a PUSH. 1990 OR 37. The rule was not always thus; see CONTINUOUS STROKE.

money ball

1. A ball, the pocketing of which causes the player to win the game or a money payoff, *e.g.*, the "9" in NINE-BALL. 1989 Koehler 257. See also PAY BALL. 2. Any billiard game played for money. "Play some money ball?"

Monte Carlo

(Bagatelle game, obs.) A game played on the PARISIAN POOL BOARD, similar to PARISIAN POOL but in which a player has only four shots in which to accumulate the highest point total. 1898 HRB 98.

A ball that moves without being struck is said to have undergone SPONTANEOUS MOTION. If a ball shifts, settles, or moves by itself, it remains in the position so attained. If a ball moves spontaneously during a stroke without fault of the STRIKER before the striker can halt

Monte Carlo

motion

A ball is said to be "in motion" if it is rolling, spinning or both. In all modern games it is a FOUL to strike while any ball is in motion. (See, for example, 1893 HRB 59). Shooting while any ball is rolling has been illegal since the time of 1674 Cotton: "He that plays a Ball, while the other runs . . . loseth an end." There is evidence that this rule was widely ignored before 1800. 1974 Hendricks 22. Up through the eighteenth century it was not a foul to strike at a SPINNING BALL.

A championship was once lost because of the rule prohibiting striking while a ball is in motion. In 1897, Frank Stewart was defending his Continuous Pool title against challenger Grant Eby. Stewart, a very fast player, needed only a few balls for victory, but he failed to wait for the cue ball to stop rolling before he made a stroke. Eby claimed a foul, went to the table and RAN OUT for the championship. 1935 NBJ (Oct).

the stroke, there is no foul and the balls are replaced as they were prior to the shot. The origin of this rule is at least as early as 1839 Kentfield 30.

If a ball drops in a pocket after having been motionless for three seconds or more, it is replaced on the table. An early version of this rule can be found at 1807 White 71. In professional play, five seconds must elapse. If a ball falls into a pocket as a player shoots at it and the cue ball passes over the spot the ball had occupied, then both object and cue ball are replaced. By extension, if a COMBINATION is being attempted and an object ball passes over that spot, it is replaced. 1982 OR 45. See also ADDRESS, IN CONTROL, TURN, VIBRATION POT, VISIT.

In Bagatelle, if the ball hovers over a hole but does not fall immediately, the adversary may say, "I challenge that ball." If the ball then drops, it must be replaced. 1878 Crawley 153. See CHALLENGE.

mouth

The opening cut in a cushion, forming the entrance to a POCKET. There is a strong tendency to name billiard table components after parts of the body. See CROTCH, ELBOW, FACE, FOOT, HEAD, LEG, LIP, NAIL, NOSE, SHOULDER.

Mouth Billiards

(game) A bizarre form of billiards in which the cue ball is projected out of the mouth. 1982 Byrne 197. Also known as BLOW POOL. The leading current practitioner of this style of game is Steve Simpson of Tennessee. It was long regarded as difficult even to take a billiard ball entirely into the mouth, and a case is known in which an unfortunately successful practitioner had to have his teeth extracted in order to remove the ball. 1901 WB (Aug 28) 438. See also NOSE. Cf. FINGER BILLIARDS.

movement of ten

(Eng. Bill.) A four-shot repetitive sequence perfected by Clark McConachy of New Zealand—a kind of RUN-NING NURSE in the English Game. 1985 Everton 107. The "ten" in the title of this maneuver comes from the number of points scored at it during one complete cycle of strokes.

MPBA

(org.) = Men's Professional Billiards Association. Formerly (until 1989) the PBA.

Mr. and Mrs. Pocket Billiards

(game) = MISTER AND MRS. POCKET BILLIARDS.

mud

(colloq.) A term used to refer to COMPOSITION BALLS, which sometimes look and feel as though they are made of dried mud. A common term during the 1930s. "They're playing with mud." See also ROCK, STONE.

Mug's Pool

(game, obs.) A game with three balls and five SKITTLES. The first player must play with white on the red. The first to score 36 points or a ROYAL is the winner. 1981c Mitchell 76.

mushroom

(colloq.) The tendency of a CUE TIP to compress and spread beyond the FERRULE after continued use. A tip that has mushroomed must be trimmed to avoid contacting the cue ball with a portion of the tip that has no solid backing. 1988 Rossman 94.

NAABP

(org.) = NATIONAL ASSOCIATION OF AMATEUR BILLIARD PLAYERS.

nail

1. = DIAMOND, DOT, RAIL MARKER, SIGHT, CUSHION SPOT or SPOT. 1850 Phelan 62, 1979 Sullivan 8. So called because nails were originally used to mark the ends of STRINGS. 2. That part of a cushion bordering a pocket. 1981 Quinn 46. See also FALL. 3. (colloq.) To hit definitively, to DRILL. "He really nailed that ball." 4. (obs.) = STRING LINE, the line defining the BAULK AREA. 1775 Annals 88. Also STRINGING NAIL. Originally, no line was drawn on the cloth, but two nails were set in the rails to mark the endpoints of the BAULK-LINE.

nail shot

(pocket games) A shot in which a ball is deliberately aimed at the pocket NAIL to effect a planned rebound. 1981 Quinn 65. See also POINT.

nameplate

= MANUFACTURER'S NAMEPLATE.

Naming Stroke Game

(game, obs.) English Billiards in which the details of each stroke, such as the ball to be struck and cushions to be contacted, must be specified before the stroke is executed, or the shot does not count. The object of this style of play is to eliminate FLUKES and cause the players to plan their shots precisely. 1889 Drayson 87. Also known as the NOMINATION GAME.

nap

A directional pile in the CLOTH that creates a favored orientation for rolling balls, namely the direction in which the fibers are pointing. A GRAIN in the cloth that runs from the BAULK END of the table to the SPOT END. For words on the effect of nap, see 1920 Levi II 146, 1933 Clifford 21, 1957 Holt 45.

Billiard cloths, particularly in England, used to be made somewhat like carpet, with fibers standing erect from a woven base and sheared off during manufacturing to the correct height. The fibers never all lie in a perfect vertical line, but are made to lean over in a particular direction. When a ball rolls down the table, its weight creates a flattened channel in the cloth. If the fibers are leaning over, the right side of the ball encounters different frictional forces than does the left side. On cloths having a nap, therefore, a moving ball tends to roll differently depending on the direction in which it is traveling, so the nap must be taken into account on long shots. In order to assist the player in doing this, cloths would be installed in a standard orientation with respect to the head and foot of the table so the player could always tell the nap direction. Modern cloths, especially those used in the U. S., are woven rather than pile and have no discernible nap, so making an adjustment for it is no longer necessary.

"Against the nap" means DOWN THE TABLE, toward BAULK. "With the nap" means UP THE TABLE, toward the SPOT. 1965 Pulman 60. In playing with the nap, right English causes the ball to curve to the right. The effect is the opposite when playing against the nap. The feel of the cloth running from baulk to the top end should be smooth, but rough in the other direction. 1990 Taylor 114. 1913 Stoddard 44 claims that the effect of nap is too small to be observed, but this certainly depends on the particular cloth. The nap phenomenon should not be confused with SWERVE, which is a partial MASSÉ stroke that does not depend on the directional properties of the cloth.

National Association of Amateur Billiard Players (NAABP)

(org.) Formed in 1899 after a dispute between billiard players and the Amateur Athletic Union. Its objective was to "guard and maintain the purity and integrity of amateur billiards, to protect the interests and conserve the rights of amateur billiard players." Its first president was Orville Oddie Jr., several times U.S. amateur Straight-Rail champion. 1899 NYDT (Oct 28) 4:2. A rival of the AMERICAN AMATEUR BILLIARD ASSOCIATION.

National Billiard Association of America (NBAA)

(org.) An organization of players and room owners formed on July 25, 1921; formerly the governing body of billiards in the U. S. By 1928, it had 35,000 members. 1928 BR (Apr) 15. Its president, Clyde A. Storer, was responsible for organizing exhibitions and instruction in more than 1500 rooms throughout the country. The body was dominated by the BBC. and, after a dispute with Willie Hoppe, became less influential during the late 1930s. It was reorganized in 1941 as the BILLIARD ASSOCIATION OF AMERICA.

National Billiard Committee

(org.) An adjudicatory body, formed in 1917, to settle disputes arising in professional carom matches. The need for such a group arose in the aftermath of a protest filed by Robert Cannefax in a three-cushion match he played against Alfredo De Oro in September 1917. The Committee members were: Thomas Foley Sr. (chairman), Harmon F. Davenport (secretary), Louis A. Bensinger, William P. Mussey, C. C. Peterson, Charles P. Miller, and Maurice Daly. It had the full power to make and amend rules, select referees and decide protests.

National Billiard Council (NBC)

(Org.) = A promotional body for the sport of billiards that coexisted and shared officers with the Billiard Congress of America during the 1940s. 1967 Polsky 26.

National Billiard News

A monthly newspaper devoted to billiards, established in 1962 by Earl Newby, now published by Ray Abrams and Conrad Burkman. Address: Box 807, Northville, Michigan 48167.

National Pocket Billiard Association (NPBA)

(org.) Organization sanctioning nationwide LEAGUE play, formed in 1964. It publishes weekly league standings, forms, statistics, and standardized rules. Address: 2635 W. Burnham Ave., Milwaukee, WI 53204.

natural

1. An easy shot, usually requiring only proper direction of the cue ball. 1941 Hoppe 75, 1992 OR 12. "You left a natural." This term was certainly in use prior to its appearance in 1910 NYT (Oct 21) 7:3. 2. = NATURAL ENGLISH, RUNNING ENGLISH. 1941 Hoppe 75. Cf. REVERSE. 3. (Pin Pool) A shot in which the player knocks down the four outside PINS with a single stroke but leaves the inside black pin standing, which wins the game. Also known as a RANCHE. Cf. ROYAL.

natural-angle stroke

(Eng. Bill.) = HALF-BALL STROKE. 1885 Cook 7, 1895 Buchanan 36, 1957 Holt 17. See also HALF-BALL ANGLE.

natural bank

An easy BANK SHOT, one that can be made merely by aiming at the center of the object ball. 1977 Fels 46. Also used in Carom Billiards, where it refers to an easy RAIL-FIRST shot.

natural bridge

An OPEN BRIDGE made with the hand, as opposed to a CLOSED BRIDGE or ARTIFICIAL BRIDGE. 1863 Phelan & Berger 11, 1864 AH 399. Also, a sightseeing attraction in Virginia. See also V-BRIDGE.

natural English

= RUNNING ENGLISH, NATURAL. 1928 Barry 3. Cf. REVERSE ENGLISH.

natural roll

1. Motion of the cue ball when no ENGLISH is applied to it. 1992 OR 10. This definition is not strictly correct, since a ball struck at its center will initially slide against the cloth before pure rolling begins. Properly, natural roll is a state in which the ball exhibits no sliding. 2. Tendency of the cue ball to curve toward the direction in which ENGLISH has been applied when the cue stick is elevated slightly.

NBAA

(org.) = NATIONAL BILLIARD ASSOCIATION OF AMERICA.

NBC

(Org.) = NATIONAL BILLIARD COUNCIL.

Near Ball

(game, obs.) A FULL RACK pocket billiard game in which the object is to sink the nine-ball. At each stroke, the player must first hit the ball that is closest to the cue ball. As might be expected, many arguments occur during the course of this game over which ball is to be hit next. Cf. HAZARDS, NEAREST BALL POOL.

nearest ball playable

(Snooker, obs.) Term used in a pre-1919 rule that allowed a player who was SNOOKERED as a result of his opponent's foul stroke to LIFT the snookering ball to permit a shot at the "nearest ball playable," which became ON for the duration of the shot. 1985 Everton 47. This rule has been supplanted by the FREE BALL rule. Cf. PLAY AGAIN RULE, TAKE UP.

Nearest Ball Pool

(game, obs.) COLOR-BALL POOL in which players must shoot at the nearest ball out of BAULK. If all are IN BAULK and the striker is IN HAND, the TOP RAIL must be struck first. 1839 Kentfield 43, 1867 Dufton 221, 1896 Broadfoot 431. Cf. HAZARDS, NEAR BALL.

negative score

In certain American games, such as 14.1 CONTINUOUS, a player's score can become negative because of a PENALTY resulting in points being subtracted from his total. For example, in the 1969 U.S. Open, Dick Baertsch beat Joe Balsis at Straight Pool by a score of 150 to minus 13, the greatest margin of victory in a 150-point game on record. In English games, points forfeited are added to the opponent's score, so no total can be negative. See OWE, PENALTY POINTS, SCORING.

net, netting

A woven container for capturing and holding balls that enter pocket holes. 1674 Cotton. Pockets, or HAZARDS, were originally simply holes cut in the table. The net was necessary to prevent balls from falling to the ground. Also POCKET NET.

nickel and dime

A 5-foot × 10-foot table. Totally unrelated to FIVE AND TEN.

nickname

An informal descriptive name, usually colorful, given to a player in place of his real name. Such names seem universal among hustlers and male tournament players but are almost never applied to women. For example, "Boston Shorty" is the nickname of Larry Johnson, a superb all-around player of both pocket and carom games. He is short, lives in the Boston area, and is probably known to more people by his nickname than by his real name.

Nicknames generally fall into five categories: they may be based on (1) geographic origin, (2) physical attributes, (3) similarity to a well-known person or character, (4) occupation, or (5) playing ability. "Boston Shorty" is a combination of the first and second types. Luther Lassiter was called "Wimpy" because of a penchant for hamburgers reminiscent of the Popeye character, which is an example of the third. Joe Balsis was "The Meatman" because of his involvement with his family's meat business. Lou Butera was named "Machine Gun" by a newspaper reporter who was stunned at the ruthless way Butera crushed an opponent. 1973 NBJ (Mar) 75. He is also a very rapid player, which makes the nickname unforgettable.

Considerable ingenuity can go into a nickname, several of which may have to be tried before a fitting monicker is arrived at. Some lesser-known but clever "handles" are Bad Eye, Close-Draw Foots, Jack the Hat, Pots 'n Pans, Rushout Red, Sure-Shot Logan, and Toupee Jay. 1989 Annigoni PC.

Nigger Pool

(game, obs.) A pocket billiard game similar to DUTCH POOL, played to 31 points with BURST. 1988 Lange PC.

night manager

The employee of a BILLIARD ROOM responsible for the night shift, usually from 6:00 or 7:00 P.M. until closing. The night manager carries greater responsibility than the DAY MANAGER because a room's principal business is generated in the evenings. See also MANAGER.

Nine-Ball

1. (game) A SHORT RACK pocket billiard game played with a cue ball and nine object balls numbered one

through nine, the goal being to pocket the nine-ball. On each shot, the cue ball must first contact the lowest-numbered ball remaining on the table. 1965 Fats 29, 1967 OR 74. The balls are RACKED in a DIAMOND pattern with the one-ball on the FOOT SPOT and the nine-ball in the center of the diamond. When the five-ball is a MONEY BALL, it is racked at the rear of the diamond. The usual custom is that the player who wins a game is allowed to BREAK in the next game. In some variations, if the nine-ball is pocketed while other balls remain on the table, the highest-numbered remaining ball becomes the GAME BALL. 1985c Game Rules.

The origin of Nine-Ball is obscure, which is surprising for such an overwhelmingly popular game. Special diamond-shaped racks for it, known as "nine-ball triangles," were being sold in the 1920s, but official printed rules did not appear until 1967. Its roots are unknown. One of its offspring is SIX-BALL. During the 1970s, Nine-Ball replaced Straight Pool as the most popular form of professional billiards. Matches are of the RACE variety; the first player to win a predetermined number of games is the winner. Tournaments generally follow the DOUBLE ELIMINATION format.

Nine-Ball is a fast, spectator-oriented game, well-suited to television coverage. One reason is that the penalty for a FOUL is that the incoming player has cue ball IN HAND anywhere on the table. It is also an easy game to HANDICAP—the superior player may SPOT his opponent the break or the eight-ball, meaning that the inferior player will win if he pockets the eight *or* the nine. For examples of such handicaps, see BANK THE NINE, EIGHT SAFE, EIGHT TO HOP, HOP THE EIGHT, LAST TWO, ORANGE CRUSH, SPOT THE BREAK, TEXAS EXPRESS, WILD. The popularity of the game has also resulted in many rule variations. See HIT THE BALL, HONEST JOHN, IN HAND, NEAR BALL, NINE-BALL BANKS, ODDBALL, OLYMPIC NINE-BALL, ONE SHOT OUT, PASS, PENETRATION NINE-BALL, PLAY AGAIN RULE, PLAY-TO-HIT, PUSHOUT, ROLLOUT, SHOOT OUT, TWO-SHOT ROLLOUT, WILD.

Variants of Nine-Ball can be produced by changing the number of balls used in the game. See THREE-BALL, SIX-BALL, SEVEN-BALL, TEN-BALL. The vocabulary of Nine-Ball is still actively evolving. See CRUSH, KICK, ORANGE CRUSH, PARK THE BALL, RUN STICK, SERIOUS FOUL, SPLIT HIT, STANDARD FOUL.

Nine-Ball is the dominant American professional game. The number of tournaments and total prize money eclipse all other forms together. The five highest-ranked male players in 1991 were Buddy Hall, Johnny Archer, Nick Varner, Earl Strickland and Jim Rempe. The top female players were Ewa Mataya,

Robin Bell, Loree Jon Jones, JoAnn Mason-Parker and Belinda Bearden. 1992 BD (Feb).

The number of different possible initial racks in Nine-Ball is 7! = 5040. 2. (Pocket Bill.) The striped yellow ball bearing the digit 9.

Nine-Ball Banks

(game) Nine-Ball in which only BANK SHOTS are legal.

Nine-Hole Snooker

(game) A Snooker-like game played with PINS on a modified Bar Billiards table having nine holes. It was advertised at 1956 BSTE 27 to be "as up to date as the latest jet plane."

nine-shot, nine-stroke

(Eng. Bill., Amer. Four-Ball Bill.) A shot that scores nine points. In English Billiards, this can be accomplished by striking the WHITE first, making a CANNON, and potting all the balls. 1890 HRB 110. In American Four-Ball, it is done by caroming on the two REDS and pocketing them both. Curiously, this legal manner of scoring is not mentioned in the list of valid shots in 1850 Phelan 22.

nip

A very short stroke used to avoid making a PUSH SHOT. Usually a close DRAW in which downward action is put on the ball by snapping the butt up against the heel of the hand with a flick of the wrist. Called at 1925 Hoppe 196 "the most difficult of all draw strokes," it is used when full draw would either result in a double hit or cause the cue ball to rebound into the cue tip, as when the cue ball lies close to the object ball. See also COUP SEC, PINCH.

no count

A style of scoring in which RUNS or BREAKS of fewer than a given number of points do not count and result in no score. For example, in a game played "10 no count," only runs of 10 or more points will be scored. Originally the phrase was "or no count," as in "10 or no count." 1979 Grissim 252. This explains why runs of 10 count, despite the phrase "10 no count," which suggests that a run of ten would not count.

No count may be used for offering a HANDICAP or simply to yield a more challenging game. When a handicap is given, the stronger player will play, for example, five no count to the weaker player's STRAIGHT-UP.

George H. Sutton, the handless player, when on exhibition tour, would play BILLIARDS 100 or no count to his opponent's STRAIGHT-RAIL. 1922 BM (May). An extreme example occurred in 1886, when Harvey Mc-

Kenna offered to play Straight-Rail against anyone in New York except Maurice Daly and William Sexton at a handicap of 1000 or no count. 1886 NYT (Aug 3) 8:4. He usually won! In Britain, no count is known as the BREAK GAME. Cf. DISCOUNT for a related method of handicapping, especially ROYAL DISCOUNT, a special case of no count in which all the points needed for game must be made in a single turn at the table.

no English system

(Three-Cushions) = DEAD BALL SYSTEM. A DIAMOND SYSTEM used to compute the path in the SHORT TABLE taken by a ball struck without ENGLISH.

no shot in

(Balkline, obs.) A name for 18.1 BALKLINE that was used by George Butler Sutton but never gained acceptance. It referred to the fact that a player facing two balls IN BALK had no shot in which to maneuver before having to drive one of them out of balk. Properly called ONE SHOT IN.

nominated

(pocket games) = CALLED, designated to be struck first or pocketed.

nominated ball

1. (Snooker) = FREE BALL; the object ball that the striker declares he will attempt to strike with the first impact of the cue ball after being SNOOKERED by his opponent's FOUL. 1957 Holt 149, 1978 BSCC 48. 2. (Pocket Bill.) A CALLED BALL; one the striker intends to pocket.

Nomination Game

(game, obs.) English Billiards in which all shots must be called (*i.e.*, NOMINATED) in advance, including any cushions that are to be contacted during a CANNON. If the player fails to make the stroke named, any points scored are credited to his opponent. 1866 Crawley 232. It is described in 1856 Crawley 97 as "slow and uninteresting." Also known as the NAMING STROKE GAME. Cf. CALL-SHOT THREE-CUSHIONS.

noncontinuous

Referring to a pocket billiard game in which scoring is by FRAME; the player who wins the most frames is the winner of the match. There is no BREAK BALL, and no score carries over from one frame to the next. Cf. CONTINUOUS POOL.

Non-Continuous Fifteen-Ball Pocket Billiards

(game, obs.) = FIFTEEN-BALL, SIXTY-ONE POOL. Failure to satisfy the OPENING BREAK requirements is equivalent to two SCRATCHES and carries a penalty of six points. 1916 RGRG 56.

Non-Cushion Game

(game, obs.) = STOP GAME. 1839 Kentfield 38, 1850c White & Bohn 38, 1867 Dufton 235. A strange contest in which the striker's INNING ends if his cue ball contacts a cushion. SLOW cloth can be helpful in this game.

Non-Pareil Cannon Game

(Bagatelle game, obs.) A version of the CANNON GAME in which failure to strike the opponent's cue ball results in one point plus the value of any CUPS in which balls have fallen being added to the opponent's score.

nonplayer interference

INTERFERENCE with a game that is caused by an agency other than one of the PLAYERS, such as a SPECTATOR. No PENALTY is assessed as a result of such interference and the balls are replaced by the referee. 1916 RGRG 10, 1986 OR 46. The rule was not always such. In England during the 1830s, if a nonplayer stopped the motion of a ball, "it must stand in the place where it was stopped." See also REPLAY. Cf. ACT OF GOD, PLAYER RESPONSIBILITY FOUL.

Some extreme examples of nonplayer interference are on record. During a championship match at American Four-Ball in San Francisco in March 1870, A. P. Rudolphe was within one point of victory over John Deery when a member of the audience ran to the table, picked up one of the balls, and tried to throw it out the window. The ball stayed in the room. The courteous Deery picked it up himself and replaced it in position so his opponent could win.

In August 1871, C. A. Frink was beating Ebenezer Francis at American Four-Ball in Newark, New Jersey. As the game drew to a close, the crowd surrounded Frink to congratulate him. As he made the winning point, a spectator nudged him, causing his cue stick to touch a ball. Frink claimed a foul, which was allowed. Frink stepped to the table and ran 82 and out to win the match! Under modern rules, there would have been no foul. Francis protested, the stake money was not paid, and a rematch was arranged, at which Francis won. 1940 NBJ (Nov) 23.

In February 1872, Frank Dion, Cyrille's brother, claimed that he had been drugged during a match by a spectator who offered him what was purportedly a glass of brandy. 1872 NYT (Mar 1) 2:6. These wild happenings of the 1870s were eventually countered by rule changes that prevent spectators from tampering with a game in progress.

nonstop play

An endurance contest in which a player continues shooting until forced to retire from exhaustion. Success

156

is measured by elapsed time before collapse occurs. This is the kind of performance engendered by the Guinness Book of World Records, which elected to glorify the activity by making it a new category of record. In 1975, Mark Quinn of New York played for 25 hours, sinking 7035 balls. Whether this was the maximum at the time is questionable, since the author and many of his associates during their collegiate days played in marathon sessions whose length approached that of the claimed record.

A closely related challenge is to pocket the greatest number of balls in a 24-hour period. Although this exercise may be mind-numbing (worse for the REFEREE than the player), at least it ends in a day, while the competition for nonstop play threatens to take much longer. In July 1980, Mike Massey sank 11,230 balls in 24 hours at an exhibition in Sacramento. At one ball every 7.69 seconds, this is a fierce pace.

nonstriker
Usually, the opponent of the STRIKER; any PLAYER who is not currently IN CONTROL of the table. 1885 Cook 11, 1916 RGRG 41, 1978 BSCC 24.

north-hander
(Brit.) A left-handed player; a southpaw. 1984 NBN (Jan) 7. This is yet another example of the difference between the British and American frames of reference.

nose
1. The beveled edge of a cushion that overhangs the table BED; the surface presented to the balls. 1992 OR 3. So named from the shape of its profile. The PBTA regulation nose height for pocket billiard tables is 1²⁹⁄₆₄″. This height is very important because a nose that is too high will partially trap the ball, causing it to bounce on rebound. If the nose is too low, balls will tend to fly off the table after striking the cushion. It is also important for a contact with the cushion not to impart any follow or draw to the ball; this is achieved when the nose height is at the ball's center of percussion. 2. A proboscis extending from the center of the human face, occasionally used to propel billiard balls in place of a cue stick. The use of the nose in this fashion is described in 1974 Lindrum 124. Herbert Roberts always chalked his nose before shooting when he was using it as a cue and could even play AROUND THE TABLE shots. Toots, a dog owned by Arthur Clayton, was trained to play pocket billiards with his nose and achieved fleeting fame at this endeavor in 1914. Herman Cohn, alias Prof. Henry Lewis, made his entire career of nose exhibitions and once made a run of 46 at STRAIGHT-RAIL. 1928 BR (Jul) 5. See FINGER BILLIARDS and MOUTH BILLIARDS for the use of different parts of the body to strike the ball.

not frozen
(Bill.) The referee's CALL in response to being asked to rule whether two balls are touching each other when, in his judgment, they are not. There is no appeal from such a call, since it is a factual assessment. 1916 RGRG 13. If the balls are indeed FROZEN, the action to be taken differs in various games. In Three-Cushions the rules formerly provided for the player whose cue ball was frozen to an object ball to set up an OPENING BREAK. The modern trend is to spot only the frozen balls. Cf. FROZEN.

not on
See OFF, ON.

notation
1. A nondiagrammatic method of specifying the positions of billiard balls, used for defining standard shots or for telegraphic purposes. See COORDINATES. See also ARTISTIC BILLIARDS, KEY SHOT BILLIARDS, TELEGRAPHIC BILLIARDS. 2. A set of abbreviations for recording the events in a billiard game, particularly Nine-Ball.

NPBA
(org.) = NATIONAL POCKET BILLIARD ASSOCIATION.

nudge
The act of hitting the cue ball accidentally during warm-up stroking. In Carom Billiards, the nudge cannot be counted by the player as a legal stroke and so constitutes a FOUL. 1976 Regulation 71. This contradicts the old rule that "a touch is a shot." 1916 RGRG 11. What happens if the player makes a carom on a nudge! See also FEATHER, FIDDLE, MISCUE, TOUCH, WAGGLE, WARM-UP.

null game
A TIE or DRAW. WBA 5. See also STALEMATED GAME, SUDDEN DEATH.

numbered ball
A BALL marked with numerals. "That game with the fifteen numbered balls is the devil's tool!" 1957 Willson *The Music Man*. During the late nineteenth century, numerals were engraved on the balls in a manner similar to scrimshaw, but this method was unsatisfactory because of the unpredictable collision that can occur when the engraving is at the POINT OF CONTACT. Numbered balls are not used in English Billiards, Snooker, or carom games.

nurse
(Bill.) A delicate sequence of shots that disturb the object balls as little as possible or that result in a repetitive position, permitting extremely long runs.

157

1857 Phelan 138, 1881 MB 26, 1941 Hoppe 75. Originally the term referred to GATHER work rather than close manipulation, but this changed as players acquired a high degree of skill at minute positioning of the balls. The history of Carom Billiards is replete with efforts to curtail nursing because of its monotonous effect on the game.

For specific nurses, see AMERICAN SERIES, ANCHOR CANNON, ANCHOR NURSE, BALKLINE NURSE, CHUCK NURSE, CLOSE CANNON, CRADLE CANNON, DION'S NURSE, EDGE NURSE, JAM CANNON, LINE NURSE, PASS NURSE, PENDULUM CANNON, RAIL NURSE, ROCKING CANNON, RUB NURSE, RUDOLPHE'S NURSE, SÉRIE AMÉRICAINE, SQUEEZE CANNON. See also BALKLINE, LIMITED RAIL, NURSERY, NURSERY CANNON, RUNNING NURSE, STATIONARY NURSE, STRAIGHT-RAIL, UNLIMITED RAIL. See also SHORT GAME.

nursery

(Eng. Bill.) = NURSE. 1869 Roberts 135, 1885 Cook 11. The original usage was in the sense of a "nursery of cannons," meaning a collection of shots. See NURSERY CANNON.

nursery cannon

(Eng. Bill.) = NURSE, NURSERY. For particular types in English Billiards, see ANCHOR CANNON, CLOSE CANNON, CRADLE CANNON, JAM CANNON, PENDULUM CANNON, ROCKING CANNON, SQUEEZE CANNON. The success of nursery play led to various rules restricting CONSECUTIVE CANNONS. In one variation, only 25 cannons could be made without causing one of the object balls to strike a cushion. 1920 Levi II 49. Later, a limit was placed on the number of successive cannons permitted without an intervening hazard.

nuts

1. (sl.) A good proposition, particularly a sure thing. "It's the nuts." 2. Insane, crazy. Frequently applied to billiard players.

object ball

A ball that is to be hit by the cue ball. 1807 White 12, 1850 Phelan 20, 1866 Crawley 17, 1941 Hoppe 75. In modern usage, any ball other than the cue ball, particularly one to be struck or pocketed. 1985 Marguglio distinguishes among the "primary," "secondary" and "ultimate" object balls. The term "passive ball" is used in 1806 Phil 11. See also CAROM BALL, FIRST OBJECT BALL, LEGAL OBJECT BALL, OBJECT WHITE, SECOND OBJECT BALL.

object white

(Bill., *esp.* Eng. Bill.) The white ball that is not the player's cue ball, but instead serves as an OBJECT BALL. 1904 Mannock I 325. See also WHITECHAPEL.

oblique stroke

(obs.) A JUMP SHOT; one that causes the ball to leave the cloth. 1807 White 25. So named because the cue stick on such a shot makes an oblique angle with the plane of the table. Such jump shots were known at least several decades before the invention of the cue tip. See also HIGH OBLIQUE STROKE, PERPENDICULAR STROKE.

obstruction

A situation in which the player cannot contact all or a portion of the ball he desires or is required to hit because of the presence of an intervening ball. Obstruction comprises four related concepts:

(1) A player is able to SEE a ball if he is able to contact any portion of it, however small, with his cue ball by a straight shot without contacting any cushions or resorting to a JUMP SHOT. (2) A player is SNOOKERED if there is any portion of the ball that he *cannot* contact. 1978 BSCC 47. See also SNOOKER. Being snookered is not the same as being unable to see a ball: If the ball is only partially obscured, the player can still see it but be snookered nonetheless. (3) A player can make a FULL BALL shot if he is able to contact its center directly. This definition is employed in ENGLISH EIGHT-BALL POOL. 1985 KTGP 31, 1986 Quinn 88. It may be possible to make a full ball shot even when one is snookered. If one can make a full ball shot one can certainly SEE the ball. (4) The last concept is that of the ANGLED BALL. The cue ball is angled if the player is snookered on every ball on by a pocket. 1987 BSCC S12. See also ANGLE, CORNER HOOKED, HOOKED, JAWED, OPEN SHOT.

A pocket is "obstructed" if its effective opening is diminished in any way with respect to a particular object ball by the presence of other balls. Note that a pocket may be obstructed for sinking one object ball and not another. *See illustration on next page.*

occupied

A SPOT is said to be occupied if a ball cannot be placed on it without touching or disturbing another ball. 1807

See. The cue ball cannot see ball 2 because it is obscured by the edge of 1.

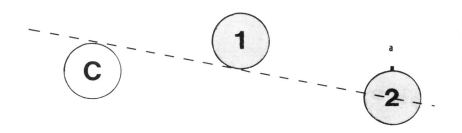

Snooker. The cue ball can see ball 2 but is snookered by ball 1 since point a cannot be hit.

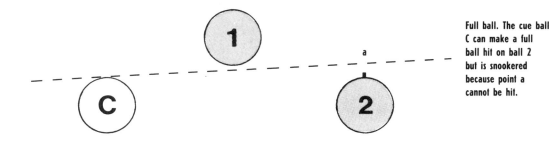

Full ball. The cue ball C can make a full ball hit on ball 2 but is snookered because point a cannot be hit.

obstruction

White 66, 1861 *Leslie's* (May 11) 411:3, 1978 BSCC 25. See COVER, INTERFERENCE, SPOTTING.

Rules vary as to what should be done when a ball needs to be placed on an occupied spot. In some games, provision is made for a different spot to be used, often the one on which the interfering ball itself would normally be placed. In other games, the ball to be spotted is held OFF THE TABLE until its spot becomes VACANT, or it may be placed at one of the other spots in a predetermined sequence.

ocean
(colloq.) The central area of a billiard table that is distant from the cushions, in which it is difficult to manipulate the balls. The term reflects the resemblance between this large green region and the high seas. Also known as the OPEN TABLE. See also GREEN.

Oddball
1. (game) A pocket billiard game for four players, played with a FULL RACK in which the one is placed on the FOOT SPOT, the two at the right rear of the TRIANGLE, the three at the left rear and the fifteen in the center. The object is to be the first player to score 21 points. The lowest-numbered ball must be contacted first on each shot. Odd-numbered balls count one point. In addition, two points are awarded to the team having the greater total of balls pocketed during the frame, both odd and even,

each ball counting for its numerical value. 1982 OR 100. 2. (game) A game, usually a variant of Nine-Ball, in which money is won by sinking odd-numbered balls.

odds

A form of HANDICAP in which the stronger player (the "odds-giver") pays more if he loses than the weaker player would if he were to lose. In the ENGLISH GAME, it was usual for the player receiving odds (*i.e.*, the weaker player) to LEAD. 1869 Kavanagh 11. The term can be used generally to refer to any handicap, such as DISCOUNT, whether or not the payoffs to the players differ.

off

1. Opposite of ON, with respect to one's stroke or shot. Not IN STROKE, not easy, not possible. "The combination is off." "He's off tonight." 2. Imperfectly aimed. "He was off on that shot." 3. Not TRUE. "The table is off." 4. = TIME OFF, meaning that a player wants to terminate his playing session at a public billiard room and pay the check. Cf. ON. See also OFF AND ON. 5. A term used in connection with a HANDICAP at Eight-Ball. In "one-off," the weaker player is permitted to remove one of his GROUP BALLS, at his choice, once the table is no longer OPEN. In "two-off," he may remove two balls, and so forth. 6. = OFF THE TABLE.

off and on

An instruction given by a player to the COUNTER MAN in a billiard room to request that a new time record be started. That is, he wants to be taken OFF the current check and placed ON another. This situation occurs when a new player enters the game and the person renting the table wishes to settle up with his previous opponent and must therefore learn the amount of his bill so far. Cf. TIME OFF, TIME ON.

off the balls

(Eng. Bill.) In one RUN or TURN at the table. 1856 Crawley 97, 1869 NYT (Aug 8) 6:1. To make "game off the balls" is to RUN OUT the game from the current position. See also CLEAN UP, GET OUT, OUT, UNFINISHED.

off the table

A ball that is not IN PLAY is said to be off the table or just OFF. 1807 White 107. It applies particularly to the opponent's white ball in English Billiards, which, when pocketed, remains out of play until the end of the striker's INNING, when it is placed in the D. See also BALL OFF, DEAD BALL, JUMP BALL, IN HAND, IN PLAY, LOSE THE WHITE, OCCUPIED, WHITECHAPEL.

offending player

A player who has committed a FOUL or other infraction of the rules. 1989 Raftis 14. It is an old principle of billiards that the offending player cannot realize any benefit from illegal behavior. See, for example, FREE BALL, INTENTIONAL MISS, PLAY AGAIN RULE, REPLACEMENT.

offense

That aspect of the game concerned with scoring, as opposed to DEFENSE or SAFETY PLAY, in which scoring opportunities are less important than preventing the opponent from advancing. See also SHOTMAKER.

oil

1. (colloq.) Extreme ENGLISH, GREASE, JUICE, SPIN, STUFF. 1912 NYT (Feb. 19) 10:4. Cf. GAS. 2. A lubricant applied to preserve ivory balls. The wisdom of the practice is questioned in 1893 HRB 27. The occasional loss of oil from a spinning ball may have resulted in the use of "oil" to mean ENGLISH. Linseed oil is sometimes applied to the shaft of a cue stick to keep it from becoming brittle. 1988 Davis 15. 3. (rare) A SAFETY. Probably derived from the idea of pouring oil on troubled waters. 1913 NYT (Nov 6) 15:3. To "play the oil" means to attempt an intentional safety, often while trying to disguise one's true intention.

Old Army Game

(game, obs.) A test of carom billiard skill in which the player must make the following shots in order: a three-cushion shot, a two-cushion shot, a CUSHION CAROM, a DIRECT CAROM, and a BANK. A shot calling for a specific number of cushions must be made using that number exactly. 1915 *Billiard News* (Aug) 3.

old man's aid

A disparaging term for the MECHANICAL BRIDGE. 1977 Martin 207. Also known as the CRUTCH, LADIES' AID, or SISSY STICK.

Olympic Nine-Ball

(game) A version of Nine-Ball scored for points. The balls are racked in clockwise order. The opening breaker has cue ball in hand and shoots under Nine-Ball rules until he misses, scoring one point for each ball pocketed. The next player then has ball in hand and continues until missing, which ends the first inning. The balls are racked again for the next inning. An arbitrary number of players may participate. Sinking the nine-ball scores nine points. Sinking the nine-ball on the break or running out an entire rack scores 10 points. The player with the highest point total after 10 innings is the winner. 1992 PBM (Jun) 26.

on

1. Possible, able to be made; said of a shot. "It's on." Properly lined up, as in "the combination is on." "Not on" means OFF or impossible. 2. Obliged to play a certain ball next, as in "you're on the five," or, "after potting a red, the player is on colors." In Snooker, the official definition is "may lawfully be struck next by the cue ball." 1978 BSCC 47. See BALL ON for the origin of this usage of "on." 3. In stroke; said of a player, as in "He's really on tonight." Cf. OFF. 4. Having backed as a bettor. "I'm on him" means "I have bet on him to win." See also GET ON. 5. Being in a particular state in the game, as "on two scratches," meaning that the player has scratched on his two immediately preceding shots. A player is "on a foul" if his previous inning ended with a foul stroke. See CONSECUTIVE FOULS, ON A FOUL. 6. = TIME ON, meaning that a player wants to begin a playing session at a public billiard room. Cf. OFF. See also OFF AND ON.

on a cribbage

(Cribbage) The state of having legally pocketed an object ball. The player is next obliged to pocket that ball's COMPANION BALL, whose numerical designation is determined by subtracting from 15.

on a foul

The state of having committed a FOUL in one's prior turn at the table. This condition is announced by the referee. 1983 Rule Book 254. Whether or not a player is on a foul is important in games that exact additional penalties for CONSECUTIVE FOULS, such as 14.1 CONTINUOUS. See also FIFTEEN-POINT PENALTY.

on ball

(Snooker) A ball that is ON, usually referred to as a BALL ON. For example, if all the REDS are DOWN, then after the BLUE is potted the on ball is the PINK.

on the hill

(colloq.) Needing one point for victory. See also CASE GAME, CASEY JONES, DOUBLE CHEESE, HILL, HILL GAME, ONE-HOLE.

on the pocket

Near the LIP or MOUTH of the pocket. 1927 Katch 50. In pocket games, a HANGER. For a discussion of what happens when a ball on the pocket happens to fall in after appearing to stop moving, see ADDRESS, MOTION.

on the wire

(colloq.) Already scored or awarded as a HANDICAP, referring to the tally beads on the SCORE STRING. A player who is given a SPOT of three games in a RACE to nine match is said to have "three on the wire."

One and Fifteen-Ball Rotation Pocket Billiards

(game, obs.) A four-handed ROTATION pocket billiard game in which teams are determined by which players sink the 1 and 15 balls. The player pocketing the 1 is paired with the player pocketing the 15 if the 15 is the last ball remaining on the table and their combined scores total at least 61 points. This team then wins the game. If their total is less than 61, the 15 is spotted and the next player attempts to pocket it. Other rules cover the case in which the 15 is not the last ball pocketed or the same player sinks both the 1 and the 15. 1925 RGRG 63. Cf. ONE AND NINE BALL.

one and fifteen in the side

(Eight-Ball) Rule variation in Eight-Ball under which the specified balls must be pocketed in designated side pockets. 1979 Grissim 252. See also ALABAMA EIGHT-BALL, LAST POCKET OPTION, MISERY, MISSOURI.

One and Nine Ball

(game) Pocket billiard game for four players, essentially team ROTATION. The teams are not determined until the rack is partially complete. The player pocketing the one-ball is the partner of the player pocketing the nine-ball. If this is the same player, then the player pocketing the ten, eleven, etc. becomes his partner. If the nine through fifteen are all pocketed by the player pocketing the one, then balls eight, seven, etc. are used, in that order. The balls are racked with the one on the FOOT SPOT, the two at the right rear, the three at the left rear, and the nine in the center of the triangle. 1965 Fats 56, 1973 Mizerak 66, 1982 OR 102. Substantially the same game as ONE AND FIFTEEN-BALL ROTATION POCKET BILLIARDS.

One and Safe

(game) A variation of ONE-POCKET in which a player who has pocketed a ball legally must play a SAFETY at his next shot and cannot receive credit for any additional balls in that INNING. This rule prevents runs and is usually played as a HANDICAP. Cf. ONE AND STOP.

One and Stop

(game) A variation of ONE-POCKET in which a player is permitted only one stroke in each INNING, regardless of whether he pockets a ball. This rule prevents runs and is usually played as a HANDICAP. It can be used in any game, especially Three-Cushions. Cf. ONE AND SAFE, STOP.

Originally, all games allowed the player only a single stroke at each turn. See FOLLOWING GAME.

one-ball

1. The solid yellow pocket billiard ball marked with the numeral 1; for this reason, also known as the ACE. 2. (game) A pocket billiard game played with a FULL RACK. The one-ball is racked in the center of the triangle. The first player to CALL and pocket the one-ball wins. 1982 OR 104.

one-ball break

(pocket games) A BREAK SHOT in which the only requirement is that the cue ball must contact a ball and at least one object ball must be driven to a cushion. This break is used in ONE-POCKET and BASIC POCKET BILLIARDS. Cf. TWO-BALL BREAK.

one continuous stroke

(pocket games) See CONTINUOUS STROKE.

One-Cushion

(game) There is no such game. The proper term in English is CUSHION CAROMS, which refers to a game in which the cue ball must hit at least one cushion before contacting the SECOND OBJECT BALL. However, the name of the game in many foreign countries is a literal translation of One-Cushion, such as Una Banda and Einband.

one-handed play

A manner of stroking in which the player shoots using only one arm, that is, by gripping the BUTT of the cue with one hand and not forming a BRIDGE. 1869 Roberts 234 warns of sharpers in this game, saying that it is not so difficult but that "altogether it is a very deceptive method of play." For shots on which it is not feasible to rest the shaft of the cue stick on a rail, the recommended method is to grasp the cue directly behind the BALANCE POINT and to follow through completely without resting the shaft on the rail. It is astounding how accurate one can be using this technique. According to Ripley, Stanley Stonik was able to achieve runs exceeding 40 in one-handed pocket billiard play. See also AMBIDEXTROUS, JACK-UP POOL.

One-handed play is not confined to ordinary stroking. Kinrey Matsuyama, U.S. National Three-Cushion champion, was able to make massé shots one-handed by grasping the shaft of his cue very near the tip and striking straight down on the ball.

one-hole

1. The state of needing one point for victory; "playing for one." 1941 Hoppe 75. "He's in the one-hole." See also CHEESE, DOUBLE CHEESE, HILL GAME, ON THE HILL. 2.

(game, colloq.) = ONE-POCKET. Also just HOLE. 3. (game) = ONE POCKET TO FIVE. 1775 Annals 111, 1807 White 50.

One Hundred and One

(game) A FULL RACK pocket game in which the pockets are numbered and the number of points awarded for sinking a ball is the number of the pocket in which it falls. The numbering scheme assigns the following values to the pockets, counterclockwise from the right head pocket: 1, 2, 3, 5, 10, 15. A player must score 100 points exactly, then win by sinking a ball in the right head pocket for another point to yield 101. 1992 BD (Feb) 85.

one-piece cue

A cue stick that has been formed from a single piece of wood without a joint. HOUSE CUES are normally one-piece because of cost considerations and the fact that there is no need to break them down for convenience. Cf. JOINTED CUE, SNEAKY PETE, TWO-PIECE CUE.

One-Player Rotation

(game) A tournament pocket billiard game for an arbitrary number of players. The balls are RACKED for each player, who breaks by hitting the one-ball and must score as many points as possible in a single inning, shooting as in Rotation.

One-Pocket

(game) A SINGLE-RACK pocket billiard game in which each player is assigned one of the FOOT POCKETS, his opponent receiving the other. A ball pocketed in one of these pockets is credited to the "owner" of the pocket, regardless of who sinks it. The first player to score eight balls wins. A ONE-BALL BREAK is utilized. A HANDICAP may be given by allowing fewer points for a victory. The game is given to long stretches of defensive play, and BANK SHOTS are common. 1965 Fats 24, 1982 OR. The game was described as early as 1869 Roberts 234, but is derived from the much earlier BAR-HOLE GAME. It was a favorite HUSTLER'S game in the U.S. for many decades before prize tournaments began to be held in JOHNSTON CITY during the 1960s. The first modern printed rules did not come on the scene until the 1967 edition of the BCA rule book, the same volume in which the Nine-Ball rules first appeared. Also known as POCKET APIECE, ONE-HOLE or just HOLE. See also EIGHT AND OUT, FRONT TO BACK, ONE AND SAFE, ONE AND STOP. Cf. ONE POCKET TO FIVE.

One-Pocket require great offensive and defensive skill. Matches may last an hour and require extreme patience, as the players may maneuver at length awaiting a

162

mistake by the opponent. Grady Mathews is acclaimed as one of the top One-Pocket players in the U.S.

The number of different possible initial racks in One Pocket is $15! = 1,307,674,368,000$.

One Pocket to Five

(game, obs.) A CRAMP GAME of English Billiards in which one player must use only one pocket, the other being free to use the remaining five. CANNONS count, and any ball going into a pocket counts to the "owner" of that pocket. 1839 Kentfield 36, 1850c White & Bohn 37, 1862 Crawley 96. 1856 Crawley 96 says that this HANDICAP is equivalent to giving 15 in 50, 1866 Crawley 229 and 1885 Cook 177 say 50 in 100. Cf. DIVIDED POCKETS, TWO POCKETS TO FOUR.

one shot in

(Balkline) Variety of game in which a player confronted with two object balls lying in the same BALK SPACE or ANCHOR SPACE must drive at least one out of the space on his first shot or forfeit his TURN. 1916 RGRG 16. Any BALKLINE game whose numerical designation ends in ".1" is of this type. See also NO SHOT IN. Cf. TWO SHOTS IN.

one shot out

(Nine-Ball) Optional rule specifying that if a player fails to hit the lowest-numbered ball on the table first, the incoming player has cue ball in hand anywhere on the table. 1979 Grissim 253. Also called "one-shot shoot-out" or HIT THE BALL. Cf. PLAY AGAIN RULE, ROLLOUT, SHOOT OUT.

open

1. (Eight-Ball) The table is said to be "open" when neither player has selected a GROUP and the STRIKER may pocket any ball other than the eight without penalty. 1992 OR 43. See FREE TABLE, OPEN TABLE. 2. Not OBSTRUCTED. Said of a shot that is not blocked and can therefore be made. "The five is open." Said of a LAYOUT in which the balls are cleanly separated. "The table is open." Also CLEAR, OPEN SHOT. 3. To commence the game, to BREAK, to play the opening shot. See also OPEN THE GAME. 4. (Bill.) Not FROZEN. Balls that are close together but not actually touching are said to be open. The significance of this is that the balls would have to be SPOTTED if frozen. 5. (Brit. games) To break apart a CLUSTER of balls. "Pot the pink and open the reds." 1984 Karnehm 92. 6. Said of a HALF-INNING in which no point is scored.

open break

1. (pocket games) A type of BREAK, required in games such as EIGHT-BALL, in which at least four object balls must be driven to cushions. 1983 Rule Book 254, 1992 OR 13. In general, credit is given for any ball pocketed on an open break even though no ball is CALLED. Examples of games utilizing an open break are BANK POOL, CRIBBAGE, EIGHT-BALL, ELIMINATION, FORTY-ONE, NINE-BALL, PEA POOL, ROTATION, SEVEN-BALL, SIX-BALL, TEN-BALL. Cf. CLOSED BREAK, FREE BREAK. Through 1930, the record number of balls pocketed on the break from a rack of 15 balls was seven, accomplished by Roy Motes in 1916. 2. (pocket games) A style of BREAK in which no attempt is made to play a SAFETY, but an effort is made to pocket one or more balls. 1946 *Atlantic Monthly* (Aug) 134. Failure to sink a ball after an open break generally leaves the opponent with an OPEN TABLE. See also FREE BREAK, KNOCK-OUT. Cf. SAFETY BREAK. 3. (obs.) The original name given to the break shot by Jerome Keogh, the inventor of 14.1 CONTINUOUS. 1910 NYT (Oct 26) 6:5. This usage stems from the fact that in this game the last ball of each rack is not pocketed but is left "open" to be used as a target on the ensuing BREAK SHOT.

open bridge, open-hand bridge

= V-BRIDGE. Cf. CLOSED BRIDGE.

open game

A money game in which anyone may participate, at his option, without being invited to do so. 1959 Tevis 108. Cf. RING GAME.

open shot

Situation in which the cue ball and at least one object ball are placed so that the player can execute a shot directly, without having to contact a rail or another ball first. 1927 Katch 50. Cf. ANGLED BALL, FREE BALL, OBSTRUCTION, SNOOKERED.

open table

1. (pocket games) A LAYOUT consisting of well-scattered balls. 2. (Bill.) That area of the table that is distant from the cushions. A region to be avoided in CUSHION CAROMS and STRAIGHT-RAIL because of the difficulty of making GATHER SHOTS there. 1879 NYT (Jan 21) 5:3. The central rectangle on a BALKLINE TABLE, in which unlimited consecutive counts are permitted. 1924 BM (Jul). The OCEAN. 3. (Eight-Ball) Situation in which neither player has pocketed a ball and no GROUP has been selected, so the STRIKER may pocket any ball (except the eight). 1979 Grissim 253, 1982 OR. See OPEN, def. 1. Also FREE TABLE. 4. (Balkline) Marker's CALL when one ball has been driven out of BALK. 1916 RGRG 16. The table is then "open" in the sense that there are no restrictions or requirements to be met on the player's next shot.

open the game

1. To LEAD or OPEN. 2. The first player who does not play a SAFETY and attempts an uncertain score is said to "open the game." 1869 Roberts 171.

opening break

The first shot of the game after the LAG. Each style of billiard game has a defined formal arrangement of the balls for the opening break and a set of requirements that must be satisfied by the striker on the first shot. Also known as the BREAK, BREAK SHOT, LEAD or LEADING STROKE.

In 14.1 CONTINUOUS, at least two object balls must contact cushions in order for the BREAK to be legal. 1977 Fels 65. The choice of which player breaks is usually determined by LAG or LOT. In sequences of games, especially SHORT RACK games, there are several options for choosing a breaker: (1) if breaking is an advantage, the winner of the previous game breaks; (2) the winner of a game has choice of break on the next game; or (3) the player behind in the scoring has the choice of breaking. If the score is tied, the winner of the last game has his choice. 1982 OR 46. In Billiards, the opening break is also called the BREAK SHOT (see also CUE-BALL SPOT). In English games it is known as the LAY-OFF.

See also BREAK, BREAKING VIOLATION, CLOSED BREAK, FREE BREAK, OPEN BREAK, PLAY OFF, SAFETY BREAK, SPOTTING.

opposing side

(Eng. Bill.) = CHECK SIDE, REVERSE ENGLISH. 1868 *London Soc.* (Apr). Also called COUNTER, HOLD-UP, or WRONG-WAY ENGLISH.

optional cue ball

(Three-Cushions) Rule variation under which the player may select either cue ball at each shot. 1912 MB 354. A tournament at this game was tried in Chicago in 1911. Also known as FREE BALL. Cf. CHOICE OF CUE BALL, STREAMLINED BILLIARDS. Sometimes billiards was played with three white balls, the striker being allowed to choose any of them as a cue ball at each inning or shot.

orange

1. (Pocket Bill.) The color of the five-ball and the thirteen-ball. 2. (Snooker Plus) A ball whose value is eight points, spotted at the beginning of a FRAME midway between the BLUE SPOT and the PINK SPOT.

orange crush

(Nine-Ball, colloq.) A SPOT in which the weaker player is given the five-ball (which is orange) and the break

(CRUSH). A powerful handicap, derived from the name of the overwhelming defensive unit of the Denver Broncos football team.

orange spot

(Snooker Plus) The SPOT on which the ORANGE is placed, midway between the BLUE SPOT and the PINK SPOT.

ornamentation

Decorative material applied to an item of billiard equipment, particularly a CUE STICK or TABLE.

out

1. To completion, as in "He ran five and out." 1979 Grissim 253. See also OFF THE BALLS, RUN OUT. A player's "hand is out" when his inning has been terminated. See HAND OUT, LOSE ONE'S HAND, OUT OF HAND, OUT SHOT. 2. The condition of being able to sink the remaining balls or score the number of points needed for game, as in, "I'm out from here." 1916 BM (Jan) 35, 1979 Grissim 253. 3. (Balkline) The marker's CALL when a required ball has been driven OUT OF BALK, possibly to return. 1916 RGRG.

out in the country

(Eng. Bill.) Said of a POSITION in which the balls are widely spread and in which close work is therefore impossible. 1896 Broadfoot 304. Cf. OPEN TABLE.

out of balk

Generally, not within the balk area. In Balkline, the two object balls are said to be out of balk when (1) they lie in different balk spaces; (2) either ball lies in the center space; or (3) in games played TWO SHOTS IN, they lie in the same balk space but at least one ball has been driven out of the balk space on the previous shot and has returned. See OUT. Cf. IN BALK.

out of hand

Said of a player who has MISSED or committed a FOUL and whose INNING has thus terminated. 1864 AH 420. See HAND OUT, LOSE ONE'S HAND. Not related to IN HAND.

out of play

Said of a ball that is not IN PLAY by reason of having been pocketed or being held OFF THE TABLE. A ball that is out of play may nevertheless not be touched by a player in a refereed game, since there is no legitimate reason for him to do so. 1992 OR 49.

out of round

Not TRUE, said of a ball that is imperfectly spherical. 1978 Byrne 9.

out of stroke

= OFF, not playing up to one's norm. Cf. IN STROKE.

out shot

A shot that, if made by the player, will cause him to win the game. "He missed his out shot and lost the game." See OUT.

outgoing player

The player whose HALF-INNING has just ended, as by a MISS, a FOUL or his having attempted the allotted number of strokes. Cf. INCOMING PLAYER.

outside

On the side of a ball nearer to the center of the table than to the cushion. Used to describe English in the direction taken by the cue ball in a type of UMBRELLA shot at Three-Cushion Billiards. Cf. INSIDE.

outside English

(colloq.) ENGLISH on the opposite side of the cue ball to the direction in which the object ball is being CUT. That is, left English if the object ball is being cut to the right. 1989 Koehler 257. INSIDE ENGLISH is just the opposite. The terms are thoroughly confusing because nobody can remember the difference between inside and outside. In fact, some players reverse the meanings of the phrases, so their use should be totally avoided.

outside red

(Snooker) One of the two REDS located at the corners of the PYRAMID. 1938 Clifford 11.

outside umbrella

See OUTSIDE, UMBRELLA.

oval table

A billiard table in the shape of an ellipse. On an oval table, a ball hit from one focus to the cushion without ENGLISH will theoretically pass over the other focus, regardless of the direction in which it is aimed. 1981c Clare 11. C. C. Peterson was so taken with this shape that he proposed tournaments be played on oval tables. He was adept at making a billiard ball HUG THE RAIL all the way around such a table. Consult the article "The Oval Billiard Table" in 1907 *Scientific American* (Jul 6) 473. (This actually describes a table that is composed of four circular arcs rather than a true ellipse.) See also TABLE for other shapes.

Oval tables are regularly revived but have never advanced beyond the fad stage. See, for example, 1992 *USA Today* (Jun 23) 2C.

overcut

(Pocket Bill.) To hit an object ball too THIN to cause it to enter the desired pocket. 1989 Koehler 259. See CUT. Cf. UNDERCUT.

over/under

A type of bet placed on the outcome of a billiard game in which the participants wager on whether the loser will score more or less than (that is, will go over or under) a certain number of points. See also GAMBLING.

oversize ball

(Bar Pool) A CUE BALL that is slightly larger (usually ⅛ inch) than the object balls, used on a COIN-OPERATED TABLE so that it can be returned to the player after it enters a pocket instead of being trapped to await the next coin. 1989 Koehler 258.

owe

(Pocket Bill.) To be obliged to relinquish points should they be scored in the future or return pocketed balls to the table by virtue of having previously FOULED. 1992 OR 64. In One-Pocket, for example, if a player fouls twice before having pocketed any balls, he is said to "owe two," and the first two balls he scores will be spotted and used to restore his score to zero. See NEGATIVE SCORE, SCORING.

There is no owing in Elimination; in that game, one may foul with impunity before having pocketed any balls.

pace

1. Speed of stroke; the strength with which a ball is struck. 1908 Mannock II 312. "You need more pace on the ball." 2. = ENGLISH, especially FOLLOW. 3. The elasticity of the cushions. 1873 Bennett 77.

pack

(Pocket Bill., Snooker) = RACK; the cluster of balls arranged in a triangular or diamond shape at the FOOT SPOT in pocket billiard games or at the PYRAMID SPOT in SNOOKER. Also BUNCH, HEAP, PYRAMID, or STACK.

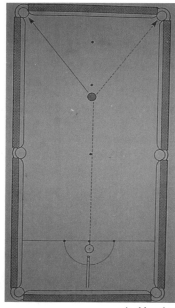

pair of breeches

pair of breeches
(Eng. Bill.) A type of SPOT SHOT in which the player makes a WINNING HAZARD and a LOSING HAZARD on the same stroke. 1807 White 37, 1866 Crawley 66, 1867

Dufton 44. So named because the path traced by the balls resembles a pair of pants. Also known as a PAIR OF SPECTACLES. A variety of DOUBLE HAZARD.

pair of spectacles
(Eng. Bill.) = PAIR OF BREECHES. 1941 Levi 46.

Pair Pool
(game) = CRIBBAGE; so called because balls have to be sunk in pairs whose numerical values total 15. 1988 PBM (Nov) 32. Also known as FIFTEEN POINTS.

panel
(Balkline) A rectangular BALK SPACE. 1912 NYT (Mar 16) 11:1.

Paper Pool
(game, obs.) A game played with paper cutouts to represent billiard balls and a table. 1898 NY Herald (Mar 6) 5:11.

Parepa
(Bagatelle game, obs.) Played on the PARISIAN POOL BOARD with colored balls numbered from 10 to 100 by tens, which are RACKED in the shape of a triangle and a white cue ball. On a WINNING HAZARD, the striker scores

166

Parepa

the value of the ball pocketed and he may remove any ball from a pocket and play again. On a LOSING HAZARD he merely has the right to continue shooting. Game is normally 500 points. 1898 HRB 113.

Parisian Pool
(Bagatelle game, obs.) = LA BARRAQUE.

Parisian Pool Board
(obs.) A playing surface consisting of a thick board of black walnut with 12 to 15 CUP holes, angled upwards similar to a BAGATELLE board. 1893 HRB 106. For games played on this device, see HIGH NUMBER POOL, LA BARRAQUE, MONTE CARLO, PAREPA, PARISIAN POOL, PIGEON HOLE AND JENNY LIND, POOL FOR 31 POINTS.

park the ball
(Nine-Ball, colloq.) To position the cue ball near the center of the table after a BREAK SHOT; in Nine-Ball, this is a favorable location. 1992 Billing 92.

Parker's box
(Balkline) A rectangular box of dimension 3½ × 7 inches, drawn in chalk on the cloth. Its long side is adjacent to a rail and is centered on a BALKLINE. In games such as 18.2 Balkline, in which four lines are used, there are eight such boxes. If both object balls lie in the same box they are considered to be IN BALK even though they may technically fall in different BALK SPACES. 1913 Daly 16.

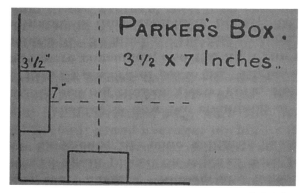

Parker's Box

The box was introduced in 1894 on a suggestion by Charles J. E. Parker, a tournament manager from Chicago, after huge runs were made by Jacob Schaefer Sr. and Frank Ives at the ANCHOR NURSE. Originally, ten shots were allowed IN ANCHOR. This was reduced to five in 1896 for 18.2. In that year, only one shot in anchor

was allowed in 18.1, and eventually only two shots were allowed in 18.2.

Although Parker's box was effective against the anchor, it was too small to prevent the CHUCK NURSE, in which one of the balls is positioned outside the box. By 1916 it had been expanded to the seven-inch-square ANCHOR SPACE.

parlor
= BILLIARD PARLOR.

Parlor Billiards
(game, obs.) = AMUSETTE, IMPROMPTU BILLIARDS.

pass
1. To relinquish a TURN at the table voluntarily. Normally, the INCOMING PLAYER must make a stroke or be charged with a FOUL. In certain rare circumstances, however, the player may decline to do so without suffering any penalty. For example, a player may pass if his opponent SCRATCHES on the BREAK SHOT in Nine-Ball. 2. (obs.) = ARCH, IRON, PASSE, PORT. 1807 White 3, 1863 Phelan & Berger 96. A wicket-like arch originally used in the ground game of Pall-Mall, then brought to the billiard table. Engravings show the pass in use as early as 1640.

pass iron
(obs.) = PASS, def. 2.

pass nurse
(Bill.) The EDGE NURSE. 1913 Daly 61, 208. A delicate two-shot NURSE sequence in which the cue ball is made to graze the edge of both object balls, moving them down the table slightly. The cue ball is then stroked in the opposite direction, and so forth, to achieve a reproducible position. The nurse is a RUNNING NURSE, but just barely. In British usage, the SQUEEZE CANNON.

167

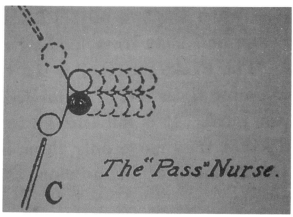

pass nurse

passe

(obs.) French term for the ARCH, PASS, or PORT. 1857 Phelan 30.

pattern

= LAYOUT. The arrangement of the balls on the table. 1979 Grissim 253. Also POSITION. Cf. LEAVE.

pattern play

(pocket games) Pocketing the balls in a particular order, as in Rotation or Nine-Ball. 1992 Billing 92. See also SET-ORDER GAME.

pay ball

1. A MONEY BALL. 2. Any game in which a player who pockets a ball receives money from each other player. 1979 Grissim 253. Particularly, a variant of American Snooker, also known as PINK BALL, in which money is won for each ball pocketed, with double stakes on the last ball.

PBA

(org.) = PROFESSIONAL BILLIARDS ASSOCIATION.

PBTA

(org.) = PROFESSIONAL BILLIARDS TOUR ASSOCIATION.

pea

A PILL or TALLY BALL. A small numbered ball used with the SHAKE BOTTLE in PILL POOL or KELLY POOL. 1976 WSD 305, 1977 Martin 216. Hence, PEA POOL.

Pea Pool

(game) = KELLY POOL, PILL POOL. 1965 Fats 30, 1974 ITP 31, 1992 OR 87.

pedestal

A table component that supports the BASE FRAME. The pedestal may touch the floor directly or may be mounted on FEET.

penalty

Forfeiture of a point or points because of an infraction of the rules. Depending on the game being played, a penalty may result in points being subtracted from a player's score or added to the opponent's score. Penalties have been imposed in billiards since the earliest days. 1674 Cotton cites more than 10 violations resulting in a loss of points.

See AWAY, COMPULSORY STROKE, DELAY, DISQUALIFICATION, FIFTEEN-POINT PENALTY, FIVE-POINT PENALTY, FORFEIT, FOUL, INTERFERENCE, LOSS OF GAME, NEGATIVE SCORE, PENALTY POINTS, PLAYER RESPONSIBILITY FOUL, SUSPENSION, UNSPORTSMANLIKE CONDUCT.

penalty ball

(Volunteer Snooker) A POOL BALL that is VOLUNTEERED out of order and whose value is forfeited by the STRIKER should he fail to pocket it. 1978 BSCC 62.

Penalty Game

(game, obs.) Game played with the balls arranged as for Snooker, but using only a single RED, worth eight points and spotted at the opposite end of the table from the BLACK and in a symmetrical position. 1924 Ogden diag. 121.

penalty points

(Snooker) Points awarded to the opponent because of a player's foul stroke. 1973 Spencer 92. These points are given in lieu of subtracting from the player's score, so a NEGATIVE SCORE is not possible. See SCORING.

pendulum cannon

(Eng. Bill.) A CANNON made with the two object balls two or three inches apart and a slight distance from and in a line parallel to the cushion; the cue ball, when struck on alternate shots, travels to and fro like a pendulum and makes contact with both balls, which remain nearly stationary. 1912 Levi 580, 1957 Holt 93, 1979 Everton 42. The stroke is said to have been invented by Walter Lovejoy in 1907. 1908 Mannock II 422. (Lovejoy once ran 100 cannons with all three balls on a small piece of paper.) Cf. RUDOLPHE'S NURSE.

pendulum cannon

pendulum swing

A smooth swing of the cue stick using the elbow as fulcrum. 1896 Broadfoot 125, 1913 Daly 27, 1977 Martin 21. This is the orthodox swing, contrasted with Willie Hoppe's sidearm stroke, which was characteristic of players who began the game at an early age, when they were too short to reach shots in any other fashion.

Penetration Nine-Ball

(game) A completely offensive and rapid form of NINE-BALL in which safety play is severely restricted. While at least four object balls remain on the table, the incoming player always has BALL IN HAND. When fewer than four object balls remain, the game is said to be IN GEAR and the cue ball is played from where it comes to rest. When the game is in gear, fouls are penalized by giving the INCOMING PLAYER cue ball IN HAND BEHIND THE HEAD STRING.

penguin

(sl.) A tournament player, so called because of the tuxedo he wears to comply with the DRESS CODE. 1990 Rushin 14.

Penny Pot

(game, obs.) Similar to LIFE POOL, but instead of playing for a stake with three lives, a penny is paid by the owner of a LIFE to its taker. WINNING HAZARDS receive a penny; LOSING HAZARDS, MISSES, and COUPS pay a forfeit. The game was invented by George Pardon, who used the name "Captain Crawley" in his extensive billiard writings. 1866 Crawley 185.

Pentathlon

(game) A form of international competition in which players engage in five types of billiard games: STRAIGHT-RAIL to 200 points, 47.1 BALKLINE to 150 points, CUSHION CAROMS to 100, 71.2 BALKLINE to 150, and THREE-CUSHIONS to 30. The mix of games and point totals may vary. The idea of a multiple-game competition is not new—a series known as the MIXED GAME was held at Mussey's in 1914 and revived at Peterson's in 1923. 1926 BM (Mar) 23. Cf. BIATHLON.

perpendicular stroke

(obs.) = MASSÉ. So called because of the nearly vertical position in which the cue stick is held, *i.e.*, perpendicular to the bed of the table, when playing a MASSÉ. 1850 Phelan. The stroke is shown but not named in 1836 Tillotson 55. See also HIGH OBLIQUE STROKE, OBLIQUE STROKE.

Perpetual Pool

(game, obs.) = EVERLASTING POOL. ENGLISH POOL in which each player has an unlimited number of LIVES. 1867 Dufton 222. Also BLACK POOL.

Pétanque, La

(game, pr. lah pay-TAHNK) Played with 12 balls (six of each of two colors) and a COCHONNET. The first player banks the cochonnet. The second player tries to maneuver one of his balls near the cochonnet or to drive away one of the opponent's, the object being to lay a ball as close as possible to the chochonnet. 1983 Malsert 169.

Peterson Pocket Billiard Contest

(game) A solitaire game developed by C. C. Peterson that is suitable for competition in which the players are unable to meet in the same place. Chalk lines are drawn on the table connecting opposite pairs of diamonds as shown. The balls are placed at the indicated positions at the start of each INNING. Each player is given five innings to score as many points as possible. As the game is offensive only, the scores of different players can be compared objectively. Cf. EQUAL OFFENSE.

petit massé

A massé performed with the BRIDGE HAND resting on the table. Likewise, "petit piqué." 1908 Mannock II 43. Cf. FREE-HAND MASSÉ GRAND MASSÉ

pigeon

An easy MARK for a SHARPER. 1775 Annals 106. A SUCKER, a FISH; one who is ripe for plucking. 1794 OED. Despite its age, this term is not at all obsolete.

Pigeon Hole and Jenny Lind

(Bagatelle game, obs.) Played on the PARISIAN POOL BOARD with one red and eight white balls. The red is placed on the CENTER SPOT; if it is pocketed on a legal stroke, the player scores double the number of points the stroke is worth. 1898 HRB 98. Cf. JENNY LIND.

Pigeon-hole Game

(Bagatelle game, obs.) A synonym for Bagatelle.

pigeon-hole table

A table having an arrangement of slots on one short rail that resemble the cavities made for pigeons in a dovecote. 1847 OED, 1876 Collender 19. Also known as a SIPPIO TABLE. *See illustration on next page.*

pigeon-hole table

Pigeon-Pool

(game) A type of BILLIARD BOARD game. 1922 BM (May) 10.

pill

A PEA used in PILL POOL. 1979 Sullivan 112. A TALLY BALL, one of a set of 15 counters whose numbers correspond to those of the pocket billiard balls. Used in games requiring secret selection of an object ball or number for each player. See also PRIVATE BALL.

pill game

A game in which PILLS are used. See, for example, BLIND, BOTTLE POCKET BILLIARDS, CHECK-CHECK, FORTY-ONE POCKET BILLIARDS, HIGH-LOW-JACK GAME, KELLY POOL, PEA POOL, PILL POOL, PIN POOL, STRAIGHT.

Pill Pool

(game) A pocket billiard game for several players played with 15 balls, a SHAKE BOTTLE, and 15 PILLS numbered 1–15. Each player selects a pill at random from the bottle without disclosing its number to the others. The one-ball is RACKED at the FOOT SPOT, the two at the right rear, and the three at the left rear. The object is to pocket the ball corresponding to one's numbered pill. A player who does this wins the game. If a player's ball is pocketed by another player, he must announce that fact and retire from the game. In one variation, the winner receives two points from each player and pocketing an opponent's ball yields one point; the owner of the pocketed ball forfeits one point. 1974 ITP 31. In another

variation, the player's score, when added to his secret number, must total 31. Also known as KELLY POOL or PEA POOL.

The number of different possible initial racks in Pill Pool is 12! = 479,001,600.

piloted joint

A cue joint in which a metal fitting is inserted into the shaft and a screw protrudes from the butt, in which metal meets metal when the cue is assembled for play. 1992 Billing 6. Cf. FLAT JOINT.

pin

= SKITTLE. A wooden target for use in billiard games.

Pin Pool

(game) A generic variety of game played with two white balls, one red ball, and five wooden PINS or SKITTLES, resembling miniature bowling pins, to be used as targets. 1850 Phelan 42, 1891 MB 339, 1916 RGRG 23. The rotation of play is determined by LOT with small, numbered balls called PILLS. Another choice of a small ball determines a player's private number. The object is to score 31 points as the total of the number of pins knocked down and the number on the player's PRIVATE BALL. Played with PRIVILEGE, LIVES and BURST.

The initial set-up is as in the SPANISH GAME, with the pins 68 millimeters apart. One white ball is spotted five inches from the lower end of the table; the red is placed on the FOOT SPOT. The first player strikes the other white from within the string at either ball. Neither caroms nor hazards count. Points are scored only by knocking over pins after hitting an object ball. The only penalty is forfeiture of stroke; no points are lost. A NATURAL or RANCHE, in which the four outside pins are knocked down leaving the center pin standing, wins the game. A BURST player may claim PRIVILEGE. 1890 HRB 93.

Pin Pool was introduced to the U.S. at Bassford's room in New York during the 1830s. 1925 BM (Jul). A prize match was played in Pittsburgh in 1872. 1891 MB 669. Maurice Vignaux was said to be the best Pin Pool player in France during the 1870s. 1974 NYT (Oct 9) 8:5. Modern versions of the game are extremely popular in Europe and Latin countries. A huge number of variations are known, including BAR BILLIARDS, BRUNSWICK TEN-PIN BILLIARD GAME, CASIN, CAROLINA, COCKED HAT, DANISH BILLIARDS, FIVE-PIN GAME, ITALIAN BILLIARDS, ITALIAN SKITTLE POOL, KEGEL-PARTIE, LITTLE CORPORAL, LITTLE MIDGET, MUG'S POOL, NINE-HOLE SNOOKER, PLANT GAME, RED WHITE AND BLUE, SENTINEL POOL, SKITTLE BILLIARDS, SPANISH GAME, TEN PINS, and TWO-PIN GAME. Details of others, with a wide variety of pin arrangements, can be found in 1971 Ardévol.

pin-pool board

(Pin Pool, obs.) A MARKING BOARD used for scoring at PIN POOL. 1876 Collender 24.

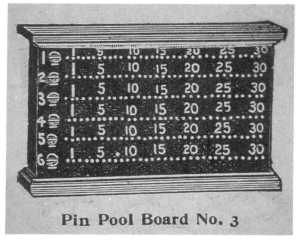

Pin Pool Board No. 3

pin-pool board

pin-pool spot

(Pin Pool) Any of the five SPOTS arranged at the center of the table for PIN POOL, each one ball diameter from the CENTER SPOT.

pinch

= NIP. 1977 Martin 215. A CLOSE DRAW in which the cue stick appears only to "nip" the cue ball, there being almost no FOLLOW-THROUGH in order to avoid a PUSH.

pink

1. (Snooker) The color of the ball valued at six points and spotted at the beginning of each FRAME on the PYRAMID SPOT (which is thus also known as the PINK SPOT). The pyramid is placed so as to be close to, but not actually touching, the pink ball. Also, the name given to the pink ball. "He's on pink." The pink is not used in Canadian Snooker. 2. (Bagatelle, obs.) To STRING for the LEAD.

Pink Ball

(game) = PAY BALL, a variant of American Snooker.

Pink Pool

(game) A game similar to BLACK POOL that was played by Joe Davis in his youth. 1986 Trelford 23. Cf. BLACK AND PINK POOL.

pink spot

(Snooker) The spot located midway between the BLUE SPOT and the TOP RAIL, on which the PINK is spotted at commencement of each FRAME. 1975a Lowe 13. Also called the DARK-RED SPOT, FOOT SPOT, PYRAMID SPOT, RED SPOT (Eng. Bill.), or WINNING SPOT.

piqué, piquet

(pr. pee-KAY) A term applied to three different types of shots performed with an elevated cue. See also GRAND MASSÉ, PETIT MASSÉ for the terms "grand piqué" and "petit piqué." 1. A shot in which the angle formed by the cue and the table exceeds 45 degrees but is not as great as in the MASSÉ. 2. A shot in which extreme BACKSPIN is applied to the cue ball by raising the cue stick into a nearly vertical position, but distinguished from MASSÉ in that side ENGLISH is not used. 1889 Vignaux 236, 1908 Mannock II 45, 1913 Stoddard 51. The ARTISTIC BILLIARDS program features numerous piqué shots. 3. A massé in which the cue ball reverses direction before striking another ball. 1896 Broadfoot 255, 1924 Ogden 272, 1977 Martin 216. The cue stick must be elevated to achieve this result, since it is physically impossible to impart sufficient backspin with the cue held horizontally, no matter how low the ball is stroked.

pit

A small depression in the CLOTH, caused by driving a ball downward into the BED of the table. Cf. BURN MARK.

pitcher

(Baseball Pocket Bill.) The name for the nine-ball. 1925 RGRG 48. If anyone knows the origin of this term, please write to the author.

plain

1. (Bill.) The unmarked white object ball. 1954 KTG 4. By extension, the player who is using this ball. "Are you spot or plain?" Also, PLAIN BALL, PLAIN WHITE, WHITE. Cf. SPOT. 2. (Eight-Ball) A SOLID. Cf. STRIPE.

plain ball

1. = PLAIN, PLAIN WHITE, WHITE, CLEAR BALL. Cf. SPOT WHITE. 2. A shot in which no side ENGLISH is used. 1957 Holt 29, 1990 French 48. Also CENTER BALL.

plain white

= PLAIN, PLAIN BALL, WHITE, CLEAR BALL. Cf. SPOT WHITE.

plant

1. (Brit. games) A shot in which two object balls are touching and an imaginary line perpendicular to their LINE OF CENTERS and radiating from the center of one ball passes through a pocket. 1957 Holt 178. When this is the case, the ball can be potted by caroming it off the ball it is touching. Also RUN OFF. In American terminology, a KISS SHOT.

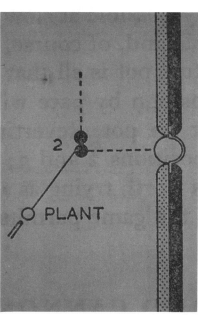

plant

Although a technical distinction is made between a PLANT and a SET, there is a strong tendency to use the terms interchangeably. Originally, the word "plant" was used to refer to what is now a set—namely, a shot in which the centers of two object balls point to a pocket; a COMBINATION. 1896 Broadfoot 106. This definition has been retained in some modern sources. 1976 Charlton 13, 1992 OR 13.

As Snooker developed, additional terminology must have become necessary, and by 1910 both "plant" and "set" were in use. 1910a Ritchie 136i. Some authors who equate plant with set employ the term REVERSE PLANT for the kiss shot. 1954 Davis 70. 1984 Williams 49 and 1991 Everton 77 use "plant" to mean a set in which the object balls are not FROZEN. In 1983 Bills 12 it is a "billiard that scores a winning hazard."

2. (Pin Pool, obs.) A tactical move in which the player voluntarily terminates his run by declaring "plant," to avoid the possibility of a BURST. 1857 Phelan 212, 1881 MB 26. Also called a "planter" in this context. See PLANT GAME.

Plant Game

(game) A variation on PIN POOL in which a player wishing to PLANT, that is, terminate his run prior to a BURST, must signify his intention in advance of the shot.

play

1. To engage in a game of billiards. 2. To attempt a shot. "I'll play the five-ball," meaning "I will try to pocket the five-ball." "Play safe." See also IN PLAY.

play across

(Eng. Bill.) To deal with a DOUBLE BAULK by hitting the side rail forward of the BAULKLINE with ENGLISH that causes the cue ball to return behind the line for a legal stroke. 1929a Davis 181. This maneuver was described in 1836 Tillotson 28, but was not named there. It is not to be confused with "play a cross," which means to play a BANK SHOT. Also PLAY BACK.

play again rule

(Pocket Bill., Snooker) A rule designed to prevent a player from gaining an advantage from an illegal stroke. The incoming player has the option of requiring the previous striker to shoot again or he may accept TABLE IN POSITION. 1965 Pulman 138. The rule is sometimes used in NINE-BALL. See also PLAY OUT, ROLLOUT, SHOOT OUT. Cf. FREE BALL, HIT THE BALL, NEAREST BALL PLAYABLE, ONE SHOT OUT, TAKE UP. The fact that this optional rule was in effect during Joe Davis's first MAXIMUM BREAK of 147 prevented official recognition of his record, even though no situation arose in which the rule would have applied. 1985 Everton 50.

play away

1. = SHOOT AWAY, def. 1. To hit the cue ball so that it does not contact an object ball to which it is FROZEN or near, thus avoiding a PUSH. In playing away from a frozen ball, it is not a foul even if the object ball moves by SETTLING. 2. = SHOOT AWAY, def. 2. To play

recklessly, attempting to make a shot at nearly every turn with little attention to SAFETY PLAY.

play back

(obs.) To play BRICOLE, hitting a cushion first to have the cue ball rebound "back." 1850c White & Bohn 61, 1858 Mardon 54. "Playing back in baulk" is a maneuver in which the striker with BALL IN HAND hits a ball IN BAULK legally by first hitting a SIDE RAIL forward of the BAULK-LINE with spin, causing it to return behind the line. 1839 Kentfield 25. The shot is pictured but not named in 1836 Tillotson 29. Also PLAY ACROSS.

play ball

(Bill., obs.) The CUE BALL that is used by a player; the one with which he "plays." 1875 NYT (Sep 21) 5:6. Also STROKE BALL.

play off

1. To resolve a tie. See PLAYOFF. 2. (obs.) To LEAD, OPEN THE GAME. 1844 Mardon 29.

play on

A ball is said to be "played on" when it has been struck by the cue ball.

play out

(Snooker) To make a fair attempt to hit a ball. A player whose opponent failed to hit the ball ON could force the opponent to "play out" of the position and try again. See PLAY AGAIN RULE.

play position

To execute shots with a view toward causing the balls to move into locations that will make successive shots possible or easy. See POSITION, POSITION PLAY.

play safe

To shoot a SAFETY. 1890 NY Herald (Mar 1) 8:1. See also SAFE, SAFETY PLAY.

play the spot ball

1. (Amer. Snooker, Eng. Bill.) To hole the red ball repeatedly off the SPOT. 1859 Phelan 69, 1881 MB 26. See also SPOT-STROKE. Note that the expression in this context has nothing to do with the SPOT BALL, but refers to the ball that is on the spot. 2. (Bill.) To use the SPOT BALL as one's cue ball. "The opening breaker must use the spot ball."

play-to-hit

(Nine-Ball) = ROLLOUT, a rule variation popular in the South. 1991 Snap (Jul/Aug) 30. Cf. TWO-SHOT ROLL-OUT.

player

1. A participant in a billiard game who is permitted to strike the cue ball and score, especially the current shooter. At any instant during the game, a player is either the STRIKER or a NONSTRIKER. Nonplayer participants include the REFEREE, MARKER, and UMPIRES or SECONDS. The SPECTATORS were formerly also participants.

The distinction between players and nonplayers is important in certain situations. See NONPLAYER INTERFERENCE, PLAYER RESPONSIBILITY FOUL.

2. A skilled cueist, as opposed to a novice or casual shooter. "She's a player" means "She plays very well."

player responsibility foul

A FOUL caused by contact between a ball and EQUIPMENT for which a PLAYER is responsible by reason of having handled it or brought it to the table, such as chalk, the cue stick, files, tools, scuffers, or the MECHANICAL BRIDGE. 1992 OR 38. See INTERFERENCE, NONPLAYER INTERFERENCE.

Player's Eight-Ball

(game) A variety of EIGHT-BALL played at the Player's Club in New York City, which was established as a theatrical club by Edwin Booth in 1887 and included Mark Twain among its members. ("Player" in this context refers to a stage performer rather than a billiard player.) The game was devised by Jack Smart, the "Fatman" of 1950s radio mystery serials. The balls are racked in the particular arrangement shown, with the one at the APEX. The breaker is assigned the GROUP of balls 1–7 (the SOLIDS) and must shoot at the lowest-numbered ball on the table. The second player has STRIPES and must shoot at the highest-numbered ball on the table. After a player sinks all the balls in his group, he wins the game by pocketing the eight-ball. A HAND-

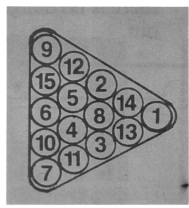

Player's Eight-Ball

ICAP can be given readily by varying the ranges of balls assigned to the players, *e.g.*, 1–9 and 10–15. 1986 BD (Dec) 30. Cf. ROTATION EIGHT-BALL.

playing

(Brit. games) Referring to the STRIKER or INCOMING PLAYER. A term used in announcing the score of a billiard game. See SCORE.

playing cue

A player's regular cue stick, his RUN STICK. Cf. BREAK CUE.

playing surface

The flat area of the table on which the balls roll, bounded by the cushions and covered with CLOTH. The playing surface is measured from the cushion NOSE, since that is the area to which the balls are confined. The playing surface must be flat, to the extent that a deviation of only 0.02 inches is allowed along its entire length. 1992 OR 2. When the table is loaded with 200 pounds at its center, the deflection must not exceed 0.03 inches. Cf. BED.

playoff

A supplemental game or match played to resolve a TIE in the standings at the end of a tournament. The players who are tied are said to PLAY OFF the tie. Sometimes multiple playoffs are required to determine a winner. At the end of regular play in the 1937 World Pocket Billiard Championship, four players were tied with identical records. A playoff was held that resulted in a tie among three of the players. A second playoff was required to crown Ralph Greenleaf the victor.

Plon-Pon

(game) Played with two white balls. The player's object is to make his cue ball hit the other ball twice. Its invention is credited to Joseph Dion and it was played in 1873, but it seems likely to be of much earlier vintage. 1887 NYT (Nov 20) 12:1. It has been reinvented many times by others. The name is onomatopoetic, imitating in French the sound made by two successive ball contacts, similar to "ping-pong." Also known as KISS-CANNONS or the TWO-BALL GAME.

plum

(pocket games, colloq.) The four-ball, so called because of its purple color. See also PURPLE.

plus system, plus-two system

(Three-Cushions) A DIAMOND SYSTEM used to calculate the path taken by the cue ball when it is first shot into a SHORT RAIL, based on the fact that a ball hit with NATURAL ENGLISH into a point on the short rail half a

diamond from the corner will return after hitting two cushions to a point on the LONG RAIL two diamonds from its starting position. 1928 Barry 17, 1941 Hoppe 70. A type of END RAIL SYSTEM.

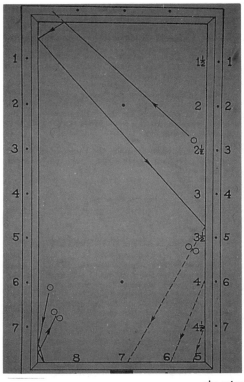

plus system

po

(Amer. college sl.) = POSITION. A horrid contraction, but one that is in actual use.

pocket

1. An opening in the table to receive balls. 1976 WSD 321. A HOLE. A ball entering a pocket is either trapped in a POCKET NET or returned through GUTTERS to the GULLY or BALL RETURN. At the time of Cotton in 1674, tables had six pockets, known as HAZARDS, and NETS or BOXES to catch the balls. These were no more than round holes cut directly into the BED of the table. The term "pocket" was used in connection with cricket as early as 1754 and in a billiard sense by 1780. Tables having one, three, four, and six pockets were used at various times. In the obsolete game of TRUCKS, eight or ten pockets were used.

British pockets have rounded corners known as ELBOWS. The pointed American pocket was invented by Michael Phelan in 1857, for which he received U.S. Patent No. 19,101. Phelan found that a curved pocket entrance made it difficult to determine a precise point of aim to cause the ball to enter, so he remedied this problem by using flat surfaces.

A ball that enters a pocket must remain there in order to be considered pocketed. If the ball rebounds out, it is not counted. See POCKETED BALL.

A pocket should be able to hold at least five balls without requiring emptying. 1856 Crawley 6. See DROP POCKET. The regulation sizes of pockets have varied throughout history. They are enlarged when it is desired to spur offense. Room owners have been known to widen the pockets of their tables to make the game easier for patrons, thus encouraging repeat business.

On a GULLY TABLE, the pockets do not lead to nets but instead to a system of troughs under the table that return all pocketed balls to a tray located under the FOOT of the table for convenience in RACKING.

In Great Britain, the size of pockets is specified by a TEMPLATE issued by the BSCC. At the time of Kentfield, all six pockets were 3¼ inches wide; there was no distinction made between corner and middle pockets. 1839 Kentfield 2. Both corner and middle pockets can now be no more than 3½ inches wide at their widest point. 1957 Holt 6. In the U. S., the BCA regulations for Pocket Billiards allow the corner pockets to measure between 4⅞ and 5⅛ inches at their widest, while side pockets may be between 5⅜ and 5⅝ inches. For American Snooker, the corner pockets may range from 3⅜ to 3⅝ inches and side pockets must be no wider than 4⁵⁄₁₆ inches. 1992 OR 2. A pocket that is unusually wide is called a BUCKET, SEWER or WASTEBASKET. See also BASKET, CUT ANGLE, DUPLEX POCKET, ELBOW, FALL, IRON, NAIL, POCKET ANGLE, POCKET DROP, POCKET LINER, POINT, UNDERCUT.

A pocket table can be converted into a CAROM TABLE by blocking the pockets with inserts. See CAROM PLUG.

2. To sink a ball in a pocket. 1780 OED, 1992 OR 21. See POCKETED BALL.

pocket angle
The angle at which the slate is cut from vertical at the FALL of a pocket. The U.S. standard is 12 degrees, with a tolerance of one degree. 1992 OR 2. An angle of zero degrees would form a vertical fall.

Pocket Apiece
(game, colloq.) = ONE-POCKET. 1965 Fats 24, 1974 ITP 24. So called because each player is assigned a pocket into which he must sink balls; thus the players have a "pocket apiece."

Pocket Billiards
(game) An ambiguous generic term for any game played on a billiard table having pockets and in which the goal is to force one or more balls into the pockets. The name

was introduced in 1911 as part of a public-relations campaign to eliminate the use of "Pool" in such compounds as BALL POOL and CONTINUOUS POOL. It generally refers to the game of 14.1 CONTINUOUS, which is still commonly known as STRAIGHT POOL in spite of 80 years of efforts to suppress the use of the word "Pool." See also POCKET GAME. It is often combined with a modifier, as in BASEBALL POCKET BILLIARDS, BASIC POCKET BILLIARDS, MISTER AND MRS. POCKET BILLIARDS.

pocket block
= BILLIARD BLOCK, CAROM PLUG, POCKET STOP.

pocket drop
The action of a ball as it falls into a pocket. 1959 Tevis. The drop should be "clean," with no rattling in the JAWS that might cause the ball to rebound back onto the table. Cf. DROP POCKET.

pocket game
Any billiard game played on a table having pockets, in which the object is to sink balls. The term usually refers to 14.1 CONTINUOUS. See also POCKET BILLIARDS.

pocket iron
A metal part used to attach a POCKET NET to the RAIL.

pocket liner
A removable insert used to reduce the width of a POCKET to sharpen a player's aim during practice.

pocket net
= NET. 1893 HRB 28. A web or bag suspended from a pocket in which balls are captured. A modern DROP POCKET may have a BASKET rather than a net. *See illustration on next page.*

pocket scratch
(pocket games) A SCRATCH in which the cue ball enters a pocket. Cf. TABLE SCRATCH.

pocket side
(Eng. Bill.) SIDE that will cause the cue ball to enter the pocket if it should hit the JAW on a LOSING HAZARD. 1889 Drayson 60, 1954 KTG 22. Pocket side makes the pocket "bigger" in the sense that it increases the player's margin of error in aiming. When shooting at a ball near the right rail, pocket side is RIGHT ENGLISH. 1924b Newman 25. Note that this is not the same English that is required to make the object ball HUG THE RAIL on its way to the pocket.

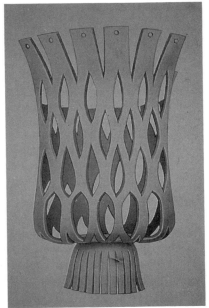

pocket net

pocket stop

= BILLIARD BLOCK, CAROM PLUG, POCKET BLOCK. A device that allows a POCKET TABLE to be used for carom games by obstructing the pockets to prevent balls from entering.

pocket table

A table having pockets, as distinguished from a CAROM TABLE, which has no pockets. A POOL TABLE. See also BILLIARD TABLE, ENGLISH TABLE, TABLE.

pocketed ball

(Pocket Bill.) A ball that enters and remains in a pocket by means of a legal stroke. 1983 Rule Book 252. If a ball enters a pocket and then comes back out (even if it leaves the table), it is not considered pocketed. 1916 RGRG 52. If a ball falls into a pocket without having been CON- TACTED by another ball, it is replaced on the table. 1916 RGRG 54. See MOTION for more details. See also SUS- PENDED BALL.

Pockets

(game, colloq.) Term for any pocket billiard game, particularly 14.1 CONTINUOUS. 1929 BM (Feb), 1946 OR 93, 1948 Mosconi 10. Cf. RAILS.

point

1. A unit of score in billiard games. 1807 White 48, 1873 Bennett 14, 1992 OR 55. Currently, one point is awarded for pocketing a ball in Straight Pool or making a carom in Straight-Rail and Three-Cushions. This was not always so. In American Four-Ball Billiards, up to 13 points could be scored on a single stroke. In English

Billiards, at least two points are earned for a successful shot. 2. The corner formed at a pocket opening on an American table. 1979 Grissim 254. British tables have rounded pocket corners; see BUMP, ELBOW, SHOULDER. See also NAIL SHOT. 3. One of the PRONGS in the BUTT of a CUE STICK. 1965 Fats 74, 1992 Billing 6. See also CROWN. 4. The tip end of the cue stick, as opposed to the BUTT. 1806 Phil 14. See also CUE POINT. 5. The ball spotted at the APEX of the TRIANGLE, the "point ball." 6. A punctuation mark used in naming billiard games, particularly in Balkline. A period, or "point," is used to separate the distance at which the lines are drawn from the number of shots that can be scored while both object balls lie in a BALK SPACE without having to drive at least one of them out. For example, "18.2," which is read "eighteen point two," means that the lines are drawn 18 inches from the cushions and two shots are allowed IN BALK.

point and point

(obs.) An old optional rule from the days of the MACE and BUTT, under which the players agreed to use only the point of the cue and the mace and not to strike with the butt. 1807 White 72.

point of aim

Point on the object ball or cushion at which the player must aim the center of the cue ball to cause a hit at the desired POINT OF CONTACT. *See illustration on next page.*

point of contact

1. Point at which two balls meet when hitting each other, as distinguished from the POINT OF AIM. 1970 Knuchell 237. 2. The location on a cushion at which the player must aim his ball to cause it to contact that cushion at the correct point. 1881 MB 68. General- ly, when playing according to the DIAMOND SYSTEM, the player is directed to aim his cue ball at a diamond, not at the point on the cushion opposite the diamond. On a ball, the point of contact and point of aim are the same only when shooting directly at the ball's center. *See illustration on next page.*

point system

(Eight-Ball) A method of scoring in which three points are awarded for winning the game plus one point for each opponent's ball remaining on the table when the game ends. 1983 Rule Book 255.

Poker Pocket Billiards

(game) A SINGLE-RACK pocket billiard game having the flavor of Poker. The object is to create poker hands by sinking specially marked balls. There are 16 object

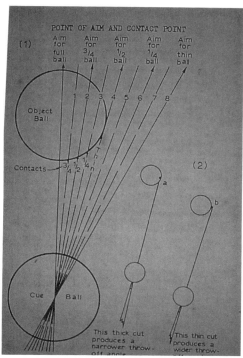

point of aim

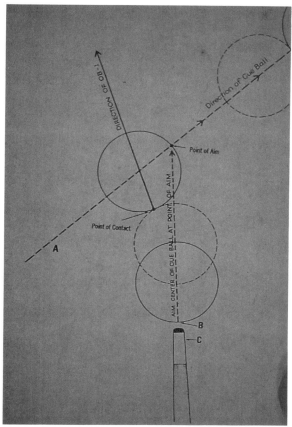

point of contact

balls—four each labeled A, K, Q, and J—that are RACKED in a diamond configuration. No player is allowed to pocket more than five balls in a game. The player who constructs the best "hand" wins the game. The highest hand is four-of-a-kind. 1900 May 100, 1916 HDB 110, 1977 OR 87. See also SIXTEEN-BALL RACK.

Poker Pool

(game) A pocket game played with an auxiliary deck of cards. The Poker Pool deck consists of 60 cards, 4 corresponding to each numbered ball in the range 1–15. Each player is dealt a poker hand (5 or 7 cards). The first player to pocket all the balls matching the cards in his hand is the winner. A single ball matches all cards of the same denomination in the striker's hand. Before pocketing the winning ball, a player must announce, "last card." After any foul, the player must draw another card from the deck and add it to his hand.

polish

A substance applied to billiard balls, particularly IVORY balls, to protect them and increase their luster. Tournament regulations were once very specific about the degree of polish acceptable on balls. For example, championship Balkline rules specified a medium-polish finish, defined as being "between a dead finish and a high polish." 1911 HRB 43a.

Pool

1. (game, U.S.) The game of POCKET BILLIARDS or any of its variations, especially 14.1 CONTINUOUS. The popular games played in the U.S. through the nineteenth century were PYRAMID POOL, SIXTY-ONE POOL, FIFTEEN-BALL POOL, and CONTINUOUS POOL.

The word "pool" is from the French *poule*, meaning a collective STAKE or ante, and it reflects the fact that players often wagered on the outcome of games by "pooling" their bets. 1979 Grissim 28. The connection between Pool and gambling was also enhanced by the fact that the game was played in betting establishments known as "pool rooms." These originally had nothing to do with billiards (public billiard halls were called BILLIARD PARLORS until late in the nineteenth century), but were places in which bettors could wager on horse races. These rooms installed billiard tables as a diversion for their patrons, and the disreputable qualities of the betting hall became linked to billiards in the public mind. 1957 Willson *The Music Man*. The confusion between the billiard and gambling meanings of "Pool" is apparent in the following newspaper headline from 1881: "The Pool Tournament . . . Pool Selling Still Carried On." 1881 NYT (Jan 14) 5:2. In this context,

177

"pool selling" referred to the practice of making book on the outcome of matches.

For a considerable time the billiard industry fought against the use of the word "Pool" to describe any billiard game. After 1900, in a series of advertisements and other public-relations efforts, it was insisted that "Pocket Billiards" was the correct term. The championship game of "Continuous Pool" had its name changed officially to "Pocket Billiards" in 1911. A statute was passed in New York State forbidding the use of "Pool" as part of the name or sign of any billiard establishment. 1925 BM (Aug). By 1931, Jack Doyle, a prominent New York room owner, felt that things had calmed down enough that he felt safe in resuming the use of "Pool." 1931 BM (Jul) 32.

Pool is not, in fact, a synonym for Pocket Billiards, although it is commonly used that way. The original game of SKITTLE POOL was played on a table without pockets. 1890 HRB 119. See also WESTERN POOL, which is a pure carom game.

The following 85 games have names incorporating "Pool": AMERICAN PYRAMID POOL, BACKWARDS POOL, BALL POOL, BANK POOL, BAR POOL, B.B.C. CO. POOL, BIG FOUR POOL, BILLIARD POOL, BLACK AND PINK POOL, BLACK POOL, BLOW POOL, BLUE POOL, BOSTON POOL, BOTTLE POOL, BOUCHON POOL, BOUNCE POOL, BUMPER POOL, CALIFORNIA POOL, CAROM POOL, CHICAGO POOL, CHINESE POOL, CHOPSTICKS POOL, COLOR-BALL POOL, CONTINUOUS POOL, CONTRA POOL, CORK POOL, COWBOY POOL, CRAZY POOL, CRIBBAGE POOL, CUE BALL POOL, DISC-POOL, DUTCH POOL, ENGLISH EIGHT-BALL POOL, ENGLISH POOL, EVERLASTING POOL, FIFTEEN-BALL POOL, FIVE-PIN POOL, FOLLOWING POOL, 14.1 CONTINUOUS POOL, GOLF POOL, HIGH NUMBER POOL, INDIAN POOL, IRISH POOL, ITALIAN SKITTLE POOL, JACK-UP POOL, KELLY POOL, KISS POOL, LIFE POOL, LIVE POOL, MUG'S POOL, NEAREST BALL POOL, NIGGER POOL, PAIR POOL, PAPER POOL, PARISIAN POOL, PEA POOL, PERPETUAL POOL, PIGEON-POOL, PILL POOL, PIN POOL, PINK POOL, POKER POOL, POOL, POOL FOR 31 POINTS, PYRAMID POOL, RACK POOL, ROTATION CONTRA POOL, RUSSIAN POOL, SCOTCH POOL, SCRATCH POOL, SELLING POOL, SENTINEL POOL, SEVEN-UP POOL, SINGLE POOL, SIXTY-ONE POOL, SKILL POOL, SKITTLE POOL, SNOOKER POOL, SOLITAIRE POOL, SPEED POOL, STRAIGHT POOL, THIRTY-ONE POOL, TWO-BALL POOL, TWO-PIN POOL, WESTERN POOL.

2. (game, Brit., obs.) The game of LIFE POOL. 1830 Mingaud, 1839 Kentfield 40, 1896 Broadfoot 408. The game is mentioned in the 1819 edition of Hoyle but not the 1817 edition; by 1825 it was one of the five most popular billiard games in England.

3. The collective bet in multiplayer games, especially LIFE POOL. 1836 Tillotson 7. The POT or STAKE. Rarely, the collection of players who have made such a bet.

4. The required score of 61 points in FIFTEEN-BALL POOL. Also, the MARKER'S call to indicate the completion of this game. 1877 NYT (Dec 14) 5:1. "Wilson again failing to count, he made pool."

Pool and Billiard Magazine

A monthly glossy publication edited by Shari Simonsen-Stauch and published by Sports Publications, Ltd., 109 Fairfield Way, Suite 207, Bloomingdale, IL 60108. It is devoted to news, instructional columns, new product announcements, and advertising. Its chief rival is BILLIARDS DIGEST; however, well-informed students of the game subscribe to both publications.

pool ball

1. A ball used in playing pocket billiard games, usually one of the 15 numbered balls. 1858 OED, 1976 WSD 328. 2. (Snooker) A COLOUR, that is, any coloured ball other than a RED. 1976 WSD 328, 1978 BSCC 47. Cf. PYRAMID BALL.

pool basket

(Brit. games) A basket having a narrow neck so that the marker can give out PRIVATE BALLS without anyone seeing their color. 1896 Broadfoot 101, 1897 Payne 34. In American games, this function is performed by the BOTTLE.

pool board

A MARKING BOARD for recording LIVES lost in LIFE POOL and related games. 1911 Roberts 19. Also called a LIFE BOARD. Cf. PARISIAN POOL BOARD.

pool counter ball rack

Device for keeping SCORE by storing balls pocketed by different players on separate shelves. 1908 Brunswick 117. *See illustration on next page.*

pool cue

= CUE STICK, particularly one that is made for playing pocket games. Cf. BILLIARD CUE, SNOOKER CUE.

Pool for 31 Points

(Bagatelle game, obs.) PARISIAN POOL played to 31 points with BURST. The first player strikes from within the STRING, and must hit one or more cushions and attempt to lodge his ball in one of the CUPS, in which case he scores the value of that cup. After a burst, the

pool counter ball rack

player may claim PRIVILEGE and pay a FORFEIT to remain in the game. 1890 HRB 107.

pool hall
= POOL ROOM.

pool pin
A PIN or SKITTLE used in PIN POOL. 1908 Brunswick 85.

pool player
One who plays pocket billiards, as opposed to a BILLIARD PLAYER, who prefers carom games.

pool room
1. A room, usually in a public establishment, in which Pocket Billiards is played. See POOL. Often just a ROOM.
2. A betting parlor, particularly for wagering on horse races. See POOL.

pool shark
= SHARK. 1936 NBJ (Mar). A HUSTLER. In 1915, W. C. Fields made a short film entitled "Pool Sharks." The term connotes an expert but unsavory player who conceals his true ability, which enables him to bet advantageously on his game.

pool spot
(American Four-Ball Game, obs.) A SPOT located five inches from the TOP RAIL, on which the white object ball is spotted at the beginning of the game. 1857 Phelan 171, 1893 HRB 30. Also known, confusingly, as the WHITE-BALL SPOT, which is placed differently in Three-Ball Billiards.

pool stop
(obs.) An accessory used to convert a Carombolette table so that balls are prevented from returning to the table once they have entered HOLES. 1898 HRB 101.

pool table
A POCKET TABLE, especially one on which POCKET BILLIARDS is played, as opposed to a BILLIARD or CAROM TABLE, which has no pockets. 1860 OED.

poolroom
= POOL ROOM.

port
(obs.) An arch, made of ivory or iron and similar to a croquet wicket, that was used as an obstacle in early billiard games. The player could score by sending the ball through the port and touching the KING, an ivory stick located at one end of the table, or by sending the opponent's ball against the king or into a HAZARD. 1674

179

port (1694)

Cotton 25. Also called the ARCH, IRON, PASS, or PASS IRON. See also FORNICATOR.

portable table

A billiard table designed to be moved easily, often having folding or detachable legs. 1830 Mingaud.

position

1. A placement of the cue ball and object balls allowing another shot to be made. "He got position." Placement of the balls through skillful play to permit an extended run of points (also called POSITION PLAY or "playing position"). 1880 NYT (Mar 26) 8:4, 1992 OR 13. Called AFTER-POSITION in 1925 Peall. See also PO, SHAPE, WALK-UP.

The significance of position play is summed up in 1807 White 94: "Nothing is of more importance in the game of billiards than to be able to foresee the course which the balls will take after their contact."

2. The LAYOUT or arrangement of the balls on the table at any given moment. Also LEAVE or PATTERN. 1875 NYT (Nov 20) 2:5. See also TABLE IN POSITION.

How many different possible positions are there? The number is theoretically infinite if the centers of the balls can be placed arbitrarily. However, minute changes in location may not yield substantially different shots. In 1931, Professor Frank G. Dickinson of the University of Illinois attempted to calculate the number of substantially different positions that can be occupied by three balls on a standard carom table. Assuming that each ball is localized within a one-eighth-inch square, he obtained the result 63 quadrillion = 6.3×10^{16}. 1931 NYT (Apr 27) 26:2.

position marker

(Brit. games) A device for marking the location of a ball that must be removed from the table for cleaning or replacement so that it may be replaced precisely in its original location. See also CLEANING, LIFTED BALL.

position play

Making strokes whose object is to achieve accurate positioning of the cue ball or object balls for subsequent shots. 1977 Fels 69. The term appears in 1879 NYT (Sep 17) 3:4. See POSITION. A "position player" is one who concentrates on or is skilled at obtaining good position, as opposed to a SHOOTER.

In CAROM BILLIARDS, the systematic development of position play began in the 1850s with work on GATHER SHOTS by Claudius Berger. In the U. S., Phelan's columns in *Leslie's* reveal that only rudimentary position play was known in 1861. The subject of position

play in STRAIGHT-RAIL and BALKLINE is treated exhaustively in 1913 Daly, one of the best-selling books on sports and games ever published.

In THREE-CUSHIONS, position play is accessible only to advanced players and has just begun to be described in the literature. 1978 Byrne, 1979 Robin, 1979 Ceulemans. The position play of Alfredo De Oro in the early decades of the twentieth century was remarked upon by reporters of the period.

In POCKET BILLIARDS, position play is essential to long runs but it was not discussed in the literature until after World War II. The undisputed master of position play is Willie Mosconi, whose record for RUNNING OUT the game in a single INNING has never been approached.

In ENGLISH BILLIARDS, where the importance of position play has always been recognized, the great positional tool was the SPOT-STROKE.

postman's knock

(Eng. Bill.) A KISS stroke in which the cue ball is aimed at an object ball that is near a cushion in such a way that the cue ball contacts the object ball twice in rapid succession, making a "rat-tat" sound reminiscent of a door knocker. 1908 Mannock II 315, 1957 Holt 16. Cf. KISS-CANNONS, PLON-PON. It is used to keep the first object ball near the cushion—the motion of the object ball is arrested by its second contact with the cue ball.

pot

1. (Brit. games) To POCKET a ball. 1860 OED. A WINNING HAZARD. 1924 Aiken 21, 1976 WSD 330. See also CUSHION POT, INDIRECT POT, POTTER. 2. A POOL or collective STAKE.

pot black

1. (Snooker) The pocketing of the BLACK, or a strategy involving alternate potting of the black ball and the REDS, desirable because of the high value (seven points) of sinking the black. 1975a Lowe 74. 2. A popular British television series giving extensive coverage to Snooker matches. This show is credited with reviving professional Snooker in the U.K. 3. A glossy British monthly magazine devoted to Snooker.

pot game

A game for three or more players who each contribute to a POT that goes to the winner. 1979 Grissim 253. A POOL in its original sense.

potter

(Snooker) A player who excels at potting rather than at defensive play. 192x Reece Snooker 1. In American usage, a SHOOTER.

potting line

(Eng. Bill.) = LINE OF CENTERS. 1924 Smith 30. The direction along which an object ball must be made to travel in order that it may be pocketed. The potting line is an approximation only, as it ignores the effect of THROW.

powder

Talc or other finely powdered substance used to dry the BRIDGE HAND and facilitate movement of the cue against the fingers. 1992 OR 13. See also HAND CHALK, TALCUM POWDER.

power draw

Extreme DRAW. See FORCE DRAW.

PPPA

(org.) = PROFESSIONAL POOL PLAYERS' ASSOCIATION.

practice

To prepare oneself for a MATCH, game, or stroke by playing real or simulated shots. Practice stroking is permitted prior to a shot, provided that no ball is contacted. See FEATHER, FIDDLE, NUDGE, WAGGLE, WARM-UP. Practicing the lag or any other shot is a foul if any ball, including the cue ball, is struck. It is also a foul to practice during a game, even if no ball in play is touched (for example, on a nearby table that is not in use). 1992 OR 49.

practice game

A game that is played before SPECTATORS but is not announced in advance to the public and hence does not qualify as an EXHIBITION.

practice room

An area set aside at TOURNAMENTS that contestants may use to warm up prior to MATCHES. The practice room is often the scene of money games involving the players.

Président, Le

(game, pr. luh PRAY-zee-DAHN) A French variation of the PROGRESSIVE CAROM GAME. 1983 Malsert 168. A player making an ordinary carom involving no cushions does not score, but is allowed to continue shooting. Otherwise, one point is awarded for each cushion contact. The game was named for A. Bruneau, president of the Club de Billard d'Orléans.

presumption of innocence

The principle that the striker is deemed to have committed a FOUL only if he is positively observed doing so. If there is any DOUBT on the issue, he is presumed innocent.

principal spot

(Bagatelle, obs.) A spot placed between the DEAD-BALL LINE and the #1 CUP, on which the red ball is spotted at the beginning of play.

private ball, private number ball

(Pill Pool) The ball having the number designated on the PILL chosen by a player. 1850 Phelan 45, 1992 OR 88. Certain games require each player to "own" a ball selected by LOT. In Pill Pool, a player is out of the game when his private number ball is pocketed by another player. See also BOTTLE, PIN POOL, POOL BASKET, TALLY BALL.

privilege

(Life Pool, obs.) The right to purchase one or more LIVES after being KILLED by virtue of having lost all one's original allotment of lives. 1857 Phelan 64. See also PURCHASE, STAR. "Privilege" is a synonym for "life" in PIN POOL. 1869 Kavanagh 19.

pro taper

= PROFESSIONAL TAPER.

professional

Anyone who derives income from the game of billiards. Although the term is used informally to refer to players who attempt to make a living by playing in TOURNAMENTS, it was originally used to distinguish pure AMATEURS who had no financial connection with the game. For example, an employee of a billiard room was considered a professional, even though he may never have touched a cue, and was therefore barred from amateur competition.

Professional Billiards Association (PBA)

(org.) Changed its name to MEN'S PROFESSIONAL BILLIARDS ASSOCIATION in 1989.

Professional Billiards Players Association

(org., Brit.) Formed in 1968, the precursor of the WORLD PROFESSIONAL BILLIARDS AND SNOOKER ASSOCIATION.

Professional Billiards Tour Association (PBTA)

(org.) An organization of leading pocket professionals formed in 1991 to compete in a regular schedule of tournaments and to secure television sponsorship for pool. Its leader, Don Mackey, is referred to as "Commissioner." The PBTA is associated with the MPBA but not the WPBA and therefore does not represent women's billiards. Address: P.O. Box 5599, Spring Hill, FL 34608.

Professional Pocket Billiard Player's Association

(org.) Formed in 1965 by tournament players to fill the void left by the absence of sanctioned title events.

Professional Pocket Billiard Player's Club

(org.) Formed in New York in 1916 to stimulate interest in pocket billiards. At the time, before the days of Ralph Greenleaf, Balkline and Three-Cushions were much more popular games.

Professional Pool Player's Association (PPPA)

(org.) A pocket billiard sanctioning organization formed by tournament players following a reduction in prize money offered at the U.S. Open pocket billiard tournament.

Professional Referee's Association

(org., Brit.) An officials' organization formed in 1979. 1985 Morrison 103. Cf. ASSOCIATION OF BILLIARDS AND SNOOKER REFERENCES.

professional taper

A TAPER in which the shaft has a constant diameter for some distance from the tip, usually about 14 inches, before widening. So called because it is preferred by professional pocket billiard players. Also DELAYED TAPER, PRO TAPER. 1990 White 2-3. Cf. EUROPEAN TAPER, KOMORI TAPER, STRAIGHT TAPER.

Professional Women's Billiard Alliance

(org.) An organization formed in 1975 to promote women's pocket billiards. Its name was changed in 1976 to the WOMEN'S PROFESSIONAL BILLIARD ASSOCIATION to avoid confusion with the Professional Women Bowlers Association, which shared the same initials, PWBA.

Progressive Carom Game

(game) Carom Billiards in which the striker who completes a carom is credited with one point for each cushion contact made by the cue ball; one point is also given for an ordinary ball-to-ball carom. 1890 HRB 62, 1913 Stoddard 148, 1916 RGRG 15. The word "progressive" indicates that the score for a shot increases as the cue ball "progresses" from one cushion to the next. In LE PRÉSIDENT, a French variation, a carom involving no cushions earns no points, but the player is permitted to continue shooting.

projecting the pocket

A technique for simplifying BANK SHOTS by selecting fixed objects in the billiard room as points of aim. An imaginary line is projected from the pocket being aimed at through the opposite pocket for a distance equal to the width of the table. The end of this line segment is the

point at which the object ball should be aimed. This method is of particular value in ONE-POCKET, where bank shots are frequent.

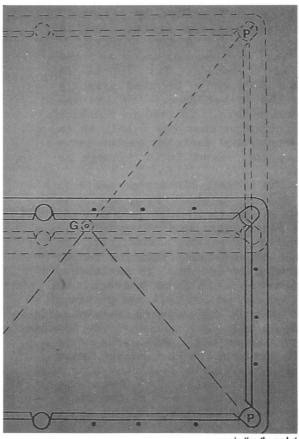

projecting the pocket

prong

A triangle of wood forming part of the CROWN in the BUTT of a cue stick. 1977 Martin 216. Also called a POINT. The prongs are claimed to be important in acting as shock absorbers during the stroke, but this assessment is challenged by cuemakers. 1965 Fats 74. See also SPLICE.

proposition bet

A proposed wager that seems too good to resist, generally offered by a HUSTLER. An example of such a bet is "50 against 2 in the side," in which the hustler claims that he will sink 50 balls at ordinary Straight Pool before the victim can sink two balls in the side pockets. His strategy will be to remove balls from the area between the two side pockets and leave the cue ball within it. Not only will the opponent have no shot, he will also find it difficult to play a SAFETY. See also PROPOSITION SHOT.

proposition shot

A shot that seems impossible and on which a SUCKER can be induced to wager. Once the bet is down, the player makes the shot and collects the bet.

protest

A complaint that a violation of the rules has occurred. 1890 HRB 35. An objection lodged to tournament officials asserting an error in a REFEREE'S ruling. The referee judges matters of fact, such as whether two balls are FROZEN, and on such issues his opinion is final and not subject to protest. A rule interpretation may be reviewed later by the authorities, however, since such a review can be made without disturbing any factual decision. A request for a rule interpretation must be made before the next shot is taken and all players must honor the request to halt play pending the decision or risk DISQUALIFICATION. 1982 OR 52. See also INSTANT REPLAY.

The first public game played under protest occurred on January 28, 1869. Joseph Dion was playing Melvin Foster at Four-Ball Billiards in Montreal and ran 103 with the balls CROTCHED in the corner. The referee forced Dion to break up the position, which he did, but under protest, as there seemed to be no authority in the rules for such an action. The protest was dropped when Dion won, 1500 to 1116. 1912 MB 224.

psych

1. (colloq.) To use psychological tactics on one's opponent. 1977 Fels 9. To "psych out" the adversary means to anticipate his strategy or to unsettle him. Because billiards requires thorough concentration as well as coordination, efforts to unnerve the opponent are often successful. Such behavior, when deliberate, can be punished as UNSPORTSMANLIKE CONDUCT.

Robert Cannefax, a brilliant but erratic THREE-CUSH-IONS player of the 1920s, had a wooden leg. To perturb his opponents during matches, he would stick a knife through his pants into the leg. During the CHALLENGE match for the World Pocket Billiard Championship in 1966, Luther Lassiter pretended to fall asleep during a long run by Cisero Murphy. When Murphy saw Lassiter dozing, he promptly missed and Lassiter, who was quite alert, ran out the game for the championship title.

Among the mundane techniques for distracting the other player are making noise by filing the cue tip, chalking the cue, or blowing one's nose. 1951 *Reader's Digest* (Feb) 12. Alfredo De Oro was a master of psychological tactics and once beat Welker Cochran just by failing to go to the bathroom during a game! (For details of this story, see 1972 Byrne.) 2. (colloq.) To

experience a sudden loss of ability or concentration in a game for no apparent reason; to CLUTCH.

Puff Billiards

= BILLARD NICOLAS. Cf. MOUTH BILLIARDS.

pull

(Brit., colloq.) = DRAW. 1926 BM (Mar) 49.

Pull-Down Game

(game, obs.) = GO-BACK GAME. 1850c White & Bohn 38. So called because the points scored by a player are "pulled down" from the scoreboard whenever he misses.

punch

A stroke in which the cue stick is forced suddenly, or punched, through the cue ball, generally with a very short FOLLOW-THROUGH and used to avoid a PUSH. See also CRAMP STROKE. Cf. NIP.

puppy

(colloq.) = CHERRY, CRIPPLE, DUCK, HANGER, MINNIE, SET-UP, SITTER. 1990 Rushin 24.

purchase

(Life Pool, obs.) To buy another LIFE; to STAR. 1856 Crawley 168. See also PRIVILEGE.

purple

1. (Pocket Bill.) The color of the four-ball and twelve-ball. See also PLUM. Purple cloth has occasionally been used in billiard matches. See CLOTH. 2. (Snooker Plus) A ball whose value is 10 points and is spotted at the beginning of a FRAME on the PURPLE SPOT.

purple spot

(Snooker Plus) The SPOT on which the PURPLE is placed, midway between the BLUE SPOT and the BROWN SPOT.

push

A stroke in which the cue stick is allowed to remain in contact with the cue ball as that ball contacts an object ball. 1881 MB 26. The American equivalent of a PUSH STROKE, it is not legal in CAROM BILLIARDS. It was formerly allowed in POCKET BILLIARDS if the motion of the cue stick was a CONTINUOUS STROKE. However, the tip of the cue may not contact any ball other than the cue ball. This standard has been replaced by the MO-MENTARY CONTACT rule. A DOUBLE HIT, in which the cue ball is struck twice by the cue tip, is always illegal but may be difficult to detect. 1992 OR 38. The REFEREE judges a push shot by the sound made by the balls and by the path of the cue ball. A push shot in which the cue ball is shoved along the table instead of being stroked is also illegal.

The following peculiar rule applies in Eight-Ball but in no other game: "If the cue ball is close, but not frozen to the object ball, the cue must be elevated to a 45 degree angle when shooting in the general direction of the line of the two balls. A level cue may be used if aiming 45 degrees or more off line of the two balls." 1992 OR 45.

The rule forbidding the double hit is of antique origin, going back to the prohibition against TRAILING with the MACE, which was already in force in the 1600s. "If you touch your ball twice it is a loss." 1674 Cotton. The problem of detecting a push is mentioned in 1806 Phil 55. The push was controversial in the U.S. in the mid-1800s, where it was finally BARRED in AMERICAN FOUR-BALL BILLIARDS temporarily in 1862 and permanently in 1868, when John McDevitt used it to run 1458 points. For the situation in England, see PUSH CANON, PUSH STROKE. Cf. HALF-PUSH, STIRABOUT.

push canon
(Eng. Bill.) A CAROM made by means of a PUSH STROKE, which was formerly legal in English Billiards. 1889 Drayson 31. Textbooks of the 1890s contained instructions on how to perform this shot.

push-on tip
A fitting consisting of a collar, usually plastic, with a TIP attached, designed to be installed over the tip end of the shaft of a cue stick and held in place by pressure.

push-out
(Nine-Ball) = SHOOT OUT, a permitted maneuver in which a Nine-Ball player may, without penalty on the shot following the BREAK, roll the cue ball with his cue to any position on the table. 1986 OR 61. The cue ball need not CONTACT either a cushion or an object ball on a push-out.

push shot
= PUSH.

push stroke
(Brit. games) A formerly legal stroke in which the cue stick remains in contact with the cue ball as the cue ball contacts an object ball. 1895 Buchanan 99. A shot in which the cue ball is placed close to the object ball and stroked smoothly through. 1873 Bennett 314. See also PUSH, PUSH CANON. Cf. HALF-PUSH, STIRABOUT.

A "push stroke" is defined in the 1978 BSCC regulations as a FOUL in which (1) the tip of the cue remains in contact with the cue ball as the cue ball makes contact with an object ball, or (2) the tip of the cue remains in contact with the cue ball after cue ball has commenced its forward motion. See 1884 *London Times* (Dec 17) for

an article discussing the merits and disadvantages of the push stroke. 1896 Broadfoot 386.

put him in
(Eng. Bill.) To pocket the opponent's cue ball. 1904 Mannock I 434. See also WHITECHAPEL.

PWBA
(org.) = PROFESSIONAL WOMEN'S BILLIARD ALLIANCE. Changed in 1976 to WPBA.

pyramid
1. (Brit. games) The PACK, especially in SNOOKER. So named because of the pyramidal visual appearance of the triangular rack of 15 balls. Also BUNCH, HEAP, RACK or STACK. 2. (game) See PYRAMID GAME, PYRAMIDS. 1850 OED. Cf. LOSING PYRAMIDS.

pyramid ball
(Snooker) A RED, one of the 15 red balls racked in the PYRAMID. 1978 BSCC 47. Cf. POOL BALL.

Pyramid Game
(game, obs.) A SINGLE-RACK pocket billiard game played with 15 red balls and a cue ball. The object is to pocket more of the balls than one's opponent. Only WINNING HAZARDS count. 1850 Kentfield 48, 1858 Mardon 396. A direct ancestor of Pocket Billiards. Cf. AMERICAN PYRAMID POOL, PYRAMID POOL.

The English version of this game is played with the BAULK SEMICIRCLE and 15 REDS. Varying numbers of balls may be used. When only one red ball remains on the table, one player uses the white ball as a cue ball while the other uses the red as a cue. If an odd number of red balls is employed, the last hazard is worth two points. 1891 MB 359. When only 14 reds are used, the ball in the middle of the back row of the PYRAMID is removed. When 16 reds are used, the last one is placed directly behind the center of the back row of the pyramid. 1893 HRB 113.

Pyramid Pool
(game, obs.) A pocket billiard game similar to AMERICAN PYRAMID POOL except that CALLING of shots is not required. The player sinking the last ball wins. 1850 Kentfield 49, 1856 Crawley 111, 1919 Hoyle 632. In 1850 Kentfield 49, the game is played with 14 red balls; the red ball in the middle of the back row of the rack is removed. Cf. PYRAMID GAME, PYRAMIDS.

pyramid rest
(Brit. games) = SPIDER. 1873 Bennett 28, 1897 Payne 33. A REST particularly useful in the game of PYRAMIDS,

184

where a cluster of balls may prevent the use of an ordinary rest.

pyramid spot

(Snooker) The spot on which the PINK is placed, midway between the CENTRE SPOT and the middle of the TOP RAIL. 1873 Bennett 83, 1895 Buchanan 2, 1957 Holt 6. Also known as the DARK-RED SPOT, FOOT SPOT, PINK SPOT, RED SPOT (in Carom Billiards), or WINNING SPOT.

Pyramiden-Partie

(game, obs.) = GERMAN PYRAMID GAME. 1850c White & Bohn 45, 1856 Crawley 106.

Pyramids

(game, obs.) = PYRAMID, PYRAMID GAME. 1850 OED, 1856 Crawley 171.

Q

quarter-ball

A term used to describe the fullness of hit by the cue ball upon an object ball. 1807 White 20, 1839 Kentfield 8, 1941 Hoppe 25. The edge of the cue ball is aimed at a point halfway between the center and the edge of the object ball. Cf. FULL BALL, HALF-BALL.

quarter ball

quarter-butt

(Eng. Bill., obs.) A short BUTT, longer and much heavier than a cue, tipped with leather at the thick end and used in playing up the table to DOUBLE on balls in BAULK. 1869 Roberts 172, 1873 Bennett 27. It is used to avoid imparting any spin to the cue ball so the rebound from the cushion will be precise.

quarter table

A COIN-OPERATED TABLE that dispenses a RACK of object balls when a quarter is inserted.

queen

One of a set of specially marked balls used in POKER POCKET BILLIARDS. 1946 OR 72.

queue

The original spelling of "cue," from the French word for "tail." 1829 Plan 1. The tail, or handle, of the MACE was used by early players to strike at a ball that lay near a cushion. The mace was turned around for this purpose. See CUE.

quick game triangle

See TRIANGLE, QUICK GAME.

quill stroke

(Eng. Bill., obs.) A LOSING HAZARD played thinly off a ball that lies just outside the BAULK-LINE but hanging

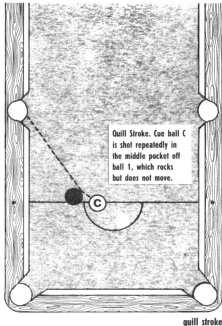

Quill Stroke. Cue ball C is shot repeatedly in the middle pocket off ball 1, which rocks but does not move.

quill stroke

partly over it. 1869 Roberts 136, 1885 Cook 11, 1889 Drayson 99. If the shot is taken softly, the object ball will only be rocked and the player will be IN HAND and able to repeat the stroke indefinitely. Also called the FEATHER STROKE. A species of JENNY, it is described but not named in both 1807 White 39 and 1844 Mardon 95. The tactic enabled even inferior players to RUN OUT the longest of games and was ultimately outlawed. Since it is based on a losing hazard, the shot is not possible in Pocket Billiards.

185

rabbit

(Brit., colloq.) A mediocre player, one who may be "chased" by the others. 1941 Levi 194.

race

A style of competition in which the player who first wins a predetermined number of games or points wins the match. 1992 OR 13. "Race to 11" means that two players will play until one has won 11 games. This will occur after at most 21 games. The usual format for NINE-BALL tournaments. Tournaments at FIFTEEN-BALL POOL in the 1870s were of the race variety, although the term was not applied at the time. See BEST OF, SESSION. Cf. AHEAD SESSION.

rack

1. (Pocket Bill.) A TRIANGLE for arranging the balls at commencement of the game. Racks are made in special shapes for games such as NINE-BALL, TEN-BALL, SEVEN-BALL, and POKER POCKET BILLIARDS. See also APRON, SKIRTED RACK. 2. (Pocket Bill.) The pyramidal grouping of balls that have been set with the TRIANGLE or other FRAME. 1878 NYT (Apr 21) 1:7. The PACK. By extension, the term can refer to the full collection of object balls used in a pocket billiard game. "He ran six racks." Also BUNCH, HEAP, PYRAMID, STACK. See also FULL RACK, SHORT RACK, SIXTEEN-BALL RACK. 3. (Pocket Bill.) To place the object balls in the triangle; to RACK UP. In tournament play, the balls are racked by the REFEREE to ensure that each ball is touching its neighbors. See also RACK 'EM. In private games, the NONSTRIKER racks the balls for the STRIKER. The origin of this custom is presumably that the successful shooter should not be interrupted and forced to rack for himself and also to prevent him from giving himself an advantage by tampering with the rack or aligning it improperly. However, this procedure provides the nonstriker with an astonishing opportunity to cripple the striker.

In an article in the *National Billiard News* in July 1987, Grady Mathews details nine different methods of MISRACKING the balls, some maddeningly difficult to detect, that interfere with the normal action of the balls. Most of these involve failing to FREEZE the balls properly, which substantially reduces the tendency of the balls to fly apart nicely. Breaker beware! See also CHEATING.

The racked balls must be placed in the triangle in a special way for games such as EIGHT-BALL and NINE-BALL, in which certain balls have particular significance. But in STRAIGHT POOL all the balls are interchangeable. Why do the BCA rules (1992 OR 55) require racking the one-ball and five-ball at the corners of the rack? In a letter to Clement Trainer dated 1979, Bruce Venzke, a member of the BCA Rules Committee, explains that these balls are solid yellow and orange, respectively, and are thus highly visible against the green cloth. They are placed at the corners to aid the referee in determining whether the two required balls contact cushions on the OPENING BREAK.

The various games impose detailed racking requirements of which many players are unaware. In Eight-Ball, for example, one corner ball must be solid, the other corner ball must be a stripe, and the eight-ball itself must be in the middle of the third row. For information on racking details, see the individual game entries.

Elaborate rules may be employed to determine what happens if racking cannot be performed because of the presence of balls in the area of the pyramid. See INTERFERENCE.

4. An apparatus for storing billiards balls (a BALL RACK) or cue sticks (a CUE RACK). See also TO THE RACK.

rack boy

An employee of a BILLIARD ROOM or club who racks the balls for the players at the completion of each FRAME. 1959 Tevis 108, 1967 Polsky 39.

rack 'em

(colloq.) Literally, "rack them," meaning to place the object balls in the rack to set them in position for the next game. Used figuratively to mean, "let's play pool." Also "rack 'em up."

Rack Pool

(game) = STRAIGHT POOL. 1978 Byrne 168. So called because the balls are repeatedly RACKED to permit continuous play. Also known as 14.1 CONTINUOUS or 14.1 RACK.

rack up

1. (Pocket Bill.) To arrange the object balls in a RACK or TRIANGLE. 2. To score points. To mark up the scored points on a score sheet, STRING or other marking device. "He racked up 23." 3. To terminate play, as by hanging up one's cue stick in a RACK. Putting away the cue is a gesture of CONCESSION.

rag

(sl.) A CUSHION, referring to the cloth with which it is covered. 1985 Marguglio 221.

rail

1. One of the borders of a billiard table, to which the CUSHIONS are attached. A CUSHION RAIL. The term SIDE RAIL is sometimes used to refer to a portion of the APRON. See LEDGE for an obsolete term. The word "rail" is used as a verb in 1674 Cotton: "it [the Table] is rail'd round."
2. A CUSHION. This use of "rail" is universal but technically incorrect because the rail is the top horizontal surface to which the cushion proper is attached, not the cushion itself. The author is flagrantly guilty of misusing the word in this book, but he is in good company. In normal play, no ball touches a rail; all contact is with the cushions. See CUSHION RAIL, END RAIL, FOOT RAIL, HEAD RAIL, HUG THE RAIL, LEDGE, LEFT RAIL, LONG RAIL, RIGHT RAIL, SHORT RAIL, SIDE RAIL, TOP RAIL, and the compounds below. See also WOOD. 3. The RAIL NURSE. 1879 NYT (Feb 7) 8:1. To "get the rail" means to obtain a favorable position from which the rail nurse can be executed. See LIMITED RAIL, STRAIGHT-RAIL, UNLIMITED RAIL.

rail billiards

(obs.) = STRAIGHT-RAIL. Carom billiards in which the RAIL NURSE can be executed, that is, in which there is no BALK SPACE. The term began to be used in the 1870s to describe a style in which players attempted to maneuver the balls as rapidly as possible into a rail nurse position. It later evolved into "Straight-Rail."

rail bird

(colloq.) A SPECTATOR; one who stands close to the RAIL of the table to watch a game.

rail bolt

A bolt used to fasten a RAIL to the BED of a table. The cap covering the bolt head is called a ROSETTE.

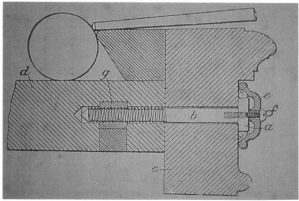

rail bolt

rail bridge

A FINGER BRIDGE that permits the player to shoot at a ball lying close to a RAIL. 1941 Hoppe 15. A common error committed by players is to make an ordinary bridge atop the rail and use it to shoot downward at the ball. It is important to position the fingers to keep the cue as level as possible to avoid unwanted MASSÉ.

rail cloth

The cloth used to cover the rubber CUSHIONS of a table. Although it is customary for the same cloth to be used to cover both the cushions and the bed, this is not necessary and some table owners use different materials for these purposes. Cf. BED CLOTH.

rail-first

Describing a shot in which the cue ball contacts a RAIL, *i.e.*, a CUSHION, before hitting any other ball. Rarely, a shot in which an object ball contacts a rail before entering a pocket. A BANK SHOT in CAROM BILLIARDS. See also BRICOLE.

rail marker

1. A scoring device with knobs and dials set in a RAIL for keeping track of the points made by each player. 1908 Brunswick 89. See also MARKER. 2. (rare) = CUSHION SPOT, DIAMOND, DOT, NAIL, or SIGHT. 1965 Mosconi 87. *See illustration on next page.*

rail nurse

(Bill.) The most important RUNNING NURSE in STRAIGHT-RAIL Billiards. 1913 Daly 166. The position is as shown. The cue ball is stroked softly to knock the first object ball to the rail and back; the second object ball is moved slightly down the rail while remaining the same distance from it. See FIVE-INCH LINE. The result is the same position shifted by a small amount. ENGLISH can be used to correct small errors made while manipulating the balls. When the end of the cushion is reached, a sequence of several shots is used for TURNING THE CORNER to reestablish the nurse on the adjacent rail. An experienced practitioner can run from this position essentially indefinitely. Some 200–300 shots are made during one complete circuit of the table. Runs in the thousands were commonplace in the late nineteenth century. Modern runs exceeding 10,000 are known in the Far East.

The rail nurse position is shown, but not named or described, at 1844 Mardon pl. xxix. The shot originated from a STATIONARY NURSE in which the two object balls were FROZEN to the cushion and the cue ball made to graze the edges of both. After a number of repetitions, one of the balls becomes dislodged from the cushion. About 1860, Joseph Dion developed the nurse with one

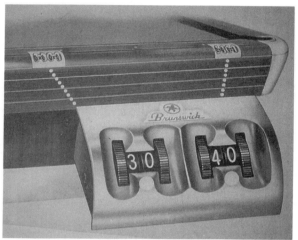

rail marker (1)

rail marker (1)

rail marker (2)

ball out in this fashion. By 1865, Louis Fox had mastered a PUSH SHOT version of it, but his technique was later barred under the rules. For his Three-Ball tournaments during the period 1873–4, Albert Garnier surreptitiously enhanced the effectiveness of the stationary form. By practicing many MASSÉ shots on the table to be used for the championship, he wore a slight gutter into the cloth next to the cushions. Any ball lodging near a cushion would thus tend to become frozen to it, making the nurse much easier to play. 1896 NY *Herald*

(Apr 6) 10:5. William Sexton used this technique to run 287 in 1876.

Sexton developed the running rail nurse in 1877–8. His style was known at the time as "Rail Billiards." 1878 NYT (Jul 9) 2:4. His success led to the introduction of the CHAMPION'S GAME in 1879, in which large CROTCH spaces defined by diagonal lines at the corners interrupted the nurse. The term "rail nurse" appears in 1879 NYT (Jan 23) 5:3. Billiard variations in which an attempt was made to restrict RAIL PLAY were known as LIMITED RAIL games. Ordinary Carom Billiards became known as the UNLIMITED RAIL or STRAIGHT-RAIL game.

Much of the development of Billiards came about because of the need to curb the rail nurse. The Champion's Game and BALKLINE are the most important examples. A lesser-known approach, tried in 1880, required the balls to be SPOTTED for a BREAK SHOT each time the striker had run 50 points. See SPOT AT FIFTY. 1912 MB 256.

The rail nurse is also known in ENGLISH BILLIARDS, where it is more difficult to play because of the need to avoid LOSING a ball in a pocket. 1908 Mannock 423. In that game, however, NURSERY breaks are limited by the rule restricting CONSECUTIVE CANNONS. Outside the United States, the rail nurse is called the AMERICAN SERIES or SÉRIE AMÉRICAINE. *See illustration on next page.*

rail play
(Bill.) That phase of the game concerned with keeping both object balls near each other and close to a cushion to permit long runs, especially at the RAIL NURSE. 1881 MB 26.

rail shot
A shot in which the cue ball lies close to a cushion, requiring elevation of the cue BUTT or the use of a special FINGER BRIDGE. Sometimes, a shot in which the SHAFT of the cue stick is rested on a rail during stroking.

railroad shot
A TRICK SHOT in which the cue ball moves along a groove formed by placing two cue sticks next to each other on the table. 1981 Margo 56. A version of the shot is shown but not named in 1902 Herrmann 92. A variation is known as the SWITCHBACK CANNON. See also CHINESE POOL. *See illustration on next page.*

Rails
(game) = THREE-CUSHION BILLIARDS. Cf. POCKETS.

rake
= MECHANICAL BRIDGE. 1977 Fels 9, 1978 Byrne 13. So named because of its visual resemblance to a gardener's

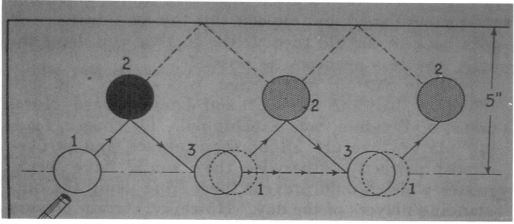

rail nurse

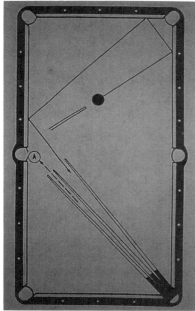

railroad shot

rake. For this reason also known as the "farmer's aid." 1991 Raftis 9.

raking
(obs.) = TRAILING. 1674 Cotton, 1974 Hendricks 10.

ranche
(Pin Pool) The act of knocking over the four outside PINS with a single stroke, while leaving the inside black pin standing, thereby winning the game. Also called a NATURAL. 1916 RGRG 25, 1919 Hoyle 648. Cf. ROYAL.

ranking
An ordering of players from best to worst, based on actual performance. The system used by the PBTA assigns ranking points to each money winner in a sanctioned tournament. The number of points is based on both the purse and the player's final standing. This method is more meaningful than tracking total winnings, since points are scaled to prevent a single large prize from skewing the results. However, because the ranking is based on play extending over an entire season, the top-ranked player is not necessarily the favorite in a particular tournament.

rapid-fire tournament
A tournament designed to be completed quickly, usually in a single night, and composed of very short games involving HANDICAPS. 1913 NYT (Apr 3) 7:4, 1926 BM (Mar) 25. See also SCRAMBLE.

rating
See TOTAL PERFORMANCE AVERAGE. Cf. RANKING.

rattle
(colloq.) To become unnerved during a game and have one's performance suffer as a consequence. 1883 NYT (May 18) 5:1, 1959 Tevis 112. A player may rattle as the result of a PSYCH.

Razzle-Dazzle
(game, colloq.) A carom game played to 25 points, each player being required to make five points each by direct caroms, one-cushion, two-cushion and three-cushion shots, in any order. The remaining five points may be made optionally by any method.

RC Marks system
(Three-Cushions) A precise version of the DIAMOND SYSTEM, perfected and published by Raymond Ceulemans (RC), the holder of the largest number of billiard titles of all time. See 1979 Ceulemans. *See illustration on next page.*

189

RC Marks system

read the table

(pocket games) To assess the POSITION of the balls in order to plan one's sequence of shots. 1988 Davis 101.

receiving

Being the recipient of a SPOT or HANDICAP of points. 1836 Tillotson 2. The "receiving player" is usually the weaker and generally BREAKS in games in which it is an advantage to do so.

recess

= INTERMISSION.

record

1. A feat is considered a record only if it is made under competitive conditions, in a CHAMPIONSHIP, a TOURNA-MENT, or an EXHIBITION. The event must have been announced in advance and the public admitted. PRAC-TICE RUNS are never taken as records, nor are perfor-mances in informal games. The commonly kept records for individual players are HIGH RUN, AVERAGE, and BEST GAME. In Nine-Ball, a recorded statistic is TOTAL PER-FORMANCE AVERAGE. See also ACCU-STATS. For a more unusual example, see NONSTOP PLAY. 2. A player's standing in a tournament, in terms of games won and lost. "He took the title with a record of 6–1."

recovery ball

(Snooker) A BALL ON that is well-positioned following an attempted SHOT TO NOTHING that results in a POT. So named because the striker must use this ball to "recover" his break, which would have terminated on a SAFETY

MISS. The shot is a safety if the striker misses because he is on COLOURS, while his opponent would be on REDS.

red

1. (Bill., Eng. Bill.) The RED BALL, one of the three balls with which the game is played. 1839 Kentfield 2. See also LIGHT RED. 2. (Snooker) One of the 15 PYRAMID BALLS. Cf. COLOUR, POOL BALL. 3. (Pocket Bill.) The color of the 3- and 11-balls. See also DARK RED.

red ball

1. An object ball used in carom games and Snooker. 1807 White 53, 1946 OR 94. Also known as just the RED. 1839 Kentfield 2.

In ENGLISH BILLIARDS the red ball is said to be always "on the table," meaning that once pocketed or having jumped from the table, it is immediately replaced. If its spot is occupied, the red is placed on the CENTER SPOT. 1836 Tillotson 3. Because it is spotted when pocketed, the red ball is sometimes known as the SPOT BALL. A player who uses the red ball as a cue ball forfeits the game.

Prior to 1771, billiards was played with white balls only—the natural color of ivory. In that year, stained balls were introduced in England, although their hue is not recorded. 1974 Hendricks 17. The red ball was certainly in use by 1795. In the AMERICAN FOUR-BALL GAME, two different shades of red were used, one for the DARK RED (or DEEP RED), a second for the LIGHT RED.

2. (game) A carom game in which the red ball must be the first object ball on each shot. 1946 OR 94. The game was popular in France around 1900. 1925 Hoppe 65. C. C. Peterson holds the world record HIGH RUN of 54 and was the champion from 1907 to 1944. 1967 OR 100. Also known as ROUGE.

3. (game, obs.) A miniature electrical billiard game introduced by the Telecoin Corporation in 1947. 1947 NYT (Nov 3) 37:6.

red hazard
(Eng. Bill.) A WINNER or LOSER off the red ball (known as a RED WINNER or RED LOSER, respectively), worth three points. 1807 White 9, 1976 WSD 206. Cf. WHITE HAZARD.

red loser
(Eng. Bill.) A LOSING HAZARD off the red ball, which scores three points. 1954 KTG 8. A type of RED HAZARD. Cf. RED WINNER, WHITE LOSER.

Red Losing Game
(game, obs.) 1807 White 137, 1839 Kentfield 33. A British game in which the striker wins points for caroms and LOSING HAZARDS, but WINNING HAZARDS cause forfeits. Called the Red Losing Carom Game in 1867 Dufton 208. Cf. RED WINNING CARAMBOLE GAME.

red spot
1. (Eng. Bill.) The SPOT located in the longitudinal center of the table and 12¾ inches from the TOP RAIL. 1895 Buchanan 2. On a METRIC TABLE, the distance from the cushion is ¹⁄₁₁ the length of the playing area. 1978 BSCC 23. Also called the BILLIARD SPOT, ENGLISH SPOT, LOSING SPOT, TOP SPOT, WINNING AND LOSING SPOT, or just the Spot.

The red ball is placed on the red spot after being potted. If the spot is OCCUPIED, the PYRAMID SPOT is used. If that spot is occupied, the ball goes on the CENTRE SPOT. Should the red be pocketed five times in succession during a single BREAK, it is placed on the centre spot. 1978 BSCC 37.

2. (Bill.) The FOOT SPOT, at which the RED is spotted. Note that the relative location of this spot differs in the English and American styles of billiards. In the AMERICAN FOUR-BALL GAME, the DARK-RED SPOT. Also the PINK SPOT, PYRAMID SPOT, or WINNING SPOT.

Red, White, and Blue
1. (game) A PIN game played on a carom table with three colored pins and three balls of corresponding colors: a white cue, a BLUE and a RED. 1890 HRB 99, 1891 MB 345, 1916 RGRG 21. At the beginning of the game the red pin is placed on the FOOT SPOT, white on the CENTER SPOT, and blue on the HEAD SPOT. The red ball is placed on the foot rail at the right diamond, the blue on the foot rail at the left diamond. The striker has the white cue ball IN HAND. The object is to knock over each pin in the order red, white, blue by driving the ball of corresponding color into the pin with the cue ball. The player who does this is the winner; caroms do not count. The game begins with a shot at the red ball. A BURST occurs if a pin is knocked down out of order. 1890 HRB 99. A variation was invented by Charles Mussey, the Chicago room owner, about 1888. 1888 NYT (Oct 21) 17:4. 2. (game, obs.) An experimental version of THREE-CUSHIONS, tried in a tournament in Chicago in 1900, in which only one (white) cue ball was used by both players; the object balls were red and blue. 1904 MB 310. 3. (game, obs.) A variation of Straight-Rail, played with red and blue object balls, in which the player is obliged to carom alternately from the red to the blue, then the blue to the red, etc. Introduced in Paris by Jacob Schaefer Sr. 1902 WB (Dec 10) 552. Also EXPERTS' GAME. 4. (game, obs.) A four-ball carom game devised around 1870 as an early attempt to suppress nursing, using a red, a blue, and two white balls. When the two object balls both fell within a certain distance of the cue ball, the player was obliged to contact the farther object ball first. The game was tried on June 1, 1870, with J. Dion beating Melvin Foster. 1904 MB 230. Also known as the EXPERTS' GAME. See AMERICAN FOUR-BALL BILLIARDS.

red winner
(Eng. Bill.) A WINNING HAZARD potting the RED and scoring three points. 1954 KTG 8. A type of RED HAZARD. Cf. WHITE WINNER.

Red Winning Carambole Game
(game, obs.) ENGLISH BILLIARDS game in which points are made by WINNING HAZARDS and CANNONS only. All LOSING HAZARDS, MISSES, and COUPS count for the adversary. 1839 Kentfield 31, 1856 Crawley 159, 1866 Crawley 155, 1867 Dufton 205. Played 18 UP. The reason the word "red" appears in the title of this game is to designate that it is a three-ball game played with a red ball, to distinguish it from the WHITE WINNING GAME, which was played with two balls. Sometimes called the Red Winning Cannon Game, it is known as the WINNING CARAMBOLE GAME in 1807 White 123.

referee
The official responsible for the conduct of a billiard game. 1983 Rule Book 251. The role of the referee has varied throughout history, and it also depends on whether he is the sole official or whether a MARKER is present. The referee decides COUNTS, MISSES, COUPS,

FREEZES, PENALTIES, and FOULS. He determines whether the balls are IN BAULK or IN ANCHOR. As to matters of fact, his rulings are final and not subject to protest or appeal. He is charged with improving play by cleaning the table and equipment when he deems it desirable, normally at the end of even innings.

The referee may respond to objective inquiries, such as whether a ball would interfere with racking, but may not offer advice or opinions. 1992 OR 53. (In earlier times, a player was responsible for his own actions and could not seek rulings by the referee.) If no marker is employed, the referee assumes his functions, such as calling the score and handing the REST to the players. A player is not protected against misstatements by the referee concerning the rules of the game, such as what the penalty will be should he foul on the next shot. He is protected, however, against erroneous statements of fact, such as whether a ball is frozen to a cushion. 1992 OR 53.

The referee must warn a player in certain situations and must *not* warn in others. For example, a player committing an INTENTIONAL FOUL must be warned by the referee that a repetition will result in a FORFEIT. He must likewise warn a player who has cue ball IN HAND BEHIND THE HEAD STRING if the cue ball is not properly placed. He must not warn a player who is about to shoot at the WRONG BALL.

In CALL-SHOT GAMES, the striker need not specify his shot if his intention is obvious. The referee makes the announcement on his behalf. If the referee calls the wrong shot, the player must correct him. However, if the player makes an erroneous call, the referee may not intervene. For example, if the player calls the five-ball in the left side pocket but is obviously aiming for the corner pocket, the referee may not warn the player or change the call.

If the referee is unable to see a shot or is uncertain whether a foul occurred, he may ask the SPECTATORS as to matters of fact. This is a very old practice in billiards, dating back at least to the late seventeenth century.

In Snooker, the referee may not answer any question not authorized by the rules. For example, he may not inform a player of the difference in scores. 1978 BSCC S24.

Referees also perform some unexpected functions. In the days of gas lamps, the referee would hold aside the gas fixture to permit a MASSÉ SHOT to be played. This was found to be necessary after Thomas Wallace seriously burned himself during a Cushion Caroms tournament in 1883. 1883 NYT (May 17) 5:3. See LIGHTING. It is still the rule in Snooker that the referee

must identify the colours of the balls for any COLOUR-BLIND player who so requests.

It is desirable for the referee to wear thin gloves to avoid putting perspiration or skin oils on the balls. In ARTISTIC BILLIARDS, cleanliness is so important that the referee is obliged to clean the balls after every group of shots.

The job of referee is exhausting and demanding. An entire book, *Le billard et l'arbitrage*, by G. Rottie (1981 Rottie), has been devoted to the subject. The referee must have his eyes on the table at all times and must always be in the correct position to judge fouls and COUNTS. This may require him to run rapidly around the table to view the tangent line between the moving cue ball and the second object ball. In Three-Cushions, because a shot may be made by an unexpected TIME SHOT or KISS, the referee must keep a mental count of the number of cushions contacted by the cue ball during the shot and which object ball was struck first. A referee who is not diligent may find himself "screened" by a player. See CHEATING, COAT. The referee may not smoke during a game.

What happens if the referee makes a mistake? The rules in such a situation are unspecified. In an 1873 match between Maurice Daly and Cyrille Dion, the prize-fighter John C. Heenan was officiating as referee. The score was 1490 to 1486 in favor of Dion with Dion at the table when a spectator claimed that the referee had miscounted and Daly actually had 1505 points, which would make him the winner. The referee ruled a DRAW after securing the agreement of the players. Pandemonium ensued among the gallery and the intervention of the police was required. The game was REPLAYED a week later, with Dion winning 1500 to 1147. 1931 BM (Mar). Videotape has somewhat reduced the risk of civil disturbance in case of an officiating error. See INSTANT REPLAY.

The British have developed a strict program for training and classifying referees, under the supervision of the ASSOCIATION OF BILLIARDS AND SNOOKER REFEREES. Apprenticeships in each category must be served for a prescribed length of time before a referee is permitted to supervise a match in a higher category. By contrast, the U. S. has neither a training program nor any published instructions on how to officiate. See also PROFESSIONAL REFEREE'S ASSOCIATION.

reflected hazard

(Eng. Bill., obs.) A WINNING HAZARD in which the object ball hits a cushion before entering a pocket. 1807 White 135. Also known as a DOUBLET hazard. In modern parlance, a BANK SHOT or DOUBLE.

regulation table

A table that conforms to official specifications, particularly with respect to size, and is thus suitable for use in TOURNAMENT play. The relevant regulations are promulgated by the appropriate sanctioning organization. In the U.K., table specifications are very strict and no record is recognized nor any match made official unless the table on which it occurred conforms to the standards both before and after the competition. See TEMPLATE. In the U.S., specifications are much less precise and are often ignored for tournament purposes.

rencontre

(Fr.) = TIME SHOT. The literal French meaning is "meeting," which describes perfectly what happens during such a shot.

rentré

(Balkline, Fr., pr. rahn-TRAY) International referee's CALL when the object balls are IN BALK, but at least one of balls had left the balk space on the previous stroke and returned. The literal French meaning is "reentered." 1981 Rottie 136. See also Á CHEVAL, DEDANS, ENTRÉ, RESTÉ DEDANS.

replacement

An act by the REFEREE to RESTORE the balls as nearly as possible to the positions they occupied prior to INTERFERENCE or a FOUL STROKE. Its purpose is to prevent a player from gaining an advantage from an infraction of the rules. See TABLE IN POSITION. The rule on replacement was first invoked by Tom Gallagher in 1879 in a three-ball championship game against George Slosson. 1919 BM (Jun) 18.

In Snooker, potted REDS are never replaced even though the result may be that a player benefits from his own foul. 1987 BSCC S11.

replay

1. The complete repetition of a game or MATCH that for some reason was not deemed to be official. Replays are extremely rare but may occur because of refereeing error or other incident whose consequences cannot be corrected. For example, if a spectator INTERFERES with the balls in such a way that they cannot be REPLACED, the game is replayed. 1992 OR 50. See also CURFEW, NONPLAYER INTERFERENCE, REFEREE. 2. See INSTANT REPLAY.

rerack

The replacement of the object balls in the RACK after a BREAKING VIOLATION or certain fouls by the STRIKER.

respot

= SPOT, def. 1. To replace a ball on the spot it originally occupied, or to place a pocketed ball on a designated spot. The term appeared in a flyer entitled "Rules for Base-Ball Pocket-Billiards," issued by Brunswick in 1912. See also SPOTTING.

rest

1. (Brit. games) = MECHANICAL BRIDGE. 1866 Crawley 10, 1974 KTG 16. Sometimes known as a CUE REST. See also CROSS REST, CUSHION REST, EXTENDED SPIDER, HIGH ARCH REST, LONG REST, REST HEAD, SPAN REST, SPIDER, SWAN NECK. Many players experience great difficulty in manipulating the rest. 1896 Broadfoot attributes this to the difference in friction presented by the rest and the human hand. For a device that increases the effective length of the rest, see EXTENSION. 2. (obs.) A FINGER BRIDGE. 1850 Phelan 17.

rest head

The part of a MECHANICAL BRIDGE on which the cue stick rests. 1978 BSCC 30. Also BRIDGE HEAD. Rest heads are usually made of metal, but this has the disadvantage that small burrs can damage the shaft of the cue as it travels back and forth. The striker must take care not to allow the rest head to touch a ball, or a PLAYER RESPONSIBILITY FOUL will result. In Snooker, if the rest head falls off accidentally and contacts a ball, there is no penalty. 1988 WPBSA. See also HEAD.

resté dedans

(Balkline, Fr., pr. ruh-STAY duh-DAHN) International referee's CALL when the object balls were IN BALK and neither was driven out of the balk space on the previous stroke. Therefore, at least one ball must be driven out by the stroker on the ensuing shot. Literal French meaning: "stayed in." 1981 Rottie 136. See also ÁCHEVAL, DEDANS, ENTRÉ, RENTRÉ.

restore

To replace the balls in the position they occupied prior to certain types of FOULS so the INCOMING PLAYER is not disadvantaged by his opponent's violation of the rules. 1988 PBA 22. In the event that the balls cannot be replaced for some reason, a REPLAY of the game may be ordered by the referee. See also INTERFERENCE, REPLACEMENT.

restricted space

(usually Bill.) = INTERDICTED AREA. A region marked on the cloth within which only a limited number of consecutive caroms may be made or points scored. See ANCHOR, BALK, CROTCH.

return

1. (Pocket Bill.) = BALL RETURN, GULLY. 2. (obs.) = DRAW. 1836 Tillotson 34.

return safety

(Pocket Bill.) A SAFETY played from the HEAD of the table in which the cue ball is made to contact a ball at the FOOT end and return to the head, preferably FROZEN to the head cushion. It is frequently played as a BANK SHOT. 1948 Mosconi 72. The goal of the shot is to leave the opponent in a position where he not only has no shot but also has difficulty answering with a safety of his own.

reverse

= REVERSE ENGLISH. Cf. NATURAL.

Reverse Billiards

(game) = BACKWARDS POOL, BILLIARD POOL, CAROM POOL, CHINESE POOL, CONTRA POOL, INDIAN POOL, IRISH POOL, KISS POOL, LOOP. 1992 Billing 42. Cf. CUE BALL POOL.

reverse English

1. Spin causing the cue ball to come off a cushion at a more obtuse angle and at a slower speed than a ball hit without ENGLISH. 1873 NYT (Jun 26) 5:3, 1881 MB 119, 1941 Hoppe 75, 1992 OR 13. Spin that tends to make a ball move in a direction contrary to its natural motion. The opposite of NATURAL ENGLISH. If a ball strikes a cushion at an angle between zero and 90 degrees (measured from a direction to the left of the contact point), then left English is reverse English. Also known as CHECK SIDE, COUNTER, HOLD-UP, OPPOSING SIDE, or WRONG-WAY ENGLISH. An anonymous 1846 French treatise contains diagrams showing extreme applications of reverse English but does not use the term. The phrase "reverse side" appears in 1862 Crawley 47. Cf. RUNNING ENGLISH.

2. (rare) DRAW, that is, English that causes the cue ball to "reverse" its direction after contacting an object ball. 1976 WSD 351.

reverse plant

(Snooker) A PLANT in which the first object ball is the one that enters the pocket. A shot in which the object ball caroms off a ball to which it is FROZEN. 1954 Davis 70. But note that this is called just a "plant" by most authorities. In American parlance, a KISS SHOT.

reverse system

(Three-Cushions) A DIAMOND SYSTEM used to predict the path taken by a cue ball that is shot into a cushion with REVERSE ENGLISH.

194

Revolution Game

(game, obs.) = AMERICAN FOUR-BALL GAME or FOUR-BALL GAME. 1825 Hoyle, 1974 Hendricks 26. Said to derive its name from the large (revolutionary) changes of fortune that may occur during its play. 1845 Hoyle 231. The reason this is possible is that up to 13 points can be scored on a single shot. See THIRTEEN-SHOT.

ricochet cannon

(Eng. Bill.) A CANNON in which the cue ball contacts the same cushion several times in succession in reaching the second ball. 1924 Ogden 272, 1957 Holt 61. A JAR STROKE, SERPENTINE MASSÉ, SMASH-IN, SNAKE SHOT, or SQUIB.

ride

1. (colloq.) To "give the ball a ride" means to drive it hard, especially in NINE-BALL and other games in which a pocket need not be CALLED, in the hope that it will enter a pocket. 2. (usually Bill.) To roll on top of a cushion. The ball is then said to "ride the rail." This motion counts as only one CONTACT in games requiring one or more cushion hits, even if the ball should bounce several times on the same cushion consecutively. 1946 OR, 1992 OR 111.

right

= RIGHT ENGLISH. Cf. LEFT.

right English

SPIN applied by striking the cue ball to the right of center, causing it to rebound to the right after hitting a cushion. See ENGLISH. Also called RIGHT. Cf. LEFT ENGLISH.

right rail

The LONG RAIL to the player's right when viewed from the HEAD of the table. 1883 NYT (Apr 7) 1:5. Cf. LEFT RAIL.

ring

A decorative component of a cue stick, usually mounted at the JOINT or AFTERWRAP. The ring is concentric with the cue and creates the visual effect of a circle surrounding the BUTT. 1990 White 2-9. A ring that has become loose can cause an annoying rattle during the stroke.

ring game

Any method of play in which as many players are allowed as the participants determine, each player being able to leave the game whenever he so elects. 1985 BD (Feb) 52. Cf. OPEN GAME.

road player

A HUSTLER who makes a living (or attempts to) by traveling from one public room to another in different towns, relying on his anonymity to secure ACTION.

rock

(sl.) A BILLIARD BALL, usually the cue ball. 1988 Rossman 34, 1990 White G-5. Also STONE. See also MUD.

rocking cannon

(Eng. Bill.) A NURSERY CANNON in which the red ball is FROZEN to a cushion, the cue ball is a few inches away and opposite the RED, and the OBJECT WHITE is next to the cue ball. The cue ball is made to KISS gently off the frozen ball to make a fine contact on the SECOND OBJECT BALL, which remains stationary although it is slightly "rocked" by the contact. 1908c Cook, 1924 Ogden 272, 1957 Holt 93. In American terminology, the CHUCK NURSE. See also ANCHOR CANNON, SETTLING. William Cook Jr. made a break of 490 at this nurse in 1908. 1978 BSCC 93. Its use today would be restricted by the rule limiting CONSECUTIVE CANNONS.

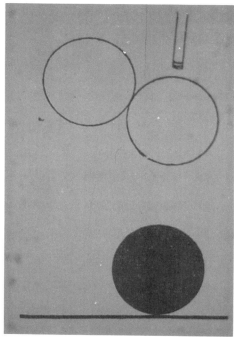

rocking cannon

roll

1. = TABLE ROLL. On seeing a ball deviate from its true path on a table that was not level, U.S. Three-Cushion champion Allen Gilbert said to the room proprietor in 1988, "I'd like coffee with that roll." See also DRIFT, LEVEL, LONG ROLL, SHORT ROLL. 2. Rotational motion of a ball about a horizontal axis, as opposed to either skidding motion or SPIN. Cf. SLIDE.

roll-up

(Snooker) An attempted SAFETY in which the cue ball slowly "rolls up" to and becomes FROZEN to an object ball that will not be ON for the INCOMING PLAYER. See CRAWL STROKE. Such a shot is not legal in U.S. pocket games because of the requirement that some ball contact a cushion after the cue ball contacts an object ball.

rollout

(Nine-Ball) A rule variation covering the situation in which the OUTGOING PLAYER has failed to hit the lowest-numbered ball on the table. The INCOMING PLAYER may compel his opponent to shoot again or may accept TABLE IN POSITION, whichever he deems more desirable. 1977 Fels 163. Because of this rule, a player who is unable to hit the BALL ON directly may "roll" the cue ball with his cue stick into a position leaving a difficult shot. In Snooker it is known as the PLAY AGAIN RULE. Cf. COMPULSORY STROKE, HIT THE BALL, ONE SHOT OUT, SHOOT OUT.

In professional Nine-Ball, the player who is shooting immediately after the break shot (the breaker, if he sinks a ball; otherwise, the opponent) may execute a rollout.

Rondo

(game, obs.) A gambling game in which balls are rolled by hand on a billiard table. A billiard version of bocce. Cf. FINGER BILLIARDS.

195

room

A BILLIARD ROOM, usually a public establishment. Famous rooms of the past include The Hub, Twentieth Century Parlors (Boston); Bensinger's (Chicago); Helm's (Cleveland); Detroit Recreation (Detroit); Kling & Allen's (Kansas City); Ames, Daly's Academy, Julian's (closed December 1992), McGirr's (New York); Plankington Arcade (Milwaukee); Allinger's (Philadelphia); McCourt-Ellis Billiards (Pittsburgh); Graney's, Palace Billiards (last managed by Tony Annigoni) (San Francisco); Peterson's (St. Louis). Also BILLIARD PARLOR or just PARLOR.

room high run

The longest HIGH RUN yet made by any player in a particular BILLIARD ROOM.

rosette

A decorative cover for the head of a RAIL BOLT. 1956 BSTE 15.

Rotation

1. (game) A SINGLE-RACK pocket billiard game in which the lowest-numbered ball must be contacted first by the cue ball and each ball pocketed is worth as many points

as its numerical value, as in FIFTEEN-BALL POOL. 1888 NYT (Jun 6) 3:5. Other variations are BOSTON, CHICAGO, and SIXTY-ONE. 1911 HRB 72, 1965 Fats 38. Since the sum of the numbers on the balls is 120, the first player to score 61 wins, since his opponent can have no further chance barring a SCRATCH. 1982 OR 65. The name of the game comes from the arrangement of the balls in the game of Chicago, in which the player had to strike at balls spotted around the table in counterclockwise order. The theory that "rotation" originally referred to the fact that the balls must be struck in numerical order lacks merit; in that case the game ought to be called "series" or "sequence." See also CALL-SHOT ROTATION, CRAZY POOL, LUCK ROTATION, ONE-PLAYER ROTATION, ROTATION BANKS, ROTATION EIGHT-BALL, TEN-BALL ROTATION.

The number of different possible initial racks in Rotation is 11! = 39,916,800.

2. The order of play in a game involving multiple players, sometimes determined by LOT. 1916 RGRG 7. "You're next in rotation."

3. SPIN applied to a ball.

Rotation Banks
(game) BANK POOL in which the balls must be pocketed in numerical order. 1987c OBG 34. A severe test even for experts.

Rotation Contra Pool
(game, obs.) CONTRA POOL in which the lowest-numbered ball on the table must be used as the cue ball. 1913 Burrowes 17.

Rotation Eight-Ball
(game) EIGHT-BALL in which each player must pocket his GROUP BALLS in numerical order. 1987c OBG 20. Cf. PLAYER'S EIGHT-BALL.

Rouge
(game) The game of RED BALL, from the French word for "red."

round
1. The preferred shape for a billiard ball. In this context, the use of the term "round" is technically incorrect, since balls are "spherical" rather than round. See also SHARP, TRUE. 2. A set of games in a tournament, usually played simultaneously, corresponding to levels of the DRAW. Sometimes a synonym of FLIGHT.

round-robin
A TOURNAMENT format in which each player plays against each other player at least once. 1916 BM (Jan) 20,

1941 Hoppe 76, 1982 OR 21. In obsolete British usage, an AMERICAN HANDICAP.

A round-robin is deemed the fairest tournament arrangement because no player has any advantage of the DRAW or SEEDING and a player does not risk being eliminated during a single bad game. Drawbacks are that the competition is lengthy and late-round matches may have no effect on the outcome, reducing audience appeal. For a time, the World Three-Cushion and 14.1 Continuous championships were DOUBLE ROUND-ROBIN tournaments, each player facing every other player *twice*. Cf. SINGLE ELIMINATION.

A "round-robin" was originally a document subscribed by mutineers in a circular fashion so that it could not be determined who had signed first, thus disguising the identity of the ringleader. It was used in this sense as early as 1731, but it is unclear how it came to apply to tournaments.

The first U.S. professional billiard tournament was in round-robin format, involving five players in New York in October, 1860. Dudley Kavanagh was the winner, earning acclamation as the first American champion at Four-Ball Billiards. 1891 MB 371.

rover
1. The pink ball in RUSSIAN POOL, spotted on the PYRAMID SPOT and with which WINNING HAZARDS and LOSING HAZARDS may be made in any pocket, scoring six points. 1924 Smith 93, 1954 KTG 36. 2. The black ball in BLACK POOL, which the striker may POT after sinking a RED. 1985 Arnold 207.

royal
A NATURAL or RANCHE in the FIVE-PIN GAME, MUG'S POOL, and ITALIAN SKITTLE POOL. 1869 Roberts 247.

royal discount
(obs.) A method of giving a HANDICAP, in which the superior player must make all the points for game in a single turn at the table. See DISCOUNT. A game at royal discount is equivalent to playing to GAME TOTAL at NO COUNT. Thus a match to 100 at royal discount is the same as playing to 100 at 100 or no count. Also GO-BACK GAME.

rub nurse
(Bill.) A nurse at CUSHION CAROMS in which the cue ball is BANKED off a cushion to graze the two object balls, which move only a fraction of an inch. 1913 Daly 162, 1979 Sullivan 188. Hints of its beginnings appear in 1881 NYT (Nov 15) 5:3, but its invention is later credited to Eugene Carter. 1898 Thatcher 239. (Carter won the

Three-Cushion title in 1900.) Jacob Schaefer Sr. and Frank Ives were prominent exponents.

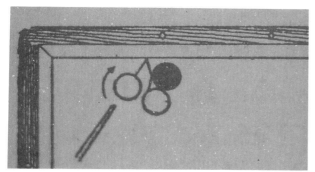

rub nurse

rub the wire

To cheat by covertly moving the wooden MARKERS on the SCORE STRING. See WIRE. 1989 Jacobs PC.

rubber

1. Material of which cushions are made. The use of rubber for this purpose began in 1835 and became practical after the discovery of vulcanization in 1839. Also GUM. See CUSHION PROFILE, NOSE. 2. Figuratively, a CUSHION. 3. (sl.) A piece of tubing used in place of a WRAP to provide the player with a firmer grip on the cue; a CONDOM.

Rudolphe's nurse

(Bill., obs.) A STATIONARY NURSE in which both object balls are touching and FROZEN to a cushion. The cue ball is made to graze both balls without disturbing their position. 1913 Daly 10. An ancestor of the PENDULUM CANNON, it is named for A. P. Rudolphe, the French player who was U.S. Three-Ball champion in 1874 and 1875. In BALKLINE, the ANCHOR SPACES prevent this nurse. *See illustration in next column.*

rule of doubt

The principle that the STRIKER is not given the benefit of the doubt in deciding whether a requirement for a shot has been complied with. See DOUBT. Cf. PRESUMPTION OF INNOCENCE.

rules

1. Regulations governing the play of the game. Sets of rules were printed in very early times, certainly by the seventeenth century, and were often displayed on the walls of billiard rooms in the form of large charts. 1674 Cotton lists 16 "orders to be observed by such who will play at Billiards," which includes many modern rules such as the requirement that at least one of the player's

Rudolphe's nurse

feet must touch the floor and prohibitions against hitting the cue ball twice, playing with the wrong ball, and shooting while a ball is in motion.

The later history of rules portrays a battle to keep the game lively and interesting. Only a small number of FOULS have been added since 1674; the majority of new rules have dealt with SAFETY PLAY and schemes for limiting long RUNS and outlawing monotonous tactics such as the PUSH SHOT and QUILL STROKE. For a current listing of rules of major billiard games, see 1992 OR.

Rules often vary based on local custom, particularly in non-tournament games. See HOUSE RULE.

2. Lines drawn on the table for BALKLINE play, usually with white tailor's chalk (1881) or pencil (1883).

run

1. A series of consecutive points scored, ending with a MISS, FOUL, or completion of the game. 1857 Phelan 153, 1858 NYT (Jan 5) 2:3, 1881 MB 26, 1992 OR 15. In English games, a BREAK. Also used as a verb, as in "He ran 73 balls." See also CLUSTER, HIGH RUN, STRING, UNFINISHED.

A RUN may extend over multiple BLOCKS, provided that the position of the balls is marked during the intermissions. A run does not extend over multiple GAMES, however. Jake Schaefer Jr. once ran out four consecutive 200-point games at 18.2 Balkline, but his sequence of 800 points without a miss did not count as a record because it was not made in a single run.

2. RUNNING ENGLISH, as in the expression, "Hit it with run."

3. To roll, as said of a ball. 1850 OED. "It's running."

4. A unit of score in BASEBALL POCKET BILLIARDS. 1925 RGRG 49, 1946 OR 51.

197

run a coup

(Eng. Bill.) To SCRATCH the cue ball in a pocket after missing the object ball and hitting no balls at all. 1976 WSD 363. See COUP. The penalty for a coup is a deduction of three points.

run off

(Brit. games) A PLANT or KISS SHOT; one in which a ball contacts another before entering a pocket. 1981 Quinn 70.

run out

To complete the game from the current position in a single INNING without missing, that is, in one RUN. 1875 NYT (Nov 20) 2:5. See also CLEAN UP, GET OUT, OFF THE BALLS, OUT, RUNOUT, UNFINISHED.

run stick

(Nine-Ball, colloq.) A CUE STICK used for normal play, as opposed to a BREAK STICK. Also PLAYING CUE.

run-through

(Eng. Bill.) = FOLLOW SHOT. So called because the cue ball seems to "run through" the position formerly occupied by the cue ball. 1873 Bennett 231, 1895 Buchanan 76, 1954 KTG 16.

198

running English

Spin that tends to favor a ball's progress, either right or left as the direction of the shot dictates. 1928 Barry 3, 1941 Hoppe 76. When the ball strikes a cushion or another ball with running English, it rebounds at a greater angle than it would if played without ENGLISH. 1976 WSD 364, 1992 OR 14. Also known as NATURAL, NATURAL ENGLISH, or RUN. In British usage, RUNNING SIDE. Cf. REVERSE ENGLISH.

If a ball strikes the cushion at an angle between zero and 90 degrees (measured from a direction to the left of the contact point as seen from the line of the approaching ball), then running English is right English. If two long or two short rails are hit consecutively, running English can effectively change to REVERSE ENGLISH and vice versa, although the direction of the ball's spin remains the same.

running nurse

(Bill.) Any NURSE in which the resting position of the balls changes as the nurse is executed, as opposed to a STATIONARY NURSE, in which the balls are not moved or are made to return to the same position after the stroke. 1913 Daly 11. See, for example, BALKLINE NURSE, LINE NURSE, RAIL NURSE, RUB NURSE. It is generally easier to maintain a running nurse because the motion of the balls on every shot permits the player to make small positional corrections that would be impossible in a stationary nurse.

running side

(Brit. games) = RUNNING ENGLISH. Spin that tends to widen the angle at which a ball rebounds when hit obliquely into a cushion. 1924 Aiken 31. Cf. CHECK SIDE.

runout

(Brit. games) The act of RUNNING OUT, that is, completing the game in a single turn at the table from the current position. The first runout in a public game occurred on August 4, 1869, when Melvin Foster ran 1000 in the first inning to beat George Stone 1000 to 19 at AMERICAN FOUR-BALL BILLIARDS. 1912 MB 227. In British usage, a BUSTAWAY.

Russian Bagatelle

(Bagatelle game, obs.) Played on a special BAGATELLE board measuring 4'6" × 2'4" with many brass obstacle pins each 1½ inches high, six arches and CUPS beneath them, a bell that rings when struck by a ball, and slots into which balls that fail to enter any cup are collected. 1878 Crawley 154, 1884 Bohn 613. Also known as COCKAMAROO.

Russian Billiards

(game, obs.) A pocket billiard game played on an English Billiards table in which the score for a successful shot varies between one and nine points and a player must score exactly 100 points to win or BURST if he exceeds that total. Played with a blue (worth 9), brown (7), green (5), and yellow (3), which are spotted in a special arrangement. Each ball must be potted in a particular pocket in order to score. 1924 Ogden diag. 119. It is similar in concept to the RUSSIAN GAME in that holing a ball in other than one of its allowed pocket results in a penalty. The game enjoyed a surge in popularity in New York in 1916, according to 1916 NYT (Sep 1) 11:6. Sometimes it is played in other variations with a red and a pink added. When the pink is used, it is known as a ROVER since it may be holed in any pocket.

Russian Carambole

(game, obs.) A carom game with WINNING HAZARDS in which the INCOMING PLAYER with BALL IN HAND may place his cue ball anywhere on the table. If the striker holes his own ball, he loses as many points as he would otherwise have scored on the stroke. 1775 Annals 112, 1807 White 55. It was one of the most popular billiard games in England in 1773. 1974 Hendricks 40.

Russian Game, Russian Pool

(game) A pocket and carom game played with five balls, usually the white, yellow, green, blue and black. Each ball may be holed only in certain pockets or a penalty results. 1837 Walker 81, 1850 Phelan 37, 1911 HRB 122, 1974 KTG 35. Scores and forfeits range up to nine points. The origin of the name of this game is unknown, but it is unlikely that it was imported from Russia. It is also called INDIAN POOL, SLOSH, or TOAD-IN-THE-HOLE Cf. CARLINE, RUSSIAN BILLIARDS, RUSSIAN CARAMBOLE.

safe

1. A SAFETY. 1807 White 36. To "play safe" means to play a safety or to take a shot involving little risk. See also DUCK, ONE AND SAFE. 2. Said of an incoming player who has no shot or of a POSITION that affords no offensive possibilities. 1807 White 155, 1844 Mardon 24. "You left him safe."

safe eight

(Nine-Ball) = EIGHT SAFE. 1988 BD (Feb) 66.

safety

1. A defensive shot in which a player sacrifices an opportunity to score in order to leave the opponent in a difficult POSITION. 1844 Mardon pl. 25, 1873 Bennett 386, 1941 Hoppe 76, 1992 OR 14. See also SAFETY PLAY.

Safeties tend to slow the game and reduce scoring, which diminishes spectator satisfaction. As a result, a large body of rules has been developed in various games for restricting safety play. In Pocket Billiards, a safety is legal only if the cue ball strikes an object ball and then some ball is driven to a cushion or an object ball is pocketed. Failure to accomplish this results in a FOUL. In 14.1 Continuous, if the object ball lies within one ball's width of a cushion, only two consecutive safeties may be played off that ball. 1992 OR 56. To prevent long sequences of illegal safety attempts, an additional penalty is imposed for CONSECUTIVE FOULS. These rules ensure that the position of the balls changes regularly, preventing a lengthy sequence of defensive moves in which the cue ball is merely touched. In Three-Cushions, a distinction is made between intentional safeties

and missed shots in which the STRIKER made a legitimate attempt to score.

In Pocket Billiards, a player may call a safety and then pocket a ball. The player's INNING ends in spite of the fact that a ball was pocketed and the ball is SPOTTED for the opponent. For a period in 1936, safeties were eliminated completely from title pocket billiard play. See CENTER STRING. They have also been banned from Three-Cushions at various times.

See also DELIBERATE SAFETY, DODGE, DOUBLE BAULK, DUCK, FINESSE, GIVE A MISS, INTENTIONAL MISS, INTENTIONAL SAFETY, MISS IN BAULK, OIL (obs.), PLAY SAFE, RETURN SAFETY, ROLL-UP, SHOOT THROUGH, SHOT TO NOTHING, Z STROKE, and the compounds below.

2. A CALL by the REFEREE announcing a safety attempt by the striker. 1946 OR 49. The result of the player's stroke is a call of either SAFETY ALLOWED or SAFETY NOT ALLOWED.

safety allowed

A CALL by the REFEREE following a SAFETY attempt by a player. "Safety allowed" means that the attempt was successful and the player's INNING has ended without a penalty. "Safety not allowed" means that the legal conditions for a proper safety were not met and the stroke is a FOUL.

safety break

(Pocket Bill.) A BREAK SHOT whose object is to leave the opponent in a difficult POSITION rather than to score points. 1881 NYT (Feb 28) 2:2. The break shot now used in 14.1 CONTINUOUS to send two balls to cushions is illustrated in 1894 *NY Herald* (Mar 25) 7, which shows a maneuver from continuous pool. Cf. OPEN BREAK, OPENING BREAK. *See illustration on next page.*

safety miss

(Eng. Bill.) A MISS taken deliberately to effect a SAFETY. 1904 Mannock I 357. The cue ball is struck but no other ball is contacted. The opponent is then said to SCORE A MISS as a result of the striker's foul. This tactic is to no avail in SNOOKER, since the INCOMING PLAYER would be awarded a FREE BALL if he were snookered as a result of such a stroke. A "safe miss" in 1865 NYT (Mar 11) 2:1.

safety not allowed

See SAFETY ALLOWED.

safety play

That phase of the game concerned with DEFENSE; the sacrifice of a scoring potential in order to leave the opponent in poor POSITION. 1867 NYT (Jun 11) 1:7, 1881 MB 26, 1913 Daly 270. The playing of SAFETIES instead

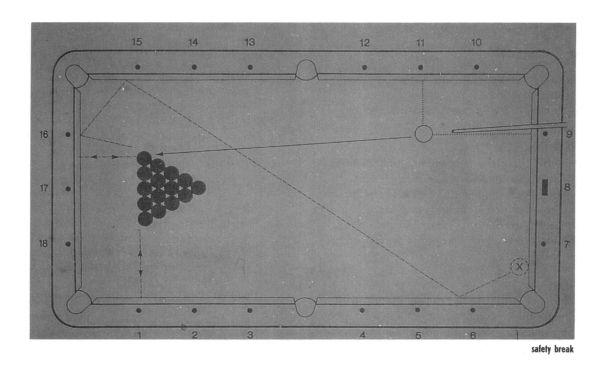

safety break

of shots intended to earn points. Safety play was well known at the time of 1807 White. He explains, for example, that in Billiards it is desirable to strike the red ball first in order not to leave one's cue ball next to the RED in case of a miss, or else the opponent will have an easy shot.

Safety play is common in Straight Pool because top professionals are capable of a RUNOUT if given an open shot. With the cost of a miss so high, players resort to safety frequently. A good play is to leave the opponent in a position from which he has no shot and cannot easily reply with another safety.

In Nine-Ball, safety play can become a powerful offensive weapon. If the opponent fails to contact the lowest-numbered ball on the table first, the incoming player is awarded BALL IN HAND. There is therefore great advantage to positioning the cue ball to prevent the opponent from hitting the required ball. See also SUCCESSIVE FOULS.

In Three-Cushions, there are a substantial number of rules of thumb to avoid leaving the opponent with an easy shot. Some are described in short phrases such as "easy up to the red, hard away from the white." (This is the opposite of the rule in 1807 White, which applies to ordinary carom billiards, not Three-Cushions.) The general idea is to leave the opponent's cue ball far from either object ball. For a summary, see 1978 Byrne 275.

sanction

A TOURNAMENT or other competition is "sanctioned" if it is authorized by a governing body that is satisfied that the event will be conducted in conformance with certain standards and will recognize the results officially. The sanctioning body may also guarantee that prize money will be paid regardless of the financial condition of the promoter or sponsor. See also WAIVER.

Sans Egal

(Bagatelle game, obs.) A French style of BAGATELLE for two players. One player uses four white balls, the other four reds. A black ball is used that counts for the player holing it. The players strike alternately, each time using another ball of his color. The opponent is credited with any ball of his color that is pocketed. The game may be played either for a fixed number of rounds or to 21 or 31 points. 1837 Walker 91, 1863 Phelan & Berger 95, 1884 Bohn 612.

Sausage Game

(game, obs.) A pocket billiard game played with 15 colored balls, of which 12 are placed in two rows. The object of the striker is to sink exactly two balls in each pocket. Each ball that is pocketed in a corner scores two points; each ball in the side pockets scores eight. Many variations exist, both as to scoring and the arrangement of the balls, including one in which the balls are lined up between the side pockets. 1850c White & Bohn 47, 1856 Crawley 106.

The name of the game is a translation of the German WURST-PARTIE, from *wurst*, meaning "sausage," referring to the appearance of the rows of balls at the start of the game, which resembles sausage links.

saver

(colloq.) An illicit agreement between two or more players in a TOURNAMENT to lower their collective risk by dividing their winnings in a certain ratio or by having the winner pay a portion of his proceeds to the loser. The effect of a saver is to reduce competitiveness, since a player will still receive money even if he loses, thereby "saving" him from being denied a share of the purse. In essence, it is an insurance policy in the form of a side bet in which a player wagers on himself to lose. Cf. APPEARANCE MONEY, DUMP.

Savile Snooker

(game, obs.) A version of SNOOKER played at the Savile and Garrick Clubs in London around the turn of the century. Its object is to POT the 15 REDS without touching any COLOURS. 1986 Trelford 16.

scatter shot

A shot whose effect is to separate the balls widely. In Billiards, one taken without any regard for GATHER. In Pocket Billiards, a shot that separates a RACK or CLUSTER. 1878 NYT (Jun 28) 5:1. See also BREAK SHOT, BURST, BUST, SPLIT SHOT.

Schaefer shot

(Three-Cushions) A particular type of BANK SHOT played with REVERSE ENGLISH. 1983 Malsert 121. Named for Jacob Schaefer Sr.

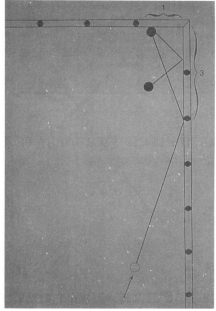

Schaefer shot

scoop shot

A JUMP SHOT made by dipping the cue tip under the cue ball to cause the ball to rise from the BED of the table. It is illegal in all cue games, even those in which jump shots are allowed, because of the erroneous belief that the shot works by lifting the cue ball with the FERRULE of the cue stick.

score

1. The total number of points or games won by the players. "What's the score?" To have points added to one's credit. 1807 White 48. "The shot scored three." See SCORING for the process of marking up points. Up to 1800, billiard games were very brief; they were usually played to 12 or 16 points, with some strokes gaining more than a single point. By 1870, the American Four-Ball Game was played to 100 points in casual games and to such totals as 1500 points in championship matches. Later, Balkline BLOCKS were played to between 400 and 600 points. Three-Cushion tournament games are normally 50 or 60 points, but may consist of several 15-point games. For devices used in keeping score, see SCORING.

The score of a game in progress is normally announced by the referee, but the manner of doing so differs in various games. In games in which runs of points are possible, such as 14.1 Continuous and Three-Cushions, the length of the current run is announced after each shot. At the end of an inning, the referee instructs the marker to add a specific number of points to the outgoing player's total by saying something like, "Score 68 for Ms. Mataya." No scoring occurs in Eight-Ball or Nine-Ball until the end of a rack. When a player nears GAME TOTAL, the referee announces, "playing for two," "playing for one," and "game" on successive shots.

In Snooker, when the incoming player steps to the table, the score is announced by stating his score first, then the word "playing," followed by the opponent's score. For example, "10 playing 33" means that the STRIKER has 10 points and the opponent 33.

2. (Bill.) A successful shot, a COUNT; also used as a verb. 1844 Mardon 94, 1873 Bennett 301. "She brought it around the table for the score." "He potted pink to score six." In the U.S., each successful shot normally counts for one point, except in unusual or obsolete contests such as the FOUR-BALL GAME. In Britain, it is common to have more than one point scored per stroke, *e.g.*, in ENGLISH BILLIARDS, at least two and at most ten points are awarded for a successful shot.

201

score a miss

(Eng. Bill.) To receive points because the opponent has committed a MISS, that is, failed to hit any object ball. See also GIVE A MISS.

score ball

(Bill.) The SECOND OBJECT BALL, contact with which will complete the CAROM and hence effect a SCORE. 1977 Gilbert 29. Also CAROM BALL.

score sheet

A document on which scoring details of a game or match are recorded, usually by an employee known as the scorekeeper, who generally has no role other than ensuring that the tally is accurate. The role of the score sheet in TOURNAMENTS is official. It must be signed by the players and the REFEREE. A losing player who refuses to sign a score sheet may be disqualified from the tournament. LINE SCORE.

score string

A WIRE on which BEADS or BUTTONS are strung to keep track of the score in billiard games. 1850 Phelan 19, 1977 Martin 218. According to Phelan, it should be at a height of 4½ feet above the table. Also called a MARKING STRING or sometimes just the STRING.

scoring

The rules and means by which points are tallied in billiard games. It would seem to be a simple matter to add up the points earned by each player, but the process is surprisingly complex. For games in which a MARKER is present, runs are announced and the details of recording the score are left to him so the problem is only one of rule interpretation. In private games, pencil and paper are rarely used, and the players must keep score with rudimentary marking devices.

The simplest score recorder is the MARKING STRING or SCORE STRING, which consists simply of two sets of beads on a wire. See also MARKING BOARD. It is usual to move the beads corresponding to the player's most recent run at once and keep them together, merging them with the developing total only when the player scores again. In this fashion, the prior run is visible and subject to verification.

A rail marker consists of numerical dials mounted in or atop a rail. The score is kept by manually moving the dials.

It is traditional to use a chalkboard to record Snooker scores because the range of points awarded for a shot varies from two to seven, and a mechanical device would be unwieldy. Chalkboards were also used in the early nineteenth century to record scores by means of tally marks. When a player suffered a penalty, his marks would be scratched out, which is believed to be the origin of the SCRATCH, meaning a loss of points.

Scoring in 14.1 Continuous in private games (without a referee) can be somewhat complicated when using rail markers instead of a score string. Because it is easy to lose track of how many points a player has made, scoring is logically divided into racks of 14 points and two scores are kept—a cumulative score and a rack score. The rack score is the number of points a player has made on the current rack. In general, the players' rack scores plus the number of balls remaining on the table must equal 15. When a player scratches without sinking a ball, a point is subtracted from his cumulative score. If he scratches but has a cumulative score of zero (for example, on the first rack), a ball must be spotted (to keep the rack total equal to 15 minus the number of balls on the table), and the player is said to OWE a ball. This means that at the end of the next inning in which he pockets a ball, one ball will be respotted to maintain the correct totals. At the end of a rack, which occurs after 14 balls have been pocketed, the rack totals are added to the cumulative scores and are then reset to zero. Totals that become negative are often kept by memory or on paper, as rail markers make no provision for a NEGATIVE SCORE.

In scoring forfeits, the rules usually provide that the winner is credited with having made GAME TOTAL and the forfeiting player receives no points. In tournaments in which ties are resolved based on average, this method causes a problem since the forfeited game cannot be counted and the winner has lost an opportunity to improve.

Billiard score sheets are relatively simple, no more complicated than in bowling. Provision is made for cumulative scores and inning-by-inning totals. The numerical list of the players' runs is called the LINE SCORE. In Nine-Ball, the number of balls pocketed does not determine the winner; the game is scored instead by recording certain critical events. See TOTAL PERFORMANCE AVERAGE.

Scotch doubles

MIXED DOUBLES in which the team members are allowed to confer for one 20-second time-out per game.

Scotch Pool

(game, obs.) A billiard board game similar to the HIGH-LOW-JACK GAME but played with a pigeon-hole board. Also called MAC'S SOLITAIRE. 1928 BR (Apr) 15.

scramble

1. A style of RAPID-FIRE TOURNAMENT in which players of differing skill are given different HANDICAPS and

charged an entry fee. The handicaps are of the RACE variety, for either games or points. That is, if a player with a 12 handicap plays against one with a 9, he must win 12 games before his opponent wins 9 in order to win the match. The players' handicaps may be adjusted based on the outcome. See also HANDICAP SWEEPSTAKES, an ancestor. 2. (colloq.) To make a difficult shot in a desperate effort to sustain a RUN. 1985 Marguglio 222. "He's really scrambling."

scratch

A shot contrary to the rules that results in loss of turn, with or without a penalty. 1976 WSD 373, 1992 OR 14. A FOUL. This meaning probably refers to the act of "scratching out" points from the chalkboard on which the score was kept. See also SCORING.

1. (Pocket Bill., Snooker) A foul stroke in which the cue ball enters a pocket. 1879 NYT (Mar 20) 2:3. See also GUTTER BALL, POCKET SCRATCH, WASTE.

2. A shot in which the cue ball fails to contact any object ball or (in Pocket Billiards) contacts an object ball but causes no ball subsequently to contact a cushion or enter a pocket. See also TABLE SCRATCH. The offense is defined in 1916 RGRG 51. A scratch has been a foul stroke since at least 1674 Cotton: "He that. . .hazards his own Ball . . . loseth one." See COUP. If the cue or object ball is FROZEN to a cushion, at least one of them must contact another cushion or the object ball must enter a pocket. This rule originated in FIFTEEN-BALL POOL in 1880 as a response to excessive SAFETY PLAY. The earlier rule permitted the cushion contact to precede any ball contact. 1880 NYT (Dec 27) 2:7. Originally in the U.S. the penalty was added to the opponent's score rather than subtracted from the offender's.

If a player in 14.1 CONTINUOUS scratches in three successive turns at the table, he suffers an additional penalty. See CONSECUTIVE FOULS.

3. (obs.) An unanticipated development as a result of a player's stroke. An unintended lucky shot, a FLUKE. 1850 Phelan 12, 1867 NYT (Dec 17) 8:1. Also called a CROW, GARBAGE SHOT, SLOP SHOT.

4. Said of a player who needs no HANDICAP. "A scratch player." 1899 Souv 16, 1925 BM (Jun), 1937 NBJ (Sep) 16.

Scratch Pool

(game) = THIRTY-ONE POOL. 1902 Burrowes 9.

screw

1. (Brit. games) = DRAW, a DRAW SHOT. 1836 Tillotson 16, 1862 Crawley 20. Screw was applied to the ball even before the invention of the cue tip, especially with a

beveled instrument called the JEFFERY. 1866 Crawley 38 instructs the reader to make "a peculiar and sudden drawback of the hand, accompanied by an indescribable turn of the wrist." But this is not necessary—better results can be obtained with a smooth stroke. Also called SCREW-BACK. Both terms refer to the backspin rotation applied to the cue ball in this stroke. See also the compounds below. 2. A threaded male portion of the JOINT of a cue stick. The screw may be part of either the BUTT or the SHAFT.

screw-back

(Brit. games) = DRAW, SCREW. 1844 OED, 1895 Buchanan 115, 1976 Charlton 12.

screw cannon

(Eng. Bill.) A CANNON performed with the use of SCREW. A DRAW SHOT. 1866 Crawley 125.

screw-on tip

A TIP for a cue stick that is fastened by a screw rather than with adhesive. The advantage of this method is that the tip can easily be replaced. A disadvantage is that such tips rarely hold securely. Cf. PUSH-ON TIP.

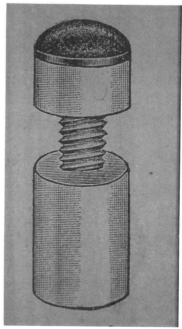

screw-on tip

Screw Your Buddy

(game, sl.) = CUT-THROAT, ELIMINATION.

seam

The boundary between two pieces of SLATE. Ideally, a seam should be as narrow as possible to avoid affecting the movement of any ball passing over it. This can be

203

achieved by machining the slates to produce sharp right angles at the edges. "Seaming" a pair of slates means filling in the seam with material to produce a smooth flat upper surface before covering the table with cloth. Seaming was formerly done with plaster of Paris or wax. Wax is not effective on heated tables, since it will melt away. Plaster of Paris tends to become pulverized after continued play. Modern technique employs epoxy resin or auto body compound. The best materials are those that do not shrink but expand slightly when setting. Any excess can then be sanded away. The term is also used as a verb, meaning to fill in the space between two pieces of slate. "Many mechanics still use paraffin to seam the slates."

second

An advisor accompanying a PLAYER to represent his interests in a competition. The second may not, however, give advice to his player while a game is in progress. The second formerly took charge of a player's cue ball during intervals in matches. 1925 Hoppe. Although it was formerly known as an UMPIRE, the position should not be confused with that of REFEREE, who is a tournament official. See also ABSENCE.

second-ball play

(Bill.) POSITION PLAY at STRAIGHT-RAIL and BALKLINE, in which the method of landing on the second object ball is important in obtaining POSITION. 1913 Daly 2. This phase of the game is crucial in executing NURSES as well as ordinary GATHER SHOTS.

second object ball

(Bill.) The second OBJECT BALL contacted by the cue ball in completing a CAROM. 1872 NYT (Sep 4) 5:5, 1941 Hoppe 76. The CAROM BALL. Cf. FIRST OBJECT BALL.

section

(obs.) = BLOCK.

see

To have a direct shot at. 1807 White 169. "Can you see the five?" Being unable to see a ball is not the same as being SNOOKERED. A ball can be seen if any portion of it can be struck. A snooker occurs if any part *cannot* be struck. See OBSTRUCTION.

seeding

Prior determination of rankings or pairings of players in a TOURNAMENT to heighten competition and, therefore, spectator interest. See BYE, DRAW. A negative side effect of seeding is that players having low rankings are paired against top players in early rounds and thus have little chance to win. A benefit is the higher probability that the final match will involve the two best players. Seeding in a round-robin tournament consists of excusing the seeded players from one or more preliminary rounds.

sell-out

(colloq.) A missed shot that leaves the opponent with a good scoring opportunity. 1978 Byrne 278. Avoiding sell-outs is one of the objectives of SAFETY PLAY.

Selling Pool

(game, obs.) = EVERLASTING POOL, PERPETUAL POOL. 1896 Broadfoot 429.

Semi-Billiards

(Bagatelle game) = BAGATELLE. This somewhat denigrating term reminds us that Bagatelle was never taken seriously as a billiard game.

semicircle

= D, BAULK CIRCLE, BAULK SEMICIRCLE, HALF-CIRCLE or STRIKING RING. In ENGLISH BILLIARDS it is the area from which a player having BALL IN HAND must put it into play. 1864 AH 419. Its radius has varied from 10 to 11½ inches and currently stands at 292 millimeters on a METRIC TABLE, almost exactly 11½ inches. In FRENCH CAROMS, its radius is six inches and it defines the region from which the striker plays a BREAK SHOT.

Sentinel Pool

(game, obs.) A game similar to PIN POOL, played with two object balls and four PINS. Pocketing a ball is worth one point, a carom two. One point is scored for each pin knocked over after an object ball has been struck. The object is to score 31 points exactly, with a BURST if that total is exceeded. 1902 Burrowes 8.

série Américaine

(Bill., Fr., pr. SAY-ree ah-MAY-ree-ken) The running version of the RAIL NURSE, which was developed by American carom players. The term is from the French, meaning literally the AMERICAN SERIES. 1889 Vignaux.

serious foul

(Nine-Ball) A FOUL that is penalized by LOSS OF GAME, normally an INTENTIONAL FOUL. 1988 PBA 20. Cf. STANDARD FOUL.

serpentine massé

A MASSÉ shot in which the cue ball repeatedly returns to the same cushion because of extreme English. See also JAR STROKE, RICOCHET CANNON, SNAKE SHOT.

session

A MATCH consisting of a series of games between two players, from which a winner is determined. For example, a match of RACE to nine may involve from nine to 17 games, the collection of which is a session. 1985 Marguglio 222. See also AHEAD SESSION.

set

1. (Brit. games) A WINNING HAZARD in which the object ball caroms off another on its way to the pocket. 1954 KTG 34. The term is frequently confused with a PLANT, and sources distinguish them in different ways. In 1924 Smith 86, "set" and "plant" are synonyms. In 1907 Levi 321, 1954 Davis 68 and 1957 Holt 178, a "set" is a shot in which the object ball struck is not the one pocketed, or, in American parlance, a COMBINATION. 1975a Lowe 94 and 1984 Williams 49 use "set" to refer to a "plant" in which the balls are FROZEN. By contrast, 1981 Quinn 69 says that a "set" is a "plant" with the balls *not* frozen. 1938 Clifford 32 explains that "set" is used in the North of England, while "plant" is employed elsewhere. Confusing? See also HIDDEN SET. 2. A collection of billiard balls matched by weight, size, and possibly color. 3. A sequence of games needed to win a match, as in tennis. 1982 OR 21, 1983 BD (Nov) 24. In a RACE match of Nine-Ball, the games played to determine the winner constitute a set. The format in international Three-Cushion matches is frequently a set of three 15-point games. 4. To arrange, as in SET THE BALLS, SET THE TABLE.

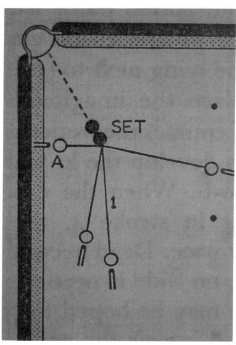

set

set-order game

(pocket games) A game in which balls must be contacted in a prescribed order, such as Nine-Ball, Rotation, Seven-Ball, Six-Ball and Ten-Ball. Cf. CALL-SHOT GAME. The order restriction is severe enough that shots usually need not be called. Therefore, only very specialized set-order games, such as Call-Shot Rotation, are also call-shot. See also PATTERN PLAY.

set the balls

Placing the balls for the commencement of the game. 1893 HRB 114. A particular form of SPOTTING. See also SET THE TABLE.

set the table

To place the balls in the formal position required for the opening shot. Also SET THE BALLS.

set up

1. To obtain POSITION for a shot. "He set up the break nicely." 2. To place the balls in a certain way, especially for a TRICK SHOT. 3. To assemble a billiard table and bring it into playing condition. 4. To assume one's STANCE at the table in preparation for a shot. 1982 BD (Sep/Oct).

set-up

1. An easy shot, a DUCK. 1873 NYT (Jul 1) 5:1, 1881 MB 26, 1974 Lindrum 140. For a time, the plural was "sets-up." Also known as a CHERRY, CRIPPLE, HANGER, MINNIE, PUPPY, or SITTER. 2. A situation in which a SUCKER is induced to make imprudent bets or is the victim of a DUMP or collusion in a THREE-HANDED GAME.

settling

Movement of an object ball that occurs when the cue ball and object ball are FROZEN and the cue ball is shot away from the object ball without touching it in the process. The object ball may "settle" into a dimple in the cloth that has been created by its own weight. See also PLAY AWAY. Even though the object ball may move, no foul occurs if there has been no impetus from the player's stroke. 1881 NYT (Apr 15) 8:3. (This was not always so; see 1807 White 69.) The success of certain NURSES such as the CHUCK NURSE and ROCKING CANNON depends on the phenomenon of settling.

Settling was the cause of a dispute in a 1925 challenge match for the 18.2 BALKLINE title between Jake Schaefer Jr. and Edouard Horemans. Schaefer was frozen to the red ball and attempted a shot so incredible that he explained it to the referee in advance. Shooting a MASSÉ away from the red, he sent the cue ball to the cushion, hit the white, and caromed back to the red to complete

205

the COUNT. It was undisputed that the red ball moved as Schaefer shot away from it. The referee disallowed the point. Schaefer continued the match under protest, agreeing to continue only if he could be assured of a return match within 30 days, then lost in a heartbreaking finish, 1500 to 1495.

Seven-Ball

(game) A ROTATION game with rules similar to NINE-BALL except that only seven balls are used. They are RACKED in the shape of a solid hexagon, with the seven ball in the center. The one ball is at the APEX; the two through six are placed in clockwise order surrounding the seven. After the OPENING BREAK, the opponent of the breaker selects the three pockets on one side of the table and must pocket the seven ball into one of the selected pockets. Likewise, the opening breaker must pocket the seven ball into one of the other three pockets. The lowest-numbered ball on the table must be contacted first by the cue ball. The first player to pocket the seven legally is the winner. A HANDICAP may be given by restricting or increasing the number of pockets into which a player may pocket the seven. 1981 BD (Sep/Oct) 24, 1992 OR 59.

The invention of the game is credited to William D. Clayton. 1985 Guinness. A version for television utilizes a special seven ball, developed by Charles J. Ursitti, that does not resemble the three ball and is thus distinguishable from the seven on the screen. (In a standard set of pocket billiard balls, the three and seven are colored with similar shades of red and are nearly indistinguishable on television.)

seven-shot, seven-stroke

(Eng. Bill., American Four-Ball Bill.) A shot in which seven points are scored. In English Billiards, this may be done by (1) hitting the white, POTTING it, making a CANNON, and potting the RED; or (2) making a cannon and holing a WHITE and a red; or (3) hitting the white and potting all the balls without making a cannon. 1830 Mingaud 14, 1890 HRB 110. In the American Four-Ball Game, this is done by caroming on red and white and pocketing both, or caroming on all the balls and pocketing white. 1850 Phelan 22.

Seven-Up Pool

(game, obs.) = HIGH-LOW-JACK GAME, BIG FOUR POOL. 1884 MB 299.

71.1 Balkline

(game) 71.2 BALKLINE with only ONE SHOT IN allowed. Cf. 71.2 BALKLINE.

71.2 Balkline

(game) A BALKLINE game in which the table is divided into six BALK SPACES by means of lines drawn approximately 71 centimeters from the cushions. (The UMB rules specify 71⅛ cm, exactly half the width of the playing surface. WBA 12.) Although 71 centimeters is the metric equivalent of 28 inches, 71.2 BALKLINE differs from 28.2 Balkline in that the latter game is ruled for four balk spaces. Neither game has a CENTER SPACE for unrestricted caroms.

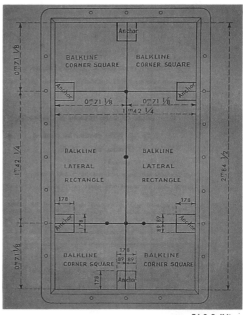

71.2 Balkline

71.2 was developed in France around 1910 by F. Ferrandin. 1974 Troffaes 125. Later, Roger Conti became its primary exponent. It was introduced in the U.S. in New York on November 29, 1937, when Willie Hoppe and Jake Schaefer Jr. played for the American championship. 1937 NYT (Nov 30) 32:1. Hoppe won, setting the world record high run of 248. The game was deemed interesting by writers and spectators but it never became popular opposite 14.1 CONTINUOUS and THREE-CUSHIONS, and competition ceased in the U.S. after only two years. The game is still played regularly in Europe, where it forms part of the PENTATHLON.

sewed up

(colloq.) = TIED UP. 1991 Raftis 39. To be grammatical, the phrase should be "sewn up."

sewer

(pocket games, sl.) = WASTEBASKET, an abnormally large or receptive pocket, *i.e.*, one into which SLOP will fall.

shaft

The thinner section of a cue stick, extending from the JOINT to the TIP, away from the BUTT end. The shaft is generally fashioned from the center of an ash or maple log. 1967 Polsky 14, 1992 OR 14. It is a debated point among players whether a stiff or a flexible shaft is preferable. See SPINE, STIFFNESS.

The shaft of the cue was not originally so named; at 1839 Kentfield 6 it is the "small end," in 1866 Crawley the "other part." 1896 Broadfoot 93 refers to "what one may call the shaft of the cue," which suggests that the term was not yet in common use.

shake ball

One of the miniature numbered balls or PILLS used in PILL GAMES. The balls are placed in the SHAKE BOTTLE to be drawn by LOT. 1908 Brunswick 85.

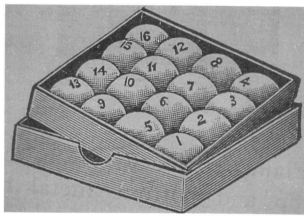

shake ball

shake bottle

A bottle used for holding PEAS, PILLS or SHAKE BALLS for KELLY POOL or PILL POOL. The pills are mixed by shaking the bottle, hence its name. 1974 ITP 30. The bottle may itself be a target in games such as BOTTLE POOL. 1976 WSD 383. *See illustration in next column.*

shape

(colloq.) = POSITION. 1875 NYT (Nov 16) 8:3, 1978 Byrne 80, 1979 Grissim 254. "He's got good shape." Also AFTER-POSITION, LEAVE, LIE. Cf. LAYOUT, PATTERN.

shark

A HUSTLER or SHARPER. A predatory player or swindler. An adept but undesirable billiard player. 1713 OED, 1973 Mizerak 83. See also POOL SHARK, SHARPER.

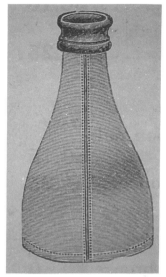

shake bottle

sharking

1. = HUSTLING. 2. Creating distractions for the opponent. 1977 Fels, 1989 Koehler 260. An infamous example of sharking occurred in the playoff game between Ralph Greenleaf and Erwin Rudolph for the 1929 World Pocket Billiard Championship in Detroit. Greenleaf, returning to the playing area while his opponent was shooting, jumped over the railing just as Rudolph was about to strike a ball. Distracted, Rudolph missed, scattering the balls. Greenleaf went on to win the game and title, but his tactic provoked much adverse comment in the press. 1930 BM (Jan) 16. Some other sharking techniques are pouring water, rattling ice, striking a match, waving one's handkerchief, and polishing the cue shaft as the opponent is shooting. 1937 NBJ (Sep). See also BUSINESS, PSYCH, UNSPORTSMANLIKE CONDUCT.

sharp

1. (obs.) = SHARPER. 1877 NYT (Jan 4) 5:3, 1881 MB 22. A term for a HUSTLER, SHARK or BLACKLEG (obs.), one who engages in "sharp" practices. It is used in a famous billiard quotation from the operetta *The Mikado*, written by William S. Gilbert in 1884:

The billiard sharp whom anyone catches
His doom's extremely hard.
He's made to dwell in a dungeon cell
On a spot that's always barred.
There he plays extravagant matches
In fitless finger-stalls.
With a cloth untrue and a twisted cue,
And elliptical billiard balls.

207

sharp (A Flat Between Two Sharps, Rowlandson, 1803)

For a full technical understanding of this quotation, see also BARRED, SPOT-BARRED GAME and UNTRUE. A "finger-stall" is a kind of splint; "fitless" means ill-fitting. Playing billiards while wearing finger-stalls would be difficult even if they fit properly. In this case the punishment indeed fits the crime. In 1959 Tevis *The Hustler*, the method of dealing with a shark was to break his thumbs.

The victim of a sharp was known in England as a "flat" around 1800. 1857 Phelan 69. This term is reflected in the title of an 1803 etching by Thomas Rowlandson, "A Flat Between Two Sharps."

2. (colloq.) A billiard table is "sharp" if it runs SHORT, that is, balls rebound from the cushions at an angle closer to perpendicular than normal. Also CRISP.

sharper

(obs.) A term for a HUSTLER, one who lives by concealing his true skill at billiards in the hope of enticing players into wagering with him. A SHARP or BLACKLEG. In modern parlance, a SHARK.

The term was in use by 1681, at least in a non-billiard context. 1775 Annals 106 describes some hustling methods: "In proportion as they advance the betts, the sharper will lug out his play, and the stranger will be astonished to find, at his cost, the worst player in the

world at first, in the end turn out one of the best." 1807 White 2 warns, "Billiards being a game of skill, is peculiarly calculated to ensure success to the predatory designs of sharpers. No billiard room of any notoriety is free from men who are gamesters by profession, and who are constantly in waiting to catch the ignorant and unsuspecting. . . . Their grand object is to conceal their skill from their adversary, and to accommodate their play to his, in such a manner, as to appear to obtain the conquest more in consequence of good fortune than good play. . . . They generally suffer their adversary to gain some few games successively, and then propose to double the stake. . . . it is well for him indeed, if he escape being fleeced of all the ready money he may happen to have about him." 1869 Roberts contains a lengthy chapter detailing the activities of sharpers.

Shell Out

1. (game) A game similar to ENGLISH PYRAMIDS. On a WINNING HAZARD, the STRIKER receives a penny from each player. On a LOSING HAZARD, MISS, or COUP, he pays a penny to each player. 1866 Crawley 200, 1896 Broadfoot 407, 1927 Clifford 53. 2. (game, obs.) = BLACK POOL. 1889 Drayson 105. So called because the other players must "shell out" money to a striker who pots the black ball.

shield

1. A LEATHER covering the outside of a pocket. 1991 Conway 53. Cf. INSIDE LEATHER. 2. A metal emblem used as a weight in a CHALK HOLDER. 1908 Brunswick 67.

shift shot

(Bill.) A maneuver in Carom Billiards to work the balls closer to a corner while maintaining their relative orientation. 1913 Daly 262. The shot is used repetitively in preparation for a GATHER. *See illustration on next page.*

shim

A thin strip of wood inserted underneath the leg of a table for LEVELING.

ship, billiards aboard

Despite the obvious difficulty of maintaining a level table, billiards has been played aboard ship for over a century. Around 1900, it was common to outfit British warships with a billiard table for officers to use while in port. The liner *Great Eastern* and the cruiser H.M.S. *Renown* carried tables. 1909 *Scientific American* (Jul 10) 41 described a special mount that could keep the playing surface of a table level even while on the ocean, though it appears to have been only a partial success.

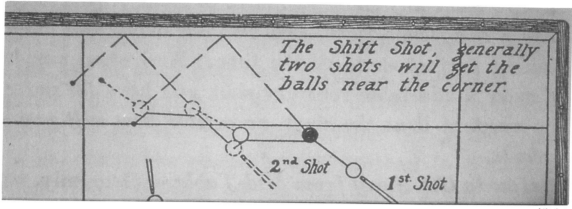

shift shot

The problem is that even very small motions of the table cause noticeable ROLL. See LEVEL. Modern cruise ships have used a table employing rounds disks instead of balls, which are much less sensitive to such deviations. Cf. DiscPool. See also AIRPLANE BILLIARDS.

shoot

1. To make a STROKE or SHOT. 2. To play billiards. "Let's shoot a game." 3. (obs.) Said of a spinning ball that moves with accelerated speed after contact with a cushion. 1873 Bennett 371.

shoot away

1. To strike the cue ball in a direction away from a ball to which it is FROZEN or near, in order to avoid a PUSH. See also MASSÉ DÉTACHÉ, PLAY AWAY, SETTLING. 2. To play boldly, risking a MISS, rather than to play safely and defensively. 1948 Mosconi 74.

shoot out

1. (Nine-Ball) Rule under which the INCOMING PLAYER after a foul has the choice of either shooting or requiring the OFFENDING PLAYER to shoot again. 1974 ITP 29. Cf. HIT THE BALL, ONE SHOT OUT, ROLLOUT, PLAY AGAIN RULE, PUSH-OUT. In professional NINE-BALL, a player may shoot out only after a legal BREAK SHOT. 2. (Three-Cushions) To attempt a shot instead of playing a SAFETY. 1942 Cochran 110. 3. (colloq.) A confrontation between two players.

shoot the lights out

(colloq.) To play very well, sink RACK after rack. 1977 Martin 218. During the 1988 U.S. National Three-Cushion championship, held at Abel's Club in New York, Harry Sims accidentally banged his cue stick against a brass light fixture above the table, making a loud noise. Frank Torres, a former U.S. champion, was standing nearby and immediately exclaimed, "He's really shooting the lights out!"

shoot through

1. To score inadvertently when attempting a SAFETY is known as "shooting through" one's safety. 1983 BD (Jan/Feb) 20. This is an error that usually results in the player leaving himself a difficult or impossible shot that was intended instead for his opponent. 2. = RUN-THROUGH. 1977 Martin 66.

shooter

1. = STRIKER, the PLAYER at the table, whose turn it is to shoot. 2. A player known for his shotmaking ability rather than for strategic or defensive skills. "He's a shooter." A SHOTMAKER. In Britain, POTTER.

shooter-stick

(Brit., colloq.) = CUE STICK. 1937 NBJ (Oct).

short

1. Said of a missed shot that could have been made if more RUNNING ENGLISH had been used off the last rail. See also SHORT ROLL, SHORT TABLE. Cf. LONG. 2. A shot in which a ball fails to travel far enough to effect a score is also said to be "short."

short-angle shot

(Three-Cushions) A NATURAL shot in which all three balls lie at the same end of the table and the cue ball CONTACTS a LONG RAIL, a SHORT RAIL, and the other long rail, in that order. The shot is "short" in the sense that the cue ball does not have to travel very far; hence the name refers not to sharpness of angle but to a short shot in the ANGLE GAME, another name for Three-Cushions. 1931 BM (Feb) 21. Thus the use of the hyphen in the name of this shot is erroneous but universal. Short-angle shots are as basic to the game as ground strokes are in tennis. See SHORT-ANGLE SYSTEM for a method of aiming them. The shot is known by the French as the "tricolore." *See illustration on next page.*

209

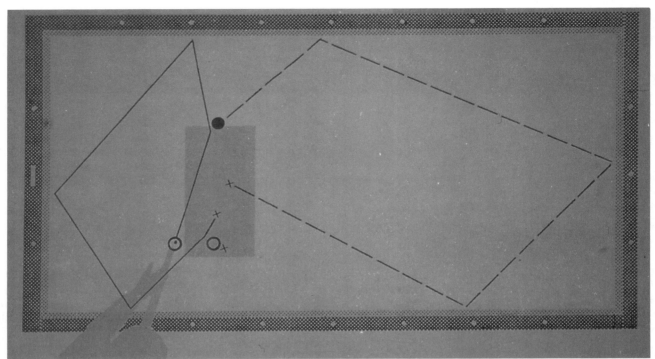

short-angle shot

short-angle system

(Three-Cushions) A DIAMOND SYSTEM for aiming SHORT-ANGLE SHOTS based on computing the point at which the cue ball must contact the second rail (that is, an END rail). 1977 Gilbert 26.

short bank

(Pocket Bill.) A CROSS-SIDE or CROSS-CORNER type of BANK SHOT in which the object ball traverses only the short dimension of the table and does not cross the CENTER STRING. 1894 *NY Herald* (Mar 25) 7:4. Cf. LONG BANK.

short bridge

1. A FINGER BRIDGE in which the player's BRIDGE HAND is close to the cue ball, permitting him more control over the shot. 1806 Phil 30, 1898 Thatcher 190. Players tend to FOLLOW THROUGH less with a short bridge. Cf. LONG BRIDGE. 2. A MECHANICAL BRIDGE whose shaft is approximately five feet in length. 1881 MB 25. Cf. LONG BRIDGE.

short game

(Bill.) NURSING; extremely close work; strokes that are confined to the SHORT TABLE. That aspect of play in which the balls are kept under control and are moved very little during each shot.

short jenny

(Eng. Bill.) A LOSING HAZARD into the MIDDLE POCKET when the object ball is near a side cushion. 1924 Aiken 32. See JENNY. Cf. LONG JENNY.

short rack

(pocket games) A RACK composed of fewer than 15 balls. 1982 OR 22. Examples of games using a short rack: BOWLLIARDS, NINE-BALL, SEVEN-BALL, SIX-BALL, TEN-BALL. Not all games employing fewer than 15 balls are considered short rack games; for example, Cowboy Pool uses only three object balls, which are not racked at all but placed on individual SPOTS. Cf. FULL RACK.

short rail

An END RAIL, so called because it is half the length of a SIDE RAIL. Cf. LONG RAIL.

short roll

Motion of a ball in which it bends toward a LONG RAIL while slowing down. See NAP, SHORT. 1978 Byrne 183. Cf. LONG ROLL.

Short Snooker

(game) Snooker played on tables six feet long or less, in which only six REDS are used instead of 15 to prevent crowding during play. Cf. SNOOKER PLUS.

short table

1. The area of the table between a STRING and the nearest END RAIL, constituting a rectangle of dimensions two diamonds by four. The area within a STRING. 1913 Daly 81, 1978 Byrne 195. Also called the END TABLE. In Billiards, it is desirable to keep all the balls within a short table, since one is then playing on a table essentially one-quarter of the size of the full playing surface. Cf. CENTER TABLE. See also SHORT GAME. 2. A table is said

to play "short" if more RUNNING ENGLISH than expected is needed to effect a score. The phrase does not imply anything about the dimensions of the playing surface; a table of regulation size may nevertheless be "short." Cf. LONG, def 1.

shortstop

A player who can be beaten only by the top players. 1970 Fensch 161. An excellent player, but one of the second rank. 1967 Polsky 10. A professional who just misses championship form, *i.e.* one who "stops short." The term was originated by J. Frawley, champion billiardist of Ohio, in 1887. 1898 Thatcher, 1899 Souv 18, 1925 BM (Mar) 22. Competitions were often designated as "shortstop tournaments" to denote the caliber of players participating.

shot

An attempt at a SCORE during which the cue ball is moved. More generally, any action by the player resulting in a FOUL or contact with a ball. 1850 Phelan 21, 1902 OED, 1976 WSD 387. In Britain, more commonly called a STROKE. See TAKE.

In professional Nine-Ball, a shot begins when the ball in contacted by the cue tip (while it is attached to the cue stick) and ends when the MOTION of all balls has ceased. 1992 OR 53. A foul is therefore not a shot unless the cue ball is struck by the tip.

There is a profusion of named shots: ANGLE SHOT, AROUND THE TABLE shot, BANANA SHOT, BANK SHOT, BEHIND-THE-BACK shot, BILLIARD SHOT, BLINDFOLDED SHOT, BOWERY shot, BREAK SHOT, CHALK SHOT, CIRCUS SHOT, CROSS-TABLE SHOT, CROSSOVER SHOT, CURVE SHOT, CUT SHOT, DEAD BALL shot, DOUBLE-CHANCE SHOT, DRAW SHOT, FANCY SHOT, FOLLOW SHOT, FOOTBALL SHOT, FORCING SHOT, FULL BALL shot, GAFF SHOT, GARBAGE SHOT, GATHER SHOT, HALF-BALL shot, JAW SHOT, JUMP SHOT, KEY SHOT, KICK SHOT, KILL SHOT, KISS-BACK SHOT, KISS SHOT, MASSÉ SHOT, NAIL SHOT, NIP shot, OPEN SHOT, OUT SHOT, POSITION shot, PROPOSITION SHOT, PUSH SHOT, RAIL SHOT, RAILROAD SHOT, SCATTER SHOT, SCHAEFER SHOT, SCOOP SHOT, SHIFT SHOT, SHORT-ANGLE SHOT, SHOT TO NOTHING, SKID SHOT, SKYROCKET SHOT, SLOP SHOT, SNAKE SHOT, SPIT SHOT, SPLIT SHOT, SPOT SHOT, SQUEEZE SHOT, STICK SHOT, STOP SHOT, STRAIGHT SHOT, STROKE SHOT, SYSTEM SHOT, THREE-CUSHION SHOT, THREE-ON-TWO SHOT, THROW SHOT, TIME SHOT, TRICK SHOT, TWO-CUSHION SHOT, TWO-WAY SHOT, UMBRELLA SHOT, WING SHOT.

The following are shots whose names do not contain the word "shot": ARTISTIC BILLIARDS, BREAK, BREAK-OFF, BREECHES STROKE, BRICOLE, BUBBLE, BUST, CANNON, CAROM, CASIN, COMBINATION, COUP, COUP FOUETTÉ, COUP SEC, CRAMP STROKE, CRAWL STROKE, CROSS, CRUSH, CUSHION CAROM, DIP, DOUBLE, DOUBLE BAULK, DOUBLE DOUBLE, DOUBLE-THE-CORNER, DOUBLE-THE-RAIL, DOUBLET, DRIVE, DROP CANNON, ESCAPE, FEATHER STROKE, FLUKE, FOUR-ON-TWO, HANGER, HAZARD, HIGH OBLIQUE STROKE, IN-OFF, JAR STROKE, JENNY, KISS-POT, KNOCK-OUT, LAG, LEAP, LONG BANK, LOSING HAZARD, MASSÉ, MISCUE, MISS, NATURAL, NURSE, NURSERY CANNON, OPENING BREAK, PERPENDICULAR STROKE, PIQUÉ, PLANT, POSTMAN'S KNOCK, PUSH-OUT, QUILL STROKE, RAIL-FIRST, RETURN SAFETY, RICOCHET CANNON, ROLL-UP, RUN-THROUGH, SAFETY, SAFETY MISS, SCRATCH, SCREW CANNON, SET, SNAP, SPOT HAZARD, SPREAD, SPREAD DRAW, SQUEEZE CANNON, SQUIB, STAB, STEEPLECHASE CANNON, STRAIGHT BACK, STUN, SWERVE, SWITCHBACK CANNON, TREBLE, UP-AND-DOWN, WINNING HAZARD, Z STROKE.

Some shots are named by the number of points scored by making them: TWO-SHOT, THREE-SHOT, FOUR-SHOT, FIVE-SHOT, SIX-SHOT, SEVEN-SHOT, EIGHT-SHOT, NINE-SHOT, TEN-SHOT, ELEVEN-SHOT, THIRTEEN-SHOT. See also TWELVE-SHOT.

shot clock

A clock used to count down time permitted for a shot when a TIME LIMIT is in effect, usually 45 seconds in professional Nine-Ball but as low as 10 seconds in WORLD TEAM BILLIARDS. Cf. GAME CLOCK.

shot diagram

A graphic representation of a shot, usually indicating the paths taken by the balls. The first extensive billiard diagrams in an English-language book appeared in 1807 White. 1827 Mingaud illustrates spinning balls by showing the paths as curled. Phelan's columns in *Leslie's Illustrated Weekly* beginning in 1861 marked an early regular appearance of shot diagrams in a newspaper. 1880 Garnier contains some of the first diagrams in color.

Shot diagrams are often confusing because it is not clear exactly what the significance of the path lines may be. Do they represent the motion of the center of the ball? If so, no path line should ever touch a cushion, since the ball's center can never do so. The modern trend, dating from the 1940s, is to take care that the lines represent only the path of a ball's center.

The English to be applied and the position of the cue when stroking are sometimes indicated by a separate legend affixed to the shot diagram. 1979 Ceulemans and 1979 Robin are meticulous in this regard.

shot to nothing

(Snooker) A shot to POT a RED and return behind the BAULK LINE. If it is made, the player is ON the COLOURS

211

and should easily be able to SNOOKER the opponent, who will be on reds, or can use a RECOVERY BALL to continue his BREAK. If he misses, a difficult shot is left for the opponent. 1954 KTG 30. A shot to nothing is a genuine attempt at a shot, which, if missed, leaves the opponent SAFE. 1976 Reardon 90. Also known as a BALL TO NOTHING. Cf. SAFETY, in which no attempt is made to COUNT.

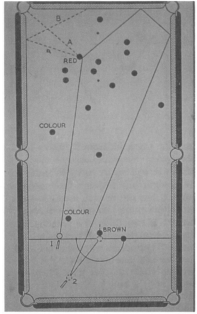

shot to nothing

shotmaker
= SHOOTER, one who excels at OFFENSE rather than POSITION PLAY or DEFENSE. 1989 Koehler 260.

shoulder
1. (Brit. games) The curved portion of the cushion surrounding a pocket opening on an English Billiards table. Also known as the ELBOW or BUMP. 1869 Roberts 173, 1904 Mannock I 321, 1911 Roberts 4. See also MOUTH, NAIL. 2. That part of the cue TIP lying between the BASE and the CROWN. 1965 Fats 77. *See illustration in next column.*

shove
1. = PUSH. 1858 NYT (Jan 5) 2:3, 1946 OR 9, 1964 Cottingham 43. 2. (obs.) A TRAILING shot made with the MACE. 1807 White.

shutout
A GAME in which one player or side scores no points or a MATCH in which one side wins no games. Also LOVE GAME, WHITEWASH. For the story of a famous shutout and the unusual circumstances that led to it, see LAG.

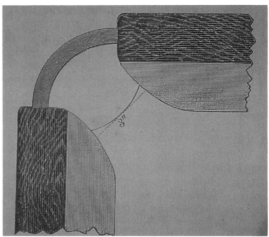

shoulder

There has never been a shutout in a Three-Cushion title game, but a number have occurred in Straight-Rail, Balkline, and Straight Pool competition.

side
1. Left or right SPIN, imparted to the ball by striking it to one side of its vertical axis. 1896 Broadfoot 191. The British term for ENGLISH. See also CHECK SIDE, COMMUNICATED SIDE, OPPOSING SIDE, POCKET SIDE, RUNNING SIDE, SIDE STROKE, SIDE-TWIST, TRANSMITTED SIDE, TWIST.

Shots requiring side are illustrated in 1829 Plan, and 1830 Mingaud gives the instruction, "strike your ball on the left side," but the term does not appear to have been used until 1836 Tillotson 3 and even there and in 1839 Kentfield 17 it is used in the compound SIDE STROKE. The first English term for spin was EFFECT, from the French *effet*.

2. "The side" refers to a SIDE POCKET, as in the CALL, "Ace in the side," meaning that the one ball is to be pocketed in the indicated side pocket. Cf. CORNER.

3. A team of two or more players who play together against a set of opponents. "Ten points for our side."

Side Against Side
(game, obs.) ENGLISH BILLIARDS in which each player is assigned three pockets on one side of the table into which he may play WINNING HAZARDS and LOSING HAZARDS. Hazards made on the opponent's side of the table score for the opponent. 1839 Kentfield 37, 1856 Crawley 98, 1867 Dufton 234. One might call this game "Three-Pocket" by analogy to ONE-POCKET.

side cushion
= SIDE RAIL, def. 1. 1806 Phil 22, 1989 Koehler 260.

side English

Right or left spin applied to a ball, as opposed to FOLLOW or DRAW. See also LEFT ENGLISH, RIGHT ENGLISH.

side pocket

(Pocket Bill.) A POCKET in the center of a LONG RAIL. 1850 Phelan 71, 1992 OR 4. Called a MIDDLE POCKET in ENGLISH BILLIARDS; rarely, a CENTER POCKET. Colloquially, just the SIDE. Cf. CORNER POCKET.

side rail

1. = LONG RAIL. A RAIL to the player's left or right side when he is facing the HEAD or FOOT of the table. 1875 NYT (Nov 17) 5:3. Cf. END RAIL, SHORT RAIL. 2. A panel hanging below the surface of a table and forming part of the APRON, as opposed to a CUSHION RAIL, one to which a cushion is attached. 1957 Holt 5.

side stroke

(Eng. Bill.) Left or right ENGLISH, that is, SIDE. 1836 Tillotson, 1839 Kentfield 4, 1856 Crawley 17. John Carr was known in the 1820s as the "father of the side stroke" for his demonstrations of spin achieved with a leather tip and chalk. 1974 Hendricks v.

side-twist

(Eng. Bill., obs.) = SIDE, def. 1. 1866 Crawley 83, 1869 Roberts 56.

sidearm stroke

A manner of holding the cue out over the table with the arm and elbow out to one side instead of directly under the shoulder as in the orthodox SWING. This technique is typically developed by players who begin the game at such an early age that they are unable to reach many shots in the normal fashion. A number of them maintain the ability to shoot this way even as adults. Willie Hoppe and Jake Schaefer Jr. had pronounced sidearm strokes.

sideboard

(pocket games, colloq.) A situation in which an object ball lies near the JAWS of a pocket, so that any other object ball shot at the pocket will fall in on a carom. 1992 Billing 92. The advantage of a sideboard is that it increases the effective width of the pocket. Also BIG POCKET.

sight

= DIAMOND, DOT, NAIL, SPOT or CUSHION SPOT. 1857 Phelan 30, 1890 HRB 14, 1975 Billiard Facts 15. A mark embedded in the RAIL of the table and used for aiming shots.

sighting

See AIMING.

Simonis

Brand name of a high-quality CLOTH made in Verviers, Belgium. Named for Iwan Simonis, who was born on January 6, 1769. Cf. GRANITO.

simultaneous hit

See BALLS STRUCK SIMULTANEOUSLY, DOUBT, SPLIT HIT.

213

sidearm stroke (Schaefer Jr.)

single average

The average number of points per INNING made by a player during a single game of a match or tournament. 1875 NYT (Nov 4) 10:4. See also AVERAGE, GRAND AVERAGE, HIGH SINGLE AVERAGE.

single baulk

(Eng. Bill.) A shot that leaves one of the two remaining balls IN BAULK when the opponent's ball is OFF THE TABLE. 1924 Ogden 268. The INCOMING PLAYER then has a difficult shot because he may not play at the ball that is in baulk. Cf. DOUBLE BAULK.

single elimination

Form of tournament in which a player is eliminated after suffering only a single loss. 1982 OR. Also KNOCK-OUT. Since each game eliminates exactly one player from the competition, a single elimination tournament with n players requires exactly $n - 1$ games to determine a winner. The number of ROUNDS required is the smallest integer not less than $log_2 n$. Cf. DOUBLE ELIMINATION.

Single elimination is not regarded as a fair method of deciding championships among more than two players and has never been used to determine the world Straight Pool title.

Single Pool

(game, obs.) The WHITE WINNING GAME played by two players only, each having a single ball, either the WHITE or SPOT WHITE. The opening striker plays at his opponent's ball from the BAULK SEMICIRCLE. Played with LIVES but no STAR, the taker of the last life being the winner. 1866 Crawley 179, 1896 Broadfoot 416. The strategy in Single Pool was to leave one's own ball as far from the opponent's as possible and to leave him FROZEN to the cushion whenever feasible.

single-rack

(Pocket Bill.) Said of a game that does not require reracking of the balls; that is, a game that ends after at most a single RACK of balls has been used. Examples of single-rack games: EIGHT-BALL, ELIMINATION, NINE-BALL, ONE POCKET, ROTATION, SEVEN-BALL.

sink

(pocket games) To POCKET. "Sink the five and get shape on the six."

Sippio table

(obs.) = PIGEON-HOLE TABLE. 1876 Collender 19.

sissy stick

(colloq.) A derogatory term for the MECHANICAL BRIDGE, wrongly implying that one who uses it must be frail in some way. One of a group of related synonyms that includes CRUTCH, LADIES' AID, and OLD MAN'S AID.

sitter

(Brit. games) A DUCK, an easy shot, one in which a ball is "sitting" on the edge of a pocket. 1924 Smith 30, 1936 Davis 54, 1957 Holt 174. Also a CHERRY, CRIPPLE, HANGER, MINNIE, PUPPY or SET-UP.

Six-Ball

(game) A SINGLE-RACK game similar to NINE-BALL, but played with six balls numbered one through six racked in a three-row triangle, with the six placed in the center of the back row. The object is to sink the six after hitting the lowest-numbered ball on the table first. 1982 OR 59.

In an explanation ascribed to Rudolph Wanderone by Wilson Lange, Six-Ball arose in the days when billiard parlors charged by the rack. Nine-Ball players, finding themselves with six balls remaining that they had paid for, would rack them and play a similar game but with the six balls numbered 10–15.

A handicapped version of Six-Ball in which the five-ball plays a special role is described in 1989 Raftis 150. The number of different possible initial racks in Six-Ball is $4! = 24$.

six-shot, six-stroke

(Eng. Bill., American Four-Ball Bill.) A stroke scoring six points. In English Billiards, this may be accomplished by hitting the RED and potting it and the striker's ball; or hitting the white, cannoning to the red, and potting both white balls. 1890 HRB 110. In American Four-Ball, this is done by pocketing a red and caroming onto the other red. 1850 Phelan 22.

sixteen-ball rack

(Poker Pocket Bill.) A special configuration of object balls arranged in a 1-2-3-4-3-2-1 diamond shape and containing four balls each of denominations A, K, Q, and J for forming poker hands. See RACK.

Sixty-One

(game) = ROTATION. It is so named because of the method of scoring, in which each ball counts for its numerical value. Since the sum of the numbers from 1 through 15 is 120, only 61 points are required to win. Cf. SIXTY-ONE POOL, in which the balls need not be struck in numerical order.

Sixty-One Pool

(game, obs.) = FIFTEEN-BALL. The game differs from SIXTY-ONE in that the balls need not be contacted in numerical order.

skid shot

A shot made using DRAG. 1978 Byrne 75. So called because the ball skids when first stroked, then assumes a rolling motion. See also SLIDE.

Skill Pool

(game, obs.) A British game, invented in 1909, that is played with the COLOURS and one RED. The BREAKER plays for a CANNON off the red to a colour, for two points. Potting the red after a cannon scores two points. He then plays for WINNING HAZARDS and LOSING HAZARDS off the colour first struck when the initial cannon was made. After scoring off a colour, a cannon off the red is played again, and so forth. 1986 Rhys 100.

skirt

= APRON.

skirt divider

A curtain approximately 24 to 30 inches high surrounding the playing area of a TOURNAMENT to separate the players from the GALLERY and to prevent motion of the SPECTATORS' feet from distracting the contestants.

skirted rack

A TRIANGLE that has been fitted with an APRON to protect the cloth as balls are being RACKED.

skittle

A PIN; a wooden object intended to be knocked down by a ball on a billiard table. 1976 WSD 399. Various shapes are employed, the most popular being that of a bowling pin. The term was in use by 1634. See KEGEL-PARTIE, PIN POOL, SKITTLE BILLIARDS.

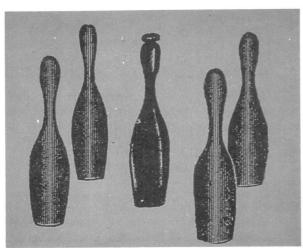

skittle

Skittle Billiards

1. (game) See CASIN, PIN POOL, SKITTLE GAME, SKITTLE POOL. 2. (game) A game played with three balls, 10 white PINS, and three black pins. 1856 Crawley 103, 1896 Broadfoot 431, 1908 Brunswick. For a modern version, see BAR BILLIARDS.

Skittle Game

(game) = SPANISH GAME, KUGEL-PARTIE. Played with three balls—one red, two white—and five wooden skittle PINS. The skittles are set up in a diamond arrangement approximately two inches apart, with the fifth pin in the center. The red ball is spotted and the first player strikes at it from one of the corner spots on the BAULK SEMICIRCLE. WINNING HAZARDS, CANNONS and knocking over skittles score points as follows: Knocking down a pin after striking a ball scores two points; knocking down two pins after striking a ball is worth four points, and so on, with two points added for each additional pin. Knocking down all pins wins the game; knocking down the middle pin only scores five points. Pocketing the red earns three points; pocketing the white two. Knocking down a pin before striking a ball loses two points for each pin. Played 21 UP. 1866 Crawley 220. See SKITTLE BILLIARDS.

Skittle Pool

(game) A game using three balls and 12 skittles (10 white, 2 black), played 31 or 62 up. Scoring is based on knocking down skittles after contacting the red ball. Cf. SKITTLE BILLIARDS. 1839 Kentfield 50, 1862 Crawley 117, 1866 Crawley 183, 1891 MB 365, 1913 Stoddard 151, 1916 RGRG 26. A variation involves ten white pins and three black pins arranged in an elaborate layout. Each white pin knocked down by a ball that has first struck another ball counts between three and ten points. Knocking down a black pin is a BURST, which resets the striker's score to zero. Each player has one stroke at a turn, whether he counts or misses. 1890 HRB 120. A modern descendant is CASIN. *See illustration on next page.*

skyrocket shot

(obs.) A fancy shot, particularly one in which the cue ball takes a curved path resembling the arc of a skyrocket. 1881 NYT (Nov 16) 5:4.

slate

A slab of stone forming the BED of a billiard table. Slate was used experimentally in 1826 to replace wooden beds. Iron had been tried but was found to be too irregular, hard and prone to rusting. Slate is still regarded as the best material for billiard tables. It is naturally flat, hard, dense, easily machined, resistant to

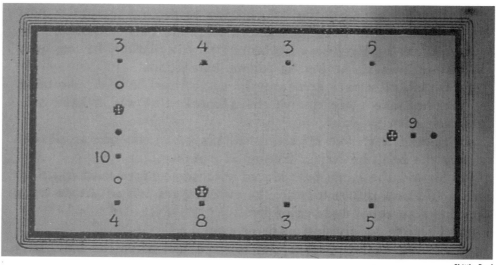

Skittle Pool

warping and sufficiently porous to prevent moisture from accumulating in the cloth.

The weight of a one-inch slate on a 4½- × 9-foot table is about 750 pounds. The UMB requires a minimum thickness of 45 millimeters for competitive play, about 1¾ inches, and thicker slates are now common in Europe. Søren Søgård uses two-inch slates, Chevillotte a whopping 2½ inches.

Italy has a near-monopoly on the world production of billiard slate. The quarries produce excellent slabs, and Italian workers are renowned for their stonecutting. Italian quarries began to mine slate around 1814. 1985 BD (Feb) 42. By the mid-1820s, it was being used for billiard tables.

Slates may be shipped whole to the table manufacturer, who will grind them further for flatness and then slice them into pieces. Most slates in the U.S. come in three portions that are fitted together with short DOWELS. There are thus two joints between the pieces, lying approximately two and a half diamonds from each end of the table. The slate on an ENGLISH TABLE may consist of up to five pieces. Seams are created where the parts meet. These are essentially straight cracks in the slate whose width depends on how well the cuts were made. A properly machined slate should have an edge as sharp as a knife. When the table is installed, the cuts are SEAMED by being filled with a setting compound that forms a firm bond. Plaster of Paris was commonly employed for this application, but it tends to become powdery under regular pounding. Resinous materials such as epoxy are now used instead.

slick

(sl.) A good player who bets on his game. 1990 White G-5. Sometimes a synonym for HUSTLER.

slide

1. Motion of a ball without rotation about its horizontal axis, that is, without rolling. 1941 Hoppe 63. A ball struck in its exact center will both slide and roll forward immediately. To eliminate sliding, it is necessary to hit the cue ball at a point approximately ²⁄₁₀ of a ball diameter above its center. In order to increase the tendency of the ball to slide, it should be hit below center. See also SKID SHOT. 2. A phenomenon observed on new cloth, by which balls tend to take a wider angle of rebound than expected after striking a cushion. The effect is lost after about 10 hours' play as the fibers are stretched and exercised by the motion of the balls.

slip stroke

A method of stroking in which the player releases his GRIP briefly and re-grasps the cue farther back before hitting the cue ball. 1974 Beverly 12. Although the stroke is not orthodox, it is used effectively by a number of players, including Allen Gilbert, many times U.S. Three-Cushion champion.

Slop

1. (game, colloq.) Any POCKET BILLIARD game without CALLED SHOTS. The game is "sloppy" in that players can receive credit for balls pocketed unintentionally. It is a favorite of HUSTLERS because they are able to conceal their playing ability by making shots appear to be the result of luck. 2. A SLOP SHOT.

slop shot

(colloq.) A shot in which the ball is pocketed inadvertently, by sloppy play or by mere LUCK. 1979 Grissim 254, 1989 Koehler 160. See also CROW, FLUKE, GARBAGE SHOT, SCRATCH, Slop.

216

Slosh

(game) = RUSSIAN POOL. 1924 Smith 92, 1954 KTG 35, 1976 WSD 365. Also, a variation of Billiards played in India, using several colored balls having various point values. 1986 Trelford 22. Sometimes called INDIAN POOL or TOAD-IN-THE-HOLE. Slosh ball sets have been sold containing white, yellow, green, blue, and black balls. 1957 BSTE 3.

slow

1. Having insufficient speed or elasticity. Said of a ball, cushion or the table itself. 1911 Roberts 3, 1913 Stoddard 8. A ball that is shot too slowly to COUNT or reach the pocket is said to lack LEGS. 2. Said of a TAPER that increases only gradually in diameter between the TIP and the JOINT. 1983 NBN (Mar) 18. Cf. FAST.

slow play

See DELAY.

slow taper

= DELAYED TAPER.

small colour

(Snooker) A BAULK COLOUR, *i.e.*, the yellow, the green, or the brown. So called because only a small number of points is scored for potting one of them. 1987 Thorburn 88.

smash

(Pocket Bill.) A hard hit at the APEX ball of the PYRAMID in order to maximize the chances of sinking a ball on the BREAK. 1866 Crawley 190.

smash-in

(obs.) A FOLLOW SHOT into a ball that is on a cushion, in which the cue ball contacts the cushion two or more times. 1898 Thatcher 52. See also JAR STROKE, RICOCHET CANNON, SNAKE SHOT, SQUIB. *See illustration in next column.*

smoking

Billiards and smoking have a coextensive history extending back to the seventeenth century. 1989 BD (Dec) 34. Currently, smoking is prohibited in matches during a player's INNING. The REFEREE may not smoke while on duty. 1981 Rottie 154.

snake shot

1. (Three-Cushions) A THREE-ON-TWO shot. 1914 Taylor 13, 1941 Hoppe 56, 1992 OR 14. A shot in which three or more cushion contacts occur using fewer than three different adjacent rails. For a DIAMOND SYSTEM useful in making snake shots, see 1928 Barry 19. 2. A shot in which ENGLISH, usually FOLLOW, is used to

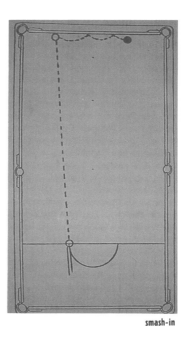

smash-in

cause the cue ball to make repetitive contacts with a rail. The phenomenon is described in 1806 Phil 41, before the invention of the cue tip! Also known as "writhing action." 1978 Byrne 202. See also JAR STROKE, RICOCHET CANNON, SMASH-IN, SQUIB, SERPENTINE MASSÉ.

snap

(Pocket Bill.) The BREAK SHOT, especially at NINE-BALL. 1984 Tevis. To win "on the snap" means to win the game on the break shot by sinking the MONEY BALL. Also CRUSH.

sneaky Pete

(colloq.) A JOINTED CUE having no COLLAR and whose JOINT has been disguised so the cue appears to be a ONE-PIECE CUE. It is used by HUSTLERS who want their victims to think they are using a HOUSE CUE, the idea being that the victim will be reluctant to play for money against a player who has invested in his own cue. A sneaky Pete is itself sometimes known as a "hustler," "trapper," or "silent partner." 1984 NBN (Apr) 23.

Snooker

1. (game) An amalgam of PYRAMIDS, LIFE POOL, and BLACK POOL, played with 22 balls on an ENGLISH BILLIARDS table. Fifteen REDS, six COLOURS and a white cue ball are used. The reds, each worth one point, are RACKED in a PYRAMID at the start of the game; the colours have numerical values from two to seven and are spotted in designated positions. The opening striker plays from the D. The object is to pot a red, then a colour, then a red again, and so forth, alternately, colours being respotted as they are pocketed. After the last red is sunk,

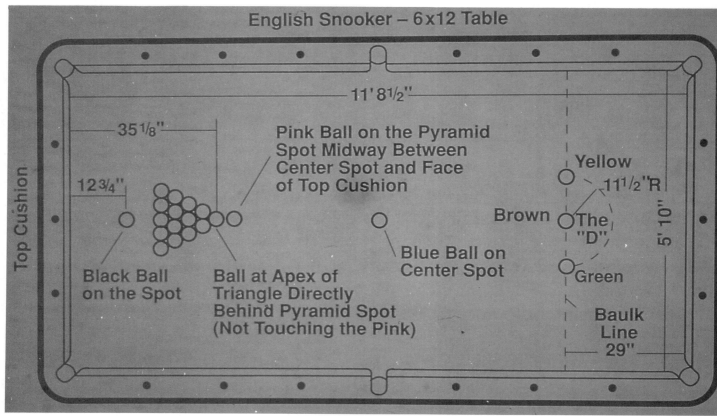

English Snooker – 6x12 Table

Top Cushion

11' 8½"

35⅛"

12¾"

Pink Ball on the Pyramid Spot Midway Between Center Spot and Face of Top Cushion

Black Ball on the Spot

Ball at Apex of Triangle Directly Behind Pyramid Spot (Not Touching the Pink)

Blue Ball on Center Spot

Yellow

11½"R

Brown The "D"

Green

5' 10"

Baulk Line 29"

the player may pot any colour, and it will be respotted. Beyond this point, the colours are to be potted in order of their numerical values. At each stroke, a player is obliged to contact first either a red, any colour, or a specific colour, depending on the situation. Failure to do so is a FOUL and is penalized by the awarding of points to the opponent. The winner is the player with the greater number of points at the end of the FRAME.

The popular legend concerning the origin of Snooker holds that it was invented around 1875 by British army officers stationed in India, who modified the game of BLACK POOL by adding several coloured balls from LIFE POOL to the normal complement of 15 reds and a black. Col. Sir Neville Francis Fitzgerald Chamberlain (not the gentleman who later became prime minister) was with the Devonshire Regiment in Jubbulpore. One day he found himself without a shot at this hybrid game when his opponent failed to hole a ball, and he called the man a "snooker," which was a term of derision applied to first-year cadets at the Royal Military Academy at Woolwich. The name stuck. Stories reached England of the new game in 1880. In 1885, Roberts visited India and brought Snooker back with him. 1976 WSD 40, 1978 BSCC 75, 1979 Everton 61. Unfortunately, there are no contemporary accounts of the

invention of the game, and the preceding story was not related until the 1930s. No description of Snooker before that time contains any mention of its genesis, and news articles concerning Chamberlain make no reference of any role he may have had in its invention.

Early versions of Snooker utilized four POOL BALLS (1889 Drayson), then five (1896 Buchanan), and later six (1896 Broadfoot 424). It was also known as SNOOKER POOL or SNOOKER'S POOL. The game was introduced into Australia in 1887 by Frank Smith Sr. The first official rules were promulgated by the Billiards Association (British) in 1903. At first, Snooker was viewed primarily as a gambling game or a change of pace from English Billiards.

The first Snooker competition was for amateurs and was not held until 1916. Sidney Fry, in 1919, was the first amateur to win championships at both Billiards and Snooker in the same year. 1986 Everton 49. The first professional tournament, sponsored by the BILLIARDS PROFESSIONALS ASSOCIATION, was held in 1923. Among professional ranks, the only player ever to hold the world Billiards and Snooker titles simultaneously was Joe Davis, beginning in 1928. By the later 1930s, Snooker had overtaken Billiards in popularity.

The world champions have been Joe Davis, who held the title from 1927–46, Walter Donaldson (1947, 1949), Fred Davis (1948 and 1951–56), John Pulman (1957–68), John Spencer (1969, 1970, 1977), Alex Higgins (1972, 1982), Ray Reardon (1970, 1973–76, 1978), Terry Griffiths (1979), Cliff Thorburn (1980), Steve Davis (1981, 1983–84, 1987–89), Dennis Taylor (1985) and Joe Johnson (1986). World championship Snooker matches are generally best of 35 frames.

The Women's World Championship was instituted in 1934 and won by Ruth Harrison eight successive times through 1948. In 1934 and 1939 she was simultaneously the women's professional champion at English Billiards. The competition has recently been dominated by Allison Fisher.

Snooker is now one of the most popular billiard games in the world. It is played to the virtual exclusion of other styles in the British Commonwealth, including Canada, and even in parts of the United States. Its enthusiastic following in the U.K. is promoted by frequent television coverage on the program POT BLACK. The highest-paid professional sports figures in England are Snooker players, with incomes from tournament winnings alone approaching $2 million annually. Steve Davis, despite his relative youth, has lifetime earnings from Snooker exceeding those of any billiard player in history.

Snooker is the only billiard game in which both offense and defense are encouraged through the direct awarding of points. In most other games, defense is suppressed by rules designed to prevent spectator boredom.

For game variations, see AMERICAN SNOOKER, CANADIAN SNOOKER, DEVIL-AMONG-THE-TAILORS, FOUR-HANDED SNOOKER, GOLF, LIABILITY, NINE-HOLE SNOOKER, PAY BALL, PENALTY GAME, PINK POOL, SAVILE SNOOKER, SHORT SNOOKER, SNOOKER BILLIARDS, SNOOKER GOLF, SNOOKER PLUS, SNOOKER ROULETTE, SNOOKERETTE, VOLUNTEER SNOOKER.

The vocabulary of Snooker is vast and includes the following: ALL ON THE BLACK, AWAY, BACK DOUBLE, BALL ON, BANANA SHOT, BAULK COLOUR, BLACK-BALL GAME, BREAK, BREAK CERTIFICATE, BREAK-OFF, BUBBLE, CENTURY, CLEAR BALL, CLEARANCE, CLIP, COCKED-HAT DOUBLE, COLOUR, CRAWL STROKE, CROSS DOUBLE, CROSSOVER SHOT, CUTBACK DOUBLE, D, DUB, ESCAPE, FRAME, FREE BALL, GET OUT, GOD BLESS YOU, HIDDEN SET, INDIRECT POT, LAY A SNOOKER, LIFT, LONG TACKLE, MAXIMUM, NEAREST BALL PLAYABLE, NOMINATED BALL, ON, ON BALL, OUTSIDE RED, PENALTY BALL, PENALTY POINTS, PLANT, PLAY AGAIN RULE, PLAY OUT, POOL BALL, POTTER, PYRAMID, RECOVERY BALL, RED,

REVERSE PLANT, ROLL-UP, SET, SHOT TO NOTHING, SMALL COLOUR, SNOOKER BALL, SPLIT, SQUEEZE SHOT, STRIKING RING, TAKE THE COLOURS, TAKE UP, TIME WASTING, TOTAL CLEARANCE, TOUCHING BALL, VOLUNTEER, WANTING A SNOOKER. 2. (Snooker) A shot that leaves the opponent SNOOKERED.

Snooker ball

(Snooker) A BALL used in playing Snooker; a cue ball, a RED or a COLOUR. The diameter of Snooker balls is 52.5 millimeters (2¹⁄₁₆ inches). 1986 KTG 6. Cf. BILLIARD BALL, POOL BALL.

Snooker Billiards

(game) A unique game played on an ENGLISH BILLIARDS table with six COLOURS, one RED and a white cue ball. The balls are SPOTTED as in Snooker, but the pink is placed on the PYRAMID SPOT with the red touching and directly in front of it. The opening striker is IN HAND and must play at BLACK. Scoring is by WINNING HAZARDS, LOSING HAZARDS, and CANNONS, but with unusual restrictions. Each of the colours is associated with one of the six pockets, and any hazard of or off a colour must be into its corresponding pocket in order to score. A cannon counts only if made from a ball to the next higher ball in numerical sequence, that is, from red to yellow, yellow to green, etc. No cannon can be made off black. After a legitimate scoring stroke, the player is allowed a single "free stroke" of a hazard of or off any ball into any pocket, after which he must again play a legitimate stroke. "The game is a good one, and provides a welcome change from billiards and snooker." 1936 Clifford 48. Cf. PENALTY GAME.

Snooker cue

(Snooker) A CUE STICK that is intended for use in playing Snooker. It is typically made of ash, 1.5 meters (59 inches) long, with a brass FERRULE and a tip diameter of 10–12 millimeters. 1986 KTG 6. Cf. BILLIARD CUE, POOL CUE.

Snooker Golf

(game) Played with the cue ball and a RED on a Snooker table. The red is spotted at the CENTRE SPOT and the cue is played from BAULK. The object is to pot the red in each of the pockets successively, in clockwise order beginning at the top left, in the least number of strokes. Also known (in Britain) as BILLIARDS GOLF. Cf. GOLF, GOLF BILLIARDS.

Snooker Plus

(game) Snooker played with the addition of two extra COLOURS: an ORANGE ball worth eight points, and a PURPLE worth ten. The orange is spotted midway between the BLUE and the PINK; the purple midway between the BROWN and the BLUE. A MAXIMUM BREAK in this game consists of 210 points. It was devised in 1959 by Joe Davis, who recorded its first CENTURY of 108. 1986 Rhys 103. The longest break made so far is one of 156 by Jackie Rea.

Snooker Pool

(game) = SNOOKER. 1896 Buchanan 57. Also SNOOKER'S POOL.

Snooker Roulette

(game) A practice game invented by Ted Lowe consisting of a predetermined sequence of six shots. 1983 Perrin 149. See also GOLF.

Snooker table

(Snooker) An ENGLISH TABLE on which SPOTS have been placed as required for the game of Snooker. Otherwise, there is no difference between the tables used for English Billiards and Snooker. See also BILLIARD TABLE, TABLE.

snookered

(Snooker) The state of being unable to hit both sides of any BALL ON directly with one's cue ball. 1889 Drayson 111, 1954 KTG 27, 1978 BSCC 56. "Directly" in this context means by a straight shot not involving any cushions. Thus a player is snookered if any part of the ball on is obstructed by a ball not on. 1949 Davis. If the snookered player is indeed unable to contact the ball on, he will suffer a penalty. If the cue ball is in hand, the striker is snookered only if he is obstructed from all cue ball positions within the D. The American equivalent is HOOKED, IN JAIL or TIED UP.

In ENGLISH EIGHT-BALL POOL, a player is snookered if he cannot hit the center of any ball in his GROUP. 1986 Quinn 88. See FULL BALL, OBSTRUCTION, SEE.

Snookerette

(game) See BAR BILLIARDS.

Snooker's Pool

(game) = SNOOKER. 1911 HRB 125, 1919 Hoyle 636. Also SNOOKER POOL.

Soft Eight

(Eight-Ball) Rule variation in which a player, upon sinking his last group ball, is not required to contact the eight-ball, but may play a SAFETY. 1990 White G-5. Cf. HARD EIGHT.

solid

(Eight-Ball) Any of the GROUP of solid-colored balls, *e.g.*, those numbered one through seven. 1989 Koehler 261. (Even though the eight-ball itself is solid black, it is not referred to as a SOLID for reasons relating to the rules of the game.) Also LITTLE, LOW, PLAIN. Cf. STRIPE.

Solitaire Pool

(game) A solo pocket billiard game in which the 15 balls are RACKED and the player's object is to sink all the balls using the least number of shots. 1908 Hood 16. Cf. (generically) EQUAL OFFENSE.

Space Game

(game, obs.) A variety of BALKLINE with the table divided into seven spaces as shown, six of which are BALK SPACES. 1883 NYT (Dec 14) 3:2, 1884 MB 308, 1890 HRB 55. In the corner spaces, three shots are allowed; in the side spaces, two. There is no restriction in the CENTER SPACE. Designed to "moderate rail nursing and prevent the nursing of balls in the corners and at one end of the table," it was introduced publicly at a tournament in Hartford, Connecticut, in January 1884 but never achieved popularity. 1883 NYT (Dec 14) 3:2. It can be regarded as a curious footnote in the development of BALKLINE. Historically, it came after 8-inch lines but before 12- or 14-inch lines were tried.

Space Game

spacer

(Brit., colloq.) = INNING. 1937 NBJ (Oct).

span rest

(Brit. games) A version of the SPIDER permitting the player to BRIDGE over several intervening balls. 1975a Lowe 15. See REST, SWAN NECK.

Spanish Game

(game) SKITTLE game played 31 UP with three balls and five PINS set up 2¼ inches apart. 1850c White & Bohn 42, also called KUGEL-PARTIE in Germany, or the Skettle game. 1839 Kentfield 47, 1850 Phelan 39, 1891 MB 354, 1916 RGRG 75, 1919 Hoyle 649. Scoring is by WINNING HAZARDS, CANONS, and knocking down pins after striking a ball. According to 1869 Kavanagh 14, it was a combination of hazard, carom, and pin games and was popular in Spain, Mexico, Cuba, California, and New Orleans. Knocking down a pin after striking a ball scores two points for each pin downed. Knocking down the middle pin alone scores five. Knocking down all pins in one stroke wins the game. Potting white or scoring a carom is worth two points; potting red counts three. 1890 HRB 108. Cf. PIN POOL.

spare

(Bowlliards) The act of pocketing 10 balls in two RUNS in a single inning, resulting in an extra score of 10 points plus the number of balls pocketed on the player's next run. Cf. STRIKE.

spectators

The crowd of people observing a billiard game; the GALLERY. Unlike in many sports, billiard spectators have an official role in administering the game when no REFEREE is present or when the referee is unable to see a disputed stroke. According to 1674 Cotton: "All Controversies are to be decided by the Standers by, upon seeking judgment." By 1773, a MARKER was in common use, but if he failed to see the shot a majority of the COMPANY decided any questionable matters of fact. 1974 Hendricks 25. The practice remained codified in printed rules until 1890. See, for example, 1845 Hoyle 225. Even today, in certain games such as Snooker and Nine-Ball, the referee is permitted to consult the crowd for assistance. 1987 BSCC S24, 1992 OR 52. See also GUEST, RAIL BIRD.

The spectators, of course, are not permitted to interfere with the game, and may be put out of the arena should they do so. However, the rules must provide for the case in which a spectator is unable to control himself. See NONPLAYER INTERFERENCE.

221

spectators (Demandez plutôt a la galerie)

For methods by which the spectators show their appreciation for good play, see APPLAUSE.

speed

1. Velocity imparted to a ball, *e.g.*, "medium speed." Measurements with a radar gun reveal that only top players are able to shoot the cue ball faster than 30 miles per hour. A good amateur should be able to BREAK at 25 miles per hour. 2. (colloq.) One's true playing ability, frequently concealed by HUSTLERS. 1865 NYT (Nov 9) 5:2, 1883 NYT (Mar 30) 5:2, 1979 Grissim 254. "He's not showing his speed."

Speed Pool

(game) Pocket billiard game in which the objective is to sink all 15 object balls in the shortest possible time by means of legal strokes, which means that the cue ball must come to rest before a shot can be attempted. Forty seconds is a world-class time at this event.

spider, spider-rest

(Brit. games) A very high REST used in PYRAMID games and SNOOKER. 1867 Dufton 18, 1885c Cook 12, 1976 Charlton 39. The device has arched legs so the entire apparatus can slide over a ball. 1954 KTG 16. It was originally known as the HIGH ARCH REST. 1866 Crawley 10. See also EXTENDED SPIDER, PYRAMID REST, SPAN REST.

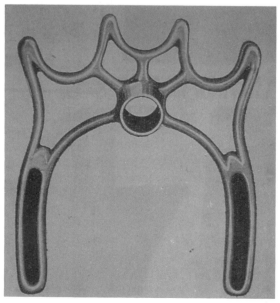

spider

spin

Rotation imparted to a ball by an off-center or glancing blow, also called ENGLISH or (by the English) SIDE. 1976 WSD 411. Extreme spin is known colloquially as GREASE, JUICE, OIL, or STUFF. See also MASSÉ, PIQUÉ.

spine

= STIFFNESS, that property of the SHAFT of a cue stick that minimizes flexing when a ball is struck. 1946 Bruns 11, 1983 NBN (Mar) 18.

spinning ball

A ball whose center is stationary but that is still spinning. A player's stroke has not ended until all balls have stopped spinning. 1897 Payne 25, 1992 OR 37. Originally, it was not illegal to strike at a spinning ball. For at least 300 years, however, it has been a FOUL to shoot while the center of any ball is moving. See MOTION.

spit shot

A TRICK SHOT or GAFF SHOT in which the (illegal) application of a small spot of saliva between the balls is required for success. 1981 Margo 46. Saliva alters the nature of the contact between the balls, greatly reducing friction, and thus lessens the effect of THROW.

splice

A joining of woods with glue, forming a bond that may be stronger than either wood alone. Cue stick BUTTS are often formed by splicing two or more woods together, often using VENEERS. A splice is used because the balance point of the cue can be positioned better if woods of two different densities are used to form the BUTT.

spliced cue

1. A cue whose butt contains a SPLICE. 2. (obs.) A ONE-PIECE CUE in which a new SHAFT has been spliced into an old BUTT. 1895 Buchanan 161.

split

(Snooker) A shot whose side effect is to separate balls in a CLUSTER, one that OPENS the balls. A type of BREAK SHOT. Cf. SPLIT SHOT.

split double elimination

A type of DOUBLE ELIMINATION tournament DRAW in which the players are divided into BRACKETS, each bracket yielding a player to compete for the championship in the final round. 1992 OR 14. See also BRACKET, LOSERS' BRACKET, WINNERS' BRACKET. All players start in the winners' bracket. After losing a game, a player is moved to the losers' bracket. After losing in the losers' bracket, a player has lost two games and is eliminated from competition. For the last match to determine the tournament winner, the winner of the winners' bracket plays the winner of the losers' bracket.

The split double draw can be confusing to SPECTATORS, since it is difficult to determine which players will be paired in the losers' bracket, which is constantly being fed with new players from the winners' bracket. A further problem is that the game between the winners of the two brackets may not produce a winner. For example, suppose A loses to B in their first match, but both go through the remainder of the tournament undefeated. A will win the winners' bracket; B will win the losers' bracket. Suppose that, when they meet in the final, B beats A. They now have identical records, with one loss apiece. Who should be the winner? In some tournaments, a third game is played to break the tie. In others, the winner of the final game is declared the winner despite the tie. The situation arises rather frequently—in the 1989 U.S. Open Straight Pool Tournament, Steve Mizerak took the winners' bracket and Oliver Ortmann won the losers' (after having lost to Mizerak). The two met in the single-game final, which was increased to 200 points and the winner (Ortmann) was awarded first prize even though the players' final won-lost records were the same.

split hit

(Nine-Ball) A shot in which the cue ball appears to CONTACT two object balls simultaneously. 1992 OR 53. In unrefereed games, if a split hit occurs, the lower-numbered ball is presumed to have been hit first. This provision is contrary to the traditional rule in billiards, more than a century old, under which the striker is not given the benefit of the doubt as to whether a rule has been complied with. See BALLS STRUCK SIMULTANEOUSLY, DOUBT.

The supposed purpose of the rule is to reduce the possibility of disputes, especially in LEAGUE play absent a REFEREE. It does not accomplish this goal—an opponent bent on cheating will simply claim that the higher-numbered ball was hit first. The solution is not to repeal the RULE OF DOUBT but to ask a neutral third person to observe the hit.

split shot

(Pocket Bill., obs.) A CAROM in which the two object balls are close to one another and the SECOND OBJECT BALL is pocketed, so called because the cue ball appears to "split" the balls apart. 1894 NY Herald (Mar 25) 7:4. Cf. SPLIT.

split the pocket

(pocket games) To pocket a ball in the very center of the pocket opening. 1977 Martin, 1979 Grissim 254.

split the time

A method of paying for TABLE TIME in a public billiard room. The players divide the bill evenly regardless of who wins. 1967 Polsky 33. Such a split was the rule in "better-class rooms." 1916 BM (Mar) 11. Cf. FOR THE TIME.

spontaneous motion

Movement of a ball without apparent reason. See MOTION.

sportsmanship

Actions not required by the rules but that ennoble the game by reflecting the ideals of honor and fairness. The history of billiards is replete with outstanding examples of sportsmanship. During the 1941 world Three-Cushion championship, Willie Hoppe became ill and was unable to play his scheduled match with Jake Schaefer Jr. Schaefer was unwilling to take advantage of the situation and refused to accept the forfeit, insisting instead that the game be postponed until Hoppe returned to the tournament. Hoppe won the title. 1941 NBJ (Feb). In his 1964 challenge match in which Arthur Cranfield took the world pocket billiard title from Luther Lassiter, Cranfield called a FOUL on himself that the referee had failed to observe and won respect for his honesty.

The fundamental rule of behavior appears at 1916 RGRG 5: "Billiards is a gentleman's game at which all contests whether for pleasure or prize, should be dominated by courtesy and sportsmanship. A spirit of equity should prevail. Trickery or unseemly tactics should not be countenanced." Cf. UNSPORTSMANLIKE CONDUCT.

spot

1. A mark on the cloth for use in placing balls accurately. 1807 White 61, 1839 Kentfield 25, 1881 MB 26. To position a ball on such a mark. 1844 Mardon 99. See SPOTTING. The spot itself, sometimes called a SPOT

223

WAFER, was first made of COURT-PLASTER, then plain silk. Under current international rules, physical spots may not be placed on the table because of possible interference with the motion of the balls. Their locations are marked in pencil or chalk. WBA 3. The mark is to consist of a cross whose arms are five millimeters in length. 1989 Salvador 90.

"The Spot" refers to the BILLIARD SPOT in British games. 1885 Cook 13. In American games, it is the FOOT SPOT. See also SHARP.

A large number of spot names and equivalents are given in the table below. 1991 BD (Feb) 64. The "Coordinates" column gives the Cartesian coordinates of the spot in units of table widths. The lower left corner is at (0.0, 0.0); the upper right corner is at (1.0, 2.0), and the center of the table is at (0.5, 1.0). The radius of a ball is denoted by r, its diameter by d. Letters in the "Key" column refer to the accompanying spot map. In some cases, it is difficult to compare spot locations because of differing games and tables sizes, so the synonyms listed are only approximate. For more information, see entries under individual spots.

2. A DIAMOND, DOT, NAIL, RAIL MARKER, SIGHT, or CUSHION SPOT. A mark on the rail to assist in aiming or to define the end of a STRING. 1807 White 61, 1964 Cottingham 137.

3. A HANDICAP. 1931 BM (Apr) 39, 1970 Fensch 162. "He received a spot of 10 points in 50." To give a handicap. During the 1870s, a spot was credited to the weaker player at the beginning of the game. That is, being given 50 in 200 meant that the game would start with the score 50–0. Later in the century, spot points were marked up at the end of the game. See also RECEIVING.

4. The marked white ball in carom or ENGLISH BILLIARDS, also known as the SPOT BALL or SPOT WHITE. Also BLACK BALL. Cf. PLAIN. Any ball highlighted with a spot in LIFE POOL, of which there may be up to six of different colours. 1919 Hoyle 640.

5. (Bill.) The player using the marked ball. OED. "Spot shoots next."

6. (Bill.) The OPENING BREAK, that is, the shot played at the spotted balls. "He ran 23 from the spot."

7. (obs.) A SPOT SHOT or SPOT-STROKE. 1869 Roberts 367.

Spot at Fifty
(game, obs.) STRAIGHT-RAIL billiards played with a rule requiring the balls to be spotted whenever the striker has made a run of 50 points. Introduced at Mussey's in St.

Louis in 1882 to counter the effect of the RAIL NURSE. 1891 MB 667.

spot ball
1. (Bill.) The marked white ball in billiards; also known as the SPOT or SPOT WHITE. 1875 NYT (Feb 23) 5:4, 1881 MB 27. The mark is applied to enable the players to distinguish between the two white cue balls. See BLACK BALL. Cf. PLAIN.

Thomas Gallagher claimed that a good player will always choose the unmarked ball because the speck on the spot ball destroys its evenness. 1900 NYDT (Dec 9) II 9:5. There may have been some justification for this view in the days of ivory balls when the spot was actually an inlay rather than merely a marking.

2. A ball that has been placed on a SPOT in accordance with the rules, as when it has been pocketed illegally. 1946 OR 94, 1976 WSD 415. Also a "spotted ball." See SPOTTING.

3. (Eng. Bill.) The RED BALL, so called because it is replaced on the SPOT when pocketed. See also PLAY THE SPOT BALL, SPOT-STROKE.

4. (game, obs.) HAZARDS as played in the U.S. in the early nineteenth century. 1866 Phelan i.

spot-barred game
(Eng. Bill.) A rule in English Billiards under which no two consecutive SPOT HAZARDS (WINNING HAZARDS from the BILLIARD SPOT) can be made into any pocket. 1885 OED, 1897 Payne 48. Two versions of the rule exist; one applies to all pockets, the other to the two TOP POCKETS only. Their purpose is to prevent long breaks at the SPOT-STROKE. The restriction became part of the official rules in 1898. 1985 Everton 93. See also BARRED. Cf. SPOT IN, TWO-POT RED RULE.

spot end
(Eng. Bill.) The END of the table nearest the BILLIARD SPOT. Also TOP OF THE TABLE.

spot-end play
(Eng. Bill.) = TOP-OF-THE-TABLE GAME. 1957 Holt 106. Play that is largely confined to the SPOT END. The TEA-TRAY GAME.

spot hazard
(Eng. Bill.) A SPOT-STROKE. 1885c Cook 13. A shot in which the red ball is potted from the BILLIARD SPOT. 1869 Roberts 137, 1911 Roberts 114.

spot in
(Eng. Bill.) The opposite of SPOT-BARRED; that is, a game in which the SPOT-STROKE is unrestricted. 1979 Everton 14.

CHART OF NAMED SPOTS			
SPOT NAME	FUNCTION, SYNONYMS	KEY	COORDINATES
American	Light-red in American Four-Ball. Also head, light-red, string, upper, white.	H	$(0.5, 1.5)$
baulk	Brown in Snooker. Also baulk-line, brown, middle spot in baulk.	B	$(0.5, 0.4)$
baulk-line	Brown in Snooker. Also baulk, brown, middle spot in baulk.	B	$(0.5, 0.4)$
billiard	Black in Snooker; red in English Billiards. Also black, English, losing, red, top, winning and losing.	E	$(0.5, 2.0 - 2/11)$
black	Black in Snooker; red in English Billiards. Also billiard, English, losing, red, top, winning and losing.	E	$(0.5, 2.0 - 2/11)$
blue	Blue in Snooker. Also center, middle.	C	$(0.5, 1.0)$
bottle	1 and 2 in Bottle Pool.	T	$(0.5 \pm 0.25, 2 - r)$
brown	Brown in Snooker. Also baulk, baulk-line, middle spot in baulk.	B	$(0.5, 0.4)$
center	Object ball in 14.1; for opponent's cue ball in Three-Cushion. Also blue, middle.	C	$(0.5, 1.0)$
Chicago	Object balls in Chicago Pool.	R, T	$(r, 0.25)$, $(r, 0.5)$, $(r, 0.75)$, $(r, 1.25)$, $(r, 1.5)$, $(r, 1.75)$, repeat above for $1 - r$, $(0.25, 2 - r)$, $(0.5, 2 - r)$, $(0.75, 2 - r)$
cue-ball	Cue ball in Carom Billiards.	3	$(0.5 \pm 6'', 0.5)$
dark-red	Dark-red in American Four-Ball. Also eight-ball, foot, pink, winning.	F	$(0.5, 1.5)$
eight-ball	Eight-Ball in English Eight-Ball Pool. Also dark-red, foot, pink, winning.	F	$(0.5, 1.5)$

CHART OF NAMED SPOTS			
SPOT NAME	FUNCTION, SYNONYMS	KEY	COORDINATES
English	Red in English Billiards. Also billiard, black, losing, red, top, winning and losing.	E	$(0.5, 2.0\text{–}^{2}/_{11})$
foot	Object ball in 14.1; red in Carom Billiards. Also dark-red, eight-ball, pink, winning.	F	$(0.5, 1.5)$
four-ball	Red balls in oriental four-ball billiard games.	4	$(0.5, 0.25), (0.5, 1.75)$
green	Green in Snooker.	G	$(^{1}/_{3}, 0.4)$
head	Object in 14.1; opponent's cue ball in carom billiards. Also American, light-red, string, upper, white.	H	$(0.5, 0.5)$
light-red	Light-red in American Four-Ball. Also American, light-red, string, upper, white.	H	$(0.5, 0.5)$
losing	Red in English Billiards. Also billiard, black, English, red, top, winning and losing.	E	$(0.5, 2.0\text{–}^{2}/_{11})$
middle	Used in English Billiards; 5 in Cowboy. Also blue, center.	C	$(0.5, 1.0)$
middle spot in baulk	Brown in Snooker. Also baulk, baulk-line, brown.	B	$(0.5, 0.4)$
orange	Orange in Snooker Plus.	O	$(0.5, 1.25)$
pin-pool	Wooden pins in Pin Pool and Casin.	P	$(0.5 \pm d, 1.0 \pm d$
pink	Pink in Snooker. Also dark-red, eight-ball, foot, pyramid, winning	F	$(0.5, 1.5)$
pool	White in American Four-Ball.	L	$(0.5, 2.0\text{–}5'')$
principal	Red ball in Bagatelle.		
purple	Purple in Snooker Plus.	Q	$(0.5, 0.7)$
pyramid	Apex of rack in Pyramids. Also, dark-red, eight-ball, foot, pink, winning.	F	$(0.5, 1.5)$

226

CHART OF NAMED SPOTS			
SPOT NAME	FUNCTION, SYNONYMS	KEY	COORDINATES
red	Red in English Billiards. Also: billiard, black, English, losing, top, winning and losing.	E	$(0.5, 2.0–\frac{2}{11})$
skittle	Balls and pins in Skittle Pool (also uses spot B). (At left, *i* is a variable ranging from 1 to 4)	S	$(3\frac{1}{2}'', 0.4i), (1.0–3\frac{1}{2}'', 0.4i), (0.5 \pm 7'', 0.4),$ $(0.5 \pm 0.25, 0.4),$ $(1.0 − 5\frac{1}{4}'', 0.8), (0.5, 1.725), (0.5, 1.7)$
string	Opponent's cue ball in Carom Billiards. Also American, head, light-red, upper, white.	H	$(0.5, 0.5)$
top	Red in English Billiards. Also billiard, black, English, losing, red, winning and losing.	E	$(0.5, 2.0 − \frac{2}{11})$
upper	Opponent's cue ball in Carom Billiards. Also billiard, black, English, losing, red, winning and losing.	H	$(0.5, 0.5)$
white	Opponent's cue ball in Carom Billiards. Also billiard, black, English, losing, red, winning and losing.	H	$(0.5, 0.5)$
white (Casin)	White in Casin.	W	$(0.5, d)$
winning	Dark-red in American Four-Ball. Also dark-red, eight-ball, foot, pink, pyramid.	F	$(0.5, 1.5)$
winning and losing	Red in English Billiards. Also billiard, black, English, losing, red, top.	E	$(0.5, 2.0 − \frac{2}{11})$
yellow	Yellow in Snooker.	Y	$(\frac{2}{3}, 0.4)$
yellow (Casin)	Yellow in Casin.	D	$(0.5, 2.0 − d)$

spot shot

1. (Pocket Bill.) A shot at a ball that has been placed on the FOOT SPOT, usually with the cue ball IN HAND BEHIND THE HEAD STRING after a SCRATCH, with the object of sinking it in one of the FOOT POCKETS. 1958 OR, 1992 OR 15. Because of the frequency with which this shot occurs, various aiming methods have been developed to assist the player in making it, as by placing the cue ball in a certain place and striking it toward a specific diamond. 2. (Bill.) The OPENING BREAK; a shot in which the balls are all positioned on spots. 1906 NYT (Dec 19) 9:1, 1946 OR 95.

spot-stroke

(Eng. Bill.) A SPOT HAZARD. 1844 Mardon, 1862 Crawley 71. A repetitive position obtained by potting the red ball and maneuvering the cue ball into position for another shot on the red, which is respotted each time it is pocketed. 1885c Cook 13, 1895 Buchanan 109. Proficient players achieved BREAKS of such magnitude at the spot-stroke that its use had to be curbed. See SPOT-BARRED GAME.

spot the break

To give a HANDICAP of the BREAK SHOT in games in which it is an advantage to break, such as NINE-BALL. This is generally a small advantage to a player who is not likely to RUN OUT, and in many cases may not even be of benefit. An even smaller handicap is LAST TWO. See SPOT.

spot wafer

A thin circle of fabric or COURT-PLASTER that is affixed to the cloth to define a SPOT. 1895 Buchanan 38, 1908 Brunswick 83. The use of wafers is prohibited in international play; chalk or pencil marks must be used to prevent interference with the motion of the balls. A spot wafer of large diameter is generally used at the foot spot on pocket tables to prevent wearing of the cloth at the APEX of the RACK. Spot wafers are generally black. This often causes unexplained black marks to appear on balls that are struck hard after being spotted.

228

spot white

(Bill.) The white cue ball that is marked with one or more small spots to distinguish it from the PLAIN WHITE. 1885c Cook 13, 1919 Hoyle 620. Two spots are sometimes placed at opposite ends of a diameter so that at least one will be visible no matter how the ball comes to rest. Also SPOT, SPOT BALL, or, occasionally, the BLACK BALL. Cf. PLAIN.

spotting

The act of placing a ball on a SPOT. 1844 Mardon 99. The rules specify how this shall be done in case multiple balls must be spotted, a spot is OCCUPIED or balls in play interfere with spotting. See 1983 Rule Book 252 and INTERFERENCE. Spotted balls are placed so that they are FROZEN to interfering balls. However, when the interfering ball is the cue ball, the spotted ball is not placed in contact with it, but as close as possible without actually touching. 1982 OR 45. A ball is not properly spotted unless it is placed by hand on its prescribed spot. 1978 BSCC 26. That is, a ball that appears to be on the proper spot cannot simply be left there but must be taken up and replaced by hand. For example, suppose in English Billiards the striker's cue ball comes to rest frozen to the red ball, which happens to lie on its spot. When the balls are separated, the red must be touched and placed on the spot again manually. See also RESPOT.

In POCKET BILLIARDS, if multiple balls are to be spotted, the lower-numbered ball of any pair is placed closer to the FOOT SPOT. 1992 OR 39. If the LONG STRING between the foot spot and the FOOT RAIL is entirely occupied, balls are placed on the line joining the foot spot and the CENTER SPOT, in decreasing numerical order toward the center of the table.

In some versions of BILLIARDS, if the cue ball is FROZEN to an object ball, the player has the option of having the object ball spotted or he may SHOOT AWAY from the frozen object ball. See MASSÉ DÉTACHÉ. In other styles, it is mandatory to spot both frozen balls. Spotting the balls every so often during a run has been used to suppress the RAIL NURSE. See SPOT AT FIFTY.

In Snooker, if a colour is to be spotted but its proper spot is OCCUPIED, it is placed on the highest value spot available. If two or more colours are to be spotted, they are spotted in order of highest value first. If all spots are occupied, the colour is placed as near as possible to its own spot, between that spot and the closest point on the TOP cushion. 1987 BSCC S17.

spread

(Bill.) A CAROM in which the angle formed by the cue ball and the two object balls is approximately 90 degrees. 1857 Phelan 102, 1913 Daly 23. See also DEAD SPREAD, SQUARE, SWING.

spread draw

(Bill.) A DRAW SHOT in which the cue ball travels to the left or right of the first object ball a considerable distance before completing the carom, that is, one in which the object balls are well spread. 1942 Cochran 111.

square

1. An ANCHOR SPACE, which is a seven-inch square. 2. (Bill., obs.) To carom off at a 90-degree angle to one's line of aim. 1836 Tillotson 24. "He squared his ball." See also SPREAD.

squeeze cannon

(Eng. Bill.) A CANNON in which the cue ball just grazes the edges of the object balls. A variety of open-table NURSE. 1957 Holt 92. The EDGE NURSE or PASS NURSE. A "squeeze-through" or "zigzag" cannon is one in which the cue ball passes between the two object balls, describing a path resembling the letter Z. 1908 Mannock II 387.

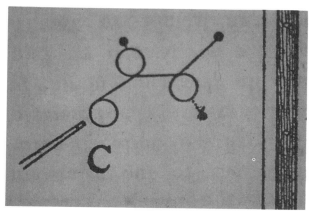

squeeze-through cannon

squeeze shot

1. A TIGHT shot in which the cue ball and an object ball must pass closely by one another. 1977 Martin 219. 2. (Snooker) A PLANT in which the object balls are not touching and are not directly in line with a pocket. In American usage, a type of THROW SHOT. 3. (Eng. Bill.) A shot in which a ball FROZEN to the rail and blocking a pocket is hit sharply to force it into the cushion and thus out of the way long enough for an IN-OFF. 1910b Ritchie 36.

squib

(Bill., obs.) A shot perfected by Jacob Schaefer Sr., in which the cue ball is made to strike full on a ball that is FROZEN to a cushion. The momentum of the cue ball is transferred to the object ball and any subsequent motion

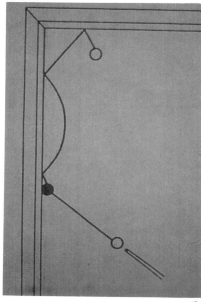

squib

of the cue ball is due primarily to spin. 1898 Thatcher 16. See SNAKE SHOT for an example. *See illustration*

squirt

The phenomenon by which a ball struck off center by the cue stick does not travel away exactly along the direction in which it is struck, but at an angle inclined slightly to the opposite side of the ball. This is caused by friction between the ball and the table which results in the point of contact with the table acting as a pivot. In 1978 Byrne 264, the term "squirt" is ascribed to Jack Leavitt of Star Billiards, Santa Rosa, California. The effect of squirt is mentioned clearly, though not named, in 1806 Phil 29, before the invention of the cue tip. See AIMING.

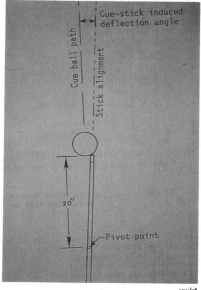

squirt

stab

1. (Brit. games) A shot in which the cue ball stops DEAD or travels only slowly after hitting the object ball, but does not recoil as in a DRAW SHOT. 1873 Bennett 192, 1895 Buchanan 71, 1954 KTG 21. This effect is accomplished by using a short, stiff stroke. Also called a STAB-SCREW. Cf. STOP, STUN. 2. (Brit. games) Use of low ENGLISH to steady the cue ball on its path; called CRAWL, DRAG, JAB, or a SKID SHOT in other sources. 1924 Smith 89.

stab cannon

(Eng. Bill.) A CANNON made with STAB. 1873 Bennett 281.

stab-screw

(Eng. Bill.) = STAB. 1873 Bennett 192.

stack

(Pocket Bill., colloq.) = PACK, meaning the racked balls. 1977 Fels 65, 1979 Grissim 253. Sometimes used to apply to a rack that has just been broken. See BREAK. 1990 Rushin 27. The BUNCH, HEAP, RACK, or PYRAMID.

stake

The cash amount wagered on the outcome of a game by its participants and sometimes held for safekeeping by an intermediary called a "stakeholder" to ensure payment. "Willie, give him the stake." 1961 *The Hustler* (film). (The line refers to Willie Mosconi, technical advisor on the film, who appears in several scenes.) See also HAZARD, POOL, POT.

stakehorse

(colloq.) A BACKER, one who provides a STAKE; a gambler who pays a player's entire losses, and often his expenses, in return for a share of his winnings.

stalemated game

A game having no winner. In EIGHT-BALL, if neither player attempts to pocket a ball after each has had three consecutive turns at the table, the game is declared stalemated and a new game is played with the same opening breaker. 1986 OR 57. In Snooker, a stalemate is a practical possibility, because there is no requirement that any ball be driven to a rail and endless SAFETY PLAY can occur. The referee therefore has the power to declare a stalemate and restart the FRAME if the players engage in such tactics. 1987 Hales 44. This puts the onus on the player who is ahead to make a legitimate attempt at a shot, or lose his advantage. Under the rules of ENGLISH EIGHT-BALL POOL, the referee may declare a stalemate under certain conditions, as when a player's only legal stroke would cause him to lose the game by potting the eight-ball. Query the wisdom of this provision, however. If the opponent possesses the skill to set up such a situation, why should he not benefit? Cf. DRAW, NULL GAME, SUDDEN DEATH, TIE.

stall

1. To cause undue DELAY. Such behavior may constitute UNSPORTSMANLIKE CONDUCT and can lead to a FORFEIT. 2. (colloq.) A HUSTLER'S term for the tactic of losing a game to keep the opponent betting, using such devices as deliberately missing or leaving oneself in poor position. 1967 Polsky 47, 1970 Fensch 162. See also DOG, DUCK, LEMON, LET UP, LIE DOWN.

stance

The position of the player's body and feet as he ADDRESSES the ball. An early description of how a player should stand at the table can be found in 1839 Kentfield 4: "stand firmly on the right leg (if a right handed player), with the left a little bent, and the trunk nearly erect, or not more inclined forward than may be necessary for the left hand to rest with ease upon the table." This method is no longer recommended. 1867 Dufton advised different stances for men and women. See also 1941 Hoppe 76, 1992 OR 17.

stand-up

(colloq.) Said of a player, particularly a HUSTLER, who is playing at his true SPEED and not attempting to conceal his ability.

standard foul

(Nine-Ball) A FOUL that is penalized by loss of one's turn at the table, after which the opponent has BALL IN HAND. 1988 PBA 19, 1992 OR 48. In general, an infraction that is not an INTENTIONAL FOUL. Cf. SERIOUS FOUL.

standard table

A REGULATION TABLE; one that conforms to the rules. 1978 BSCC 22.

star

(Life Pool, obs.) The right to purchase additional LIVES and thus avoid being eliminated from the game. 1836 Tillotson 4, 1839 Kentfield 42, 1924 Smith 109. The player who is the first one to be KILLED may pay into the POOL another ante, for which he receives the least number of lives remaining on the MARKING BOARD. The name of this option stems from the early custom of placing a small star on the board opposite the name of the player who made the purchase. Only one star was allowed in any pool.

states, names of

The following billiard games incorporate names of states: ALABAMA EIGHT-BALL, CALIFORNIA POOL, MISSISSIPPI, MISSOURI, TEXAS EXPRESS. Cf. CITIES, NAMES OF and COUNTRIES, NAMES OF.

stationary nurse

(Bill.) Any NURSE in which the position of balls does not change with respect to the table at each shot, giving a repetitive position that is maintained as long as the player's skill and the rules permit. 1913 Daly 11. For examples, see ANCHOR NURSE, CHUCK NURSE, DION'S NURSE, EDGE NURSE, ROCKING CANNON, RUDOLPHE'S NURSE. Cf. RUNNING NURSE.

steeplechase cannon

(Eng. Bill.) A cannon made by a JUMP SHOT. 1900 WB (Dec 26) 107, 1909 BA Rules, 1910a Ritchie 124. The term usually refers to the illegal variety of this stroke, in which the cue stick digs under the cue ball and lifts it off the table. Also LEAP. The origin of the term is the steeplechase, a horse race in which the entrants must leap over hurdles.

steer man

(colloq.) One who sets up billiard games on which money is risked by "steering" bettors or players to one another in return for a fee or percentage of the winnings. Also WHEEL MAN. See GAMBLING.

stick

1. A CUE STICK. 1775 Annals 93. A BILLIARD STICK. 2. Figuratively, one's game, *e.g.*, "to shoot a good stick," meaning to play a good game of billiards. 3. (colloq.) A good player. "Dozens of the nation's top sticks convened." 1982 BD (Sep/Oct) 4. 4. ENGLISH that causes the cue ball to stop after contacting the object ball. 1982 Mizerak 48. STOP BALL. In 1895 Buchanan 71, the cue ball may travel slowly after contact. 5. (obs.) When the balls are hit very hard and made to fly in all directions, the player is said to have given them "stick." 1869 Roberts 174. 6. (obs.) A MACE. 1674 Cotton, 1734 Seymour *Compl. Gamester.*

stick bridge

= MECHANICAL BRIDGE. 1976 WSD 425.

stick shot

= STOP SHOT. A shot made using STOP or STICK.

stiff

1. (Three-Cushions) A position in which no reasonable shot is possible. A bad LEAVE, a DOG. "He left me a stiff." 2. A player of low skill.

stiffness

The rigidity of the SHAFT of a cue stick, which tends to prevent it from flexing during a shot. 1806 Phil 49. Also known as SPINE.

still cue ball

(Bill.) The cue ball that was not used as a cue ball by the previous STRIKER. The concept is important in describing the rules of three-handed play, in which the INCOMING PLAYER uses the still cue ball. 1946 OR 5.

stirabout

(obs.) A bizarre stroke in which the PUSH and MASSÉ are combined. The cue stick is held nearly vertically and is used in a continuous motion to roll the cue ball to a position from which a push shot can be executed. Now completely illegal, it was used when the cue ball and object ball were close to a pocket but not lined up for a shot. 1919 Hoyle 629. The word "stirabout" referred to a type of porridge made by stirring oatmeal into boiling water or milk with a motion resembling this shot.

stone

(colloq.) A ball. Also ROCK. See also MUD.

stop

1. = STOP BALL. 2. A handicap requiring the stronger player to relinquish his inning after making a certain number of points, to prevent a long RUN. See ONE AND STOP, SAFE. See also DUCK. Cf. NO COUNT, the opposite handicap, in which a player scores in an inning only if he makes at least a minimum number of points. 3. A device for blocking up pockets to prevent balls from falling in. See POCKET STOP, POOL STOP.

stop ball

ACTION applied to the cue ball by hitting it in the center or slightly below center with FOLLOW-THROUGH, which causes it to stop after a FULL contact with the object ball. 1948 Mosconi 46. Used in performing a STOP SHOT. See also DRAG, HOLD, STAB, STICK SHOT.

Stop Game

(game, obs.) A CRAMP GAME in which the STRIKER's ball must not touch any cushion; if it does, he loses a point and his turn, except that he may contact no more than one cushion when IN HAND and shooting at a ball IN BAULK. A LOSING HAZARD counts even if the cue ball touches the edge of the cushion as it enters the pocket. 1856 Crawley 99. (This is the origin of the concept of INCIDENTAL CONTACT.) This HANDICAP is said by 1850c White & Bohn 40 to be equivalent to giving about half the points. It is also called the NON-CUSHION GAME. 1839 Kentfield 38, 1862 Crawley 98, 1867 Dufton 233.

stop shot

(Pocket Bill.) A shot in which the cue ball stops immediately after contacting the object ball. 1931 BM (Feb) 39, 1965 Fats 73, 1976 WSD 427. This is accomplished by striking the cue ball at or very slightly below center and hitting the object ball FULL. The cue ball is then said to have been hit with STOP BALL. Also called a STICK SHOT. In English Billiards, a STOP-STROKE.

stop-stroke

(Eng. Bill.) A shot in which the cue ball stops dead at the point of impact with the object ball. 1866 Crawley 80. In American usage, a STICK SHOT or STOP SHOT.

231

stopped

A ball is considered to have "stopped" if it remains motionless for five seconds. 1988 PBA 23. See MOTION.

straight

1. (game) STRAIGHT POOL, 14.1 CONTINUOUS POCKET BILLIARDS. 2. (game) STRAIGHT BILLIARDS, STRAIGHT-RAIL. 3. = STRAIGHT-UP. 4. A "straight" shot is one that can be made by striking the object ball FULL. 1807 White 134. "It's a straight bank." 5. Pure, unadorned, with no embellishments or special rules. "Let's play straight Nine-Ball." 6. Consecutive, consecutively. "He won eight straight games." 7. Honest, honestly. "Play it straight." 8. (game) A ROTATION game, played in Hawaii, using PILLS numbered 10-20. The object is to have the total of one's run plus the number on a pill equal 31 exactly. Cf. BLIND, in which a player does not draw a pill until after his run. 1991 Masui PC.

straight back

(Pocket Bill.) A LONG BANK. 1978 Fels 50. Sometimes used as a CALL for such a shot; *e.g.*, "the five straight back."

Straight Billiards

(game) = STRAIGHT-RAIL.

232

Straight Pool

(game) = 14.1 CONTINUOUS POCKET BILLIARDS. 1946 *Atlantic Monthly* (Aug) 134, 1976 WSD 39. The term was used in 1911 NYT (Apr 21) 9:5 to mean a straightforward style of play in which fancy shots and COMBINATIONS were avoided. It eventually became used as the name of the game itself. The game replaced Continuous Pool in championship events beginning in 1912, when Edward I. Ralph won the first national tournament. The runs listed in the table below include both tournament and exhibition play.

AMERICAN HIGH RUNS AT STRAIGHT POOL				
RUN	YEAR	PLAYER	LOCATION	OPPONENT
46	1912	De Oro	Philadelphia	T. I. Wilson
59	1913	De Oro	New York	J. Maturo
70	1913	Taberski	New York	—
74	1868	M. Philips	Decatur, IL	—
78	1868	Layton	Chicago	—
94	1914	Harry Hart	Brooklyn	—
98	1914	B. Allen	—	—

AMERICAN HIGH RUNS AT STRAIGHT POOL				
RUN	YEAR	PLAYER	LOCATION	OPPONENT
141	c1915	Blankenship	Cleveland	—
152	1917	Rudolph	Cleveland	—
155	1919	Greenleaf	Danbury, CT	R. Stone
200	1921	Taberski	Stuttgart, AR	S. Sharock
206	1922	Greenleaf	Logansport, IN	G. Kelly
208	1934	F. Broughton	—	—
267	1935	Greenleaf	—	—
272	1935	Greenleaf	Norfolk, VA	—
277	1935	Rudolph	—	—
309	1939	Crane	Layton, UT	—
309	1945	Mosconi	Perth Amboy, NJ	—
322	1953	Mosconi	Platteville, WI	—
355	1953	Mosconi	Milwaukee	—
365	1953	Mosconi	Wilmington, NC	—
526	1954	Mosconi	Springfield, OH	—

Straight-Rail

(game) A synonym for CAROM BILLIARDS or the THREE-BALL GAME; that is, ordinary Billiards in which the object is to make a carom with one's cue ball, there being no BALK restrictions or minimum number of cushion contacts required. 1899 Souv 49, 1941 Hoppe 76. The phrase "straight-rail" is considerably younger than the game it describes, and its origin, explained below, is somewhat obscure. See 1988 BD (Oct) 54.

The game is just the carom portion of English Billiards but with pockets removed from the table. It was popularized by the French—in the mid-nineteenth century it was known as FRENCH CAROMS. The first public stake match in the U.S. took place on a 6-foot × 12-foot table in San Francisco between Michael Phelan and a Monsieur Damon of Paris on April 13, 1855. After seven hours of play, the HIGH RUN (by Phelan) was nine.

Phelan won two out of three games and the $500 stake. 1891 MB 472.

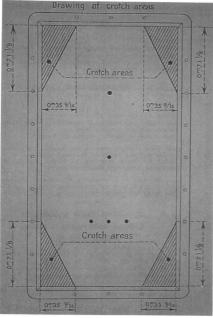

Straight-Rail

The carom game became progressively more popular during the 1860s. The first tournament in the U.S., for the world title, was held in New York in June 1873. Albert Garnier won with an AVERAGE of 12 and a high run of 113. Players worked assiduously for the next several years on RAIL NURSE technique, achieving rapid success. (See the table below for the progress of Straight-Rail high run records.) This nurse was sometimes itself called the "straight rail." 1912 MB 261. It was occasionally known as the "straight-forward rail," describing the way in which the balls are pushed forward as the nurse progresses. 1928 BR (Sep) 22.

In 1878, the phrase "rail billiards" was used to describe the manner of play in which the rail nurse was used for long periods. 1878 NYT (Jul 9) 2:4. The demise of the game was also being predicted correctly that year: "it will

then be for the professionals . . . to determine on a game to take its place." The high run record had reached 690 by 1879, when the CHAMPION'S GAME was introduced to curb rail play. The span of the professional game in the U. S., therefore, lasted only six years, from 1873 to 1879.

The Champion's Game, which employed long diagonal lines at the corners to define restricted spaces, became known as the "limited-rail" game, since it limited the rail nurse. The phrases "straight rail" and "unlimited rail" were used to distinguish ordinary billiards, in which the rail nurse was permitted, from the Champion's Game. The term "straight rail" was used in 1881 NYT (Mar 23) 5:6. "Straight Billiards" appeared in 1888 NYT (Jan 31) 1:4.

After 1879, no player of the top rank competed in Straight-Rail tournaments in the U.S. Maurice Vignaux ran 1531 in Paris in 1880, and amateurs continued with the game as the professionals moved on to Balkline. George Spears ran 5041 in 1890 and there were several players who could essentially run points until they dropped from exhaustion. Runs greater than 10,000 have reliably been reported, but it is probably more difficult for the marker to stay awake to keep an accurate count than it is for the player to make such a run.

Straight-Rail is called the FREE GAME in Europe because of the absence of balk restrictions. It is still popular there; it forms part of the PENTATHLON competition and is regarded as excellent practice for Balkline and Three-Cushions.

See also AIRPLANE, AMBIDEXTROUS, AMERICAN SERIES, COVER, DELAY, FREE GAME, FRENCH BILLIARDS, GATHER, LINE-UP, NO COUNT, NURSE, RAIL NURSE, SPOT AT FIFTY. Cf. BALKLINE, CHAMPION'S GAME, ENGLISH BILLIARDS, THREE-CUSHIONS. The table below illustrates the progress of U.S. high runs in Straight-Rail. The marks are not necessarily official records, since some were made in exhibition matches, but were the highest runs recorded up to that time. In 1874, Edward Daniels lost the game despite his world record high run of 249.

233

AMERICAN HIGH RUNS AT STRAIGHT-RAIL BILLIARDS					
RUN	YEAR	PLAYER	LOCATION	OPPONENT	TABLE SIZE
9	1855	Phelan	—	Damon	12′
11	1863	Kavanagh	—	Gayraud	12′
19	1863	Carme	New York	Kavanagh	11′
30	1868	Rudolphe	—	Deery	11′

AMERICAN HIGH RUNS AT STRAIGHT-RAIL BILLIARDS					
RUN	YEAR	PLAYER	LOCATION	OPPONENT	TABLE SIZE
40	1868	Foster	New York	Deery	11'
41	1870	Stone	New Haven	Hewins	—
85	1870	Carme	New Orleans	H. Miller	10'
107	1871	Rudolphe	New Orleans	H. Miller	10'
113	1873	Garnier	New York	—	10'
117	1873	Ubassy	—	—	10'
153	1873	Daly	Chicago	—	10'
212	1874	Daly	New York	C. Dion	10'
249	1874	E. Daniels	—	—	10'
251	1876	Sexton	Philadelphia	Rudolphe	10'
287	1876	Sexton	Philadelphia	—	10'
311	1876	Slosson	New York	Garnier	10'
417	1877	Sexton	New Orleans	Slosson	10'
429	1878	Schaefer	St. Louis	C. Dion	10'
441	1879	Slosson	New York	Sexton	10'
464	1879	Slosson	New York	Schaefer	10'
476	1879	Slosson	Boston	Stone	10'
690	1879	Schaefer	Chicago	Slosson	10'
942	1884	McLaughlin	Chicago	Catton	10'
2572	1887	McKenna	Boston	Eames	10'
2996	1890	Schaefer	San Francisco	McCleery	9'
5041	1895	Spears	—	—	—
10,232	1931	C. Peterson	—	—	—

234

straight taper

A TAPER in which the diameter of the shaft increases linearly from TIP to JOINT. Also EUROPEAN TAPER. Cf. DELAYED TAPER, KOMORI TAPER, PROFESSIONAL TAPER.

straight-up

With no HANDICAP. Describes a game in which each player needs the same number of points to win as any opponent. See also LEVEL, UP.

Straights

(game, sl.) = STRAIGHT POOL. 1959 Tevis 38.

Streamlined Billiards

(game) THREE-CUSHION BILLIARDS with the following rule variation, introduced in 1942: A player who COUNTS successfully on the first stroke may use either cue ball for his second shot but then must continue using that ball for the remainder of his INNING. The

INCOMING PLAYER shoots with the STILL CUE BALL. Cf. CHOICE OF CUE BALL, OPTIONAL CUE BALL.

stretcher

A board used to support the SLATE of a table. OBG 64. Cf. MARKER STRETCHER.

strike

1. To hit a ball with an instrument. 1674 Cotton 27. In 1806 Phil, a distinction is drawn between "strike," which refers to contacting a ball with the cue stick, and "hit," which means a contact between two balls. 2. (Bowlliards) The act of pocketing 10 balls at a player's first opportunity in an INNING. This results in a bonus of 10 points plus the number of balls pocketed in the player's next two RUNS. 1982 OR 82. Cf. SPARE.

striker

The PLAYER whose turn it is to shoot. 1775 Annals 89, 1807 White 32. The SHOOTER. Ponder, if you will, at what point the INCOMING PLAYER becomes the striker. Cf. NONSTRIKER.

striker's ball

(Bill.) The cue ball belonging to the PLAYER who is shooting. 1866 Crawley 7.

striking point

1. The point on the cue ball contacted by the cue stick. 2. (Eng. Bill., obs.) = the D. 1807 White 3. The area from which the cue ball may validly be struck when it is IN HAND.

striking ring

(Eng. Bill., Snooker, obs.) = D. So called because it is a ring-shaped area resembling a D in shape, from which the striker must play when the cue ball is IN HAND. 1814 OED. Called the STRIKING POINT in 1807 White. Also, the BAULK CIRCLE, BAULK SEMICIRCLE, HALF-CIRCLE, or SEMICIRCLE.

string

1. A RUN of points made during a single INNING, so named because the points were tallied by means of beads threaded on a wire, known as a MARKING STRING. 1871 NYT (Apr 27) 1:5. Also called a BREAK or CLUSTER. 2. A MARKING STRING. A row of counters mounted on a stretched wire for scorekeeping. The American strings typically had 100 counters, the English 50, and the European 25. 1869 Kavanagh 67. 3. A line or imaginary line on the table bed, usually the HEAD STRING. 1857 Phelan 30, 1869 Kavanagh 5, 1992 OR 4. See also CENTER STRING, FOOT STRING, LONG STRING, STRING LINE. Rarely, a BALKLINE. 1976 WSD 430. How did "string" come to be used in Billiards? The answer is

unclear, but actual strings were once part of the table accessories. "Some instead of a King use a string and a bell." 1674 Cotton 30. 4. To LAG. 1814 Hoyle 373, 1839 Kentfield 29, 1954 KTG 6. Both players strike their cue balls simultaneously from behind the BAULK-LINE, or STRING to the TOP cushion, with the object of leaving the ball as close as possible to the BOTTOM cushion. The player who wins the string obtains a tactical advantage by being permitted to elect whether or not to play first. In Bagatelle, to string for the LEAD is to PINK. In 1674 Cotton, to "string" means to place the ball in position for the lag.

string line

An imaginary line on the table passing through a SPOT and running parallel to a RAIL to define a STRING, usually the HEAD STRING. 1806 Phil 22, 1884 MB 269.

string spot

= HEAD SPOT, LIGHT-RED SPOT. 1916 RGRG 14. The SPOT located at the center of the HEAD STRING. Also the AMERICAN SPOT, UPPER SPOT, WHITE SPOT, and, in the Three-Ball Game, the WHITE-BALL SPOT. Sometimes known as the STRINGING SPOT.

stringing

A process used to determine who will LEAD, in which both players strike their balls from within the STRING toward the opposite end cushion with the object of having them land as close as possible to the HEAD cushion. 1836 Tillotson 1, 1857 Phelan 66, 1942 Cochran 110. See LAG.

stringing nail

(obs.) = STRINGING SPOT. 1788 OED, 1845 Hoyle 224. So called because the limits of the string line were marked by nails driven into the rails.

stringing spot

(obs.) One of the two SPOTS defining the STRING LINE. 1839 Kentfield 29. On modern tables, the second spot on the LONG RAIL away from the HEAD RAIL.

stripe

(Eight-Ball) A ball having a stripe of color around its circumference. One of the GROUP of balls numbered 9 through 15. 1989 Koehler 261. Also called a BANDED BALL, BIG, HIGH. Striped balls were in use by 1889. 1891 MB 655. Cf. PLAIN, SOLID.

Stripes and Solids

(game) = EIGHT-BALL, so called because one player must pocket the SOLIDS and the other the STRIPES. 1974 ITP 26. Also BIGS AND LITTLES.

235

stroke

1. An attempt at a shot, in which there is contact between the cue stick and the cue ball. The action of moving the cue stick through the position occupied by the cue ball, thus propelling the ball. 1674 Cotton. A stroke is not complete until all balls on the table have become motionless; that is, until they are no longer rolling or spinning. 1982 OR. The stroke is preceded by a BACKSWING. Unlike in the game of golf, a motion of the cue stick that does not result in contact with any ball does not count as a stroke, regardless of the player's intention. See IN CONTROL, INNING, MOTION. See also COMPULSORY STROKE, COUP, FAIR STROKE, FOUL STROKE, LEADING STROKE, TEN-STROKE, THIRTEEN-STROKE. 2. A type of shot or particular technique used in hitting the cue ball. See BREECHES STROKE, CONTINU-OUS STROKE, COUP SEC, CRAMP STROKE, CRAWL STROKE, DRAW stroke, FEATHER STROKE, FOLLOWING STROKE, FRENCH STROKE, HALF-BALL STROKE, HARPOON STROKE, HIGH OBLIQUE STROKE, HIGH STROKE, JAR STROKE, KISS STROKE, LONG STROKE, LOW STROKE, NATURAL-ANGLE STROKE, OBLIQUE STROKE, PERPENDICULAR STROKE, PUSH STROKE, QUILL STROKE, SIDE STROKE, SIDEARM STROKE, SLIP STROKE, SPOT-STROKE, STOP-STROKE, STROKE BALL, STROKE SHOT, Z STROKE. The term "stroke," when used as a suffix, is primarily British; the U.S. equivalent is SHOT. 3. A player's "stroke" refers to the style in which he swings the cue and follows through the ball. See also DEAD STROKE, FREE STROKE, IN STROKE, OUT OF STROKE, SLIP STROKE. The straightness of one's stroke can be verified by a method credited to Frank Callen, using the boundary between the cloth and the top of the rail as an aiming line. Form a bridge on the rail atop the line and pretend to strike at an imaginary ball also lying on the line. If the tip of your cue winds up over the line, your stroke is straight. 1991 Everton 55.

stroke ball

(Bill., obs.) One's own cue ball; the ball that is about to be stroked with the cue stick. 1897 NYT (Dec 4) 4:5. One's PLAY BALL.

stroke shot

A FANCY SHOT requiring an outstanding STROKE, usually involving extreme English. The primary U.S. exponent of such shots is Mike Massey.

Stroklet

(game, obs.) A drawing-room billiard game played on a square table whose sides measure 30 or 36 inches and played with small MACES and SKITTLES.

Stroklet

stuff

1. (colloq.) = ENGLISH, GREASE, JUICE, OIL, SPIN. 1924 Smith 14. 2. (colloq.) Playing skill. "Show me your stuff."

stun

1. (Brit. games) A stroke causing the cue ball to move very slowly after hitting an object ball. Similar to DEAD BALL. 1908c Cook Jr. 92, 1978 Byrne 63. "When the pot is not straight, the 'stop' shot becomes a stun." 1976 Reardon 66. This refers to the fact that the cue ball cannot be made to stop dead unless it hits the object ball FULL. Cf. STAB. 2. (Brit. games) DRAW applied to slow the progress of the cue ball. 1924 Ogden 273.

stun through

(Brit. games) = STUN. A stroke in which the cue ball moves ahead slowly after contacting the object ball. 1976 Charlton 12. The cue ball remains near the object ball after the stroke. 1954 KTG 21.

substitute bridge

= MECHANICAL BRIDGE. WBA 5.

successive fouls

(Pocket Bill.) = CONSECUTIVE FOULS, that is, fouls on consecutive shots, not simply in consecutive INNINGS. Three successive fouls results in LOSS OF GAME in SIX-BALL, SEVEN-BALL, NINE-BALL, TEN-BALL, ROTATION, ONE POCKET, COWBOY POOL, CRIBBAGE, and MISTER AND MRS. POCKET BILLIARDS. In BOTTLE POOL, fouls in three successive innings result in loss of game.

suck

(sl.) To apply DRAW to a ball. 1990 White G-6.

sucker

(colloq.) A player of lower skill who is easily enticed by a HUSTLER into a losing game. Also called a FISH, MARK, or PIGEON. 1857 Phelan 72, 1979 Grissim 255. See also THROUGH-TICKET.

sudden death

A situation in which the first player to score or pocket a ball will win the game. This is always true of a HILL GAME but is rare in other billiard situations. In Bowliards and Equal Offense, if the players are TIED after each has played the prescribed number of INNINGS, the game is decided by sudden death. For a related case in Snooker, see ALL ON THE BLACK.

Super Billiards

(game) = 28.2 BALKLINE. So called by the French, who popularized the game and regarded it as the supreme test of Balkline skill. 1937 NYT (Jan 7) 25:8. Cf. 71.2 BALKLINE.

suspended ball

A ball that has come to rest above the table BED, usually atop balls that are JAWED. 1983 Rule Book 252. A suspended ball is not a JUMP BALL. When confronted with a suspended ball, the referee projects its center (visually or physically) directly downward from the jawed position. If the ball lies above the pocket, it is removed and considered pocketed, and play continues. 1982 OR 45. Any suspended ball not deemed to be pocketed is replaced on the table bed at the discretion of the REFEREE.

suspension

1. Withdrawal of a player's privilege of entering TOURNAMENTS for a prescribed period. A severe sanction imposed by a LEAGUE or tournament authority for a particularly noxious violation of the rules of the game. For the story of a famous suspension, see CLOTH. 2. Temporary delay in the progress of a game, declared by the REFEREE and usually brought on by an unusual event such as a power failure or trouble with the EQUIPMENT. See also INTERMISSION.

swan neck

(Brit.) An EXTENDED SPIDER or SPAN REST. 1988 Davis 10.

sweator

(colloq.) One who is nervous during a billiard game, possibly because he has placed a bet on the outcome. 1990 White G-6. See GAMBLING. The spelling "sweator" is used instead of "sweater" to avoid confusion with a garment of the same name. See DRESS CODE.

sweep

1. The act of winning all of one's games in a match or tournament. One of the most famous sweeps in billiard history occurred in the 1940 World Three-Cushion Championships, in which Willie Hoppe swept all 20 games he played, although his margin of victory in one of his games against Joe Chamaco was but a single point. 2. (obs.) A TRAILING shot made with the mace. 1807 White.

swerve

(Brit. games) A stroke that causes the cue ball to follow a slightly curved path. 1912 Levi 759. A CURVE SHOT. A partial MASSÉ performed by tilting the cue stick vertically at an angle and hitting the cue ball off center. 1925 Peall 83, 1954 KTG 23. The shot is shown but is not named in 1830 Mingaud. An "immature masse," according to 1924a Newman 143. It is offered in 1954 Davis 80 as a method for getting out of SNOOKERS. Joe Davis himself was an expert at the swerve.

swing

1. Motion of the arm that holds the BUTT end of the cue stick preparatory to and during the STROKE. The orthodox method is to use a PENDULUM SWING, which results in a steady, reproducible movement. Players who began the game as children and were not tall enough to reach ordinary shots, such as Willie Hoppe, attained skill with the unorthodox SIDEARM SWING, in which the player's eyes are not directly over the cue stick during the stroke, making this technique the virtual equivalent of shooting a gun from the hip. 2. (Brit.) A shot in which the cue ball takes a wide angle after contacting an object ball, akin to a SPREAD. 1986 Everton 88.

switchback cannon

(obs.) = RAILROAD SHOT. 1899 Stancliffe.

system

A method of aiming shots, often based on the DIAMONDS, generally in THREE-CUSHIONS. 1928 Barry, 1941 Hoppe 75. See also DIAMOND SYSTEM and BANK SHOT. A "system player" is one who adheres to a manner of play and methodically applies principles to his play without being tempted by easy or flashy shots. A "system

237

player" in Three-Cushions is usually one who relies on one or more diamond systems or other standardized schemes for aiming shots. Some players are known to possess hundreds of such systems; Nobuaki Kobayashi, former world champion, is said to use over a thousand.

system shot

A shot played by means of a SYSTEM, particularly in Three-Cushions.

table

A flat surface, covered with cloth, surrounded by resilient cushions and elevated above the floor, on which billiards is played. 1976 WSD 439. The table is the arena in which the drama of the game unfolds.

Billiards was played principally on the ground until the mid-1400s, when it was moved indoors to a table. Green cloth was used to simulate grass. It is reported that King Louis IX of France owned a billiard table in 1469. Tables were originally fitted with pockets, usually three or six, but the number varied from zero to ten. Various targets and obstacles were placed on the surface, most often an arch known as the PORT and an upright stick called the KING—implements borrowed from the game of croquet.

Few changes were made during the next 350 years, although tables became more sturdy during the 1600s. 1674 Cotton 23 reports that "The form of a Billiard-Table is oblong, that is something longer than it is broad; it is rail'd round, which rail or ledge ought to be a little swel'd or stuft with fine flox or cotton: the superficies of the Table must be covered with green-cloth, the finer and more freed from knots the better it is: the Board must be level'd as exactly as may be, so that a Ball may run true upon any part of the Table without leaning to any side thereof." This paragraph lays down the basic requirements: flat, level and cushioned. Neither the dimensions nor the ratio of length to width was fixed at

238

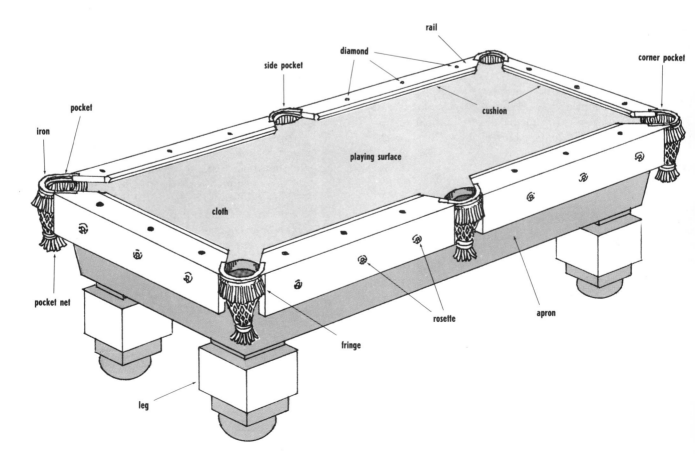

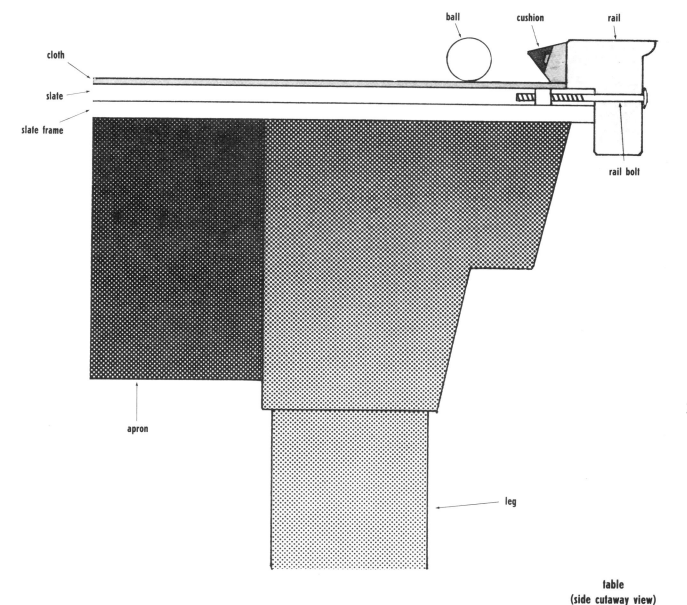

**table
(side cutaway view)**

this time; the two-to-one ratio did not become standard until the middle of the next century, though even at the time of White in 1807 there was considerable flexibility in sizes. A bit later, 1839 Kentfield listed various table sizes, with "the width being always one-half of the length."

The Industrial Revolution produced technological advancements in rapid succession that caused a striking improvement in table quality. Machines for cutting and grinding stone slabs allowed SLATE to be polished for use in billiard tables. Vulcanization of rubber, discovered in 1839, gave rise in 1845 to reliable rubber cushions.

By 1850, the table had assumed its modern form. Many tables from the 1870s are still in excellent condition.

Carom tables began to be manufactured in greater numbers in 1810 and became dominant in France and the U.S. after 1850, but have never been common in the U.K. The four-pocket table was introduced in the U.S. in 1863 but was used in tournaments for only about 10 years. See AMERICAN FOUR-BALL BILLIARDS. Kavanagh and Decker in New York could produce three tables a day in 1869 at a retail price of $525 each. Adjusted for inflation, the price of tables has not increased in 150 years.

DIMENSIONS OF VARIOUS STANDARD TABLE SIZES				
EXTERIOR SIZE (FEET)	PLAYING SURFACE (INCHES)	PLAYING AREA (SQUARE FEET)	CORNER POCKET WIDTH (INCHES)	SIDE POCKET WIDTH (INCHES)
3 × 6	32 × 64	14	—	—
3½ × 7	38 × 76	20	—	—
4 × 8	44 × 88	27	—	—
4½ × 9	50 × 100	35	4⅞–5⅛	5⅜–5⅝
5 × 10	56 × 112	43.5	—	—
6 × 12	68 × 136	64	3⅜–3⅝	4¹/₁₆–4⁵/₁₆

METRIC TABLES have lengths of 2.5, 2.6 (8 feet), 2.8 (9 feet), 3.1 (10 feet), and 3.5 (12 feet) meters. A table is set up and leveled by an INSTALLER or MECHANIC. See also LEVEL.

The dimensions of the playing surface are taken from the covered nose of the cushion rubber. Note that a 12-foot table is almost twice as large as a 9-foot table in area. The usual table size in the U.S. and the U.K. was 6 feet by 12 feet until about 1850. For the next 20 years, a table measuring 5½ feet by 11 feet was used in professional competition. The 10-foot table was first used by top players at Platt's Hall in San Francisco on January 12, 1871. 1928 BR (Aug) 4. This size remained standard for both pocket and carom games until the 4½ × 9 pocket table became official in 1949.

The largest billiard table ever constructed is believed to be 10½ feet by 18 feet, approximately four times as large as a regulation table. It was made entirely of wood and could be taken down and assembled without the use of a single nail or screw. It was first exhibited in Pittsburgh on December 6, 1986.

The height of the table has remained fixed within narrow limits for at least 200 years. BCA standards specify that the distance from the table bed to the bottom of the leg be 29¼ inches to within a tolerance of ¼ inch. International rules require a height of 79 to 80 centimeters, which is approximately 31 inches. WBA.

Tables were made by numerous manufacturers, many of which were small, local shops. The most famous makers were Phelan and Collender, Kavanagh & Decker, J. M. Brunswick & Balke, Burrowes, National, and A. E. Schmidt. Well-known British manufacturers were Thurston, Burroughes & Watts, and E. J. Riley. Table styling and ORNAMENTATION has generally lagged behind furniture design trends by at least a decade. 1990 M. Fish PC.

Old tables are objects of considerable veneration by players and collectors alike. There is intense interest in refinished and replica tables based on classic Brunswick designs such as the Monarch, an unusual table with a cast-iron base having lions for legs, the Brilliant Novelty, the Arcade, the Kling, and the Centennial, a deco table issued in 1945 for the 100th anniversary of the founding of Brunswick. A restored Monarch may bring $40,000; other specialty tables have recently sold for $100,000, and rare examples from the eighteenth century over $200,000.

Tables have been manufactured in numerous shapes, including circular, octagonal, oval, and square (1807 White 3, 1866 Crawley 7, 1981c Clare 11), racetrack (having straight sides but curved ends), scalloped (with cushions composed of arcs), and triangular (1827 Mingaud). Some of these shapes, particularly oval, are periodically—but only temporarily—revived. The circular and oval tables have been made in several forms, including pocketless, with six pockets, and with a single pocket cut into the bed of the table.

Tables have been made for shipboard use. See SHIP, BILLIARDS ABOARD. Tables are often disguised as other pieces of furniture or designed to be transformed quickly from a dining table to a billiard table, for example. See CONVERTIBLE TABLE.

See also BAGATELLE, BALKLINE TABLE, BAR TABLE, BAR-TABLE GAME, BILLIARD BOARD, BUMPER POOL, CAROM TABLE, CAROMBOLETTE, COIN-OPERATED TABLE, COMBINATION TABLE, COMMERCIAL TABLE, CONVERTIBLE TABLE, ENGLISH TABLE, GULLY TABLE, HOME TABLE, METRIC TABLE, NICKEL AND DIME, OVAL TABLE, PARI-

SIAN POOL BOARD, PIGEON-HOLE TABLE, POCKET TABLE, POOL TABLE, PORTABLE TABLE, QUARTER TABLE, REGULATION TABLE, SIPPIO TABLE, SNOOKER TABLE, STANDARD TABLE.

For table parts, see APRON, BAIZE, BALL RETURN, BAND, BANK, BASE, BASE FRAME, BED, BUMP, BUMPER, CLOTH, CUP, CUSHION, CUSHION FACING, CUSHION NOSE, CUSHION PROFILE, DIAMOND, DROP POCKET, DUPLEX POCKET, ELBOW, FEATHER STRIP, FOOT, FRAME, GULLY, GUTTER, HAZARD, HEATING, IRON, LEG, MANUFACTURER'S NAMEPLATE, NAIL, NET, NOSE, PEDESTAL, PLAYING SURFACE, POCKET, POINT, RAIL, RAIL BOLT, ROSETTE, RUBBER, SHOULDER, SKIRT, SLATE, STRETCHER, TROUGH, UNDERCUT, WOOD.

For table markings, see ANCHOR SPACE, BALK, BALKLINE, BAULK, BOX, CENTER SPACE, CROTCH, D, DEE, END TABLE, FOOT STRING, HEAD STRING, INTERDICTED AREA, KITCHEN, PARKER'S BOX, SEMICIRCLE, SHORT TABLE, SPOT, STRING. For different table styles, see AMUSETTE, IMPROMPTU BILLIARDS, PARLOR BILLIARDS.

For table accessories, see ANCHOR BLOCK, ARCH, BALKLINE MARKER, BILLIARD BLOCK, BRIDGE, BRIDGE-HOOK, BRUSH, BUTT HOOK, CAROM PLUG, CHALK, COUNTING STRING, COVER, EQUIPMENT, IRON, KING, MECHANICAL BRIDGE, PASS, PASS IRON, POCKET STOP, POOL STOP, PORT, RAIL MARKER, SHIM, TABLE COVER, TEMPLATE, WIRE.

Portions of the table include the BAULK CUSHION, BOTTOM, CENTER TABLE, CORNER, END RAIL, END TABLE, FOOT, HEAD, POCKET, SHORT TABLE, SIDE, SIDE RAIL, TOP, TOP OF THE TABLE, UPPER TABLE, UPTOWN. See also OCEAN.

For properties of a table, see DRIFT, FAST, LONG, ROLL, SHORT, SLOW, TABLE ROLL, TRUE, UNTRUE.

The term "table" appears in the expressions AROUND THE TABLE, CLEAN THE TABLE, CLEAR THE TABLE, CROSS-TABLE SHOT, FREE TABLE, LEAVE THE TABLE, OPEN TABLE, TABLE IN POSITION, TABLE SCRATCH, TABLE TIME.

table cover

A blanket, usually of thin plastic, used to protect the cloth and rails when a table is not in use. A COVER.

table in position

A term that describes the state of the table confronting an INCOMING PLAYER, indicating that he must play the balls as they lie, without any being moved, spotted or replaced. After an INTERFERENCE foul in certain games, the incoming player has the option of accepting the "table in position" ("as is") or having the balls replaced at

the locations they occupied before the interference. Also used to indicate that the object balls have not been moved during a shot. 1986 OR 23. See also REPLACEMENT.

table roll

The phenomenon in which a billiard ball fails to roll in a straight line because of some component of EQUIPMENT that is UNTRUE, such as an unbalanced table, poor cloth or an uneven slate. 1989 Koehler 261. Also DRIFT, ROLL.

table scratch

A SCRATCH committed by the player's failure to DRIVE a ball to a rail after contacting an object ball, as required by the rules, or by failure to contact or pocket any ball. So called because the cue ball remains on the *table* but the shot is treated as a *scratch* nonetheless, except that the cue ball is not IN HAND (except in games, such as modern NINE-BALL, in which all fouls result in BALL IN HAND). The term predates the 1960s but the earliest printed reference located was 1992 Billing 44. Cf. POCKET SCRATCH.

table time

A charge for the use of a billiard table measured by the length of time it has been occupied. "Who's paying the table time?" The idea of charging by time used rather than by games played began in the U.S. in 1867. 1867 NYT (Aug 23) 5:5. It was based on the common practice in England of paying for time in certain games. 1807 White 51. See FOR THE TIME, OFF AND ON, SPLIT THE TIME, TIME.

take

To attempt a shot. "Take a five-rail bank." To try to pocket a ball. "I'll take the five." See also TAKE A HAZARD, TAKE THE COLOURS.

take a hazard

(Brit. games, obs.) An optional action in LIFE POOL or TWO-BALL POOL whereby a NONSTRIKER, certain of making a HAZARD that the STRIKER prefers not to attempt, will try it himself under the penalty of losing as many LIVES as he would gain if successful. 1857 Phelan 65, 1891 MB 35. Cf. VOLUNTEER.

take the colours

(Snooker) To POT all the COLOURS in numerical order from yellow (value 2) to black (value 7), thereby scoring 27 points. 1954 KTG 34.

take up

(Snooker) To remove a ball from the table temporarily so that the INCOMING PLAYER is not left SNOOKERED by his opponent's FOUL stroke. The rule permitting this originated with LIFE POOL. 1836 Tillotson 3. The ball is replaced immediately after the stroke is completed. The purpose of taking up is to ensure that a player is not put at a disadvantage by his opponent's violation of the rules. See LIFT, LIFTED BALL. Cf. FREE BALL, NEAREST BALL PLAYABLE, PLAY AGAIN RULE, POSITION MARKER.

taker

(Brit.) The COUNTER MAN, one who "takes" the patrons' money. 1937 NBJ (Oct).

talcum powder

Powder used for drying the hands and reducing the friction between the BRIDGE HAND and the SHAFT of the cue stick. 1989 Koehler 261. See also HAND CHALK.

tally ball

= PEA, PILL. 1979 Sullivan 112. Used with the SHAKE BOTTLE to determine the order of player ROTATION or to select a PRIVATE NUMBER BALL for each player in games such as KELLY POOL.

taper

The profile of the SHAFT of a cue stick as it widens in diameter from the TIP to the JOINT or BUTT. A taper is said to be "fast" or "slow," depending on how rapidly this increase occurs. A FAST TAPER is thought to be more effective in transferring force to the cue ball and is currently in favor among THREE-CUSHION players. 1983 NBN (Mar) 18. See also DELAYED TAPER, EUROPEAN TAPER, KOMORI TAPER, PROFESSIONAL TAPER, STRAIGHT TAPER.

tapping

The seating of a ball on a SPOT or other location on the table by rapping it from above with another ball. A small pit in the cloth is thereby created in which the positioned ball tends to remain. Although this method is not recommended for ordinary spotting, it can be useful for placing balls precisely for TRICK SHOTS. 1992 OR 52.

target pocket

1. The pocket in which the STRIKER intends to pocket a ball on a particular stroke. 2. (One Pocket) One of the two FOOT POCKETS, into which balls may be legally pocketed. 1992 OR 64.

Tavern Eight-Ball

(game) Eight-Ball as played on a BAR POOL table.

tea-tray game

(Eng. Bill.) = TOP-OF-THE-TABLE GAME. 1895 Buchanan 94. The term stems from a remark by William Cook,

the champion of England, who, when told that the size of the pockets was about to be reduced in order to restrict the SPOT-STROKE, reputedly said that he did not care and could play on a tea tray. 1900 WB (Nov 24) 40.

telegraphic billiards

1. A method of competing by telegraph to permit competition between players who cannot meet at the same table for some reason. Since it is impractical to use this medium to communicate the position of the balls after every shot, stylized versions of the game were developed to allow less frequent reporting.

The first match by telegraph was played on March 26, 1901. It was a game of 14.2 Balkline between Wayman McCreery and Martin Mullin, in which each player shot from the spot and then used the STILL CUE BALL for five innings, after which the balls were again spotted. The positions were not telegraphed; only the run lengths were. McCreery was the victor, 500–471. 1904 MB 284. Such a contest is, of course, purely offensive. See also DUPLICATE BILLIARDS, KEY SHOT BILLIARDS. Billiards has also been played by mail, but this must prove to be excruciatingly slow. It would seem hard to stay IN STROKE for so many months! 1943 NYT (Dec 15) 34:4. Cf. EQUAL OFFENSE for a related pocket billiard game. 2. A method of relaying match positions by geometric COORDINATES. Early newspaper accounts of matches were obtained by telegraphing the position of the balls to the home office so that shot diagrams could appear in the paper the next morning.

telescoping cue

A cue stick having a BUTT of adjustable length. See EXTENDIBLE CUE. Cf. EXTENSION.

television

The most extensively televised billiard game is Snooker, which seems to have been tailored to the needs of the medium. The layout is colorful and the FRAME as a unit of play seems to be just the right length to maximize viewer interest. Defense adds to the tactical nature of the game and permits commentary of an analytical nature. The widespread popularity of Snooker can be traced largely to television viewership. See POT BLACK.

The requirements of television have caused significant changes in American pocket games. It is chiefly responsible for the replacement of Straight Pool by Nine-Ball as the primary competitive professional game. In Straight Pool, a single player may dominate the table for an entire television time slot, which makes the game appear boring. Nine-Ball racks are short, permitting frequent commercial breaks, and interesting. The audience, which may have trouble understanding the positional nuances of Straight Pool, is easily able to follow the numerical sequence of shots in Nine-Ball.

The most recent Nine-Ball sets use colored but unnumbered balls, with shades chosen to be readily distinguishable on television. The nine-ball, for example, is orange with a black stripe. The game of SEVEN-BALL was specifically designed for television. Even in other games, the rules have been altered for television. In professional Nine-Ball, it is not a foul to touch an object ball accidentally, *unless the game is being televised.* For the use of television in refereeing, see INSTANT REPLAY.

template

1. (Brit. games) A pattern used to determine whether the pockets of a table are of regulation shape, including size, UNDERCUT and FALL. The use of templates dates from the late nineteenth century. 1985 Morrison 135. 2. A device used in ARTISTIC BILLIARDS to set up predefined shots precisely. See COORDINATES. The term can also describe any tool whose outline is traced in order to draw shapes on the table, such as the D.

tempo

(Three-Cushions) An advanced phase of the game concerned with POSITION PLAY and avoidance of KISSES by controlling the relative speeds of the cue ball and first object ball. 1979 Ceulemans 360. A kiss occurs when the paths of the cue ball and object ball intersect and the balls approach the intersection point at the same time. By altering their speeds, the player is able to cause one ball to pass through the intersection before the other, thus eliminating the kiss.

Ten-Ball

1. (game) A ROTATION game similar to NINE-BALL, but in which 10 balls are racked in a 1-2-3-4 pattern. The 10-ball is placed in the center of the third row of balls. The break is less of an advantage in this game than it is in Nine-Ball because it is more difficult to RUN OUT in Ten-Ball. 1982 OR 63.

The number of different possible initial racks in Ten-Ball is 8! = 40,320. 2. (game) A game similar to FIFTEEN-BALL POOL, but played with only 10 balls; the first player to score 28 points wins. This is not a Rotation game, but each ball counts for its numerical value. 1985c Game Rules. Cf. TEN-BALL ROTATION.

Ten-Ball Rotation

(game) ROTATION played with 10 balls instead of 15, the first player to score 28 points winning. 1985c Game Rules. Cf. TEN-BALL.

Ten Pins

(game) A game similar to bowling but played on a billiard table. Ten wooden PINS are set up three inches apart in a triangular arrangement, with the head pin on the HEAD SPOT and the point of the triangle oriented toward the FOOT. A player has three shots in each INNING in which to knock over the pins after banking the cue ball first against the FOOT RAIL. Any number of cushion contacts is allowed, but no pins may be credited after the cue ball touches the HEAD RAIL. Scoring is as in bowling. 1902 Burrowes 20. See also BOWLLIARDS, BRUNSWICK TEN-PIN BILLIARD GAME, COCKED HAT.

ten-shot, ten-stroke

(Eng. Bill., Amer. Four-Ball Bill.) A stroke scoring 10 points, the maximum for a single shot at ENGLISH BILLIARDS. This can be accomplished by potting the RED, cannoning on WHITE, potting the white, and holing the cue ball. The LOSER is deemed to be IN-OFF red, the first ball contacted, and is thus worth three points. 1890 HRB 111, 1985 Arnold 224. In American Four-Ball, this is accomplished by caroming on all the balls, pocketing a white and a red. 1850 Phelan 22.

tenon

A cylindrical projection from the TIP end of the cue stick, to which the FERRULE is fastened. 1979 Sullivan 189. See CUE STICK for an illustrative diagram.

Texas Express

(game) Nine-Ball played with the rule that all balls pocketed (except the nine-ball) remain DOWN even if they have been pocketed illegally, and the INCOMING PLAYER has ball IN HAND after a scratch on the OPENING BREAK. This game proceeds more rapidly than ordinary Nine-Ball, hence the term "express." 1992 BD (Feb) 31. For a list of other states named in billiard games, see STATES, NAMES OF.

thick

A ball is said to be hit "thick" when it is hit FULL. See also FULL BALL. Cf. FINE BALL, THIN.

thin

A ball is said to be hit "thin" when it is just grazed. See also CLIP, CUT, CUT POT, FEATHER, FINE BALL, UNDERCUT. Cf. FULL, THICK.

thirteen-shot, thirteen-stroke

(Amer. Four-Ball Bill., obs.) A shot scoring 13 points, the maximum obtainable by a single stroke, accomplished by caroming on and pocketing all the object balls. 1850 Phelan 22. Cf. TEN-SHOT.

Thirty-Eight

(game, obs.) A predecessor of COWBOY POOL played with two cue balls and the two-, three-, and five-balls, placed on the FOOT, HEAD, and CENTER SPOTS, respectively. Thirty-eight or more points may be made by any combination of caroms and HAZARDS; there is no BURST. A carom is worth one point; a hazard is worth the value of the ball pocketed. A shot on which a SCRATCH occurs cannot result in the scoring of points, but none are deducted. A player wins by holing his cue ball off an object ball after he has scored 38 points. The game was introduced as a change of pace from regular pocket and carom games. 1885 NYT (Jan 21) 2:6. Cf. BULL DOG GAME, SCRATCH POOL, THIRTY-ONE POOL.

38.2 Balkline

(game) The scaled equivalent of 47.2 BALKLINE as played on a 2.5-meter table instead of a regulation 3.1-meter (10-foot) table. 1981 Rottie 135. Cf. 39.2 BALKLINE.

39.2 Balkline

(game) The scaled equivalent of 47.2 BALKLINE as played on a 2.6-meter (8-foot) table instead of a regulation 3.1-meter (10-foot) table. 1983 Malsert 105. Cf. 42.2 BALKLINE, 38.2 BALKLINE.

Thirty-One Pool

(game, obs.) A hybrid game similar to COWBOY POOL, played with the one-, two-, and three-balls placed on the HEAD, CENTER, and FOOT SPOTS, respectively. A carom on two balls counts one; a carom on three balls, two; and a hazard scores the value of the ball pocketed. The player must score 31 points exactly to win and will BURST if he exceeds that total. 1902 Burrowes 9. Also known as SCRATCH POOL. Cf. BULL DOG GAME, THIRTY-EIGHT.

Three-Ball, Three-Ball Game

1. (game) = CAROM BILLIARDS, FRENCH CAROM GAME, STRAIGHT-RAIL. 1857 Phelan 191, 1869 Kavanagh 9. When played on a POCKET TABLE, only caroms count; balls that are pocketed are respotted. 2. (game) A pocket billiard ROTATION game in which the three balls numbered one through three are racked in a triangle. The object is to sink the three-ball, with rules as in NINE-BALL. A very fast game in which luck is a significant component.

Three-Cushion Banks

(game) THREE-CUSHION BILLIARDS in which the cue ball must contact a rail before hitting any other ball. It is not an overstatement to describe this game as difficult. Between equally strong players, the player who must

bank as a HANDICAP should be able to score five or six points to his opponent's twenty.

Three-Cushion Billiards

(game) CAROM BILLIARDS in which the cue ball must make at least three distinct cushion CONTACTS before hitting the second object ball for the first time. 1890 HRB 61, 1916 RGRG 19. The game is also called THREE-CUSHIONS, THREE-RAIL, RAILS, or the ANGLE GAME.

The origin of the game remains shrouded in mystery. Dudley Kavanagh stated in the 1890s that it was unknown in his time, which was the 1860s. It was popularized by Wayman C. McCreery, the Internal Revenue Collector of the Port of St. Louis, who was the equal of Jacob Schaefer Sr. at it. 1898 Thatcher 11. The first Three-Cushion tournament was held at Mussey's Room in St. Louis in 1878, with Leon Magnus the victor. The HIGH RUN was six, the best AVERAGE 0.75. 1912 MB 343. It is safe to conclude that Three-Cushions developed in the U.S. in the 1870s. It was not immediately popular—tournaments were held only occasionally before 1907. Not all top players of that era were fond of the game; George Slosson did not favor it and complained that there was no use for the massé shot. 1900 NYT (Sep 2) 17:6. Press coverage of the game was intense from 1907, when the Lambert Trophy was introduced, until 1952, when interest in the U.S. declined after Willie Hoppe's retirement. It remains extremely popular in Europe, Korea, Japan, and the Latin countries. Three-Cushions has never enjoyed any substantial following in Britain.

Three-Cushions is difficult. An average of 0.75 is excellent for an amateur; 1.0 is solidly professional, and 1.5 is at the top rank among the world's players. Raymond Ceulemans, winner of more than 100 tournaments and many times world champion, and Torbjorn Blomdahl are the present leading exponents. For many years the U.S. EXHIBITION high run was 25, accomplished by Willie Hoppe in a match against Charles C. Peterson at Wright's Room in San Francisco in 1918. Jacob Schaefer Sr. performed a three-cushion NURSE involving a DOUBLE-THE-RAIL position at which he ran 36. 1931 BM (Sep) 32. The world record tournament high run is 30, achieved by Yoshio Yoshihara in 1988. Ceulemans has reportedly run over 40 on a 7-foot table. The 1992 champion, determined by a ranking system, is Torbjorn Blomdahl of Sweden, who occasionally averages 2.0 in tournaments.

The record for BEST GAME of 50 points U.S. championship play is 16 innings, achieved by Otto Reiselt on March 10, 1926 and equalled by Sang Lee in a non-championship game in 1992. Reiselt's LINE SCORE was

9-2-3-14-4-0-0-5-3-0-0-1-2-5-1-1. His average after five innings was 6.40. See also AVERAGE, MARGIN. Former American champions include Robert Cannefax, Joe Chamaco, Welker Cochran, Alfredo De Oro, Willie Hoppe, Augie Kieckhefer, Johnny Layton, and Reiselt. Author Robert Byrne names Jay Bozeman, who came in second in the world tournaments of 1933, 1939, and 1953 and third in 1941, 1944, 1947, and 1952, "the best player who never won the world's championship." The top modern American players include Allen Gilbert, Carlos Hallon, Sang Lee, Eddie Robin, Billy Smith, and Frank Torres. Besides Ceulemans and Blomdahl, present leaders in world play are Sang Lee, Richard Bitalis, Ludo Dielis, Dick Jaspers, Nobuaki Kobayashi, Junichi Komori, Rini Van Bracht, and Marco Zanetti.

Because of the difficulty of the game, lack of scoring threatened it as a spectator sport and it was necessary to encourage offense and restrict defense. This situation should be contrasted with that of BALKLINE, which was made progressively more difficult because of the advancing skill of the players. The DELIBERATE SAFETY in Three-Cushions was restricted, and, in 1911, players were allowed to shoot with either cue ball at each shot in order to improve the chance of a COUNT. This experiment has been repeated at various championship events. Sometimes a TIME LIMIT has been imposed to speed the game. The aiming of shots is facilitated by a variety of mathematical aids known collectively as the DIAMOND SYSTEM.

Many game variations are played. One difficult style requires hitting the red object ball first. Korean rules award an extra point for a rail-first shot.

See also AMATEUR; BEAT THE BREAKER; CHOICE OF CUE BALL; CROSS-TABLE SHOT; DIAMONDS COVERED; DOUBLE-THE-CORNER; DOUBLE-THE-RAIL; EQUAL INNINGS; FOUR-ON-TWO; FROZEN; GOOD HIT; HELP; INTENTIONAL SAFETY; MAXIMUM ENGLISH; OPTIONAL CUE BALL; PLUS SYSTEM; RC MARKS SYSTEM; RED, WHITE, & BLUE; SCHAEFER SHOT; SHORT-ANGLE SHOT; SNAKE SHOT; STIFF; STREAMLINED BILLIARDS; TEMPO; THREE-CUSHION BANKS; THREE-ON-TWO; TICKY, TRACK; UMB; UMBRELLA; UNITED STATES BILLIARD ASSOCIATION; WILD BALL BILLIARDS.

AMERICAN HIGH RUNS AT THREE-CUSHION BILLIARDS				
RUN	YEAR	PLAYER	LOCATION	OPPONENT
14	1885	F. Petersen	St. Louis	—
15	1910	G. Moore	New York	T. Gallagher

AMERICAN HIGH RUNS AT THREE-CUSHION BILLIARDS				
RUN	YEAR	PLAYER	LOCATION	OPPONENT
18	1914	P. Maupome	St. Louis	C. Peterson
18	1915	Jess Lean	Chicago	—
18	1915	C. Morin	St. Louis	F. Bensen
18	1917	De Oro	New York	—
19	1914	Kieckhefer	Chicago	F. White
25	1918	Hoppe	San Francisco	C. Peterson

Three-Cushions

(game) = THREE-CUSHION BILLIARDS.

three-four system

(Three-Cushions) A DIAMOND SYSTEM permitting the player to predict where the cue ball will strike the third and fourth cushions after being shot AROUND THE TABLE. 1977 Gilbert 44.

Three-Handed Game

(game) Any game for three players, particularly applied to a version of the AMERICAN GAME. 1869 Kavanagh 8. The presence of three players introduces the possibility of collusion between two of them to the disadvantage of the third. 1869 Roberts 233 warns against playing three-handed against strangers, since it "admits of sharp practice."

three-on-two

(Three-Cushions) A shot in which the three required cushion contacts are obtained using only two different cushions, especially two adjacent cushions. This can be accomplished by shooting at a narrow angle into a rail with REVERSE ENGLISH. The ball hits the rail, then the adjacent rail and returns to contact the original rail again. Also DOUBLE-THE-RAIL, SNAKE SHOT. Cf. DOUBLE-THE-CORNER, FOUR-ON-TWO. *See illustration on next page.*

three-pool

(Life Pool, obs.) MARKER'S call to indicate that only three players remain in the game when one of four remaining players has been KILLED. 1896 Broadfoot 415.

Three-Rail

(game) = THREE-CUSHION BILLIARDS.

245

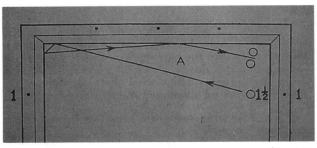

three-on-two

three scratches

(14.1 Continuous) See CONSECUTIVE FOULS, FIFTEEN-POINT PENALTY. In tournament Nine-Ball, three successive scratches or FOULS cause LOSS OF GAME.

three-shot, three-stroke

(Eng. Bill., American Four-Ball Bill.) A stroke on which three points are scored. In English Billiards, this can be done by potting the RED or by potting the striker's ball off the red. 1856 Crawley, 1890 HRB 110. In American Four-Ball, it is done by pocketing a red or caroming on both reds. 1850 Phelan 21.

through-ticket

(colloq.) A variety of FISH; a gambler who continues to play, even when losing, until his entire bankroll is gone.

throw

1. The name for the directional effect on the object ball of ENGLISH applied to the cue ball. The object ball is "thrown" in the direction opposite that of the English used. That is, a cue ball struck with RIGHT ENGLISH will throw the object ball farther to the left than if it were hit at the same POINT OF CONTACT but with no English. Formerly called "throw-off." 1894 NY Herald (Mar 25) 7:4, 1948 Mosconi 56, 1978 Byrne 84. 2. The tendency of an object ball to be pushed forward while it is in contact with a moving ball. Because the collision between the balls is not perfectly elastic, they remain in contact as they deform slightly from spherical shape. During this time, the balls move in tandem. By the time the contact is broken, the object ball has moved from its original position, making the planned line of aim inaccurate. This phenomenon requires balls to be CUT finer than aiming along the LINE OF CENTERS would dictate. 1990 Byrne 23. 3. To lose deliberately; to DUMP.

This may be done to defraud bettors or to conceal one's ability. Two players were barred from championship tournaments for life in 1877 after throwing one of their games. 1877 NYT (Jan 4) 5:3. Albert Frey was accused of throwing a game during the national tournament at Fifteen-Ball Pool. 1881 NYT (Jan 5) 5:5. He apparently regarded the charge seriously and altered his play to avoid any such suggestion in the future.

throw shot

1. A shot in which a ball is made to move off along a line other than the LINE OF CENTERS through the use of THROW. 1978 Byrne 84. A shot in which ENGLISH is used to alter the direction of the object ball's travel. 1982 OR. 2. (Pocket Bill.) A COMBINATION whose direction is altered by an off-center hit. 1978 Fels 55a, 1982 OR. In British parlance, a SQUEEZE SHOT.

Thurston's

The first major English manufacturer of billiard tables. In 1799, John Thurston established a business as cabinetmaker and builder of billiard tables. In 1814, he devoted his entire establishment to billiard tables and related items. Prior to that time, billiard tables were built to order by custom furniture makers. Thurston was responsible for the introduction of most of the technological improvements made to tables in England during the nineteenth century, including the slate bed, rubber cushions, and table heating. King William IV granted Thurston a royal warrant in 1833. 1985 Clare 11. Thurston died in 1850, but his firm's successors thrive to this day. Since the sales records of Thurston's date back to 1818, they are an invaluable source of historical information. Its London showrooms (but not its records) were destroyed by bombing during World War II.

ticky

(Three-Cushions) A particular type of RAIL-FIRST shot, in which the cue ball contacts a rail, a ball, and the same rail again in rapid succession before going on to hit another cushion to complete the COUNT. 1978 Byrne 212. The earliest ticky diagram known to the author is from 1829 Plan, in which the shot is shown but not named. The idea was hinted at, but not developed, in 1807 White fig. 65. The origin of the name is not known, but it appears to be recent, raising the question of what the shot was called before "ticky" came into use. *See illustration on next page.*

tie

1. A DRAW, NULL GAME or STALEMATED GAME. See also SUDDEN DEATH. 2. A situation in which two or more players have identical won-lost records at the close of regularly scheduled tournament play. Ties for first place

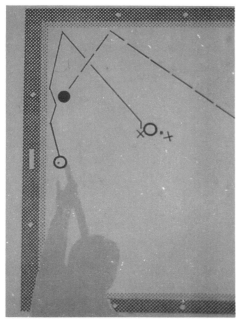

ticky

are nearly always resolved by PLAYOFF; ties for lesser prizes may be divided or broken based on AVERAGE or other statistic, such as most balls pocketed or TOTAL POINTS. Ties can be a source of great discomfort for tournament organizers and spectators alike. At a tournament in Chicago around 1900, all five entrants finished with 2–2 records. In St. Louis in 1887, 12 out of 13 contestants were involved in ties in the standings.

tie-up

(Bill.) = LINE-UP, COVER. 1913 Daly 123. A situation in which the striker is unable to make an easy carom in spite of the fact that the object balls lie close together.

tied up

Said of a striker who has no direct shot or when the path of a ball is blocked by another ball or a pocket. Also HOOKED, IN JAIL, SEWED UP. Cf. SNOOKERED, which has a similar but technically different meaning.

tight

1. Narrow. Said of pockets, or a table possessing them, on which scoring is difficult because the pocket openings are small. 1973 Spencer 120, 1988 Rossman 97. Cf. LOOSE. 2. Having little margin for error. Said of a shot that must be aimed precisely, because of the angle of approach to a pocket, the thickness of HIT required, or the presence of interfering balls. "It's tight on the nine." 3. Close. Said of a game or match in which two or more players' scores differ by only a small amount. 4. Uncomfortable, nervous. Said of a player who is not stroking well. "He's tight." Cf. LOOSE.

timber-lick

(colloq., obs.) A shot in which balls played at are jarred together along with the cue ball. A PUSH. 1865 Phelan 67. The origin of this term is obscure. The shot is also called a BOWERY SHOT or GERMAN-TOWNER.

time

1. A CALL by the REFEREE, made on his own initiative or at the request of a player, denoting that play is suspended so that the balls may be examined or a question put to the referee. 1890 HRB 38. It is essential to halt play so that the examination or ruling can be made prior to the next stroke. See also DELAY. 2. = TABLE TIME. "Winner pays the time."

time, for the

See FOR THE TIME.

time limit

A restriction imposed on the amount of time within which a player must attempt a shot or lose his INNING. See also DELAY, GAME CLOCK, SHOT CLOCK, TIME WASTING.

For the 1918 world Pocket Billiard championship, a limit of one minute was suggested to hamper Frank Taberski, a painfully slow but talented player who had won 10 straight title matches. The proposal was not implemented, and no tournament was held that year. 1918 NYT (Feb 24) II 8:4. However, the time limit was introduced in the 1919 championship, and Taberski refused to compete, thus starting the reign of Ralph Greenleaf. At the 1944 world Three-Cushion tournament in New York, one minute was allowed, with the referee required to warn the striker after 45 seconds. 1945 NBJ (Jan).

A different type of time limit tournament is one in which there is no limit on each shot, but the player scoring the most points within a given total time is the winner. A Three-Cushion tournament of this variety was held in Mexico in 1975.

Under the old championship Three-Cushion rules, a player was permitted to leave the playing area only once during a game, during his own inning, and then for no more than eight minutes. 1925 RGRG 22.

In Nine-Ball, time begins for the INCOMING PLAYER 10 seconds after the balls stop moving at the end of the outgoing player's inning. 1992 OR 50. See also WORLD TEAM BILLIARDS.

time off

A direction by a player to the COUNTER MAN at a public room, indicating that he is finished playing and wants to

247

pay for the TABLE TIME. See also OFF. Cf. OFF AND ON, ON, TIME ON.

time on

A direction by a player to the COUNTER MAN at a public room, indicating that he wants to begin play and that clocking of TABLE TIME should be started. See also ON. Cf. OFF, OFF AND ON, TIME OFF.

time shot, timed shot

(usually Bill.) An intentional KISS; a shot in which a player deliberately sets both object balls in motion to effect a score later. 1937 NYT (Feb 5) 24:5, 1978 Byrne 184. A shot in which an otherwise stationary ball is made to change position before the score is completed. A KISS-IN. Occasionally known as a "calculation shot" or COMBINATION (in a rare and obsolete usage). 1898 Thatcher 37. In French, the term is RENCONTRE, which expresses the idea precisely—the balls meet up with one another later in the shot. Time shots in pocket games are extremely rare and are most often played in exhibition as FANCY SHOTS.

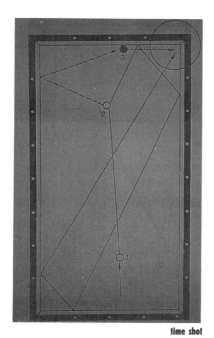

time shot

time, split the

See SPLIT THE TIME.

time wasting

(Brit.) = DELAY. 1988 WPBSA. The Snooker referee may disqualify, after warning, a player who takes an "abnormal amount of time" over a stroke. 1987 BSCC S22. See also TIME LIMIT.

tip

1. A rounded patch of material, usually leather, affixed to the narrow end of the cue stick. 1873 Bennett 9. The tip is needed to prevent the cue from slipping off the ball as it is being struck. It increases the friction between the two surfaces and, because it is compressible, increases the amount of time the stick and ball are in contact, which permits more English to be applied to the ball. Application of CHALK further increases the friction.

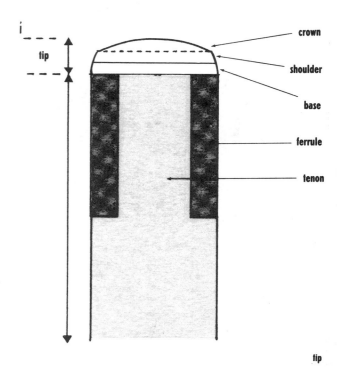

tip

Maces were sometimes "tipped" with ivory at the broad end, and Cotton cautioned in 1674: "note, if the heads happen to be loose, you will never strike a smart stroke, you will easily perceive that defect by the hollow deadness of your stroak [sic] and faint running of your Ball." This phenomenon can be observed in any modern cue having a loose tip or FERRULE.

There is confusion in the literature between two uses of the term "tip." It originally meant the uncovered narrow wooden end of the cue stick (def. 2, below). Cue ends were rounded and chalked before leather was used to cover them. Cues were also tipped with other materials, such as ivory, prior to the discovery of leather for this purpose. Therefore, a reference to a tip in an antique book does not necessarily mean a leather tip.

The leather tip is said to have been invented by Captain François Mingaud, a French political prisoner, while he was in jail. The first tip was cut out of a leather harness. The date of this experiment is uncertain, but it was sometime between 1807 and 1823, probably close to 1818, judging from notes left in Mingaud's handwriting. Mingaud was so successful in using the tip to put spin on the ball that he was accused of being a sorcerer for the amazing shots he was able to execute, including the MASSÉ. Mingaud's 1827 book of trick shots makes it clear that his skill was considerable—many of the shots are extremely difficult even today. The records of Thurston's indicate that the firm was tipping cues in 1818, but it is not certain that leather was used. 1974 Hendricks 36.

Whatever the date of its invention, the tip did not become popular very quickly. In 1829, a pamphlet appeared with the title, *Plan of the 44 Strokes at the Game of Billiards to Teach the Use of the Queue Tipped with Leather*, which suggests that use of the tip was not widespread and so had to be specially taught. The advantages of the tip are explained: "by means of the leather, which should be rubbed with chalk, the Player is enabled to strike the Ball on any particular point, whether above, below, or on the sides without any fear of erring." The tip was intended only for advanced players: "It is recommended that beginners should in the first instance make use only of the plain Queue. The use of the leather tipped Queue will be more appropriate, when the beginner has acquired the power of striking the ball with some degree of certainty on the desired point."

1839 Kentfield discusses various kinds of tips, with instructions on how to attach them to the shaft. A few drops of shellac were spread on the end of the shaft (not the tip), which was then held in a candle flame, but "not so long as to ignite it." The cue was then ready to use in about a minute without the need for a CLAMP. Later in the century, two pieces of leather were cemented together to form a tip; a hard BASE that is attached to the shaft, and a softer CROWN portion that contacts the ball.

Alternative methods of mounting tips are known. Wax was occasionally used, as was the CUE WAFER, a disk of adhesive placed between the tip and the end of the shaft. Sometimes tips were made with tacks and intended to be hammered into the shaft or with screws to be screwed into a fitting. See SCREW-ON TIP. For temporary and inexpensive repairs, a PUSH-ON TIP may be used. It is usual now to attach tips with fast-setting cement that forms a bond stronger than the leather itself.

The frequent need to replace tips has encouraged the development of a variety of tools and machines for preparing the ferrule, trimming the tip to size after gluing, shaping the tip, and roughening its surface to retain chalk.

Immense effort has been expended in an unsuccessful attempt to find a tip material superior to leather. Much experimentation has gone into development of a tip that will not require chalking. Such an item would have to be permanently abrasive, yet not so hard that it would scratch the balls. Combinations of rubber and carborundum have been tried, without useful results.

It is recommended that the tip be shaped to have the curvature of a nickel. 1982 BD (Sep/Oct). See DRESS. Tips are available in different diameters, usually from 11 to 15 millimeters, and in different degrees of hardness. The debate is unceasing over whether a hard or soft tip is preferable; it appears to be a matter of personal taste. See also FRENCH TIP. Regular maintenance is required to ensure that the tip has the proper roughness and shape. See MUSHROOM.

The tip is the only portion of the cue stick that may contact the cue ball during a stroke, and then only while it remains attached to the shaft. While using the cue stick to position the cue ball, as when the player has BALL IN HAND, the player may *not* touch it with the tip. A tip is important if the cue ball is to be hit at other than its center, but is not essential otherwise. A. P. Rudolphe once played at long odds with a tipless cue after his tip fell off, and he won nonetheless. 1898 Thatcher 191. It is doubtful under present rules whether a tipless cue would be legal.

2. The narrow end of the cue stick, at which the ball is contacted, as opposed to the BUTT. 3. A unit describing the amount of ENGLISH being applied to the cue ball. "Two tips" of English means that the ball is being struck as the outer edge of the cue tip is aimed at the cue ball two tip diameters from the center.

Tivoli

(game, obs.) A version of BAGATELLE.

to the rack

A phrase denoting the utter defeat of a player, causing him to stop play and return his cue to the RACK. 1941 Hoppe 76.

Toad-in-the-Hole

(game) = RUSSIAN POOL. 1924 Smith 92, 1954 KTG 35, 1976 WSD 365. Also called INDIAN POOL, SLOSH. "Toad in the Hole" is a British dish of meat baked in a crust. 1787 OED, 1992 Ronca PC. For a recipe, see Morris, *British and Irish Cooking*, New York: Round the World (1972), p. 39. What connection this may have with a

249

billiard game is obscure; the author would appreciate enlightenment.

token

A counter in the form of a coin, bought for cash and used to pay for games in a public billiard room. Also TRADE CHECK. A wonderful benefit for the room owner, since the purchaser of a token may lose it or never use it. In any event, some time will elapse before it is redeemed, and the house will have enjoyed a loan of the customer's money.

tool

(colloq.) One's cue stick, also known as the WAND or WEAPON.

top

1. (Brit. games) The END of the table farthest from baulk. 1836 Tillotson 1, 1839 Kentfield 25, 1913 Stoddard 8. To Americans, the FOOT OF TABLE. 2. FOLLOW, so called because the cue ball is stroked near its top. 1901 OED, 1957 Holt 42. Also CARRY-THROUGH. The term was not used before 1896, since it does not appear in the encyclopedic 1896 Broadfoot nor any other work of that vintage.

top of the table

(Brit. games) The area of the table near the TOP RAIL. The SPOT END. "Top" here does not refer to the flat playing surface of the table, which is known as the BED, nor to the tops of the rails, but to the portion of the table at which the SPOT-STROKE is played. See also FLOATING WHITE TECHNIQUE, TOP-OF-THE-TABLE GAME.

top-of-the-table game

(Eng. Bill.) That component of the game concerned with making long BREAKS at the TOP OF THE TABLE—that is, the SPOT END—with the red ball being spotted as often as possible, the white remaining within a few inches of the spot, and the player behind the two object balls. H.W. Stevenson's 1906 book is devoted entirely to this manner of play. See also TEA-TRAY GAME.

top pocket

(Brit. games) A pocket at the TOP end of the table. In American games, a FOOT POCKET. Cf. BOTTOM POCKET.

top rail

(Brit. games) The rail nearest the BILLIARD SPOT. Cf. BOTTOM RAIL.

top side

(Brit. games) = TOP, obtained by hitting the cue ball as high as possible above its center. 1904 Mannock I 163.

top spot

(Eng. Bill.) The BILLIARD SPOT, BLACK SPOT, ENGLISH SPOT, LOSING SPOT, RED SPOT, WINNING AND LOSING SPOT, or just "the Spot." The SPOT at the TOP end of the table.

top twist

(Brit. games, obs.) = TOP, HIGH.

total clearance

(Snooker) A CLEARANCE during which all 21 object balls are potted. The minimum possible score for a total clearance occurs by potting a red followed by yellow 15 times for 45 points, then TAKING THE COLOURS for an additional 27, yielding a total of 72 points. Murt O'Donoghue of New Zealand is generally credited with the first total clearance in 1929, a break of 134; he even potted a RED on the BREAK-OFF. The first official total clearance was also a break of 134 by Sidney Smith in 1936. 1985 Morrison 16.

total performance average

A numerical measure of performance in Nine-Ball, developed by Pat Fleming of ACCU-STATS. A method of RATING professional players. Abbreviated TPA.

A player's AVERAGE in balls per inning is not a good predictor of success at Nine-Ball, since no points are awarded for balls and there is therefore no direct connection between average and performance. Pat Fleming invented a new statistic, known as the "total performance average," which can be computed easily for any number of players in a Nine-Ball tournament. It is calculated by dividing the number of balls made by a player by the number of balls plus the number of "errors" committed by the player. There are five types of errors: (1) a miss, that is, failing to pocket a ball if the player can SEE it and intends to pocket it; (2) a SCRATCH on the BREAK; (3) a bad HIT, in which the player was unable to see the required object ball and was not able to hit it; (4) a bad SAFETY, in which the player attempted to play a safety but the next player was able to pocket a ball at his next turn other than by a kick shot; and (5) bad position, in which the player scratches (except on a kick or the break) or the player pockets at least one ball on the break but fails to win the rack. Note that a TPA must always lie between 0.000 and 1.000. In many ways it resembles a baseball player's fielding average.

total points

The accumulated number of points scored or balls pocketed by a player during a tournament. This quantity is sometimes used to break a TIE when two or more players have identical won-lost records.

250

touch

1. Finesse, delicacy of STROKE. 1895 Buchanan 30. 2. Contact between the cue stick and a ball. "A touch is a shot." 1916 RGRG 11. Touching a ball during aiming was neither a FOUL nor a stroke in 1836—the ball could be replaced in position by the player and he might strike again without penalty. 1836 Tillotson 7. See NUDGE. Cf. HIT.

touching ball

1. (Snooker) Verbal CALL by the referee to indicate that the cue ball is touching the BALL ON or a ball that can be designated as ON. 1978 BSCC 51. The player must PLAY AWAY from the ball or the stroke will be a PUSH. 1985 Arnold 208. If he plays away, he will be deemed to have hit the ball on. If he NOMINATES another ball and plays away, he will not be deemed to have hit the ball on unless he also hits the nominated ball. If the cue ball is touching a ball not on, the striker will not be considered to have contacted it if he plays away. The rule was introduced in 1927. 1985 Everton 47. See FREEZE. 2. (Eng. Bill.) A situation in which a player's cue ball is FROZEN to an object ball. Since March 1898, the rule has been that in such a case the red ball is spotted on the BILLIARD SPOT, the white on the CENTRE SPOT, and the player strikes from the D. 1912 Levi 577.

tough break

1. (colloq.) A situation in which the cue ball rests in such a position as to prevent the STRIKER from making another shot. 1927 Katch 51. 2. (Pocket Bill.) A difficult BREAK SHOT.

tour de cue

(from Fr., meaning literally, "trick of the cue") A FANCY SHOT, a billiard *tour de force*.

tournament

A competitive contest involving more than two players and consisting of several MATCHES. For different types, see DOUBLE ELIMINATION, DOUBLE ROUND-ROBIN, FLITE, KNOCKOUT, MIXED DOUBLES, RACE, ROUND, ROUND-ROBIN, SCOTCH DOUBLES, SCRAMBLE, SINGLE ELIMINATION, SPLIT DOUBLE ELIMINATION. The first professional tournament held in the U. S. took place in New York in 1860 at the AMERICAN FOUR-BALL GAME. 1860 *Leslie's* (Nov 10) 393.

Being expensive to organize, tournaments were not common during the nineteenth century. A much more common mode of competition was the challenge match, which involved only two players. So dominant was this format that only 16 of the first 117 occasions on which the pocket billiard championship was contested were tournaments.

tout

(colloq.) An individual who professes to be able to pick winning players for a gambler in return for a percentage of any winnings. See GAMBLING. Sometimes the tout does not pretend to predict the future but implies that the outcome has been predetermined and the result is known to him.

TPA

= TOTAL PERFORMANCE AVERAGE.

track

(Three-Cushions) A concept useful in playing the DIAMOND SYSTEM. A track consists of a predictable path followed by a ball when hit in a prescribed fashion, usually with NATURAL ENGLISH. Once a ball is stroked properly into a track, it will take a known course around the table. 1964 Cottingham 142.

trade check

(obs.) = TOKEN. A counter used to pay for billiard games. 1908 Brunswick 106.

trail, trailing

1. To be behind in the score. 2. (obs.) A method of cheating with the MACE in which the cue ball was shoved with the mace for such a distance that the shot became easy. Employed by unscrupulous players. The term was in use by 1740. The tactic was denounced by 1807. See also DEAD TRAIL, LONG TRAIL, RAKING, SHOVE, SWEEP, TURN-UP. 1775 Annals 105, 1807 White 22.

transmitted side

(Brit. games) Spin transferred to the object ball from the cue ball. Also known as COMMUNICATED SIDE. It is a source of great controversy among the British authorities as to whether the phenomenon exists. A. Newman-Mond wrote a 100-page manuscript entirely devoted to the subject. Interestingly, the debate has not crossed the Atlantic to the U. S., where transmitted English has long been recognized as essential in various NURSES.

The following sources endorse the concept of transmitted side: 1913 Daly 39, 1925 Hoppe 250 (explaining how to perform the LINE NURSE), 1935 Smith 48. According to 1920 Levi III, Cook, Sidney Fry, and Charles Roberts also support it. 1941 Levi 113 states that Walter Lindrum is a proponent.

These sources claim that it is either impossible to transmit side or that any amount of spin transferred is too small to be detected: 1856 Crawley 46, 1929a Davis, 1935 Newman, 1941 Levi 113, 1986 Davis 53. Some of these references are quite vehement on the issue. According to 1866 Crawley 59, "side is never communicated." In 1920 Levi III 167, the following players are said to deny the possibility of transmitted side: Dawson, George Gray, Melbourne Inman, John P. Mannock, Arthhur F. Peall, Tom Reece, John Roberts, H. W. Stevenson. 1896 Broadfoot is equivocal on the issue.

To leave the reader with no doubt as to my position: Transmitted side not only exists but is most useful to position play at carom billiards and bank shots in pocket billiards. The fact that there can be any equivocation on the issue is itself astounding, for not only can English be transferred from one ball to another by friction, but a ball struck without English and aimed at an off-center point on an object ball will acquire English by virtue of the oblique contact.

traveler

(Brit., colloq.) = FORCER; a ball that has been hit hard. 1937 NBJ (Oct).

treble

(Brit. games) = A DOUBLE DOUBLE; a particular type of two-cushion BANK SHOT in which the object ball crosses the table twice before entering a pocket. 1936 Newman 55. A DOUBLE BANK. Cf. TRIPLE.

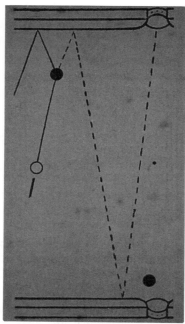

treble

treble discount

(obs.) A method of granting a HANDICAP, in which the superior player loses three points for every point scored by his opponent. 1857 Phelan 66. See DISCOUNT.

triangle

(Pocket Bill.) = A FRAME or RACK, used for setting balls in position on the table. 1881 NYT (Jan 11) 2:5. It may be made in many shapes, some not necessarily triangular, for racking balls in various games such as NINE-BALL. Used by extension to mean the PACK itself. See also SKIRTED RACK and TRIANGLE, QUICK GAME.

triangle

triangle, quick game

(Pocket Bill.) A TRIANGLE having a flattened appendage that is lined up flush with the FOOT RAIL in order to assist in accurate placement of the balls. It is intended to solve the problem of being unable to see the FOOT SPOT when racking, thereby making it difficult to ensure that the base of the triangle is aligned parallel to the foot rail. 1908 Brunswick 93. The alignment problem is currently eliminated by marking the position of the RACK with a pencil line on the cloth so the triangle may be placed accurately and quickly. *See illustration on next page.*

triangular balkline

(Bill., obs.) A diagonal line joining the end and side rails and defining a space within which the number of caroms is restricted unless the player drives at least one

QUICK GAME TRIANGLES

Used by Professionals
Makes Games More Rapid
Puts Balls on the Spot

In ordering specify size of
your table

Each $1.50

triangle, quick-game

ball out of the space. Used in the CHAMPION'S GAME.
1881 MB 27, 1891 MB 35.

Triathlon

A form of competition in which a player must partici-
pate in Cushion Caroms, Three-Cushions. and 47.2
Balkline. 1989 Salvador 93. Cf. BIATHLON, PENTATH-
LON.

trick shot

A shot that is inordinately difficult or flashy, requiring
extreme force, ENGLISH, or fine aim. It may involve
pocketing multiple balls or some unexpected behavior
by the cue or object balls, sometimes demanding the use
of such props as the RACK, a hat, a handkerchief (for
so-called BLINDFOLDED SHOTS), an extra cue, or the
application of saliva or chalk to the balls. See CHALK
SHOT, GAFF SHOT, SPIT SHOT. See also TAPPING.

Many trick shots violate the rules of billiards, which
renders them useless in actual play but they are nonetheless entertaining to spectators. Sometimes synonymous with FANCY SHOT, although a shot may be fancy or
difficult without being a trick shot. Otto Reiselt probably achieved some sort of record for trick shot complex-
ity when he performed a six-cushion bank shot for
cartoonist Robert ("Believe It Or Not") Ripley that
involved placing 123 obstacles on the table! 1931 BM
(Feb).

1807 White 5 relates stories of trick shots performed as
early as 1789, considerably before the invention of the
leather cue tip. The first book devoted to trick shots was
Mingaud's 1827 French treatise, elaborately produced
with hand-colored plates. It was translated into English
by Thurston in 1830 and shows a variety of jump and
massé shots. A large number of fancy Three-Cushion

shots appear in 1898 Thatcher. 1899 Stancliffe, 1902
Herrmann and 1908 Hood contain pocket billiard
tricks, many involving props. 1948 Caras is largely an
updated compilation of these shots. 1965 Mosconi
explains a number of shots invented by Mosconi himself. 1982 Byrne is an astounding compendium of
pocket and carom tricks that traces the origin of a host of
specific shots.

A number of practitioners specialize in trick and fancy
shots, devoting much of their playing careers to trick
shot exhibitions. The most prominent U.S. artist is
Mike Massey, whose repertoire includes a number of
finger shots. Trick shot tournaments are held occasionally; interest in this form of competition is currently
increasing because of its appeal to spectators. The BCA
now sponsors "artistic pool" competition, in which
players attempt a fixed series of trick shots of varied
difficulty.

trickle

(Brit.) To roll the cue ball slowly up against another for
defensive purposes. 1990 French 48. A ROLL-UP. This
maneuver cannot be used in American games because a
TABLE SCRATCH would result.

triple

(obs.) To cause a ball to contact three cushions. 1830
Mingaud 37. Cf. TREBLE.

tripod bridge

1. A three-point support for the cue stick in which the
middle finger of the BRIDGE HAND is folded so as to be
nail-down on the table. 1965 Fats 6, 1978 Fels. This
bridge is called the "orthodox" bridge in 1941 Hoppe 16.

2. A MASSÉ bridge formed by making a tripod out
of the last three fingers of the bridge hand. 1925
Hoppe 242. *See illustration on next page.*

Troll Madame, Trou Madame

(Bagatelle game) Similar to MISSISSIPPI, except that the
balls are played from the end of the BAGATELLE board
through the bridge. 1837 Walker 92, 1863 Phelan &
Berger 95. The words "troll," "troule" and "trou" are
equivalent and mean "to play jovially." The game was
originally intended as a ladies' pastime using wood or
metal balls—its name literally means "ladies' play."
1572 OED.

trough

(Pocket Bill.) = GUTTER. 1908 Brunswick 90.

253

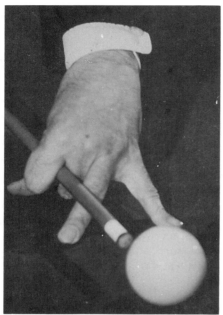

tripod bridge (Hoppe)

Trucks

(game, obs.) An old Italian game similar to billiards, played on a large table with three or more holes at each end in addition to the corner holes. It was played with accessories known as the "Sprigg" and "Argolis," which played the role of the KING and PORT. The balls used were larger than billiard balls, propelled by sticks known as "tacks." The strategy of the game was highly developed by 1674. 1588 OED, 1674 Cotton 39. Sometimes known as TRUNKS. In Italian, the game is known as "Il Trucco." 1866 Crawley 5.

true

Generally, having the proper shape or direction. Cf. UNTRUE.

1. Perfectly round; said of billiard balls. 1895 Buchanan 35. They "require much art in their rounding, for otherwise they will never run true." 1674 Cotton 41. 2. Perfectly flat; said of a table or cloth. 1674 Cotton. See also LEVEL.

truing

The process of TURNING a ball into a round shape or leveling a slate.

Trunks

(game, obs.) = TRUCKS.

turn

1. An opportunity to shoot. A HALF-INNING. All strokes made by a player during one trip to the table are said to constitute his "turn." See also ADDRESS, IN CONTROL,

INNING, VISIT. 2. To grind a billiard ball into a round shape, making it TRUE. One who does this is known as a "turner." 3. (rare) Mild SWERVE in which the ball turns in the direction of its SIDE in going with the NAP or on a napless cloth, or away from its side going against the nap. 1925 Peall 48.

turn-up

(obs.) A TRAILING shot made with the MACE. 1807 White.

turning the corner

(Bill.) A maneuver in playing the RAIL NURSE in which several strokes are used to cause the balls to progress past a corner from one rail to an adjacent rail, but remaining in position so the nurse can be continued. 1875 NYT (Nov 18) 5:4, 1913 Daly 182. It is also performed in ENGLISH BILLIARDS, where the process is complicated by the presence of pockets. 1896 Broadfoot 356, 1912 Levi 574.

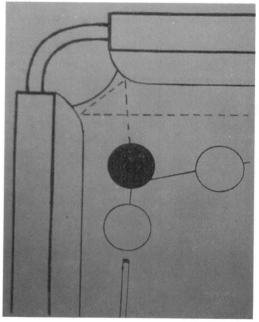

turning the corner

TV game

A game in which the players are tied with one point or game remaining in the match. An exciting situation, perfect for television because the audience is not inclined to tune away until the match is completed. See also CASE GAME, CASEY JONES, DOUBLE CHEESE, HILL GAME.

Tweeten's Four-Ball Billiard Game

(game, obs.) A game devised in 1940 to revive interest in carom billiards, played with one white cue ball and three red object balls. Each player has nine innings, each consisting of four shots, in which to score. For the break position, the three red balls are placed on the HEAD, CENTER, and FOOT SPOTS. The cue ball is struck from the D. Differing numbers of points are awarded depending on how the carom is made, ranging up to four points for a three-cushion billiard. A perfect game scores 144 points for calling and making four three-cushion shots in each of nine innings. 1940 NBJ (Dec). This game was not successful at its goal and quickly passed out of existence. See also TWEETEN'S POCKET BILLIARD FOUR-BALL GAME. Tweeten's is a long-time manufacturer of billiard supplies, particularly cue tips and tip cement.

Tweeten's Pocket Billiard Four-Ball Game
(game, obs.) A pocket game with scoring suggested by bowling. Four object balls are racked in a diamond arrangement centered on the FOOT SPOT. Each player is given nine innings, each consisting of a break and four called shots. Sinking four balls in four shots is a STRIKE (def. 2); four balls in five shots is a SPARE. 1938 NBJ (Oct). See also TWEETEN'S FOUR-BALL BILLIARD GAME.

12½.2 Balkline
(game, obs.) 14.2 BALKLINE scaled down proportionately for a 9-foot table. A 10-foot table has a playing surface that is 112 inches long; a 9-foot table is 100 inches long, exactly in the ratio 14:12½. A tournament was actually held at this obscure game in 1891.

twelve-shot, twelve-stroke
(Amer. Four-Ball Bill.) There is no such thing, since there is no legal way to score exactly 12 points in a single stroke. But see ELEVEN-SHOT and THIRTEEN-SHOT.

28.2 Balkline
(game) BALKLINE played with lines drawn 28 inches from each rail, dividing the table into four rectangles as shown, each of which is a BALK SPACE. 1977 OR 38. There is no CENTER SPACE in which to make unrestricted caroms. The game was invented in Chicago in 1894 but was popularized in France, where it was known as SUPER BILLIARDS because of the extreme test of skill it presents to the players. The American title was contested in 1937 by Willie Hoppe and Jake Schaefer Jr., with Schaefer the victor. 1937 NYT (Jan 31) V 1:3. The high run is 132 by Schaefer. Cf. 71.2 BALKLINE, a similar game with a different method of marking the lines.

Twenty-One Ball
(game, obs.) A ROTATION game played with 21 balls racked in the shape of a triangle with six rows. Played

beginning in the 1930s, this was a betting game in which the player had a chance to win money from the HOUSE, or room owner. 1981 BD (Sep/Oct) 17.

twice around system
(Three-Cushions) A DIAMOND SYSTEM used for aiming shots in which the cue ball travels AROUND THE TABLE twice. 1928 Barry 15, 1977 Gilbert 36.

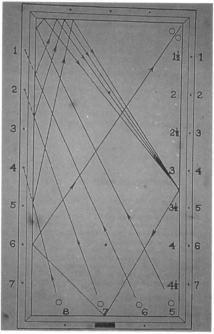

twice around system

twist
1. (obs.) = DRAW, SCREW. 1806 Phil, 1830 Mingaud 39, 1862 Crawley 20. The use of "twist" preceded the American term "draw" (not used in the U.K.) by about 60 years. 2. (obs.) = ENGLISH. 1850 Phelan 62 (also mentions correctly that twist can be acquired in rebound from a cushion), 1881 MB 27, 1896 Broadfoot 191. 3. (obs.) = SWERVE. 1859 *Leslie's* (Apr 2) 283:1.

twisting powder
(obs.) = Powder that, when rubbed on the cue tip, enables TWIST, or DRAW, to be applied to the ball. See CHALK for the legend of Jack Carr and his twisting powder.

two-ball
1. (Pocket Bill.) The SOLID blue ball marked with the numeral 2, informally known as the DEUCE. 2. (game) A game invented by George Fels, played with a cue ball and two object balls. The goal is to make a CAROM and sink one of the object balls on the same shot. 1982 BD (Nov/Dec) 30.

Two-Ball Billiards

(game) Played with two cue balls on a CAROM TABLE. The object is to bank one's cue ball off three cushions and then hit the other ball. 1913 Burrowes 28.

two-ball break

(pocket games) A BREAK SHOT in which the only requirement is that the cue ball must contact a ball and at least two object balls must be driven to cushions. The two-ball break with CALL is used in 14.1 CONTINUOUS, HONOLULU, and LINE-UP. The two-ball break without CALL (that is, it is not necessary to call any ball on the break, but all balls pocketed are credited) is used in FIFTEEN-BALL. Cf. ONE-BALL BREAK.

Two-Ball Game

1. Generally, any game in which only two balls are used. 2. (game, obs.) A game, popular in Latin countries, played on a CAROM TABLE with only two balls, the object being to BANK one ball off at least two cushions to contact the other ball. 1896 Cady 35. 3. (game, obs.) = KISS-CANNONS, PLON-PON. A game played with two balls in which the object is to cause one's ball to hit the other ball twice.

Two-Ball Pool

1. (game, obs.) A game, popular around 1850, played with a red and a white ball on a POCKET TABLE. A NONSTRIKER who believes a hazard may be made in a given position may claim the stroke and "take the hazard" if the striker does not wish to attempt it, under penalty of losing a LIFE if he misses. 1857 Phelan 200, 1890 HRB 90, 1916 RGRG 69. The striker plays with the ball that was the object ball on the previous stroke, unless a ball has been pocketed, in which case there is a new LEAD. (Thus in this game the red ball may be struck.) Cf. VOLUNTEER. 2. (game, obs.) A variant of LIFE POOL for any number of participants but played with only two balls; the players alternate strokes. 1839 Kentfield 40.

Two-Cushion

(game) A carom game in which the cue ball must make at least two cushion contacts before contacting the SECOND OBJECT BALL. It is more difficult than CUSHION CAROMS but lacks the depth of THREE-CUSHIONS. Theoretically, a cue ball BANKED off two perpendicular cushions should return on a course parallel to its original line. 1925 Hoppe 218. This fails to happen in practice because a ball banked into a rail obliquely acquires ENGLISH in the process. This game is rarely played and no tournaments of record have been held, but it is excellent practice for all carom games.

256

two-piece cue

A JOINTED CUE having a BUTT and a SHAFT that screw together so it may be broken down for ease of carrying. Cf. ONE-PIECE CUE.

Two-Pin Game, Two-Pin Pool

(game) A SKITTLE game played with a black PIN, a white pin, two white balls, and a red ball on a CAROM TABLE. 1891 MB 344, 1916 RGRG 28. Caroms do not count, and if the game is played on a POCKET TABLE then HAZARDS do not count. (Scoring is accomplished only by knocking over pins.) The balls are spotted as in the FIVE-PIN GAME. The black pin is placed on the CENTER SPOT, the white pin to the right of the center spot and five inches from the black pin. The red ball is placed on the FOOT SPOT, the white nine inches from the FOOT RAIL. The object is to play at the object ball and knock down the white pin. If the black pin is knocked over, there is a forfeit. There is a financial settlement after each ball. The striker continues to shoot until he fails to score. 1890 HRB 98. Cf. PIN POOL, SKITTLE POOL.

Two Pockets to Four

(game, obs.) A CRAMP GAME of ENGLISH BILLIARDS in which one player has two pockets in which to play HAZARDS and the other has four. The odds between equal players were said to be about 10 in 50, but this depends on the particular pockets chosen. 1862 Crawley 97. Cannons count. 1839 Kentfield 36, 1856 Crawley 98. Cf. DIVIDED POCKETS, ONE POCKET TO FIVE.

two-pot red rule

(Eng. Bill.) A rule requiring the RED to be placed on the CENTRE SPOT if it is potted twice in succession from the BILLIARD SPOT by the STRIKER. If it is potted from the centre spot, it is returned to the billiard spot and the two-pot rule is again in effect. See SPOT-BARRED GAME.

two-shot, two stroke

(Eng. Bill., Amer. Four-Ball Bill.) A stroke on which two points are scored. In English Billiards, this is the minimum number of points that can be scored by the STRIKER for a successful stroke. It is accomplished by potting the opponent's ball, making a cannon, or pocketing one's own ball off the opponent's. 1890 HRB 110. In the American Four-Ball Game, it is done by caroming on a white and a red or holing the white. 1850 Phelan 21.

two-shot rollout

(Nine-Ball) A variation on the ROLLOUT rule, popular in the northern U.S. If a player fouls on two consecutive

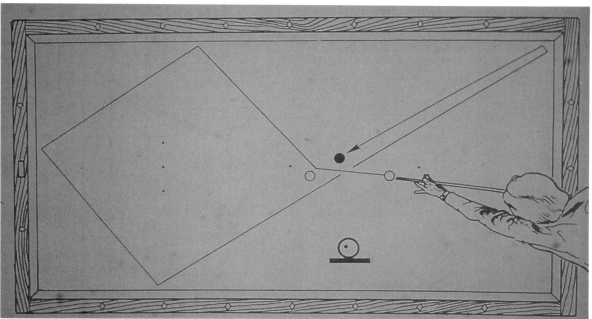

two-way shot (3 or 5 cushions)

shots, his opponent has BALL IN HAND. 1991 *Snap* (Jul/Aug) 30.

two shots in

(Balkline) Variety of game in which a player confronted with both object balls in the same BALK SPACE or ANCHOR SPACE has two shots in which to drive one of them out or lose his turn at the table. 1916 RGRG 17. The ball must leave the space on or before the second shot but may return. Any balkline game whose numerical designation ends in ".2" allows two shots in, as 18.2 BALKLINE. Cf. ONE SHOT IN.

two-way shot

(usually Bill.) A shot in which the player has two opportunities to score. If the cue ball misses the SECOND OBJECT BALL on its first pass, it may have another chance after rebounding off one or more cushions. 1978 Byrne 191, 1984 BD (Dec) 20. Also DOUBLE-CHANCE SHOT.

UMB

(org.) UNION MONDIALE DU BILLARD, the World Billiard Union.

umbrella

1. (Three-Cushions) A difficult shot in which the cue ball strikes two or more cushions before hitting the FIRST OBJECT BALL, then hits another cushion before completing the COUNT. So called because the shot seems to open up like an umbrella, although the image can be difficult to spot . 1929 BM (Jul) 38, 1941 Hoppe 76, 1978 Stone 69, 1978 Byrne 219. Umbrella shots are classified as INSIDE or OUTSIDE, depending on which side of the first object ball is contacted by the cue ball. See also UMBRELLA SYSTEM. 2. An instrument for protecting pedestrians from the rain but occasionally used as a cue stick. John Roberts is said to have used an umbrella for a cue, but he in fact used a walking stick and would challenge all comers with it in public rooms. His opponents could use cues. 1908 Roberts 72. In 1939, Raymond Miller of Adelaide, Australia, used an umbrella as a cue stick for three months, though his purpose in so doing is unclear. 1974 Lindrum 124. *See illustration on next page.*

umbrella system

A DIAMOND SYSTEM for umbrella shots developed by Clarence Jackson, one of the originators of diamond systems. He classified umbrellas as either "back-door" or "front-door," which correspond to the modern designations "inside" and "outside." 1931 BM (Nov).

umpire

A player's advisor or SECOND, one who looks out for his interests. In an earlier day, the umpires appointed the

257

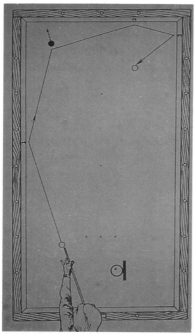

umbrella

umbrella (outside)

REFEREE. 1858 NYT (Jan 5) 2:3, 1864 AH 434. Only an umpire was permitted to make an appeal to the referee; the player himself had to remain silent. 1890 HRB 41.

See also ASSISTANCE. Players may still employ umpires, but their role is now entirely unofficial.

unbanded ball

(Pocket Bill., rare) A SOLID, one of the pocket billiard balls numbered one through eight and not bearing a BAND. 1977 Martin 220. See also BALL. Cf. BANDED BALL, STRIPE.

under the cushion

FROZEN to a cushion. 1807 White 82, 1897 Payne 29. At the time of White, cushions were flat vertical walls whose height was greater than the diameter of the balls. The phrase now reflects the fact that a portion of a ball that is in contact with a cushion actually lies under the nose of the cushion. See also GUM.

undercut

1. (Pocket Bill.) To fail to hit an object ball sufficiently THIN to cause it to enter the desired pocket. See CUT. Cf. OVERCUT. 2. That portion of a cushion that is cut away at an angle from the top of the cushion to the table BED to form the NOSE.

underwrap

The portion of the butt of a cue stick that is covered by the WRAP. 1983 NBN (Mar) 18.

unfair conduct

(Brit. games) = UNSPORTSMANLIKE CONDUCT. In Snooker, a player who engages in willful or persistent unfair conduct loses the game and is liable to be further disqualified from sanctioned competition. 1987 BSCC S23.

unfinished

Said of a RUN or BREAK that is not terminated by a MISS or a FOUL but is halted voluntarily or because the required GAME TOTAL has been reached. In tournament play, the striker must cease play when game is reached and further scoring is not counted for any purpose. In EXHIBITION, players are frequently exhorted by the audience to continue a run to break a record. In awarding a prize for HIGH RUN in a competition, an unfinished run is superior to a completed run of the same length. 1956 BSTE 18. See OUT.

Union Mondiale du Billard

(org.) The World Billiard Union, or UMB. Formed in 1928, for decades it was international governing body for carom games and sanctioning organization of the world amateur Three-Cushion championship. The members of the UMB are billiard organizations of various countries; there are no individual members.

United States Billiard Association (USBA)

(org.) Formed in 1988 by the merger of the AMERICAN BILLIARD ASSOCIATION and the BILLIARD FEDERATION OF THE USA to consolidate rival U.S. Three-Cushion titles.

United States Pool Players' Association (USPPA)

(org.) An organization of approximately 7000 members sponsoring handicapped league play, founded in 1968 by Gene Stary. Its computerized handicapping system is based on a mathematical model developed by Mike Pascual and divides players into 10 categories, from Professional and Semi-Professional, through AAA, AA, and A–F (for beginners). 1992 European Billiard News (Sep) 62.

unlimited rail

(Bill., obs.) A name for STRAIGHT-RAIL Billiards, a game in which there is no restriction limiting the RAIL NURSE. 1883 NYT (Mar 18) 14:1. Cf. LIMITED RAIL.

unsanctioned

As applied to a competition, not approved by a governing body. The results of an unsanctioned match or tournament are unofficial, no title can be awarded, and any record-breaking performances count as EXHIBITION records only. Sometimes the appropriate sanctioning organization imposes a penalty on any player who plays in an unsanctioned event without permission. See WAIVER.

unscrew

To disconnect the SHAFT from the BUTT of a TWO-PIECE CUE. For the consequences of unscrewing the joint of one's cue stick during a match, see CONCESSION.

unsportsmanlike conduct

An act that is embarrassing, disruptive or detrimental to the other players, officials, hosts or the sport in general. The referee may penalize or disqualify a player who engages in such behavior. See DISQUALIFICATION, INTERFERENCE. Principles of etiquette and fair play made their way into the rules of billiards before the invention of the cue tip. One of White's 1807 rules of English billiards reads: "The striker has a right to command his adversary not to stand facing him or near him, so as to annoy or molest him in his stroke." Later rules allowed the marker or referee to declare the game drawn for persistent violations. By the 1940s, referees in professional tournaments could assess a penalty of up to five points for a single infraction or impose a forfeit for a

repetition. See FIVE-POINT PENALTY, PSYCH. In Britain, UNFAIR CONDUCT.

untrue

1. Out of round, said of billiard balls that do not roll accurately. Cf. TRUE. 1895 Buchanan 35. 2. Said of a cloth that is not TRUE or of a table that is not flat. For a relevant quotation from *The Mikado*, see SHARP.

up

1. At the number or limit agreed upon as the score or game. In a game played "500 up," each player must score 500 points to win. 1680 OED, 1807 White 85. In this sense, "up" means "done' or "finished," as in "the game is up." 2. Ahead in the scoring. "He's up by 25." 1894 OED. 3. Being next to shoot. "You're up." 4. = STRAIGHT-UP; without a HANDICAP. 5. (Brit. games) Toward the TOP of the table. Cf. DOWN.

up-and-down

A shot that travels the length of the table twice. In English Billiards, an up-and-down cannon is one in which the cue ball travels toward one short cushion then back past its original position toward the other. 1904 Mannock I 321. In Pocket Billiards, an up-and-down shot is a BANK SHOT into a corner pocket off a SHORT RAIL. 1985 Marguglio 224.

up the table

Toward the HEAD RAIL, UPTOWN. 1970 Knuchell 246. But in English games, toward the TOP RAIL (the opposite meaning). Cf. DOWN THE TABLE.

upper cushion

The HEAD RAIL. 1850 Phelan 28.

upper spot

The HEAD SPOT. 1850 Phelan 47. Also called the AMERICAN SPOT, LIGHT-RED SPOT, WHITE SPOT and, in the Three-Ball Game, WHITE-BALL SPOT.

upper table

(Brit. games) The BAULK end. 1807 White 3. Cf. LOWER TABLE.

uptown

(Pocket Bill., colloq.) UP THE TABLE, toward the HEAD RAIL. In most pocket billiard games, uptown is a bad place to find oneself, since most of the object balls usually lie at the other end of the table. Cf. DOWNTOWN.

U.S. Open

(org.) The United States Open Pocket Billiards Tournament. Traditionally a SPLIT DOUBLE ELIMINATION Straight Pool Tournament with men and women par-

259

ticipating in separate divisions. It is truly an open tournament because any player may qualify by winning regional tournaments. The 16 men's tournaments have been won by nine different players: Joe Balsis, Jimmy Caras, Irving Crane, Tom Jennings, Luther Lassiter, Steve Mizerak, Oliver Ortmann, Mike Sigel, and Dallas West. The 15 women's tournaments have been won collectively by only three women: Dorothy Wise (5 times), Jean Balukas (7), and Loree Jon Jones (3). The men's high run record in U.S. Open play is 150, held by several people. The women's high run is 68, by Ewa Mataya in 1992.

USBA

(org.) = UNITED STATES BILLIARD ASSOCIATION.

USPPA

(org.) = UNITED STATES POOL PLAYERS' ASSOCIATION.

V-bridge

An OPEN BRIDGE, named for the shape made by the thumb and forefinger in forming such a bridge. Also NATURAL BRIDGE. Cf. BRIDGE BOUCLÉE, CLOSED BRIDGE.

vacant

Said of a SPOT that is not OCCUPIED, on which the center of a ball may be placed without moving any ball or the RACK.

vacuum cleaner

A device for cleaning dirt and chalk dust from the cloth of a table. Unless removed, these materials become ground into the cloth and lodge between it and the SLATE, affecting the roll of the balls. At Sang Lee's room, SL Billiards in Queens, New York, the tables are vacuumed after each use. See also BRUSH.

Vaso amendment

(pocket games) A rule, adopted in 1985 but of much earlier origin, that all balls CALLED on a shot must be pocketed, or no balls at all are credited. Under this restriction, it is never advisable to call more than one ball on any shot.

vee-bridge

= V-BRIDGE.

veneer

A thin strip of wood used as a decoration on the BUTT of a cue stick. Unlike an INLAY, a veneer generally runs through the entire thickness of the butt.

vibration pot

(Brit. games) A situation in which an object ball lying near a pocket falls in without any action being taken by the player IN CONTROL. 1985 KTGP 28. See CHALLENGE, MOTION, SPONTANEOUS MOTION.

visit

A TURN at the table; a HALF-INNING. 1986 Quinn 88. See also ADDRESS, IN CONTROL. After a foul in ENGLISH EIGHT-BALL POOL, a player loses his next visit to the table. 1985 KTGP 31.

volunteer

(Volunteer Snooker) To elect to play at a POOL BALL that is not ON. 1978 BSCC 62. This is an old idea; see TAKE A HAZARD. See also PENALTY BALL.

Volunteer Snooker

(game) SNOOKER with a relaxed rule as to the order of potting balls after a RED and a COLOUR. The striker may "volunteer" to pot a colour out of its usual order, with a penalty if he fail to pot it, but no ball may be volunteered more than three times in succession. 1924 Smith 91, 1954 KTG 35.

wad

1. (sl.) A bankroll, a STAKE of money to be used for gambling. One's AMMUNITION, ARMY or CHEESE.

2. (obs.) An early type of TIP made of leather, reportedly dating from about 1806. 1868 *London Soc.* vol. XIII.

wafer

See CUE WAFER, SPOT WAFER.

waggle

To make short practice strokes prior to attempting a shot. 1949 Davis 55. Also FEATHER, FIDDLE, NUDGE, WARM-UP.

waiver

Permission from a sanctioning organization for a professional player to enter an UNSANCTIONED event. 1987 WPBA 13. The usual penalty for participating in an unauthorized competition is a fine or suspension from sanctioned tournaments. See SANCTION.

walk-up

(Brit., colloq.) To play POSITION. 1937 NBJ (Oct).

wand

(colloq.) A player's cue stick; his TOOL or WEAPON.

wanting a snooker

(Snooker) The situation in which one player cannot win except by making his opponent FORFEIT points; that is, when the total value of all balls remaining on the table is less than the difference in the players' scores. 1954 KTG 34.

War Game

(game, obs.) = A LA GUERRE, JEU DE GUERRE. A French game for eight or nine players described as early as 1665. 1974 Hendricks 25.

warm-up

1. PRACTICE in advance of a match. 2. A practice SWING preparatory to a stroke. "He accidentally touched the ball during his warm-up."

warning

Notification by the REFEREE that a player is about to commit an infraction of the rules. 1988 PBA 22. Certain warnings, known as MANDATORY WARNINGS, *must* be given, or no infraction results. Others may never be given, such as the fact that the player is aiming at the WRONG BALL. Warnings are not to be given by the SPECTATORS or the striker's coach, SECOND, or teammate. See also ASSISTANCE, REFEREE, SERIOUS FOUL.

waste

(Brit. games) To POT the opponent's ball, which remains off the table and is thus unavailable for use during the remainder of the player's BREAK. To pot one's own ball off another. 1988 Conlon PC. See also LOSE THE WHITE, PUT HIM IN, WHITECHAPEL.

wastebasket

(pocket games, sl.) An abnormally wide POCKET that accepts balls that would refuse to fall on other tables. Also BUCKET, SEWER.

WBSA

(org.) = WOMEN'S BILLIARD AND SNOOKER ASSOCIATION.

WCBS

(org.) = WORLD CONFEDERATION OF BILLIARD SPORTS.

weapon

(colloq.) A player's cue stick; his TOOL or WAND.

weight

1. The heaviness of the cue stick, generally 15 to 22 ounces. Also, material inserted in the BUTT to increase its mass or alter the BALANCE POINT. 1984 Karnehm 19. 2. HANDICAP points given away as a SPOT. 1869 Roberts 278, 1970 Fensch 162, 1979 Grissim 255. "He can't give away that much weight." 3. Playing ability. 1970 Fensch 162. This term is used in this sense with great effect in the film *The Color of Money*. Fast Eddie, played by Paul Newman, is hustled by a chubby character named Amos, played by Forest Whittaker. At the end of their SESSION, when Eddie has lost a considerable sum, Amos asks him, "Do you think I need to lose some weight?" (Meaning: "Maybe you could beat me if I didn't play as well.") The line is an inside joke to pool players but is taken by laymen to refer only to Amos's girth.

Western Pool

(game, obs.) A carom game, not a pocket game, in which a ball is placed in each corner of a CAROM TABLE. A triangle is drawn in chalk in the center of the table the same size as a pocket billiard RACK. The object is to drive all the balls into the triangle in the least number of strokes, using one of the balls as a cue ball. Even when the cue ball itself enters the triangle, the game does not end unless it contacts another ball. 1884 MB 298. Cf. CALIFORNIA POOL.

wheel man

(colloq.) A STEER MAN, one who "drives" one bettor to meet another, thus creating ACTION. See GAMBLING.

white

(Bill.) Any white cue ball used in a billiard game. 1856 Crawley 29, 1873 Bennett 213. The PLAIN ball. "I'm shooting white." The player using the white ball. See also LOSE THE WHITE. Cf. RED, SPOT, SPOT WHITE.

white ball

(Bill.) Any unmarked white ball used in a billiard game. The WHITE.

White Ball Against the Red

(game, obs.) CRAMP GAME of English Billiards in which one player plays at the white, the other at the red. 1839 Kentfield 39. Since RED HAZARDS score three but the WHITE HAZARDS score only two, the red player has an advantage that according to 1850c White and Bohn 38 is about 6 or 7 in 16.

white-ball spot

1. (Bill.) The HEAD SPOT, on which the white ball is placed. Also the AMERICAN SPOT, LIGHT-RED SPOT, STRING SPOT, UPPER SPOT, or WHITE SPOT. 2. (Amer. Four-Ball Bill.) The POOL SPOT, on which the white ball is spotted, five inches from the FOOT of the table. 1890 HRB 30.

white hazard

(Eng. Bill.) A WINNING HAZARD in which the WHITE is pocketed for two points. 1807 White 9, 1976 WSD 481. A WHITE WINNER or WHITE LOSER. Cf. RED HAZARD.

white loser

(Eng. Bill.) A LOSING HAZARD off the white ball, scoring two points. 1954 KTG 8. A type of WHITE HAZARD. See also WHITECHAPEL. Cf. RED LOSER, WHITE WINNER.

White Losing Game

(game, obs.) A predecessor of English Billiards, played to 12 points with two white balls only. LOSING HAZARDS score for the striker, WINNING HAZARDS for the opponent. DOUBLE HAZARDS (that is, both a winning and losing hazard on the same stroke) score for the striker. 1807 White 48, 1839 Kentfield 52, 1850c White & Bohn 33, 1866 Crawley 130. Cf. WHITE WINNING GAME.

white spot

(Bill.) The HEAD SPOT, AMERICAN SPOT, LIGHT-RED SPOT, or STRING SPOT. The SPOT on which the white ball is placed in Carom Billiards.

white winner

(Eng. Bill.) A WINNING HAZARD potting the white ball and scoring two points. 1954 KTG 8. A type of WHITE HAZARD. Cf. RED WINNER, WHITE LOSER.

White Winning and Losing Game

(game, obs.) A game played with two balls that was a predecessor of English Billiards. Both WINNING HAZARDS and LOSING HAZARDS count for the striker. Caroms do not count. 1807 White 48, 1850c White & Bohn 33.

White Winning Game

(game, obs.) A forerunner of English Billiards, played 12 up with two white balls only. The object is to score by pocketing the opponent's ball. 1807 White 48, 1839 Kentfield 29, 1866 Crawley 130. Cf. WHITE LOSING GAME.

Whitechapel

(Eng. Bill.) To "play Whitechapel" is to pot the white ball (the opponent's cue ball). 1866 OED, 1897 Payne 31. The white is not respotted, so once it has been pocketed the player must continue his INNING with only two balls on the table. 1957 Holt 69. The player who does this is said to LOSE THE WHITE, POT the white, WASTE the white or to have PUT HIM IN. ("Him" refers to the opponent, whose ball is now OFF THE TABLE.) The white is, of course, spotted for the INCOMING PLAYER at the end of the striker's BREAK. 1878 Crawley 10.

For some unknown reason, potting the opponent's ball was not considered to be fair play, although it was permitted by the rules and despite the fact that the player who loses the white leaves himself with only limited scoring opportunities. Whitechapel is an area of London with a historically unsavory reputation.

whitewash

(colloq.) A SHUTOUT in the scoring; to make all the points for GAME before the opponent has made any. 1878 NYT (Apr 21) 1:7, 1985 Morrison 164. See also LOVE GAME.

whitey

(Pocket Bill., colloq.) The CUE BALL, so called because it is pure white. 1983 BD (Jan/Feb) 18, 1988 Rossman 175. The WHITE. Cf. SPOT.

whiz wheel system

(pocket games) An aiming system developed by Billie Billing and explained in 1992 Billing. It permits the player to determine the fullness of hit required to pocket an object ball. See also AIM.

wicker bottle

A SHAKE BOTTLE used in English LIFE POOL to dispense small numbered balls randomly for the assignment of PRIVATE NUMBER BALLS. 1908 Brunswick 98.

wild

1. (Nine-Ball, colloq.) Term describing a HANDICAP in which the game may be won by pocketing a ball without having to CALL a pocket. For example, in "Wild 8," the weaker player wins by sinking the eight or nine in any pocket at any time without calling. 2. The striped ball used in HI-CUE.

Wild Ball Billiards

(game) A handicapped variation of Three-Cushions in which each player is allotted a number of INNINGS equal to his handicap and may play each shot after the BREAK with either cue ball. The cue balls are therefore "wild." The player scoring the greater number of points in his total of innings is the winner. The game was popularized by Otto Reiselt at Allinger's in Philadelphia in 1931, although it had been played earlier in other cities. 1931 BM (Jun) 27.

window

A decoration, usually applied to the AFTERWRAP portion of the BUTT of a cue stick, whose appearance resembles a rectangular window. 1983 NBN (Mar) 18.

windy

(colloq.) To BREEZE by an object ball but *without* hitting it. A locution from Chicago, the "Windy City." 1980 LeBar 19. Also called a BARBER. See also AIR BALL, FEATHER, FIELD GOAL.

wing shot

(Pocket Bill.) A FANCY SHOT in which the cue ball is shot at a moving object ball. 1901 WB (Apr 10) 344, 1977 Martin 220. (The object ball is "on the wing," so to speak, when it is struck.) In Pocket Billiards, the object ball is usually CUT into a corner pocket. 1941 NBJ (May-Jun), 1979 Grissim 254. This shot is a specialty of Willie Mosconi, who has made 30 consecutive wing shots without a miss. It is of entertainment interest only, since it is illegal in all games to shoot at a moving ball. See MOTION. Wing shots are also possible in Three-Cushions.

winner

1. (Brit. games) A WINNING HAZARD. See also RED WINNER, WHITE WINNER. Cf. LOSER. 2. The successful player in a game, MATCH, or TOURNAMENT. 1967 Polsky 61.

winner breaks

A convention that the winner of one game in a series is permitted to BREAK for the next game. 1992 OR 47. This is an advantage in games in which the break is desirable, such as Nine-Ball. Cf. ALTERNATING BREAK, LOSER BREAKS.

winner stops on

(Brit. games) A rule in British pubs whereby a player desiring to play may register his intention by placing money on the table or chalking his name on a board. He will then play against the winner of the game just completed when his turn arrives. 1981 Quinn 30. See also WINNERS.

winners

A term by which a person announces his intention to challenge the winner of the game currently in progress, sometimes accompanied by placing stake money on the table. "I have winners." Used particularly in BAR POOL. See also WINNER STOPS ON.

winners' bracket

A grouping of players in a SPLIT DOUBLE ELIMINATION tournament, consisting of those competitors who have not yet lost a game. After one loss, a player moves to the LOSERS' BRACKET. The final game of the tournament pits the winners of the two brackets against each other.

Winning Against the Winning and Losing

(game, obs.) A CRAMP GAME in which the superior player may score by WINNING HAZARDS only; the weaker may score by both winning and LOSING HAZARDS. 1839 Kentfield 33, 1866 Crawley 234. It is said by 1850c White & Bohn 35 to be equivalent to giving 10 points in 24.

Winning and Following Game

(game, obs.) The WINNING GAME in which the striker is permitted to shoot as long as he continues to score. 1839 Kentfield 2. See FOLLOWING GAME.

Winning and Losing Carambole Game

(game, obs.) = ENGLISH BILLIARDS. 1807 White 53, 1856 Crawley 161. The name reflects the fact that the game is an amalgam of the WINNING GAME, the LOSING GAME, and the CARAMBOLE GAME. The term is obsolete, but the game is still played.

Winning and Losing Game

(game, obs.) An early form of ENGLISH BILLIARDS in which points could be made by WINNING HAZARDS (POTS) and LOSING HAZARDS (IN-OFFS). Introduced around 1770. 1979 Everton 10. It was played 21, 24, 30, 42, 50, 63, 100 UP, but usually to 24 points. 1773 *Covent Garden*, 1775 Annals 94, 1839 Kentfield 33. The modern form, established by 1807, allowed scoring by caroms also. Cf. WINNING AND LOSING CARAMBOLE GAME.

winning and losing spot

(Eng. Bill.) The BILLIARD SPOT. 1866 Crawley 7. Also known as the BLACK SPOT (Snooker), ENGLISH SPOT, LOSING SPOT, RED SPOT (Eng. Bill.), TOP SPOT, or just "the Spot." The location for the WHITE in LIFE POOL. 1836 Tillotson 1.

263

Winning Carambole Game

(game, obs.) ENGLISH BILLIARDS in which only CAN-NONS and WINNING HAZARDS count. 1807 White 54. Sometimes called the Winning Hazard and Carambole Game. 1856 Crawley 86.

Winning Game

1. (game, obs.) The WHITE WINNING GAME, played with two balls, in which only WINNING HAZARDS counted. 1773 *Covent Garden*, 1775 Annals 93. 2. (game, obs.) Three-ball billiards, played on a POCKET TABLE, and with scoring only by caroms and WINNING HAZARDS. 1850c White & Bohn 34.

winning game hazard

(obs.) = WINNING HAZARD. A scoring HAZARD in the WINNING GAME.

winning hazard

(Eng. Bill.) A shot on which an object ball enters a pocket; a hazard in the WINNING GAME. 1807 White 30, 1839 Kentfield 10, 1866 Crawley 78. So called because it is a HAZARD on which points were originally *won* in early versions of billiards. Cf. LOSING HAZARD, a hazard of the cue ball off another, on which points were formerly lost or forfeited. A red winning hazard (RED WINNER) is one in which the red is pocketed; similarly, white winning hazard (WHITE WINNER). 1836 Tillotson 2.

Winning Hazards Against All Hazards and Canons

(game, obs.) A CRAMP GAME of ENGLISH BILLIARDS in which the superior player can COUNT only with WINNING HAZARDS. 1856 Crawley 98. The odds were said to be 2-1 between otherwise equal players.

winning spot

(Eng. Bill.) = PYRAMID SPOT. 1856 Crawley 5, 1873 Bennett 19. The SPOT on which the POTTED ball is SPOTTED after a WINNING HAZARD if the BILLIARD SPOT is occupied. Also the DARK-RED SPOT, FOOT SPOT, PINK SPOT, or RED SPOT (Eng. Bill.)

wire

(colloq.) The SCORE STRING, which consists of a metal wire on which BUTTONS are strung. See ON THE WIRE, RUB THE WIRE.

WLBSA

(org.) = WORLD LADIES BILLIARDS AND SNOOKER AS-SOCIATION.

women in billiards

Women have played billiard since the earliest times. There is a 1426 account in the *Journal de Paris* of Margot, a Frenchwoman who could beat the best

players, including men. The game was played by royalty, but women were compelled to use the MACE, out of fear that they would tear the cloth with the pointed cue (which had no tip until the early 1800s). During the mid-nineteenth century, billiards became a polite accomplishment for ladies; it was taught in finishing schools and was socially acceptable if practiced in an all-female environment.

Women players have labored under a double standard for centuries. Either they were poor players, not to be taken seriously, or were brazen tarts, courting the attention of men by intruding on the male domain. Neither role won them respect, which is why genuine playing achievement by women should be an object of deep admiration, considering the difficulty of attaining it.

Men have debated at length what the proper role of women in the game should be, considering virtually every facet of the issue except the viewpoint of the women themselves. It was felt, at various times, that they were biologically incapable of wielding the cue, temperamentally unsuited to competition, inattentive to serious instruction, or too susceptible to male advances to be serious players.

The women's era really began about 1900, when Alice Howard Cady wrote the first American book on pocket games (and the first book by a woman on any aspect of billiards). Soon thereafter, informal women's competitions were held in both Britain and the U.S., usually resulting in the crowning of champions by general acclamation rather than by sanctioned tournaments. The number of skilled women players was too small then to provide an adequate field of tournament entrants. The most notable women's champion of the period was Ruth McGinnis, who rose to prominence during the 1930s as an exhibition companion of Willie Mosconi. She was unbeatable by women until her retirement and was the first woman invited to play in a men's professional tournament, the New York State championship of 1942. Masako Katsura participated in the world Three-Cushion tournaments of 1952–54.

The revival of pocket billiards in the 1960s brought forth a small number of dedicated women willing to play for prizes much smaller than those offered to men. Dorothy Wise won the first five U.S. Open championships, beginning in 1967. Jean Balukas, an exceptional all-around athlete, won the next seven Opens. She dominated women's billiards completely before withdrawing from competition in 1988. Wise and Balukas firmly established women's professional competition as a fixture of major U.S. tournaments. The absence of Balukas has opened the door for many other players, the most prominent of whom are Ewa Mataya, Loree Jon Jones, Robin Bell, JoAnn Mason-Parker, Peg Ledman, Jeanette Lee, Belinda Bearden, Mary Kenniston, Kelly Oyama, Laura Smith, Gloria Walker, Vivian Villarreal, and Nikki Benish.

A number of women are not only players but also organizers, contributing their time to the Women's Professional Billiard Association. These include Billie Billing, Peg Ledman, Fran Crimi, Shari Simonsen-Stauch and Vicki Paski. See also WOMEN'S PROFESSIONAL BILLIARD ASSOCIATION.

For an extensive treatment of the subject of women in billiards, see 1992 BD (Apr).

Women's Billiard and Snooker Association (WBSA)
(org.) A British association of women players. Abbreviated WBSA.

Women's Professional Billiard Association (WPBA)
(org.) A U.S. association of women tournament players. Abbreviated WPBA. It was formed in 1976 as the PROFESSIONAL WOMEN'S BILLIARD ALLIANCE by Palmer Byrd, Madelyn Whitlow, and Larry Miller. Its executives have been Billie Billing (president, 1977–81), Fran Crimi (president, 1982–83), Barry Dubow (managing director, 1983–85), Belinda Bearden (president, 1985–87), Peg Ledman (1987–91) and Vicki Paski (1992–93). The organization sanctions tournaments and represents the interests and media participation rights of female professional players. Address: 219 E. Jefferson St., Grand Ledge, MI 48837.

wood
The upper portion of a RAIL, to which a CUSHION is attached. A ball that has left the table and contacted the wood is considered a jump ball under modern rules, even if it then returns to the BED.

World Billiard Union
(org.) The UNION MONDIALE DU BILLARD, the UMB.

World Billiards and Snooker Council
(org.) Formerly the world amateur governing body of English Billiards and Snooker, its name was changed to the INTERNATIONAL BILLIARD AND SNOOKER FEDERATION in 1973.

world championship
See CHAMPIONSHIP.

World Confederation of Billiard Sports (WCBS)
(org.) Formed in 1990 as the parent of the UMB, WPA and Snooker organizations. Supervised by the International Olympic Committee.

World Ladies Billiards and Snooker Association (WLBSA)
(org.) British organization formed in 1981. The world governing body of ladies' snooker.

World Pool Association (WPA)
(org.) A subordinate organization to the WORLD CONFEDERATION OF BILLIARD SPORTS that exercises authority over pocket games.

World Professional Billiards and Snooker Association (WPBSA)
(org.) British governing body for the professional game, formed in 1968 and known prior to 1971 as the PROFESSIONAL BILLIARDS PLAYERS ASSOCIATION. 1983 Bills 11. Cf. BSCC, the former governing body of amateurs.

World Straight Pool Association (WSPA)
(org.) Formed in 1976 to obtain recognition of world Straight Pool champions.

World Team Billiards
A form of Nine-Ball competition in which teams of four players compete against the clock. The team that wins the greatest number of games before time expires is the victor. The SHOT CLOCK allows 10 seconds for a BREAK SHOT, 25 seconds for the INCOMING PLAYER to take his first shot, and 20 seconds for each subsequent shot of the HALF-INNING. The format is suitable for television because the competition is of highly predictable length. See TIME LIMIT.

WPA
(org.) = WORLD POOL ASSOCIATION.

WPBA
(org.) = WOMEN'S PROFESSIONAL BILLIARD ASSOCIATION. Formerly the PWBA.

WPBSA
(org.) = WORLD PROFESSIONAL BILLIARDS AND SNOOKER ASSOCIATION.

wrap, wrapping
A covering for that portion of the BUTT of a cue stick that is grasped by the player. See also GRIP. The function of the wrap is to improve the player's hold on the cue and, in the case of cloth and CORK wraps, to absorb perspiration. Materials used include IRISH LINEN, nylon and LEATHER to provide friction and comfort. 1965 Fats 76. A current fashion, particularly among billiard players, is to use a sleeve of rubber that can be rolled onto the butt. Its use avoids the need to turn down and cover the beautiful PRONGS of the butt to apply a traditional wrap. See also AFTERWRAP, FOREWRAP, RUBBER, UNDERWRAP.

Wrapping is a relatively recent innovation, considering that cues were in use by the year 1680. In the 1870s, Albert Garnier found that he was unable to control the cue to his satisfaction during delicate NURSE shots, so he rubbed the butt with beeswax to prevent it from slipping through his hand. 1879 NYT (Feb 9) 12:2. This was the first true wrap.

wrong ball

(Bill.) The NONSTRIKER'S cue ball. In games that use more than one cue ball, it is possible for a player deliberately or inadvertently to shoot with the wrong ball, *i.e.*, the cue ball belonging to his opponent. 1807 White 148, 1845 Hoyle 222. Shooting with the wrong ball is a FOUL, but the rule varies as to when and by whom this foul may be CALLED and how many points are to be forfeited. In general, the striker is credited with all points scored on strokes prior to the one on which the foul is discovered. A player who himself has used the wrong ball may not call this foul against the incoming player who has thereby been misled into also using the wrong ball. 1916 RGRG 9.

In some games, the referee may alert the player that he is about to shoot with the wrong ball; in others, the referee may not call such a foul himself after it has been committed, but must wait for the opponent to complain. See WARNING. What should the rule be if a *spectator* warns a player? Must the player be penalized for something he never did? If so, this might result in enemies of a player "helping" him by such a warning, expecting a penalty to be assessed. The issue was commented upon without resolution by the editor of *World of Billiards* in 1901. See also CHANGED BALL.

wrong-way English

(colloq.) = REVERSE ENGLISH. 1978 Byrne 77. So called because the cue ball appears to go the "wrong way" after contact with a cushion, that is, in a direction contrary to that expected with NATURAL ENGLISH or no ENGLISH. See also CHECK SIDE, COUNTER, HOLD-UP, OPPOSING SIDE.

WSPA

(org.) = WORLD STRAIGHT POOL ASSOCIATION.

Wurst-Partie

(game, obs.) = SAUSAGE GAME. 1850c White & Bohn 47, 1856 Crawley 106. From the German *Wurst*, meaning "sausage," which refers to the shape formed by the balls when arranged for play at this game.

yellow

1. (Snooker) The color of the ball that is valued at two points and is spotted at the beginning of a FRAME on the right corner of the D. Also, the name given to that ball: "the yellow." For an aid in remembering where to spot the yellow, see GOD BLESS YOU. 2. (Pocket Bill.) The color of the balls numbered one and nine. 3. The color of one of the cue balls in international Carom Billiards, used to distinguish the two cue balls by color. The yellow is frequently referred to as the BLACK BALL for historical reasons related to the black dot on the SPOT BALL. 4. Color of a ball used in RUSSIAN POOL, CARLINE, and various other games.

yellow spot

(Snooker) The SPOT on which the YELLOW is placed, at the right intersection of the D and the BAULK-LINE. Cf. GREEN SPOT. In CASIN, a spot on the long string one ball diameter from the foot rail.

Yotsudama

(game) A Japanese four-ball CAROM game played in many variations with two white and two red balls. One version requires the player to hit the two red balls

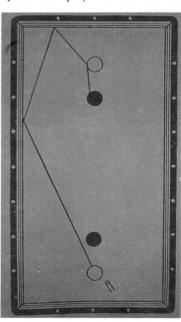

Yotsudama

without touching the other white. Cf. AMERICAN FOUR-BALL GAME, KOREAN GAMES. The name is from the Japanese *yotsu*, "four," and *tama*, "ball." An obsolete Japanese word for billiards is *tamatsuki*, or "ball-hit." The modern Japanese word for billiards is *biriaado*, with "aa" pronounced as "aah."

Z stroke

(Eng. Bill.) A SAFETY stroke in which the cue ball traces out the shape of the letter Z before coming to rest IN BAULK. 1986 Buchanan 46. (Americans note: The pronunciation is "zed-stroke.") *See illustration in next column.*

zigzag ball

A pocket billiard ball introduced in the 1920s by Hyatt. Each OBJECT BALL is marked with a zigzag border around its circumference to provide the player with a visual reference point for aiming regardless of how the ball may be lying on the table.

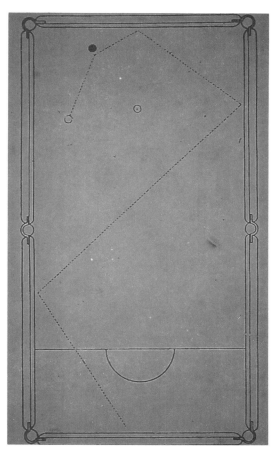

Z stroke

267

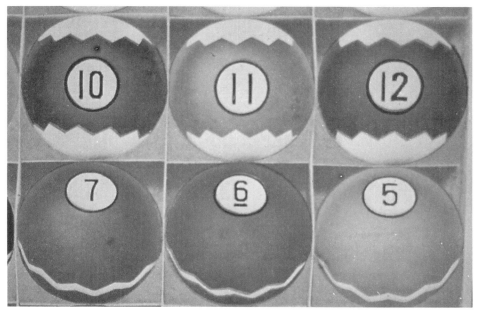

zigzag ball

Appendix A:
Billiard Numbers

Billiards is a mathematical game.
—1881 MB 12.

Following is a selection of billiard concepts and events indexed by numerical value. It should take but a few minutes to become familiar with its contents and method of ordering. A term in small caps refers to an entry in the main text. A numerical citation refers to this table.

−13	Ralph Greenleaf's score in his worst defeat in a 125-point game of Straight Pool, at the hands of Willie Mosconi. Curiously, also the score attained by Joe Balsis when he was beaten by Dick Baertsch by 163 points in the 1969 U.S. Open—a record victory margin in a 150-point match. See MARGIN, NEGATIVE SCORE.
0	Number of points scored by Erich Hagenlocher in his 400-point match of 18.2 Balkline against Jake Schaefer Jr. in February 1925. See DRAW.
0.005	Maximum permissible vertical deviation between adjacent slates of a table BED, in inches. Diameter tolerance of BALLS for pocket, carom, and Snooker games.
0.02	Maximum permissible deviation in flatness along the length of the PLAYING SURFACE of a table, in inches. See 0.03.
0.03	Maximum permissible deviation in flatness along the length of the PLAYING SURFACE of a table, when loaded with 200 pounds at its center, in inches. See 0.02.
0.05	Maximum permissible upper deviation in diameter permitted of a Snooker ball, in millimeters. 1984a BSCC S8. See also 0.08. Maximum deviation from regulation weight permitted for an entire English Billiards set, in grams. 1984a BSCC S8.
0.08	Maximum permissible lower deviation in diameter permitted of a Snooker ball, in millimeters. 1984a BSCC S8. See also 0.05.
1/11	(Brit. games) Distance of BILLIARD SPOT from top cushion, as a fraction of table length.
1/8	Distance between adjacent DIAMONDS, as a fraction of table length.
1/6	(Brit. games) Radius of the D, as a fraction of table width.
1/5	(Brit. games) Distance of BAULK-LINE from bottom cushion, as a fraction of table length.
1/4	Distance of HEAD STRING from head cushion, as a fraction of table length.
1	Value of a RED ball in Snooker, solid YELLOW in Pocket Billiards.

1.27   Width of PLAYING SURFACE on a small CAROM TABLE, in meters. See 2.54.

1.42   Width of PLAYING SURFACE on a regulation CAROM TABLE, in meters. See 2.84.

1²⁹⁄₆₄   = 1.453125. PBTA regulation CUSHION NOSE height, in inches.

1.5275   Exterior width of a small CAROM TABLE, in meters. See 2.80.

1.6775   Exterior width of a regulation CAROM TABLE, in meters. See 3.10.

1.75   Width in meters of a METRIC TABLE.

2⅓   Value of the YELLOW in Snooker, solid BLUE in Pocket Billiards.

+2   A DIAMOND SYSTEM. See PLUS-TWO SYSTEM.

2¹⁄₁₆   Diameter of Snooker balls, in inches. 1992 OR 92.

2¼   Diameter of pocket billiard BALLS, in inches. 1992 OR 3.

2⅓   =⁷⁄₃. Length of side of the regions used to position balls for ARTISTIC BILLIARDS, in inches. See COORDINATES.

2²⁷⁄₆₄   Diameter of carom BALLS, in inches. 1992 OR 3.

2.54   Length of PLAYING SURFACE on a small CAROM TABLE (8-foot), in meters. See 1.27.

2.80   Exterior length of a small CAROM TABLE (9-foot), in meters. See 1.5275.

2.84   Length of PLAYING SURFACE on a regulation CAROM TABLE, in meters. See 1.42.

3   Value of the GREEN in Snooker, solid LIGHT RED in Pocket Billiards.
Maximum tolerance of the deviation in length or width of a 3.5-meter METRIC TABLE, in millimeters.
Maximum deviation from regulation weight permitted for an entire Snooker set, in grams.

3.10   Exterior length of a regulation CAROM TABLE (10-foot), in meters. See 1.6775.

3.125   Record AVERAGE until 1992 for a 50-point tournament game of Three-Cushions, by Otto Reiselt in 1926 and Sang Lee in 1992. See also 12.5.

3⅜   Minimum width of an end pocket on a SNOOKER TABLE, in inches.

3.5   Width in meters of a METRIC TABLE.
Height of PARKER'S BOX, in inches.

3⅝   Maximum width of an end pocket on a SNOOKER TABLE, in inches.

3¹¹⁄₁₆   Distance from center of DIAMOND to tip of CUSHION NOSE, in inches, according to PBTA specifications.

4   Value of the BROWN in Snooker, solid PURPLE in Pocket Billiards.
Minimum penalty for a FOUL at SNOOKER. See 7.
Minimum point value for a shot at ARTISTIC BILLIARDS. See 11.

4¹⁄₁₆   Minimum width of a middle pocket on a Snooker TABLE, in inches.

4½   Size of the CROTCH, in inches.

4⅝   Maximum width of a middle pocket on a Snooker TABLE, in inches.

4⅞ Minimum width of a corner pocket on a 9-foot table, in inches.

5 Value of the BLUE in Snooker, solid ORANGE in Pocket Billiards.

Maximum distance between cue ball and object ball on force follow shots in ARTISTIC BILLIARDS, in millimeters. See COUP FOUETTÉ.

Regulation length of the penciled crossed lines used as SPOTS, in millimeters.

Penalty for ungentlemanly conduct in 14.1 Continuous. See FIVE-POINT PENALTY.

Minimum weight of a Snooker ball, in ounces.

5⅛ Maximum width of a corner pocket on a 9-foot table, in inches.

5⅜ Minimum width of a side pocket on a 9-foot table, in inches.

5½ Minimum weight of a BALL in Pocket Billiards, in ounces.

Maximum weight of a Snooker ball, in ounces.

A DIAMOND SYSTEM. See FIVE-AND-A-HALF SYSTEM.

5⅝ Maximum width of a side pocket on a 9-foot table, in inches.

6 Value of PINK ball in Snooker, solid GREEN in Pocket Billiards.

Distance in inches within which the center of the cue ball must lie from the head spot on the OPENING BREAK in carom games.

Maximum weight of a pocket billiard BALL, in ounces.

7 Value of BLACK ball in Snooker, solid dark red in Pocket Billiards.

Maximum penalty for a FOUL at Snooker.

Minimum weight of a carom BALL, in ounces.

7½ Maximum weight of a pocket billiard BALL, in ounces.

8 Value of solid black ball in Pocket Billiards, orange ball in SNOOKER PLUS.

8.2 Balkline game. See 8.2 BALKLINE.

9 Value of striped YELLOW ball in Pocket Billiards.

9⅜ Radius of the D in American Snooker. 1992 OR 97.

10 Value of striped BLUE ball in Pocket Billiards, PURPLE ball in Snooker Plus.

Maximum number of points that can be scored in a single stroke at ENGLISH BILLIARDS.

Number of seconds permitted for a break shot in WORLD TEAM BILLIARDS.

10.2 BALKLINE game.

10½ Distance in inches from the BLACK SPOT to the FOOT RAIL in American Snooker. 1992 OR 97.

11 Value of striped RED ball in Pocket Billiards.

Number of balls lying between the FOOT SPOT and the foot cushion on the LONG STRING (inclusive).

Maximum number of points that can be scored in a single stroke at COWBOY POOL.

Maximum point value for a shot at ARTISTIC BILLIARDS. See 4.

11½ Radius of the D in Snooker.

12 Value of striped purple ball in Pocket Billiards.
Incline of POCKET ANGLE, in degrees.

12.2 Balkline game.

12½.2 Balkline game. See 12-½.2 BALKLINE.

12¾ Distance in inches from the BLACK SPOT to the TOP RAIL in Snooker.

13 Value of striped ORANGE ball in Pocket Billiards.
Maximum number of points that can be scored in a single stroke at AMERICAN FOUR-BALL BILLIARDS.
Number of times Irving Crane was runner-up for the title at 14.1 Continuous, a record.

14 Value of striped GREEN ball in Pocket Billiards.
Distance between adjacent DIAMONDS on a 10-foot table, in inches.

14.1 Balkline game. See 14.1 BALKLINE.
Pocket game. See 14.1 CONTINUOUS.

14.2 Balkline game. See 14.2 BALKLINE.

15 Number of red balls used in SNOOKER.
Value of striped dark red ball in Pocket Billiards.
Number of object balls used in pocket billiards: a RACK.
Former penalty for three consecutive scratches in Pocket Billiards.
Maximum number of HAZARDS that may be played in succession in ENGLISH BILLIARDS. See CONSECUTIVE HAZARDS.

16 Maximum number of points that can be scored at one stroke in Snooker. To learn how, see FREE BALL.
Number of object balls used in POKER POCKET BILLIARDS.
Record 1930 high run by Gus Copulos at CALL-SHOT THREE-CUSHIONS.

16.30 Distance in centimeters between the foot and center spots on a small metric CAROM TABLE.

18 Number of DIAMONDS on a pocket table.

18.1 Balkline game. See 18.1 BALKLINE.

18.2 Balkline game. See 18.2 BALKLINE.

18.25 Distance in centimeters between the foot and center spots on a regulation metric CAROM TABLE.

20 Number of DIAMONDS on a carom table.
Centimeter equivalent of 8-inch Balkline.
Penalty for three consecutive fouls in 14.1 Continuous, as a percentage of GAME TOTAL.
Number of seconds permitted between consecutive shots in WORLD TEAM BILLIARDS.

22 Number of balls used in Snooker and BASEBALL POCKET BILLIARDS, including the cue ball.

23½ Distance of HEAD RAIL to BALK LINE in American Snooker, in inches. 1992 OR 97.

24 4!, the number of different racking arrangements in SIX-BALL.

25 Record U.S. high run at THREE-CUSHIONS (exhibition), by Willie Hoppe in 1918.
Number of seconds allowed for the first shot of an inning in WORLD TEAM BILLIARDS.

27   (Snooker) Number of points scored in TAKING THE COLOURS.

28   Distance of APEX BALL to TOP CUSHION in American Snooker, in inches. 1992 OR 92.

Winning score at TEN-BALL ROTATION.

28.2   Balkline game. See 28.2 BALKLINE.

29   Distance from BAULK-LINE to bottom cushion in Snooker, in inches. 1992 OR 92.

29¼   Distance in inches from the BED to the bottom of the leg of a regulation table.

30   World competitive high run at THREE-CUSHIONS, by Yoshio Yoshihara in 1988.

Current penalty for three CONSECUTIVE FOULS in a 150-point game of 14.1 Continuous. See 20.

31   Number of points required for victory at Pin Pool and other BURST games.

Game. See THIRTY-ONE POOL.

32   Width of PLAYING SURFACE on a 6-foot table, in inches. See 64.

33   Record number of consecutive victories by a player in 14.1 CONTINUOUS league play, Frank Taberski, 1925 season.

35   Centimeter equivalent of 14″ Balkline.

Maximum number of frames in a world championship SNOOKER match (best of 35). See 145.

36–37   Distance from the cloth to the cushion NOSE on a carom table, in millimeters.

38   The name of a game. See THIRTY-EIGHT.

Width of PLAYING SURFACE on a 7-foot table, in inches. See 76.

38.2   Balkline game. See 38.2 BALKLINE.

39.2   Balkline game. See 39.2 BALKLINE.

40   Thickness of SLATE required in European carom tournaments on 2.8-meter tables, in millimeters. 1989 Salvador 89.

Usual game total in preliminary rounds of THREE-CUSHION tournaments.

41   GAME TOTAL in FORTY-ONE POCKET BILLIARDS.

42.2   Balkline game. See 42.2 BALKLINE.

44   One of two legal widths of PLAYING SURFACE of an 8-foot table, in inches. See 46, 88.

45   Thickness of SLATE required in UMB tournaments, in millimeters.

Angle to which the cue stick must be elevated to avoid a PUSH in Eight-Ball.

Angle in degrees erroneously thought to be the HALF-BALL ANGLE.

Game. See FORTY-FIVE.

45.1   Balkline game. See 45.1 BALKLINE.

45.2   Balkline game. See 45.2 BALKLINE.

46   Apparent run record by Prof. Henry Lewis at NOSE billiards.

One of two legal widths of PLAYING SURFACE of an 8-foot table, in inches. See 44, 92.

47.1 Balkline game. See 47.1 BALKLINE.

47.2 Balkline game. See 47.2 BALKLINE.

47.416 Official distance from the BALKLINES to the cushion in 47.2 BALKLINE, in centimeters.

50 Usual GAME TOTAL in final rounds of Three-Cushion tournaments.
Minimum thickness of slate required for ARTISTIC BILLIARDS, in millimeters. 1989 Salvador 95.
Width of PLAYING SURFACE on a 9-foot table, in inches. See 100.

51 GAME TOTAL in FORTY-FIVE.

52.5 Diameter of regulation Snooker BALLS, in millimeters.

53 Record high run at CUSHION CAROMS (American match). Willie Hoppe v. C. C. Peterson, 1933. 1946 OR 10. See also 199.
Record high run at RED BALL, by C. C. Peterson, 1915.

56 Width of PLAYING SURFACE on a 10-foot table, in inches. See 112.

57.2 Balkline game. See 57.2 BALKLINE.

61 GAME TOTAL at Fifteen-Ball Pool or ROTATION. See 120.

61–61.5 Diameter of regulation carom BALLS, in millimeters.

63 Game total at CORONATION CORK POOL BILLIARDS. See 126.

64 Length of PLAYING SURFACE on a 6-foot table. See 32.

65.5 Diameter of Korean carom BALLS, in millimeters.

68 Women's U.S. OPEN high run in Straight Pool by Ewa Mataya, 1992.
Number of shots in the official ARTISTIC BILLIARDS program.

70 Width of regulation Snooker playing surface, in inches. See TABLE.

71.1 Balkline game. See 71.1 BALKLINE.

71.125 Distance from balklines to cushion in 71.2 BALKLINE, in centimeters.

71.2 Balkline game. See 71.2 BALKLINE.

72 (Snooker) Minimum number of points scored during a TOTAL CLEARANCE.

74 The greatest point deficit that any Snooker player has ever overcome for victory in a professional frame. 1991 Everton 18.

75 Maximum number of CANNONS that may be played in succession without a HAZARD in ENGLISH BILLIARDS. See CONSECUTIVE CANNONS.
Regulation CUSHION FACING angle, in degrees, according to PBTA specifications.
Number of times the pocket billiard title has changed hands in New York City. Chicago is runner-up with 17.

76 Length of PLAYING SURFACE on a 7-foot table, in inches.
See 38.

79–80 Regulation height of table BED, in centimeters.

81 Alfredo De Oro's tournament high run at CONTINUOUS POOL, 1910.

85 hrs., 49 min.	Length of time required for Tom Reece's BREAK of 499,135 at the ANCHOR CANNON, spread over five weeks.
88	One of two legal lengths of PLAYING SURFACE of an 8-foot table, in inches. See 44, 92.
90	Theoretical angle of separation between cue ball and object ball paths, in degrees. See SQUARE.
92	One of two legal lengths of PLAYING SURFACE on an 8-foot table, in inches. See 46, 88.
97	William Clearwater's exhibition high run record on a 10-foot table at CONTINUOUS POOL.
100	A CENTURY. Length of PLAYING SURFACE on a 9-foot table. See 50.
101	Number of points required for victory at COWBOY POOL. Game. See ONE HUNDRED AND ONE.
103	Number of tables formerly at Detroit Recreation, once the largest billiard room in the U.S.
105	CUT ANGLE of side pocket, in degrees; PBTA specifications.
112	Length of PLAYING SURFACE on a 10-foot TABLE, in inches. See 56.
113	Length of first CENTURY at Snooker, by Con Stanbury in 1922.
118	William Clearwater's exhibition high run record on a 9-foot table at CONTINUOUS POOL.
120	Sum of the numerical values of the balls 1 through 15. One more than half this total is 61, GAME TOTAL in Rotation.
123	Number of obstacles used by Otto Reiselt in a six-cushion carom TRICK SHOT (probably a record).
125	Formerly, the length of tournament STRAIGHT POOL games, in points.
126	Game total at CORONATION CORK POOL BILLIARDS. See 63.
127	Record championship tournament high run (125-point games) at 14.1 CONTINUOUS.
132	Jake Schaefer Jr.'s record high run at 28.2 Balkline, 1937.
133	Length of first unofficial TOTAL CLEARANCE at Snooker by Murt O'Donoghue, 1929.
134	Length of first official TOTAL CLEARANCE at Snooker by Sidney Smith, 1948.
140	CUT ANGLE of corner pocket, in degrees; PBTA specifications.
140.5	Regulation length of Snooker PLAYING SURFACE, in inches. 1992 OR 92.
141	Highest official break by an amateur in Snooker, by G. Thompson in 1953. See MAXIMUM BREAK.
142.25	Width of the playing surface of a metric CAROM TABLE, in centimeters.
144	A perfect score at TWEETEN'S FOUR-BALL BILLIARD GAME.
145	Length of world championship Snooker matches in the years after World War II, in frames (best of 145). See 35.

147 MAXIMUM BREAK at Snooker. 1965 Pulman. See also 152, 155.

150 Present length of tournament STRAIGHT POOL games, in points.
Record exhibition high average at 18.1 Balkline, by Welker Cochran, 1927.

152 Highest Snooker break on record, by Kirk Stevens in 1984. See MAXIMUM BREAK. Cf. 147, 155.

154 Official high run at LINE-UP, by Emmett Blankenship, 1916. See 284.

155 MAXIMUM BREAK at Snooker with FREE BALL. 1941 Levi 257. See also 147, 152.

159 Minimum possible final score of a player who makes a MAXIMUM BREAK of 155 at Snooker.

178 Length of a side of the ANCHOR SPACE, in millimeters.

182 Tournament record high run at 14.1 CONTINUOUS, by Joe Procita, 1954.

199 Francis Connesson's record high run at CUSHION CAROMS.

200 Score in a perfect game of EQUAL OFFENSE.
(Eng. Bill.) Maximum number of points that may be scored without having the cue ball cross the BAULK-LINE. See LINE RULE.

205–215 Range of weights of regulation carom BALLS, in grams.

210 Maximum break at SNOOKER PLUS.
Length in millimeters of the CROTCH on a regulation CAROM TABLE.

212 Tournament high run at 18.1 BALKLINE, by Jake Schaefer Jr., 1926.

224 Length of 1941 world championship league season, in games, 14.1 CONTINUOUS.

231 Highest possible individual score in BASEBALL POCKET BILLIARDS.

248 Willie Hoppe's U.S. high run at 71.2 Balkline, 1937.

272 Roger Conti's world record high run at 71.2 Balkline, 1938.

284 Unofficial record high run at LINE-UP, by Abner Finn, 1930. See 154.

290–292 Radius of the D on a METRIC TABLE, in millimeters.

300 A perfect game at BOWLLIARDS.

303 Willie Hoppe's world record high run at 14.1 Balkline, 1914.

307 Record for consecutive match victories at 14.1 Continuous, by Frank Taberski, ending in 1921.

320–324 Distance between the SPOT and the TOP CUSHION on a METRIC TABLE, in millimeters.

322 Fourth highest run at 14.1 CONTINUOUS, by Willie Mosconi, 1953.

329 Record high run by Maurice Vignaux at 8.2 Balkline, 1884.

334 feet, 2 inches Longest drive of a billiard ball on a level surface, by C.C. Peterson at the Navy Pier, Chicago, 1935.

353 Exhibition high run at 18.1 Balkline, by Welker Cochran, 1927.

355   Third highest run at 14.1 CONTINUOUS, by Willie Mosconi, 1953.
Size in millimeters of the 32 large squares into which the playing surface is divided for ARTISTIC BILLIARDS.
Record ARTISTIC BILLIARDS score in world title competition, by Raymond Steylaerts, 1984. See 404.

365   Second highest run at 14.1 CONTINUOUS, by Willie Mosconi, 1953.

398   George Slosson's record high run at the CHAMPION'S GAME against Maurice Vignaux, Paris, 1882.

400   Jake Schaefer Jr.'s run from the SPOT at 18.2 BALKLINE against Erich Hagenlocher, 1925.

404   Record competitive score at ARTISTIC BILLIARDS, by Jean Reverchon, 1991. See 355.

416   Roger Conti's record high run at 47.1 BALKLINE.

432   Jake Schaefer Jr.'s high run, title match, 18.2 BALKLINE.

450   Former length of 14.1 continuous matches, in points.

487   Frank Ives' run at the ANCHOR NURSE in 1894 that led to the introduction of PARKER'S BOX.

500   Maximum possible score in ARTISTIC BILLIARDS. See 404.

520   Minimum allowable table illumination under international rules, in lux. See LIGHTING.

526   Willie Mosconi's record exhibition high run at 14.1 CONTINUOUS, 1954.

531   Cure's run at 18.2 BALKLINE in 1912.

566   Record high run by Jacob Schaefer Sr. at 14.2 BALKLINE, 1893.

600   Maximum allowable table illumination under international rules, in lux. See LIGHTING.
Former length of continuous pool matches, in points.

622   Willie Hoppe's run at 18.2 BALKLINE in 1912.

625   Mike Eufemia's claimed high run at 14.1 CONTINUOUS, 1965. Not recognized as a record.

684   Welker Cochran's high run at 18.2 BALKLINE.

690   Jacob Schaefer Sr.'s great run at STRAIGHT-RAIL in 1879 that led to the introduction of the CHAMPION'S GAME.

740   Distance in millimeters between the BAULK-LINE and the BOTTOM CUSHION on a METRIC TABLE.

837   Roger Conti's high run at 18.2 BALKLINE. 1929 NYT (Oct 19) 15:7.

850   Minimum height of table BED, in millimeters.

875   Maximum height of table BED, in millimeters.

910   (Brit. games) Minimum CUE STICK length, in millimeters.

1000   NO-COUNT game of Straight-Rail offered by Harvey McKenna to all comers except Maurice Daly and William Sexton, 1886.

1010   Record UNFINISHED high run at the CHUCK NURSE in 18.2 BALKLINE, by William A. Spinks, 1912.

1152   Number of squares into which the table is divided by the coordinate system of ARTISTIC BILLIARDS.

1214	Roger Conti's record high run at 45.2 BALKLINE.
1458	McDevitt's run at Four-Ball in 1868 that led to the barring of the PUSH stroke.
3360	Number of distinct locations at which balls may be placed in ARTISTIC BILLIARDS. See COORDINATES.
5040	Number of different racking arrangements in Nine-Ball; = 7!
5041	U.S. high run at STRAIGHT-RAIL, by George Spears, 1895.
11,230	World record for number of balls pocketed in a 24-hour period, by Mike Massey, 1980. See NONSTOP PLAY.
20,000	Number of elephants killed annually for billiard balls in the 1920s.
40,320	Number of different racking arrangements in Ten-Ball; = 8!
42,746	William Cook Jr.'s official high run record at the ANCHOR CANNON.
499,135	Tom Reece's unofficial high run record (UNFINISHED) at the ANCHOR CANNON, 1907.
3,628,800	Number of different racking arrangements in Bowlliards; = 10!
39,232,000	Number of people in the U.S., age six and older, who played BILLIARDS at least once in 1991.
39,916,800	Number of different racking arrangements in Rotation and Mr. and Mrs.; = 11!
479,001,600	Number of different racking arrangements in Pea Pool; = 12!
958,003,200	Number of different racking arrangements in Elimination; = 2 × 12!
6,227,020,800	Number of different racking arrangements in 14.1 and LINE-UP; = 13!
46,942,156,800	Number of different racking arrangements in Eight-Ball; = 2 × 7 × 7 × 12!
134,120,448,000	Number of different racking arrangements in Cribbage; = 14 × 12 × 10 × 2 × 11!
1,307,674,368,000	Number of different racking arrangements in Bank Pool, One-Pocket, Basic Pocket Billiards, Equal Offense, Honolulu; = 15!
63,000,000,000,000,000	Number of different possible three-ball billiard POSITIONS, computed by Professor Frank G. Dickinson of the University of Illinois in 1931 by dividing the table into squares of side 1/8 inch.

Appendix B:
Billiard Games

The names of all games (over 400) appearing in the text are listed below. Because of synonyms, not all the games listed are distinct. For example, 14.1 Continuous and Straight Pool refer to the same game. Synonyms can be located by referring to the corresponding text entries.

A la Guerre
A la Royale
Action Eight-Ball
Alabama Eight-Ball
All-In Game
American Four-Ball Game
American Game
American Pyramid Pool
American Snooker
Amusette
Angle Game
Apple
Around the Clock
Around the Horn
Around the Table
Artistic Billiards
Backwards Pool
Bagatelle
Balkline
Ball Pool
Bank Billiards
Bank Pool
Bank-Shot Game
Bank the Nine
Banks
Banks, Kisses and Combinations
Bar Billiards
Bar-Hole Game
Bar Pool
Bar-Table Game
Barraque, La (Bagatelle game)
Baseball
Baseball Pocket Billiards
Basic Pocket Billiards
B.B.C. Co. Pool
Beat the Breaker
Biathlon
Big Four Pool
Bigs and Littles

Biliardino (Bagatelle game)
Billard Nicolas
Billiard Bowls
Billiard Pool
Billiards
Billiards Golf
Black and Pink Pool
Black Ball
Black Pool
Blazz
Blind
Blow Pool
Blue Peter
Blue Pool
Boston
Bottle Pool
Bouchon Pool
Bounce Pool
Bowlliards
Box Billiards
Boy Meets Girl
Break Game
Bricole Game
Brunswick Ten-Pin Billiard Game
Bull Dog Game
Bumble-Puppy
Bumper Pool
Bumpers
Bumps
California Pool
Call-Shot Rotation
Call-Shot Three-Cushions
Canadian Snooker
Cannon Game (Bagatelle game)
Canons Against Hazards and Canons
Carambole Game
Carline
Carolina. See CARLINE.
Caroline

Carom Billiards
Carom Pool
Carombolette (Bagatelle game)
Casin
Champion's Game
Championship Game
Check-Check
Chicago
Chicago Pool
Chinese Billiards
Chinese Pool
Choice of Balls
Chopsticks Pool
Cockamaroo (Bagatelle game)
Cocked Hat
Color-Ball Pool
Commanding Game
Common Game
Continuous
Continuous Balkline
Continuous Pocketings
Continuous Pool
Contra Pool
Cork Pool
Corner Game
Coronation Cork Pool Billiards
Cowboy Pool
Crazy Eight
Crazy Pool
Cribbage
Cue Ball Pool
Cue Roque, Cue-Roquet
Cushion Caroms
Cushion Game
Cut-Throat
Danish Billiards
Devil-Among-the-Tailors
Diamonds Covered
DiscPool
Divided Pockets
Doublet Game
Duplicate Billiards
Dutch Pool
Eight and Eight
Eight-Ball
Eight-Ball Pyramid
8.2 Balkline
18.1 Balkline
18.2 Balkline
Elimination
English Bagatelle (Bagatelle game)
English Billiards
English Eight-Ball Pool
English Game

English Pool
English Pyramids
Equal Offense
Everlasting Pool
Experts' Game
Fantaisie Classique
Fantasy Billiards
Fifteen-Ball
Fifteen-Ball Continuous Pocket Billiards
Fifteen-Ball Pool
Fifteen Points
57.2 Balkline
Finger Billiards
Five Ahead
Five and Ten
Five-Pin Game
Following Pool
Football Pool
Fortification Billiards
Forty-Five
45.1 Balkline
45.2 Balkline
Forty-One Pocket Billiards
47.1 Balkline
47.2 Balkline
42.2 Balkline
Four-Ball Caroms
Four-Ball Game
Four Game
Four-Handed Snooker
Four Match
Four Pockets
14.1 Balkline
14.1 Continuous
14.1 Rack
14.2 Balkline
Free Game
French Billiards
French Carom Game
French Caroms
French Corner Game
French Following Game
French Game
French Game (Bagatelle game)
French Pocket Billiards
French Winning Game
Front to Back
Game of Three
Gentleman's Call
German Pyramid Game
Go-Back Game
Golf
Golf Billiards
Golf Pool

Ground Billiards
Hand Billiards
Handicap Sweepstakes
Hard Eight
Hazards
Hi-Cue
High-Low-Jack Game
High Number Pool (Bagatelle game)
Highs and Lows
Hole
Honolulu
Hot Eight
Impromptu Billiards
Indian Billiards
Indian Pool
Indirect
Indirect Game
Intercollegiate Billiards
Irish Cannon Game (Bagatelle game)
Irish Pool
Italian Billiards
Italian Skittle Pool
Jack-Up Pool
Jenny Lind
Jeu de Guerre
Keeley
Kegel-Partie
Keilley Game
Kelly Pool
Key Shot Billiards
Killer
Kiss-Cannons
Kiss Pool
Klondike
Kugel-Partie
La Barraque
La Pétanque
Last Player
Last-Pocket Eight-Ball
Le Président
Liability
Liberty Billiards
Life Pool
Limited Game
Line-Up
Little Corporal
Little Midget
Live Pool
Loop
Losing Carambole
Losing Game
Losing Game of Pyramid
Losing Hazard Pyramid
Losing Pyramids

Luck Rotation
Mac's Solitaire
Man-of-War Game
Match of Four
Metric Balkline
Mexican Rotation
Misery
Mississippi (Bagatelle game)
Missouri
Mister and Mrs. Pocket Billiards
Mixed Game
Monte Carlo (Bagatelle game)
Mouth Billiards
Mr. and Mrs. Pocket Billiards. See
   MISTER AND MRS. POCKET
   BILLIARDS
Mug's Pool
Naming Stroke Game
Near Ball
Nearest Ball Pool
Nigger Pool
Nine-Ball
Nine-Ball Banks
Nine-Hole Snooker
Nomination Game
Non-Continuous Fifteen-Ball Pocket
   Billiards
Non-Cushion Game
Non-Pareil Cannon Game (Bagatelle
   game)
Oddball
Old Army Game
Olympic Nine-Ball
One and Fifteen-Ball Rotation
One and Nine Ball
One and Safe
One and Stop
One-Ball
One-Hole
One Hundred and One
One-Player Rotation
One-Pocket
One Pocket to Five
Pair Pool
Paper Pool
Parepa (Bagatelle game)
Parisian Pool (Bagatelle game)
Parlor Billiards
Pay Ball
Pea Pool
Penalty Game
Penetration Nine-Ball
Penny Pot
Pentathlon

Perpetual Pool
Pétanque, La
Peterson Pocket Billiard Contest
Pigeon Hole and Jenny Lind (Bagatelle game)
Pigeon-hole Game (Bagatelle game)
Pigeon-Pool
Pill Pool
Pin Pool
Pink Ball
Pink Pool
Plant Game
Player's Eight-Ball
Plon-Pon
Pocket Apiece
Pocket Billiards
Pockets
Poker Pocket Billiards
Poker Pool
Pool
Pool for 31 Points (Bagatelle game)
Président, Le
Progressive Carom Game
Puff Billiards
Pull-Down Game
Pyramid Game
Pyramid Pool
Pyramiden-Partie
Pyramids
Rack Pool
Rails
Razzle-Dazzle
Red Ball
Red Losing Game
Red, White, and Blue
Red Winning Carambole Game
Reverse Billiards
Revolution Game
Rondo
Rotation
Rotation Banks
Rotation Contra Pool
Rotation Eight-Ball
Rouge
Russian Bagatelle (Bagatelle game)
Russian Billiards
Russian Carambole
Russian Game
Russian Pool
Sans Egal (Bagatelle game)
Sausage Game
Savile Snooker
Scotch Pool
Scratch Pool

Screw Your Buddy
Selling Pool
Semi-Billiards (Bagatelle game)
Sentinel Pool
Seven-Ball
Seven-Up Pool
71.1 Balkline
71.2 Balkline
Shell Out
Short Snooker
Side Against Side
Single Pool
Six-Ball
Sixty-One
Sixty-One Pool
Skill Pool
Skittle Billiards
Skittle Game
Skittle Pool
Slop
Slosh
Snooker
Snooker Billiards
Snooker Golf
Snooker Plus
Snooker Pool
Snooker Roulette
Snookerette
Snooker's Pool
Soft Eight
Solitaire Pool
Space Game
Spanish Game
Speed Pool
Spot at Fifty
Spot Ball
Stop Game
Straight
Straight Billiards
Straight Pool
Straight-Rail
Straights
Streamlined Billiards
Stripes and Solids
Stroklet
Super Billiards
Tavern Eight-Ball
Ten-Ball
Ten-Ball Rotation
Ten Pins
Texas Express
Thirty-Eight
38.2 Balkline
39.2 Balkline

Thirty-One Pool
Three-Ball
Three-Ball Game
Three-Cushion Banks
Three-Cushion Billiards
Three-Cushions
Three-Rail
Tivoli (Bagatelle game)
Toad-in-the-Hole
Triathlon
Troll Madame (Bagatelle game)
Trou Madame (Bagatelle game)
Trucks
Trunks
Tweeten's Four-Ball Billiard Game
Tweeten's Pocket Billiard Four-Ball
   Game
12½.2 Balkline
28.2 Balkline
Twenty-One Ball
Two-Ball
Two-Ball Billiards
Two-Ball Game
Two-Ball Pool

Two-Cushion
Two-Pin Game
Two Pockets to Four
Volunteer Snooker
War Game
Western Pool
White Ball Against the Red
White Losing Game
White Winning and Losing Game
White Winning Game
Wild Ball Billiards
Winning Against the Winning and
   Losing
Winning and Following Game
Winning and Losing Carambole Game
Winning and Losing Game
Winning Carambole Game
Winning Game
Winning Hazards Against All Hazards
   and Canons
World Team Billiards
Wurst-Partie
Yotsudama

Appendix C:
Billiard
Organizations

Following is a list of the 110 billiard organizations that appear in the text. Many more exist. For example, many countries operate billiard federations that are not enumerated here.

AABA = American Amateur Billiard Association
AAU = Amateur Athletic Union
ABA = American Billiard Association
ACA = American Cuemakers Association
ACU-I = Association of College Unions International
AEBF = Australian Eight-Ball Federation
Amateur Athletic Union (AAU)
American Amateur Billiard Association (AABA)
American Billiard Association (ABA)
American Cuemakers Association (ACA)
American Pocket Billiard League
American Poolplayers Association (APA)
American Three-Cushion Billiard League
APA = American Poolplayers Association
APBU = Asian Pocket Billiards Union
Asian Pocket Billiards Union (APBU)
Association of Billiards and Snooker Referees
Association of College Unions International (ACU-I)
Association of Snooker Writers (ASW)
ASW = Association of Snooker Writers
Australian Eight-Ball Federation (AEBF)
BAA = Billiard Association of America
BACC = Billiards Association and Control Council
BAPTO = British Association of Pool Table Operators
BBIA = Billiard and Bowling Institute of America
BCA = Billiard Congress of America
BFUSA = Billiard Federation of the USA
Billiard and Bowling Institute of America (BBIA)
Billiard Archive
Billiard Association of America (BBA)
Billiard Congress of America (BCA)
Billiard Federation of the USA (BFUSA)
Billiard Players Association (BPA)
Billiard Room Proprietor's Association of America (BRPAA)
Billiards and Snooker Control Council (BSCC)
Billiards and Snooker Foundation
Billiards and Snooker Trades Association
Billiards Association
Billiards Association and Control Council (BACC)

Billiards Control Club
Billiards Professionals Association
Billiards Worldcup Association (BWA)
Billiard Players Association (BPA)
British Association of Pool Table Operators (BAPTO)
BPA = Billiard Players Association
BRPAA = Billiard Room Proprietor's Association of America
BSCC = Billiards and Snooker Control Council
BWA = Billiards Worldcup Association
CEB = Confédération Européenne de Billard
Champion Billiard Player's League
CIBA = Commission Internationale de Billard Artistique
Colored Amateur Billiard Players' Association
Commission Internationale de Billard Artistique (CIBA)
Confédération Européenne de Billard (CEB)
DBU = Deutsche Billard Union
Deutsche Billard Union (DBU)
EPBF = European Pocket Billiard Federation
European Pocket Billiard Federation (EPBF)
Fédération Française de Billard (FFB)
Fédération Luxembourgeoise des Amateurs de Billard (FLAB)
Federation of Billard Players
FFB = Fédération Française de Billard
FLAB = Fédération Luxembourgeoise des Amateurs de Billard
IBSF = International Billiard and Snooker Federation
Interclub Billiard League
International Billiard and Snooker Federation (IBSF)
International Pocket Billiards Association (IPBA)
Interstate League
IPBA = International Pocket Billiards Association
Men's Professional Billiards Association (MPBA)
MPBA = Men's Professional Billiards Association
NAABP = National Association of Amateur Billiard Players
National Association of Amateur Billiard Players (NAABP)
National Billiard Association of America (NBAA)
National Billiard Committee
National Billiard Council (NBC)
National Pocket Billiard Association (NPBA)
NBAA = National Billiard Association of America
NBC = National Billiard Council
NPBA = National Pocket Billiard Association
PBA = Professional Billiards Association
PBTA = Professional Billiards Tour Association
PPPA = Professional Pool Player's Association
Professional Billiards Association (PBA)
Professional Billiards Players Association
Professional Billiards Tour Association (PBTA)
Professional Pocket Billiard Player's Association
Professional Pocket Billiard Player's Club
Professional Pool Player's Association (PPPA)
Professional Referee's Association
Professional Women's Billiard Alliance (PWBA)
PWBA = Professional Women's Billiard Alliance
UMB = Union Mondiale du Billard

Union Mondiale du Billard (UMB)
United States Billiard Association (USBA)
United States Pool Players' Association (USPPA)
USBA = United States Billiard Association
USPPA = United States Pool Players' Association
WBSA = Women's Billiard and Snooker Association
WCBS = World Confederation of Billiard Sports
WLBSA = World Ladies Billiards and Snooker Association
Women's Billiard and Snooker Association (WBSA)
Women's Professional Billiard Association (WPBA)
World Billiard Union
World Billiards and Snooker Council
World Confederation of Billiard Sports (WCBS)
World Ladies Billiards and Snooker Association (WLBSA)
World Pool Association (WPA)
World Professional Billiards and Snooker Association (WPBSA)
World Straight Pool Association (WSPA)
WPA = World Pool Association
WPBA = Women's Professional Billiard Association
WPBSA = World Professional Billiards and Snooker Association
WSPA = World Straight Pool Association

Appendix D:
Index of Names

References to the names of individuals, cities, and companies appear throughout the text. Each name appears below, followed by a list of entries in which the name is mentioned. Numbers at the end of an entry refer to the table of numbers in Appendix A.

291

293

McKenzie, Lawrence A.
FOOTBALL POOL
McLaughlin, Edward
STRAIGHT-RAIL
Meo, Tony
MAXIMUM BREAK
Mexico
DIAMOND SYSTEM, SPANISH GAME,
TIME LIMIT
Miller, H.
STRAIGHT-RAIL
Miller, Larry
WOMEN'S PROFESSIONAL BILLIARD
ASSOCIATION
Miller, Raymond
UMBRELLA
Milwaukee
ROOM, STRAIGHT POOL
Mingaud, François
CUE LEATHER, MASSÉ, MINGO, TIP
Minneapolis
EIGHT AND EIGHT
Mizerak, Steve
14.1 CONTINUOUS, HALL OF
FAME, SPLIT DOUBLE ELIMINA-
TION, U.S. OPEN
Moore, George
INTERSTATE LEAGUE, THREE-CUSH-
ION BILLIARDS
Morningstar, Ora
18.1 BALKLINE, 18.2 BALKLINE, FLY,
IVORY
Mosconi, Willie
COMBINATION, CROSSOVER PLAYER,
DOUBLE ROUND-ROBIN, EXHIBI-
TION, 14.1 CONTINUOUS, LEAGUE,
HALL OF FAME, POSITION PLAY,
STRAIGHT POOL, WING SHOT,
WOMEN IN BILLIARDS; Appendix A:
−13, 322, 353, 526
Motes, Roy
OPEN BREAK
Mullin, Martin
TELEGRAPHIC BILLIARDS
Murphy, Cisero
AFRICAN-AMERICAN PLAYERS, CHAL-
LENGE, PSYCH
Mussey, Charles
RED, WHITE, AND BLUE
Mussey, William P.
NATIONAL BILLIARD COMMITTEE
Mussey's
PENTATHLON, SPOT AT FIFTY, THREE-
CUSHION BILLIARDS
Napoleon
FINGER BILLIARDS
Nartzik, Benjamin
HALL OF FAME
National Billiards
TABLE

National Three-Cushion Billiard League
CLOTH
Navarra, Juan
FINGER BILLIARDS
New Haven, CT
STRAIGHT-RAIL
New Orleans
STRAIGHT-RAIL
New York
AFRICAN-AMERICAN PLAYERS, AM-
ATEUR, AMBIDEXTROUS, AMERICAN
GAME, AMERICAN THREE-CUSHION
BILLIARD LEAGUE, BALKLINE, BALL,
BILLIARD MARKER, BILLIARD ROOM
PROPRIETOR'S ASSOCIATION OF AMER-
ICA, BOWERY SHOT, CHAMPIONSHIP,
CHURCH, COLORED AMATEUR
BILLIARD PLAYERS' ASSOCIATION,
CROTCH, DOUBLE ROUND-ROBIN,
DUPLICATE BILLIARDS, 18.1 BALKLINE,
18.2 BALKLINE, FIFTEEN-BALL, FINGER
BILLIARDS, FOUL, HIGH-LOW-JACK
GAME, JENNY LIND, LEAGUE, LIGHT-
ING, NO COUNT, NONSTOP PLAY, PIN
POOL, PLAYER'S EIGHT-BALL, PROFES-
SIONAL POCKET BILLIARD PLAYER'S
CLUB, ROUND-ROBIN, RUSSIAN BIL-
LIARDS, 71.2 BALKLINE, SHOOT THE
LIGHTS OUT, STRAIGHT POOL,
STRAIGHT-RAIL, TABLE, THREE-CUSH-
ION BILLIARDS, TIME LIMIT, TOUR-
NAMENT, VACUUM CLEANER,
WOMEN IN BILLIARDS; Appendix A: 75
Newby, Earl
NATIONAL BILLIARD NEWS
Newman, Paul
COLOR OF MONEY; HUSTLER, THE;
WEIGHT
Newman, Tom
ENGLISH BILLIARDS
Norfolk, VA
STRAIGHT POOL
Northville, MI
NATIONAL BILLLIARD NEWS
Norwich, CT
AMBIDEXTROUS
Oddie Jr., Orville
AMATEUR, NATIONAL ASSOCIA-
TION OF AMATEUR BILLIARD PLAY-
ERS
O'Donoghue, Murt
MAXIMUM BREAK, TOTAL CLEAR-
ANCE; APPENDIX A: 133
Ortmann, Oliver
14.1 CONTINUOUS, SPLIT DOUBLE
ELIMINATION, U.S. OPEN
Oxford
INTERCOLLEGIATE BILLIARDS
Oyama, Kelly
WOMEN IN BILLIARDS

Palace Billiards
ROOM
Panozzo, Michael E.
BILLIARDS DIGEST
Paris
BILLARD NICOLAS; BOUCHON POOL;
CHAMPION'S GAME; 8.2 BALKLINE; 18.1
BALKLINE; 18.2 BALKLINE; LIBERTY
BILLIARDS; RED, WHITE, AND BLUE;
STRAIGHT-RAIL; Appendix A: 398
Parker, Charles J. E.
BALKLINE, PARKER'S BOX
Parker, Frank
AMERICAN FOUR-BALL GAME
Pascual, Mike
UNITED STATES POOL PLAYERS' AS-
SOCIATION
Paski, Vicki
WOMEN IN BILLIARDS, WOMEN'S PRO-
FESSIONAL BILLIARD ASSOCIATION
Perth Amboy, NJ
STRAIGHT POOL
Peter the Great
BILLIARDS
Petersen, F.
THREE-CUSHION BILLIARDS
Peterson, Charles C.
AIRPLANE BILLIARDS, BEHIND THE
EIGHT-BALL, BILLIARD ASSOCIATION
OF AMERICA, CROSS CUE TOURNA-
MENT, CUSHION CAROMS, FANCY
SHOT, GRIP, HALL OF FAME, LIBERTY
BILLIARDS, NATIONAL BILLIARD COM-
MITTEE, OVAL TABLE, PETERSON
POCKET BILLIARD CONTEST, RED
BALL, STRAIGHT-RAIL, THREE-CUSH-
ION BILLIARDS; Appendix A: 53
Peterson's
ROOM
Phelan, Michael
BILLIARD CUE, BRUNSWICK, DIA-
MOND, DRAW, POCKET STRAIGHT-
RAIL
Phelan, Rev. John A.
CHURCH
Phelan & Collender
AMERICAN FOUR-BALL BILLIARDS,
BRUNSWICK, TABLE
Philadelphia
GERMAN-TOWNER, ROOM, STRAIGHT
POOL, STRAIGHT-RAIL
Philips, M.
STRAIGHT POOL
Pittsburgh, PA
BILLIARD ARCHIVE, PIN POOL, ROOM
Plankington Arcade
ROOM
Platteville, WI
STRAIGHT POOL
Player's Club
PLAYER'S EIGHT-BALL

Ponzi, Andrew
CROSSOVER PLAYER, 14.1 CONTINU-
OUS, HALL OF FAME, LEAGUE
Procita, Joe
CROSSOVER PLAYER, 14.1 CONTINU-
OUS; Appendix A: 182
Pulman, John
SNOOKER
Quinn, Mark
NONSTOP PLAY
Ralph, Edward I.
CURFEW, STRAIGHT POOL
Rambow, Herman J.
CUE STICK, HALL OF FAME
Ransom, J. Clinton
FOR THE TIME
Rea, Jackie
SNOOKER PLUS
Reardon, Ray
SNOOKER
Reece, Tom
ANCHOR CANNON, CRADLE CANNON;
Appendix A: 85 hrs., 49 min., 499,135
Reims
AMATEUR
Reiselt, Otto
AVERAGE, DIAMONDS COVERED,
DOUBLE ROUND-ROBIN, LEAGUE,
THREE-CUSHION BILLIARDS, TRICK
SHOT, WILD BALL BILLIARDS; Appen-
dix A: 3.125, 123
Rempe, Jim
14.1 CONTINUOUS, NINE-BALL
Reverchon, Jean
ARTISTIC BILLIARDS; Appendix A: 404
Ribas, Isidro
FANCY SHOT, FINGER BILLIARDS
Riley Co., E. J.
TABLE
Ripley, Robert
TRICK SHOT
Roberts, Herbert
NOSE
Roberts, Louis
DEATH
Roberts Jr., John
ANCHOR CANNON, BILLIARDS AS-
SOCIATION, ENGLISH BILLIARDS
Roberts Sr., John
BILLIARDS ASSOCIATION, ENGLISH
BILLIARDS, FINGER BILLIARDS, FOUR-
HANDED GAME, SNOOKER, UM-
BRELLA
Robin, Eddie
THREE-CUSHION BILLIARDS
Rochester, NY
FLY
Roig, Louis
FANTAISIE CLASSIQUE
Rossman, Tom
BANK SHOT

Bibliography

This section contains a bibliographic reference to each book cited in the text. Individuals who provided information by private communication are also listed. References that are abbreviated in citations are listed under both full and abbreviated titles. Identifying numbers of the form "CR A317" indicate entries in 1983 Craven, a lengthy bibliography of billiard books. For books that do not appear in Craven, the International Standard Book Number (ISBN) has been provided where possible. The abbreviation n.c. indicates that the reference was examined during the research for this book, but no citations to it appear in the text[1].

(ABC) *ABC's of Billiards*. 1948c. Chicago: Billiard and Bowling Institute of America. 24 pp.

AH. See *American Hoyle*.

Aiken, Tom. 1924. *Plain Talks to Billiard Players*. 120 pp. CR A138.

Amateur Billiard Championship of America, Souvenir (abbrev. Souv). 1899. 71 pp. New York: J. J. Little. CR A20.

American Hoyle (abbrev. AH). 1864. New York: Dick & Fitzgerald. 491 pp.

(Annals) *Annals of Gaming*. 1775. London. CR A2. (A microfilm copy is held by the New York Public Library.)

Annigoni, Tony. Room owner, San Francisco, California.

(Ardévol) Ardévol Dous, Javier. 1971. *ABC . . . XYZ de Billar*. Barcelona: Editorial Sintes. CR A455.

Arnold, Peter. 1985. *The Book of Games*. New York: Exeter. 256 pp. ISBN 0-671-07732-5

Aveline, Claude. 1961. *Le code des jeux*. Paris: Hachette. 641 pp. n.c.

BA Rules. See *Billiard Association Rules of Billiards, Pool, Pyramids, Snooker's Pool and Russian Pool*.

BABP. See "Billiards and Billiard Players."

Backman, Sue. Room owner, Emeryville, California.

(Balukas) Balukas, Jean and Joel Cohen, Joel. 1980. *Jean Balukas's Pocket Billiards*. New York: Atheneum. 197 pp. CR A374.

Barry, Edward H. 1928. *System Play in Three-Cushion Billiards*. New York. 23 pp. CR A143.

———. 1934. *System Play in Three-Cushion Billiards*. New York. 22 pp. CR A144.

BBM. Bowling and Billiard Magazine.

BD. Billiards Digest

Bennett, Joseph. 1872. *The Spot-Stroke*. London: De La Rue. 28 pp. CR A29.

———. 1873. *Billiards*. London: De La Rue. 483 pp. CR A23.

Beverly, Richard P. 1974. *The Pocket Billiards Textbook*. Privately printed. 147 pp.

Billiard Association Rules of Billiards, Pool, Pyramids, Snooker's Pool and Russian Pool (abbrev. BA Rules). 1909. Billiard Association. 80 pp. CR A34.

Billiard Facts. 1975. Chicago: National Sporting Goods Association. 39 pp.

Billiard Year-Book for 1910 (abbrev. BYB). 1909. London: Black. 116 pp.

"Billiards and Billiard Players" (abbrev. BABP). 1868. In *London Society*, vol. XIII.

Billiards and Snooker Control Council (abbrev. BSCC). 1978. *Handbook and Rules of English Billiards, Snooker, Volunteer Snooker*. West Yorkshire. 144 pp.

———. 1984a. *Handbook and Rules of English Billiards & Snooker*. Leeds. 192 pp

———. 1984b. *Rules of English Billiards*. Liverpool. 20 pp.

———. 1987. *Rules of Snooker*. Liverpool. 24 pp.

[1]*The Billiard Archive, 605 Devonshire Street, Pittsburgh, PA 15213 will provide a photocopy of any book listed (except microfilm) that is not under copyright for a prepaid charge of $20.00 plus $0.50 per page, based on the number of pages listed.*

Billiards and Snooker Teasers Explained (abbrev. BSTE). 1956. London: Burroughes and Watts. 32 pp.

———. 1957. London: Burroughes and Watts. 32 pp.

Billiards Magazine (abbrev. BM).

Billiards Simplified or How to Make Breaks. 1889c. Burroughes and Watts. 217 pp. CR A39. n.c.

(Billing) Billing, Billie and Megan Ratner. 1992. *Pool Pointers.* New York: Avon. 92 pp. ISBN 0-380-76136-X.

Bills, Peter. 1983. *Sportsviewer's Guide Snooker.* Newton Abbot: David & Charles. 64 pp. ISBN 0-7153-85-6-2.

BM. *Billiards Magazine.*

Bogumil, Cz. 1876. *Das Billardbuch.* Leipzig: Weber. 393 pp. CR A463.

Bohn. H. G. ed. 1884. *The Handbook of Games.* London: Bell. 617 pp.

(BOR) 1993. See Meurin, Dawn.

(Bottema) Bottema, O. and S. C. Van Veen. 1947. "Kansberekeningen bij het biljartspel," *Nieuw Archief voor Wiskunde,* 2d Ser., 22:15.

BR. *Official Billiard Reporter*

Broadfoot, William. 1896. *Billiards.* London and Bombay: Longmans, Green (Badminton Library of Sports and Pastimes, v. 4) 455 pp. CR A44.

(Brunswick). Brunswick-Balke-Collender Co. 1897. Catalog.

———. 1908. Catalog.

———. 1915. Catalog.

———. 1928. Catalog.

———. 1935. Catalog.

———. 1946. *Brunswick's Quick Easy Way to Play Straight-Rail and Three-Cushion Billiards.* Chicago: Brunswick. 31 pp.

BSCC. See Billiards and Snooker Control Council.

BSTE. See *Billiards and Snooker Teasers Explained.*

Buchanan, John P. 1895. *Hints on billiards.* London: Bell. 208 pp. CR A54.

———. 1896. *Pyramids and Pool Games with a Chapter on Winning Hazards.* London and New York: Routledge. 83 pp. CR A55.

Bullock, Thomas R. 1884. *Bullock's Billiard Manual and Handbook of References.* Philadelphia: Bullock. 96 pp. CR A56. n.c.

Burrowes Co., E. T. 1902. *Rules for Twenty-Six Games.* Portland. 21 pp.

———. 1913. *Thirty Games of Pool and Billiards.* Portland. 29 pp.

Burwat. 1930. *Burwat Billiards View,* v. 1.

BYB. See *Billiard Year Book for 1910.*

Byrne, Robert. 1972. *McGoorty. The Story of a Billiard Bum.* Secaucus, NJ: Lyle Stuart. 229 pp. CR A382.

———. 1978. *Byrne's Standard Book of Pool and Billiards.* New York: Harcourt, Brace. 332 pp. ISBN 0-15-115223-3. CR A380.

———. 1982. *Byrne's Treasury of Trick Shots in Pool and Billiards.* New York: Harcourt, Brace. 293 pp. ISBN 0-15-115224-1. CR A381.

———. 1990. *Byrne's Advanced Technique in Pool and Billiards.* New York: Harcourt, Brace. 238 pp. ISBN 0-15-614971-0.

Cady, Alice Howard. 1896. *Billiards: a Brief Record of the Game.* New York: American Sports Publishing Co. 38 pp. CR A57.

Caras, Jimmy. 1948. *Trick and Fancy Shots in Pocket Billiards Made Easy.* Springfield, PA: Caras. 74 pp. CR A331.

Ceulemans, Raymond. 1979. *Mister 100.* Brussels. 471 pp. A389.

Charlton, E. 1976. *Winning Snooker with Eddie Charlton.* Melbourne: Macmillan of Australia. 113 pp. A385.

———. 1977. *Eddie Charlton's Trick Shots.* Melbourne: Macmillan of Australia. 80 pp. A384.

Chin, Marvin. 1982. *Billiards Accuracy.* Hicksville, NY: Exposition Press. 168 pp. A387.

Christopher, Bruce. 1975. *The Godplayer.* Privately printed. 80 pp. n.c.

Cilione, Antonio. 1958. *Billar: Teoria de los diamantes.* Buenos Aires: Albatros. 187 pp.

Clare, Norman. 1981c. *A Short History of Billiards and Snooker.* Liverpool: E. A. Clare & Son. 16 pp.

———. 1985. *Billiards and Snooker Bygones.* Aylesbury: Shire. 32 pp. ISBN 0-85263-730-6.

Clifford, W. G. 1927. *Billiard Table Games for Tables of All Sizes.* London: Foulsham. 64 pp. CR A175.

———. 1933. *Billiards through the Centuries.* London: Printing Craft, Ltd. 37 pp. CR A177.

———. 1936. *Billiard Table Games for Tables of All Sizes.* London: Foulsham. 64 pp.

———. 1938. *How to Play and Win at Snooker*. London and New York: Foulsham. 62 pp. CR A178.

———. 1981. *Winning Snooker*. London: Foulsham. 64 pp. ISBN 0-572-01148-2.

Cochran, Welker. 1942. *Scientific billiards*. Chicago: Ziff-Davis (Little Technical Library). 111 pp. CR A336.

Collender Co., H. W. 1876. *Collender's Standard American Billiard Tables* (catalog).

Conlon, Carl. Three-Cushion instructor, Ann Arbor, Michigan.

Conway, Alan D. 1991. *Pool Tables Sales and Service*. Porterville: author. 100 pp.

Cook, William. 1885c. *Billiards*. London: F. Warne. 332 pp. CR A61.

Cook Jr., William. 1908c. *The Game of Billiards*. London: World of Billiards. 124 pp.

Coriolis, G. G. 1835. *Théorie Mathématique des Effets du Jeu de Billard*. Paris: Carilian-Goeury. 174 pp. CR A471.

Cottingham, Clive. 1964. *The Game of Billiards*. Philadelphia: Lippincott. 165 pp. CR A337.

Cotton, Charles. 1674. *The Compleat Gamester*. Reprint. London: Cornmarket Reprints. 232 pp. CR A7.

(Crane) Crane, Irving and George Sullivan. 1964. *The Young Sportsman's Guide to Pocket Billiards*. Comden, NJ: Thomas Nelson. 95 pp. CR A369.

Craven, Robert. 1980. "Billiard, Pool and Snooker Terms in Everyday Use." *American Speech* (Summer, 1980), 93-100.

Craven, Robert. 1983. *Billiards, Bowling, Table Tennis, Pinball, and Video Games: A Bibliographic Guide*. Westport: Greenwood Press (1983). 163 pp. ISBN 0-313-23462-0. 1983. Craven is not listed in 1983 Craven, although it could have been unless it had taken pains to list every bibliography that did not mention itself. 1993 Shamos is not listed in 1993 Shamos because it contains no self-references (except this one).

Crawley, Captain. 1859. *Billiards: Its Theory and Practice*. 1st ed. London: C. H. Clarke. 164 pp. CR A95.

———. 1862. A *Handbook of Billiards*. London: Routledge. 96 pp.

———. 1866. *The Billiard Book*. London: Longmans, Green. 261 pp. CR A91.

———. 1876. *Billiards: Its Theory and Practice*. 10th ed. London: Ward, Lock, & Tyler. 154 pp.

———. 1878. *Billiards: Its Theory and Practice*, 11th ed. London: Ward, Lock. 154 pp. CR A98.

Cut-Cavendish. 1919. *The Beginner at Billiards*. London: T. W. Laurie. 120 pp. CR A141.

Daly, Maurice. 1913. *Daly's Billiard Book*. Chicago: A. C. McClurg. 276 pp. CR A179. Reprinted by Dover, 1971.

Davis, Fred. 1983. *Talking Snooker*. London: Black. 123 pp.

Davis, Joe. 1929a. *Billiards Up To Date*. London: J. Longmans. 228 pp. CR A188.

———. 1929b. *My Snooker Book*. London: J. Longmans. 160 pp. CR A191. n.c.

———. 1936. *Improve Your Snooker*. London: Methuen. 93 pp. CR A190.

———. 1949. *How I Play Snooker*. London: Country Life. 176 pp. CR A341.

———. 1954. *Advanced Snooker*. London: Country Life. 112 pp.

———. 1974. *Complete Snooker*. 1974. 301 pp. CR A394.

Davis, Steve. 1986. *Successful Snooker*. London: Letts. 95 pp.

———. 1988. *Matchroom Snooker*. London: Pelham. 168 pp.

Dawson, C. 1904. *Practical Billiards*. Surbiton, Eng.: author. 233 pp. CR A192.

de Rivière, Arnous. 1891. *Traité Populaire du Jeu de Billard*. Paris: Flammarion. 310 pp. CR A536. n.c.

(Des Moines) Des Moines Billiard Supply Co. 1930. Price list.

Dizionario Enciclopedico Italiano. 1975.

Drayson, Maj. Gen. A. W. *Billiards*. 1889. 115 pp. CR A64.

Dufton, William. 1867. *Practical Billiards*. London: Routledge. 242 pp. CR A67.

Duteil, Jean. 1976. *Le Billard*. Paris: Bornemann. 47 pp. CR A478.

Egan, Pierce. 1820. *Sporting Sketches*.

(Ency. Brit.) *Encyclopedia Britannica*.

Everton, Clive. 1979. *The Story of Billiards and Snooker*. London: Cassell. 192 pp. CR A397.

———. 1985. *Snooker: the Records*. Enfield: Guinness. 160 pp. ISBN 0-85112-448-8.

———. 1986. *The History of Snooker and Billiards*. Haywards Heath: Partridge Press. 192 pp. ISBN 1-85225-013-5.

———. 1991. *Snooker & Billiards*. Swindon, Wiltshire: Crowood Press. 128 pp. ISBN 1-85223-480-6.

Fats, Minnesota. 1965. *Minnesota Fats on Pool*. M. F. Enterprises. 120 pp. CR A371.

———. 1966. *The Bank Shot and Other Great Robberies*. Cleveland: World Publishing. 232 pp. CR A372.

303

Fels, George. 1977. *Mastering Pool*. Chicago: Contemporary Books. 188 pp. CR A398.

————. 1978. *Pool Simplified—Somewhat*. Chicago: Contemporary Books. 97 pp. CR A399.

Fensch, Thomas. 1970. *The Lions and the Lambs*. South Brunswick: A. S. Barnes. 167 pp. CR A400.

Fish, Marilyn. Student of billiard room decorating and design, Roseland, New Jersey.

French, Liz. 1990. *How to Play Snooker*. Norwich: Jarrold. 48 pp. ISBN 0-7117-0504-6.

Fry, Sidney. 1922c. *Billiards for Amateurs*. London: Hodder & Stoughton. 233 pp.

(Game Rules) *Game Rules for Six-Pocket*. 1985c Niles: WICO. 5 pp.

Garnier, Albert. 1880. *Scientific Billiards*. New York: Appleton. 109 pp. CR A69.

————. 1891. *Nouveau traité de billard destiné aux amateurs*. Toulouse: B. Sirven. 109 pp. CR A488.

Gilbert, Allen. 1977. *Systematic Billiards*. California. 64 pp. CR A403.

Gomis Lluch, Pedro. 1952. *Historia del billar*. Barcelona: Juventud. 127 pp.

Griffiths, Terry. 1984. *Complete Snooker*. London: Pelham. 128 pp. ISBN 0-7207-1502-4.

Grissim, John. 1979. *Billiards*. New York: St. Martin's. 255 pp. CR A404.

Grote & Hubbell. 1925c. Catalog.

(Guinness) *Snooker: The Records*. 1985. Enfield, Middlesex: Guinness Books. 160 pp. ISBN 0-85112-448-8.

Hales, Geoff. 1987. *Snooker Rules OK*. London: A. & C. Black. 72 pp.

Handbook of Rules of Billiards (abbrev. HRB). Brunswick-Balke-Collender Co. 1890 CR A53

————. 1892. Brunswick-Balke-Collender Co.

————. 1893. Brunswick-Balke-Collender Co.

————. 1898. Brunswick-Balke-Collender Co. CR A51

————. 1908. Brunswick-Balke-Collender Co.

————. 1911. Brunswick-Balke-Collender Co.

Hardy, F. 1866. *The ABC of Billiards*. London: Warne (Warne's Bijou Books). 95 pp. CR A72.

HDB. See *History and Description of Billiards*.

Hendricks, W. 1974. *William Hendricks' History of Billiards*. Roxana, IL: author. 54 pp. CR A405.

Herrmann, F. 1902. *Fun on the Pool Table*. New York: Tricks Pub. Co. 95 pp. CR A345. Reprint issued by Dover, 1967.

History and Description of Billiards. Billiards the King of Games and the Game of Kings (abbrev. HDB). Toronto: Samuel May & Co. 101 pp.

Holiday, Johnny. 1973. *Position Play for Hi-Runs*. West Palm Beach, FL: Golden Touch Enterprises. 114 pp. CR A407. n.c.

————. 1977. *Encyclopedia of Pocket Billiards*. Port Richey, FL: Jo-Ned Ltd. 209 pp. CR A406. n.c.

————. 1984. *Continuous Hi-runs*. Port Richey, FL: Caldwell. 117 pp. n.c.

Holmes, Elizabeth. Author, Healdsburg, California.

Holt, Richard. 1957. *Teach Yourself Billiards and Snooker*. London: English Universities Press. 214 pp. CR A346.

Hood, Joe. 1908. *Trick and Fancy Pool Shots Exposed*. Roxbury, MA: Expose Publishing Co. 96 pp. CR A208.

Hoppe, Willie. 1925. *Thirty Years of Billiards*. New York and London: Putnam. 255 pp. CR A209.

————. 1941. *Billiards as it Should Be Played*. Chicago: Reilly & Lee. 78 pp. CR A347.

Hotine, Frederick. 1906. *The Whole Art of Billiards*. Edinburgh: Sands. 117 pp. CR A211. n.c.

Howlett, Richard. 1680. *The School of Recreation*. 1680. CR A9.

Hoyle. 1775. *Hoyle's Games*.

————. 1779. *Hoyle's Games*.

————. 1817. *Hoyle's Games Improved*. C. Jones, ed.

————. 1845. *Hoyle's Games*. Philadelphia: Anners. 277 pp.

————. 1919. *Foster's Complete Hoyle*. New York: Stokes. 701 pp.

HRB. See *Handbook of Rules of Billiards*.

Inman, Melbourne. 1924c. *Billiards*. London and New York: Foulsham. 108 pp. CR A217.

International Tournament Pool (abbrev. ITP). 1974. 120 pp. CR A412.

ITP. See *International Tournament Pool*.

Jacobs, Bob. Labor leader, Chicago, Illinois. Son of Jess Jacobs, competitor in world Three-Cushion tournaments during the 1930s.

Jewett, Robert. 1987. *The Shots of Artistic Billiards*. Privately printed. 95 pp.

Karnehm, Jack. 1984. *Understanding Billiards and Snooker*. London: Pelham. 127 pp.

Katch, George. 1927. *How to Play at Pocket Billiards*. Pittsburgh, PA: Confey Sales. 56 pp. CR A219. (A microfilm copy is available at the New York Public Library)

Kavanagh, Dudley. 1869. *The Billiard World*. New York: Kavanagh and Decker. 94 pp. CR A74.

Kentfield, Edwin. *Kentfield on Billiards*. 1839. 29 pp, 77 pl. CR A75.

———. 1850. London: J. Thurston. 5th ed. 45 pp. CR A77.

———. 1886. London: J. Thurston. 6th ed. 94 pp. CR A78.

Know the Game Billiards and Snooker (abbrev. KTG). 1974. East Ardsley, Yorkshire: EP Group. 8th ed. 36 pp.

———. 1986. London: A. & C. Black. 36 pp. ISBN 0-7136-2570-8.

Know the Game Pool (abbrev. KTGP). 1985. London: Black. 32 pp.

Knuchell, Edward. 1970. *Pocket Billiards with Cue Tips*. Cranbury, NJ: A. S. Barnes. 256 pp. CR A418.

Koehler, Jack. 1989. *The Science of Pocket Billiards*. Laguna Hills, CA: Sportology. 262 pp. ISBN 0-9622890-0-0.

KTG. See *Know the Game Billiards and Snooker*.

KTGP. See *Know the Game Pool*.

Lange, Wilson, Player and correspondent.

(Lassiter) Lassiter, Luther and George Sullivan. 1965. *Billiards for Everyone*. New York: Grosset & Dunlap. 96 pp. CR A349.

LeBar, Kenneth R. 1980. *Official Rules and Directives to Billiard "Golf."* Privately printed, 1980.

Levi, Riso. 1904. *Billiards: the Strokes of the Game*. Vol. 1. Manchester: author. Pp. 1–264. CR A225.

———. 1907. *Billiards: the Strokes of the Game*. Vol. 2. Manchester: author. Pp. 265–500. CR A225.

———. 1912. *Billiards: the Strokes of the Game*. Vol. 3. Manchester: author. Pp. 500–786. CR A225.

———. 1920. *Billiards for the Million*. Vol. 1. Manchester: author. 248 pp. CR A222

———. 1924. *Billiards for the Million*. Vol. 2. Manchester: author. 248 pp. CR A222.

———. 1928. *Billiards for the Million*. Vol. 3. Manchester: author. 280 pp. CR A222.

———. 1935. *Billiards for All Time*. Wilmslow, Cheshire: author. 244 pp. CR A221.

———. 1941. *Billiards and Snooker Strokes*. Wilmslow, Cheshire: author. 260 pp.

———. [n.d.] *Billiards in the Twentieth Century*. Manchester: author. 268 pp. CR A224.

Lindrum, Horace. 1974. *Pool, Snooker & Billiards*. Sydney and New York: Hamlyn. 144 pp. CR A421.

Linhard, Peter. 1983. *How to Get by Without Working*. Bryn Mawr: Dorrance. 77 pp. ISBN 0-8059-2849-9.

Lowe, Ted. 1975a. *Play Snooker*. Toronto: Coles. 110 pp.

———. 1975b. *Snooker*. East Ardsley: EP Publishing. 111 pp. ISBN 0-7158-0585-1. n.c.

———. 1984. *Between Frames*. London: Black. 161 pp. ISBN 9-7136-2446-9. n.c.

Macmillan, A. D. 1925. *Everybody's Billiards Book*. London: Collins. 230 pp. CR A230.

Malsert, Philippe. 1983 *Le Guide Marabout du Billard*. Verviers: Marabout. 192 pp. ISBN 2-501-00340-3.

Mangin, Eugène. 1880. *Complément du nouveau traité du jeu de billard*. Paris. 175 pp. CR A516.

Mannock, John P. 1904. *Billiards Expounded*. Vol. 1. London: G. Richards. 437 pp. CR A232.

———. 1908. *Billiards Expounded*. Vol. 2. London: G. Richards. 434 pp. CR A232.

Mardon, Edward. 1844. *Billiards: Game, 500 Up*. Brighton, Eng.: Leppard. 116 pp. CR A80

———. 1858 3rd ed. *Billiards: Game, 500 Up*. London: Houlston & Wright. 431 pp. CR A82

(Margo) Margo, Pete and Robert Cherin. 1981. *Trick Shots for Fun and Blood*. Mt. Kisco, NY: Eleven Publishing. 80 pp. CR A427.

Marguglio, Ben W. 1985. *How to Shoot Pool*. Jackson, MI: Quality Press. 224 pp.

(Martin) Martin, Ray and Rosser Reeves. 1977. *The 99 Critical Shots in Pool*. New York: Quadrangle. 220 pp. CR A428.

Masui, Warren. Room owner, Honolulu, Hawaii.

May & Co., Samuel (abbrev. HDB). 1900. *A History and Description of the Game of Billiards*. Toronto: Samuel May & Co. 101 pp.

MB. See *Modern Billiards*.

McGinley, Lee. 1973. *Pocket Billiards Simplified*. Hicksville, NY: Exposition Press. 52 pp. CR A425. n.c.

(Meadowcroft) Meadowcroft, Jim and Joe Hennessey. 1988. *Play to Win Snooker*. London: Octopus. 80 pp. ISBN 0-7064-3158-8.

Meurin, Dawn, 1993. *Billiards: Official Rules, Records & Player Profiles*. New York: Spi Books. 164 pp. ISBN 1-56171-210-8.

Mingaud. 1827. *Le Noble Jeu de Billard*. Brussels: Jobard. 2 pp., 40 pl. CR A524.

———. 1830. *The Noble Game of Billiards*. London: John Thurston. 7 pp., 40 pl. CR A84.

Mitchell, J. R. [n.d.] *Billiards and Snooker—A Trade History*. British Sports and Allied Industries Publication. 97 pp. ISBN 0-9507442-0-1.

Mizerak, Steve. 1982. *Steve Mizerak's Pocket Billiards Tips and Trick Shots*. Chicago: Contemporary. 161 pp. ISBN 0-8092-5779-3.

(Mizerak) Mizerak, Steve and Joel Cohen. 1973. *Inside Pocket Billiards*. Chicago: Regnery. 83 pp. CR A429.

———. 1984. *Steve Mizerak's Winning Pocket Billiards*. Chicago: Contemporary. 180 pp. ISBN 0-8092-5777-7.

Modern Billiards (abbrev. MB). 1881. New York: B.B.C. Co.

———. 1884. New York: B.B.C. Co.

———. 1891. New York: B.B.C. Co.

———. 1904. New York: B.B.C. Co.

———. 1908. New York: B.B.C. Co.

———. 1912. New York: B.B.C. Co.

Morin, Pierre. 1978. *Techniques du billard*. Montreal: Editions de l'homme. 198 pp. CR A525.

Morrison, Ian. 1985. *The Hamlyn Encyclopedia of Snooker*. Twickenham: Hamlyn. (1985) 176 pp.

———. 1988. *Play the Game Billiards and Snooker*. London: Ward Lock Ltd. (1988) 80 pp. ISBN 0-7063-6658-1.

Morrison, Ian and Terry Smith. 1988. *Snooker, Billiards and Pool*. London: Hamlyn. 32 pp.

Mosconi, Willie. 1948. *Willie Mosconi on Pocket Billiards*. New York: Crown. 143 pp. CR A357.

———. 1965. *Winning Pocket Billiards*. New York: Crown. 139 pp. CR A359.

Mott. 1938. *A History of American Magazines* 1850–1865. Cambridge: Harvard Univ. Press, p. 203.

NBJ. National Bowlers Journal.

NBN. National Billiard News.

Newman, Stanley. 1936. *How to Play Snooker*. London: Pitman. 81 pp. CR A243.

Newman, Tom. 1924a. *Advanced Billiards*. London: John Long Ltd. 312 pp. CR A244.

———. 1924b. *Billiard Do's and Don'ts*. London: Methuen. 56 pp. CR A245.

———. 1935. *How to Play Billiards*. 3rd ed. London: Methuen. 219 pp. CR A248.

NYDT. *New York Daily Tribune*.

NYT. *New York Times*.

OBG. See *Official Billiard Games Rule Book*.

O'Donoghue, Murt. 1986. *Advanced Billiards*. Victoria, Australia: Richter. 81 pp. ISBN 1-86252-160-3. n.c.

OED. *Oxford English Dictionary*.

Official Billiard Games Rule Book (abbrev. OBG). 1987c. Chicago: D&R Industries. 64 pp.

Official Rule Book for All Pocket & Carom Billiard Games (abbrev. OR). 1945. Chicago: Billiard Association of America. 114 pp.

———. 1946. Chicago: Billiard Congress of America.

———. 1948. Toldeo: Billiard Congress of America.

———. 1958. Toldeo: Billiard Congress of America.

———. 1967. Toldeo: Billiard Congress of America.

———. 1974. Chicago: Billiard Congress of America.

———. 1977. Chicago: Billiard Congress of America.

———. 1982. Chicago: Billiard Congress of America.

———. 1986. Iowa City: Billiard Congress of America.

———. 1992. Iowa City: Billiard Congress of America.

Ogden, James H. 1924. *English Billiards Made Easy*. Toronto: Brunswick-Balke-Collender Co. of Canada. 273 pp. CR A249.

One Hundred Years of Recreation. 1945. Chicago: Brunswick-Balke-Collender Co. 49 pp. n.c.

OR. See *Official Rule Book for All Pocket & Carom Billiard Games*.

Orme & Sons. 1905. Catalog.

Payne, A. G. 1897. *Billiards*. London: Routledge. 95 pp.

PBA. See Professional Billiards Association.

PBM. Pool and Billiards Magazine.

PC. Private communication. See entry under name of individual contributor.

Peall, Arthur F. 1925. *All About Billiards*. London: Ward, Lock. 252 pp. CR A251.

Perrin, Reg. 1983. *Pot Black*. London: BBC. 183 pp.

Phelan, Michael. 1850. *Billiards Without a Master*. New York: D. D. Winant. 127 pp. CR A103.

———. 1857. *Game of Billiards*. 1st ed. New York: Appleton. 237 pp. CR A104.

———. 1859. *Game of Billiards*. 4th ed. New York: Appleton. 267 pp. CR A107.

———. 1865. *Game of Billiards*. 6th ed. New York: Appleton. 264 pp. CR A109.

————. 1866. *Game of Billiards*. 8th ed. New York: Dick & Fitzgerald. 264 pp. CR A110.

————. 1870. *Game of Billiards*. 10th ed. New York: Dick & Fitzgerald. 264 pp. CR A112.

Phelan, Michael and Claudius Berger. 1863. *The Illustrated Handbook of Billiards*. New York: Phelan & Collender. 104 pp. CR A115.

Phelan and Collender. 1860. *The Rise and Progress of the Game of Billiards*. 41 pp. CR A118. n.c.

(Phil) *Philosophical Essay on the Game of Billiards, A*. 1806. Bath, England. 59 pp. CR A19.

(Plan) *Plan of the 44 Strokes at the Game of Billiards to Teach the Use of the Queue Tipped with Leather*. 1829. London. 12 pp.

Polsky, Ned. 1967. *Hustlers, Beats and Others*. Chicago: University of Chicago Press. 220 pp. CR A364.

Professional Billiards Association (abbrev. PBA). 1988. *Tournament Promoter's Handbook*. Roseland, NJ. 43 pp.

Pulman, John. 1965. *Tackle Snooker*. London: Stanley Paul. 144 pp. CR A437.

Quinn, Peter. 1981. *Tackle Pool*. London: Stanley Paul. 117 pp. CR A438.

————. 1986. *Winning Pool*. London: Stanley Paul. 88 pp. ISBN 0-09-166131-5.

Raftis, Chris. 1989. *Cue Tips*. Detroit: C.R. Billiards. 186 pp. ISBN 0-9625197-9-0.

————. 1991. *Teach Your Self Pool*. Detroit: C.R. Billiards (1991). 326 pp. ISBN 1-880135-00-0.

Reardon, Ray. 1976. *Classic Snooker*. Newton Abbot: David & Charles. 128 pp. CR A439.

Reece, Tom. 1925. *Dainty Billiards*. London: C. Arthur Pearson. 108 pp. CR A258.

————. [n.d.] *Snooker*. 8 pp.

Reece, Tom & Clifford, William. *Billiards*. 1915. 312 pp. CR A259.

(Regulation) *Regulation Rule Book for Pool and Billiards*. Delevan, WI: Ajay Enterprises. 72 pp. CR A441.

RGRG. See *Rules Governing the Royal Game of Billiards*.

Rhys, Chris. 1986. *The Book of Snooker Disasters and Bizarre Records*. London: Stanley Paul. 119 pp. ISBN 0-09-166000-9.

Ritchie, Wallace. 1910a. *Billiards in 12 Lessons*. London: Burroughes & Watts, Ltd. 143 pp. CR A264.

————. 1910b. *Useful Strokes for Billiard Players*. London: Routledge. 101 pp. CR A268.

Roberts, Charles. 1901. *Billiards for Everybody*. 1st ed. London: Simpkin, Marshall, Kent & Co. 128 pp. CR A272.

————. 1908. *Billiards for Everybody*. 3rd ed. London: Routledge. 129 pp. CR A274.

————. 1911. *The Complete Billiard Player*. London: Methuen. 284 pp. CR A276.

————. [n.d.] *Billiards for Everybody*. 7th ed. London: Routledge. 88 pp.

Roberts, John. 1869. *Roberts on Billiards*. London: Stanley Rivers & Co. 368 pp. CR A121.

Robertson. 1974. *Book of Firsts*.

Robin, Eddie. 1979. *Position Play in Three-Cushion Billiards*. Los Angeles: author. 339 pp. ISBN 0-936362-00-6. CR A442.

Ronca, Ted. Attorney, Westbury, NY. Associate Curator for Acquisitions, The Billiard Archive.

Rossman, Tom. 1988. *Rack Up a Victory*. Minonk, IL: author. 182 pp.

Rottie, Georges. 1981. *Le billard et l'arbitrage*. Brussels: van Belle. 167 pp. ISBN 90-70252-10-4.

(Rule Book) *Rule Book, The*. 1983. New York: St. Martin's Press. 431 pp.

Rule Book for French or Carom Billiards (abbrev. WBA). [n.d.] Brussels: World Billiard Association. 15 pp.

Rules Governing the Royal Game of Billiards (abbrev. RGRG). 1916. Chicago: Brunswick-Balke–Collender Co. 80 pp. CR A169.

————. 1925. Chicago: Brunswick- Balke–Collender Co. 64 pp. CR A170.

Rushin, Steve. 1990. *Pool Cool*. New York: Pocket Books. 132 pp. ISBN 0-671-69138-4.

Russell, H. H. 1910. *Practice Billiards*. Portland, ME: author. 32 pp.

Salvador, Jean. 1989. *Le Billard*. Paris: De Vecchi. 110 pp. ISBN 2-7328-0572-6.

Schmidt Company, A. E. 1960. Catalog.

Scriven, B. 1938. *Billiards and Snooker*. London: Universal Publications. 90 pp. CR A294.

Segal, Daniel S. A player from Clarendon Hills, Illinois.

Shamos, Mike. 1991. *Pool*. New York: Mallard Press. 128 pp. ISBN 2-8307-0160-7.

Smith, Willie. 1924. *How to Play Snooker and Other Pool Games*. London: C. Arthur Pearson. 122 pp. CR A298.

————. 1935. *Billiards in Easy Stages*. London: Pitman. 92 pp. CR A295.

Souv. See *Amateur Billiard Championship of America, Souvenir*.

Spencer, John. 1973. *Spencer on Snooker*. London: Cassell. 137 pp. CR A443.

Stancliffe. 1899. *Fun on the Billiard Table*. London: C. Arthur Pearson. 114 pp. CR A302.

Stevenson, H. W. 1906. *The Top-of-the-Table Game*. London: Cox & Yeman. 64 pp. CR A304.

Stoddard, J. T. 1913. *The Science of Billiards*. Boston: Butterfield. 160 pp. CR A305.

Stone, Joe. 1979. *The Master's Book of Pool and Billiards*. New York: Crown. 96 pp. CR A444.

Storer, Clyde. 1934. *The Complete Fundamentals of Billiards*. Chicago: National Billiard Association. 112 pp.

Sullivan, George. 1979. *The Complete Beginners Guide to Pool and Other Billiard Games*. New York: Doubleday. 196 pp. CR A445.

Taylor, Al. 1914. *Billiards for Beginners*. Milwaukee: Tate (1914). 21 pp. n.c.

(Taylor) Taylor, Dennis & Clive Everton. 1990. *Play Snooker with Dennis Taylor*. London: BBC (1990). 119 pp.

Tevis, Walter. 1959. *The Hustler*. New York: Dell (1959). 223 pp.

———. 1984. *The Color of Money*. New York: Warner (1984). 294 pp. ISBN 0-446-32353-5.

Thatcher, J. A. 1898. *Championship Billiards*. Chicago: Rand McNally. 244 pp. CR A125.

Thorburn, Cliff. 1987. *Cliff Thorburn's Snooker Skills*. Scarborough: Prentice-Hall. 127 pp. ISBN 0-13-136730-7.

Tillotson, J. 1836. *The Game of Billiards*. London: author. 62 pp. CR A127.

Trainer, Clement F. 1971. *History of the 18.2 Balk-Line Game of Billiards in the United States*. Privately printed. 54 pp. CR A344.

Trelford, Donald. 1986. *Snookered*. London: Faber & Faber. 200 pp. ISBN 0-571-13640-0.

Troffaes, Georges. 1974. *Le billard et l'histoire*. Paris: Laguide. 149 pp. CR A547.

Trumps. 1899. *The American Hoyle*. New York: Dick & Fitzgerald. 529 pp.

Varner, Nick. 1981. *The World Champion on Winning Pool and Trick Shots*. Owensboro, KY: author. 141 pp. CR A447.

Vignaux, Maurice. 1889. *Le billard*. Paris: Delarue. 414 pp. CR A551.

Walker, Donald. 1837. *Games and Sports*. London: Thomas Hurst. 388 pp.

WB. World of Billiards.

WBA. See *Rule Book for French or Carom Billiards*.

Webster's Sports Dictionary (abbrev. WSD). 1976.

White, E. 1807. A *Practical Treatise on the Game of Billiards*. London: W. Miller. 212 pp. CR A132.

White, Jack and Dale Griffin. 1990. *Come Let Us to Billiards Away*. Farmington, UT: Expressed Publishing. 254 pp. ISBN 0-9625666-0-8.

White & Bohn. [n.d. 1856c] *The Billiard Player's Handbook*. Philadelphia: Anners. 100 pp.

Williams, Rex. 1984. *Snooker—How to Become a Champion*. London: Luscombe. 144 pp. CR A450.

Willson, Meredith. 1957. Song " 'Ya Got Trouble," from *The Music Man*.

(WPBA) Women's Professional Billiard Association. 1987. *Player Manual*. Hollandale, WI: WPBA. 22 pp.

(WPBSA) *WPBSA Official Diary Yearbook 1988/9*. Hove: WPBSA (1988).

Wright, Rick. 1983. *Trick Shot Wizardry in Pocket Billiards*. Privately printed. 120 pp. n.c.

WSD. See *Webster's Sports Dictionary*.